REFORMED
LUTHERAN
WESLEYAN
BAPTIST
ANGLICAN
ANABAPTIST
PENTECOSTAL
DISPENSATIONAL

Exploring
Protestant
Traditions

AN INVITATION TO
THEOLOGICAL HOSPITALITY

W. David Buschart

IVP Academic
An imprint of InterVarsity Press
Downers Grove, Illinois

InterVarsity Press
P.O. Box 1400, Downers Grove, IL 60515-1426
World Wide Web: www.ivpress.com
E-mail: mail@ivpress.com

*InterVarsity Press® is the book-publishing division of InterVarsity Christian Fellowship/USA®, a student
movement active on campus at hundreds of universities, colleges and schools of nursing in the United States
of America, and a member movement of the International Fellowship of Evangelical Students. For
information about local and regional activities, write Public Relations Dept., InterVarsity Christian
Fellowship/USA, 6400 Schroeder Rd., P.O. Box 7895, Madison, WI 53707-7895, or visit the IVCF website at
<www.intervarsity.org>.*

Scripture quotations, unless otherwise noted, are from the New Revised Standard Version of the Bible,
copyright 1989 by the Division of Christian Education of the National Council of the Churches of Christ in the
USA. Used by permission. All rights reserved.

Design: Cindy Kiple

ISBN-10: 0-8308-2832-X
ISBN-13: 978-0-8308-2832-6

Printed in the United States of America ∞

Library of Congress Cataloging-in-Publication Data

Buschart, W. David.
 *Exploring Protestant traditions: an invitation to theological
 hospitality / W. David Buschart.*
   p. cm.
 Includes bibliographical references and index.
 ISBN-13: 978-0-8308-2832-6 (pbk.: alk. paper)
 ISBN-10: 0-8308-2832-X (pbk.: alk. paper)
 1. Theology, Doctrinal. I. Title.
 BT77.B97 2006
 230'.044—dc22

                                                                                    2006013028

P	18	17	16	15	14	13	12	11	10	9	8	7	6	5	4	3	2	1
Y	20	19	18	17	16	15	14	13	12	11	10	09	08	07	06				

To Nancy,

as we journey together

in Christ and in the Christian tradition.

Contents

Acknowledgments

Congregations of varied traditions, in both the United States and Canada, have enriched my understanding of Christ and his church through welcoming me to worship with them. Many people have shared with me the gift of Christian fellowship in the spirit and style of their respective traditions. For these individuals and churches I am thankful.

The genesis of this book lies in interaction with students. I am indebted to students of Canadian Theological Seminary and Denver Seminary for the questions they raised in their "first course" in theology and their keen interaction in seminars based on some of the material in this book. A number of students provided both research and technical assistance, including Paul Collier, Joe Fortna and Norton Herbst.

I greatly appreciate the ready reception of the concept for this book by the people of InterVarsity Press. Daniel Reid, my editor, has been encouraging since our first conversation. He has been a patient, gracious and wise guide throughout the process. Joel Scandrett and Allison Rieck provided timely assistance during a well-earned sabbatical for Dan.

The research for this book once again confirmed that libraries and the people who staff them are undervalued resources. My good friend Sandy Ayer of Canadian Theological Seminary and Heather Clark, Randy Kemp and Tom Jacobs of Denver Seminary provided expert and gracious assistance in identifying and obtaining materials.

This book would not have been completed apart from two sabbaticals that provided opportunities for sustained research and writing. I thank the faculty, board and administration of Canadian Theological Seminary and the faculty, board and administration of Denver Seminary for these special times. The first of these sabbaticals was spent at the Institute for Ecumenical and Cultural Research, St. John's University, Collegeville, Minnesota. During one of the best years of my professional life, Patrick Henry, then director, and the other scholars-in-residence were wonderful colleagues through the foundational phase of research and writing.

Colleagues and friends have provided varied forms of indispensable aid. Danny Carroll R., Cynthia McDowell and Don Payne helped with the form and the substance of several chapters, Chris Sandifer provided timely computer assistance, and Jeanette Freitag provided helpful secretarial support. Jim Beck gave insightful critique of numerous chapters, wise counsel about the process of writing, and the use of his quiet office while he was at the farm. Members of the covenant group to which my wife and I belong, members of the Vernon Grounds reading group, Dianne McReynolds, and other friends have prayed and encouraged.

The shortcomings that remain in this book are not attributable to any of these good people. Errors and weaknesses are mine alone, and I welcome readers' correspondence regarding these.

Throughout the process of research and writing I have been mindful of what a privilege it is to stand within the Christian tradition—the transgenerational community of life in Christ. I was blessed with a Christian heritage through my paternal grandparents, William L. and Elizabeth M. Buschart, and through my parents, William A. and Margaret P. Buschart. Though none of them lived to share directly in this present work, their faithful lives are for me a special part of both the Christian tradition and the spirit in which I write about it.

My daughters, Amanda and Meredith, have provided both heartfelt support and delightful diversion. I celebrate their journeys with Christ and look forward to watching their journeys unfold.

Nancy, my wife, and I shared most of the experiences reflected in the vignettes at the beginning of the chapters, and she helped with recounting them here. With respect to this project, she has given me time and given of her own time. She is my companion in all of life. I cherish our exploration together of life in Christ and the riches of the Christian tradition and its traditions.

1 ■ Introduction

I'm a plain simple Christian.
                    Motto on a T-shirt

One cannot be a "Christian in general." Christians are earthed saints.
                    Alan P. F. Sell, in *Major Themes in the Reformed Tradition*

When I was about ten years old, I had a very brief conversation with my mother that turned out to be far more significant than either of us could have imagined. After playing with some neighborhood friends, I came home and told her that Danny was Roman Catholic, Chuck was Methodist, and Larry was Presbyterian. Then I asked, "What are we?" My mother paused, thought a bit, and said, "Well, I guess we're just Christians."

I have recalled this exchange many times over the years, and I have come to view my mother's response as beautiful and exemplary. In her own mind and heart, my mother was "simply" a Christian. Her theology was uncomplicated, and her faith was simple. She trusted in Jesus as Savior and was guided by a desire to live a life that honored him. Furthermore, my parents, who were charter members of a denominational Protestant congregation, never spoke in a disparaging way about another Christian tradition. This is the beauty of my mother's response. Without arrogance or uncharitable criticism of Christians who differed from us in certain matters of doctrine, worship, polity or lifestyle, she articulated something of the identity that all followers of Jesus Christ have and must claim: we are, first and foremost, *Christi*ans.

By the time I reached my twenties, however, I found the viewpoint summarized in my mother's response less than satisfying, less than adequate. In the years since that early exchange, I continued, by God's grace, in the Christian faith and, by my own choice, in the denominational tradition of my childhood home. I also had the opportunity to study the history of Christianity and to have substantive interactions with Christians from a variety of traditions. Among the phenomena I observed was that some groups of Christians, both past and present, have tried to occupy an ecclesiastical or spiritual high ground, claiming to be—unlike other churches—nothing other than the descendants of Jesus Christ and "the New Testament church." Over the course of time, however, it repeatedly has become clear that each of these groups is the same as all other Christian groups in a fundamental way: they are a tradition of like-minded Christians, not necessarily any more or any less authentically Christian than any other tradition. They seek to follow Jesus, to believe and obey the Bible, and to be a genuine expression of the church. Furthermore, Christians—including, of course, Protestants—have historically believed and worshiped in the context of specific ecclesio-theological traditions, and my mother's response had left me without any idea as to where we fit, where we belonged.[1] I was confident that I was a Christian, but had little, if any, idea where I was located in the landscape of the diverse expressions of Christianity. Increasingly, this troubled me. As Susan Felch notes, "One does not simply live in tradition abstractly considered but within specific traditions, among distinctive voices, entangled in concrete ways of talking, acting, and being in the world."[2]

I was also troubled by questions of Christian tradition and identity shortly after I began to teach theology. Two episodes will serve to illustrate. In one instance, a student from a Wesleyan-Holiness tradition expressed curiosity about Dispensational theology. She had some contact with Dispensational teachings on "the end times," and over the years she had several friends who belonged to independent Bible churches that nurtured them in Dispensational theology. I loaned her a copy of Charles Ryrie's book *Dispensationalism Today* and suggested that she read it as an example of Dispensational thought. The next week, when the student returned the book, she stated with considerable relief and surprise, "They aren't heretics after all. They're very serious about studying and following the Bible." As the chapter below on Dispensationalism will show, it is an understatement to say that Dispensationalists are very serious about studying and following the Bible, and whatever disagreements one may have with Dispensational theology, it is not heretical.

In another instance, a Mennonite student indicated that he was interested in doing some reading in Calvinist theology. So, with the qualifying observation that not all Calvinists agree with everything John Calvin wrote, I gave the student the first volume of Calvin's *Institutes of the Christian Religion* and identified selected portions to read. Several weeks later the student said, almost in a confessional tone, "I haven't 'converted,' but I sure enjoyed reading this." He went on to tell me that he had obtained his own copy of the *Institutes* and was reading it in conjunction with his daily devotions.

With such eager and interested students, what troubled me? Obviously, it was not their curiosity or their readiness to study for better understanding. Rather, what was troubling were the sincere yet uninformed stereotypes and postures of criticism—and fear—that these and other students held prior to their modest investigations into primary sources. This was troubling because I had enough experience in "the Christian world" to know that such ignorance of and apprehension toward traditions outside one's own are far too common. Most Christians have a rather restricted view of the rich and diverse landscape of Christianity. Protestants' posture toward Roman Catholicism often is based on second-hand stories or on someone's rather extreme reaction against the experience of having been raised in a Roman Catholic home. Similarly, despite the fact that Eastern Orthodoxy has made significant inroads into North America in recent decades, Orthodoxy is by and large still a mystery to most North American Protestants, often being viewed as a more exotic version of Roman Catholicism. Many Protestants would do well to acquaint themselves, firsthand, with the liturgical, devotional and theological resources of these Christian traditions. If the reader does not already have a firsthand acquaintance with Roman Catholic Christianity and Eastern Orthodox Christianity, some well-chosen reading[3] and, more important, several visits to Roman Catholic and Eastern Orthodox churches undertaken in conversation with the clergy of these churches will more than reward the time and energy invested.

At the same time, there is also the need for many, perhaps most, Protestants to acquaint themselves with even nearer neighbors: other Protestants. Many Mennonites and other Anabaptists do not understand why anyone, such as Anglicans or Episcopalians, would, in the name of Christ, baptize infants. Many Lutherans are puzzled how anyone, such as Wesleyans, can preach salvation by grace alone and at the same time call upon people to constantly work toward greater personal holiness. Many Dispensationalists cannot comprehend how anyone, such as Reformed Christians, can take promises and practices given to God's Old Testament people and directly apply them, perhaps in a spiritualized form, to today's New Covenant church. Many Baptists are troubled when some Christians, such as Pentecostals, so assertively pray to God in expectation of quick and miraculous healing of a physical illness. In these and dozens of other ways, Protestants simply do not know, understand or learn potentially valuable lessons from one another. This book seeks to address in some small measure this lack of knowledge, understanding and appreciation.

Eight Traditions

The chapters that follow introduce eight traditions of Protestant theology that have provided orienting landmarks on the Protestant Christian landscape for the better part of the past five centuries: Lutheran, Anabaptist, Reformed, Anglican,

Baptist, Wesleyan, Dispensational and Pentecostal. These eight traditions will be presented in this order, which approximates the chronological sequence of the historical emergence of these movements as distinct traditions.[4] This list is not to be regarded as exhaustive. There are Protestant churches and denominations that would not explicitly identify with any one of these theological traditions. However, most major Protestant ecclesiastical and theological traditions are linked, either directly or indirectly, to one or more of these traditions.

Some of the traditions examined here are related historically in their origins, with one emerging from another. These would include, for example, the Wesleyan tradition in England emerging from the Anglican Church, or the Pentecostal tradition in North America emerging, both directly and indirectly, from the Wesleyan. Other traditions considered here, such as the Anabaptist and Dispensational, have no substantive historical relation with respect to their origins. Christians in some of these traditions prefer not to be described as "Protestant," because the term connotes to them principles or historical events with which they do not want to be associated. For example, the persecution of early Anabaptists by "Reformed" Christians contributes to many Anabaptists' hesitancy to be associated with "Protestantism," and the nearly four centuries of what Pentecostals regard as the failure of Protestants to fully embrace the person and work of the Holy Spirit leads some Pentecostals to view themselves as standing outside of Protestantism. Nonetheless, each of these traditions traces its origins either directly (Lutheran, Anabaptist, Reformed, Anglican) or indirectly (Baptist, Wesleyan, Dispensational, Pentecostal) to the European reform movements outside of the Roman Catholic Church in the early-to-middle sixteenth century.

There is considerable theological diversity not only among the traditions presented here but also within each of them. In most, if not all, cases, diversity was evident in the early stages of the tradition. For example, by the middle of the sixteenth century, three major groups were seeking to lead the Lutheran movement: the Gnesio-Lutherans, who sought to preserve the integrity of Martin Luther's teachings; the Philippists, who advanced the more conciliatory views of Philipp Melanchthon; and a third, moderating group led by Martin Chemnitz. Similarly, three subtraditions emerged early in the development of the Baptist tradition, and each of these is still manifest today: Particular Baptists are Calvinistic in their theological orientation, General Baptists are Arminian in orientation, and Seventh-Day Baptists continue to observe Saturday as the sabbath. This kind of diversity is found in both the history and the present expressions of each of the traditions presented in this book. In some cases, the diversification that has developed in recent decades has been so great that there is increas-

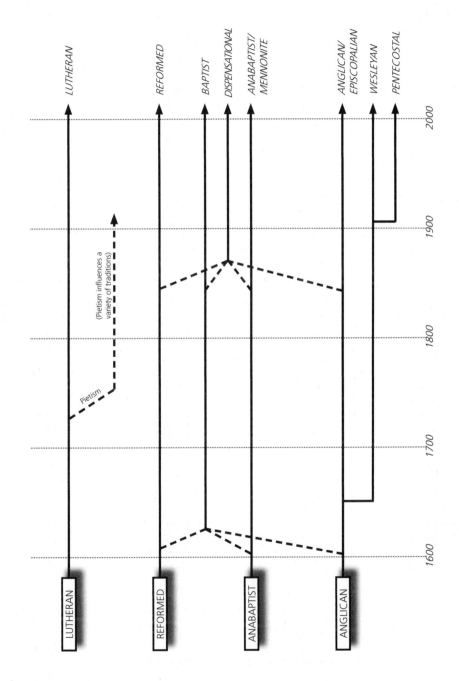

STREAMS OF PROTESTANT TRADITIONS

ing discussion of "identity" and even of "identity crises" in publications with titles such as *Anabaptist-Mennonite Identities in Ferment,* "Debating Reformed Identity," "The Rise and Fall of the Thirty-Nine Articles: An Inquiry into the Identity of the Protestant Episcopal Church in the United States," and "Conflict and Identity in the Southern Baptist Convention: The Quest for a New Consensus."[5] As will be observed in the chapters that follow, the development of diversity within each tradition is part of the story of the traditions.

At the same time, continuities and commonalities abide amidst the diversity, and the handing-on of these continuities and commonalities from one generation of Christians to the next has constituted various traditions. Even the discussion of diversity itself takes place among people and within publications that bear descriptors such as "Lutheran," "Mennonite," "Reformed," or "Baptist."[6] *Tradition* in its most fundamental sense refers to the handing-on of beliefs or practices from one generation to the next. *Christian tradition* simply refers to the handing-on of beliefs with respect to God in Christ and practices associated with life in Christ, both individual and corporate. Thus, in at least a minimal sense, any group of people, ecclesiastical organization or set of beliefs that endures more than one generation constitutes a tradition. The traditions considered in this book have helped to sustain millions of Christians through many generations, and they continue to do so today. Each tradition has provided context and community, guidance and grace. Furthermore, theology at its best is closely related to the life of the church and its churches, and each of the *theological* traditions considered here has been closely related to the life of specific *ecclesiastical* traditions. Many theological schools of thought that arose in the nineteenth and twentieth centuries emerged from the halls of the academy. However, most of the theological traditions considered here arose in conjunction with the emergence of specific ecclesiastical traditions, and these theological traditions subsequently nourished and guided these ecclesiastical traditions. To be sure, sometimes denominations merge or form new subtraditions. And, there are examples, such as the United Church of Canada, of churches of differing traditions entering into ecclesiastical unity. Yet, by and large, the theological traditions discussed here have helped to sustain, and have themselves flourished in conjunction with, specific ecclesiastical traditions.[7] For example, Reformed theology is one of the historically defining components of Presbyterian and Reformed churches, while Wesleyan theology has provided the framework for Wesleyan and most Methodist churches. Baptist churches are the ones that have most consistently taught and embodied distinctively Baptist theology, while Mennonite, Brethren and related groups are the ones that have continued to develop theology in the Anabaptist spirit. Though most, if not all, of the theological traditions considered here emerged in a context of reaction against or separation from an existing church, each of these theological traditions has nonetheless drawn life from and contributed to the life of specific churches.

A word is in order about one of the traditions included here that may be completely foreign to some readers. Historically speaking, Dispensationalism is relatively young, and dispensational theology has not been a prominent school of thought in what can be regarded as "mainstream" academic and ecclesiastical circles. Personally, I do not subscribe to Dispensational theology. And, although my appreciation for the tradition is enhanced by a familial connection to it (as I will note below), this indirect lineage does not explain the inclusion of Dispensationalism in this book. It is included because any book that seeks to survey, without undue prejudice, major Protestant theological traditions with particular attention to North America would be incomplete without it. Dispensationalism entails a comprehensive and integrative approach to interpreting the Bible. It is informed throughout by attention to the relationship between Israel and the church, and thus also the relationship between the Old and New Testaments. As an identifiable theological tradition, it is older than the youngest tradition considered here—Pentecostalism—and the full-scale assessment of its influence has yet to be adequately calculated.[8] Although Dispensational theology has not been predominant in certain corridors of power, through scores of Bible institutes, Bible churches, independent churches, media broadcasts, study Bibles, popular books and several seminaries, it has been, and continues to be, a widespread, distinctive and influential tradition of Protestant theology. In short, for the purposes of this book, Dispensationalism should not be left behind.

Structure of the Chapters

This book explores eight traditions of Protestant theology by considering each one under three headings—historical, methodological and doctrinal. First, the historical story is told, describing the origins and development of the tradition. Where did it come from? Who were the people that began the tradition? What were the events and beliefs that help explain why and how it came into existence? Once established, how was it handed on from one generation to the next? As it was handed on, what type of unity and diversity developed within the tradition, and what have been its most prominent ecclesiastical homes?

Second, having observed where the tradition has come from, we examine the approach to theology taken within the tradition. How important is formal theological reflection, and what role does theology play? What are the sources of authority for theology, and how are these sources viewed and used in relation to one another? What are the principles and practices that are employed in reading and interpreting the Bible?

Third, against this historical and methodological backdrop we examine the theological beliefs that flow from the particular history and the particular method. What are some of the defining theological beliefs of the tradition? How does a consideration of two illustrative doctrines illuminate the distinctive character of the tradition? A comprehensive description of all of the fundamental tenets of each tradition is not possible here. Rather, we focus on two doctrines within each tradition that illustrate the distinctive character or emphases of the tradition. In some cases, the doctrine is unique to the tradition, such as the Pentecostal belief that speaking in tongues is the initial sign of baptism in the Holy Spirit, and that this baptism is normative for the life of all Christians. In other cases, such as the Lutheran doctrine of justification by faith, the doctrine is not unique to the tradition, but it is formulated and emphasized in such a way that one cannot fully understand or appreciate the tradition without understanding its distinctive approach to this doctrine. Thus, *illustrative* and *distinctive* do not necessarily refer here to beliefs held exclusively, or virtually so, by one tradition alone; rather, they suggest beliefs that are formulated in a distinctive way and beliefs without which one cannot understand or appreciate the particular tradition being considered. While this approach highlights distinctive theological beliefs, it is pursued in the context of a firm commitment to the unity of the church. Indeed, as will be advanced later in this introduction and more fully in the concluding chapter, a proper understanding of and appreciation for this type of diversity is a necessary part of a greater realization of Christian unity.

Clarification is also in order with regard to the theological resources that are in focus here. Theologians of many persuasions recognize that there are multiple levels of theology. For example, Clodovis Boff, a South American liberation theologian, identifies "professional," "pastoral" and "popular" liberation theologies.[9] Similarly, North American theologians Stanley Grenz and Roger Olson delineate a spectrum of five levels of theology, from "folk" through "lay," "ministerial," and "professional" to "academic."[10] And these theologians rightly affirm the respective value and contribution of each level. The nature and scope of this book are such that, for the most part, the descriptions of theologies reflect what would be regarded as professional theology and, to a lesser degree, ministerial or pastoral theology. Comprehensive systematic theologies, books and articles on discrete theological topics, and doctrinal statements of various sorts weigh heavily among the sources cited in the notes.[11] Such documents usually are the work of theological scholars, educators or pastoral ministry professionals. Historians and theologians also recognize that until relatively recently in the history of Christianity, women and persons of color in North America were by and large deprived of the specialized formal education and the professional opportunities ordinarily needed to write and publish these kinds of theological works.[12] "We must admit," writes Anthony Carter, "that American theology has lacked cultural or racial diversity and has been the poorer for it."[13] This should be borne in mind as the theologies presented here are described and assessed.

Furthermore, the historical and theological descriptions of the traditions explored here give particular attention to the early history and the eventual North American expressions of these traditions.[14] Each of the traditions has a rich history, the most recent of which (the history of Pentecostalism) extends for over one hundred years. These histories brim with interesting people, events, movements and ideas—and these are only the ones that historians have recovered to date. Thus, the development and dissemination of a tradition is best understood in conjunction with a comprehensive and contextually informed history of the tradition. For example, some knowledge of the violent Russian revolution in the first quarter of the twentieth century combined with an understanding of the historically agrarian character of the Mennonite movement can shed light on why and how Mennonite colonies came to be established in Argentina. More comprehensive history such as this is beyond the scope of this book. Additionally, as also suggested by this Mennonite example, each of the traditions explored here has been carried to many places around the world. Some Christians are surprised to find that there are Anglicans in Singapore, or large Baptist churches in Russia, or the aforementioned Mennonite communities in Argentina. Yet the fact is that each of the traditions represented in this book is found on every continent, and in an increasing number of cases denominations within these traditions are now numerically larger outside the Euro-American arena. Although the historical and theological surveys in the chapters here can be neither geographically nor chronologically comprehensive, the tradition-specific bibliography at the end of each chapter directs the reader to resources that can help with a more historically and geographically comprehensive introduction.

Finally, we should note the rationale for the particular threefold structure employed here. This structure—history, method, theology—is employed not only because it offers a representative description of each tradition, but also because it serves to highlight a coherence that exists within traditions. Once one knows about (1) the historical origins and development of a tradition and (2) the role and method of theology in that tradition, then (3) characteristic theological beliefs of the tradition often make perfect sense. By "make perfect sense" I do not mean to suggest that the validity or truthfulness of the theological beliefs is logically proven, but rather that whether or not one agrees with a tradition, one can readily understand how and why someone within a particular tradition can hold beliefs and engage in practices that might seem strange or wrong to those outside that tradition. The theological beliefs that characterize a tradition are conclusions that one could readily expect, given the particular historical background and methodological approach of the tradition. This is not to suggest some kind of theological determinism whereby any particular group of Christians, given their history and method, have no choice but to believe as they do. It is, however, to suggest that there is an internal coherence in the traditions presented here—an existential or phenomenological coherence. This combination of historical development, theological method and characteristic beliefs goes a long way toward elucidating the content and character of Christian traditions.

"Classical" Traditions of Theology

As we have noted, each tradition is marked by both unity and diversity. The unity, consisting in commonalities shared in historical continuity, is what primarily gives identity to the tradition. The diversity, usually consisting in either long-held differences or diversifying developmental changes, can pose a challenge—sometimes real, sometimes only perceived—to that identity. This *combination of both unity and diversity* is one of the characteristics that distinguish genuinely Christian traditions from cultic distortions of Christianity. One of the marks of a cult is enforced conformity and lack of diversity; one of the marks of authentic Christianity is genuine diversity (see 1 Cor 12:4-26). Recognition of this diversity informs the chapters that follow. The story of the history of each tradition, told in the first section of each chapter, reflects some of the diversities that have developed within each tradition. In noting this diversity there is a recognition that, for example, Reformed Christians do not agree on everything, nor do Dispensationalists. And the same must be said for each of the traditions. This past and present diversity serves as a caution against making generalized statements that, for example, all Wesleyans or all Pentecostals hold to a particular belief.

At the same time, there is unity within the traditions such that they do exist as identifiable schools of Christian belief. There are denominations, churches, organizations and publications that bear descriptors in their names such as "Lutheran" or "Reformed" or "Anglican." There are commonalities and continuities that can be identified, and these are most readily observable in what can be referred to as "classical" expressions of the traditions. These classical expressions will be in focus in the second and third sections of each chapter, dealing with the approach to theology and characteristic doctrines.

Patrick Henry rightly cautions that the designation "classical" can become a synonym for "what I like best."[15] Harold T. Lewis, an African American writing from within the Anglican tradition, asks, "Who determines . . . what should be classified as a Christian classic? If the sermons of Donne and Andrews, why not the sermons of Absalom Jones or George Freeman Bragg? If the writings of Calvin, why not the writings of Martin Luther King?"[16] There is a tendency for one's personal preferences or biases to dictate what one recognizes as a standard. Furthermore, no clear scholarly consensus exists as to what the terms "classic" and "classical" mean with respect to theology. Consequently, it will be helpful here to make explicit the understanding of "classical" that guided the selection of material for inclusion in the sections on the approach to theology and characteristic doctrines of the traditions.

First, classical expressions of theological traditions are characterized by a continuity that extends back to the origins and early expressions of the tradition. Just as all traditions are marked by a combination of unity and diversity, so too the historical path of all traditions consists of a combination of continuity and change. Change is an inevitable part of the church's earthly existence, and over the course of time theological traditions change. Classical theological traditions are not static. They undergo change. Complex theological constructions are elaborated and informed by new contexts, challenges and ideas. At the same time, a classical expression of a theological tradition also will be marked by significant continuity.[17] This is inherent in the notion of tradition—a handing-on from one to another. And, continuity is also inherent in the notion of the classical. It refers to something that has been held in high regard by many people over an extended period of time.[18] Thus, in combination with change, there is a substantial sameness, a substantial constancy. There is continuity. This does not mean that consistent or unbroken historical development always exists, but whenever and wherever classical theological expressions occur, they are recognizably related to a defining theological tradition of the past. This continuity extends back to the earliest expressions of the tradition as identified by those who stand within the tradition. A tradition per se is as old as its earliest proponents— it is neither older nor younger. Continuity with "the founders" of a tradition, as identified by those who stand within it, does not constitute a proof of the truthfulness of the tradition's beliefs, but it does constitute a key component of identity. If one claims certain persons, events, documents or ideas as marking the beginning of a tradition, then a classical expression of that tradition will bear a substantial resemblance to those persons, events, documents or ideas. It would be rather odd for a theological belief that categorically contradicts defining beliefs of, for example, Luther and Melanchthon to be described as embodying classical Lutheran theology, or for a school of thought that overturns John Wesley's foundational teachings regarding the Christian life to be referred to as an example of classical Wesleyan theology. Classical expressions of theological traditions are identified with the early expressions that have proved over time to be formative and, to varying degrees, determinative for that tradition.

Second, the continuity in classical expressions of theological traditions is primarily one of substance, and secondarily one of aim and form. Marva Dawn suggests, "The faith always needs to be rethought in each age and modified in some particulars, but not in essence."[19] Some scholars suggest that continuity and change in Christian thought should be analyzed in terms of the degree to which change or development is congruent with the "aim" or "goal" of an earlier set of beliefs.[20] By this criterion, the substance of belief (*what* is believed) can change as long as the guiding intent of the belief (*how* and/or *why* it is believed) is congruent with the intent of the earlier belief. However, the understanding of theological continuity that informs the chapters that follow has to do with the substance of what is believed. Thus, from the perspective of the contemporary classical expression of the tradition, fundamental theological beliefs that characterized the early expressions of the tradition are substantially, abidingly true. They are not of "mere" historical interest. The substance of what was believed significantly corresponds to what is believed today, and vice versa.[21]

Third, classical expressions of theological traditions may articulate what is currently "a minority view."[22] Classical theological traditions are not constituted by a contemporary majority vote. In the historical development of a tradition it is possible that a classical expression may have occupied "minority" status within the tradition. As indicated above, "classical" as used here refers to a continuity of substance going back to the earliest manifestations of the tradition. Such a view may or may not be the "majority" position today.

In accord with this working understanding of the term *classical,* the descriptions and analyses that follow are contemporary, although no attempt is made here to describe all of the changes or to analyze all of the exploratory proposals being considered in each tradition. Certainly, significant changes have been and are being explored in the traditions, as indicated by the "identity crises" noted above. However, the fact that such changes are being talked about in this way is itself indicative of the fact that there *are* identities to be challenged. The histories and approaches to theology recounted here continue to shape today the traditions to which they belong. The doctrinal beliefs described here continue to constitute within each tradition, at the least, reference points for interacting with and assessing new proposals and developments within each tradition.

Purpose and Agenda
This book is intended to help people who do not identify themselves as Chris-

tians to better understand Christianity through studying major theological traditions within one of Christianity's main streams—Protestantism. It is also intended to help Christians better understand and appreciate the theological and ecclesiastical traditions through which many other Christians pursue life in Christ. Such understanding and appreciation strengthens the church. This strengthening need not be equated with "converting" to one of the traditions described here, nor does it come about through well-intended but misguided attempts to ignore or do away with multiple and diverse traditions. Rather, the body of Christ is strengthened through increased mutual learning, charity and cooperation among Christians. It is strengthened through continuing to develop a more complete apprehension of the truth through learning the truth set forth in other traditions. These virtues can be substantially increased through better understanding and appreciation of traditions different from one's own. (And, whether recognized or not, each Christian *does* stand within some tradition.) Thus, the following chapters are primarily descriptive and affirmative rather than polemical or defensive. They are an exercise in theological hospitality.[23]

I have made every attempt to present the history, theological method and selected beliefs of the traditions in a way that accurately represents them as understood by people who stand within these traditions. With only a few exceptions, the sources cited here are primary sources—that is, sources written by people who stand within the tradition being considered. No attempt is made either to present critiques of a tradition by those who stand outside that tradition or to anticipate and respond to such external critiques on behalf of a tradition. Rather, each tradition is presented in such a way that it might stand on its own before the reader. Of course, reading alone does not fully introduce one to a religious or theological tradition, and readers are encouraged to follow up reading this book by personally engaging with people and churches that stand within the traditions considered here.

In light of this agenda and the spirit of theological hospitality it encourages, it is fair and fitting for me to identify at the outset my own theological location. The church in which I had the privilege of being nurtured from the cradle through my twenties, a congregation of the Evangelical Free Church of America, was one of those that did not explicitly claim identification with any particular theological tradition, claiming, rather, to be a church "for all believers, but believers only." In conjunction with a teaching appointment following graduate school, my wife and I fellowshiped and served for ten years in the context of a denomination that shares some ecclesiastical affinities with Presbyterianism and some theological affinities with Charismatic and Holiness traditions: the Christian and Missionary Alliance. Throughout this sojourn, including my formal education, I have always been appreciative of and drawn to the Reformed tradition, and for some years now we have been members of congregations in the Evangelical Presbyterian Church. We are thankful for and deeply appreciative of our church home.

To the Reader

Some readers come to this book possessing a clear sense of identification with a particular Christian tradition, whether or not it is among the traditions considered here. I hope that these readers will be both deepened in their commitment to their own tradition through a comparison with other traditions and enriched in their faith through an increased understanding of and appreciation for other traditions. Other readers do not come with this clear sense of identification. Increasingly, Protestant Christians in North America do not have a clear or strong sense of identification with a particular Christian tradition, and many are quite cynical about the very notion of "tradition" or identifying with a particular ecclesiastical heritage.[24] I hope that these readers will both cultivate an increased appreciation for the potential value of "tradition" and be deepened and enriched in Christian faith by the diversity of beliefs and practices represented in the traditions discussed here. (Perhaps some of these readers will even take particular interest in and further explore one of these traditions.) Thus, all readers are encouraged to look for lessons that might be learned from these traditions with respect to Christian faith and life.

Some of these lessons will involve dissent, while others will take the form of assent. Lessons of dissent reflect the spirit of George Santayana's well-worn, yet nonetheless wise, adage that those who are ignorant of history are doomed to repeat it. Thoughtful study can clarify through leading one to identify beliefs and practices that one will *not* accept, and each reader will find in the chapters that follow beliefs and practices that they do not accept. Thus, it is important to ask questions such as, "What beliefs or practices in this tradition are erroneous and, if embraced, harmful?" At the same time, there are affirmative lessons to be learned. This follows the way of the humble recognition that all traditions of Christianity contain an admixture of truth and error, of wisdom and weakness. The fact that one's own theology or tradition contains some error and weakness means that each of us has room to grow, gaps to fill and lessons of assent to learn. And, the fact that other traditions contain some truth and wisdom means that potentially we can grow, fill gaps and learn constructive lessons from them. Thus, in studying other traditions, one should also ask, "What beliefs or practices are true and, if embraced, would enrich Christian faith and life?"

Each tradition bears the potential for both types of lessons—lessons of dissent and lessons of assent. Both types of questions should be asked of each tradition. Without denying the need to stay critically alert for lessons of dissent, I encourage all readers to be humbly receptive to lessons of assent. (In the epilogue I describe some of the lessons I have learned, lessons of both dissent and assent.) Each of the traditions presented here has made and is making enriching contributions to the body of Christ, to the lives of individual Christians and the lives of Christian communities. Resources that contribute to the enrichment of all Christians can be found in each tradition.

Most of the creeds and confessions cited in the chapters that follow are available from multiple sources, both hardcopy and online digital. For each citation here, reference is made to a standard hardcopy source. Some of these sources are books published by or under the auspices of ecclesiastical denominations. When such a source is not used, reference is made to a readily available collection of creeds and confessions, J. Gordon Melton, ed., *The Encyclopedia of American Religions: Religious Creeds,* 2 vols. (Detroit: Gale Research, 1988-1994). References to articles or sections of confessional documents guide the reader regardless of the particular form in which a document is consulted; references to page numbers direct the reader in the specific hardcopy source cited.

FOR FURTHER STUDY

Reference Works
Atwood, Craig D., Frank S. Mead and Samuel S. Hill. *Handbook of Denominations in the United States.* 12th ed. Nashville: Abingdon, 2005.

Melton, J. Gordon, ed. *Encyclopedia of American Religions.* 7th ed. Detroit: Gale Research, 2003.

Collections of Primary Source Documents
Melton, J. Gordon, ed. *The Encyclopedia of American Religions: Religious Creeds.* 2 vols. Detroit: Gale Research, 1988-1994.

Pelikan, Jaroslav, and Valerie Hotchkiss, eds. *Creeds and Confessions of Faith in the Christian Tradition.* 3 vols. New Haven: Yale University Press, 2003.

Williamson, William B., ed. *An Encyclopedia of Religions in the United States: One Hundred Religious Groups Speak for Themselves.* New York: Crossroad, 1992.

Survey
Campbell, Ted A. *Christian Confessions: A Historical Introduction.* Louisville: Westminster John Knox, 1996.

On Tradition and Traditions

Congar, Yves M.-J. *Tradition and Traditions: An Historical Essay and a Theological Essay,* translated by Michael Naseby and Thomas Rainborough. New York: Macmillan, 1966.

Pelikan, Jaroslav. *Credo: Historical and Theological Guide to Creeds and Confessions of Faith in the Christian Tradition.* New Haven: Yale University Press, 2003.

Roozen, David A., and James Nieman, eds. *Church, Identity, and Change: Theology and Denominational Structures in Unsettled Times.* Grand Rapids: Eerdmans, 2005.

Williams, Daniel H. *Retrieving the Tradition and Renewing Evangelicalism: A Primer for Suspicious Protestants.* Grand Rapids: Eerdmans, 1999.

2 ■ A Gospel of Grace

Lutheran Theology

In the Lutheran self-understanding . . . the Reformation has been from the beginning essentially a matter of the true preaching of the gospel and the right administration of the sacraments.

Carl Braaten, *Principles of Lutheran Theology*

Plainly . . . both the Bible and Confessions wish to stress the triumph of God's love in the Gospel.

Horace Hummel,
"Are Law and Gospel a Valid Hermeneutical Principle?"

Lutheranism has never embraced a "decision theology" where conversion is quick and certain and fueled by enthusiasm. Good things take a long time. . . . It takes an entire life to figure out how to respond to God's grace.

David Morgan, in *The Lutheran Reader*

When our two daughters were six and nine years old, our family enjoyed a wonderful sabbatical in Minnesota for the academic year. Each of us pursued an agenda for the year: the girls attended school and made new friends, Nancy audited graduate school courses, and I worked on research and writing. We wanted to engage together the geography, culture and religious heritage of our temporary home. We were particularly interested in experiencing a church tradition different from our own, and the first Lutheran church that we visited gave us a warm welcome. Sunday morning worship services were enriching, and our children participated in Sunday school. Among the memorable events of those Sunday mornings was a baptismal service. At the invitation of the minister, the parents carried their infant daughter to the front of the sanctuary, where the child's godparents joined them. There the minister delivered words of instruction and asked them questions about their understanding of what was about to take place and about their commitment to raising this child in the ways of Christ and his church. They responded affirmatively. Then the minister took the baby in his arms and instructed the parents and godparents to gather around the baptismal font, prominently located near the altar. He said a prayer of blessing and then three times dipped his hand into the font and poured water onto the forehead of the little girl, baptizing her "in the name of the Father and the Son and Holy Spirit. Amen." After gently dabbing the water from the baptized baby's face, he gently lifted the child into the air, walked up and down the aisles of the sanctuary, and, with a look of pleasant assurance of God's gracious work, invited the congregation to "welcome our newest member."

Context: Historical and Ecclesiastical Background

Historical origins and development. Observers have identified three different events as possible starting points for Lutheranism: the posting of ninety-five theses by Martin Luther (1483-1546) on the door of the University of Wittenberg chapel, on October 31, 1517; Luther's "tower experience," sometime between 1514 and 1518; and the ratification of the Augsburg Confession in 1530. Whichever event one chooses, Luther is viewed as the originating figure, and his theological thought, particularly as developed by his close associate Philipp Melanchthon (1497-1560), is regarded as the origin of distinctively Lutheran ideas.[1] One of the differences between Lutherans and most other Protestants is that the latter believe that although Luther may have started well in his challenges to the Roman Catholic Church of his day, he did not bring the job to completion; Lutherans, on the other hand, think that fundamentally Luther got it right.

The occasion for Luther's initial confrontations with the church was the selling of indulgences, but this disagreement was not at the heart of his dissent. Over time it became evident that Luther's disagreements with the church revolved around more fundamental concerns: his understanding of salvation and the Christian life, and his understanding of the authority of Scripture. In the preface to his commentary on the book of Galatians, Luther writes, "If the doctrine of justification is lost, the whole of Christian doctrine is lost."[2] And, he tenaciously held to this belief because he understood it to be the teaching of the written Word of God, the Bible.

It is important to observe the ecclesiastical context from which Luther and subsequent Protestant Reformers arose. Lutheran historian Eric Gritsch offers this description of the Roman Catholic Church in the early sixteenth century:

The papacy now demanded greater obedience from both clergy and laity; the distance between church leaders and the people widened. The laity sank into a mire of superstition, often fueled by fear of punishment after death. The sacrament of penance became the principle tool by which the hierarchy ruled. . . . Life was based on the "if-then" condition: if I do such and such for God—that is, for the church— then I will endure less punishment, both now and after death, for sins I commit.[3]

It was in this context that Luther and those who embraced his new theology "sought to rebuild their lives by renewed attention to Christianity's constituting message, the 'gospel.'"[4] For Luther, the gospel was the offer of justification by grace through faith alone. He did not arrive hastily at this conclusion. With his parents wanting him to become a lawyer, Luther received a solid, traditional education, completing his bachelor's degree in 1502. He completed a master's degree in 1505 and proceeded to law school at the University of Erfurt. However, while traveling to Erfurt in July of that year, he became terrified by a violent storm and vowed to become a monk. Several weeks later, he entered a monastery of the Hermits of St. Augustine at Erfurt. Although Luther embraced the practices of monastic life, the spiritual fear and anxiety that troubled him before continued unabated. In time, what he described as *Anfechtung,* or oppressive despair, increased. He was terrorized by the unrelenting sense that he could never adequately satisfy the demands of divine righteousness, nor that he could know that he was acceptable to God. As a result of following the guidance of Johannes von Staupitz (1460-1524), who oversaw the Augustinians in Saxony, and an in-depth study of Scripture, particularly the book of Romans,[5] Luther concluded that "faith alone makes a person righteous and fulfills the law. For out of the merit of Christ, [faith] brings forth the Spirit."[6]

Luther debated Johannes Eck (1486-1543), representative of the Roman Catholic Church, at Leipzig in 1519. By the time these debates were completed, the differences between Luther and Rome clearly were irreconcilable. The pope ordered Luther to recant many of his views. In December of 1520, Luther joined others in a protest at Wittenberg, burning the papal disciplinary documents issued to him as well as other Roman Catholic writings. Less than four weeks later, Luther learned of his condemnation as a heretic, and that he was no longer recognized as priest or professor. His books were slated for destruction, and his followers were told to recant the views they had embraced through Luther. These events proved to be seminal not only for Lutheranism, but also for much of the larger phenomenon that we know as Protestantism.

As for Lutheran theology, the debates and controversies of the decade following Luther's excommunication culminated in two catechisms that Luther published in 1529, and in the Confession of Faith resulting from the Diet of

Augsburg in July 1530. Next to the Bible, Luther's Small Catechism, originally intended for children, and the Augsburg Confession are today the two most widely recognized and authoritative sources among Lutherans worldwide.[7] Nonetheless, in the decades following 1530 the Lutheran movement was troubled by serious and heated intramural controversies over the interpretation and theological implications of the Augsburg Confession, and by the end of the sixteenth century three groups vied to guide the movement: the Gnesio-Lutherans, who viewed themselves as preserving the pure teachings of Luther[8]; the Philippists, who followed the more conciliatory lead of Philipp Melanchthon; and a moderating group between these two, led by Martin Chemnitz (1522-1586).[9] Differences among these groups were expressed and elaborated in a series of theological controversies.

The Antinomian controversy dealt with what role, if any, Old Testament law should play in the lives of New Testament Christians. Luther and Melanchthon affirmed that there is a place for the law; John Agricola (1494-1566) denied this. The Adiaphorist controversy dealt with the identification of what could and could not be regarded as "adiaphora"—that is, matters that are not essential to salvation and that, as such, are matters concerning which there should be a considerable measure of freedom. For example, Melanchthon and the Philippists asserted that liturgical ceremonies and ecclesiastical structures were largely adiaphora, and therefore some "Roman" practices could be followed. Matthias Flacius (1520-1575) and the Gnesio-Lutherans rejected this view as a capitulation to Rome. The Osiandrian controversy was prompted by Andrew Osiander's (1498-1552) view of justification as "the indwelling of Christ's essential nature" in the Christian, in contrast with the Gnesio-Lutheran view that salvation results from "the forensic application of Christ's righteousness" grasped through faith and obedience.[10] The Majoristic controversy pitted the view of George Major (1502-1574), who maintained that as a complement to faith, good works are necessary for salvation, against the view of Nicholas von Amsdorf (1483-1565) and Matthias Flacius, both Gnesio-Lutherans, who asserted that good works are harmful to salvation. In the Crypto-Calvinist controversy, Albert Hardenberg (1510-1574), a Philippist, was accused by John Timann (1500-1557), a Gnesio-Lutheran, of denying the "real presence" of Christ in the Lord's Supper. Because Melanchthon remained largely uninvolved in this controversy, he was accused of being a crypto-Calvinist—that is, secretly holding a Calvinistic view of the Lord's Supper that did not affirm real presence in a Lutheran sense. Finally, manifesting "all the basic features of future Lutheran academic infighting," the Synergistic controversy debated the relationship between divine providence and human freedom, with the Gnesio-Lutherans accusing the Philippists of giving too much credence to human ability as it pertains to salvation.[11]

Precipitated most immediately by the Synergistic controversy and drafted under the leadership of Chemnitz, the Formula of Concord addresses all the major issues raised in these six controversies, as well as several others. The Formula was set forth in 1577 as a "Final Restatement and Explanation of a Number of Articles of the Augsburg Confession on Which Controversy Has Arisen for a Time."[12] As such, this document helped preserve unity within the Lutheran movement and marked the passage toward Lutheran orthodoxy.[13] Three years later it was included along with all other foundational Lutheran confessional documents in *The Book of Concord*. This book, also known as *Concordia,* contains the three ecumenical creeds (Apostles', Nicene, Athanasian), the Augsburg Confession (1530), Melanchthon's Apology of the Augsburg Confession (1531), Luther's Smalcald Articles (1537), Melanchthon's *Treatise on the Power and Primacy of the Pope* (1537), Luther's Small Catechism (1529) and Large Catechism (1529), and the Formula of Concord (1577). Gathered together in *The Book of Concord* in 1580, and acknowledged by both civil authorities and many theologians, these documents constituted the confessions of the Lutheran church near the end of the sixteenth century.

The seventeenth century saw the emergence of Lutheran "orthodoxy" or "scholasticism." The scholastic dogmatic theologians sought to preserve and advance Lutheranism's doctrinal gains of the sixteenth century in elaborate, rationally sophisticated theological works. Martin Chemnitz responded to the Roman Catholic Church's Council of Trent in his *Examination of the Council of Trent.* Johann Gerhard (1582-1637), bishop of Coburg and professor at the University of Jena, published a comprehensive nine-volume *Loci Theologici,* and the theologian Abraham Calov (1612-1686) wrote a twelve-volume *Systema Locorum Theologicorum.* In these and similar works correct Lutheran teaching was set forth against erroneous teaching in Roman Catholicism, in other Protestant traditions (particularly Calvinism and Arminianism), and within Lutheranism itself (notably Syncretism). In the latter part of the seventeenth century, Pietism emerged in reaction to this rationally oriented scholasticism. The Pietists also reacted against the combative spirit of the scholastic's debates and the carnage of the Thirty Years' War (1618-1648) between Protestants and Roman Catholics. Under the successive leadership of Philip Spener (1635-1705), August Franke (1663-1727) and Ludwig von Zinzendorf (1700-1760), Pietism called upon Lutherans to be less concerned with doctrinal details and more concerned with living the Christian life, less concerned with winning theological battles and more concerned with studying the Bible and demonstrating Christian charity. In sum, Pietism pursued a Lutheranism with a little less head and much more heart.

In the eighteenth century, some Lutheran scholars in Europe embraced the principles of the Enlightenment, and others followed Friedrich Schleiermacher (1768-1834). For the most part, however, European Lutherans remained solidly anchored in either the confessional assertions of Lutheran orthodoxy or the spiritual fervor of Pietism. Eric Gritsch observes, "Most pastors taught either 'pure doctrine' or propagated the conversion of the individual to a more obviously Christian life by way of a 'rebirth.'"[14] Nineteenth-century Lutheranism in Europe came to reflect theological forces emanating from German universities. Theories of historical development, practices of historical criticism, and emphasis on personal experience began to shape European Lutheran theology. The so-called Erlangen school, under the leadership of Johann von Hofmann (1810-1877), resisted some of these influences and continued to uphold the inspiration of Scripture and the abiding authority of the Lutheran Confessions.[15]

Lutherans began immigrating to America in 1623. Most of the earliest immigrants were from the Netherlands and Sweden, and they tended to settle along the Hudson and Delaware Rivers and in Pennsylvania. Unlike some who came largely to escape religious persecution (e.g., many Anabaptists and Baptists), these early Lutherans came from lands where Lutheranism was favored, and they came to America primarily to realize hopes for growth and prosperity.[16] Immigrants formed the first Lutheran congregation in America in 1649 in New Amsterdam (the location of present-day New York City), but a century passed before Lutheranism became firmly established in the United States. The substantive establishment of Lutheranism during the eighteenth century was primarily due to the number and dispersion of Lutheran immigrants, largely from Germany, and the work of Henry Melchior Muhlenberg (1711-1787). Between 1727 and 1775, more than sixty-five thousand Germans, Swedes and Austrians, the majority of whom were Lutheran, entered the United States through Philadelphia. Many settled in Pennsylvania, while many others moved on to Maryland, Virginia, North Carolina and Georgia.[17] In 1748, Lutherans formed the first Lutheran synod in America, the Ministerium of Pennsylvania. The synod included pastors and churches from New Jersey, New York, Maryland and Pennsylvania. The primary agent in bringing this to pass was Henry Muhlenberg, sometimes referred to as "the Patriarch of the Lutheran Church in America."[18]

Muhlenberg was well suited by both skills and outlook to serve as a founding leader of Lutheranism in America. He arrived from Germany in 1742, and his motto was *ecclesia plantanda,* "the church must be planted." For him this entailed the Lutheran church in America being independent of ties to the "Old World."[19] Largely due to this pastor's energetic leadership and brokering of controversies, by the end of the eighteenth century Lutherans in America had "become American Lutherans."[20] Furthermore, Muhlenberg embodied in his own person a blend of "orthodoxy and Pietism," a combination that continues to shape American Lutheranism today.[21] This blend was important because "part of the Lutheran immigration luggage included the continental controversies between the 'orthodoxists' (strict adherents to the Lutheran Confessions) and the Pietists, who stressed the born-again experience over 'pure doctrine.'"[22] Because of his own appreciation for and reservations about both impulses, he was able to work with persons and churches across the spectrum of early American Lutheranism.

Throughout the eighteenth century, many Lutherans in America "gradually drifted away from their confessional moorings," and this process of cutting European ties continued into the nineteenth century.[23] This drift was in part the result of the migration of German and Scandinavian Lutherans to southern and western regions of the United States, where it was more difficult to maintain links with the Old World, and by the formation of the General Synod of Lutheran churches in 1820.[24] With this latter event, "the last real bonds with Europe began to break, and American Lutheranism was increasingly on its own."[25] This breaking away included a certain theological independence, as the constituting documents of the General Synod did not include a specific confessional basis.[26] Yet, although the ties to Europe continued to be broken, the power of ethnic loyalties remained. Immigrants continued to pour into America, and synods generally were "formed along ethnic lines."[27] The pattern of ethnic distinction included the first and only African American synod, the Alpha Synod of the Evangelical Lutheran Church of Freedmen in America, which was established in May 1889 but "died" in 1891.[28]

During the middle of the nineteenth century, theological evolution continued such that by 1875, "the confessional movement was in full swing in American Lutheranism, and the theological climate supported a conservative and traditional point of view."[29] Foremost in contributing to this climate was the work of C. F. W. Walther (1811-1887) and the influence of the Lutheran Church—Missouri Synod. Walther emigrated from Saxony, Germany, in 1839, and more than anyone else he was responsible for the formation of the Missouri Synod and its staunchly conservative and aggressively confessional character. Abdel Wentz describes the founders of the Synod as "imbued with a double portion of the spirit of confessionalism," having a "fiery zeal for the whole body of Lutheran doctrine . . . made even more intense by the ardor of their piety."[30] Walther served as the founding president of the Missouri Synod (1847-1850, and 1864-1878) and also as president of the Synod's seminary, Concordia Seminary, St. Louis (1854-1887). He was succeeded as president of Concordia by Franz O.

Pieper (1852-1931; president, 1887-1931), who published a three-volume work in German that became the standard theological textbook of American confessional Lutheranism: *Christlich Dogmatik* (1917-1924).[31] Many theological controversies arose in the latter half of the nineteenth century, including battles over historical-critical methods of studying the Bible, evolutionary theory and predestination. The specifically Lutheran dimensions of the controversies entailed issues such as the extent to which the *Book of Concord* was authoritative, and which confessional documents were most authoritative. For example, Lutherans of Finnish and Swedish origins tended to embrace the *Book of Concord* in its entirety, while those of Danish and Norwegian origins embraced the creeds, the Augsburg Confession and Luther's Small Catechism. Those of German origin made a point of affirming both the entire *Book of Concord* and the Bible.[32] These controversies pitted the "Neo-Lutherans" or "American Lutherans," who increasingly sought to adapt Lutheranism to the American religious context, against the "Old Lutherans" or "Confessional Lutherans," who stringently maintained fidelity to the Lutheran Confessions of European origin.[33] To a significant degree, "the history of Lutheranism in America is the history of its interpretation of the Lutheran Confessions."[34]

These theological debates entailed controversies concerning the character and identity of Lutheranism,[35] and such debates were going on in other parts of the world. Throughout the early part of the twentieth century, the identity of Lutheranism was a focal point of a series of Lutheran World Conventions convened in Europe beginning in 1923. These were succeeded by the formation in Sweden in 1947 of the Lutheran World Federation. The Federation, a free and voluntary association, affirmed the Bible as the source of and norm for teaching and practice, and the Lutheran confessions, with special attention to the Augsburg Confession and Luther's Small Catechism, as setting forth the proper interpretation of the Bible.[36]

Lutheranism in America in the twentieth century was characterized by moves toward denominational unification.[37] Historic ethnic ties, including linguistic ones, became less and less powerful, and the spirit of consolidation led to many mergers. Some of the denominations formed by these mergers were the National Lutheran Church (1918), the American Lutheran Church (1930), the Lutheran Church in America (1962), the Evangelical Lutheran Church in Canada (1968) and the Evangelical Lutheran Church of America (1988). Another factor in some of the more recent mergers has been declining membership. Yet, even the pattern of many of the mergers betrays the fact that the old divisions between Neo-Lutherans and Old Lutherans continued, and many of the most hotly debated theological issues echoed the debates of the nineteenth century: experience as a source for theology, critical study of the Bible, evolution.[38] In addition to these particular theological issues, from the 1930s onward, theological debate within Lutheranism has often revolved around "varying definitions of confessional unity" within Lutheranism itself.[39] The question is, "Does confessional unity require theological uniformity?"[40] Neo-Lutherans say no, while Old Lutherans say yes. These fundamental theological differences continue into the present, and they are embodied denominationally in the two largest Lutheran denominations in America: the Evangelical Lutheran Church in America (ELCA) and the Lutheran Church—Missouri Synod (LCMS).

Diversity. "Although Lutherans share a common confessional heritage," writes Charles Arand, "they have not always agreed about what fidelity to their symbolical writings means."[41] Missouri Synod scholar David P. Scaer observes, "Quite clearly any unanimity in Lutheran theology that might have been evident in the sixteenth-century confessions, and then in the classical dogmatics of the sixteenth and the seventeenth centuries, is lacking today."[42] Lutheran theologian Carl Braaten comments, "Pluralism, like specialization, is one of the telling features of present-day theology. Among Lutherans alone we have almost every kind of modern label: Erlangen, Lundensian, eschatological, process, existentialist, hermeneutical, language analysis, secular, liberation, feminist, and what not."[43] There is little question that a substantial, sometimes troubling, diversity has developed within Lutheran theology. Lutheran theologians as different as Scaer and Braaten agree on this fact. However, they just as clearly disagree in their respective assessments of this diversity. From Scaer's perspective, a variety of forces in the modern era—from Pietism and Rationalism, to the denial of the inspiration of Scripture and a "formal" rather than "real" affirmation of the Lutheran Confessions—have "devastated the classical Reformation Lutheran understanding of theology."[44] By contrast, Braaten celebrates the "creative efforts of Lutheran theologians" that "have contributed to a positive correlation of Christianity with the modern world since the Enlightenment."[45]

George Lindbeck describes two different approaches to the Lutheran confessional heritage.[46] One approach views documents such as the Augsburg Confession as providing "a precedent." The confessions are not binding, but they do provide guidance. The other approach views the confessional documents as "constitutive." They declare abiding truths and solicit allegiance. Samuel Nafzger, writing from a Missouri Synod perspective, suggests that major doctrinal differences within Lutheranism are ultimately rooted in "disagreement on the meaning of *sola scriptura.*"[47] A more complete understanding of theological differences within Lutheranism consists in acknowledging both Lindbeck's and Nafzger's analyses. Underlying most, if not all, of the significant theological di-

versities within Lutheranism are differing views of the authority and interpretation of Scripture and differing postures toward the Lutheran confessions. Furthermore, according to Lindbeck, "This conflict . . . is not likely to be resolved
in the foreseeable future. It reflects a cleavage between two comprehensive, coherent, and fundamentally irreconcilable construals of much the same range of
data."[48]

As we noted earlier, the two largest denominations are the ELCA and the
LCMS, which together represent more than 90 percent of Lutherans in America.
The ELCA was formed in 1988 by a merger of the American Lutheran Church
and the Lutheran Church in America. It pursues "a vision of inclusiveness"—
theological, cultural and gendered inclusiveness—within its understanding of
Lutheran confessionalism, and participates in the Lutheran World Federation,
the World Council of Churches and the National Council of Christian Churches.[49]
The LCMS is the oldest continually existing Lutheran church body in America,
having been established in 1847. Rocked by theological controversies in the
1970s over the authority of Scripture and the ordination of women, the LCMS
continues to uphold an "Old Lutheran," conservative approach. It is a member
of the International Lutheran Conference (ILC). The ILC, formed in 1952 under
the leadership of the LCMS, provides "a sustained confessional fellowship and
. . . mutual supportiveness."[50] The third largest church body, though considerably smaller than the LCMS, is the Wisconsin Evangelical Lutheran Synod
(WELS). The WELS is similar to the LCMS in theology. The small percentage of
Lutherans who do not belong to one of these denominations belong to independent Lutheran church bodies, including the American Association of Lutheran
Churches, the Association of Free Lutheran Congregations and the Evangelical
Lutheran Synod.[51] The theology of most of these groups is of the more conser-
vatively confessional character.[52]

Approach: Theological and Hermeneutical Method

Role of theology. Theology is highly important to Lutherans. Theodore Bachmann suggests that the theological controversies woven into the history of Lutheranism show that "theology will have itself taken seriously, and not simply
taken for granted. . . . Lutheranism is not an organizational label but a faith-filled
life."[53] From Luther's Small Catechism and Large Catechism (1529), to Calov's
twelve-volume *Systema locorum theologicorum* (1655-1677), Heinrich Schmid's
Doctrinal Theology of the Evangelical Lutheran Church (ET, 1875),[54] Franz
Pieper's *Christian Dogmatics* (1950-1953), Carl E. Braaten and Robert W. Jenson's *Christian Dogmatics* (1984)[55] and the *Confessional Lutheran Dogmatics*
series (1989-),[56] Lutherans have considered it important to invest themselves in

THE LUTHERAN TRADITION

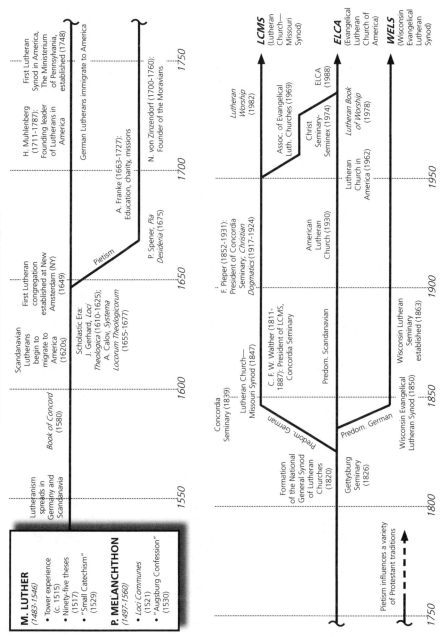

M. LUTHER
(1483-1546)
- Tower experience (c. 1515)
- Ninety-five theses (1517)
- "Small Catechism" (1529)

P. MELANCHTHON
(1497-1560)
- *Loci Communes* (1521)
- "Augsburg Confession" (1530)

Lutheranism spreads in Germany and Scandinavia

Book of Concord (1580)

Scandanavian Lutherans begin to migrate to America (1620s)

Scholastic Era: J. Gerhard, *Loci Theologica* (1610-1625); A. Calov, *Systema Locorum Theologicorum* (1655-1677)

First Lutheran congregation established at New Amsterdam (NY) (1649)

Pietism

P. Spener, *Pia Desideria* (1675)

H. Muhlenberg (1711-1787): Founding leader of Lutherans in America

German Lutherans immigrate to America

A. Franke (1663-1727): Education, charity, missions

N. von Zinzendorf (1700-1760): Founder of the Moravians

First Lutheran Synod in America, The Ministerium of Pennsylvania, established (1748)

1550   1600   1650   1700   1750

Pietism influences a variety of Protestant traditions

1750   1800   1850   1900   1950

Formation of the National General Synod of Lutheran Churches (1820)

Gettysburg Seminary (1826)

Concordia Seminary (1839)

Lutheran Church—Missouri Synod (1847)

Predom. German

C. F. W. Walther (1811-1887): President of LCMS, Concordia Seminary

Predom. Scandanavian

F. Pieper (1852-1931): President of Concordia Seminary; *Christian Dogmatics* (1917-1924)

American Lutheran Church (1930)

Lutheran Church in America (1962)

Assoc. of Evangelical Luth. Churches (1969)

Christ Seminary-Seminex (1974)

ELCA (1988)

Lutheran Worship (1982)

Lutheran Book of Worship (1978)

LCMS (Lutheran Church—Missouri Synod)

ELCA (Evangelical Lutheran Church of America)

Wisconsin Evangelical Lutheran Synod (1850)

Wisconsin Lutheran Seminary established (1863)

WELS (Wisconsin Evangelical Lutheran Synod)

rigorous, in-depth theological work. Yet, even the history of dogmatic and systematic theological work by theologians does not sufficiently communicate the depth of Lutheran regard for theology.

Samuel Nafzger observes, "Lutheran churches are creedal churches. . . . Lutherans define themselves not by organizational structures . . . or by rite or ceremony . . . but by written confessions of what they understand the Bible, which alone can determine doctrine, to teach."[57] Classical Lutheran theology is creedal and confessional theology.[58] Within a generation of Luther's posting of his ninety-five theses, all of the documents eventually brought together in *The Book of Concord* (1580) had been formulated, including the Augsburg Confession, the Apology of the Augsburg Confession, the Smalcald Articles and the Formula of Concord. Moreover, since *The Book of Concord* was first published, Lutherans have not left their confessional documents to gather dust, but have continuously studied and reflected upon them.[59] Wherever one stands within the varieties of Lutheran theology, the confessions are part of the definition of Lutheranism and the articulation of Lutheran theology.[60]

Much of the motivating force behind Lutheran investment in theological work emanates from taking truth seriously. As the title of an article by J. A. O. Preus III puts it, "Lutheran identity is insistence on truth."[61] Moreover, in Lutheran theology, theological truth is saving truth. The burden that propels Lutheran theology is soteriological. The "ultimate purpose of theology *(finis ultimus),"* writes Pieper, is *"salus aeterna"* (eternal salvation).[62] This being assured to one who has faith in Christ, theology is also to foster sanctification and good works. Thus, "the purpose of sacred theology is not academic or speculative, but intensely and absolutely practical *(habitus practicus)."*[63]

Theological method. The guiding principles of the Lutheran reformation are often identified as the formal principle and the material principle. The formal principle consists in the affirmation of Scripture as the supreme source and authority for theology; the material principle consists in the affirmation of justification by grace through faith. These principles are embodied in the *"solae"* of classical Lutheran theology: *sola scriptura, sola gratia, sola fide, solus Christus.*[64] The material principle will be considered in the third section of this chapter, but the formal principle of *sola scriptura* is a fitting place to begin a consideration of Lutheran theological method.

The Lutheran Confessions do not contain articles that explicitly affirm *sola scriptura.* However, such an affirmation is clearly, according to Carl Braaten, "presupposed and applied."[65] In *Theology of the Lutheran Confessions,* Edmund Schlink writes, "The sole norm for dogmatics is the Holy Scripture of the Old and New Testaments. All dogmatic statements must be derived from God's revelation in his Word."[66] Similarly, the Brief Statement of the Doctrinal Position of the Missouri Synod (1932) affirms Scripture as "the sole source from which all doctrines proclaimed in the Christian Church must be taken and therefore, too, the sole rule and norm by which all teachers and doctrines must be examined and judged."[67] The fundamental reason for this confidence in the Bible is the belief that it is the written Word of God. Pieper writes, "Holy Scripture, in con-tradistinction to all other books in the world, is God's own infallible Word and therefore the only source and norm of Christian doctrine."[68] Again, the Missouri Synod's Brief Statement affirms that "the Holy Scriptures differ from all other books in the world in that they are the Word of God" (citing 2 Tim 3:16; 2 Pet 1:21; Jn 10:35; Rom 3:2; 1 Cor 2:13).[69]

This understanding of *sola scriptura* has implications for the roles given (or not given) to what some traditions regard as sources for theology: tradition, rea-son, experience. Henry Jacobs asks, "Is Christian experience . . . a standard for doctrine?" He answers, "Never."[70] For Pieper, employing religious experience as the starting point for theology is "ruinous and forbidden."[71] Scripture alone is the source of and standard for theology. As for reason, it may properly have an "instrumental" role, but not a "normative" one. When reason is kept subordinate to faith, "sanctified" and guided by the Holy Spirit, it can assist in formulating the relationship between various spiritual truths, but it is never to be regarded as the determining arbiter in matters of faith.[72] Thus, in classical Lutheran theol-ogy, "The *sola scriptura* principle means that in approaching the Scriptures the experience of the interpreter and the use of reason cannot be used against its plain meaning or sense. . . . The reason, experience, and even the common sense of the theologian are simply unacceptable as sources."[73]

Although the principle of *sola scriptura* excludes reason and experience as sources per se for theology, tradition and historical sources have a greater role to play. As we noted earlier, classical Lutheran theology is confessional theol-ogy. Thus, although Scaer rejects reason and experience as "simply unaccept-able sources," he allows that "historical precedents . . . may confirm or supple-ment the Scriptures as the sole source of theology."[74] Tradition in the form of the Lutheran Confessions plays a highly significant role in the doing of theology. In fact, the confessions constitute the proper starting point for theology. The first question the theologian asks is "What do the confessions say and mean?"[75] Al-though this may at first appear to subvert Scripture's role as sole source, it does not. Scripture is the source of and norm for all of theology. Scripture is author-itative because it is the written Word of God. The confessions, on the other hand, are authoritative because they expound the teaching of Scripture. The constitution of the Missouri Synod asserts that "all the symbolical Books of the

Evangelical Lutheran Church" are "a true and unadulterated statement and exposition of the Word of God."[76] Gassmann and Hendrix indicate that the confessions are "vehicles for handing on the gospel as the central message of Scripture," and Arand states that the confessions are normative by virtue of their claim to "restate in summary fashion the message and content of Scripture."[77] Thus, the authority of the confessions is derivative; it is derived from Scripture. And, by virtue of the confessions' faithfulness to Scripture, theology consists not only in "what the Scriptures teach and allow but also what can be demonstrated from the confessions."[78]

Establishing the confessions as the starting point for theology is also classical Lutheranism's foundation for biblical hermeneutics. That hermeneutic reflects a recognition of hermeneutics as a perspectival endeavor and a commitment to theology as a churchly endeavor. Schlink writes, "Since we live, hear, and pray in the church, we already have our continuous point of departure from the Confession, whether we do so in conscious clarity or in a temporally conditioned lack of clarity. None of us interprets Scripture as an individual but as a member of the church."[79] Everyone who reads Scripture comes to it with a particular perspective or frame of reference, and for classical Lutheran theology that frame of reference is the confessional heritage of the Lutheran church. The confessions provide the "chart and compass" for exegetical work.[80] They articulate the church's interpretation of Scripture, which then serves as a guide to proper interpretations and a guide away from improper interpretations.[81] Scripture retains its unique role as source and authority because the confessional heritage is subject to scrutiny and correction by Scripture. Theological statements are formulated and tested "against both the Scriptures and the Lutheran Confessions."[82] This view of the authority and function of the confessions leads some Lutherans to discount such an approach as "repristination confessionalism."[83] This "repristination" approach, it is suggested, views theology as simply repeating the theological formulations of the sixteenth century. Instead of "really listening to God's Word," the theologian is "imprisoned within an ecclesiastical monologue."[84] However, Scaer indicates that classical Lutheran theology does not require "blind submission" to the confessions, for "the first task of the Lutheran theologian is to test the Confessions" against the biblical documents.[85] Furthermore, there is the recognition that many theological issues not addressed by the confessions have arisen since the sixteenth century. Regarding such issues, classical Lutheran theology seeks to formulate responses that are logically derived from and consistent with the confessions.[86]

For Lutherans, "a non-confessional Christianity is a contradiction in terms"; theology is confessional theology.[87] The confessions constitute a doxology, giving praise and thanks to God for his work in Jesus Christ, proclaimed in the gospel. The confessions provide identification, communicating the beliefs and principles that guide the church. And, most important for theological method, the confessions provide a hermeneutical framework for interpreting Scripture, assessing faith claims and formulating a contemporary expression of the gospel message.[88]

In addition to the commitment to a confessional interpretive framework, several other principles are characteristic of classical Lutheran hermeneutics. One of these is a "literal" approach to interpretation.[89] The interpreter is to discern the "intended sense *(sensus literalis)*" or meaning "in the text" itself, taking into account the original historical setting. The reader is to seek the Bible's "ordinary, uncomplicated sense."[90] This literal approach is to be distinguished from a "literalistic" one, the latter failing sufficiently to take into consideration factors such as historical setting and literary genre.[91] Even so, the assumption is that texts are *not* to be interpreted figuratively or metaphorically unless there are "compelling reasons" to do so.[92] Consequently, as will be seen below, the Scripture passages most often cited as the basis for the Lutheran understanding of the Lord's Supper (Mt 26:26-28; Mk14:24; Lk 22:19-20) are to be interpreted "not as flowery, figurative, or metaphorical expressions, as they appear to our reason, but we [Lutherans] must accept them in simple faith and due obedience in their strict and clear sense, just as they read."[93] "This is my body" means "This *is* my body."

Another principle that guides classical Lutheran hermeneutics is application of the *analogia fidei* or "the rule of faith." The Missouri Synod's Brief Statement declares, "The 'rule of faith' *(analogia fidei)* according to which the Holy Scriptures are to be understood are the clear passages of *Scriptures themselves* which set forth the individual doctrines."[94] Simply put, Scripture interprets Scripture. The clearer passages guide the interpretation of less clear passages. Undergirding this principle is belief in the unity of Scripture, a "unity of authorship, content, and purpose."[95] That content and purpose is, above all, soteriological.[96] Thus, Harold Ditmanson writes, "The massive soteriological content and purpose of Scripture gives it a unity which dictates that in the act of listening the reader will respect the principle that Scripture interprets Scripture."[97]

This soteriological content and purpose are nowhere more clearly evident than in the canonical writings of the apostle Paul, and Pauline texts play a determinative role in the Lutheran application of the *analogia fidei* principle. In discussing some of the tensions between Pauline texts and the book of James with reference to justification by faith, one theologian states that Romans and Galatians would have interpretive priority over James by virtue of the fact that the former books deal with justification "professedly and in extended argu-

ment," and thereby they are "the norms whereby to judge mere incidental allu-
sions in other passages," in this case the book of James.[98] Gritsch states that the
doctrine of justification by faith, which is central to all of Lutheran theology, is
"oriented to an essentially Pauline appropriation of Israel's prophetic tradition."[99] Historically, Lutheran interpreters have viewed the unity of the Bible
"from a Pauline perspective, regarding Paul's exposition of justification as the
most profound theological reading of the gospel."[100] Thus, "for Lutherans, the
radical Pauline understanding of the grace of God is the central interpretive key
to the meaning of the whole."[101]

Furthermore, this grace of God is properly understood only in the context of
the distinction between law and gospel, a third principle that guides Lutheran
hermeneutics. The law-gospel distinction is central to Lutheran theology and
biblical hermeneutics. The Apology of the Augsburg Confession states, "All
Scripture should be divided into these two main topics: the law and the promises."[102] In accord with this model Pieper states, "Holy Scripture, the Word of
God, is divided into Law and Gospel. The theologian must teach both, without
curtailment or alteration," and the theologian also must always keep them "separate."[103] Citing the Apology of the Augsburg Confession, Horace Hummel says
that the law-gospel distinction, though not the only hermeneutical principle,
constitutes "a hermeneutical master key," an "indispensable" hermeneutical
principle.[104] The law-gospel distinction is essentially synonymous with what
Lutheran scholars also refer to as "the Gospel principle" or "the Christological
principle," which in turn are synonymous with the doctrine of justification by
grace through faith.[105] The law does not and cannot justify sinful persons, but
instead "always accuses and terrifies consciences." By contrast, the message of
the gospel is "the promise of the forgiveness of sins and justification on account
of Christ," obtained through faith alone.[106] That which is law must not be misread as gospel, and that which is gospel must not be misread as law. Maintaining this distinction, while also maintaining their interrelationship, is necessary if
the salvific message of the Scriptures—the message of the provision of justification by the gracious work of God in Christ, obtained through faith in this God
and his work—is to be understood and proclaimed. Indeed, "The principle of
law and gospel," observe Gassmann and Hendrix, "governs the confessional
theology of repentance and faith that form the rhythm of Christian life."[107]

Theology: Characteristic Beliefs

Lutheranism is often described by Lutherans in such a way as to stress continuity
with catholic Christianity. Thus, Lutherans conceive of themselves as "evangelical catholics" and their faith as being synonymous with "Christianity," albeit

with a Protestant twist. From such a perspective, Lutheranism is "a theological movement of renewal within the historically continuous structures of the catholic churches."[108] David Scaer writes, "To be 'Lutheran' is simply to be one who adheres to the ancient faith of the catholic and apostolic church, revived and restored at the time of the Lutheran Reformation."[109] Indeed, continuity with the ancient and medieval catholic Christian tradition is one dimension of Lutheranism and Lutheran theology.[110] And, to the degree that Lutheran theology is characterized by this continuity, there are, properly speaking, no Lutheran "distinctives." However, although continuities with ancient catholic Christian faith are essential to genuinely Lutheran theology, there are also theological beliefs that set Lutheranism apart from Roman Catholicism and from other Protestant theological traditions.

There is widespread agreement among Lutherans that the doctrine of justification constitutes the *articulus stantis et cadentis ecclesiae,* the doctrine by which the church stands or falls.[111] Justification by grace through faith, apart from works of the law, is emphasized in a way and to a degree that is distinctive of Lutheran theology. Furthermore, the doctrine of justification includes within it two of the "three *solae*": *sola gratia, sola fide, sola scriptura* (implicit here is a fourth: *solus Christus*). These provide an "outline of what Lutherans believe."[112] Carl Braaten suggests that in addition to these, the "classical elements" of Lutheranism include eschatological hope in Christ, sacramentalism, the law-gospel distinction and the "two kingdoms" doctrine.[113] Others would add to this list the doctrine of *simul justus et peccator,* "at once justified and a sinner." Some of these distinctives, such as *sola scriptura* and the law-gospel distinction, have been considered above. Others, such as eschatological hope in Christ, the doctrine of the two kingdoms, and *simul justus et peccator,* certainly are important to Lutheran theology but are not as central as is justification by faith. Thus, for the purposes of illustrating classical Lutheran theology, we will consider here justification by grace *(sola gratia)* through faith *(sola fide),* and two of the means of grace through which justification and its benefits become a reality in one's life: the sacraments of baptism and the Lord's Supper.

The hinge of grace: Justification.

The center of Lutheran doctrine. As we have noted, in classical Lutheranism the doctrine of justification constitutes the doctrine by which the church stands or falls.[114] Simply put, it is "the cardinal article upon which all others hinge"[115] and "*the* criterion of the gospel."[116] In his commentary on Galatians Luther writes, "As I often warn . . . the doctrine of justification must be learned diligently. For in it are included all the other doctrines of our faith; and if it is sound, all the others are sound as well."[117] This emphasis is found also in the Lutheran Confessions. "The message and doctrine of justification," observe Gassmann and Hendrix, "are at the center of the Christian faith and the Lutheran confessions."[118] According to the Augsburg Confession, the fact is that "we receive forgiveness of sin and become righteous before God out of grace for Christ's sake through faith when we believe that Christ has suffered for us and that for his sake our sin is forgiven and righteousness and eternal life are given to us."[119] In keeping with this, J. A. O. Preus III writes, "The article of justification serves as a kind of hermeneutical principle in the light of which we understand all else that God has revealed in Scripture. All theological talk begins and ends with it."[120] "Justification is not a separate topic apart from which still other topics could be discussed," says Oswald Bayer; rather, it is "the starting point for all theology, and it affects every other topic."[121] Franz Pieper extends this conviction to the assertion that the "integration and correlation" of all Christian belief around the doctrine of justification "was not devised by Luther and the Lutheran dogmaticians, but is set down in Holy Scripture as a fact."[122]

Definition of justification. In justification, God "accounts" the sinner "as righteous."[123] God takes away the condemnation under which we are rightly condemned and "ascribes" to us Christ's perfect merit. This transaction is a "forensic or judicial" act.[124] Justification is an act in which sin is forgiven. In fact, "forgiveness of sins" and "justification" are synonyms in the Lutheran vocabulary. Justification is also an act in which divine favor is bestowed, for Christ's righteousness is "imputed" to the sinner.[125] Romans 4:5 promises that "to one who without works trusts him who justifies the ungodly, such faith is reckoned as righteousness," and Romans 5:1 reads, "Therefore, since we are justified by faith, we have peace with God through our Lord Jesus Christ." Thus, "The word through which God forgives sins is at the same time the judgment by which God declares the sinner righteous. . . . As forgiveness of sins is nonimputation of sins for Christ's sake . . . so justification is the imputation of Christ's righteousness."[126]

Although justification pronouncing the sinner righteous is judicial, it is nonetheless "a re-creative act." In justification, the Word of God "creates as it speaks; it does what it says. It makes sinners righteous as it pronounces them righteous."[127] As Schlink says, "God's justifying verdict is never 'merely' a verdict; this verdict posits a reality"; the sinner "is not only regarded as righteous; he *is* righteous."[128] And, it must never be forgotten that this comes to pass only by grace.

Justification sola gratia. Sinners are justified by grace alone. "Justification involves dying and rising in Christ," writes Wanda Deifelt. "Sin dies and grace rises."[129] Romans 3:24 teaches that sinners "are now justified by his grace as a gift, through the redemption that is in Christ Jesus." Sinners are saved neither because of who they are nor because of anything they do, but solely because God, by gracious election, "creates, effects, aids, and promotes our salvation."[130] And this God does "for Christ's sake." We are saved in Christ alone, because of who Christ is and what Christ has done. God's grace is not something that we merit, but neither is it "grace bestowed upon the sinner by a fiat of the divine sovereign will"; rather, God's grace is "mediated through Christ, or grace in or for the sake of Christ." It is only because of Christ's perfect atoning work, a gift from God, that we can be saved.[131] Nafzger writes, "The basis for the grace of God that alone gives hope to sinners is the life, death, and resurrection of Jesus Christ."[132]

Sinners have nothing to offer and can do nothing to merit or earn God's favor. This lesson is learned from the law. The law condemns. The law teaches us that neither who we are nor what we do can rescue us from the just condemnation of God. We are told in Romans 3:20 that, far from providing a way of justification, "through the law comes the knowledge of sin." Paul indicates that "if it had not been for the law, I would not have known sin" (Rom 7:7). But the Bible contains more than law. The gospel is "at the heart of Scripture."[133] The gospel proclaims the good news of God's provision for forgiveness of sin. The gospel communicates God's promise of grace. In the gospel, God's gracious "absolution" of sinners by virtue of Christ's work is pronounced.[134] In the law, the sinner comes to long for the grace of God, and in the gospel, the sinner comes to know the grace of God. Through the law and the gospel, the Christian comes to know and experience the fact that "the whole Christian life rests on God's gracious disposition, the attitude and expression of his favor, toward us."[135] But how does God's favor come to rest on us?

Justification sola fide. Sinners are justified through faith alone. Faith takes hold of grace. Enabled by the Holy Spirit, the sinner responds to the gifts of justification and reconciliation with "complete receptivity"—that is, with faith. Faith accepts and trusts in God's promise of mercy.[136] As Paul says in Galatians 3:22, "What was promised through faith in Jesus Christ [is] given to those who believe." Faith "believes that we obtain grace and forgiveness of sin through Christ."[137] Indeed, it "receives" or "lays hold" of the forgiveness for sin.[138] It is "an instrument, or organ" through which forgiveness is apprehended.[139] Grace is "appropriated . . . only through faith."[140] Genuine faith is "not merely a knowledge of history."[141] True faith is "a knowledge of Christ coupled with trust *(fiducia cordis)* in the forgiveness of sins merited by Christ."[142] It is "trust that consoles and encourages" with assurance of God's grace, promised to us in the gospel.[143] It is "the true knowledge of Christ; it uses the benefits of Christ, it renews hearts, and it precedes our fulfillment of the law."[144] It is "firm acceptance" of God's promise of forgiveness of sins, God's promise of justification, based on the work of Christ.[145] As Galatians 2:16 says, "A person is justified not by the works of the law but through faith in Jesus Christ."

Though faith believes, takes hold, accepts and receives, it is not a work. In accord with Romans 3:28, Lutherans hold that "a person is justified by faith apart from works prescribed by the law." As Romans 4:5 indicates, faith is "reckoned as righteousness" to the person who "without works trusts him who justifies the ungodly." It is not "a moral achievement," required as a part of salvation.[146] As Karl L. Barth puts it, "There are not three operating forces working for the salvation of men: the Spirit, the Word, and man's consenting will. There are only two cooperating forces, and these are the Spirit and the Word."[147] The Spirit "creates our trust" in Jesus Christ, and God the Father "graciously grants us the ability to believe in Christ."[148] Conversion consists in "the kindling of faith" by God (see Acts 26:18; Eph 5:8; Col 2:12; 1 Jn 5:1).[149] In faith, sinners "let themselves be helped."[150] Schlink comments that "daring reliance and clinging is the extent of our activity."[151] This does not mean that the sinner is active, but that God in his free mercy is at work in us.[152] In the Lutheran vocabulary, *faith* is not an action verb. Having been given faith, the Christian is to demonstrate thankfulness for the grace of God through good works, works that "are the outgrowth of a good disposition, well pleasing to God, and proceed from the faith of one who is reconciled to God."[153] For, as Paul says, "by grace you have been saved through faith, and this is not your own doing; it is the gift of God—not the result of works, so that no one may boast. For we are what he has made us, created in Christ Jesus for good works, which God prepared beforehand to be our way of life" (Eph 2:8-10). Our entry into this way of life and continuance in it are intimately related to two mysteries: the sacraments of baptism and the Lord's Supper.

Means of grace: The sacraments.

Means of grace, sacraments and the Word of God. The grace of God comes to us through God-ordained instruments, "the means of grace." These are "the outward means through which the Holy Spirit enables faith and through which God's justification is given and received by this faith."[154] The means of grace are the Word of God and the sacraments. God has chosen these as the instruments through which to convey saving grace, and God "does not want to deal with us human beings except by means of his external Word and sacrament."[155] God's saving grace comes to us through the Word of God rightly preached and heard in the church, and through the sacraments properly administered in the church.[156] Thus the primary effect of the means of grace is to awaken and confirm faith in God's gracious gospel promises. Secondary yet important effects include providing a memorial wherein the people of God recall the work of God, and promoting community among Christians as God's grace is received corporately through the appointed means.[157]

Edmund Schlink observes that in the Lutheran confessions the theology of the specific sacraments, baptism and the Lord's Supper, is not derived from "a general sacramental concept."[158] Nonetheless, there is a theology of sacramentality in classical Lutheran theology.[159] The sacraments are "effective signs that participate in the reality to which they point. They communicate the reality signified; as signs of salvation they are saving signs as instruments of the saving work of the trinitarian God."[160] The saving grace that is imparted, or concerning which reassurance is given, is nothing other than the gospel promise of the forgiveness of sins in Christ.

In and of themselves, neither the physical elements nor the rites are means of grace. The physical elements and the rites are sacramental by virtue of being joined with the Word of God. Their meaning and impact "are determined by the Word alone, that is, by God's word of promise, grace, and forgiveness. Only together with the Word do the elements become means of grace."[161] The sacraments "convey forgiveness and life through the joining of Word and physical element," as God has ordained.[162] Consequently, neither the moral state nor the intention of either the administrator or recipient renders the elements or rites sacramental. Words of instruction and institution for both baptism and the Lord's Supper are given in Scripture, and if the Word of God is joined with the physical elements in accord with these directives, the elements and the rite will become sacramental and the rite will have its intended effect: the nourishment of life-giving faith.[163] Thus, a sacrament has three essential characteristics: institution by God in Christ; visible, physical element(s) identified in the institution; and the Word of God, communicated in the administration of the sacrament.[164]

Entering into grace: Baptism. According to the Augsburg Confession, baptism is "necessary." God's saving grace is bestowed through baptism.[165] In the uniting of Word and water, baptism is "the promise of salvation."[166] Yet baptism is not merely the offer of grace or the promise of salvation. As Mark 16:16 indicates, in and through baptism God brings people into the church and adopts them as his children. In baptism God grants forgiveness of sins and eternal salvation.[167] In sum, "Baptism saves."[168] Jesus said, as recorded in John 3:5, that "no one can enter the kingdom of God without being born of water and Spirit." The Holy Spirit is God's agent in creating the faith through which we are justified, and baptism is the means used by the Spirit in this creative work.

Baptism is a divinely appointed means of grace. Jesus instructs his follow-ers to "make disciples of all nations, baptizing them in the name of the Father and of the Son and of the Holy Spirit" (Mt 28:19). It is the means of grace that employs water. Paul tells us that God "saved us, not because of any works of righteousness that we had done, but according to his mercy, through the water of rebirth and renewal by the Holy Spirit" (Tit 3:5), and Peter says that baptism "now saves you—not as a removal of dirt from the body, but as an appeal to God for a good conscience, through the resurrection of Jesus Christ" (1 Pet 3:21). Baptism is not simply water, but water joined with the Word of promise—the promise that God the Father, through the agency of his Spirit and the avenue of faith, works salvation on the basis of the work of his Son.[169] As Luther reminds us in his Small Catechism, Jesus says, "Whoever believes and is baptized will be saved, but whoever does not believe will be damned" (see Mk 16:16).[170]

Because baptism is the means of grace through which God saves, it should not be withheld from infants. To the contrary, the Augsburg Confession states that it is "necessary to baptize children." Infants are in need of God's saving grace, and in baptism they are "entrusted to God and become pleasing to him."[171] Just as salvation is "offered to all," so too, in accord with the reference to "all nations" in Matthew 28:19, baptism is "offered to all—men, women, chil-dren and infants."[172] Infants inherit the "wages of sin," and if God so chooses, they can be given "the free gift of God" (Rom 6:23). There is no indication that they are exempt from Jesus' statement that the only way to enter the kingdom of God is through "being born of water and Spirit" (Jn 3:5).

In affirming the baptism of infants, Lutheran theology stresses that baptism is "God's action," not "a human response to God."[173] Through material ele-ments chosen for this use, God brings the Word and divine power to bear upon the one who is baptized. God is the Lord of life and has chosen to do this work in this way. We should not attempt to seize baptism as an action that we offer to God, or to withhold baptism until we can understand it in our own terms. The "psychological aspects of faith," particularly adult faith, should not be imposed on or expected of infants.[174] Obviously, as Kolb states, "infants do not express a 'faith' in the same way in which adults do." But that ought not be the determining factor in one's view of baptism. Rather, as Scrip-ture and the confessions testify, "God has commanded Baptism. God acts in Baptism" (see Ps 51:5; Mt 19:14; Mk 16:15-16; Acts 2:38-39; 16:15, 33; Rom 5:12; 6:3-11; Eph 2:1, 3).[175] Our responsibility is to believe and obey, by God's grace. In commenting on infant baptism, Samuel Nafzger gives voice to the triumph of grace in Lutheran theology:

Lutherans believe that it is precisely in the baptism of infants, who are included in Christ's great commission, that we can see the full meaning of "through faith alone." Those who deny that God gives faith to infants through baptism in effect deny salvation by grace alone. To say that faith depends on a person's ability to understand and to make a decision makes faith a human work rather than a pure gift of God through which alone he gives us salvation.[176]

Regardless of the recipient, either infant or adult, the specific mode of applying the water is "not the important thing."[177] What is important is that in baptism, through the water joined with God's Word, God's saving grace is given. In baptism, we who were dead are given new life, a life washed in baptism. It is eternal life, which comes from being united with the resurrected Christ (see Col 3:1-3). It is the spiritual life about which Jesus told Nicodemus (Jn 3:1-15).[178] Schlink suggests that the life of the Christian is to be lived "between the sacraments," daily orienting oneself by reference back to one's baptism and forward to the Lord's Table.[179] This means that the new life is lived "in the shadow of" baptism, regularly repenting of sin and remembering God's gracious gift of salvation.[180] Indeed, baptism is "a free and heavenly medicine, the most precious jewel for body and soul."[181]

Sustained in grace: The Lord's Supper. The life that is lived in the shadow of baptism is also to be lived in anticipation of the celebration of the Lord's Supper, for Christ is present there. From the time of Luther's battle with Zwingli at Marburg (1529) over the Eucharist, the heart of the Lutheran doctrine of the Lord's Supper has been belief in the "real presence" of Christ. The Augsburg Confession states, "The true body and blood of Christ are truly present under the form of bread and wine in the Lord's Supper and are distributed and received there."[182] Likewise, the Apology of the Augsburg Confession affirms that "in the Lord's Supper the body and blood of Christ are truly and substantially present and are truly offered with those things that are seen, bread and wine." The affirmation of the real presence was so clear and strong that in its response to the Augsburg Confession the Roman Catholic Church did not take issue with this point of Lutheran teaching.[183] Real presence has continued to be affirmed from the sixteenth century to the present.[184]

This belief is rooted in several presuppositions, most notably christological beliefs, and the literal interpretation of several passages of Scripture.[185] Schlink indicates that the doctrine of the Lord's Supper "derives from the presupposition of the incarnation of the Son of God."[186] In Christ's resurrection, ascension and current session at the right hand of the Father, he continues to possess both the divine and the human natures that were joined in his incarnation. By virtue of the "communication of attributes between the two natures," the body and blood associated with Christ's human nature can be present wherever and however God wills.[187] Christ is still present on earth in both natures. Jesus' promise "I am with you always, to the end of the age" is not limited to one or the other nature; rather, it is the promise of Jesus Christ the God-Man (Mt 28:20). "The *whole Christ*" is "truly, really, essentially and substantially present" in the Lord's Supper. And this bodily presence is "a presence for our salvation."[188]

Lutherans find in the words of divine institution the most important scriptural basis for belief in the real presence. According to Matthew 26:26-28, Jesus said, referring to the bread, "Take, eat; this is my body," and, referring to the cup, "Drink from it, all of you; for this is my blood of the covenant." In accord with Luther's interpretation, "is" means precisely what it says in this passage, as well as in parallel passages in Mark 14:22-24 and Luke 22:19-20. "This is my body" and "This is my blood" are to be interpreted literally. The Formula of Concord instructs, "The words of the testament of Christ are not to be understood in any other way than the way they literally sound, that is, not that the bread symbolizes the absent body and the wine the absent blood of Christ."[189] Likewise, references to "the body" and "the blood" of Christ in the Pauline passages of institution are to be interpreted literally (1 Cor 10:16; 11:27-29). These passages are not unique with respect to this type of "literal" teaching. For example, when Jesus said, "I am the resurrection and the life" (Jn 11:25; cf. 6:63), that is precisely what he meant—he *is* the resurrection and the life. He did not mean that he symbolizes or represents resurrection and life.[190] The reading of these texts seeks to follow "the time-honored hermeneutic rule that we must not depart from the literal meaning of the text unless the text itself compels us to do so."[191] Lutherans do not believe that these passages instituting the Lord's Supper compel such a departure.

In affirming this reading of the texts, Lutherans do not presume to explain in detail *how* this can be so, preferring to emphasize *that* it is so.[192] As described above, christological beliefs about the union of the divine and human natures and the communication of attributes between these natures provide partial explanation. And, it is asserted that the real presence results from "the sacramental union" of the Word of God with the physical elements, not from transubstantiation as traditional Roman Catholicism teaches. By virtue of this sacramental union, the bread is the body of Christ and the wine is his blood.[193] This real presence is affirmed in keeping with an understanding of the Lord's Supper as a "sacrament"—that is, as a "mystery."[194] It is not necessary to comprehend fully how Christ *can be* present in order to believe and affirm the teaching of Scripture that he *is* present.

Christ is present by virtue of the presence of the Word of the Lord, not by the faith of the recipient. Kolb says, "Faith does not make Christ's body and blood present in the Sacrament, any more than the infant's appetite makes the oatmeal present in the dish."[195] This being the case, the Smalcald Articles indicate that the body and blood of Christ are "not only offered to and received by upright Christians but also by evil ones."[196] There is, however, a difference. In eating the body and blood of Christ in an "unworthy" manner, those who do not have repentant faith receive "judgment and damnation" (cf. 1 Cor 11:27-29).[197] Those who possess genuine faith—that is, recognizing that "worthiness" to receive the sacrament "is and consists alone in the most holy obedience and perfect merit of Christ" that becomes ours only in faith—receive through the Lord's Supper the forgiveness of sins and the confirmation and strengthening of faith.[198] Schlink says that the Lord's Supper is "comfort, refreshment, and invigoration for faith and the new obedience."[199] Just as baptism is the means by which the grace of faith is initiated, the Lord's Supper is the means by which the grace of faith is nourished and strengthened.[200] Thus, like baptism, the Lord's Supper is "pure gospel." It is "a most gracious work, by which Christ deals with men, offering to all communicants the grace and merits which He obtained for the world by His death on the cross."[201] In the theology of the Lord's Supper, as in other loci, classical Lutheran theology announces a gospel of grace.

Conclusion: A Gospel of Grace

The first of the distinctively Protestant traditions proclaims, with a theology and a way of Christian life centered in a particular way upon it, a reality that other Protestant traditions also proclaim, each in its own way: God's grace. For Martin Luther and Philipp Melanchthon, and for those who consciously draw upon their thought, salvation for lost humankind is pure gift, the gracious gift of salvation by faith. This gospel of grace is at the heart of the belief and the practices of the Lutheran tradition.[202] Justification by faith is the hinge on which all of Christianity turns, and this justification occurs *sola gratia*. God gives the gift of faith. And, the gracious work of God does not stop here. God adds to this gift by offering sustaining grace through the ongoing celebration of the work of Christ his Son, who is present in the Lord's Supper. From beginning to end, in both faith and life, the Christian gospel is a message of grace.

FOR FURTHER STUDY

The endnotes for this chapter contain citations of many useful resources, most of them written from within the Lutheran tradition. A brief list of resources for further study follows here. Some of these resources consider Lutheranism in general, while others focus on Lutheran history and/or theology.

Bibliographies

Huber, Donald L. *World Lutheranism: A Select Bibliography for English Readers.* ATLA Bibliography Series 44. Lanham, Md.: Scarecrow Press, 2000.

Wiederaenders, Robert C. *Historical Guide to Lutheran Church Bodies of North America.* St. Louis: Lutheran Historical Conference, 1998.

Reference Works

Bachmann, E. Theodore, and Mercia B. Bachmann. *Lutheran Churches in the World: A Handbook.* Minneapolis: Augsburg, 1989.

Bodensieck, Julius, ed. *The Encyclopedia of the Lutheran Church.* 3 vols. Minneapolis: Augsburg, 1965.

Gassmann, Günther, ed. *Historical Dictionary of Lutheranism.* Lanham, Md.: Scarecrow, 2001.

Survey Resources

Gassmann, Günther, and Scott Hendrix. *Fortress Introduction to the Lutheran Confessions.* Minneapolis: Fortress, 1999.

Gritsch, Eric W. *A History of Lutheranism.* Minneapolis: Fortress, 2002.

Lagerquist, L. DeAne. *The Lutherans.* Denominations in America 9. Westport, Conn.: Greenwood Press, 1999.

Primary Historical and Theological Resources

Kolb, Robert, and Timothy J. Wengert, eds. *The Book of Concord: The Confessions of the Evangelical Lutheran Church.* Translated by Charles Arand et al. Minneapolis: Fortress, 2000.

Luther, Martin. *Luther's Works.* Edited by Jaroslav Pelikan. 55 vols. American ed. St. Louis: Concordia, 1958-1986.

Recent and Current Theological Explorations

Burgess, Joseph A., and Marc Kolden, eds. *By Faith Alone: Essays in Honor of Gerhard O. Forde.* Grand Rapids: Eerdmans, 2004.

Cimino, Richard, ed. *Lutherans Today: American Lutheran Identity in the*

Twenty-first Century. Grand Rapids: Eerdmans, 2003.

Forde, Gerhard O., Mark C. Mattes and Steven D. Paulson, eds. *A More Radical Gospel: Essays on Eschatology, Authority, Atonement, and Ecumenism.* Grand Rapids: Eerdmans, 2004.

Gregersen, Niels Henrik, ed. *The Gift of Grace: The Future of Lutheran Theology.* Minneapolis: Fortress, 2005.

3 ■ Faith for Radical Community

ANABAPTIST THEOLOGY

*We use the term "radical" not in its popular sense, which refers to that which is
extreme, spectacular, or violent, but in its literal one, which derives from radix,
and means root.*

John Driver, *Radical Faith*

He who would follow Christ in life
Must scorn the world's insult and strife,
And bear his cross each day.
For this alone leads to the throne;
Christ is the only way.

Jörg Wagner, "Wer Christo jetzt will folgen noch"
(trans. David Augsburger)

The Anabaptists emphasized separation from the "world," meaning the mass
of unregenerate men together with all their sinful ways and life. And they expected
a certain amount of opposition and persecution from the world. They spoke
much about bearing "the cross," of being faithful unto death, of being willing to
shed their blood for their testimony to the truth.

John Christian Wenger, *The Doctrines of the Mennonites*

Frank, a friend from college days, was proudly giving our family a walking
tour of his Pennsylvania farm. It was a place of peaceful rural beauty on this
weekday evening. The sights and sounds of city life seemed far away, even
though nearby stood more clusters of newly built suburban-style houses than
when I had visited several years earlier. As we walked along the fields near the
road, a small caravan of vehicles drove past. Clean, rather plain, black cars and
large vans, each one was full to capacity. The men and boys wore dark jackets

with white shirts. Some of the men wore wide-brimmed hats and had beards. The women and girls wore bonnets and rode in the back. They were Amish, and Frank indicated, with respect, that they were probably headed to a gathering at their meetinghouse. He said that in addition to the plain, black vehicles that drove past his farm, the parking lot at the meetinghouse would have both a few horse-drawn wagons and late-model cars of many kinds and colors.

Context: Historical and Ecclesiastical Background

Historical origins and development. More so than is the case in many other traditions, scholars from both within and outside Anabaptism have devoted much attention to the task of properly identifying and describing the origin(s) of the Anabaptist tradition. In the late-nineteenth and early-twentieth centuries, political theorist Friedrich Engels, social historian Max Weber and historian of religion Ernst Troeltsch, each in his own way, interpreted Anabaptist origins in terms of "revolutionary" figures such as the Zwickau prophets and Thomas Müntzer.[1] At the end of the 1920s, a new interpretation by an Anabaptist named Harold Bender emerged, an interpretation that was predominant among scholars into the 1970s and continues to be influential among many Anabaptists.[2] Bender led the recovery of what he called "the Anabaptist vision."[3] In contrast with previous interpretations that identified Anabaptism almost exclusively with extreme and violent revolutionaries and "prophets," the Bender school of thought, also known as the Goshen school (Bender taught at Goshen College), gave a more positive depiction of Anabaptist origins.[4] For Bender, and for several subsequent generations of Anabaptists, the movement was viewed as the logical extension of the sixteenth-century Protestant Reformation, one that emanated from Switzerland and emphasized brotherhood, rigorous discipleship and peaceful nonresistance to persecution.

At mid-century, a third interpretation emerged as church historians outside the Anabaptist tradition described a broader collection of movements under the banner of what John T. McNeill and Roland Bainton called "the left wing" of the Reformation and what George Williams referred to as "the Radical Reformation."[5] The tradition was viewed as "radical" not in the sense of being extreme or spectacular or violent, but rather, in accord with the Latin word *radix*, which means "root," the Anabaptists were viewed as going back to the roots of earliest Christianity, bypassing "established views, values, and institutions, both Roman Catholic and Protestant."[6] This broader conceptualization included movements such as the Spiritualists, who followed the inner promptings of the Holy Spirit, and the Evangelical Rationalists, who emphasized reason and its illumination by the Holy Spirit.

Further developing this recognition of diversity, Anabaptist scholars in the latter part of the twentieth century embraced a "polygenesis" reading of early Anabaptism.[7] In a 1975 article titled "From Monogenesis to Polygenesis," James Stayer, Werner O. Packull and Klaus Depperman argued that three subtraditions (hence, *polygenesis*) of Anabaptism developed from three geographical regions: the Zwinglian-humanist tradition from Switzerland, the mystical-humanist tradition from southern Germany, and the sacramentarian-apocalyptic tradition from the Netherlands and northern Germany.[8] According to Anabaptist scholar C. Arnold Snyder, this polygenesis paradigm of Anabaptist origins "has won the day among professional historians because it is, to date, the most adequate and fruitful description."[9] From these polygenetic beginnings a variety of subtraditions developed within Anabaptism, including the Hutterite, Mennonite, Amish, Brethren in Christ and Brethren traditions.[10] Snyder has also, however, further developed the polygenesis approach by combining it with the identification of a shared theological core.[11] The present chapter reflects this modified polygenesis interpretation, informed also by the Bainton-Williams approach, and focuses on the Mennonite expression of Anabaptism.[12]

The Anabaptist movement arose early in the sixteenth century and, like many other Christian movements of the time, sought dramatic religious and social change. However, unlike the other movements that came to be called "Protestant," Anabaptism was a "grassroots movement," and one that was "driven underground, where it survived in more or less clandestine fashion (depending on the level of official or unofficial toleration in a given locale)." Not surprisingly, then, within this emergent movement there existed "a bewildering variety of unique local teachings and practices."[13] Yet, there were also persons, ideas and events of sufficient significance and commonality to be regarded as important parts of the story of a tradition called Anabaptism.

Late in 1522, a Roman Catholic priest who had arrived at many of the same "new" theological conclusions as Martin Luther and other reformers resigned his appointment and assumed a post as preacher under the auspices of the city council of Zürich, Switzerland. In this post, Ulrich Zwingli (1484-1531) deliberately and gradually worked for religious and social reform by directing grassroots pressure upon the city council. By the time of Zwingli's assumption of this post, other people in Zürich who had welcomed the new theology had begun to pursue an even more radical path toward reform, "a wholesale effort at scriptural church reform."[14] This path included breaking the Lenten fast, refusing to pay tithes, disrupting celebration of the Mass, and "purifying" church sanctuaries by removing and destroying statuary and other images. By October 1523, the disruption to life in the city was such that the city council convened a disputation on images and the Mass. Having advocated that the Mass be replaced with a celebration of "the Lord's Supper," free of the words and symbols of Roman Catholic belief in transubstantiation, Zwingli agreed to delay making this change for a little over a year, in the interest of preparing people for the change. However, what was to Zwingli a pastorally and politically prudent course of action was to the "radicals" a betrayal of the cause of reform. Zwingli was wrong to have allowed the city council to determine the outcome of a spiritual, and therefore churchly, matter.[15]

Soon after, the radicals pressed to the forefront another spiritual, churchly matter: baptism. Early in 1524, influenced by the preaching of Wilhelm Reublin (1480/84-ca. 1560) and Johannes Brötli, the residents of two towns near Zürich refused to have their newborn babies baptized. Within Zürich itself, two leaders of the radicals, Conrad Grebel (1498?-1526) and Felix Mantz (ca. 1498-1527) pressed for the cessation of infant baptism, on the grounds that the practice lacked a scriptural basis.[16] Following a second disputation, this time on baptism, the radicals definitively separated themselves not only from the Roman Catholic Church and the Zürich city council, but also from the reforms of Zwingli. As with the Lord's Supper, so with baptism, they rejected Zwingli's willingness to continue for a time an unscriptural practice, in this case paedobaptism, and pursued their own course. On January 21, 1525, a group gathered at the house of Felix Mantz, and adults who had professed Christian faith were baptized. Georg Blaurock (ca. 1492-1529) asked Conrad Grebel to baptize him. Grebel did. Then, Blaurock baptized the other adults who were present, including preachers Reublin and Brötli.[17] They then pledged to live separated from the world, to witness to the gospel, and to remain true to the faith.[18] Within six months the Anabaptist movement had spread to other regions of the Swiss Confederation and into towns such as Waldshut, Schaffhausen and Hallau in southern Germany.[19]

Although all of these people had undergone a ritual of being sprinkled with water when they were infants, the events of January 21 did not constitute for them (though it did for their opponents) a *re*baptism ("*ana*baptism"); rather, on that day they for the first time underwent genuine Christian baptism. Based on passages such as Matthew 28:18-20, Mark 16:15-16 and several passages in Acts (including Acts 2:38; 9:17-19; 16:17-34; 19:1-5.), they believed that baptism is to be administered to people who have heard, understood and affirmed the gospel, and who are, as a result, committed to living a new life in Christ. Infants are incapable of such acts and decisions, and therefore they are not fit for baptism.

In the village churches surrounding Zürich, where the city council's control was limited, reforms were unfolding even more quickly, and the Anabaptist movement began to spread to the west, east and north.[20] To the north, in Waldshut, Balthasar Hubmeier (ca. 1480-1528) was leading religious reforms. In 1524, after several years of increasingly reformational preaching, he directed the removal of images and relics from the church at Waldshut and began to celebrate the Mass in the vernacular (that is, in German rather than Latin). On Easter Sunday, 1525, Hubmeier was baptized by Reublin. In the coming months several hundred adult citizens of Waldshut were baptized, and the city came to be regarded as an "Anabaptist city."[21] As the movement spread northward from Zürich, it came into contact with increasing social and civil unrest among peasants, and Waldshut was one of the cities that supported and supplied them.[22] The Anabaptists and peasants shared in common the role of being "outsiders" in relation to established religious, civil and socioeconomic systems. Unlike other Christian groups, Anabaptist leaders demonstrated Christian charity and "sympathetic solidarity" with the peasants, and "when attempts at dialogue and evangelical moderation failed, violence erupted and was repressed with even greater violence."[23] In May 1525, in the city of Franckenhausen, unrest boiled over into a fierce uprising, and violence was met with violence. Beginning at Franckenhausen and culminating with the defeat of the peasants at Waldshut late in 1525, thousands of peasants were killed during the Peasants' War, with the result that the Anabaptist movement found itself with "no political centre of support anywhere at all in the Swiss territories."[24]

At the same time, faced with increasing opposition from civil authorities, some Anabaptists chose a path of nonresistance combined with separatism. Early among these was a former Benedictine monk, Michael Sattler (1490-1527). By the summer of 1526, Sattler embraced Anabaptist principles, and he began to preach and practice accordingly. In addition to baptizing adults, he became one of the first within Anabaptism to teach that "all manner of armed resistance or governmental involvement ('the sword') was rejected as 'outside the perfection of Christ,'" a view that soon became a defining characteristic of Swiss Anabaptist beliefs.[25] These beliefs were set forth in the Schleitheim Confession (February 24, 1527). The first three articles (on baptism, the ban[26] and the Lord's Supper) articulate views that were widely held by Anabaptists, while the other four articles (on separation from the world and evil, election of the congregational shepherd, disavowal of "the sword"[27] and rejection of swearing oaths) formulated beliefs that were developing in Swiss Anabaptism but were not affirmed by all Anabaptists in other regions.[28] Nonetheless, "There can be no doubt," writes C. Arnold Snyder, "that after the failure of the Peasant's Revolt in late 1525, and with the spread of the Schleitheim Confession of 1527, the Swiss Brethren assumed a strongly separatist and pacifist stand."[29] And this stand came at a bloody cost. Mantz was sentenced to death and was drowned on January

5, 1527. Blaurock, who was beaten and expelled from Zürich the same year, was recaptured and burned to death two years later. Within three months of the creation of the Schleitheim Confession in February 1527, Sattler, his wife and a number of other people associated with the confession were martyred. Hundreds of Anabaptists were executed or killed in skirmishes from 1527 onward. Their rejection of infant baptism, which was a mark of membership in civil society, and their posture of separation brought the "near-universal condemnation of Anabaptism in western Europe." Anabaptist historian Frank Epp observes that civil and ecclesiastical authorities "probably assessed the situation correctly," recognizing that "the new baptism was an anarchical threat to the maintenance of a united, homogeneous, obedient and serene society."[30] Though not the only Christian group to experience persecution, they "faced more systematic persecution, with its accompanying physical suffering and martyrdom, than was the case for other Christian groups."[31] Moreover, their posture of nonresistance made them more vulnerable to violent persecution.

In southern Germany and Austria a similar yet distinct story was unfolding. The roots of this story lie in the carnage of the Peasants' War and the theological thought of Hans Denk (ca. 1495-1527) and Hans Hut (ca. 1490-1527). Denk was a humanistically trained teacher in Nuremberg when he came under the influence of the revolutionary Thomas Müntzer (ca. 1490-1525) and the reformer Andreas Karlstadt (ca. 1477-1541). Expelled from Nuremberg in 1525, Denk spent the next two years traveling to a number of German cities, teaching and pressing for radical reform. In his teaching he emphasized the inner word and listening to the voice of the Spirit, thereby reflecting the influence of late medieval mysticism, perhaps mediated to him by Müntzer. He also stressed the ethical dimensions of salvation, cautioning against an excessive reliance on imputed righteousness and calling for living a sanctified life in the power of the Spirit.[32] On Pentecost Sunday in 1526, Denck baptized Hans Hut, a bookbinder and bookseller. For the next year and a half Hut undertook an itinerate ministry, establishing Anabaptist congregations in southern and central Germany. Like Denck, Hut was influenced by Müntzer, though even more so. He blended Müntzer's apocalypticism with Anabaptist ideas, transforming the violent apocalyptic into "a more modest and non-violent missionary zeal."[33] Hut also emphasized God's nearness in and to all of creation, and the Christian's union with the indwelling Christ. His stress on union with Christ led Hut to "less emphasis on sin and greater emphasis on becoming like [Christ] through suffering."[34] While sharing many beliefs with Swiss Anabaptism (e.g., believer's baptism, separatism), the southern German stream manifested greater spiritualistic and mystical tendencies, including a stress on the inner work of the Spirit, more apocalyptic motivation and, rooted in both of these, greater emphasis on suffering in this world as a way of being conformed to Christ.[35]

A third Anabaptist story was written in northern Germany and the Netherlands. Unlike the others, this story has its defining origins largely in the thinking of one person: Melchior Hoffman (1495/1500-1543). Hoffman, a furrier by trade, entered the Anabaptist movement via Lutheranism. Having served for several years as a Lutheran lay missionary, he broke from Lutheranism in the spring of 1529, primarily due to his rejection of the Lutheran understanding of the Lord's Supper. Later that year, Hoffman went to Strasbourg, where he had contact with Anabaptists. He came to embrace many Anabaptist beliefs, but rather than joining an existing Anabaptist group, he formed his own. In his teaching Hoffman emphasized the prophetic books of the Bible and the imminent onset of apocalyptic events, including the return of Christ to lead his people in armed victory over the godless. In 1530, Hoffman fled to Emden in northwest Germany, where the desperate circumstances of the people—including poverty, hunger and recent war—created a receptivity to his message of hope grounded in the eschatological solution to their problems.[36] These eschatological expectations were such that Hoffman and many of his followers believed that they could help usher in the end times. Thus, in May 1533, Hoffman allowed himself to be arrested and imprisoned, thinking that this would contribute to hastening the end. Ten years later, he died in prison.

Eschatological expectations also shaped the course of events in Münster, Germany. With Anabaptists having achieved a majority on the city council in February of 1534, the Roman Catholic bishop initiated a siege against the city, requiring all persons not baptized by the Roman Catholic Church to either receive baptism or leave the city. The Anabaptists rejected both alternatives and, under the influence of recently arrived "prophet" Jan Metthijs, embraced the notion that they were establishing the eschatological New Jerusalem in Münster. However, in June of 1535 the siege came to a bloody end, with thousands of Münsterites being killed. In the wake of the fall of Münster, the movement led by Hoffman "disintegrated into several factions."[37] One of these groups grew steadily, and by the 1550s, the majority of Anabaptists in northern Germany and the Netherlands belonged to this group, while the other groups declined.[38] David Joris (ca. 1501-1556) and Obbe Philips (ca. 1500-1568) are properly regarded as the founders of this group. However, one of their followers, Menno Simons (1496-1561), emerged to give such strong and strategic leadership that his name came to be associated with the group, known as the Mennonites.[39]

Although the latter half of the sixteenth century was a time of relative peace for Swiss Anabaptists, the end of the century brought renewed harsh repression of Anabaptist civil and religious "heresy." Periodically, throughout the seventeenth and eighteenth centuries, Swiss Anabaptists were violently persecuted, in part because their beliefs and practices—such as refusal to baptize their children, to serve in the military and to swear oaths—were seen as a threat to both the ecclesiastical and, no less, the civil orders. In contrast, by the mid-seventeenth century, the Mennonites of northern Germany and the Netherlands were "entering more fully" into public life such that "Mennonite cultural, social, and even political influence in the Netherlands grew stronger than Mennonites have enjoyed anywhere else at any time."[40] These favorable circumstances afforded an unusual opportunity for theological reflection,[41] and such reflection is found in the Dordrecht Confession (1632), which continues to this day to occupy an honored place among Mennonites. However, as Cornelius Dyck reports, "In spite of these developments, or perhaps because of them, a decline set in among the congregations."[42] From the mid-sixteenth to the early-nineteenth centuries, Anabaptism experienced "a general numerical decline."[43] Factors contributing to this, especially during the first half of this period, included martyrdom, such as that experienced by the Swiss, and an undermining "accommodation to their environment," such as that experienced in northern Germany and the Netherlands.[44] Yet over this same period of time the Anabaptist movement prospered in a variety of ways. Many Anabaptists proved to be efficient and effective farmers and business people.[45] Furthermore, owing to the influence of some wise leaders, a spirit of tolerance encouraged by the emerging "enlightenment" in Europe, and a new commitment to seeking unity, stimulated by the Pietist emphasis on Bible study, prayer and mission, Anabaptists overcame many of their earlier divisions.[46]

Although political and cultural changes that encouraged toleration and discouraged violent persecution moved across much of Europe by the nineteenth century, "Mennonites were still second-class citizens whose privileges were restricted beyond those of others in most of Europe. Because of this they had withdrawn to isolated rural areas, where they remained unmolested as 'the quiet in the land.'"[47] Those who chose not to remain in these areas migrated eastward into Russia and Prussia, and westward across the ocean to North America. The earliest records of Mennonites in America indicate that they began to settle on the central eastern coast by the 1640s, and between three and five thousand continued to immigrate to America until 1756, at which time the Seven Years' War and other forms of upheaval in Europe put an end to immigration to America until around 1815.[48] Although the earliest Mennonite immigrants were not theologically separatist, they "gradually tended to prefer isolation, either because of the dynamics of sectarianism or the legacy of persecution, and tried to preserve [isolation] through geographic and language boundaries."[49] A growing separatist impulse, combined with factors such as the need for more farmland, prompted Mennonites to disperse rather quickly across the North American landscape. By the 1760s, many Mennonites and Amish had settled in southwestern Pennsylvania. By 1799, there were settlements in Ohio, and from there many moved on to Indiana or Illinois. In the wake of the American Revolution some Mennonites, perhaps those with loyalist tendencies toward the British cause, migrated across the border into Canada, settling in southern Ontario.[50]

The nineteenth century proved to be one of considerable stress and strife among Mennonites in the United States and Canada.[51] Through the middle of the nineteenth century, revivalism touched every major Christian tradition, including the Anabaptist tradition. As in other traditions, the enthusiasm, dramatic conversionism and "frequent theological oversimplification" of revivalism were embraced by some and rejected by others.[52] Moreover, these differing responses to revivalism were but one instance of an increasing diversity within Anabaptism, "a widening of the spectrum from the most conservative to the most progressive groups."[53] J. Howard Kauffman and Leo Driedger observe that by the end of the nineteenth century, "the more progressive Mennonites adopted Sunday schools, four-part singing, revival meetings, conference organization, church-operated high schools and colleges,[54] foreign missions, and church periodicals, none of which have been accepted by the Old Orders to this day."[55] Many of these "more progressive" adaptations represent what Rodney Sawatsky refers to as the "denominationalization" of Mennonitism, a late-nineteenth century shift "from a more sectarian to an increasingly denominational identity."[56] In 1860, a Mennonite denomination, the General Conference Mennonite Church, was formed, consisting largely of immigrants from southern Germany who were now settled in Illinois and Iowa, and a smaller number of Mennonites who had broken away from the "Old" Mennonites in and around Pennsylvania.[57] Immigrants were a particularly significant part of the Anabaptist story in North America between 1873 and 1950. Over fifty thousand Mennonites emigrated from Russia, with thirty-six thousand going to agricultural prairie provinces of Canada (Manitoba and Saskatchewan), and the rest settling in prairie states of the United States (Minnesota, South Dakota, Nebraska and Kansas).[58]

In the twentieth century, a number of factors contributed to "a crisis in Mennonite identity . . . a crisis of historical depth and increasing intensity."[59] First, from the earliest history of Anabaptism in the sixteenth century, Anabaptists had often been, as Dyck notes, "pilgrims and strangers in a hostile world," repeatedly forced to migrate due to persecution.[60] This changed as they settled in the United States and Canada. Although often on the margins of society (and this,

often at their own doing), they no longer had to move due to violent persecution. They were no longer clearly defined as a persecuted minority. Second, from
at least the seventeenth century onward, Anabaptists had been associated with
agricultural communities. "For 300 years," writes Dyck, "farming was thought to
be *the* Mennonite way of life and the rural community the indispensable form of
organizing their common life."[61] As increasing numbers became engaged in other
forms of commerce and moved out of rural settings, this rural-agricultural identity also changed. Increasingly equipped with higher levels of formal education,
Anabaptists became more involved with the institutions and structures of mainstream North American society.[62] Third, since its beginnings, Anabaptism had a
largely sectarian character. However, in the twentieth century many Anabaptist
groups were "shedding their sectarian skin for a larger and more comfortable
denominational one."[63] This denominationalization was embodied in a variety
of developments. Various Anabaptist groups became strongly committed to
higher education, and this manifested itself in the establishment of colleges and
seminaries. For example, Goshen College (Goshen, Indiana) was established in
1903, and Tabor College (Hillsboro, Kansas) in 1908. A Mennonite seminary was
established at Goshen in 1946. In Canada, three colleges were established in
Winnipeg, Manitoba, and a liberal arts college was established in Waterloo, Ontario. Anabaptists also began to publish journals and periodicals such as *The
Mennonite Quarterly Review* (1927) and *Sword and Trumpet* (1929). More energy was also being devoted to formalized theological reflection. In 1921, the
Mennonite Church adopted a statement of Christian Fundamentals, and the
church replaced this with a new statement, the Mennonite Confession of Faith,
in 1963. Developments such as these have led some Anabaptist scholars to
speak of the "accommodation" of Anabaptists to North American culture over
the course of the twentieth century.[64]

There has also been a similar change in Anabaptism's relationship to evangelical Protestantism. Wilbert Shenk observes that beginning in the nineteenth
century, "as Mennonites began to mingle more widely with other Christians and
accommodate to the dominant culture, they have taken their cues in theology
and piety largely from the evangelical mainstream."[65] These accommodations
were significant enough that, with an effect similar to that of the violent perse-
cutions suffered in the past, they prompted some Anabaptists to migrate to
places where they could preserve their religious identity, where they could live
as they believed that God intended. This time, they went from the United States
and Canada to Central and South America.[66] Those who remained in North
America continued to adapt to mainstream urban culture, concretely symbolized
in, for example, leaving the German language behind in favor of English. More-

over, Mennonites in Canada became increasingly involved in government and politics. In some sectors of Anabaptism, by the end of World War II social action and social service became "the dominant form of mission," spurred on by a combination of the historical Anabaptist commitment to nonresistant love and the harsh realities of the major wars of the twentieth century.[67]

Diversity. Today, Mennonites and other Anabaptist traditions in the United States are concentrated in Pennsylvania, Ohio, Indiana and Kansas, while they are more widely settled throughout many provinces in Canada. Over the course of the late-nineteenth and early-twentieth centuries, one of the ways in which the diversity within Anabaptism came to be embodied was in denominations. The Mennonite Church, sometimes still called "Old Mennonites," is the largest group, with most churches located in Midwestern states and Pennsylvania. Its roots are in the Anabaptist movements of Switzerland and southern Germany. In 1860 the General Conference Mennonite Church was organized at West Point, Iowa. The General Conference is generally regarded as the most theologically liberal of all the major Mennonite groups, though it engages in extensive cooperation with the Mennonite Church.[68] For ten years the Mennonite Church and the General Conference church collaborated on the formulation of *Confession of Faith in a Mennonite Perspective,* which both groups adopted in 1995. These two groups then merged in 2001.

The Mennonite Brethren, established in the United States in 1879, have been "slower to cooperate with other Mennonites" and "more open to link with other Evangelical Christians."[69] The majority of members are in Canada and in the western United States. Like the Mennonite Brethren, the Brethren in Christ Church is a member of the National Association of Evangelicals. The Brethren in Christ, located largely in the eastern United States and in Ontario, trace their roots to Pietist influences on Anabaptism in the late-eighteenth century. Other Anabaptist denominations include the Evangelical Mennonite Church, the Beachy Amish Mennonite Churches, the Church of God in Christ—Mennonite, the Conservative Mennonite Conference, the Older Order Amish Church, the Old Order (Wisler) Mennonite Church, the Reformed Mennonite Church, the Hutterian Brethren and the Church of the Brethren. The Mennonite Central Committee, established in 1920, and the Mennonite World Conference, established in 1925, facilitate fellowship and cooperation among Mennonite groups. Mennonite Disaster Services and the Mennonite Health Service Alliance focus on cooperative relief and medical efforts.

Approach: Theological and Hermeneutical Method

Role of theology. Anabaptists are not generally known for complex or highly

THE ANABAPTIST TRADITION

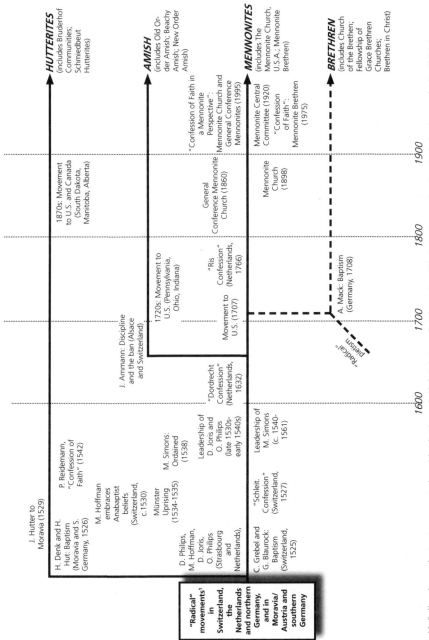

HUTTERITES
(includes Bruderhof Communities; Schmiedbeut Hutterites)

AMISH
(includes Old Order Amish; Beachy Amish; New Order Amish)

MENNONITES
(includes The Mennonite Church, U.S.A.; Mennonite Brethren)

BRETHREN
(includes Church of the Brethren; Fellowship of Grace Brethren Churches; Brethren in Christ)

"Confession of Faith in a Mennonite Perspective": Mennonite Church and General Conference Mennonites (1995)

Mennonite Central Committee (1920)

"Confession of Faith": Mennonite Brethren (1975)

1900

1870s: Movement to U.S. and Canada (South Dakota, Manitoba, Alberta)

General Conference Mennonite Church (1860)

Mennonite Church (1898)

1800

1720s: Movement to U.S. (Pennsylvania, Ohio, Indiana)

"Ris Confession" (Netherlands, 1766)

Movement to U.S. (1707)

A. Mack: Baptism (Germany, 1708)

1700

"Radical" pietism

J. Ammann: Discipline and the ban (Alsace and Switzerland)

"Dordrecht Confession" (Netherlands, 1632)

1600

J. Hutter to Moravia (1529)

H. Denk and H. Hut: Baptism (Moravia and S. Germany, 1526)

P. Reidemann, "Confession of Faith" (1542)

M. Hoffman embraces Anabaptist beliefs (Switzerland, c.1530)

Münster Uprising (1534-1535)

M. Simons: Ordained (1538)

D. Philips, M. Hoffman, D. Joris, O. Philips (Strasbourg and Netherlands)

Leadership of D. Joris and O. Philips (late 1530s-early 1540s)

C. Grebel and G. Blaurock: Baptism (Switzerland, 1525)

"Schleit. Confession" (Switzerland, 1527)

Leadership of M. Simons (c. 1540-1561)

"Radical" movements[1] in Switzerland, the Netherlands and northern Germany, and in Moravia/Austria and southern Germany

[1] *Radical* here does not denote extreme or spectacular or violent, but, in accord with the Latin term *radix*, it denotes "root." The Anabaptists were viewed as going back to the roots of earliest Christianity, bypassing established and predominant ecclesiastical views, values and institutions.

formalized theology.[70] One Anabaptist scholar bemoans the tradition's "lack of formal theological history,"[71] and James McClendon suggests that his fellow "sharers of the Radical vision have produced little that deserves the name theology."[72] From its beginnings in the sixteenth century, the tradition was marked by what Walter Klaassen describes as "hostile distrust of traditional and contemporary theologians, theology, and theologizing,"[73] and the subsequent history is largely characterized by "an ambivalence toward formal theology."[74] According to J. Denny Weaver, "Mennonites began exploring systematic theology as a genre only in the 1980s."[75]

The reasons for this are not found primarily in a lack of competence among the founding generation of Anabaptists. Although it is true that besides Balthasar Hubmeier there were no formally trained theologians among the earliest Anabaptist leaders and writers, many of these people were university educated and also had prepared for the priesthood in the Roman Catholic Church.[76] The explanation for the relative lack of attention given to formal theological reflection is found in the combination of two factors: the circumstances of their lives and the substance of their thought. First, as was described in the preceding section, Anabaptists often were the target of severe persecution, and the life circumstances of a person or a community living under the threat of persecution, much less the realization of that threat, are not particularly conducive to the luxury of formal education or extended theological study and reflection. Indeed, many of the most educated leaders of the early Anabaptist movement were martyred.[77] In part as a result of this, the early Anabaptist movement was a dynamic yet "often uncoordinated movement and not a carefully reasoned theological-ethical position."[78] McClendon observes that for much of its history, the radical tradition has been "preoccupied with the harsh struggle to survive and [has] not had the leisure for theological reflection."[79]

Second, in its substance Anabaptist thought has been, as noted above, ambivalent about highly formalized theological analysis and formulation. As Marlin Jeschke points out, Anabaptists were not oblivious to the fact that educated theologians often were the ones who engineered their persecution.[80] This contributed to ambivalence about the value, at least in principle, of formalized theology.[81] Furthermore, the Anabaptists' conscious commitments were predominantly practical or applied rather than theoretical. As Robert Friedmann observes, "To the early Anabaptists it was precisely the lack of . . . spiritual immediacy which made the Reformers predominantly 'theologians,' that is, discursive thinkers on religious questions instead of doers of divine commandments."[82] Anabaptists have always placed a premium on "doing." They have "stressed *living* the faith, giving more weight to Christian practice than to standardized doctrinal formulations."[83] This is the spirit, then, embodied in Walter Klaassen's counsel that "ultimately God does not judge men for the theology they hold but for the attitudes they reflect and for the deeds they do,"[84] and in Thomas Finger's report that in the minds of many Mennonites, "immersion in books takes time from deeds of mercy."[85] Another dimension of this ambivalence toward formalized and academic theologizing is the Anabaptists' radical commitment to the belief that all Christians, regardless of education or profession, are indwelt by the Holy Spirit and thus legitimately can and ought to interpret the Bible. There is no assumption that theological scholars ought to have the last word in matters of faith and life.[86]

None of this, however, should lead to the conclusion that Anabaptism ignores theology or that it is without written formulations of theology. Although there is some dispute among Anabaptist scholars regarding the role of formal theological reflection and formulation in the tradition,[87] theology clearly is integral to Anabaptism in at least two ways. First, even those who deny that formal or "explicit" theology has had a significant role within the tradition recognize that there is "an underlying implicit theology."[88] And this implicit theology has been nothing less than "a set of firm convictions" for which those who believed "risked, and sometimes paid, their lives."[89] Moreover, these "semiconscious theological insights and ideas" eventually find expression in confessional documents,[90] and in this, one sees a second way in which theology is integral to the Anabaptist tradition. Despite ambivalence toward theology, the Anabaptist tradition possesses a rich and continuing confessional heritage. Testimony to this is found, for example, in Howard Loewen's *One Lord, One Church, One Hope, and One God: Mennonite Confessions of Faith,* which contains twenty-seven confessions issued from 1527 (Schleitheim Confession) to 1975 (Confession of Faith of the Mennonite Brethren Church).[91] As A. James Reimer observes, "The doctrinal and confessional genre of theological thinking . . . is a long-standing and integral part of our heritage."[92] A recent exercise in such theological thinking, noted earlier, is found in the extensive confessional document titled *Confession of Faith in a Mennonite Perspective,* jointly researched and composed over a ten-year period by the General Conference Mennonite Church and the Mennonite Church.[93]

We have noted that Anabaptists' conscious commitments have been predominantly practical or applied—they have placed a premium on "doing." This orientation has influenced the nature of theology as they understand it. In the words of Walter Klaassen, theology is characterized by "the fusion of theology and ethics."[94] Theology is rooted most fundamentally not in the intellect, but in life. More than finely tuned reasoning, "openness and . . . abandonment to God and his will" is the key to a true understanding of the truth of God.[95] And, the norm to which a disciple of Jesus Christ turns to discern the truth of God is Scripture.

Theological method. The Bible constitutes the stated norm for Anabaptist theological formulation. Commenting on early Anabaptists, Friedman observes, "The overwhelming rank and file of Anabaptists . . . were simply students of the Scriptures and hardly of anything else."[96] Anabaptism has "historically rejected the creedal orientation of classical theology," writes Loewen, "claiming to be biblical rather than creedal or philosophical in its hermeneutical understanding of the theological task."[97] Daniel Kauffman asserts that the Bible is "THE BOOK, because there is none other of like authority, of like authorship."[98] The *Confession of Faith in a Mennonite Perspective* states, "The Bible is the essential book of the church." All beliefs and practices are to be examined in light of the teaching of Scripture, for it is the written Word of God.[99]

Yet in doing theology there are subordinate sources to which Anabaptists closely attend. Although it is true that in principle Anabaptists historically have sought to formulate their theology based on Scripture alone, in practice and more recently also in principle, Anabaptists have acknowledged a role for tradition.[100] Early Anabaptists were "rather unaware of tradition,"[101] if not assertively hostile to it.[102] It would be a mistake, however, to conclude that tradition does not function as a source for theology. Anabaptists have thought it important to set forth in writing summary statements of their beliefs, beginning with the Schleitheim Confession in 1527 and continuing to the *Confession of Faith in a Mennonite Perspective* of 1995. Many Anabaptists are careful to distinguish between creedal theology and confessional theology.[103] From an Anabaptist perspective, creeds are mistakenly regarded as universally binding documents that are not genuinely open for revision. Confessions, by contrast, are "statements of the working consensus of the group, and they are open to revision by ongoing consensus."[104] Understood in this way, confessional tradition can be incorporated into theological reflection without necessarily undermining the authority of Scripture.[105] In addition to confessions, the Anabaptist tradition has produced a number of catechisms, such as the Shorter Catechism of 1690 and the Waldeck Catechism of 1778.[106] Thus, although it is not inaccurate to describe Anabaptism as "noncreedal," it would be mistaken to assume that it is unaffected by tradition.[107] The traditions drawn upon and generated by early Anabaptists may have differed from the other sixteenth-century reform movements, but the traditions they generated "were no less influential on subsequent generations of Anabaptist interpreters." Throughout their history Anabaptists have looked to and drawn upon the methods and beliefs of Anabaptists of preceding generations, while at the same time wrestling with the "challenging memory" of "the initial protest against tradition's binding influence."[108]

Like other Protestant traditions, Anabaptism affirmed the principle of *sola scriptura*. Yet J. Denny Weaver notes that, while recognizing the primacy of Scripture, early Anabaptists were distinctive not because "they owned Bibles and read them," but rather because of "the way they read the Bible."[109] There are five characteristics of the way Anabaptists approach reading the Bible worth noting here.[110] Three of these pertain to those who do the interpretation, while the other two characteristics have to do with the object of interpretation, the Bible. First, biblical interpretation is carried out in and from the context of Christian community. The interpretation of Scripture is a corporate undertaking. It is, as the *Confession of Faith in a Mennonite Perspective* indicates, a work of the church, the faith community that tests individual's hermeneutical understandings and interpretations.[111] Furthermore, in this, as in other tasks, the interpretive community is to be "egalitarian," manifesting genuine respect for the communion of the saints.[112] In addition to protecting disciples from "the tyranny of individualist interpretation," this communal approach to reading Scripture helps guard against "the tyranny of the specialized knowledge and equipment of the scholar."[113] Every disciple, formally educated or not, has a right and a capacity to contribute to the community's interpretation of the Bible.[114] As Barbara MacHaffie notes, however, although historically it has been "claimed that all who had been saved were spiritual equals . . . most leaders were reluctant to give real voice to women."[115]

Second, this interpretive community must be characterized by obedience to God. "Evangelical Anabaptists insisted," notes A. J. Klassen, "on the obedience of the listening disciple in the hermeneutic community."[116] Obedience is inextricably linked with rightly reading the Scriptures. "Many Anabaptists saw obedience," observes Murray, "not only as the goal of hermeneutics but as its crucial prerequisite."[117] A. J. Klassen writes, "Only he who is committed to obeying Christ can really know the truth of the Scripture as God intended it to be understood"; in fact, "Access to correct knowledge is specifically limited to those who are willing to obey the Word no matter what the cost."[118] Readiness to obey Christ's teachings is, according to Walter Klaassen, "prerequisite to understanding them."[119] Indeed, "the true interpreter of Scripture is known by the outward witness of that interpreter's life," the "outer manifestations of inner, spiritual renewal."[120]

These two commitments—to community and obedience—are in turn rooted in a third characteristic of Anabaptist hermeneutics: it is pneumatological.[121] Disciples' reading of the Bible is enabled, both individually and corporately, by the same Spirit that guided the writing of the Scriptures. Thus, "if one comes to the

Scriptures with an honest and searching heart, the Spirit of God will illumine the mind and remove hindrances to understanding."[122] Furthermore, although, as noted above, male leaders often have been reluctant to invest women with prominent leadership roles, MacHaffie also observes that the Anabaptist emphasis on the illuminating work of the Spirit has sometimes enabled more women to assume more varied roles than in traditions where such a pneumatological emphasis is not as prominent.[123]

In addition to these three characteristics of the interpreting community, the Anabaptist view of the Bible shapes the Anabaptist reading of Scripture in two ways. First, inspired Scripture consists in all sixty-six books of the Bible,[124] but the twenty-seven books of the New Testament are given priority over the Old Testament.[125] From the sixteenth century into the twentieth, Mennonites have focused on the New Testament, particularly the Gospels.[126] Walter Klaassen indicates that at least portions of the Old Testament are "superseded by" the New Testament, and that at these points the Old Testament is "no longer authoritative for Christians."[127] Not all Anabaptists state the contrast this sharply. John Howard Yoder, for example, suggests that "when the Anabaptists rejected the Old Testament as a final standard for Christian obedience, this did not mean that they paid no attention to it or denied its authority. The relationship of the New Testament to the Old is not one of rejection but of fulfilment."[128] This is perhaps more representative of Anabaptist understanding, namely, that the New Testament is the fulfillment of the Old Testament. The Old Covenant was "preparatory," and its institutions were "temporary," but the New Covenant in Christ is the "fulfillment" of, not the categorical rejection of, the Old Covenant.[129] Nonetheless, the New Testament is given priority and precedence over the Old Testament.[130]

Second, this priority of the New Testament is best understood in light of the last of the five hermeneutical characteristic considered here: Christocentricity. Walter Klaassen observes that among early Anabaptists, Jesus was "moved unquestionably into the centre" of the interpretation of the Bible.[131] Jesus was "a hinge, a watershed. Before him had been one kind of historical reality; after him, another kind."[132] Before him were the Old Covenant and Old Testament; after him, and superseding the Old, are the New Covenant and New Testament. Thus, Jesus, in both his life and teachings, is the interpretive principle for both the New Testament and the Old Testament. As the *Confession of Faith in a Mennonite Perspective* exemplifies, Anabaptists "seek to understand and interpret Scripture in harmony with Jesus Christ as [they] are led by the Holy Spirit in the church." This approach is pursued because "Scripture as a whole has its center and fulfilment in him." Consequently, "his life, teachings, death, and resurrection are essential to understanding the Bible as a whole."[133] The theological distinctives of Anabaptism flow not from their affirmation of *sola scriptura,* but rather from their distinctive hermeneutical approach to the Bible and the theological conclusions to which this, in conjunction with their history, have led them.

Theology: Characteristic Beliefs

As noted at the beginning of this chapter, Anabaptist scholars have been increasingly drawn to a polygenetic understanding of the origins and development of the movement because this acknowledges the diversity within Anabaptism. Yet this diversity manifests itself within a context of "shared belief."[134] The distinctively Anabaptist commitment to a New Testament–based, noncreedal approach to following Christ includes the beliefs that humans possess free will, that the church is a separate, alternative community, that this community is characterized by obedient discipleship to Jesus, and that this obedient following includes sacrificial service to the world and refraining from all forms of violence. Here we will consider some of these by focusing on the community of discipleship and nonresistance to illustrate Anabaptist theology.

Community of discipleship.

Nachfolge *(Obedience).* The first question of the Shorter Catechism of 1690 is, "What induces [you] to desire to unite with the communion of believers and be baptized?" The answer is, "I am impelled by faith, to separate myself from the world and its sinful lusts, and to submit in obedience to my Lord, Redeemer, and Saviour, for the salvation of my soul."[135] In Anabaptist thought and life, discipleship and following Jesus are synonymous with obedience. For generations of Anabaptists, Christianity has been thought of as "discipleship . . . a faithful 'following after' (Nachfolge) of Christ, a resolute obedience to the ethical demand of the New Testament."[136] "The visible 'shape' of Anabaptist spirituality," writes Snyder, "is discipleship, the 'following after Christ' (Nachfolge Christi) in life."[137]

As Harold Bender observes, "The great word of the Anabaptists was not 'faith' as it was with the reformers, but 'following' *(nachfolge Christi)*."[138] And this obedience is not simply a theological belief to affirm; it is a virtue that is essential to genuine Christianity. "It is faith that saves, and faith alone," writes Wenger, *"but where there is no discipleship there is no saving faith."*[139] Similarly, Daniel Kauffman says that obedience is "essential to our right standing before God. It is coupled with our justification,"[140] and Robert Friedmann observes, "Once the reborn person comes to know that God has revealed to him His will, there is but one thing for him to do: to obey."[141] As Acts 5:32 indicates, the Spirit of God is given to "those who obey him," and Jesus himself identifies

turn faith into obedience

his friends as those who do what he commands (Jn 15:14; see also 1 Jn 2:3-4; Rom 5:19).

Absonderung *(Separation)*. Obedience will lead to separation from the world. J. Howard Kauffman writes, "Our only justifiable attitude toward God is that of willingness to do just as He wishes that we shall do, even though we may be the only ones under the sun who obey Him thus."[142] Again, the response to the first question of the seventeenth-century Shorter Catechism includes the statement "I am impelled by faith, to separate myself from the world and its sinful lusts."[143] In an article titled "Separation," the Christian Fundamentals reads, "We believe that we are called with a holy calling to a life of separation from the world and its follies, sinful practices, and methods; further that it is the duty of the Church to keep herself aloof from all movements which seek the reformation of society independent of the merits of the death of Christ and the experience of the new birth."[144] More recently, in the opening paragraph of the article on "Discipleship and the Christian Life," the *Confession of Faith in a Mennonite Perspective* states, "We become conformed to Christ, faithful to the will of God, and separated from the evil in the world."[145] It is "the mission of the Anabaptist-Mennonite church . . . to proclaim and practice liberation from the many shackles of the world's institutions and systems."[146]

The apostle Paul instructs Christians to "come out from among them" (2 Cor 6:17), and Anabaptists take heed of this and other New Testament teachings regarding separation, such as John 17:14; Romans 12:1-2; Colossians 1:13; Titus 2:14; 1 Peter 2:9. The world is characterized by evil. The world is characterized by rebellion against the will of God. Thus, there is "a line of demarcation" between the church and the world.[147] There is "an uncompromising ontological dualism."[148] Historically, Anabaptists have believed that obedience to the claims of Christ necessarily leads to nonconformity to the world, and the only way to realize this nonconformity is to separate from the world. Christians are to practice "a certain 'withdrawal' . . . a certain 'abandonment' of non-Christian society to its own management."[149] Yet, this is not separation simply for the sake of separation. Christians separate from the world so that they might live, both as individuals and as an alternative community, in accord with God's designs for human beings. In separation, Anabaptists often have gathered into "their own Christian society where Christ's way could and would be practiced."[150] Far from constituting a restraint or limitation, appropriate separation from the world provides a context of freedom in which God's will and ways may be pursued.

Separation, properly understood, is not intended to lead to isolation. For this reason, among others, some Anabaptist writers prefer to speak of "nonconformity" rather than "separation." "Rather than privatizing the spiritual life and divorcing it from life in the world," writes Arnold Snyder, "the Anabaptists insisted on applying the rules of the Kingdom to all of life"; thus, today Anabaptist life is marked by "hidden conviction *and* public behaviour."[151] Christian communities are "always in dialogue with their cultures," yet "the source and meanings of their beliefs and practices originate from beyond these contexts."[152] A community marked by disciplined obedience to Christ, made possible in part by an appropriate separation from the world, is God's primary means of witnessing to the people of the world. A community characterized by obedience to God, humility, charity, temperance, self-sacrifice, integrity and peace is a light that shines into the darkness of a world characterized by disobedience to God, pride, covetousness, intemperance, dishonesty and strife.[153] A community that provides "a wholesome example" of life as God intends it to be functions as "a sort of spiritual antibiotic" in a sin-sick world.[154] "We witness to the nations," states the *Confession of Faith in a Mennonite Perspective*, "by being that 'city set on a hill' which demonstrates the way of Christ."[155] Witnessing to God in Christ, whether by telling of God's love in Christ through words or by incarnating God's love through social action and relief work, is among the highest priorities of Anabaptists.

Sadly, when obedience to Christ demands it, the call to separation or nonconformity must be implemented with reference to others who are Christians. "Unfortunately the church has tended in every era of its existence," writes Wenger, "to allow its members to sink too largely to the level of contemporary society." Because "much of Christendom has too largely accommodated its life and ethic to the sub-biblical standards of the contemporary world," those who would be genuine followers of Christ must establish their own communities where God's standards rule.[156] This spirit is reflected in the title of Walter Klaassen's book *Anabaptist: Neither Catholic nor Protestant*. Protestant reformers did much to recover the truth of salvation through faith in Christ alone, but they did not go far enough. They are not radical enough. Although well-intended, too many Protestants, as well as Roman Catholics, attempt to realize God's reign on earth through collaborating with people and institutions of this world rather than establishing the kingdom of God on its own terms. Each Christian, as a disciple of Jesus Christ, is to pursue God's kingdom on earth through living in focused obedience to Christ. Yet, individual Christians cannot do this alone. The nonconforming and obedient life can be lived only when the Christ-follower is rooted in a community of other Christ-followers who also are pursuing nonconforming and obedient lives.

Gemeinde *(Community)*. As we noted above, the world is hostile to the ways of God. Consequently, individual believers need the support of Christian com-

munity in order to live as obedient disciples in the world. The personal or individual is inextricably "intertwined," says Thomas Finger, with the communal.[157]
Snyder notes, "It is in the communal setting of the Body of Christ that one can
profess one's faith openly, and pledge to live according to that faith, with the
help of other members." In this community "the 'habits of heaven' are practiced
and acquired" in order to live lives "in uncompromising obedience, in face of
any opposition presented to it by the powers of 'the world.'"[158] The *Gemeinde,*
or brotherhood-church, is "greatly needed to give strength for this fight."[159] Separation is pursued not as an end in itself; rather, it is pursued so that the church,
or Christian community, might be realized. God's design is that his people live
together in community. God's people are, as Paul says, a body. And separation
is the only way that genuine Christian community can be realized. The church
is to be "a body of committed and practicing Christians pledged to the highest
standard of New Testament living," and for many Anabaptists this has necessi-
tated "the gathering of true Christians into their own Christian society where
Christ's way could and would be practiced."[160] "The Anabaptist vision is inherently corporate," writes Finger, and "turning from the world to Christ involves
joining a body that seeks to wholly follow Christ."[161]

By New Testament definition (e.g., 1 Cor 12:12-31; Eph 4:11-16), a body that
seeks to wholly follow Christ is composed only of disciples of Christ. Christian
community as envisioned within Anabaptism consists solely of demonstrably
committed Christians. This view of community determines Anabaptist baptismal
practices, not vice versa. Their concern is not with rebaptizing, as the name
given by their opponents, *Ana*baptist, suggests; nor is their primary concern
with refraining from baptizing infants, though they indeed do so. Rather, their
concern is for the integrity and authenticity of the Christian community. This
community consists of those, and only of those, who have consciously committed their lives to Jesus Christ. Consequently, only believers—those who have
made this conscious commitment and demonstrate this commitment in both
word and deed—are baptized.[162]

What does a community of nonconforming, obedient followers of Christ look
like? What are the characteristics of this *Gemeinde* that make it "the essential
context for the practice and transmission of Christianity"?[163] The *Gemeinde,* or
community, is the context in which the Scriptures are read with the benefit of
interpretation by the priesthood of believers. The community is a source of
shared strength in the "never-ending fight against sin and temptation."[164] Holiness of life is modeled and encouraged. And, when individual believers are disobedient and succumb to temptation, the community provides discipline, in accord with Matthew 18:15-18.[165] The community constitutes a collective witness

to the society in which it lives by embodying a foreshadowing of the kingdom of God. This witness includes caring for the physical and material needs of both the members of the priesthood of believers and the people of the world. In a word, this community is to be characterized by love. "Christ calls us to love," writes Finger, "to servanthood, to humility—to virtues which cannot be practiced by isolated individuals. These can blossom only in communities which seek to direct their entire existence in accord with them. And one cannot consistently behave in this way toward the world—a world which is often hostile—without the community's assistance and encouragement."[166] Furthermore, the assistance and encouragement of the community in living in love is all the more needed because the hostility of the world is always to be responded to in a spirit of peace, a spirit of nonresistance.[167]

Peace.

Nonresistance. Jesus instructed his followers, "Do not resist an evildoer. But if anyone strikes you on the right cheek, turn the other also; and if anyone wants to sue you and take your coat, give your cloak as well; and if anyone forces you to go one mile, go also the second mile" (Mt 5:39-41; cf. Lk 6:27-31). When he was mocked and beaten by soldiers and then led to his cross, Jesus practiced what he preached (Mt 27:27-31; Mk 15:16-20). Those who would be obedient followers of Jesus are called to follow him in word and deed. This includes imitating him in love and nonresistance.[168]

This commitment to peace and nonresistance has been woven into the teaching and practices of Anabaptists from their earliest days.[169] At the conclusion of an article on separation from the world, the Schleitheim Confession instructs, "Thereby shall also fall away from us the diabolical weapons of violence—such as sword, armor, and the like, and all of their use to protect friends or against enemies—by virtue of the word of Christ: 'you shall not resist evil.'"[170] Citing Matthew 5:39, 44, Isaiah 2:4 and Micah 4:3, the Dordrecht Confession states, "The Lord Jesus has forbidden his disciples and followers all revenge and resistance, and has thereby commanded them not to 'return evil for evil, nor railing for railing'; but to 'put up the sword into the sheath,' or, as the prophets foretold, 'beat them into ploughshares.'"[171] Anabaptists were the most violently persecuted Christian movement of the sixteenth century, being pursued by both Roman Catholic and Protestant forces, in conjunction with civil authorities. Consequently, Anabaptists were confronted by the demand to practice in the most radical ways this principle of nonresistance, and many practiced the principle to the point of suffering a martyr's death.

The commitment to nonresistance flows from a number of the Anabaptist theological and methodological commitments noted earlier. The Old Testament is not neglected,[172] but the New Testament is given a certain priority. J. C. Wenger states, "What was permitted in the Old Testament," notably taking up arms and pursuing warfare, "could now [following Jesus] be forbidden."[173] Walter Klaassen indicates that nonresistance is based on "the distinction between the old and new covenants. The use of the sword was allowed in the old, but was not taken into the new covenant under Christ."[174] "Probably the most important principle of interpretation," writes John Roth, "is a basic distinction between the Old Testament—with its themes of promise, law, and warfare—and the New Testament, with its parallel motifs of fulfillment, grace, and self-giving love."[175] Furthermore, while not neglecting other portions of the New Testament, the call to nonresistance emphasizes the teachings of Jesus, in both word and deed, as these are recorded in the Gospels (including Mt 5:36-45; 16:24; 20:25; 23:1-36; 26:52; Lk 2:14; 12:13; Jn 2:13-22; 8:22; 14:27; 18:36). "The supreme example of nonresistance is the Lord Jesus Himself," instructs the Mennonite Confession of Faith. "The teaching of Jesus not to resist him who is evil requires the renunciation by His disciples of all violence in human relations."[176] Daniel Kauffman describes Jesus as one who was "mighty in His conflict with sin, but gentle as a lamb and harmless as a dove in the matter of exerting physical power in overawing His enemies."[177] Jesus' love expressed itself in peaceful nonresistance. Those who follow him must likewise live lives of peaceful nonresistance flowing from God's love. They are to embody "defenseless love."[178] This love can be manifest in accepting verbal assault "without retort," or suffering loss of property "without commensurate revenge," or experiencing financial exploitation "without litigation."[179] And, in order to follow Jesus in this way, individuals must find strength for nonresistance in and through the community of disciples. While nonresistance may mean that the follower of Jesus stands against and outside of the power structures of the world, he or she stands with and inside the Christian community. Jesus' disciples model the peace of love both among themselves and between themselves and the world. Nonresistance is not a characteristic of individual Christians only, nor is it to be regarded as a characteristic of just some of the traditions of Christianity; it is a mark of the people of God.[180]

Finally, the commitment to nonresistance flows from the call to obedience that marks both the Anabaptist biblical hermeneutic and the understanding of community. When they study the Scriptures, disciples of Jesus must be prepared to follow wherever the Bible or, more to the point, Jesus leads. Nonresistance is one manifestation of *Nachfolge* (obedience). The community provides the context not only for studying the Scriptures, but also for obeying the Scriptures, and that obedience includes nonresistance. The community of disciples is a community of obedience, and the obedient community will respond to evil with good, respond to violence with peace, and respond to hatred with love. Yet this peace and love should not be equated with quietism or pacifism. The peace and love of nonresistance are active, not passive.

Service. Just as separation is not intended to lead to isolation from the world, so nonresistance is not to be equated with noninvolvement. The pursuit of peace and nonresistance entails not only refraining from evil, but also doing good. Peaceful nonresistance is "a totally new life orientation in which all human relationships are governed by patience, understanding, love, forgiveness, and a desire for the redemption even of the enemy. It is part of the new way of ordering human relationships under the new covenant."[181] Peace entails not only the absence of conflict but also "the restoration of right relationship." This includes right relationships with God, among people, among nations and with the created order.[182] The *Confession of Faith in a Mennonite Perspective* teaches, "Led by the Holy Spirit, we follow Christ in the way of peace, doing justice, bringing reconciliation, and practicing nonresistance."[183] Anabaptists are known around the world for their good works on behalf of the materially and spiritually poor, the materially and spiritually hungry.[184]

Conclusion: Faith for Radical Community

It is not surprising that a movement whose origins entailed severe persecution is one that stresses the importance of Christian community. It may be surprising, though it is all the more commendable, that this same movement, having suffered violent persecution, embraces peaceful nonresistance and service to the world. Anabaptists read the Bible together, and while they formulate comprehensive statements of faith, their greatest concerns lay in doing what they believe the Bible teaches. In seeking guidance for what they are to do, they pay particular attention to the Gospels and the rest of the New Testament. Here, in the life and teachings of Jesus, they find the guidelines for their own faith and life. And, as disciples of Christ, they place a priority on obediently following him. They follow him in separation into genuine community. They follow him in peaceful nonresistance. They follow him in service to the world.

FOR FURTHER STUDY

The endnotes contain citations of many useful resources, most of them written from within the Anabapist tradition. A brief list of resources for further study follows here. Some of these resources consider Anabaptist or Mennonite traditions in general, while others focus on history and/or theology.

Bibliographies

A number of general bibliographies of Anabaptist and Mennonite resources have been published in languages other than English. In English, two journals periodically publish extensive bibliographies on selected persons or themes in Anabaptist and Mennonite history and theology: *The Conrad Grebel Review* and *The Mennonite Quarterly Review*.

Reference Works

Bender, Harold S., et al., eds. *The Mennonite Encyclopedia: A Comprehensive Reference Work on the Anabaptist-Mennonite Movement*. 5 vols. Hillsboro, Kans.: Mennonite Brethren Publishing House; Scottdale, Penn.: Herald, 1955-1990.

Durnbaugh, Donald F., ed. *The Brethren Encyclopedia*. 3 vols. Philadelphia: The Brethren Encyclopedia, 1983-1984.

Kraybill, Donald B., and C. Nelson Hostetter. *Anabaptist World USA*. Scottdale, Penn.: Herald, 2001.

Mennonnite World Handbook, 1990. Carol Stream, Ill.: Mennonite World Conference, 1990.

Survey Resources

Dyck, Cornelius J. *An Introduction to Mennonite History*. 3rd ed. Scottdale, Penn.: Herald, 1993.

Snyder, Arnold. *Anabaptist History and Theology: An Introduction*. Kitchener, Ont.: Pandora, 1995.

Primary Historical and Theological Resources

Loewen, Howard J., ed. *One Lord, One Church, One Hope, and One God: Mennonite Confessions of Faith*. Text-Reader Series 2. Elkhart, Ind.: Institute of Mennonite Studies, 1985.

Recent and Current Theological Explorations

Biesecker-Mast, Susan, and Gerald Biesecker-Mast, eds. *Anabaptists and Postmodernity*. C. Henry Smith Series 1. Telford, Penn.: Pandora; Scottdale, Penn.: Herald, 2000.

Kraus, C. Norman. *Using Scripture in a Global Age: Framing Biblical Issues*. Occasional Papers 24. Telford, Penn.: Cascadia; Scottdale, Penn.: Herald, 2006.

Liechty, Daniel. *Reflecting on Faith in a Post-Christian Time*. Living Issues Discussion Series 3. Telford, Penn.: Cascadia; Scottdale, Penn.: Herald, 2003.

Reimer, A. James. *The Dogmatic Imagination : The Dynamics of Christian Belief.* Scottdale, Penn.: Herald, 2003.

Roth, John D., ed. *Engaging Anabaptism: Conversations with a Radical Tradition.* Scottdale, Penn.: Herald, 2001.

Weaver, J. Denny. *Anabaptist Theology in the Face of Postmodernity: A Proposal for the Third Millennium.* C. Henry Smith Series 2. Scottdale, Penn.: Herald, 2000.

4 ■ To the Glory of God and God Alone

Reformed Theology

God, the great Creator of all things, doth uphold, direct, dispose, and govern all creatures, actions and things, from the greatest even to the least, by his most wise and holy providence, according to his infallible foreknowledge and the free and immutable counsel of his own will, to the praise of the glory of his wisdom, power, justice, goodness, and mercy.

Westminster Confession of Faith

Calvinism understood that the world was not to be saved by ethical philosophizing, but only by the restoration of tenderness of conscience. Therefore it did not indulge in reasoning, but appealed directly to the soul, and placed it face to face with the Living God, so that the heart trembled at His holy majesty, and in that majesty, discovered the glory of His love.

Abraham Kuyper, *Lectures on Calvinism*

Calvinism has a message. . . . It reminds every man who will hearken to reflect that always, in good or evil circumstances, he has to do with God.

John T. McNeill, *The History and Character of Calvinism*

My wife and I had just moved to the East Coast, and we wanted to find a local church home. People in the area frequently commended to us a Presbyterian congregation in a nearby town. The name of the church was New Providence Presbyterian Church, and it was located in the town of New Providence. The building was quite old. A cemetery with well-weathered grave markers, some beyond legibility, lay adjacent to the oldest part. Two pulpits stood in the sanctuary, one for preaching the Word and one for other liturgical functions. The pulpit for preaching was the larger and higher of the two. A balcony surrounded three sides of the sanctuary above the main floor, and, according to local legend, the legacy of the balcony, or what became of the balcony, is reflected in the name of the town and the church.

Just after the worship service dismissed one Sunday morning, more than a century before my wife and I visited, the congregants heard loud cracking noises coming from the building. A moment later the balcony collapsed, crashing down upon the pews on the main floor. Fortunately—or more to the point, providentially—everyone had just left the sanctuary. This potentially tragic episode proved to be disruptive and expensive, but little more. No one was hurt. And, in recognition of God's sovereign watchcare over his people, the place was named New Providence.

Context: Historical and Ecclesiastical Background

Historical origins and development. From the 1560s into the 1590s, the term *Reformed* was roughly equivalent to *evangelical* and was taken to include a variety of "protest" movements within the church, including Lutheranism.[1] By the 1590s, the diversity among these evangelical and often protesting Christians was increasingly manifest, and subtraditions were becoming increasingly distinct.[2] One of these, rooted in the work of Martin Luther and centered in Germany, came to be known as "Lutheranism." Another group was chided as "Anabaptists," because they "rebaptized" people who had been baptized when infants. Yet another major subgroup came to be known as the "Reformed" tradition. This tradition has its origins in reforming movements of sixteenth-century Switzerland and Strasbourg.[3] Characteristic emphases among these movements included commitment to the reforming of the church in accord with the written Word of God and to simplicity in worship and discipline, both individual and corporate.[4] John Hesselink expresses the "Reformed" mind when he says, "The word denotes more than an accomplishment. *Ecclesia reformate semper reformanda est!* 'A Reformed church must ever be reforming itself'—in accordance with the Word of God."[5]

There is considerable overlap in usage between the terms *Reformed, Calvinist* and *Presbyterian*, and for some people two or more of these terms function as synonyms.[6] However, there are nuances and distinctions worth noting. The theology of John Calvin (1509-1564) certainly is seminal and central to the development of the Reformed tradition, though it is not exclusively so.[7] Other figures who had significant formative influence early in the history of the tradition include John Oecolampadius (1482-1531), Ulrich Zwingli (1484-1531), William Farel (1489-1565), Martin Bucer (1491-1551), Heinrich Bullinger (1504-1575), John Knox (ca. 1513-1572) and Theodore Beza (1519-1605). Similarly, Presbyterianism constitutes an important part of the Reformed tradition, but it does not embody the entirety of the tradition. Whereas "Calvinism" tends to highlight theology, "Presbyterianism" tends to highlight church government and polity. In the present chapter we will consider the Calvinist theological tradition within the larger context of the Reformed tradition.

The origins of the Reformed tradition are found in reformational ideas and events in Zurich, Switzerland, in the years following Luther's posting of his theses in 1517. As reform unfolded in the 1520s, "the Swiss reformers were more radical than Luther. Luther wanted to eliminate from the life of the church everything condemned by Scripture, but the Swiss insisted that every Christian practice should have positive warrant in Scripture."[8] Ulrich Zwingli, John Oecolampadius and Heinrich Bullinger pressed for a church that believed and did only that which had specific endorsement from the Bible. Zwingli often is regarded as the first representative of the Reformed tradition, and its beginning often is associated with his 1519 lectures on the New Testament while he was People's Preacher at the Great Minster.[9] In these lectures and his sermons he attacked the doctrine of purgatory, the invocation of saints and monasticism. Under Zwingli's leadership throughout the 1520s, application of a "negative" test of Scripture—beliefs and practices that are not specifically authorized by the Bible must be rejected—reformed the worship and teaching in the church. Images, shrines and organs were removed from sanctuaries, singing was eliminated from services, and the Mass was replaced by a simple celebration of the Lord's Supper.[10] Upon Zwingli's death while in retreat from the Battle of Cappel in 1531, Bullinger succeeded him as People's Preacher at the Great Minster, where he remained until his death in 1575.[11] Among Bullinger's greatest contributions to the Reformed movement was his leadership in the formulation of statements of faith. He was the primary author of the First Helvetic Confession (1536), which was the first extensive and distinctively Reformed confession, and the Second Helvetic Confession (1566). The Reformed movement in Switzerland was not confined to Zurich. Oecolampadius, a contemporary of Zwingli, led the cause from his post as a pastor in Basel. Although a bit more cautious than Zwingli and not as able theologically as Bullinger, Oecolampadius contended for the Reformed faith in public disputations and provided the leadership necessary for the implementation of Reformed changes in the churches of Basel.[12]

In addition to reforming the church in these German-speaking regions of Switzerland, the Reformed movement took hold in French-speaking Geneva, Switzerland, and in France. The best-known and influential figure here, and eventually elsewhere, was John Calvin. Calvin is correctly viewed as a "second generation reformer," continuing in the spirit of work by people such as Luther, Zwingli, Bucer, who was one of Calvin's teachers, and William Farel, Calvin's predecessor at Geneva. As such, Calvin was in a position to provide "positive solutions to problems which had only been defined" by his reformational predecessors.[13] Having studied both theology and then law, Calvin, in 1533 or 1534, had a profound religious experience. Some refer to this experience as his "conversion," and it left him with a burden to see the purity of the church restored. As a result of his efforts to bring about purification of the church, opposition to Calvin's efforts was such that he fled France and went to Strasbourg, Germany. Within two years he went to Geneva, where he worked on landmark contributions to both ecclesiastical and theological reform. His outline for ecclesiastical, as well as social, reform is set forth in "Articles Concerning the Organization of the Church and of Worship at Geneva," and it was the principles articulated here that guided Calvin in the institutional reforms he implemented in Geneva.

In 1536, Calvin wrote the first edition of his *Institutes of the Christian Religion.*[14] This work, which underwent a number of expansions and revisions culminating in the 1559 edition, has become synonymous with the name of Calvin and has proved to be an abiding resource within the Reformed tradition. "Although Reformed theology is not synonymous with Calvinism," observes David Fergusson, "the writings of John Calvin—especially the *Institutes*—provide the clearest index into the theological characteristics of the Reformed movement."[15] However, the political winds were such that by the spring of 1538, Calvin and Farel essentially were driven from Geneva due to opposition to their agenda for reform. Once again Calvin retreated to Strasbourg. And, once again, in 1541, under a sense of obligation to God, he reluctantly returned to Geneva. This time he and Farel succeeded in implementing many of their desired reforms in both church and civil society. For example, behaviors such as drunkenness and wifebeating were harshly suppressed among the populace of Geneva, and dancing and theater were curtailed. Preaching based explicitly on Scripture became the norm, rigorous church discipline was implemented, and the Lord's Table was no longer regarded as a sacrifice and a good work but rather as participation in the mystery of union with Christ.[16] Geneva proved to be a laboratory in which Calvin formulated a shape for the church that came to influence "a whole constituency of Reformed churches, everywhere indebted to his doctrine, his discipline, and his worship."[17]

From the 1540s onward, the Reformed movement in France was overseen largely from Switzerland because Geneva was not under the political control of France.[18] By 1559 there were enough Protestant churches in France to form a national synod. This synod was "staunchly Calvinist in theology" and influential politically because at this point it incorporated virtually every group that opposed the Roman Catholic Church.[19] From the sixteenth century until the French

Revolution, the story of the Huguenots, as French Calvinists are known, is a story of alternating and varying degrees of religious war and peace, of governmental suppression and freedom.[20] In Germany, the Peace of Augsburg (1555), while denying individual religious freedom, permitted princes to choose between Roman Catholicism and Lutheranism as the religion of their territories. Thus, Calvinism was in effect outlawed in Germany. Nonetheless, Elector Frederick III of the Palatinate, in southwest Germany, welcomed Calvinistic ideas, and Calvinism, including Covenant (or Federal) theology, flourished there into the seventeenth century.

Covenant theology was a variation on Calvin's theology that emerged from theological controversy between Lutheran and Reformed Christians in the Palatinate region. According to covenant theology, divine election is based upon an agreement or covenant between God and Christ or between God and the elect.[21] Also formed in Germany and influenced by Calvin's theology was the Heidelberg Catechism (1563). Drafted by Zacharia Ursinus (1534-1583) and Caspar Olivianus (1536-1587), it became by some estimates "the most popular and enduring confessional contribution of the Reformed Churches."[22] In a nation that was increasingly Lutheran, Ursinus and Olivianus were commissioned to draft a document that would be "basically Calvinistic" yet would "avoid offending the moderate Lutherans," namely, those who followed Phillipp Melanchthon.[23] They succeeded. Although Calvinist in what is affirmed, the Heidelberg Catechism contains no reference to limited atonement or to double predestination, nor does it speculate on the nature of Christ's presence in the Lord's Supper.

Reformed ideas readily spread from French-speaking and German-speaking regions to the Low Countries, and there "the Reformed type of Protestantism was firmly entrenched" by the middle of the sixteenth century. The strength of the Reformed tradition was further enhanced by "the alignment of the Reformed community" with the nationalist battle for freedom from Spain.[24] By the time this freedom was realized in 1581, the Dutch church had emerged as a productive and influential center of theological thought.[25] One of the standard confessional documents of the Reformed tradition, the Belgic Confession of Faith, was produced in 1561.

The Reformed movement spread to England and Scotland. Among the sources of Reformed influence in England were Martin Bucer, who spent the final years of his life in England, and John à Lasco (1499-1560), a Reformed minister of Polish birth who served as pastor of the Church of the Strangers in London from 1550 to 1553. John à Lasco often is credited with bringing a Reformed influence to bear upon the 1552 edition of the Church of England's *Book of*

Common Prayer.[26] This edition excluded all copes and vestments, and it rejected the hearing of confessions by clergy. Most important, this edition also changed the emphasis on the celebration of the Lord's Supper from sacrifice and the real presence of Christ to commemoration and communion.[27] With the rise of Elizabeth I to the throne in 1558, Reformed theology increasingly shared the Church of England with other theological perspectives. The Church of England became even more comprehensive. As John Leith observes, "Reformed theology lived with the worship of the *Book of Common Prayer,* with episcopal polity, and with divergent theologies, such as Arminianism."[28]

Protestantism emerged as a movement in Scotland in the wake of the arrival of William Tyndale's English translation of the New Testament in 1526.[29] The Reformed tradition, which came to be the predominant form of Protestantism in Scotland, was first advanced by George Wishart (ca. 1513-1546), an educator and preacher who was well acquainted with Lutheran and Zwinglian ideas. In the wake of Wishart's martyrdom, John Knox advanced the Reformed expression of the Reformation with significant force and effectiveness in Scotland. In part through the influence of Wishart, Knox came to embrace a prophetic sense of vocation and Bucer's doctrine of the Lord's Supper. For example, he referred to "the table" rather than "the altar," and he viewed what transpired at this table as being a memorial to the death of Christ rather than a sacrifice. He accepted a call to preach at St. Andrews Castle, but shortly thereafter the castle fell to the French. Knox was captured and enslaved for almost two years. Upon being freed in 1549, he became preacher at Berwick, where he served until Mary Tudor assumed the throne in 1553 and proceeded to restore Roman Catholicism. Knox fled to the continent, serving in Frankfurt, Germany, and then Geneva, Switzerland. During this time he obtained counsel and guidance from Calvin and Bullinger, among others. By the time Knox returned to Scotland in 1559, he had become "in most respects a Calvinist."[30] His Reformed theology came to bear upon the Kirk of Scotland through, among other means, his active role in the formulation of the Kirk's liturgy and *Book of Common Order* (1564), which was significantly Presbyterian in character.[31] *The Genevan Service* was based largely upon Calvin's *Form of Prayers.*[32] Knox was also one of six drafters, possibly chief among them, of the Calvinistic Scottish Confession of Faith (1560).

The seventeenth century saw a number of important Reformed theological developments, though as Richard Muller has convincingly shown, these developments are marked by far more continuity with the Reformation of the sixteenth century than has often been recognized.[33]

As was the case with Lutheranism, Reformed theologians vigorously debated among themselves and produced books of theology and confessional documents that have proved to be abiding standards within the tradition. François Turretin (1623-1687), of Geneva, published a comprehensive theology, *Institutio theologiae elenchticae* (1679-1685), and William Ames (1576-1633), of England, published *The Marrow of Theology* (1627), both of which Reformed theologians draw upon today. In the Netherlands a group known as the Remonstrants, followers of Jacobus Arminius (1560-1609), challenged a number of theological tenets set forth in the Belgic Confession and the Heidelberg Catechism. The culminating response to this challenge took place at the Synod of Dordt (1618-1619). Participation in the synod extended beyond the Dutch church, with representatives from Germany, the Palatinate, Switzerland and England in attendance. The formulations of the synod were somewhat tempered, largely through the influence of the international participants, constituting "a middle road" between the hyper-Calvinists, such as Francis Gomarus (1563-1641), and the Remonstrants.[34] It was here at the Synod of Dordt and in opposition to the Remonstrants that the so-called five points of Calvinism were corporately articulated for the first time: unconditional election, limited atonement, total depravity, irresistible grace, perseverance of the saints.[35]

Another landmark Reformed confessional statement emerged from the seventeenth century. Against the backdrop of British civil war between King Charles I and Parliament, the latter convened an assembly at Westminster in 1643 to formulate both a theology and a polity that would be—unlike that of the Church of England—in full accord with the Bible. After almost three years of deliberation, in 1646 the Westminster Confession was issued. From the first article on Holy Scripture to the thirty-third and final article on the Last Judgment, this confession, along with the Westminster Catechism, is a classic statement of scholastic Calvinism and has proven to be among the most influential and widely used documents within the Reformed tradition, particularly within Presbyterianism.[36] By 1660, Reformed theological influences faded from the Church of England, with the Reformed tradition in England surviving largely through the "dissenting" churches: the Baptists, Congregationalists and Presbyterians.[37]

At the same time, Puritans from England were among those who brought Calvinist theology and the Reformed tradition to North America. The first permanent Reformed settlement on the continent was formed by Puritans at Plymouth in 1620.[38] By the mid-1620s, Dutch Reformed believers were immigrating to New Amsterdam (later to be named New York), and by 1640, approximately twenty thousand Puritans had arrived from England. Many of them settled at the second Reformed settlement, founded at Massachusetts Bay in 1628.[39] From this foundation, "Reformed orthodoxy was retained in most New England pulpits for at least a century and a half, to the time of the Revolution."[40] The Presbyterian

expression of the Reformed tradition became formally organized in the early decades of the eighteenth century. The first presbytery, the Presbytery of Philadelphia, was formed in 1706, and in 1717 it was joined by three other presbyteries
to form the Synod of Philadelphia. This synod eventually adopted the Westminster standards as its confessional basis. Although Westminster generally provided
a theologically and ecclesiastically unifying platform for Presbyterianism in
America, significant divisions emerged within the Reformed tradition at large. "At
the height of the first surge of the Great Awakening in America, around 1740,"
writes George Marsden, "the classic patterns for American Reformed divisions
began to emerge." For example, revivalist "New Side" Presbyterians broke away
from Scottish "Old Side" Presbyterians, who did not encourage or embrace the
Awakening.[41] New England Presbyterianism was characterized by an emphasis
on experiential, or "experimental," piety, while Presbyterians rooted in the Scots-
Irish tradition were "more confessional."[42]

The eighteenth century also produced the most influential American Calvinist
thinker of all time, and some would say the greatest American theologian of any
theological tradition. Jonathan Edwards (1703-1758) was one of the preachers
through whom the Great Awakening spread throughout New England. After
holding pastorates in Northampton (1726-1750) and then Stockbridge (1751-
1757), Massachusetts, in 1757 Edwards reluctantly accepted the presidency of
Princeton College, founded by Presbyterians as The College of New Jersey in
1746. He died one month after his inauguration, in March 1758. His most influential theological writings, which continue to be studied, include *On the Freedom of the Will, On Original Sin* and *On the Religious Affections.*[43]

Edwards's theological legacy was advanced by Samuel Hopkins (1721-1803),
Joseph Bellamy (1719-1790) and Jonathan Edwards Jr., and what came be
known as the "New Divinity" movement. This school of thought further developed a number of Edwardsian notions that were regarded by some Calvinists as
too extreme, including the absolute sovereignty of God, the radically selfish nature of sin and the corresponding need for a rigorous Christian morality. Often
overlooked in this regard is the significance of this expression of Reformed theology in the African American experience. Through the work of the Puritan pastor Lemuel Haynes (1753-1833) and other African American Calvinists, the connection was made between New Divinity theology and the evils of slavery. John
Saillant writes, "Calvinism helped to convince Haynes and his generation of
black authors that liberty must be accompanied by virtue and social harmony."
"Acknowledging the divine providence both of evil and of good," he notes, "the
black Calvinists insisted upon the human obligation to shun sin (which was displayed in the slave trade and slavery) and to further God's benevolent design

(which was exemplified in a free and harmonious society)."[44]

By the beginning of the nineteenth century, Presbyterianism was established in Ohio, Illinois, Michigan and Kentucky.[45] Predominantly British, Irish and Scottish in its Old World ties, Presbyterianism was not the only stream of the Reformed tradition that was flourishing. In 1792 a church that was to become the Reformed Church in America organized independently of the Dutch church. Rooted in the Heidelberg Catechism, the Belgic Confession and the Canons of the Synod of Dordt, the Reformed Church in America "Americanized" Dutch Reformed thought through embracing the principles of "the separation of church and state . . . the primacy of the individual conscience, and . . . the voluntary principle for church membership."[46] Additionally, portions of Calvinist theology—particularly those related to the doctrine of God and soteriology, but not those related to the sacraments, ecclesiology and polity—were carried forward in traditions that were not otherwise Reformed, most notably the Baptists.[47]

In the nineteenth century, the Reformed tradition on the European continent, with the exception of the Netherlands, prospered largely through participation in confederations and other joint endeavors with other Protestant traditions. Furthermore, through a widespread phenomenon of revival, often referred to as the *Réveil,* innovations that were characteristically British and American, such as Christian schools and foreign missions societies, as well as distinctively American notions, such as the separation of church and state, began to influence European Protestantism, including the Reformed tradition. These widespread influences led to a considerable blending of the Reformed tradition with European Protestantism more generally.[48] In the Netherlands, however, neither other Protestant traditions nor the *Réveil* had the influence that they did elsewhere on the continent. In the latter third of the nineteenth century, Abraham Kuyper (1837-1920) led a "neo-Calvinist revival" that included influential initiatives in many spheres of society, including university education and national government.[49] Kuyper was a scholar and writer, while his colleague Herman Bavinck (1854-1921) was "the seasoned systematic theologian of the neo-Calvinist movement."[50] Bavinck's magnum opus is the four-volume *Gereformeerde Dogmatiek* (*Reformed Dogmatics* [1895-1901]), which proved to be foundational for succeeding generations of Dutch Reformed thinkers in North America.[51]

Much of the story of the Reformed tradition in North America in the nineteenth century revolves around higher education and theological controversies, some of which had fractious institutional results. John McNeill reports that in the early part of the nineteenth century, "Presbyterianism was visited with new and injurious divisions, which again grew for the most part out of revivalism, and opposition to it, both in the ministry and in the seminaries."[52] By mid-century a number of new seminaries were established: Princeton (1812), Union in Virginia (1812), Auburn (1818), Western in Pennsylvania (1827), Hartford (1834) and Union in New York (1836). The founding character of a number of these was shaped by one perspective or another in various theological controversies. For example, Hartford Seminary was founded largely in reaction against the "New Haven Theology," or "Taylorism," that developed at Yale under the leadership of Congregationalist theologian Nathaniel W. Taylor (1786-1858). New Haven thought posed a liberal challenge to traditional Westminster Calvinism by proposing alternatives to doctrines such as original sin and total depravity. This controversy persisted and became part of a subsequent larger division between "Old School" and "New School" theologies.[53] The Old School held closely to "strict confessionalism," such as the Westminster documents; the New School was "an alliance of more strongly pietist or prorevivalist Presbyterians with New England Congregationalists." The New School was, says Marsden, "more typically American," being "more tolerant of theological innovation and variety."[54] By virtue of "the southern mind-set of simple trust in the Bible," "Southern Presbyterianism was essentially Old School in character," though many southern denominations "remained generally aloof from the Old School–New School controversy."[55] When the presbyteries of the southern United States eventually did separate from the north, in 1861, it was not solely the product of Old School–New School issues, though certainly those were present. The separation was fueled also by social and political issues such as slavery and states' rights, which were dividing the entire country and many Christian traditions at mid-century.[56] In 1863 the Presbyterian Church in the United States was formed through a union of the southern branch of New School Presbyterianism with the Presbyterian Church of the Confederate States. In the north, New School and Old School Presbyterians united in 1869 to form the Presbyterian Church, U.S.A.[57]

Princeton Seminary was among the most significant venues for the formulation of nineteenth-century American theology. Particularly noteworthy among the Princeton scholars who promulgated a conservative Calvinist theology were Archibald Alexander (1772-1851), Charles Hodge (1797-1878) and Benjamin Breckenridge Warfield (1851-1921).[58] Alexander was the first professor of Princeton Seminary.[59] Hodge's three-volume *Systematic Theology* (1872-1873) became a standard, and he, along with others such as Warfield, extended his influence through *The Princeton Theological Review*. At the same time, the American Dutch theological tradition continued to develop, embodied by the churches and institutions of the Reformed Church in America and later the Christian Reformed Church. Whereas the Princeton school was more rationalistic in matters of faith and reason, the Dutch Reformed tradition, advanced by people such as Kuyper and Bavinck, took a more fideistic stance.[60] Furthermore, Dutch thought was marked by emphases on covenant and kingdom. James Bratt observes, "Covenant was arrayed against revivalism as a model of Christian initiation and against dispensationalism as a view of history; and kingdom stood over against individualism as the scope of God's purpose, and against mere soul-saving as the end."[61]

As with a number of other traditions, the Reformed tradition was marked in the twentieth century by a combination of divisions and mergers. Westminster Theological Seminary (Philadelphia) and the Presbyterian Church of America illustrate the impact of the early twentieth-century fundamentalist-modernist controversy. In the wake of a confrontation between the "old" Princeton theology of Hodge and Warfield and the "new" theology of Modernism, J. Gresham Machen (1881-1937), who had studied under Warfield, resigned from his teaching post at Princeton and with several others formed Westminster Theological Seminary in 1929. Later, in 1936, Machen provided leadership in the formation of the Presbyterian Church of America, again in response to the dominance of liberal theology in the Presbyterian Church (U.S.A.).[62] Some denominations were formed not through division, but through mergers. In 1925 the United Church of Canada was formed by the merger of many Presbyterian, Congregationalist and Methodist churches.[63] Although the United Church's "Basis of Unity" is not exclusively Reformed, it is informed by Reformed theology and polity. In 1957 the United Church of Christ was formed in the United States through the merger of two denominations that were the products of mergers that had taken place in the 1930s: the Congregational-Christian Churches and the Evangelical and Reformed Church.

A number of influential Reformed systematic theologies were produced in America in the latter part of the nineteenth century and the first half of the twentieth century. As noted above, Presbyterian scholar Charles Hodge published his influential systematic theology text in 1872-1873. A three-volume Baptist theology in the Calvinist tradition was published by Augustus Hopkins Strong (1836-1921) in 1886.[64] Louis Berkhof (1873-1957) was a theologian and educator in the Christian Reformed Church who spent much of his professional life at Calvin Seminary, in Grand Rapids, Michigan. In 1941 Berkhof published his *Systematic Theology,* which "made the deepest and most long-lasting impact on the present-day Reformed community in North America" of any American systematic theology published in the twentieth century.[65] In addition to drawing upon Calvin and sixteenth-century Reformed confessions, Berkhof's theology is influenced by the Dutch tradition as expressed in Kuyper and even more so in Bavinck.[66] A number of European theologians came to have influence in North

America, largely through the translation of portions of their works into English. This literature included works by Herman Dooyeweerd (1894-1977), a philosopher at the Free University, Amsterdam; Herman Hoeksema (1886-1965), whose *Reformed Dogmatics* was published posthumously in 1966;[67] and Gerrit Cornelius Berkouwer (1903-1996), whose series of monographs on theology was translated in fourteen English-language volumes under the title *Studies in Dogmatics* (1952-1976).[68]

Neoorthodoxy is an important part of the story of Reformed theology in the middle of the twentieth century. "In many respects," writes Dennis Voskuil, "neoorthodoxy should be interpreted as a Reformed movement." He notes that nearly all of its early exponents, including major figures such as Karl Barth (1886-1968) and Emil Brunner (1889-1966), were "drawn from denominations that cherished Reformed confessions of faith" and "emphasized many of the central themes of Reformed thought," such as divine transcendence and human depravity.[69] In America there was a wide variety of responses among Reformed theologians to the neoorthodoxy of Barth and others. It was adapted to the American scene and advanced through the theological and cultural thought of Reinhold Niebuhr (1893-1971) and H. Richard Niebuhr (1894-1962), and the influence of seminaries such as Lancaster, Union (New York) and Princeton.[70] Conservative Reformed theologians such as Louis Berkhof and Cornelius Van Til (1895-1987) of Westminster Theological Seminary responded to neoorthodoxy with concern, if not opposition.

Diversity. Although those who stand outside the Reformed tradition may view it as monolithic or homogeneous, considerable diversity exists within the community. To some Reformed observers, the nature and degree of diversity is such that they speak of "fragmentation" and a lack of cohesion within the tradition.[71] Others celebrate the diversity as "a rich abundance of confessions from the most various times and contexts over four-and-a-half centuries."[72] Whether viewed with disappointment or celebration, the diversity of the Reformed tradition reflects, as Alan Sell suggests, its rich history and "multifaceted nature"— doctrinal, ecclesiological, liturgical, linguistic and cultural.[73] Yet the same observers who recognize this diversity also speak of "the Reformed faith" and "the Reformed family," recognizing commonality amidst this diversity.[74] Elements of this commonality will be considered in the third section of this chapter. Here it will be helpful to offer a summary description of the diversity that has come to characterize the Reformed tradition, particularly in North America.

In *Reformed Confessions Harmonized,* Joel Beeke and Sinclair Ferguson analyze the Reformed tradition with reference to its diverse historical origins. They portray it with reference to its Swiss, Scottish-English and Dutch-German substreams.[75] Jean-Jacques Bauswein and Lukas Vischer, in *The Reformed Family Worldwide,* set forth a typology that includes these substreams yet more adequately reflects theological and organizational developments.[76] The primary lines of lineage here are the Reformed, Presbyterian, Congregational and United churches. The "Reformed" subtradition includes denominations such as the Reformed Church in America, the Christian Reformed Church and Churches of God—General Conference. These groups largely embody the Dutch-German heritage within the larger Reformed tradition and are rooted theologically in the Heidelberg Catechism, the Belgic Confession and the results of the Synod of Dordt. Seminaries that serve these denominations include Western Theological Seminary (Holland, Michigan) of the Reformed Church, Calvin Theological Seminary (Grand Rapids, Michigan) of the Christian Reformed Church and Winebrenner Theological Seminary (Findlay, Ohio) of the Churches of God.

The Presbyterian members of the Reformed family are descendants of Scottish-English Reformed origins. Characterized by governance by "presbyters," or elders, Presbyterian denominations in North America that often are referred to as "mainline" include the Presbyterian Church in Canada and the Presbyterian Church (U.S.A.). Presbyterian denominations that are more theologically conservative include the Presbyterian Church in America, the Orthodox Presbyterian Church, the Reformed Presbyterian Church in North America and the Evangelical Presbyterian Church.

Like the Presbyterians, Congregational churches are descendants of the Scottish-English—particularly the English—roots of the Reformed tradition. However, unlike Presbyterianism whose English ancestors include the Puritans, Congregationalism is rooted in the life and work of English "Separatists," who pursued the "gathered church" principle rather than a national, state-sponsored church. The United Church of Christ is illustrative of the more liberal stream of Congregationalism, while, as the name suggests, the Conservative Congregational Christian Church represents the more theologically conservative congregational heritage.

The United Church of Christ is also illustrative of another subgroup within the Reformed tradition, that of "United" churches. United churches typically were formed by a denomination that was historically Reformed merging with non-Reformed groups.[77] The United Church of Christ was formed in 1957 by a merger between the Evangelical and Reformed Church and the Congregational-Christian Churches. Perhaps the most prominent of these "United" denominations is the United Church of Canada, which was formed in 1925 by the merger of Presbyterian, Congregational and Methodist denominations.

THE REFORMED TRADITION

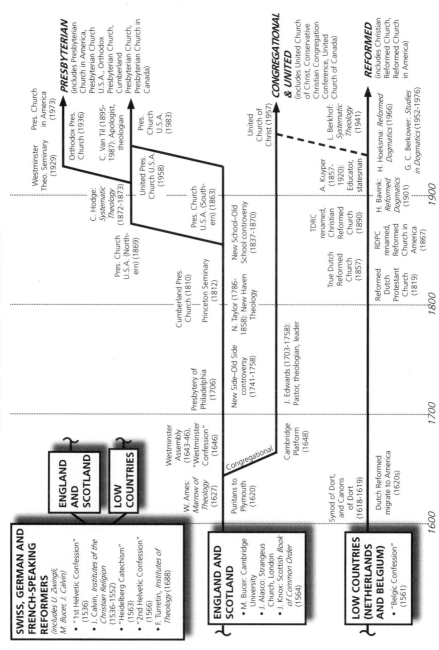

SWISS, GERMAN AND FRENCH-SPEAKING REFORMERS
(includes U. Zwingli, M. Bucer, J. Calvin)
- "1st Helvetic Confession" (1536)
- J. Calvin, *Institutes of the Christian Religion* (1536-1552)
- "Heidelberg Catechism" (1563)
- "2nd Helvetic Confession" (1566)
- F. Turretin, *Institutes of Theology* (1688)

ENGLAND AND SCOTLAND
- M. Bucer: Cambridge University
- J. Alasco: Strangeus Church, London
- J. Knox: Scottish *Book of Common Order* (1564)

LOW COUNTRIES (NETHERLANDS AND BELGIUM)
- "Belgic Confession" (1561)

PRESBYTERIAN
(includes Presbyterian Church in America, Presbyterian Church U.S.A., Orthodox Presbyterian Church, Cumberland Presbyterian Church, Presbyterian Church in Canada)

CONGREGATIONAL & UNITED
(includes United Church of Christ, Conservative Christian Congregation Conference, United Church of Canada)

REFORMED
(includes Christian Reformed Church, Reformed Church in America)

ENGLAND AND SCOTLAND

W. Ames: *Marrow of Theology* (1627)

Puritans to Plymouth (1620)

Westminster Assembly (1643-46); "Westminster Confession" (1646)

Presbytery of Philadelphia (1706)

Cambridge Platform (1648)

Congregational

New Side–Old Side controversy (1741-1758)

J. Edwards (1703-1758): Pastor, theologian, leader

Cumberland Pres. Church (1810)

Princeton Seminary (1812)

N. Taylor (1786-1858): New Haven Theology

New School–Old School controversy (1837-1870)

Pres. Church U.S.A. (Northern) (1869)

United Pres. Church U.S.A. (1958)

Pres. Church U.S.A. (Southern) (1863)

C. Hodge: *Systematic Theology* (1872-1873)

Westminster Theo. Seminary (1929)

Orthodox Pres. Church (1936)

C. Van Til (1895-1987): Apologist, theologian

Pres. Church U.S.A. (1983)

Pres. Church in America (1973)

United Church of Christ (1957)

LOW COUNTRIES (NETHERLANDS AND BELGIUM)

Synod of Dort, and Canons of Dort (1618-1619)

Dutch Reformed migrate to America (1620s)

Reformed Dutch Protestant Church (1819)

True Dutch Reformed Church (1857)

RDPC renamed, Reformed Church in America (1867)

TDRC renamed, Christian Reformed Church (1890)

A. Kuyper (1857-1920): Educator, statesman

H. Bavinck: *Reformed Dogmatics* (1901)

L. Berkhof: *Systematic Theology* (1941)

H. Hoeksma: *Reformed Dogmatics* (1966)

G. C. Berkower: *Studies in Dogmatics* (1952-1976)

1600 1700 1800 1900

There are a number of ecumenical organizations that facilitate interaction among, and common action by, Reformed churches. The oldest international association is the World Alliance of Reformed Churches, established in 1875. Other international bodies that represent various segments of the Reformed community include the Reformed Ecumenical Council (Presbyterian churches and Reformed churches), the International Federation of Free Evangelical Churches (Free churches and Covenant churches), the International Congregational Fellowship (a fellowship of individual persons in Congregational churches), the International Council of Christian Churches (Fundamentalist churches), the International Conference of Reformed Churches (conservative Reformed churches) and the World Fellowship of Reformed Churches (Presbyterian churches and Reformed churches).

Approach: Theological and Hermeneutical Method

Role of theology. There is little dispute either within or outside the tradition that disciplined theological work has always been highly important to those who identify themselves as Reformed.[78] There is more to Reformed theology than Calvinism, but the seminal and abiding significance of Calvin's *Institutes of the Christian Religion* is symbolic of the prominent place theology has always held in the Reformed tradition.[79] John Leith goes so far as to suggest that part of the uniqueness of the Reformed tradition is not just "that it insists that everyone is a theologian," for many traditions in some way acknowledge this, "but that it insists that everyone should be a responsible theologian who can speak intelligibly about the faith."[80] The "claim" of theology upon the life of the Christian, observes Gordon Spykman, "rests as an abiding task"; indeed, doing theology constitutes part of living out the call to a sanctified life.[81] At the same time, it is less well known that the Reformed tradition is concerned with theology because it is "useful and profitable," because theological truth "produces holiness."[82] "Theology is," as Alisdair Heron observes, "a practical discipline" that calls people to "glimpse and serve the glory of God displayed in Jesus Christ."[83] Fully understood, theology is "a matter of the heart; it affects the whole person, intellect, will, and emotions."[84] Thus, doing theology is not an end in itself; it is to "result in godliness and the edification of the church."[85] Theology is not to dominate, but rather, as Fred Klooster indicates, to "serve."[86] And, it serves by shaping intellect, will and emotion in such a way that they bring glory to God.

Theological method. Early in the first book of the *Institutes,* Calvin writes, "In order that true religion may shine upon us, we ought to hold that it must take its beginning from heavenly doctrine and that no one can get even the slightest taste of right and sound doctrine unless he be a pupil of Scripture."[87]

Beginning in the sixteenth century, Reformed theologians "adopted without question the view that the Scriptures furnish authoritative and final direction for the Church with respect to doctrine, discipline, and worship."[88] In accord with the goal of bringing glory to God, a genuinely Reformed method of theology is one in which Scripture is the uniquely supreme source and authority, for Scripture provides as no other source can the divine self-revelation of God.[89] "The Reformed faith has always emphasized," writes Donald McKim, "that God is made known to us in and through the Holy Scriptures."[90]

This commitment to the authority of Scripture is not ultimately the result of rational argumentation or rational proof regarding the character of Scripture; rather, the authority of Scripture is established fundamentally through the witness of the Holy Spirit. Calvin writes, "If we desire to provide in the best way for our consciences . . . we ought to seek our conviction in a higher place than human reasons, judgments, or conjectures, that is, in the secret testimony of the Spirit."[91] Subsequent Reformed thinkers share this view. For example, Otto Weber writes, "Whoever has heard God's Word in Scripture can no longer place his question the way he has until then."[92] Stephen Smallman states that Reformed Christians "finally submit to the Bible because the Holy Spirit within a Christian bears witness to it as a spiritual Book."[93] It is spiritual in that the Spirit speaks of this book and through this book. It is spiritual in that it is the Word of God written.[94] The Bible offers nothing less than "the whole counsel of God concerning all things necessary for his own glory, man's salvation, faith, and life."[95] The teachings of Scripture, and these alone, are to be binding on the conscience of the Christian.[96] Thus, as Fred Klooster indicates, "in all facets of theological investigation . . . Scripture must have priority for a genuinely Reformed theologian."[97]

The first chapter of the Westminster Confession affirms that "nothing at any time is to be added" to the whole counsel of God revealed in Scripture, "whether by new revelations of the Spirit, or traditions of men."[98] For some Reformed theologians, this priority is such that the Bible is, properly speaking, the only source for theology. Writing in 1965, J. F. Peter commented, "Reformed thinkers today continue to be generally at one in rejecting the idea of tradition."[99] Among the historical and theological reasons given for this rejection, Peter cites the concern that "the giving of any authority to tradition results in disparagement of the authority of scripture."[100] However, other Reformed thinkers, such as George S. Hendry, suggest that those who in principle reject tradition have in fact "concealed their debt to tradition."[101] Louis Berkhof, a staunch advocate of the supremacy of Scripture, observes that "the theologian is always the theologian of a particular church" and approaches the reading of Scripture with "a bias" constituted by the traditional teaching of that church.[102] Peter notes

that Calvin and other Reformers "retained tradition of the very best kind," recognized "the need for the exposition of scripture," and advocated the ongoing
observance of various liturgical seasons and practices.[103]

Reformed Christianity has long been a confessional and catechetical tradition.
Hendry posits, "Tradition in the Reformed Church takes the form of confession."[104]
Rooted in the belief that the Bible can be studied and understood, Reformed
churches have set forth in confessional and catechetical documents the teachings
of Scripture.[105] Thus, according to Berkhof, "the Creeds contain the testimony of
the Church respecting the truth revealed in the Bible,"[106] and Edward Dowey
states that confessions represent "a normative consensus of the church about the
meaning of Scripture."[107] This is the view in the confessions themselves. For example, the conclusion of the Canons of the Synod of Dordt states, "This doctrine
the Synod judges to be drawn from the Word of God."[108] Having drawn upon
Scripture in the formulation of confessions, the church then employs the confessions as guides in the subsequent interpretation of Scripture. Reformed confessions are "hermeneutical . . . designed to assist the church to elicit from the written
word the living word of the gospel."[109] Thus, when reading the Scriptures, theologians "not only compare Scripture with Scripture," observes Hodge, "but they
should also pay the greatest deference to the faith of the Church."[110] Scripture constitutes the norm of norms, and because of respect for Scripture, the voice of the
church, particularly as articulated in Reformed confessions, needs to be heeded
when one studies Scripture.

Although Reformed theologians use terms such as "crucial,"[111] "normative"[112]
and "integral"[113] to describe the role of confessions, this role is also marked by
what Abraham Kuyper refers to as "the free character of Calvinism."[114] Not
bound by ecclesiastical hierarchy or a magisterial doctrinal authority, the tradition is free to develop in many and varied forms. According to the Presbyterian
Church (U.S.A.), "In the Reformed tradition confessional statements do have authority as statements of the faith of Reformed Christians at particular times and
places." Thus, "for Reformed Christians all confessional statements have only a
provisional, temporary, relative authority."[115] There are, to be sure, differing
views among Reformed theologians regarding the relative degree to which confessions are at once historically particular and abidingly valid.[116] This circum-
stantial character of confessions means that in some Reformed circles they are
open to being "corrected or even dropped, or be supplemented or replaced by
a new one."[117] In other Reformed contexts there is a greater confidence in the
abiding truthfulness and accuracy of the affirmations in classical confessional
documents. Jan Rohls suggests that Lutheran confessional development "came
to a conclusion" with the Formula of Concord (1577) and *The Book of Concord*

(1580), but that the Reformed tradition has "nothing that corresponds to this conclusion."[118] And, the fact is that there is no "global Reformed confession."[119] Thus, like the church itself, Reformed theology is *reformata et semper reformanda* (reformed and ever in need of reform).

The Reformed tradition also manifests an enthusiastic yet qualified role for reason in theology. The life of the mind has always been highly regarded in the Reformed tradition. In this respect, the tradition is a legitimate heir of the humanistic scholars—such as Calvin, Zwingli and Bucer—who shaped its beginnings. Reformed theologians were at the forefront of the seventeenth-century era of Protestant "scholasticism," and Reformed theologians have devoted themselves to the life of the mind. As one observer puts it, "The Calvinist has the reputation of being a strong logical reasoner."[120] Berkhof indicates that the theologian constructs a logical theological system, in part, by "supplying whatever links may still be missing in the confession of the Church from the Bible as the fountain-head of religious truth."[121] Nonetheless, "because he makes the Bible his ultimate foundation, [the Reformed theologian] does not hesitate to include in his system ideas difficult for reason to harmonize, ideas which seem to be logical opposites, as long as the Bible gives him reason for doing so."[122] Reformed theologians seek to employ reason within the bounds of biblical religion.[123]

By and large, the Reformed tradition has rejected the notion that experience constitutes a source or guiding norm for theology. Howard Rice suggests that Reformed Christians often have been "almost afraid of their experiences."[124] Louis Berkhof acknowledges that the theologian's "personal appropriation of the truths of revelation will naturally be reflected in his construction of the truth." Yet he also clearly states that "Scripture never refers to the Christian consciousness as a source and norm of the truth." Reformed theologians generally are committed to the principle that experience is to be guided and interpreted by the revealed truth of Scripture, not vice versa.[125] The power of God and the significance of revealed truth are to be experienced, but experience is not the gateway into a right interpretation of God's revelation. One exception to this was the Puritans, who "gave greater recognition to the importance of experiential and pastoral issues than many of their continental Reformed colleagues."[126] More recently, African Americans within the Reformed tradition have noted that "a black theology that is both biblical and culturally credible will take the experiences of black people seriously and address a theology in which experience is viewed not above but concomitant with Scripture and community."[127]

The Reformed approach to interpreting the Bible is consistent with the view of tradition, reason and experience described above. Reformed confessional documents provide essential guidance for rightly understanding the biblical text.

For example, the Presbyterian Church (U.S.A.) has stated that "faithful members of a Reformed church . . . are not free to interpret Christian faith and life (or even Scripture itself) however seems best to them personally, but are committed to submit themselves to the authority and guidance of the confessional standards of their church."[128] Given that the confessions are open to correction, they provide the basis for what Dowey calls "the lively process of biblical interpretation."[129] Thus, the Reformed tradition reads the Bible under the tutelage, though not the tyranny, of confessional tradition.

Remembering that the confessions themselves are distillations of the teaching of Scripture, Reformed biblical interpreters also use the principle of the analogy of faith or the analogy of Scripture. The principle that Scripture be used to interpret Scripture was central to Reformation hermeneutics, and it has continued to be an important principle with the Reformed tradition. The Westminster Confession teaches, "The infallible rule of interpretation of Scripture is the Scripture itself; and therefore, when there is a question about the true and full sense of any Scripture . . . it must be searched and known by other places that speak more clearly."[130] Richard Gaffin argues that the principle that Scripture interprets Scripture should be characteristic of all biblical exegesis and is thus fundamental to biblical and systematic theology.[131] In *Principles of Biblical Interpretation,* Louis Berkhof highlights this principle and states that "the interpreter must study the particular teachings of the Bible in light of its fundamental truths."[132] There has never been universal agreement within the Reformed tradition as to what these fundamental truths in the Bible are, but there are a number of biblical loci and themes that have frequently been appealed to in various sectors of the Reformed tradition. In the Reformation era, the biblical notion of justification by faith constituted a hermeneutical key.[133] Subsequently, the biblical theme of covenant served as an interpretive key for many Reformed thinkers, with covenant and covenants providing a conceptual link between the Old and New Testaments and the unifying theme of salvation history as set forth in Scripture.[134] In these and other Reformed applications of the analogy of faith there is usually a tendency to give particular attention to Pauline writings.[135]

In applying these hermeneutical principles, Reformed theologians have pursued a coherent and comprehensive understanding of all that the Bible teaches. Their reading of the Bible has not consisted in an attempt merely to compile an extensive list of biblical beliefs; rather, with the understanding that the Bible constitutes "an organic unity of which all parts are mutually related,"[136] Reformed theology has pursued "an all-comprehensive system of thought," unified, organic and whole.[137] Guided by the confessions and using Scripture, particularly Paul's writings, to interpret Scripture, theologians in the Reformed tradition strive for a thoroughly biblical and biblically thorough worldview or "a faith of the grand design."[138]

Theology: Characteristic Beliefs

As we noted above, there is considerable theological diversity within the Reformed tradition. No one confessional document has attained universally supreme status within Reformed Protestantism, and, as the editors of the *Historical Dictionary of Reformed Churches* point out, "There is no absolute agreement on the specific doctrines that constitute Reformed theology."[139] Nonetheless, there is sufficient continuity and commonality among these Christians that there is, as John Hesselink demonstrates, "a definite and distinctive Reformed approach to the Christian faith."[140] Hesselink suggests that the Reformed tradition seeks to be centered on God, submitted to Scripture, living in and through a properly ordered church, committed to godliness and edification, and guided in all of life by a coherent theological worldview.[141]

A number of other Reformed authors also advance summaries of the distinctives of the tradition. In some cases, these summaries are more comprehensive than theology alone, attempting to distill the ethos of and life within Reformed Protestantism; in other cases, the summaries are specifically and exclusively theological in nature.[142] With respect to theology, the following beliefs and emphases, taken together, are characteristic of the Reformed tradition. Reformed theology is theocentric. "More than anything else, what distinguishes the Reformed faith from all others," writes R. C. Sproul Jr., "is that it strives to understand all things in such a way that God alone receives the glory."[143] It is marked by a pervasive focus upon the trinitarian God, particularly his sovereignty and salvific work on behalf of humankind. Carter notes that a black Reformed theology is "a glory-saturated, God-focused theology" that "has the primary goal of glorifying God."[144] Reformed theology is Word-based. Reformed Christians are "a people of the Word."[145] Reformed theology is soteriologically oriented. Although the so-called TULIP, or "five points of Calvinism," does not in itself constitute either the core or a summary of Reformed theology, it is indicative of the emphasis on God's gracious redemption that pervades Reformed thought.[146] Furthermore, for many Reformed theologians these soteriological matters are rightly understood only in terms of biblical teaching regarding covenant, and they are rightly proclaimed and applied only in the context of a properly ordered church. Reformed theological reflection is comprehensive in that it seeks to provide "a faith of the grand design" that articulates a distinctively Christian understanding of God "in the wider realms of state and culture, in nature and in the cosmos"; Reformed theology is not just about theology, but is concerned with "raising the banner of Christ's lordship over the whole of life," informing and guiding Christians, individually and collectively, in all arenas of life.[147] Here we will take our cue from Bavinck's observation that the doctrine of salvation and the doctrine of God are "inseparably related to each other. The doctrine of God is at the same time a doctrine of the eternal salvation of souls, and the second of these also includes the first."[148] Thus, the discussion below is devoted to the Reformed understanding of the sovereign God and his grace.[149]

The sovereign God. The importance of the doctrine of God is not necessarily made manifest by the length or contents of Reformed discussions of "the doctrine of God" in systematic theology texts; rather, it is more clearly indicated by the way thinking about God is viewed in relation to other doctrines. "It is, I believe, in its doctrine of God," writes Thomas F. Torrance, "that the really fundamental character of any church tradition becomes revealed. . . . [and] the theologians of the Reformed church laid great emphasis upon the sovereign majesty of the mighty, living, active God."[150] The Presbyterian Church (U.S.A.) states that "central" to the Reformed tradition is "the affirmation of the majesty, holiness, and providence of God who creates, sustains, rules, and redeems the world in the freedom of sovereign righteousness and love."[151] "The whole doctrine of faith," writes Bavinck, "in its entirety and in its parts, becomes a proclamation of the praise of God, an exhibition of His excellences, a glorification of His name."[152] Calvin's biographer Emile Doumergue observes, "The doctrine of God is the doctrine of doctrines, in a sense the only doctrine."[153] And in the *Encyclopedia of the Reformed Faith,* Catherine Gonzalez suggests that the doctrine of God "is so basic, one could incorporate much of Christian doctrine into this single issue."[154] Simply put, "In everything, faith has to do with God."[155]

Reformed theologians caution that any exposition of this doctrine will fall short of complete definition or explanation, for, as Berkhof writes, "God in His inmost Being is the Incomprehensible One."[156] "To say that we can define God," observes Herman Hoeksema, "is to deny His very Godhead."[157] Nonetheless, while recognizing that we can arrive at neither an exhaustive description of God nor an adequate definition of his essence, we can—indeed, we must—come to know the revealed attributes of God and his relationship to the created order. Each of three common Reformed descriptors of God contributes to an exalted view of God as sovereign: God is Creator, Sustainer-Ruler, Redeemer.[158]

God the Creator. In accord with the ancient creeds, Reformed confessions affirm God as Creator.[159] Spykman comments that the Bible "arrests us at the very beginning with its most fundamental affirmation: God is absolutely Prior, wholly Other, the Source and Origin of all that is."[160] Hodge states that the affirmation of God as Creator in Genesis 1 is "the foundation of all subsequent revelations concerning the nature of God and his relation to the world."[161]

Reformed theology proclaims the sovereign God in its affirmation that God created everything out of nothing, and that he did so freely. Bavinck is careful to point out that "God is not solely He who *formed* the world but also He who *created* it."[162] He cites Hebrews 11:3, "By faith we understand that the worlds were prepared by the word of God, so that what is seen was made from things that are not visible," and Revelation 4:11, "You are worthy, our Lord and God, to receive glory and honor and power, for you created all things, and by your will they existed and were created." Put negatively, that which was created "was not formed out of any preexistence or substance," including God himself; put positively, God brought something—namely, all that is—into existence from nothing. God created *ex nihilo.*[163] Spykman describes this as "a fixed and immoveable sovereign act of inauguration."[164] The origin of all that exists is attributable to God and God alone. Furthermore, God engaged in this work freely, without compulsion from without or within. Hodge writes, "It was free to God to create or not to create, to create the universe as it is, or any other order and system of things, according to the good pleasure of his will." The work of creation was "not necessary."[165] The Westminster Confession states that "it pleased God" to create.[166] Of this free act, Bavinck writes, "the cause of the creation is simply and solely the free power of God, his eternal good pleasure, his absolute sovereignty."[167] By sovereign will, God was pleased to create as he did, and in sovereign power, God was free and able to create as he did.[168] God and his sovereignty are clearly manifest in creation. And, "once He had created it, He did not let it go."[169]

God the Sustainer-Ruler. The affirmation of God as Creator is inextricably linked with the affirmation of divine providence. God "does not abandon the world which creatively he called into existence, but takes care of it in such a way that it is and remains on the way to the goal which he has in mind."[170] God is the sole Sustainer-Ruler of that which he created.[171] "Where God's creating activity leaves off," writes Spykman, "there his providential care takes over. . . . Creation moves on naturally and directly into providence, with no gap between them."[172] The Belgic Confession states, "We believe that the same God, after he had created all things, did not forsake them, or give them up to fortune or chance, but that he rules and governs them, according to his holy will."[173] God sovereignly sustains and rules, for his own honor, everything he has created. Thus, "just as everything is from God," observes Bavinck, "so also everything is through him and to him (Rom. 11:36)."[174]

God's sustaining work consists in the maintenance or preservation of creation. This maintenance is "not a passive supervision. The point is not that He *lets* the world exist but that He *makes* it exist."[175] God's ruling work consists in the governance or purposeful control over that same creation. God is proclaimed to be "King of kings" and "Lord of lords" (1 Tim 6:15; cf. Rev 17:14; 19:16). In this spirit, the Westminster Confession affirms that "God, the Creator of all things, doth uphold, direct, dispose, and govern all creatures, actions, and things . . . by His most wise and holy providence, according to His infallible foreknowledge, and the free and immutable counsel of His own will, to the praise of the glory of His wisdom, power, justice, goodness, and mercy."[176] Although these two roles—sustaining and ruling—can and should be distinguished, Reformed theologians are careful to point out that they should not be separated. "Sustenance is related toward an end," notes G. C. Berkouwer. "It is not related to Divine government merely as that which preserves the stuff to be governed. It is also purposeful. . . . Sustenance has to do with the entire process in which all things move toward God's arranged end."[177] Sustenance is goal-oriented, and the goal—God's new creation—will be achieved through God's governing rule.[178] Thus, sustaining and ruling together constitute the Reformed understanding of divine providence. God created in the beginning, has sustained and governed into the present, and will sustain and govern to the sovereignly chosen and perfectly good culmination of history. As Spykman says, "Providence not only relates to the creative beginning of all things, but also points teleologically to the goal of creation in the final coming of the kingdom."[179] In this eschatological understanding of the goal of God the sovereign Sustainer-Ruler, one also sees God the Redeemer.

God the Redeemer. Reformed theology proclaims God alone as the Redeemer of fallen creation. As already noted, in Reformed theology God's creating work is related to his sustaining and ruling work. Likewise, creation is related to redemption. And, the link between them is nothing and no one other than God himself. "There is no wedge or gap between the God who created 'all things' and the God who will ultimately redeem the cosmos and be 'all in all' (1 Cor. 15:28)," writes McKim. "The God who created is the same God who redeems in Jesus Christ."[180] The structure of Calvin's *Institutes* reflects something of this, with Book One devoted to "The Knowledge of God the Creator," and Book Two devoted to "The Knowledge of God the Redeemer in Christ." Spykman states, "Redemption is analogous to creation. Each in its own way is a work of God *ex nihilo*. . . . Christian theology stresses the absolute independence and self-sufficiency and unconditional freedom of the Creator-Redeemer in his covenant faithfulness toward his creation."[181] The One who made the world is and will be faithful to work redemptively in and for the redemptive good of the world.

This covenant faithfulness means that God will not abandon the fallen creation, but rather will sustain and govern it to the fulfillment of his redemptive purposes. The knowledge of God the Redeemer is related not only to creation, but also to sustaining and ruling. "The faith in providence," writes Bavinck, "stands in the most intimate of relationships with the faith in redemption."[182] In sovereign control of the created order, God the Father brought about his redemptive work in and through Jesus Christ; and, in sovereign control of the created order, God can and will bring to fruition his redemptive work in and through Jesus Christ.[183] For example, "We see in the development of the African-American church a testimony to the sovereignty of God. He orchestrates and conducts the affairs of human history so as to accomplish his determined plan in bringing a people to himself."[184] Both Calvin and the Westminster Confession advance what has become the classically Reformed threefold understanding of Christ the Redeemer: the offices of Prophet, Priest, King.[185] The office of King embodies the link between sovereign rule and eternal redemption. Because Christ is King, he can be Redeemer, and because he is Redeemer, he is the perfect King. Those who submit to Christ's perfect rule are the beneficiaries of the blessings of redemption, which are bestowed in the sovereign grace of God.[186]

The grace of God. George Marsden remarks, "The genius of the Reformed faith has been its uncompromising emphasis on God's grace, with the corollary that our own feeble efforts are accepted, not because of any merit, but solely due to God's grace and Christ's work."[187] In the *Encyclopedia of the Reformed Faith,* George Stroup observes, "In most forms of Reformed theology, God's grace is understood as the foundation for all things."[188] "Scripture emphasizes everywhere," Hoeksema declares, "that God is gracious. He is the God of all grace, the all gracious God."[189] Just as their understanding of Christ's work as Redeemer led the Reformers to proclaim, *"Sola Christi"* (salvation in Christ alone), so too their recognition of redemption as a free gift from God led them, and now leads their Reformed descendants, to proclaim, *"Sola gratia"* (salvation by grace alone). The sovereign God, who is Creator, Sustainer-Ruler and Redeemer, is gracious, and his grace in no way violates his sovereignty. Indeed, God's sovereignty constitutes part of the basis of his grace, for grace is *freely exercised* favor or love. Grace is "God's free, sovereign, undeserved favor or love to man, in his state of sin and guilt."[190] "Grace is always sovereign and free," notes Hoeksema; "always it has its basis only in God."[191] These Reformed convictions are grounded in texts such as Ephesians 2:8-9, "For by grace you have been saved through faith, and this is not your own doing; it is the gift of God—not the result of works, so that no one may boast," and Romans 3:23-24, "All have sinned and fall short of the glory of God; they are now justified by his grace as a gift." God gives all good gifts—from earthly existence to eternal salvation—freely through his own perfect, gracious will, without any necessity or compulsion.

Common grace. Abraham Kuyper observes God's grace "extends itself, not only as a special grace, to the elect, but also as a common grace *(gratia communis)* to all mankind."[192] The Reformed tradition possesses a keen awareness of Jesus' assurance that God the Father feeds the birds of the air, clothes the grasses of the field, makes the sun rise on the evil and on the good, and sends rain to sustain both the righteous and the unrighteous (Mt 5:45; 6:26-30). This kind of Fatherly care is often referred to as "common grace."[193] As Jesus' sermon indicates, this grace operates both in the realm of nature in general and in the realm of human affairs. From the stars in the sky and the waters on the mountains to the birds of the air and the grasses of the field, God's grace is manifest in his creation of and sustaining of the natural order.[194] And this work of making and sustaining is even more profound with respect to humankind. God's life-sustaining care is "granted to all men indiscriminately," both those who thank God for gracious gifts and those who do not. God gives life and then sustains it. God gives life through creative work and sustains it both through restraining the destructive forces of evil and through maintaining, enriching, and developing humankind in general.[195] By virtue of the common grace of divine restraint, "we never experience the unrestrained outpouring of iniquity," and life, though corrupted, is livable.[196] This common grace is not in itself salvific, but its gifts are, nonetheless, genuinely good. Thus, as Richard Mouw recalls, "He shines in all that's fair."[197] And the grace of God shines even more clearly in his saving work on behalf of those human beings chosen for eternal salvation.

Saving grace. The apostle Paul celebrates the fact that God the Father chose to adopt some, including Paul himself, as spiritual children in Christ, and that the Father did so "to the praise of his glorious grace that he freely bestowed on us in the Beloved" (Eph 1:5-6). God's grace is not limited to those good gifts that he gives to the human race in general, but is exercised even further in making spiritually alive some of those who were spiritually dead (Eph 2:1-5). Reformed theologians refer to this work of God as "saving grace," "special grace" or "efficacious grace." It is deemed special because it is saving, and it is referred to as "efficacious" because it *does* unerringly save. Louis Berkhof describes saving grace as "those gracious operations of God which aim at, and result in, the removal of the guilt, the pollution, and the punishment of sin, and the ultimate salvation of sinners."[198] The Heidelberg Catechism teaches that "God, without any merit of mine, of mere grace, grants and imputes to me the perfect satisfaction, righteousness, and holiness of Christ, as if I had never committed nor had any sin."[199] Salvation is by grace, and grace alone. It is of God, and God alone.

Some of the richness of this theology of saving grace is expressed in those beliefs known as the "five points of Calvinism": unconditional election, limited atonement, total depravity, irresistible grace, perseverance of the saints. Roger Nicole states, "The five points of Calvinism are, in reality, not five separate doctrines that we assert almost as disjointed elements, but rather articulation of one point, which is the grace of God."[200] Hesslink concurs, indicating that these five affirmations are "all about *grace*."[201] Thus, these five beliefs provide a helpful introduction to the Reformed understanding of saving grace.

Having determined to create the world and permit the human race to fall into sin, God chose some members of the human race for redemption in Christ.[202] Those who are chosen are "by nature neither better nor more deserving than others," and "the good pleasure of God is the sole cause of this gracious election." God "softens the[ir] hearts" and "inclines them to believe" in Christ, while "he leaves the non-elect in his just judgment to their own wickedness and obduracy." This election and the divine work that accompanies it are "the fountain of every saving good; from which proceed faith, holiness, and the other gifts of salvation, and finally eternal life itself."[203] This is unconditional election, or what the Canons of the Synod of Dordt repeatedly refer to as "the grace of election." In the Reformed understanding, this is the grace spoken of by the apostle Paul in Romans 8:30: "Those whom he predestined he also called; and those whom he called he also justified; and those whom he justified he also glorified." And Paul goes on to alert those who are inclined to question the graciousness of this work that just as the clay does not instruct the potter, so too human beings are not to instruct the sovereign God (Rom 9:19-24). Those who know and acknowledge this electing grace of God thereby enter into the benefits of all the blessings of God's salvation, including the benefits of Christ's atonement.

"In this is love," writes the apostle John, "not that we loved God but that he loved us and sent his Son to be the atoning sacrifice for our sins" (1 Jn 4:10). Jesus Christ died for the salvation of the elect. His death is, according to the Synod of Dordt, "the only and most perfect sacrifice and satisfaction for sin" and is "of infinite worth and value."[204] Calvin writes, "To take away all cause for enmity and to reconcile us utterly to himself, [God] wipes out all evil in us by the expiation set forth in the death of Christ."[205] Christ the Priest appeased a just and holy God by providing satisfaction for the sins of God's children.[206] Through his death, Christ purchased salvation and bestowed upon the elect the gifts of faith, cleansing from sin and eternal joy in his presence. He provided atonement. And, in accord with God's gracious will and purpose, Christ determined to "effectually redeem out of every people, tribe, nation and language, all those, and those only, who were from eternity chosen to salvation, and given to him by the Father."[207] As the New Testament indicates (Jn 10:11-15; 15:13; Eph 5:25-27; Acts 20:28; Rom 8:33), this atonement of infinite worth and value was, in God's wisdom, made for Christ's "sheep," his "friends," his "church"—that is, "God's elect." Thus, the salvific intention and effect of the atonement was limited to those chosen by God the Father. This atonement manifests, say Reformed theologians, the grace of God.[208]

The apostle Paul teaches in Romans 5:8 that God proved his love through sending Christ to die for sinners. Observing this, Calvin rhetorically asks, "How could he have given in his only-begotten Son a singular pledge of his love to us if he had not already embraced us with his free favor?" "Thus he is moved," Calvin continues, "by pure and freely given love . . . to receive us into his grace. . . . By his love God the Father goes before and anticipates our reconciliation in Christ."[209] God must go before and anticipate in order for reconciliation to occur, because all those who would be saved are, as Paul states, "dead through trespasses and sins" (Eph 2:1). In the Reformed tradition this state of spiritual death often is referred to as "total depravity." The minds of those for whom Christ died were blind, vain and perverse; their hearts and wills were wicked, rebellious and hard; and all of their inclinations were impure.[210] The Westminster Confession summarizes this by saying that human beings became "dead in sin, and wholly defiled in all the faculties and parts of soul and body."[211] Once this is recognized, the glorious grace of God becomes even more evident. God not only freely takes the initiative to save by sacrificing his own Son in suffering and death, but also chooses to do this for those who are rightfully the objects of his wrath. In divine love, God graciously chooses to provide a way of salvation.[212] Given the state of humankind, there is only one way anyone could be saved: *sola gratia.*

Having determined to give the gift of salvation, the sovereign Lord would let nothing and no one thwart his gracious intentions. God's saving grace is irresistible. The irresistible (or efficacious) grace of God works on the hearts of the elect in such a way that they "are certainly, infallibly, and effectually regenerated, and do actually believe."[213] Those whom God chooses he makes alive or regenerates. And, "if the special work of regeneration . . . be the effect of almighty power," writes Hodge, "then it cannot be resisted."[214] The dead can do nothing. Those who are spiritually dead can do nothing to ultimately thwart or supplement the loving work of the almighty God. Stroup writes, "The Holy Spirit is able, when he so chooses, to overcome all human resistance and so cause his gracious work to be utterly effective and ultimately irresistible" (see Acts 16:14; 2 Cor 4:4-6; 2 Tim 2:24-25; Eph 1:17-19).[215] This does not mean that every work of the Spirit is irresistible, as is clearly implicit in Paul's warning against quenching the Spirit (1 Thess 5:19). The person who is regenerated "cooperates, or, is active in what precedes and in what follows the change," but regeneration itself is "something experienced, not something done" by the person. Those who are regenerate actively participate in conversion, sanctification and perseverance, but they are "passive" with respect to regeneration, being made alive.[216] The elect are made alive; they do not make themselves so. John 1:13 describes those who are regenerate as "born not of blood or of the will of the flesh or of the will of man, but of God" (see also Ezek 36:26-27; Jn 3:8; Eph 2:5; Jas 1:17-18). Regenerating grace is irresistible, and thereby it is pure gift.

Finally, God will preserve in faith and into eternity those whom he has chosen, for whom Christ has died and who have been regenerated and called through the gracious working of the Spirit. This is sometimes referred to as the "perseverance of the saints" or "preservation of the faithful." Reformed theologians point out that Jesus promises his followers eternal life, and that "they will never perish." "No one will snatch them out of my hand," he says; "What my Father has given me is greater than all else, and no one can snatch it out of the Father's hand" (Jn 10:28-29). In Philippians 1:6, Paul expresses confidence that "the one who began a good work among you will bring it to completion by the day of Jesus Christ" (see also Rom 11:29; 2 Thess 3:3; 2 Tim 1:12). Louis Berkhof describes it this way: "They whom God has regenerated and effectually called to a state of grace can neither totally nor finally fall away from that state, but shall certainly persevere therein to the end and be eternally saved."[217] Furthermore, as the Canons of the Synod of Dordt indicate, "those who are converted could not persevere in a state of grace if left to their own strength. But God is faithful, who having conferred grace, mercifully confirms and powerfully preserves them . . . even to the end."[218] "Our wavering faithfulness is upheld on all sides by God's unwavering faithfulness," writes Hendrikus Berkhof. "That faithfulness is not dependent on our faith; instead, our faith depends on that faithfulness of God."[219] Because God is almighty and faithful, those who have entrusted themselves to Christ ultimately will remain faithful.

Reformed theologians often cite Romans 8:29 as indicating that nothing— absolutely no thing—can ultimately separate the Christian from God in Christ, who bestows the gift of faith. This does not mean that the faithful cannot or necessarily will not, from time to time, commit grievous sins or grieve the Holy Spirit or distort and violate conscience. It does mean, however, that the faithful cannot and will not fall *totally or finally* from the saving grace of God. Just as they did not have the ability to bestow new life on themselves in the first place, neither do they have the ability to utterly destroy the gracious gift of eternal life in Christ. Commenting on Philippians 2:12-13, Hesselink observes that there is never a denial of the need to "work out your own salvation with fear and trembling," but the Reformed tradition emphasizes that such work is possible only because "it is God who is at work in you, enabling you both to will and to work for his good pleasure."[220] For example, the affirmation of perseverance in the Canons of the Synod of Dordt is immediately followed by an exhortation to "be constant in watching and prayer" in order not to be led into temptation. This exhortation is, in turn, followed by a reaffirmation of the mercy of God, who does not "suffer [fallen believers] to proceed so far as to lose the grace of adoption and forfeit the state of justification, or to commit the sin unto death."[221] From beginning to end salvation is of God, and God is gracious from beginning to end.

Conclusion: To the Glory of God and God Alone

God is great, God is good, and *theo*logy is ultimately and finally about God. Theology proclaims the sovereignty of this great God, and those who identify themselves with God will acknowledge and submit to him. This submission will be manifest in one's beliefs and conduct of life. And, this submission can be enthusiastically embraced because this great God is also good. God is Creator and Sustainer-Ruler, sovereignly extending common grace to all of his creatures, including those who neither acknowledge nor submit to him. God is Redeemer, reclaiming for himself the creation and creatures he graciously calls to himself. Shirley Heegs sums it up well: "The essence of being Reformed is to remember that God is the subject of the verb. It is God who has reformed us, and it is God who is reforming us still."[222] *Soli deo gloria:* Glory to God alone.

FOR FURTHER STUDY

The endnotes contain citations of many useful resources, most of them written from within the Reformed tradition. A brief list of resources for further study follows here. Some of these resources consider the Reformed tradition in general, while others focus on history and/or theology.

Bibliographies

Beeke, Joel R. *A Reader's Guide to Reformed Literature: An Annotated Bibliography of Reformed Theology.* Grand Rapids: Reformation Heritage, 1999.
Maltby, William S., ed. *Reformation Europe: A Guide to Research, Part II,* pp. 75-103. Reformation Guides to Research 3. St. Louis: Center for Reformation Research, 1992.

Reference Works

Hart, D. G., ed. *Dictionary of the Presbyterian and Reformed Tradition in America.* Downers Grove, Ill.: InterVarsity Press, 1999.

McKim, Donald K., ed. *Encyclopedia of the Reformed Faith.* Louisville: Westminster John Knox, 1992.

————, ed. *The Westminster Handbook to Reformed Theology.* Louisville: Westminster John Knox, 2001.

Survey Resources

Hesselink, I. John. *On Being Reformed: Distinctive Characteristics and Common Misunderstandings.* Ann Arbor, Mich.: Servant Books, 1983.

Leith, John H. *An Introduction to the Reformed Tradition: A Way of Being the Christian Community.* Rev. ed. Atlanta: John Knox, 1981.

Primary Historical and Theological Sources

Beeke, Joel R., and Sinclair B. Ferguson. *Reformed Confessions Harmonized.* Grand Rapids: Baker, 1999.

Calvin, John. *Institutes of the Christian Religion,* edited by John T. McNeill; translated by Ford Lewis Battles. 2 vols. Philadelphia: Westminster Press, 1960.

Recent and Current Theological Explorations

Alston, Wallace M., and Michael Welker, eds. *Reformed Theology: Identity and Ecumenicity.* Grand Rapids: Eerdmans, 2003.

Gerrish, B. A., ed. *Reformed Theology for the Third Christian Millennium.* Louisville: Westminster John Knox, 2003.

Pauw, Amy Plantinga, and Serene Jones, eds. *Feminist and Womanist Essays in Reformed Dogmatics.* Louisville: Westminster John Knox, 2006.

Willis-Watkins, David, and Michael Welker, eds. *Toward the Future of Reformed Theology: Tasks, Topics, Traditions.* Grand Rapids: Eerdmans, 1999.

5 ■ The Spirit of a *Via Media*

ANGLICAN THEOLOGY

It was in establishing a certain "direction" and in avoiding premature fixation
that Anglican theology in its formative period showed at once its character and
wisdom and its underlying consistency.

Paul E. More, in *Anglicanism*

Anglicanism . . . refuses to affirm as de fide and necessarily part of its identity any
doctrine not so qualified in or by Scripture and by the Primitive Church. This
deliberate travelling light is the expression of the Anglican desire to preserve and
propagate the whole Gospel and nothing but the Gospel.

H. R. McAdoo, *Anglican Heritage*

Anglican theology is a method, not a system.

D. R. G. Owen, in *The Future of Anglican Theology*

The Chicago metropolitan area is home to a rich diversity of theological seminaries, and during my days as a student I enrolled in a course offered by an
ecumenical consortium of some of these schools. Our studies for this course
were enriched through meeting for class sessions at a different campus each
week. This week we were meeting at an Episcopal seminary. In addition to the
class session, there was time to visit the campus bookstore and participate in a
chapel service prior to sharing a meal together. While I was browsing in the
bookstore, a title caught my eye: *The Book of Common Prayer.* I had no time
right then to survey the contents, but I liked the title and was attracted to the
idea that prayer could (should?) be shared in common with all Christians. I
bought a copy of the book. Time for the service arrived, and we made our way
to the campus chapel. It was rather dark, yet pleasingly warm. Wooden beams
were softly illuminated by a combination of lights and candles. Prompted to si-

lence by the candlelight and the setting, we sat quietly, waiting for the vespers service to begin. I noticed that in the bookrack on the pew in front of me were a hymnal and a copy of the book I had just purchased, *The Book of Common Prayer.* Just then, the priest entered, dressed in colorful liturgical garb, her hands gently clasped above her waist. She raised both arms, greeted us in the name of Jesus Christ, and then prayed. She acknowledged God's presence among us and asked for his blessing on our time together. She then directed us to a page in *The Book of Common Prayer* and indicated that we would be following the service set forth there. In the moments that followed, those of us gathered—students from a variety of Christian theological seminaries—recited the same words, read the same Scripture texts, prayed the same prayers . . . together.

Context: Historical and Ecclesiastical Background

Historical origins and development. As with many aspects of Anglican theology, the identification of a *terminus ad quo* is couched in ambiguity. More than any other Protestant tradition, Anglican theology has been informed by "antiquity"—that is, the first five centuries of the Christian church. Not surprisingly, then, some suggest that the history of Anglicanism is properly traced "back to the patristic period historically and to the New Testament doctrinally."[1] Based on the history of the usage of the term *Anglicanism,* others suggest a starting point in the 1830s.[2] However, most Anglican scholars agree that the origins of Anglicanism as a "separate and distinct" tradition are found in the sixteenth century.[3]

Anglican theologians from the sixteenth and subsequent centuries consistently claim that they live "in continuity with the undivided Church of the early centuries," and in modern times that the Anglican Church "does not constitute or cultivate a separate denominational identity."[4] Nonetheless, as Stephen Sykes and John Booty indicate, "one is bound to *observe* that the *de facto* distinctness of Anglicanism begins in the sixteenth century."[5] It emerged in England as Christians there embraced, to varying degrees, the movements of reformation and counterreformation that swept western Christendom.[6] The path of reform and counterreform differed significantly from that of continental Europe, as did the ecclesiastical and theological traditions that developed in the course of British history.

As on the continent, reform movements were stirring in England well before the sixteenth century.[7] For example, both Lollardy and humanism harshly critiqued the established ecclesiastical and theological structures of the fourteenth and fifteenth centuries.[8] Yet, whereas the Reformation on the continent began with Luther's theological debates and subsequently entailed political machinations, the first clear manifestations of reformation in England are those of "a *po-litical* occurrence"; subsequently, theological developments emerged.[9] The governmental actions that culminated in the English church's break from Rome began in the 1530s, with Parliament declaring in 1534 that the king is "the only supreme head in the Church of England, called *Anglicana Ecclesia*."[10] But at the earliest, a distinctive theology began to take shape with the work of Thomas Cranmer (1489-1556), archbishop of Canterbury, who oversaw the composition of the first edition of *The Book of Common Prayer* in 1549. This being the case, the first two editions of *The Book of Common Prayer* (1549 and 1552) may be regarded as having "established the fundamental outline and spirit of Anglican theology and practice."[11] Some Anglicans suggest that Anglican theology per se did not begin to emerge until the publication of the first volume of Richard Hooker's (ca. 1554-1600) *Of the Laws of Ecclesiastical Polity* in 1594.[12] In either case, in comparison with the continental Reformation, "an articulation of the stance of the English Church came toward the end, rather than the beginning, of its reformation."[13]

This analysis should not be taken as a denial of the significance of events prior to Cranmer's *Book of Common Prayer* or Hooker's *Of the Laws of Ecclesiastical Polity*. By 1539, Henry VIII (1491-1547; ruled 1509-1547) saw to it that there was an English-language Bible in parish churches. In so doing, he supplied a key element of the basis for new theology and piety: the Bible began to be available in the language of the people. At the same time, Henry staunchly reasserted six key Roman Catholic teachings in the Six Articles Act (1539): transubstantiation, communion in one kind, clerical celibacy, vows of chastity, private Masses, sacramental confession. This document "not only dictated to people what they should believe, but made doubt or heresy a felony."[14] Furthermore, the Six Articles Act was followed in 1543 by a book titled *A Necessary Doctrine and Erudition for Any Christian Man,* known as "The King's Book," which diverged only slightly from Roman Catholic belief.[15]

With the ascension of Edward VI (1537-1553; ruled 1547-1553) to the throne upon his father's death in 1547, an opportunity for doctrinal reforms arose. Edward was only nine years old at the time. Making use of the freedom that this afforded, Edward's uncle Edward Seymour (ca.1506-1552), Duke of Somerset, and Thomas Cranmer, archbishop of Canterbury, set about reformational changes. Clearly, the accomplishment from this period that has done the most to shape Anglicanism and Anglican theology was the creation and publication of *The Book of Common Prayer.* Anglicans believed that in this book they embraced "a liturgy true to the Scriptures, consonant with the practice of the early Church, unifying to the Church, and edifying to the people."[16] From the sixteenth century into the twentieth, *The Book of Common Prayer* has been "defin-itive" for Anglicanism.[17] And, as will be seen below, by virtue of the relationship between liturgy and theology in Anglicanism, *The Book of Common Prayer* has a defining role not only in worship, but also in theology.

The pace of reformational change accelerated when, in 1550, the crafty Earl of Warwick, soon to be Duke of Northumberland, imprisoned the Duke of Som-erset and seized power, establishing an alliance with even more assertive re-formers, Nicholas Ridley (ca. 1500-1555) and John Hooper (d. 1555). Clergy were allowed to marry, and nonreform-minded bishops were replaced with those who advanced the cause of reform. A second edition of *The Book of Common Prayer* was issued in 1552. This edition was "considerably more Protestant" than the first, and it included a clear affirmation of justification by grace through faith.[18] Furthermore, forty-two articles of religion and a catechism were com-posed, both of which articulated common Protestant beliefs.[19]

This tide of Protestant reform was turned back when the sickly Edward VI died at the age of sixteen, and Mary I (1516-1558; ruled 1553-1558) assumed the throne. The five years of her reign, from 1553 to 1558, can aptly, though perhaps too timidly, be summarized as "a return to full-bodied Roman Catholicism."[20] Parliament repealed the reforming legislation passed during Edward's reign, the vernacular Bibles were withdrawn, and bishops were ordered to restore the former liturgy and to suppress priests who were married or held Protestant-like views. Many reform-minded people were jailed, approximately eight hundred fled from England, and nearly three hundred others, of both meager and lofty standing, were executed. Cranmer, the father of *The Book of Common Prayer,* Hugh Latimer (1485-1555), the reformist bishop of Worcester, and Nicholas Rid-ley, a prominent scholar and the bishop of London, were among those burned at the stake for their steadfast adherence to reformational views.[21] Despite the intensity with which Mary pursued her course, she failed to reestablish obedi-ence to the Roman Catholic Church. In addition to resenting the means by which she sought her ends, many English people resented what they perceived to be submission to foreign powers, notably the papacy in Rome and the Span-ish king Philip, whom Mary had married. As was the case at the close of the Edwardian period, the Marian period came to an unresolved end in the midst of an agenda for change—in this case, change away from Protestantism and back toward Roman Catholicism.

When Elizabeth (1533-1603; ruled 1558-1603), Mary's half-sister, became queen upon Mary's death in 1558, she inherited a difficult and dangerous po-sition. In the political arena, Mary's "tyranny and brutality at home combined with an unpopular and unsuccessful foreign policy had bred much dissatisfaction." In the ecclesiastical arena, the years of shifting tides between Roman Catholic and Protestant impulses produced an English church rendered into three groups: those, including bishops, who supported the Marian return to the Roman Catholic Church; those who had fled the country and were now waiting to see whether or not the next monarch would create a climate receptive to reform; and "a middle party who wished to see . . . a Church of England truly catholic in all essentials and yet cleansed and reformed from the abuses which had gathered round it during the Middle Ages."[22] A distinctive approach to addressing this history of competing Roman Catholic and Protestant impulses emerged over the course of Elizabeth's forty-five year reign. The Elizabethan Settlement, as it came to be called, was a political, ecclesiastical and theological approach to Christianity that came to indelibly mark Anglicanism and Anglican theology.

Two acts of the British Parliament, both passed in 1559, constitute the legislative core of the Elizabethan Settlement. The Act of Supremacy essentially returned the church to the form of Protestantism that had developed prior to Mary's reign, including the reinstatement of English royal supremacy in the church and the administration of the Eucharistic sacrament to the laity in both kinds, bread and wine. The Act of Uniformity of 1559, though a bit less radical than a similar act passed in 1552, laid down various Protestant stipulations for the "uniform" conduct of church life and worship, including adherence to a third edition of *The Book of Common Prayer* (1559), which essentially upheld the Protestant character of the 1552 edition.[23] A set of royal injunctions, or proclamations, regarding church affairs soon accompanied these two acts. These injunctions, very similar to those issued by Edward VI in 1547, required additional reforms of a Protestant nature.[24] For example, there is a repudiation of the role of "all foreign power" (namely, the papacy) in ecclesiastical affairs, the abolishment of (Roman Catholic) "images, relics, or miracles," the establishment of the use of the English language in worship, and an encouragement of Bible reading by the laity.[25] The acts of supremacy and loyalty, the royal injunctions, and the revised *Book of Common Prayer* were foundational for religious policy throughout Elizabeth's reign.[26]

As Michael Ramsey points out, "the Elizabethan Settlement was not the product of theology," but rather an address to a combination of practical, political and ecclesiastical issues. "That being so," Ramsey writes, "there still remained something to theologize about. Anglican theology followed the Elizabethan Settlement, rather than the other way around."[27] The theological developments of the Elizabethan period must not be overlooked. For example, the revision of the forty-two Edwardian Articles of Religion (1552) into the Thirty-Nine Articles of Religion (1563) is "of very great importance indeed as a statement of where the Church of England stood at the beginning of its independent existence," constituting something of a doctrinal "charter or title-deeds" of the Anglican Church.[28] The Thirty-Nine Articles are "uncompromisingly Protestant,"[29] and according to G. W. H. Lampe, they "represent the mind of the Church at the most crucial moment of its history and they therefore set the pattern for subsequent development of its authentic tradition."[30]

Furthermore, while the reforms of the Elizabethan era clearly moved the church in a Protestant direction, they also engendered a fundamental characteristic of the Anglican tradition: they intentionally sought a *via media,* a "middle way." Elizabeth sought an *English* church, one that was indigenous and subservient to neither the Roman Catholics of Rome nor the Protestants of Wittenberg and Geneva. In addition to navigating waters between Roman Catholic and Protestant influences from outside of England, the reforms of the Elizabethan era reflect responses to pressures in England from those who remained attached to many Roman Catholic practices and ideas and from those who continually pressed for even more radical Protestant reforms, the Puritans. In this context, the Anglican Church of a *via media* became a church that was catholic but reformed, a church rooted in Christian antiquity but free of those medieval practices and teachings that were considered to be corrupted and corrupting.[31]

With the death of Elizabeth in 1603, a new dynasty, the Stuarts, assumed the English throne. Shortly after becoming king, James VI (1566-1625; ruled 1603-1625) convened a conference at Hampton Court. Puritans were hoping that their calls for more radical Protestant reforms would be supported by James, who had come to the throne from Scotland, where Presbyterianism was entrenched. However, the Hampton Court conference led to only minor concessions to the Puritans, largely consisting in some revisions to the 1559 edition of *The Book of Common Prayer* (1604). Of more lasting significance, not only for Anglicanism but also for the history of Protestantism, was the plan for an English translation of the Bible that issued from Hampton Court. In 1611 the *Authorized Version,* or what came to be known as the "King James Version" of the Bible, was published.[32] Throughout the seventeenth century, this Bible, along with *The Book of Common Prayer* and the Thirty-Nine Articles, provided the foundations and guidelines for Anglican theology.[33]

James was succeeded by Charles I (1600-1649; ruled 1625-1649) in 1625. Four years later, Charles dissolved Parliament, which did not meet again until 1640, and then convened only briefly. During this time, Charles essentially committed the oversight of the Church of England to William Laud (1573-1645), then bishop of London. When Laud became archbishop of Canterbury in 1633, he

aggressively persecuted dissenters, mainly Puritans. Political and religious controversies flourished, culminating in a civil war that broke out in 1642 and ended
with the defeat of Charles I in 1646. The new Parliament that emerged from this
war "believed in Presbyterianism and was utterly intolerant of everything else,"
including monarchy and the Anglican Church.[34] The Parliamentarian and Presbyterian causes found an aggressively able champion in Oliver Cromwell (1599-
1658), who as both a military leader and eventually Lord Protector of the Com-
monwealth promoted the rule by Parliament, rather than absolute royalty, and
the reorganization of the Church of England along presbyterian, rather than
episcopal, lines. Shortly after the Presbyterians gained power, a process of doctrinal revision and formulation, begun at the Westminster assembly in 1643, culminated in the ratification of the Westminster Confession (1647). This confession, a work of Puritan Calvinism, came to be a standard expression of Calvinist
theology in the English-speaking world into the present.

However, with the restoration of the monarchy under Charles II (ruled 1660-
1685) in 1660 came the restoration of episcopal, rather than presbyterian, oversight of the church, and the conduct of worship in accord with *The Book of Common Prayer* (1604). The 1662 revision of *The Book of Common Prayer* reaffirmed
the Elizabethan spirit of the *via media,* seeking to maintain "the wisdom of the
Church of England, ever since the first compiling of her public liturgy, to keep
the mean between the two extremes."[35] This 1662 edition embodied "the independent position" of Anglicanism "against both Puritanism and Rome,"[36] and it
"remains normative" in the Church of England to the present.[37]

The theological legacy of the seventeenth century also includes the work of
two contrasting groups. The Caroline Divines upheld a "high church" emphasis
on ritual and order, and they opposed both the Protestant theology of Calvinists
and the rationalism of the Latitudinarians. The Cambridge Platonists, on the
other hand, enlarged the role of reason in theology.[38] Nonetheless, although the
place given to reason alongside Scripture and tradition increased in the seventeenth century, at the end of the century Anglicanism was "firmly established on
the two-fold basis of Scripture and ancient tradition," and the Anglican divines
regarded both the practice and the theology of the Church of England "as Catholic and as Protestant, as ancient and as reformed."[39]

In America, a Eucharistic worship service was held in accord with *The Book
of Common Prayer* as early as June 21, 1579.[40] Due largely to the strength of
Congregationalism in New England, Anglicans found Virginia and southern regions more hospitable with respect to religion.[41] The first permanently organized church of the Anglican tradition in America was established in Jamestown,
Virginia, in 1607.[42] By the end of the seventeenth century, Anglicanism had

made its way north, having established churches in Boston, Philadelphia and New York. By the middle of the eighteenth century, Anglican churches existed in all of the colonies.[43] The Anglican tradition in the United States began as "an extension of the Church of England and under its jurisdiction."[44] Churches of the Anglican tradition in the United States came to be called "Episcopal," referring to the Anglican form of polity in which bishops *(episkopos)* oversee the church,[45] while in Canada the term "Anglican" was retained.[46]

The theological climate in eighteenth-century England was characterized by a rather strong rationalism, most notably in the prominence of deism, which rejected notions such as the Trinity, miracles, the incarnation and special revelation. At the same time, however, there was an evangelical revival. In addition to those evangelicals who chose to follow the Arminian Methodism of John Wesley or the Calvinist Methodism of George Whitefield, there were those who reasserted, within the Church of England, Reformation Protestant emphases such as conversion, the supremacy of Scripture and the preaching of the gospel.[47] Typically, their theology was a moderate Calvinism, affirming total depravity but refusing to "make predestination a central tenet or to teach predestined reprobation."[48] By the end of the eighteenth century, evangelicals "had become a definite and confident Church party" in the Church of England, and the early decades of the nineteenth century are regarded by some as the "golden age" of evangelical Anglicanism in England.[49]

The eighteenth century was also a time of geographic expansion beyond England. Two important mission agencies were established in England at the turn of the century: the Society for the Promotion of Christian Knowledge in 1698, and the Society for the Propagation of the Gospel in 1701. Both sent missionaries to America in the early 1700s. In the United States, as in England, political and governmental forces played a significant role in shaping the Anglican tradition. (And it is not presumptuous to suggest that Episcopalianism influenced the shape of government in the United States, as two-thirds of the signatories of the Declaration of Independence were Episcopalians.) By the time of the American Revolution, Anglicanism was the legally established religion in Virginia, Maryland, Georgia, North Carolina, South Carolina and some counties of New York.[50]

The War for Independence precipitated many changes in the life of the Anglican Church in America. Prior to the war, American Anglican churches were supported and nurtured by missionary societies such as the Society for the Propagation of the Gospel; after the war, English missionary societies withdrew support, as did the bishop of London, leaving the churches in "an orphaned and impoverished condition."[51] Many Episcopalian clergy in northern states remained loyal to England and opposed the revolution; however, clergy in the south and most laypeople in both the south and the north supported it.[52] By war's end, Anglicanism was "literally almost destroyed as an ecclesiastical organization as well as a tradition."[53] Following the war, Anglicanism initially regained strength in northern and middle states, reinvigorated in part by the Great Awakenings. The Episcopal Church that emerged after the war was "independent and autonomous of the Church of England,"[54] and by 1782, it was preparing for the formation of an American church in the United States.[55] The second General Convention of the Episcopal Church, convened in 1789, constituted the official founding of the Protestant Episcopal Church in the United States of America[56] and established "an Anglican Church for which the Church of England was no longer the superior legislator."[57] Anglican doctrine, discipline and worship required that there be bishops to oversee the churches and to ordain priests. In accord with this, the Anglican episcopacy was formally passed to America in 1792 via the ordination of Thomas Claggett of Maryland.[58]

The distinctly American character of the Episcopal Church was evident at the first General Convention, held in Philadelphia in 1785. For example, in addition to clergy, laity attended the Convention, "a democratic arrangement without precedent in England."[59] Furthermore, the constitution adopted at the second Convention (1789) established "a constitutional episcopate preserved by democratic elections in place of the monarchical episcopate continued by royal appointment."[60] On the other hand, the Episcopal Church preserved "the continuity of the historic episcopate and conciliar principle" of the Anglican and Roman Catholic Churches,[61] and the first American edition of *The Book of Common Prayer,* officially adopted at the second Convention, contained very few substantive changes from the British edition of 1662.[62] The Anglican Church in America also preserved much of the cultural ethos of its counterpart in England, being "a literate, low-keyed, and hopeful approach to religion" that proved particularly attractive to Americans who "considered themselves modern, rational, moderate, enlightened—in a word, English."[63] In contrast to populist and "enthusiast" expressions of Christianity, the Episcopal tradition was marked by learned "moderation."[64]

While the mission thrust from England that began in the eighteenth century flourished for most of the nineteenth century, these evangelically motivated initiatives were confronted by several significant ecclesial and theological developments. The Oxford Movement was the most visible manifestation of a Catholic revival, which "effectively distanced Anglicanism from the Reformation, emphasizing its Catholic rather than Protestant heritage," stressing, for example, sacramental doctrines and the historic continuity of apostolic succession among bishops.[65] The movement was vigorous in the late 1830s, but it was significantly weakened by the activities of some "aggressively pro-Roman" proponents in the 1840s and by the resignation of prominent vicar John Henry Newman from his clerical duties as an Anglican in 1843, followed by his conversion to Roman Catholicism in 1845. The early eighteenth century also saw the continuing influence of Latitudinarianism. This movement emphasized the role of reason in theology and tolerance, or "latitude," with respect to a broad range of theological beliefs. In the mid- and later-nineteenth century, theological liberalism flourished, not least through the influence of Latitudinarian views. In 1860, seven Oxford scholars, six of whom were clergy, published a book titled *Essays and Reviews,* which included the adoption of recently formulated critical methodologies for the study of Scripture and tradition. This controversial book proved to be a landmark, indicative of the fact that liberal theology was "firmly rooted" in the Anglican Church.[66] A different manifestation of liberalism is found in *Lux Mundi: A Series of Studies in the Religion of the Incarnation,* published in 1889. Led by Charles Gore (1853-1932), these Oxford Anglican teachers sought to unite the Catholic dimensions of Anglican thought, in this respect being similar to the Oxford Movement, with modern critical scholarship, in this respect being similar to the liberal outlook of *Essays and Reviews.*[67]

Similarly, a range of theological viewpoints was being explored within the Episcopal Church. The General Convention of 1801 adopted a slightly abridged form of the Thirty-Nine Articles, with most of the deletions and revisions touching upon matters of polity. Yet neither laity nor clergy were required to subscribe to the Articles. Three years later, the next General Convention adopted Gilbert Burnet's *Exposition of the Thirty-nine Articles* (1699), in which he argued that the Articles allow for either a Calvinist or an Arminian theological viewpoint. In addition to this, by the middle of the nineteenth century, reactions in the United States to the Oxford Movement, both for and against, were evident within Episcopalianism.[68] For example, an investigation into charges of "an underground pro-Roman conspiracy" at the General Theological Seminary, New York, was conducted and led to a heresy trial for Bishop Benjamin T. Onderdonk (1791-1861), a professor of ecclesiastical polity and law at the seminary. The General Convention of 1844 was marked by "feverish discussion" of the Oxford Movement, and in the end it was "unwilling to rule" for or against it.[69] Albright observes, "The net result was a standard of tolerance, fraught with all the dangers of indifferentism but with the possibilities of fruitful and constructive theological development as well, a spirit that has characterized Episcopal Church polity since 1844."[70] In the middle and later part of the nineteenth century, there was a decline in the regard with which the Articles of Religion were held, and, as in England, an increase in the influence of Latitudinarian and liberal views.[71]

One of the most significant theological landmarks of nineteenth-century Anglicanism is the adoption of the Chicago-Lambeth Quadrilateral. In 1867, prompted by a desire to foster mutual encouragement and cooperation among the churches of the Anglican communion, the first Lambeth Conference was held in England at Lambeth Palace, the residence of the archbishop of Canterbury.[72] The Lambeth Conference has since become "the great symbol of Anglican unity."[73] Approximately every ten years the archbishop of Canterbury convenes this worldwide conference of Anglican bishops. Although only "a deliberative body" with "no canonical nor constitutional status,"[74] the discussions and resolutions of Lambeth do, as Stephen Neill indicates, "carry great weight" within the Anglican communion.[75] At the third Lambeth Conference, in 1888, the bishops adopted, with some revisions, a four-point statement of affirmations essential to Anglican unity with other Christian communions.[76] This document was a slightly revised version of one previously adopted by United States bishops at a meeting in Chicago in 1886, which was, in turn, based largely on the work of William Reed Huntington (1838-1909), an influential Episcopalian priest from New England.[77] This significant contribution to Lambeth's deliberations, combined with the first major revision of the American *Book of Common Prayer* (1892), contributed to an increasing sense within American Episcopalianism of being "a tradition in its own right" in relation both to the Anglican Church in England and to other American traditions of Christianity.[78] Both the outcomes of the Lambeth Conference and the revision of the prayer book reflected an increased acceptance of pluralism or "divergence of opinion on Anglican doctrine" that had emerged throughout the 1870s and 1880s.[79]

Over the course of the twentieth century, having achieved an increased clarity of American identity, the Episcopalian tradition cultivated "much closer and more cooperative" relations with the Church of England and has actively pursued ecumenical cooperation with other Christian traditions.[80] The influence of liberalism continued in the twentieth century, manifest in, for example, the fundamentalist-modernist controversies of the 1920s[81] and challenges to the status of the Thirty-Nine Articles.[82] In the 1920s, Episcopalianism reached what Robert Prichard calls "a working agreement about diversity of opinion" with respect to the content of the faith, and this doctrinal compromise "helped maintain the peace" in the Episcopal Church until the 1960s.[83] By mid-century, neoorthodox theology provided the "theological framework" for many Episcopalians, and "radical" theology and "the death of God" movement were challenging others.[84] Throughout the latter half of the twentieth century, each of the "legs"

of Richard Hooker's often-cited three-legged stool of Anglican authority—
Scripture, tradition, reason—increasingly came to be regarded by some Episcopalians as being of equal authority, rather than Scripture having preeminence.[85]

About this same time, charismatic renewal also emerged within the Episcopal
Church, under the leadership of people such as Rev. Dennis Bennett.[86] In addition to the growth of this and other renewal movements and the continuance of
ecumenical endeavors, the Episcopal Church in the latter part of the twentieth
century was the scene of heated controversies, in particular those focused on
the ordination of women, the 1979 revision of *The Book of Common Prayer* and
the 1982 revision of the *Hymnal.* One of the responses to the developments that
led to these changes was what Hein and Shattuck refer to as "traditionalist resurgence."[87] The most dramatic expressions of this resurgence took the form of
the establishment of new denominational groups within Anglicanism (to be
described briefly below), while initiatives such as the Prayer Book Society,
which works to preserve the integrity of *The Book of Common Prayer* as understood from a traditionalist perspective, constituted less dramatic but no less fervent expressions of a historical-theological conservativism. Harold Lewis goes
so far as to contend, "The legs [of Hooker's 'stool'] have now been wrested from
the seat and are being used as weapons." "We must," he writes, "rediscover the
via media."[88] Within the largest American Anglican church body, the Episcopal
Church, the voices calling for the ordination of women and substantive changes
in *The Book of Common Prayer* and the *Hymnal* have carried the day. More recently, the Episcopal Church consecrated its first openly homosexual bishop,
Rev. Gene Robinson. However, not all Episcopalians have accepted these
changes, with some evangelicals and some conservative Anglo-Catholics establishing new denominations and institutions devoted to the continuance of more
traditional Anglican theology, polity and worship. Whether these differences
constitute diversity and pluralism or what one Episcopal observer regards as
"theological anarchy," they do reflect the convergence of traditional Anglican
principles with distinctively American "egalitarian sentiments" whereby "everyone is entitled to an opinion" and has "a right to private judgment" regarding
Christian truth.[89] The pursuit of a *via media* continues.

Diversity. More than probably any other tradition represented in this
book, Anglicanism is committed in principle to embracing a diversity of theological viewpoints. Anglican theology characteristically seeks to "include
rather than exclude."[90] Consequently, descriptions of Anglicanism often refer
to its "ambiguity," or "tolerance" of a wide range of theological perspectives,
or the value placed on "catholicity," or the pursuit of "comprehensiveness."
Witness, for example, the subtitle of W. S. F. Pickering's book *Anglo-Catholi-*

cism: A Study in Religious Ambiguity, in which he states, "If ambiguity is re-solved, religion itself disappears."[91] One Anglican observer describes the tra-dition as "suspicious of any call for doctrinal conformity."[92] Yet they jealously guard their liturgically based unity. Reflecting on a sermon by E. B. Pusey (1800-1882), a leader of the Oxford movement, A. M. Allchin says, "The way towards unity is to be found through entering more deeply into the spirit of the liturgy, by letting the one Holy Spirit pray in us and through us."[93] From within the American context, David Sumner observes, "Unity for Episcopalians arises not so much from a common theology as from a common worship. The Episcopal Church is a *worshipping* church, and the source for that worship is its *Book of Common Prayer.*"[94] Theology and liturgy *are* closely related. Yet they are not one and the same, and Sumner's observation is accurate: for An-glicans, including Episcopalians, unity does not consist primarily in a com-monly articulated theology.

One way to describe the diversity observed in the history of Anglican theol-ogy is to consider the following four types: Evangelical Reformed, Broad Church/Latitudinarian, High Church and Anglo-Catholic.[95] The theology of some Anglicans can be described as Evangelical-and-Reformed. This theology is char-acterized by a stress on Scripture rather than on tradition; the affirmation of a generally Augustinian-Calvinist soteriology, including total depravity and pre-destination; an emphasis on conversion and justification by faith; and, in some cases, a reduced emphasis of the sacraments. Other Anglicans can be described as Broad Church or Latitudinarian. Although Latitudinarians often are sympa-thetic to Arminian theology, they are not particularly concerned with the theo-logical issues that differentiate Calvinists and Arminians, and they celebrate the fact that the Thirty-Nine Articles can be legitimately interpreted in accord with either view. In fact, Latitudinarians often are more concerned with theological temper and method than with specific doctrinal formulations. They typically give a significant place to reason and reasonableness in theology and gladly af-firm that Anglicanism should embrace a broad latitude of theological perspec-tives. High Church Anglicans stress the catholic continuity of the church and its beliefs, while maintaining a respectful appreciation for the Protestant character of Anglicanism. The catholic continuity is embodied and expressed in the sac-raments and the liturgy of the Anglican Church. High Church theology tends to be Arminian. Like High Church Anglicans, Anglo-Catholics stress the catholic continuities of the church and its theology, but with a greater readiness to min-imize or set aside altogether the more stringently Protestant dimensions of An-glicanism.[96] There is a tendency among Anglicans to think that, other than issu-ing in a liturgy conducted in vernacular language, "the Reformation was on the

THE ANGLICAN TRADITION

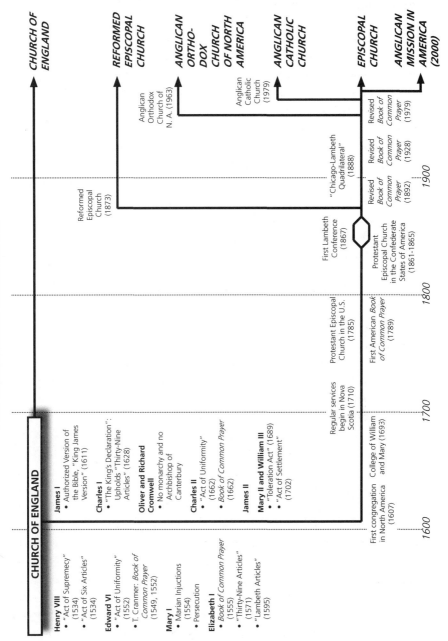

whole a bad thing."[97] Like Evangelical Anglicans, they are characterized by conservativism, but it is a conservativism primarily "in relation to church tradition."[98]
Some of these four major types have engaged varieties of Anglican thought that
emerged largely in the mid-to-late twentieth century, such as charismatic, feminist, process and environmentalist theologies.

The Anglican communion does not have a "regulated hierarchical organization," but rather is "a kinship of faith, government and worship through mutual
association with the mother church in England."[99] By far the largest Anglican
denominations in North America are the Episcopal Church in the United States
of America (until 1979, the Protestant Episcopal Church in the United States of
America)[100] and the Anglican Church of Canada. Both denominations are part
of the worldwide Anglican communion and are members of the World Council
of Churches. Within both the Episcopal Church and the Anglican Church of Canada, most, if not all, of the historical and contemporary diversity of the theologies described above can be found.

The Reformed Episcopal Church was formed in 1873, seceding from the Protestant Episcopal Church. Among the reasons for the secession were the Reformed Episcopal rejection of sacramental theology and the exclusivity of the
clerical "priesthood." The Reformed Episcopal Church produced a revised edition of *The Book of Common Prayer*, removing sacerdotal elements and references to clergy as "priests."

In the twentieth century, a number of Anglican denominations were formed
by persons who left the Episcopal Church over theological differences. These
differences typically centered on revisions to the 1928 edition of the Episcopal
Church's version of *The Book of Common Prayer*, the ordination of women
(which the Protestant Episcopal Church officially adopted in 1976), the theological "liberalism" of the Protestant Episcopal Church, or some combination of
these three. For example, the Southern Episcopal Church (established in 1962)
and the Anglican Catholic Church (established in 1979) retain the use of the
1928 edition of *The Book of Common Prayer* and do not ordain women to the
priesthood. The American Episcopal Church does not have women priests and
upholds an Anglo-Catholic view of the sacraments. Other denominations include the Anglican Orthodox Church, the Holy Catholic Church—Anglican Rite
Jurisdiction of America, the United Episcopal Church of America and the recently formed Anglican Mission in America.

Approach: Theological and Hermeneutical Method

Role of theology. In *The Integrity of Anglicanism*, Stephen Sykes analyzes the
role that systematic theological reflection has (and does not have) within Angli-

canism. At the beginning of the book, Sykes quotes the following observation by a character in a Thomas Hardy novel: "There's this to be said for the Church [of England], a man can belong to the Church and bide in his cheerful old inn, and never trouble or worry his mind about doctrines at all."[101] "Anglican links," observes Robert Hannaford, "are as much familial and historical as doctrinal."[102] As we noted earlier, unity within Anglicanism often is conceived primarily in terms of a shared liturgical tradition rather than a shared system of theology or explicitly delineated body of doctrinal belief. Perhaps it can be said that, in the Anglican tradition, liturgical worship is primary and theology per se is second-ary.[103] Louis Weil suggests, "Primary theology is what the whole Church does in its liturgical prayer," while theology in the sense of "systematic reflection upon faith" is "theology in a derived sense."[104] There undoubtedly is an intimate, though sometimes indeterminate, relationship between Anglican liturgy and theology, and this relationship is one of the keys to understanding theological method in Anglicanism.

Theological method. It is commonly said of and among Anglicans that al-though they do not have a distinctive theology, they do have a distinctive theo-logical method.[105] And, as already noted, one of the distinctive dynamics of that method is the relationship between liturgical worship and theology. This rela-tionship is denoted in the adage *"lex orandi, lex credendi"* (literally, "law of prayer, law of belief"). Much of the distinctiveness of Anglican theology, writes W. Taylor Stevenson, "lies in the stress upon worship. *Lex orandi* does precede *lex credendi.*"[106] As Weil puts it, "What is prayed is . . . what is believed." Weil goes on to suggest that "corporate prayer has shaped belief through the impact of *The Book of Common Prayer,* not only in shaping Anglican piety but theology as well," and that "it is in corporate worship that Anglicans find the common ground of their profession of faith."[107]

The liturgically informed theology of Anglicanism is a scripturally based the-ology. Sykes points out that "it is of the essence of the Anglican view of author-ity that . . . the means of judging matters concerning the faith are in the hands of the whole people of God by reason of their access to the Scriptures; and, further, that it is distinctively Anglican that this means is given to them in the liturgy of the church, backed by canon law."[108] Theological discernment is de-termined by Scripture, and one of the primary functions of the liturgy is to com-municate Scripture to the faithful. *The Book of Common Prayer* and the liturgy set forth therein are not authorities in themselves; rather "the accepted norms of authority are located first in the faith declared in Scripture."[109] Article 6 of the Thirty-Nine Articles states, "Holy Scripture containeth all things necessary to sal-vation."[110] The Catechism of the Episcopal Church instructs, "We call [the Holy

Scriptures] the Word of God because God inspired their human authors and because God still speaks to us through the Bible."[111] In being ordained, a bishop declares, "I do believe the Holy Scriptures of the Old and New Testaments to be the Word of God, and to contain all things necessary to salvation."[112] Scripture is the guide to God's saving ways. In both the Old and New Testaments "everlasting life is offered to Mankind by Christ."[113] Article 6 of the Articles of Religion states that "whatsoever is not read therein, nor may be proved thereby, is not to be required of any man, that it should be believed as an article of the Faith, or be thought requisite or necessary to salvation."[114] Herein is an entrée into the Anglican toleration for differences and ambiguity in theological belief, and the concern that one "beware of seeking to define the indefinable."[115] To think that the church must find in Scripture specific warrant for everything it affirms or practices is, for many Anglicans, a "narrow and impossible view of the function of Scripture."[116] Against such a view, which was characteristic of the Puritans, Anglicanism affirmed and continues to affirm that "whatever is needed for our salvation we find in Scripture, but we do not necessarily have to follow Scripture for rules concerning the details of the life of the church."[117]

With regard both to these details of the life of the church and to the interpretation of Scripture, tradition has a significant role to play. Article 34 of the Thirty-Nine Articles (itself a significant instance of tradition) instructs, "Whosoever, through his private judgment, willingly and purposely, doth openly break the Traditions and Ceremonies of the Church, which be not repugnant to the Word of God, and be ordained and approved by common authority, ought to be rebuked openly (that others may fear to do the like)."[118] Genuine tradition is in accord with the teachings of Scripture and is officially identified as such by the church. One seventeenth-century Anglican divine writes of Scripture as "the fountain and lively spring, containing in all sufficiency and abundance the pure Water of Life," and of the "consentient and unanimous testimony of the true Church of Christ" as "*Canalis,* a conduit pipe, to derive and convey to succeeding generations the celestial water contained in Holy Scripture."[119] Of particular importance for Anglicans is "ancient tradition" or the "appeal to antiquity."[120] This usually is associated with sources from the first five centuries after the apostles, and the authors of these sources are commonly referred to as "the Fathers." The Apostles' Creed and the Nicene Creed are affirmed as "statements of our basic beliefs about God" and are an integral part of the rites in *The Book of Common Prayer.*[121]

In addition to informing the rites and practices of the church, tradition, particularly ancient tradition, is to play an important role in the interpretation of Scripture. Article 20 of the Thirty-Nine Articles identifies the church as "a witness and a keeper of Holy Writ." The church is both responsible for rightly interpret-ing Scripture and accountable to Scripture.[122] Commenting on this article, Michael Ramsey writes, "The Anglican divines looked increasingly to the Fathers of the ancient church as guides to the understanding of Scripture."[123] The early Christian creeds, says Henry Chadwick, provide a "safeguard of interpretation" for the Bible.[124]

Anglicans often identify "the rule of faith" and various "standards of faith" as the authoritative sources for theology. The rule of faith is Scripture. The stan-dards of faith are the sources that constitute the documentary tradition. There is some variation among lists of the "standards," but the following is representa-tive:[125] creeds (especially the Apostles' and Nicene Creeds), *The Book of Com-mon Prayer,* the Thirty-Nine Articles, the Homilies,[126] the ordinals,[127] the cate-chism,[128] the "standard divines,"[129] the official decisions of councils and conferences (including the Lambeth Conference of Bishops) and canon law.[130]

In addition to Scripture and tradition, Anglicanism has always given reason a significant role in theology. "The fact is," writes H. R. McAdoo, "that from Hooker [sixteenth century] onwards the stress on reason and on a certain liber-ality is endemic in Anglicanism."[131] A. S. McGrade notes, "Reason has served An-glicans, and has often been explicitly invoked by them, as a counterpoise to un-thinking biblicism or unthinking conformity to historical precedent."[132] "Anglicanism has always been hospitable to rigorous theological enquiry," ob-serves Paul Avis; "it attempts the bold experiment of combining the traditional disciplines of personal devotion, liturgical worship and creedal orthodoxy with the most radical questioning in pursuit of truth."[133] Against this description of the critical character of the role of reason, it is considerably more difficult to give a description of its constructive role. As noted above, Anglicanism affirms the sufficiency of Scripture with regard to matters soteriological and views the ex-plicit teachings of Scripture as essentially delimited to these matters. Thus, while affirming Scripture as the rule of faith, this delimitation allows considerable room for tradition and reason to have significant roles as sources for theological thought. The creeds affirm that God is the "creator of heaven and earth," and Anglicans are confident that, in addition to God's imprint on the created order, the divine *logos* is at work in the world, informing human reason and con-science.[134] Consequently, in the interpretation of Scripture and in the testing of tradition, reason is not to be feared. It should, indeed it must, be used. This is what God intended in making us reasoning beings. "Both Scripture and tradition are interpreted by means of reason, which is understood, not in the spirit of the Enlightenment, as an individualistic and analytical instrument, but in a cultural, sapiential sense, as the light of God diffused, albeit imperfectly, through human knowledge and experience and to be exercised humbly, collectively and prayer-fully."[135] As one seventeenth-century divine put it, "The spirit in man is the can-dle of the Lord."[136]

How Scripture, tradition and reason are to be related to one another is not clear.[137] (This is not surprising when one notes that some Anglican theologians are reluctant even to use the word *method* because it "suggests something clear-cut and well-defined," preferring instead to describe Anglican theology by cer-tain "qualities which are themselves somewhat vague and elusive."[138]) Recalling a report from the 1948 Lambeth Conference, Sykes describes the combination of sources in Anglicanism as constituting a "dispersed authority" that is "a mu-tually supporting, and mutually checking life-process." This authority is embod-ied in the succession of bishops and in *The Book of Common Prayer,* and "sig-nificantly . . . the crucible in which these elements of authority are fused [is] liturgy."[139] Thus, to anyone who wants to understand Anglican theology, the in-vitation is extended to examine the Thirty-Nine Articles and then to "come and pray with us, come and worship with us, and that is how you will understand what we stand for."[140] Frederick H. Borsch summarizes Anglican method as an "intricate dance" within the Christian community: "Led in teaching by its bishops as the visible representatives of the tradition's continuity and unity of the Church, using experience and reason, and with the Bible as its canon of model stories, the community of disciples seeks to know and to do God's will."[141]

The literature of classical Anglican theology contains little discussion of Angli-can biblical hermeneutics per se. However, a number of principles that shape the reading of the Bible can be discerned in Anglican theological literature. First, Scripture is viewed as being internally coherent and authoritative in all its parts. Therefore, Scripture is to be used to interpret Scripture. Article 20 of the Thirty-Nine Articles says, "It is not lawful for the Church to . . . so expound one place of Scripture, that it be repugnant to another."[142] Second, the church is at once responsible for and accountable to the proper understanding of the teaching of Scripture. The article just cited explicitly asserts that the church has "power to decree rites or Ceremonies, and authority in Controversies of Faith." It continues, "And yet it is not lawful for the Church to ordain anything that is contrary to God's Word written." The church is subordinate to Scripture. Its doctrine and practice are to be in accord with the teaching of Scripture. And, mindful of this accountability, the church is to authoritatively explicate the teaching of Scripture. Francis Hall refers to this interpretive responsibility as part of the "priestly" office of the church.[143] Flowing from "the consensus of the community," the church's leadership in the interpretation of Scripture "avert[s] mere arbitrariness and indi-vidualism in interpretation."[144] Third, the church is not on its own in this important task. The catechism teaches, "We understand the meaning of the Bible by the help of the Holy Spirit, who guides the Church in the true interpretation of the Scriptures."[145] Recalling Jesus' promise of the guidance of the Holy Spirit, Anglicans have a confidence that, however humans may err, "by the office of the Holy Ghost the truth in its simplicity should not be lost or ever utterly obscured, and the Church as the instrument of Grace should not fail from the earth."[146] Fourth, the church looks to tradition for guidance in the interpretive task. Tradition consists of more than the liturgical tradition, but in keeping with the spirit of *lex orandi, lex credendi,* the liturgy provides one of the formative contexts in which Scripture is interpreted. Stevenson writes that the Scriptures "are only transmitted, read, and continually reappropriated by the ritually-formed community of the Church."[147] In this process, the liturgy is also interpreted in the light of Scripture. Sykes notes, "The scriptures are interpreted by the performance of the liturgy, but it is also true that the liturgy is interpreted by what the worshipper hears read from scripture."[148] This is one example of the "mutually supporting, and mutually checking life-process" among the sources of Anglican theology. Fifth, the Scriptures are read first and foremost in soteriological terms. Throughout the Anglican tradition there is the affirmation of the Scriptures as "containing all things necessary to salvation." God's redemptive work on behalf of humankind constitutes the motive and the message of the Bible. And at the center of that motive and message is Jesus Christ.[149] As the Thirty-Nine Articles affirm, "Both in the Old and New Testament everlasting life is offered to Mankind by Christ, who is the only Mediator between God and Man, being both God and Man."[150] Thus, the classical Anglican reading of the Bible is soteriologically and christologically informed. Ramsey says, "The Old Testament reveals Christ by pointing the way to him as the fulfiller, while the New Testament reveals Christ as the one who fulfills what is shadowed in the Old," and "everything that lies with both the Old and New Testaments is a part of that drama of salvation of which Christ is the head and the climax. In that sense it is true indeed that the Scriptures are a unity to which Christ is the key."[151]

Theology: Characteristic Beliefs

Paul Avis suggests that it is a "fallacy of misplaced modesty" to "play down the claim that there is a distinctive set of Anglican beliefs."[152] Yet, as noted above, Anglican unity and the distinctive characteristics of the Anglican communion are not typically talked about in terms of doctrine or theology. And, when doctrine or theology is mentioned, it can be in the context of a disclaimer. Stephen Neill states, "There are no special Anglican theological doctrines, there is no particular Anglican theology."[153] Commenting on Episcopalianism, William Williamson observes, "There is no separate 'Episcopalian doctrine.' Episcopalians adhere to the Christian Apostle's and Nicene Creeds and to the Holy Scriptures, which are said to be 'profitable for doctrine.'"[154] Instead of referring to "doctrine," many Anglican theologians are likely to use terms such as "attitude," "ethos" or "spirit" to denote the distinctives of their tradition.[155] Neill writes, "In the strict sense of the term there is . . . no Anglican faith. But there is an Anglican attitude and an Anglican atmosphere. This defies analysis. It must be felt and experienced in order to be understood."[156] "There is clearly 'something' distinctive about Anglicanism," Stevenson says, and "it is intractable because it is an ethos. . . . An ethos is made up of the predominant assumptions of a group."[157] D. R. G. Owen suggests that it is best to speak of "the spirit in which Anglicans generally conduct their theological arguments; this way of doing theology is characterized not by features that can be rigidly defined, but by qualities that are themselves somewhat vague and elusive."[158]

While the distinctives of Anglicanism may be a bit "vague and elusive," there is a considerable degree of convergence among the descriptions of those who describe the ethos or spirit of contemporary classical Anglicanism. First, Anglicanism is episcopal. Based on their understanding of the church and its oversight, as indicated in Scripture and history, the Anglican communion is overseen by *episkopoi,* or bishops. Second, Anglicanism and Anglican theology are liturgical. As Michael Ramsey says, Anglicans do their theology "to the sound of church bells."[159] Third, Anglicanism is "tolerant," not least in the realm of theology. By virtue of its belief in "the greatness of truth" and its *"confidence in"* that truth, Anglicanism is characterized by a "willingness *to tolerate for the time being* what appears to be error."[160] Rowan Williams refers to this as "passionate patience."[161] This tolerance or patience is due not to "any indifference to truth," but rather to confidence that in God's economy "no mistake is beyond repair."[162] Fourth, Anglicanism seeks to be "comprehensive." Manifesting the posture of tolerance just described, Anglicanism seeks to encompass a wide variety of theological perspectives, with a goal of being an instrument for the realization of a greater visible unity of the church catholic.[163] As Henry Chadwick puts it, the "most characteristic expression" of Anglican theology is "seeking to include rather than exclude."[164]

There is, then, some irony in attempting to discuss "characteristic" Anglican beliefs. Yet, as noted earlier, Anglican theology is liturgical and Anglican liturgy is theological, and both are revealed in, among other sources, *The Book of* Common *Prayer.* There are commitments that Anglicans hold in common. Thus, although no one doctrine or particular doctrines contain in themselves defining elements of Anglican theology, consideration of the doctrines of the church, including episcopacy, and of the sacraments provides excellent windows into the world of Anglican theology.[165] The importance of these two areas of doctrine is indicated in, for example, the fact that they constitute two of the four points of the Chicago-Lambeth Quadrilateral, the other two being Scripture and the creeds. Several twentieth-century Anglican scholars have identified one or both of these doctrines as being among the most fundamental to Anglican theology.[166] Furthermore, these two loci of doctrine—the church and the sacraments—are vitally related to each other. Francis Hall writes, "Both [the church] and its apostolic ministry are integral and fundamental elements in the Christian sacramental regimen."[167]

Ecclesiology. "Men are by nature social beings," observes Hall, "and no really vital human interest can be effectively cultivated and developed on an individualistic basis."[168] Reaching out to human beings in accord with the way he made them, God provides "a divinely created society"—the church. From its earliest days, notes Marianne Micks, the church "understood itself to be created by God's action."[169] The church is of utmost importance because it provides a corporate or social context for the life of faith, which is the kind of context within which human beings are intended to live and grow, and because it is "the antecedent medium through and from which the Holy Spirit causes all sacramental grace to flow."[170] Furthermore, as Stephen Sykes indicates, the comprehensive, tolerant ethos of Anglicanism is inextricably related to an Anglican theology of the nature of the church.[171] Thus, an understanding of Anglican ecclesiology will further our grasp of the sometimes elusive ethos of Anglicanism.

Nature and marks of the church. Article 19 of the Thirty-Nine Articles states, "The visible Church of Christ is a congregation of faithful men, in which the pure Word of God is preached, and the Sacraments be duly ministered according to Christ's ordinance, in all those things that of necessity are requisite to the same."[172] Although there was an antecedent community of belief among the Jews, the church of Christ is "the community of the New Covenant."[173] It is fundamentally a spiritual reality, brought into existence through the life and work of Jesus and in the coming of the Holy Spirit on the Day of Pentecost. In the New Testament this community is referred to as "*ecclesia,* ἐκκλησία, because it is made up of those who have been called of God into the assembly of His adopted children. It owes its origin to a divine ingather of the elect, and not to human organization."[174] It is Christ's church. It is "organic."[175] It is nothing less and nothing other than the body of Christ, "closely knit together in organic interdependence of its parts, but in total dependence on the head."[176]

Christ's church is both visible and invisible.[177] Yet, while acknowledging that there are "those whose faith is known to [God] alone,"[178] Anglicans are particularly concerned that the visibility of the church be affirmed.[179] Its members are visible, its organization is visible, and its institutions (such as the sacraments, corporate worship, discipline) are visible (see Eph 2:20; Acts 2:42; 20:7; 1 Cor 16:2; Heb 10:25; Rev 1:10).[180] In his *Laws of Ecclesiastical Polity,* Richard Hooker writes, "By the Church . . . we understand no other than only the visible Church. . . . The Church is alwaies a visible society of men, not an assembly, but a so-cietie."[181] Citing Matthew 18:17; 16:18; Ephesians 5:25-27; and John 13, Hall asserts, "The Church which Christ teaches that men should hear is obviously a visible one, and He mentions no other. It is clear that the visible Church is the subject of the promises of the New Testament."[182]

In affirming the visible church, Anglicans also acknowledge the mixed character of this church. Article 26 of the Thirty-Nine Articles states that "in the visible Church the evil be ever mingled with the good, and sometimes the evil have chief authority in the Ministration of the Word and Sacraments."[183] One seventeenth-century divine likens the visible church to "a drag-net, which is cast into the sea and fetches up much variety, not of great and little fishes only, but of stones and seaweed and shells and mud, altogether."[184] Yet, this mixed state does not render the church either unworthy or incapable of its God-given functions. Having acknowledged the "mingled" character of the church, Article 26 continues, "Yet forasmuch as [clerical ministers] do not [act] in their own name, but in Christ's, and do minister by his commission and authority, we may use their Ministry, both in the hearing of the Word of God, and in receiving the Sacraments."[185] This mixed church is *Christ's* church, and it carries out *his* ministry, employing the means that *he* ordained for *his* own purposes. No evil can thwart him. The church may, indeed must, tolerate error, including doctrinal error, at least for a time, though it cannot ever approve or endorse such error.[186]

Following the Nicene Creed, classical Anglican theology also describes the church as one, holy, catholic and apostolic. The Catechism teaches that the church is "one, because it is one Body, under one Head, our Lord Jesus Christ," it is "holy, because the Holy Spirit dwells in it, consecrates its members, and guides them to do God's work," it is "catholic, because it proclaims the whole Faith to all people, to the end of time," and it is "apostolic, because it continues in the teaching and fellowship of the apostles and is sent to carry out Christ's mission to all people."[187] According to Ramsey, the visible signs of the church include baptism, the Eucharist, teaching and apostolic ministry. Since the earliest days of the church, these signs or marks "both proclaimed and manifested the grace of God, and also helped to define [the church's] own identity."[188] Baptism is the sign of incorporation into the body of Christ (Rom 6:23; 1 Cor 12:13), and the Eucharist is the sign of abiding in the body of Christ (1 Cor 10:17). The church's teaching, described in 1 Corinthians 15:3-5, is the sign of the gospel message of the church, being "based on and derived from the Lord's death and resurrection,"[189] and the ministry of the Church is the sign of the continuation of the ministry of the apostles, as authorized by the risen Christ (1 Cor 14:36). "Apostleship is a permanent function of the Church," writes T. A. Lacey, "serving as the basis on which the whole fabric permanently rests. The title of those serving the function may vary, but the function remains the same."[190]

Mission and work of the church. The mission of the church is "to restore all people to unity with God and each other in Christ."[191] Toward this end, the Anglican communion prays, "O God, who hast made of one blood all the peoples of the earth, and didst send thy blessed son to preach peace to those who are far off and to those who are near: Grant that people everywhere may seek after thee and find thee, bring the nations into thy fold, pour out thy Spirit upon all flesh, and hasten the coming of thy kingdom."[192] Toward the fulfillment of this mission, the work of the church includes praying and worshiping, teaching Scripture and proclaiming the gospel, administering the sacraments and spiritual discipline, and promoting peace and justice among people.[193] The work of the church is overseen by and organized under a threefold episcopal order of ministry.

Order of ministry in the church. The Episcopal Catechism teaches that "the Church carries out its mission through the ministry of all its members," including laypersons, who are listed first in the enumeration of "ministers of the church."[194] The other three categories of ministers are bishops, priests (or presbyters) and deacons. Anglican theology teaches that three God-appointed orders of ordained ministry have characterized the church since its New Testament beginnings.[195] Bishops "carry on the apostolic work of leading, supervising, and uniting the Church." Priests work with the bishops, governing, doing missionary and pastoral work, preaching, and administering the sacraments. And, deacons assist the bishops and priests in all this work, and they have "a special responsibility . . . to minister in Christ's name to the poor, the sick, the suffering, and the helpless."[196] Of particular importance for understanding Anglican ecclesiology are the office of bishop and apostolic succession.

In the rite of ordination a bishop is charged, "You are called to guard the faith, unity, and discipline of the Church; to celebrate and to provide for the administration of the sacraments of the New Covenant; to ordain priests and deacons and to join in ordaining bishops; and to be in all things a faithful pastor and wholesome example for the entire flock of Christ."[197] The bishops fulfill the highest role within the ecclesiastical hierarchy of the Anglican tradition, representing Christ and the church, "particularly as apostle, chief priest, and pastor of a diocese," and acting "in Christ's name for the reconciliation of the world and the building up of the Church"; furthermore, the bishop "ordain[s] others to continue Christ's ministry."[198] Bishops, and only bishops, ordain priests, deacons and other bishops. This is the embodiment of Anglican belief in "the historic episcopate" or "apostolic succession."[199] A bishop is "a living sign of the continuity of the Church, and of its unity."[200]

Apostolic succession is sometimes described as "the handing down of grace."[201] This apostolic continuity is manifest in the liturgy, the sacraments and the faith of the church. Yet, it is also manifest in and uniquely "secured" through the successive ordination of bishops.[202] According to Paul More, the classical divines of the seventeenth century rightly believed that "the spiritual function of the priesthood was proved by experience to depend for its higher and purer efficacy on the Apostolic Succession of the bishops. And from this pragmatic argument they could go on to infer that episcopacy . . . was sanctioned by Providence to be the means of preserving the Church as the channel of Grace."[203] Citing Deuteronomy 34:9; Acts 6:6; 13:3; 20:28; and 2 Timothy 1:6, one of the divines, William Beveridge, teaches that the apostles "transferred" or "transmitted" to others, "by laying their hands upon them," the same Holy Spirit whom they had received when Christ breathed the Spirit into them.[204] The 1929 Episcopal *Book of Common Prayer* instructs the presiding bishop at the ordination of a new bishop to pray, "Receive the Holy Ghost for the Office and Work of a Bishop in the Church of God, now committed unto thee by the Imposition of our hands."[205] Ramsey recognizes the importance both of the bishops and of the ecclesiological context when he writes, "The church's full and continuous life in grace does depend upon the succession of bishops, whose work, however, is not isolated but bound up with the whole Body."[206] There are at least four ways in which apostolic succession is conceived in Anglican theology. Bishops are viewed as "being in continuity of life with the apostles of Christ," or "having that same mission from Christ the apostles had," or "maintaining the faith the apostles taught," or as "possessing a ministry and an authority in continuity with the apostles."[207] As Sykes suggests, no "particular theological interpretation of episcopacy" is "essential" to Anglicanism,[208] but at the very least, "the Anglican tradition's adherence to episcopacy is in the interests of its own catholicity of order and an expression of its intended faithfulness to the early undivided church."[209] As already noted, in addition to the episcopacy, the apostolicity of the church is made manifest in a number of other ecclesial realities, not least the sacraments.

The Sacraments.
The sacramental principle.[210] The Thirty-Nine Articles describes sacraments as "badges or tokens of Christian men's profession" and "certain sure witnesses,

and effectual signs of grace, and God's good will towards us, by which he doth work invisibly in us." They "quicken . . . strengthen and confirm" our faith.[211] The catechisms in both the 1929 and the 1978 Episcopal *Book of Common Prayer* refer to them as "outward signs of inward and spiritual grace."[212] These are the two parts of a sacrament: the outward, visible sign, and the inward, spiritual grace.[213] Strictly speaking, the term "sacrament" *(sacramentum)* refers to the outward sign. This outward sign is not simply a memorial or a testimony to grace received in the past;[214] rather, it is the God-ordained "means" and "pledge" by which God bestows the sacramental grace upon the Christian.[215] The sign possesses no supernatural attributes or powers in itself, but when administered in accord with Christ's ordinance (Mt 26:26-29; Mk 14:22-25), it becomes the instrument "by which we receive" God's grace.[216] When "ministered with unfailing use of Christ's words of Institution, and of the elements ordained by Him," God gives his grace.[217] Through the sacraments, God gives and nurtures our faith in him. And many within the Anglo-Catholic subtradition further believe that "the sacraments are not just communicating grace but are mysteries by which we are made partakers of Christ in his deeds of salvation, and in particular of his death and resurrection."[218]

The efficacy of the sacraments "flows . . . from the will of God in Christ who has seen fit to institute and employ them, and from the operation in them of the Holy Spirit."[219] The efficacy of a sacrament is not contingent on the moral state of the minister. As noted earlier, even when "the evil have chief authority in the Ministration of Word and Sacraments," we may readily partake of hearing the Word and receiving the sacraments so long as they are administered not in the name of the minister, "but in Christ's" name and "by his commission and authority."[220] The character of the effect on the recipient, however, is related to "certain moral dispositions" of the recipient. The spiritual state of the recipient neither validates nor invalidates the sacrament as a sacrament, but it may determine the "subjective benefits" that are or are not received.[221] Article 25 of the Thirty-Nine Articles states, "In such only as worthily receive the [sacraments], they have a wholesome effect or operation; but they that receive them unworthily, purchase to themselves damnation, as Saint Paul saith."[222] In this respect, the efficacy of the sacraments is "conditional," being conditioned upon "worthy reception."[223] As James cautions, "The doubter . . . must not expect to receive anything from the Lord" (Jas 1:8).

The two sacraments of the Anglican tradition are baptism and the Eucharist (Lord's Supper). Although five other rites—confirmation, ordination, holy matrimony, reconciliation, unction—are regarded with varying degrees of respect among Anglicans, baptism and the Eucharist are the two that fully and with widespread agreement qualify as sacraments.[224] Linda Moeller observes that baptism and the Eucharist "are essential to the self-identification of the Episcopal Church," and that "the relationship between baptism and eucharist is at the core of how Episcopalians understand themselves to stand in the catholic tradition while exhibiting the finest theological and liturgical foundations laid by the Reformers."[225]

Baptism. The seventeenth-century Anglican divine John Hacket suggests that "the whole life of a Christian man and woman should be a continual reflection how in Baptism we entered into covenant with Christ."[226] Baptism is a lifelong point of reference for the Christian. In it, the catechism teaches, "God adopts us as his children and makes us members of Christ's body, the Church, and inheritors of the kingdom of God."[227] Jesus instituted baptism when he instructed his disciples, as recorded in Matthew 28:19, to "make disciples of all nations, baptizing them in the name of the Father and of the Son and of the Holy Spirit." "Baptism makes us members of God's people," writes David Edwards.[228] Article 27 of the Thirty-Nine Articles states that baptism is both "a sign of profession" and "a sign of Regeneration or New-Birth."[229] This new birth entails both the forgiveness of sin and the bestowal of new spiritual life. When they recite the Nicene Creed, Anglicans state, "We acknowledge one baptism for the forgiveness of sins." The 1928 catechism teaches that the inward spiritual grace of this sacrament is "a death unto sin, and a new birth unto righteousness," while the 1979 catechism teaches that it is "birth into God's family the Church, forgiveness of sins, and a new life in the Holy Spirit."[230] The 1979 baptismal rite expresses thanks that those who receive baptism "are cleansed from sin and born again."[231] There are a variety of other blessings that accompany regeneration. This spiritually regenerate life also includes being "grafted into the Church," receiving "our adoption to be the sons of God by the Holy Ghost," and having our faith "confirmed."[232] These blessings are bestowed on the one baptized by virtue of the "union with Christ in his death and resurrection" that takes place, and is sealed by the Holy Spirit, in baptism.[233]

The sacrament of baptism and its benefits are available to both old and young. As Hall says, "Any unbaptized and rational human being is a proper subject of Baptism, if he offers no obstacle to baptismal grace."[234] According to the Catechism, receptivity to baptismal grace is associated with renouncing Satan, repenting of sins, and accepting Jesus as Lord and Savior.[235] This does not prevent young children and infants from validly receiving baptism; in fact, infants and children should be baptized.[236] The Catechism teaches that "infants are baptized so that they can share citizenship in the Covenant, membership in Christ, and redemption by God." As for renouncing Satan, repenting of sins, and accepting Jesus as Lord and Savior, these commitments are "made for them by their parents and sponsors, who guarantee that the infants will be brought up within the Church, to know Christ and be able to follow him."[237] Baptizing infants and children is in keeping with the analogy between circumcision in the Old Covenant and baptism in the New Covenant (Rom 4:11), the scriptural precedent of little children being included in covenants with God (Num 3:28; Deut 29:10-12), Jesus' attitude toward little children as recorded in the Gospels (Mk 10:13-16), and, most important, with Jesus' institution of the sacrament.[238] As recorded in John 3:5, Jesus says, "No one can enter the kingdom of God without being born of water and Spirit."[239] In the case of persons who have been baptized as infants or as young children, it is important that their parents and sponsors see that they receive proper confirmatory instruction, and that the baptized have opportunity as matured, accountable persons to affirm the commitment to renunciation of sin and faith in Christ.

The Eucharist. The Eucharist[240] was instituted by Christ when, with "thanksgiving" (Greek, εὐχαριστία), he celebrated the Passover meal with his disciples the night before his arrest (see Jn 6:30-59; 1 Cor 11:23-26; Mk 14:22-25; Lk 22:19-20; Mt 26:26-28.).[241] He commanded that his followers perpetuate the memory of his sacrificial death, suffered the day after this meal, by continuing to take such a meal together until he returns.[242] Long before that last supper with the disciples, Jesus had stated, "I am the bread of life" (see Jn 6:30-59). Each of the Synoptic Gospels records Jesus' meal with the disciples and his instructions to them regarding their celebration of it (Mt 26:26-28; Mk 14:22-25; Lk 22:19-20). Paul indicates that in instructing the Corinthians regarding the Eucharist, he was handing on to them what Jesus had handed on to him (1 Cor 11:23-26).

The celebration of the Eucharist constitutes both a commemorative and a sacramental rite. It is a commemorative rite in that the community witnesses to the sacrificial death of Christ, which death makes salvation possible. It is a sacramental meal in that the community is nourished, individually and corporately, by the body and blood of Christ. The reception of his body and blood constitutes the "inward and spiritual grace" of this sacrament.[243] Thus, recipients are "partakers of his most blessed Body and Blood."[244] At the breaking of the bread the priest prays, "The Gifts of God for the People of God. Take them in remembrance that Christ died for you, and feed on him in your hearts by faith, with thanksgiving."[245] This is a spiritual feeding on "spiritual food."[246] Article 28 of the Thirty-Nine Articles states, "The Body of Christ is given, taken, and eaten, in the Supper . . . after an heavenly and spiritual manner."[247] The nourishment provided thereby for the life of faith includes cleansing—that is, the soul is "washed through his most precious blood."[248] Sins are forgiven, and the union with Christ and with other members of his body is strengthened.[249] The recipient is also nourished by the assurance of God's "goodness towards us," our membership in the body of Christ, and eternal life as citizens of Christ's "everlasting kingdom."[250]

All of this is possible because Christ is present in the Eucharist. Although Anglicans do not affirm the Roman Catholic view of transubstantiation, the fact that the presence is a spiritual presence makes it no less real.[251] Christ is genuinely present. At the institution he said, "This is my body" and "This is my blood," and then he said, "Do *this* in remembrance of me." He did not offer an explanation or elaboration, and so classical Anglican theology likewise offers no explanation of Christ's presence. Scripture affirms *that* Christ is present, and so do recipients of the Lord's Supper. However, Scripture does not give an explanation as to *how* he is present, and recipients should not require assent to a particular explanation. Thus, Ramsey says, "how wrong it is to ask too many questions when we are faced with the joy of his wonderful and mysterious gift."[252] Christ's presence is a mystery—a wonderful, life-imparting mystery.

At the same time, although an analytical understanding of the mechanics of Christ's presence is impossible, those who would receive the sacrament of the Eucharist must do so with a proper disposition of mind and heart. In the rite for the Holy Eucharist, recipients are instructed that they "must remember the dignity of that holy Sacrament." This is necessary if one is to "share rightly in the celebration of those holy Mysteries, and be nourished by that spiritual Food." Recalling Paul's exhortation and warning in 1 Corinthians 11:27-30, recipients are to "prepare themselves carefully before eating of that Bread and drinking of that Cup." One is to examine one's life and conduct "by the rule of God's commandments, that you may perceive wherein you have offended in what you have done or left undone, whether in thought, word, or deed." Neither the faith (or lack thereof) nor the attitude (be it respectful or presumptuous) of the recipient determines whether or not Christ is mysteriously yet genuinely present in the sacrament. It is God's sacrament. It is God's chosen venue for his grace. However, "as the benefit is great, if with penitent hearts and living faith we receive the holy Sacrament, so is the danger great, if we receive it improperly, not recognizing the Lord's Body."[253] The sacrament is efficacious regardless of the spiritual state of the recipient. However, the recipient's repentant faith, or lack thereof, is a significant factor in determining whether the effect is one of spiritual nourishment or spiritual chastisement.

The faithful, including theologians (perhaps especially theologians), are to refrain from asking too many questions and are to gratefully receive in faith God's "wonderful and mysterious gift" of his Son in the Eucharist.[254] The faithful need to heed Paul's warning to avoid "a morbid craving for controversy and for disputes about words" (1 Tim 6:4) and to accept the fact that although "the revealed things belong to us and to our children forever," it is also true that "the secret things belong to the LORD our God" (Deut 29:29). Participants need to accept Christ's statements, "This is my body" and "This is my blood," and in faith receive the grace that is theirs in God's sacrament of the Holy Eucharist.

Conclusion: The Spirit of a *Via Media*

This chapter began by noting that Anglican theology is concerned with "establishing a certain 'direction' and in avoiding premature fixation." That "direction" is intended to find a *via media,* a middle way, through the theological landscape. From the Elizabethan era to today, Anglican theologians have, in the spirit of Anglicanism, sought to articulate theological beliefs that strike a middle way between Roman Catholicism and Protestantism, and a tolerant way amidst the variety within Protestantism. This has been accomplished not by formulating some sort of theological synthesis or hybrid, but by embracing ambiguity and inclusion, and by emphasizing the liturgical character of theology. On many doctrinal topics, there simply is no "Anglican" theology; rather, there is a wide range of theological views that flow from the Anglican way of being Christian, the Anglican way of doing theology.

FOR FURTHER STUDY

The endnotes contain citations of many useful resources, most of them written from within the Anglican tradition. A brief list of resources for further study follows here. Some of these resources consider the Anglican or Episcopalian traditions in general, while others specifically focus on history and/or theology.

Bibliographies

Caldwell, Sandra M., and Ronald J. Caldwell. *The History of the Episcopal Church in America, 1607-1991: A Bibliography.* Garland Reference Library of the Humanities 1635; Religious Information Systems 13. New York: Garland, 1993.

Griffiths, David N. *The Bibliography of the Book of Common Prayer, 1549-1999.* New Castle, Del.: Oak Knoll, 2002.

Hein, David, and Gardiner Shattuck Jr. "Bibliographic Essay," in *The Episcopalians,* pp. 333-48. Denominations in America 11. Westport, Conn.: Praeger, 2004.

Reference Works

Armentrout, Don S., and Robert B. Slocum, eds. *An Episcopal Dictionary of the Church: A User-Friendly Reference for Episcopalians.* New York: Church Publishing, 2000.

Rosenthal, James. *The Essential Guide to the Anglican Communion.* Harrisburg, Penn.: Morehouse, 1998.

Wall, John N. *A Dictionary for Episcopalians.* Rev. ed. Cambridge, Mass.: Cowley, 2000.

Survey Resources

Prichard, Robert W. *A History of the Episcopal Church.* Harrisburg, Penn.: Morehouse, 1991.

Sykes, Stephen, and John Booty, eds. *The Study of Anglicanism.* London: SPCK; Philadelphia: Fortress, 1988.

Primary Historical and Theological Resources

Armentrout, Don S., and Robert B. Slocum, eds. *Documents of Witness: A History of the Episcopal Church, 1782-1985.* New York: Church Hymnal, 1994.

The Book of Common Prayer and Administration of the Sacraments and Other Rites and Ceremonies of the Church; Together with the Psalter or Psalms of David, According to the Use of the Episcopal Church. New York: Church Hymnal, 1979.

Bray, Gerald, ed. *Documents of the English Reformation.* Minneapolis: Fortress, 1994.

Evans, G. R., and J. Robert Wright, eds. *The Anglican Tradition: A Handbook of Sources.* London: SPCK, 1991.

Recent and Current Theological Explorations

Douglas, Ian T., and Kwok Pui-lan, eds. *Beyond Colonial Anglicanism: The Anglican Communion in the Twenty-first Century.* New York: Church Publishing, 2001.

Douglas, Ian T., Paul F. M. Zahl and Jan Nunley. *Understanding the Windsor Report: Two Leaders in the American Church Speak Across the Divide.* New York: Church Publishing, 2005.

Slocum, Robert B., ed. *A New Conversation: Essays on the Future of Theology and the Episcopal Church.* New York: Church Publishing, 1999.

6 ■ Freedom for Immediacy

BAPTIST THEOLOGY

Baptists believe that God gave to man the innate competency in spiritual matters, to avail himself of the richness and blessedness which come as the fruitage of the free and full exercise of these rights; to make a direct approach to God for redemption and to make use of all available divine aids whereby he may keep his soul unto eternal life.

Ellis Fuller, "Why Baptists?"

Baptists indeed stand for individualism above institutionalism, for the reforming prophet more than the conforming priest, for a pietism that is private and personal before it can properly become public and social.

Edwin S. Gaustad, in *Discovering Our Baptist Heritage*

Religion is a personal matter between the soul and God.

Edgar Mullins, *The Axioms of Religion*

The man in the suit held an open Bible in his left hand as he spoke from the pulpit. He cared deeply about what he believed, and because he loved us, he taught us what was in the Bible. This particular Sunday morning he directed a portion of his sermon specifically to the "the young people." "The most important decision a person ever makes," he said, "is the decision as to whether or not to follow Jesus." He emphasized the fact that this is a personal, individual decision: it makes no difference whether or not your parents are Christians; it makes no difference whether or not you are a churchgoer. What matters, indeed the only thing that matters, is what *you* decide to do about Jesus. And, if you decide to follow Jesus, he will always be there for you. You can always talk with him, pray to him, no matter where you are. You do not need to be in a church building. You do not need a minister to pray for you. Anytime, anywhere, you can speak directly with Jesus. Furthermore, he assured us that all that he was saying was true because it was in the Bible, the Word of God, and here followed an important instruction. "If you want to follow Jesus, it's important to read your Bible every day. It's important to have a daily quiet time, just you and God, to read the Bible and pray." And, I suspect that many of the people in that service did just that on Monday morning.

Context: Historical and Ecclesiastical Background

Historical origins and development. According to Baptist historians, there are, generally speaking, three views of the origins of the Baptist tradition.[1] An older, "successionist" view claims that "an unbroken line of 'Baptistic' churches may be traced back to Jesus and the Apostles (or even John the Baptist!)."[2] A modified version of this view distinguishes between the Baptist "denomination," originating in the seventeenth century, and Baptist "faith" or "viewpoints," dating from the time of the apostles.[3] A second view locates the origins of the Baptist tradition in its links to Anabaptist movements of the sixteenth century.[4] A third, more recently proposed view emphasizes English Puritanism and Separatism as the primary contexts from which the Baptist tradition emerged.[5] Along with this emphasis is a recognition of the influence of sixteenth-century Protestant reform movements, both Magisterial and Radical, on the European continent.[6] It is this latter Puritan-Separatist approach that is adopted here.

Baptist scholars Duane Garrett and Richard Melick Jr. state, "We have many founding fathers but no single, towering figure—a Luther, Calvin, or Wesley—to whose writings we look to help establish the bounds of our tradition and orthodoxy."[7] John Smyth (ca. 1554-1612) may not be a towering theological figure, but his theology and ministry provide a viable starting point for the history of the Baptist tradition. Smyth was educated at Christ College, Cambridge, and ordained a priest in the Church of England in 1594. In 1606, Smyth and a number of others withdrew from the Church of England, separating from the impurity in doctrine and life that they believed characterized the Anglican Church. "Bypassing tradition altogether," they covenanted "with God Himself" to follow wherever God would lead them.[8] Before the end of 1607, Smyth went to Amsterdam in order to avoid persecution. There he established a church based on what he considered to be a simple, literal rendering of the church as depicted in the New Testament.[9] This included an "egalitarian" approach wherein each local church chooses its own leaders. In 1609, Smyth baptized himself and several other people who had been "baptized" as infants, including Thomas Helwys (ca. 1570-1616). If there is a single event that marks the beginning of the modern Baptist movement, this is it. As William Brackney says, "John Smyth's baptismal audacity gave birth to the Baptist movement."[10] Until this point in time, other Separatists had avoided rebaptizing, in part because of fear that they would be viewed as Mennonites or members of other Radical movements. Indeed, Smyth was sympathetic to Mennonite thought and practice, being influenced by Mennonite leader Hans de Ries, and eventually he joined a Mennonite group.[11] By 1611, Helwys led a group out of Smyth's church in part because of Helwys's rejection of Mennonite views, particularly with respect to Christology.[12] Whether or not the charges were fully accurate, Smyth was accused of holding to a docetic view of Christ, then common among some Mennonites, wherein Jesus' full and genuine humanity was implicitly denied.[13] With the exception of this revised Christology, which emerged around 1610, Smyth's central convictions have proven to be "written indelibly into the Baptist heritage." "The Baptists, allowing for wide differences and points of view within their fellowship, still stand," writes James Tull, "for convictions which Smyth stood for in his own time."[14] These include his belief in a regenerate church membership, the self-government of the church, and religious freedom, as well as his beliefs that baptism is the badge of faith and the constituting principle of church membership, and that infant baptism is invalid because infants cannot exercise faith.[15]

The following year, Helwys returned to England and established the first Baptist church in Britain, at Spitalfields near London. He is credited with transmitting Smyth's teachings and practices to England. The church that he established reflected a synthesis of elements of Mennonite belief (including commitments to believer's baptism, autonomous local congregations, human free will and religious freedom) and elements of Puritan faith (such as original sin, traditional Christology and observation of the sabbath).[16] Frequently imprisoned for his defiance of the government and its Church of England, Helwys called not only for a church consisting of regenerate and baptized persons, but also for genuine religious freedom for all. For example, the church at Spitalfields and four like-minded congregations were "theologically isolated" because of their rejection of the Calvinistic understanding of predestination and their lack of trained clergy. Because of their affirmation of a universal or general understanding of the atonement, as opposed to a limited atonement, these congregations came to be known as General Baptists. These General Baptists asserted an Arminian theology with respect to the work of Christ, and they engaged in Anabaptistic practices, particularly with reference to the (re)baptism of adults. As a result, the Church of England regarded them as a threat to order and unity, both ecclesiastical and civil.[17]

Another stream flows into the early English Baptist river. Some Baptists affirmed a Calvinistic understanding of the atonement as limited or particular, and they were called Particular Baptists. They emerged about one generation later than the General Baptists, and initially they were more moderate in their Separatist views. This more moderate approach is manifest in the thought and work of Henry Jacob (1563-1624). Jacob was non-Separatist in principle yet Separatist in his practices, ministering in congregations that functioned independently of the Church of England.[18] Around 1605, he went to Holland, where he served as pastor of an independent church near Leyden. Upon returning to England in 1616, he organized a congregation at Southwark, London. Under the leadership first of Jacob and then his successor, John Lathrop (d. 1653), the Southwark congregation proved to be the forerunner from which the first Particular Baptists descended. Over the years several small groups left the Southwark church to form other congregations, usually because of disagreement over some aspect of the administration or the subjects of baptism. Some members left in 1633, forming a congregation under the leadership of Samuel Eaton. In 1638, another group left Southwark and joined this congregation, which now was under the leadership of John Spilsbury (1593-1668). Spilsbury was a Calvinist, and his congregation became the first Particular Baptist church. By 1644, there were seven Particular Baptist congregations in and around London.[19] During this same period of time, many among the Particular Baptists became convinced that the proper mode of baptism was immersion rather than sprinkling or pouring, and this gradually came to be the practice in Particular Baptist congregations. It was several more years, though no later than 1660, before General Baptists adopted the practice of immersion. Seven Particular Baptist congregations issued the London Confession in 1644. Its fifty-two articles included an affirmation of baptism by immersion, Calvinist soteriology (including limited atonement) and a call for religious liberty.[20] This document proved to be the first of many confessions produced within the Baptist tradition through the centuries.[21]

A third stream of the early Baptist tradition, in addition to the General Baptists and the Particular Baptists, emerged in the mid-seventeenth century. Seventh Day Baptists were committed to sabbatarianism. They believed that the church was to gather on the sabbath—that is, Saturday. The details of their origins are not clear, though it is likely that Seventh Day Baptist congregations were formed by members of independent churches or already established Baptist congregations that left these groups in order to keep the sabbath. Seventh Day Baptists chose not to formally relate with other Baptists, refraining from signing confessional statements and from participating in Baptist associations. Because they were judged by civil authorities and leaders of the Church of England to be even more extreme and therefore more dangerous than other Baptists, they were more heavily persecuted.[22]

All Baptists in England faced increased persecution in the years following 1660, as the Church of England gained power with the restoration of the British monarchy under Charles II. With the adoption of the Act of Toleration by Parliament in 1689, religious liberty was realized in England, and this, according to Baptist historian Leon McBeth, was a victory for which "no group can take more credit" than the Baptists. By the end of the seventeenth century, the English Baptists, both General and Particular, had "worked out their theology" and guidance for the practice of faith.[23] Throughout the seventeenth century, the organization of Baptist church congregations often was accompanied by the adoption of confessions of faith and church covenants. The confessions of faith delineated theological beliefs, and the covenants described how adherents should live. Among these confessions, the Second London Confession (1677) proved to be, according to Timothy George, "the most influential" in Baptist history.[24] This document was largely "a Baptist adaptation of" the Presbyterians' Westminster Confession, with alterations concentrated in matters pertaining to church governance and the sacraments. These confessions, along with more modest theological writings by individual authors, constitute "the rudiments of a systematic theology."[25] The covenants provided guidance with respect to matters such as family worship, prayer, care for fellow Christians, financial support of the church and church discipline.[26]

The Baptists of colonial America had their roots in the English Baptist movements. At the outset, the Americans "struggled with the same identity issues and followed basically the same patterns of evolution" as their English counterparts.[27] For example, the most basic division among Baptists in America was between the Arminian General Baptists, who affirmed a universal atonement and were predominant in New England and southern states, and the Calvinist Particular Baptists, who held to a limited or particular atonement and were more numerous in the mid-Atlantic region, particularly Pennsylvania and New Jersey. Particular Baptists tended to be better educated and better organized. They also were more willing and able to enter into alliances with other dissenting groups.[28] Other differences among Baptists, which were reminiscent of England, could be seen between the worship practices of Seventh Day Baptists, who gathered on Saturday, and those of other Baptists, who gathered on Sunday. Nonetheless, the American churches were not simple duplicates of their British counterparts. William Brackney writes, "Baptist identity in the colonies was not so much a matter of a particular view of the atonement or practice of believer's baptism as it was a united front against religious persecution."[29] Furthermore, as

Timothy George observes, "the diversification of the Baptist tradition that began in England was accelerated in America where the great fact of national life was the frontier—a seemingly endless expanse of space that offered limitless opportunities for escaping the past."[30] Yet neither Puritan-led New England nor the Anglican-led southern colonies would grant genuine freedom of worship to Baptists, and as a result they suffered persecution in the New World analogous to that of the Old World.[31] William Brackney describes his colonial Baptist forerunners as "despised, persecuted, hole-in-the-corner dissenters within the established state-church colonies."[32]

Most of the Baptist churches established in the colonies prior to 1700 were located in New England. Under the pervasive influence of often "militant" Puritans, the Congregational Church was established as "the state-sponsored religion in most of New England." Consequently, the story of the first Baptists in North America is, according to McBeth, a story of "progress amid persecution."[33] The first church in the colonies to be organized according to Baptist principles was established in Providence, Rhode Island, in 1639, under the leadership of Roger Williams (ca. 1603-1684) and Ezekiel Holliman. Over the course of time, this church manifested something of the diversity of Baptist thought and life, alternating between General and Particular Baptist views in its preaching and teaching.[34] Other congregations, such as those at Newport, Rhode Island, and Swansea and Boston, Massachusetts, also played significant roles in the establishment and growth of the Baptist tradition in America.[35] These churches manifested the diversity and struggles of early Baptists: splits over differences between General and Particular Baptists,[36] divisions between seventh-day (Saturday) and first-day (Sunday) Baptists, and opposition from hostile civil and ecclesiastical authorities. As a result of opposition, often aroused by Congregational and Anglican influences, some Baptists moved southward to the middle and southern colonies beginning in the late seventeenth century.[37] Even with the migration of some Baptists southward to avoid persecution, the Baptist movement in America did not experience significant growth until the middle of the eighteenth century. By the end of the eighteenth century, however, it "came of age."[38]

The experiences and enthusiasm generated by the First and Second Great Awakenings (ca. 1730s-1740s and ca. 1787-1805) brought thousands of people, including many Congregationalists, into the Baptist fold.[39] The flourishing of the Baptist tradition was also the result of peoples' appreciation for Baptist faith in and commitment to the democratic form of civil government.[40] The experience of state-associated persecution contributed to the Baptist advocacy, beginning in the 1740s, of the separation of church and state. Isaac Backus

(1724-1806) was among the Congregationalists who converted to the Baptist tradition, and he became "the most influential spokesperson for religious freedom in New England."[41] The Baptist commitment to the autonomy of local congregations meant a freedom in faith and worship that appealed to many slaves and former slaves who attended and joined Baptist churches when they were free to do so.[42] And Baptist respect for individual conscience "affirmed the right of black persons to hear the drumbeats of a denied past and to feel the rhythms of a promised, consecrated future."[43] The first African American Baptist church was formed by George Leile (ca. 1750-ca. 1800) in Georgia in 1778, and the first such church in New England was formed in Boston in 1809 under the leadership of Thomas Paul (1773-1881).

The Baptist ideal of an autonomous, democratic congregation expressed itself in varied ways as the tradition indigenized in American culture. Two examples, though by no means comprehensive, illustrate the range of outcomes. Whether grounded in biblical interpretation, cultural sensibilities, or both, belief in the autonomy and democracy of the local church did not always result in the full inclusion of women in the corporate life of congregations. Speaking of churches in the Baptist and Anabaptist traditions, Barbara MacHaffie observes, "When groups outside the Protestant mainstream vested authority in the individual congregation and when they claimed that all who had been saved were spiritual equals, they had to confront the possibility of female participation in the government of the congregation. Most leaders were reluctant to give a real voice to women."[44] At the same time, Gayraud Wilmore observes, "The Baptists, with a much less centralized control over individual congregations, put fewer obstacles in the way of separating [black and white] memberships, and several independent black congregations were formed in the South and the border states before the turn of the eighteenth century."[45] As was the case with other traditions, Baptist beliefs found varied incarnations in the New World. All in all, particularly when compared with Europe, says William Estep, "the English Baptist legacy of freedom found its fullest expression in the American experience. In the new nation its liberating ideas took root, providing its citizens with freedom of conscience without which all other freedoms are meaningless."[46]

The eighteenth century was also a period during which Baptists in America were maturing theologically. The first American Baptist confession, the Philadelphia Confession, was issued in 1742, and the first Baptist theological school in the United States opened in Philadelphia in 1807 under the leadership of William Staughton.[47] These were followed by a significant history of American confessions and educational institutions, as will be seen below.

In the nineteenth century, overseas missionary work was a major catalyst to and expression of growth for the Baptists. Under the leadership of William Carey (1761-1834), and inspired by his example, the first Baptist missionary society was formed in England in 1792. Eight years later, the first Baptist missionary society in the United States was formed in Boston, largely due to the work of a layperson, Mary Webb (1779-1861).[48] The first missionary convention for African American Baptists, which placed greater emphasis on mission to Africa, convened in 1840. In addition to carrying the Baptist message overseas, mission work served as a catalyst for cooperation among Baptist congregations in the United States. Brackney suggests that the convening of the General Missionary Convention of the Baptist Denomination in the United States for Foreign Missions, May 18, 1814, constitutes the "birth of a truly united Baptist denomination in America."[49] Leaders such as Luther Rice (1783-1836), Richard Furman (1755-1825) and William Staughton (1770-1829) encouraged and worked for cooperation among Baptist churches on a national scale, and by the early nineteenth century, collaborative undertakings such as mission work, the drafting of confessional statements and the formation of conventions flourished. In fact, there was so much cooperative activity that another group of Baptists emerged, protesting against the idea of extrachurch societies (i.e., societies that transcended individual local congregations).[50] Baptists were no longer persecuted or oppressed. They now prospered and flourished, becoming one of the most important denominations in America.[51]

In 1833, the Baptist Convention of New Hampshire adopted a new confession of faith. The New Hampshire Confession articulates a much more moderate Calvinism than many earlier confessions, such as the Philadelphia Confession.[52] This is reflected in, for example, the repeated explicit references to "voluntary" actions on the part of human beings.[53] This softening of Calvinist theology was largely due to the increased influence in New England of Free Will Baptists, who rejected the Calvinist doctrine of predestination. State conventions were voluntary groups of representatives of local Baptist churches within a state, gathered to facilitate fellowship among the churches, fundraising for missions, and mutual encouragement in and planning for church ministry.[54] The formulation and adoption of the New Hampshire Confession in 1833 was a striking indication that state conventions had established themselves as part of Baptist life in America. However, cooperation did not stop at state borders. Conventions embracing entire regions, and eventually the entire country, emerged during the nineteenth century. For example, the majority of Baptist churches in the northern United States formed the General Missionary Convention in 1814. The convention largely disintegrated in 1845 over the issue of slavery, or, as Leroy Fitts refers to

it, a "great paradox." "How could a people who supported the freedom of conscience," he asks, "fail to recognize the evils of an institution styled to enslave
both body and conscience of a people?"[55] Some recognized the evil, while others did not. At this time the Southern Baptist Convention, "the first comprehensive Baptist organization" in the United States, was formed, and, in the north the
American Baptist Missionary Union (1846-1907) continued some of the functions of the General Missionary Convention.[56] In the 1880s, African American
Baptists began to establish their own churches and organizations, often including "National" in their organizational names and plans. In 1907, the Northern
Baptist Convention was formed. Voluntary cooperation among Baptists went beyond even the national level with the founding of the Baptist World Alliance, in
London, in 1905. Not least among its commitments has been the pursuit of religious freedom.

By the middle of the nineteenth century, Baptists in the United States,
amidst their diversity, had developed "a theological consensus," and around
the turn of the century there emerged what Timothy George refers to as "an
orthodox Baptist consensus, represented in the North by Augustus H. Strong,
in the South by E. Y. Mullins."[57] At the same time there was an undercurrent
of tension developing. Despite cooperative efforts, "there were major divisions along regional, racial/ethnic, and theological lines."[58] Some of the theological tensions were not unique to Baptists. They, like Christians of other traditions, wrestled with new social and theological thought coming out of
Germany, including various forms of biblical criticism, the turmoil of the
fundamentalist-modernist controversy, and the debates over the Social Gospel
movement of the early twentieth century. A number of Southern Baptist scholars, including theologian E. Y. Mullins (1860-1928), contributed to *The Fundamentals: A Testimony to the Truth,*[59] while Walter Rauschenbusch (1861-1918),
an American German Baptist, propounded *A Theology for the Social Gospel.*[60]
A number of Baptist conventions split, merged or were founded as a result of
"conservative-liberal" disagreements.[61] In 1925 the Southern Baptist Convention adopted a confession, the Baptist Faith and Message, at a time when, by
contrast, Northern Baptists chose not to adopt a confession. George also
points to another, often overlooked factor. "The communitarian character of
Baptist life, exemplified by covenants, confessions, and catechisms," he
writes, "was undermined by the privatization of Baptist theology and the rising
tide of modern rugged individualism that swept through American culture in
the early twentieth century."[62]

As was the case with many traditions, the twentieth century was in many
respects a turbulent one for Baptists. By the 1960s, the differences among Bap-

tists became more clearly delineated, as illustrated by the Southern Baptist Convention's revision of the Baptist Faith and Message in 1963, prompted in large part by a perceived need to address changing views of the Bible and its authority. Yet, this did not settle the matter, and it proved to be but "the first round of a prolonged controversy which would convulse the convention over the next three decades."[63] The controversy was largely centered around theological disagreements between "conservatives," who sought close adherence to the Baptist confessional heritage, and "moderates," who sought to maintain greater theological latitude under the Baptist principles of the supreme authority of the Bible (rather than tradition) and freedom of individual conscience.[64] As the century came to its close, the dust was still unsettled from heated and visible controversies, and from battles for control of organizations and institutions within the Southern Baptist Convention. Yet, amidst all the battles, Baptists throughout the twentieth century continued to champion the Bible as the supreme authority for faith and practice, the autonomy of local churches, believer's baptism and the imperative of mission work. And, in keeping with the Baptist tradition of freedom, they understood and applied these affirmations in a wide variety of ways.[65]

Diversity. As the history reveals, considerable diversity of theological viewpoints is found among Baptists. David Dockery observes, "From the beginning Baptists have been a varied group with a complex history and no single theological tradition."[66] Dwight A. Moody's review of the work of seven contemporary Baptist theologians confirms that the diversity that developed early in Baptist history persists into the present. He notes the commonalities among them, but he goes on to conclude that "the diversity may itself be a chief distinction of the Baptist tradition, witnessing as it does to the notion of freedom imbedded so deeply in the Baptist consciousness."[67] Furthermore, commitment to the principle of freedom means that theological differences are often "not between Unions and Conventions but between individual Baptists. No single Baptist Convention can be readily characterized by one theological label."[68] Consequently, references to the theological characteristics of associations or conventions can be made only in terms of the historical origins of or tendencies within the associations or conventions.[69]

Theological differences among Baptists on matters related to soteriology, particularly free will and the extent of atonement, can be located along a spectrum between Arminian and Calvinist theologies. The first Baptists were Arminian-minded, believing that Christ died for all human beings. In America, another Arminian-minded group emerged in the eighteenth century, affirming both universal atonement and human free will. This Arminian-minded Baptist theology is sustained today in groups such as the National Association of Free Will Baptists, the General Conference of Original Free Will Baptists, the United Free Will Baptist Church, the General Baptist Church, the General Conference of the Evangelical Baptist Church and the General Association of Separate Baptists.[70]

Calvinistic theology, however, soon became prominent among the earliest Baptists in America,[71] and a number of Baptist scholars suggest that Calvinist theology has been the predominant influence throughout Baptist history.[72] A strict adherence to five-point Calvinism is found among Reformed Baptist churches, as well as in the Primitive Baptists and the National Primitive Baptist Convention of the U.S.A. A more moderate Calvinism, reminiscent of the New Hampshire Confession, characterizes the General Association of Regular Baptist Churches, the North American Baptist Conference and the Southern Baptist Convention.[73] Other groups, such as the Baptist General Conference, the United Baptist and the Conservative Baptist Association of America, are more generically "conservative" or "evangelical."[74]

As noted earlier, the Seventh Day Baptist General Conference sustains the belief that the seventh day of the week (i.e., Saturday) is the sabbath. Another Baptist group, the Landmark movement, arose in the mid-nineteenth century and espoused a radically Baptistic theology of the church. Landmark Baptists assert that there is an unbroken succession of Baptist churches from the New Testament onward, and in principle they affirm the absolute autonomy of each local church. The American Baptist Association and the Baptist Missionary Association carry on Landmarkism. A number of other associations and fellowships are generally characterized as fundamentalist, being "militantly anti-modernist,"[75] and, for the most part, were established in reaction against liberal trends in the early twentieth century. These groups include the General Association of Regular Baptists, the Baptist Bible Fellowship and the Southwide Baptist Fellowship. The World Baptist Fellowship functions as an umbrella organization for these fundamentalist groups.

The Baptist tradition is the single largest Christian tradition among African Americans. Under the theological leadership of "preachers/pastors," African American Baptists have a theological heritage that "has definite genetic traces of Baptist identity, while within its own context producing arguably the most creative forms of Baptist thought."[76] The influence of these theological expressions of the Baptist tradition is by no means limited to African American churches, as is witnessed in, for example, the widespread influence of Martin Luther King Jr. However, distinctively African American Baptist thought is most fully embodied in groups such as the National Baptist Convention of America, Inc., and the Progressive National Baptist Convention.

THE BAPTIST TRADITION

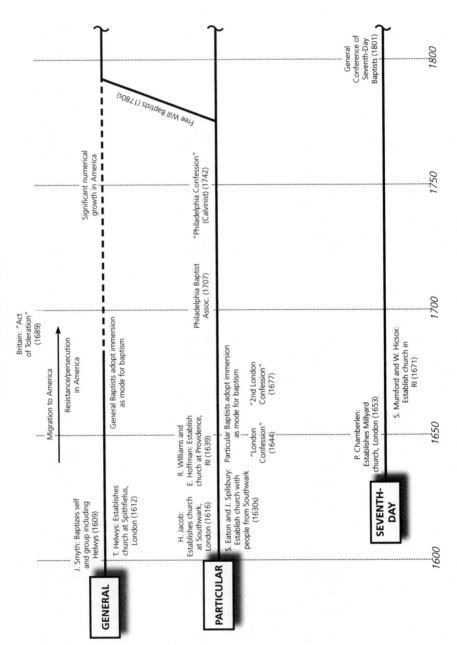

THE BAPTIST TRADITION (CONTINUED)

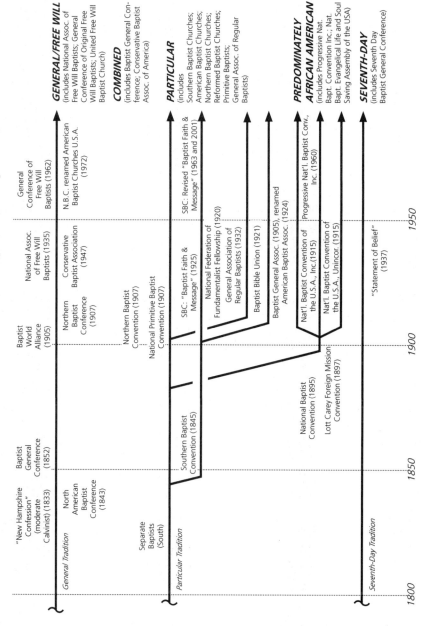

GENERAL/FREE WILL
(includes National Assoc. of Free Will Baptists; General Conference of Original Free Will Baptists; United Free Will Baptist Church)

COMBINED
(includes Baptist General Conference; Conservative Baptist Assoc. of America)

PARTICULAR
(includes Southern Baptist Churches; American Baptist Churches; Northern Baptist Churches; Reformed Baptist Churches; Primitive Baptists; General Assoc. of Regular Baptists)

PREDOMINATELY AFRICAN AMERICAN
(includes Progressive Nat. Bapt. Convention Inc.; Nat. Bapt. Evangelical Life and Soul Saving Assembly of the USA)

SEVENTH-DAY
(includes Seventh Day Baptist General Conference)

General Tradition

"New Hampshire Confession" (moderate Calvinist) (1833)

North American Baptist Conference (1843)

Baptist General Conference (1852)

Baptist World Alliance (1905)

Northern Baptist Convention (1907)

National Assoc. of Free Will Baptists (1935)

Conservative Baptist Association (1947)

General Conference of Free Will Baptists (1962)

N.B.C. renamed American Baptist Churches U.S.A. (1972)

Northern Baptist Conference (1907)

National Primitive Baptist Convention (1907)

Separate Baptists (South)

Particular Tradition

Southern Baptist Convention (1845)

SBC: "Baptist Faith & Message" (1925)

National Federation of Fundamentalist Fellowship (1920)

General Association of Regular Baptists (1932)

Baptist Bible Union (1921)

SBC: Revised "Baptist Faith & Message" (1963 and 2001)

Baptist General Assoc. (1905), renamed American Baptist Assoc. (1924)

National Baptist Convention (1895)

Lott Carey Foreign Mission Convention (1897)

Nat'l. Baptist Convention of the U.S.A., Inc.(1915)

Nat'l. Baptist Convention of the U.S.A., Unincor. (1915)

Progressive Nat'l. Baptist Conv., Inc. (1960)

Seventh-Day Tradition

"Statement of Belief" (1937)

1800   1850   1900   1950

Approach: Theological and Hermeneutical Method

Role of theology. Baptists often are portrayed as being uninterested in disciplined theological work. One contemporary Baptist theologian, Dwight A. Moody, writes, "There is one significant characteristic of those within the Believer's Church movement, namely, the reticence to write and publish systematic theologies."[77] Furthermore, Baptists have always prided themselves on rejecting one of the most common forms of theological work in the Christian tradition: creeds. Baptists are staunchly anticreedal. As one Baptist scholar observes, "The phrase 'Baptists are not a creedal people' has become an axiom within our tradition."[78] Yet, such observations should not lead one to conclude that Baptists are unconcerned about disciplined theological reflection.

Since the first days of the movement, Baptists have cared about theology. The earliest Baptists separated from the churches that they originally were associated with not because of particular practices, such as infant baptism, but because of the theological understanding of those practices. As we saw earlier, one encounters two groups when tracing the early history of the Baptists: the General and the Particular Baptists. And their differences were essentially theological, having to do with beliefs about matters such as God's sovereignty, human free will and salvation. The Landmark and Downgrade controversies of the nineteenth century were essentially theological in nature.[79] Landmark Baptists, as noted above, held to a radical view of the absolute autonomy of local churches, rooted in a belief that there is an unbroken succession of Baptist churches from the New Testament onward. The Downgrade controversy was a heated dispute between two prominent British Baptists, John Clifford and C. H. Spurgeon, at the end of the nineteenth century. Clifford advocated various then-modern forms of biblical criticism and theological method, and the preacher Spurgeon roundly rejected these as ill founded and harmful. In the twentieth century, the intramural battles within the Baptist tradition, not unlike other traditions, have undoubtedly had their "political" dimensions, but the issues at the root of many of these battles were clearly theological in nature, including such loci as biblical authority, hermeneutics and ecumenism. While Moody wishes that Baptists had written and published more systematic theologies, he describes a recent flourish of publications among Baptist theologians—and this is not surprising in light of the history of the Baptists. The book *Baptist Theologians,* edited by Timothy George and David Dockery, has chapters on thirty-three Baptist theologians, and in the concluding chapter Dockery surveys the history of Baptist theology and theologians, demonstrating that Baptists have been and are theologians.[80]

Many of these theologians have published theology texts and set forth the case for the importance of theology.[81] Underlying many of the reasons given for the importance of theology is the Baptist belief in the importance of truth— that is, correctly apprehending theological truth. Baptists are to work toward an ever greater unity "based upon the truth."[82] Millard Erickson suggests that although some people would deny the connection between truth and experience, the fact is that "in the long run the truth will affect our experience."[83] Stanley Grenz says, "By its very nature, the conceptual framework of a faith community contains an implicit claim to represent the truth about the world and the divine reality its members have come to know and experience. For this reason, theology necessarily entails the quest for truth."[84] In addition to viewing the theological enterprise as entailing a quest for truth, as do most traditions, Baptists put special emphasis on the role of truth in the transformation of human beings. John Dagg says that truth is "like the Spirit of God, brooding over the original chaos, bringing order out of confusion, and infusing light and life where darkness and death has previously reigned." He describes "Christian truth" as "exerting . . . new-creating power."[85] According to Augustus Strong, "At the moment of regeneration, the soul is conscious only of the truth and of its own exercises with reference to it."[86] And, among the regenerate, truth "thoroughly digested" is "essential" to the maturation of individual Christians and of churches.[87] This regard for truth manifests itself in serious theological work, and we will now consider how Baptists go about doing theology.[88]

Theological method. William Brackney writes, "The Baptist self-understanding begins with Scripture."[89] Emphasis on the authority of Scripture is clearly documented in the history of Baptist confessions. The affirmation of the character and authority of Scripture was placed as the first article in the Second London Confession (1677) and, in its American revision, the Philadelphia Confession (1742). The opening sentence of the Second London Confession reads, "The Holy Scripture is the only sufficient, certain, and infallible rule of all saving Knowledge, Faith, and Obedience."[90] These two confessions set the dominant pattern for subsequent Baptist confessional statements, both in England and in the United States.[91] As James Leo Garrett notes, "Baptist confessions of faith that have dealt specifically with the source or sources of authority clearly agree as to the supremacy of the scriptures and tend toward the sole authority of the scriptures."[92] Garrett himself holds that "the Bible is to be reckoned as the supreme standard or highest ranking channel of religious authority for Christians," and that this authority is nothing less than "that of the sovereign God."[93] Gordon Lewis and Bruce Demarest believe that "what the Bible teaches remains the primary source and final court of appeal" for theology.[94] Similar affirmations of the sole or the supreme authority of Scripture are found throughout the writings of Baptist historians and theologians.[95]

In light of this emphasis on the authority of Scripture and of the earlier observations that Baptists are anticreedal, it may seem odd to cite confessional documents (even surprising to have confessional documents to cite) to illustrate Baptist views. However, formal confessional documents, as well as covenants and catechisms, have played a significant role in the theological life of the Baptist tradition.[96] There has not always been, and there is not now, agreement among all Baptists regarding the role of confessions. "There are confessional Baptists," observes William Brackney, "and there are those who hold to the importance of religious experience in defining religious character." The latter "see little disciplinary, liturgical, or educational value" in confessions and place "a high priority upon liberty of conscience."[97] Representative of the former, Timothy George comments that Baptists were not "doctrinal anarchists who boasted of their 'right' to believe in anything they wanted to. Instead of flaunting their Christian freedom in this way, Baptists used it to produce and publish *confessions* of faith both as a means of declaring their own faith to the world and of guarding the theological integrity of their own fellowship."[98] To understand the role of confessions in Baptist thought, an important distinction must be noted: the distinction between creed and confession. Creeds are viewed by Baptists as "authoritative . . . final, unalterable, and binding statements of faith,"[99] and as such they are rejected because they may usurp the authority of the Bible or hinder the believer's freedom to interpret the Bible under the Holy Spirit's guidance. Confessions, on the other hand, do not have binding authority, nor are they final or unalterable. Rather, they are "abstracts of biblical truth" that "set forth . . . an accurate summary" of the faith of a Baptist church or group.[100] They are "revisable in the light of the Bible, God's infallible, unchanging revelation."[101] As William Lumpkin puts it, "Baptist confessions have a moral rather than a legal force in Baptist history."[102] Commitment to a confession consists in "voluntary, conscientious adherence"—but it is a commitment.[103] Confessions, properly understood, do not undermine the authority of the Bible, but rather articulate "a consensus of opinion of some Baptist body" providing "general instruction and guidance . . . concerning those articles of the Christian faith which are most surely held" among the group.[104] Without usurping the primacy of Scripture, confessions serve as hermeneutical guides to a proper reading of the Bible.[105]

Baptists often describe themselves as "people of the Book."[106] Thus, theology begins with, focuses on and leads to the exposition of the Bible. The theologian's primary task is to identify and rightly interpret all of the Scripture passages pertinent to any given topic.[107] Whatever else theology might entail, this comprehensive Scripture study is at its center. The earliest Baptists saw themselves as differing from Anglican and Presbyterian Protestants in that they, Baptists, sought to formulate their theology based directly on Scripture alone—not on Scripture *and* tradition or, in some instances, reason.[108] More recently, Dwight A. Moody, reflecting on the work of contemporary Baptist theologians, observes that theology is "obviously understood as the effort to discern, describe, and defend what the Bible has to say about certain religious topics."[109] From a Baptist perspective, most, if not all, Protestant traditions uphold *in principle* the authority of Scripture; however, Baptists view themselves as distinct in consistently *implementing* the principle that the individual Christian is able to, and must, interpret the Bible "on the Bible's own terms" and "submit directly" to the authority of the teaching found therein.[110] Thus, properly speaking, the Bible alone—not tradition or reason or experience or culture or any combination of these—is the authoritative source for theology.[111]

Because the Bible is the source for theology, the principles and methods of biblical interpretation are crucial for Baptist theology. Baptist scholars have written books on biblical interpretation, but they have written virtually nothing that explicitly addresses distinctively "Baptist" hermeneutics per se.[112] One Baptist scholar surmises that there has not been more self-conscious hermeneutical reflection because Baptists simply "accept the biblical text in its most obvious sense," seeking nothing more or less than "the straightforward interpretation of Scripture."[113] This is sometimes referred to as the "literal" method of interpretation, understood as "nothing more than the traditional grammatical-historical method in which meaning is found by normal interpretive rules."[114] These rules are not uniquely Baptist, but there are two tendencies, if not principles, that further shape the Baptist reading of the Bible.[115]

First, the New Testament is granted a measure of priority over the Old Testament. "A so-called flat bible approach," writes Dale Moody, "is a distortion of historical revelation."[116] It is common for affirmations of the Scriptures as the source of Baptist life and thought to mention only the New Testament, while there is simply no explicit reference to the Old Testament.[117] John Kiwiet remarks that the early Baptists "gave priority to the New Testament in interpreting the message of the Bible."[118] And Justice Anderson observes that "the Baptist denomination has rooted its faith and order in the New Testament, thereby avoiding the errors of other denominations which have carried over certain Old Testament rules and regulations in their ecclesiologies."[119] Furthermore, the New Testament is read with a christological emphasis. According to W. T. Conner, "The bible finds its center and unity in Jesus Christ. . . . First and fundamental is the record of his life, death, resurrection, and ascension as given in the Gospels."[120] For other Baptist theologians, the life and teachings of Jesus Christ provide "the theological model and the hermeneutical criterion" for theology.[121]

Second, Baptists tenaciously affirm each believer's right and obligation to read and interpret the Bible directly—that is, free from restraints imposed by any ecclesial or secular authority.[122] This right to and responsibility for "private interpretation" or "private judgment" is one aspect of soul competency. Soul competency refers to the "unhindered access to receive or to reject a personal, individual relationship with God," and, upon entering into this relationship, the similarly unhindered pursuit of Christian life before God.[123] "The authority of Scripture for Baptist faith and practice," writes C. Penrose St. Amant, "is matched by the competence of the individual believer in the fellowship of the church and under the guidance of the Holy Spirit to understand it."[124] Thus, interpretation is not "private" in some absolute sense, for it is pursued in the context of the church and in relationship with the God of the Bible. The Holy Spirit illumines the mind of the interpreter as the book, inspired by the Holy Spirit, is read and interpreted. Although this freedom of interpretation is not absolute,[125] Baptists seek to avoid, at all costs, a required adherence to anything other than the teaching of Scripture, thus "not bowing to the decisions of any fallible master."[126]

Theology: Characteristic Beliefs

The Baptist emphasis on individual soul competency and the freedom of the local church (both of which will be discussed below) contributed to the development of what William Brackney describes as "a variegated form of theology that reflected a wider variety of sources than the Scholastic and magisterial theologians."[127] Fisher Humphries makes a distinction between "the majority tradition" (i.e., Baptist) and numerous "minority traditions" within (i.e., Anabaptist, Calvinist, Landmark, Deeper Life, Fundamentalist, Progressive) and predicts that one of the minority traditions (most likely, the Fundamentalist or Calvinist or Landmark) could become the majority tradition, at least within the Southern Baptist Convention.[128] A number of Baptist scholars even refer to an "identity crisis" among Baptists.[129] Despite the truth in these observations, threads of continuity run through the story of the Baptist movement. Brackney observes, "From [the Baptist tradition's] earliest stages, genetic theological connections can be identified. Ideas pass from one pastor to another, or from a tract to a treatise. These enduring ideas are the 'genes' of Baptist thought."[130] With Scripture as their guide, Baptists do characteristically emphasize particular doctrines and confidently assert distinctively Baptist beliefs about them.[131] These include (1) the sufficiency and supreme authority of the Bible; (2) the autonomy of the local church in relation to both ecclesiastical and civil institutions; (3) church membership as including only those whose words and conduct manifest regeneration and conversion; (4) a democratic form of church life in which each member has the freedom of individual belief and a voice in the life of the church; and (5) observance of the ordinances of believer's baptism by immersion and the Lord's Supper.[132] Although not comprehensive of all of these theological topics, ecclesiology and baptism will serve here to illustrate Baptist theological belief.[133]

Ecclesiology. The doctrine of the church (or churches) is highly important to Baptists. In fact, some Baptist scholars contend that the doctrine of the nature of the church constitutes the core of Baptist identity.[134] Baptist historians often warn against allowing the name "Baptist" to distort a proper understanding of the Baptist movement.[135] As Timothy George asserts, "More than any other doctrine," including baptism, "early English Baptists' understanding of the church led them to separate from the established religious structures of their country and also set them apart from other dissenting groups, such as Presbyterians, Congregationalists, and Methodists."[136] Baptists did not separate from other churches to escape infant baptism per se; they separated from other churches in a quest for "a pure church," a church ordered and functioning in accord with the instructions set forth in the New Testament, which call for believer's baptism, not infant baptism.[137]

Form of churches: Local and democratic. Baptists emphasize the distinction between the church "universal" and the church "local." Belief in the universal church, "the whole company of those who are saved by Christ,"[138] is based on passages in the New Testament where ἐκκλησία refers collectively to all Christians (e.g., Eph 1:22; 3:10, 21; Mt 16:18; 1 Cor 15:9; Gal 1:13; Phil 3:6). The unity of this church universal is "spiritual." The universal church does not have, and should not be expected to have, a visible or "external organization" (see Acts 4:32; Jn 15:19; Gal 5:22; 1 Jn 3:14; 4:7, 21; 1 Thess 4:9; Col 3:14).[139] Consequently, "for all Baptists the most vivid expression of the Christian community is the local congregation."[140] The emphasis in the Baptist understanding of the form of the church is clearly on local churches.

"There is no such thing as 'the Baptist church,'" writes James Draper; "There are only local Baptist churches. The local Baptist church is 'Baptist headquarters.'"[141] In local congregations "the universal takes local and temporal form, and . . . the idea of the church as a whole is concretely exhibited."[142] In the New Testament, ἐκκλησία refers mainly to local assemblies of believers (e.g., Mt 18:17; Acts 8:1; 9:31; 13:1; 1 Cor 1:2; 14:23; 16:1; 2 Cor 8:1; Gal 1:2; Rev 2:1), and this "local" emphasis characterizes Baptist ecclesiology. The Baptist Heritage Commission states that a local church "represents in any place the church in that locality; it is fully the church, not a branch of some national or wider institution."[143] Citing 1 Corinthians 1:2 and 2 Corinthians 1:1, Millard Erickson states that an individual local congregation "is never regarded as only a part or component of the whole church. The church is not a sum or composite of the individual local groups. Instead, the whole is found in each place."[144] John Dagg writes, "The Holy Scriptures contain no proof that the followers of Christ, after the dispersion of the church at Jerusalem, ever acted together as one externally organized society. They constituted separate local churches which acted independently in their distinct organizations, but never formally united in counsel or in action as one body."[145]

The so-called Jerusalem Council, as described in Acts 15, is no exception. Churches from outside Jerusalem sent messengers who participated in the discussion, but the decision reached was that of the church at Jerusalem, not of the church universal. This is indicative of the fact that "there is no jurisdiction of one church over another, but all are on equal footing." Acts 5:29 reports that Peter and the apostles said, "We must obey God rather than any human authority." Thus, "each local church is directly subject to Christ."[146] This does not mean that each local church is to function without regard for other churches. The Baptist Heritage Commission instructs, "Each local church is free, and indeed dutybound by the concerns of the gospel, to enter into covenant relationship with other Christians, both nationally and locally."[147] From the early years of the Baptist movement, individual Baptist churches associated with other local churches for mutual encouragement and ministry. Today, this cooperation is embodied in the various national and international "associations," "conventions," "conferences," "federations" and "unions" of Baptist churches. However, Baptists emphasize the autonomy of the local church, with African American Baptist churches tending, according to James Washington, to be even "more militantly congregational."[148] Cooperative relationships are always voluntary, and no such organization can ever exercise binding authority over any of the participating churches.[149] Each local congregation of believers is free to be directly related to Christ as head of the local church. No ecclesiastical body, such as a denomination, nor individual person, such as a bishop, is to have authority over a local congregation; rather, the leadership of a local church is located and functions from within that local church.

Similarly, within each local church, each individual member is seen as relating directly to Jesus Christ.[150] As Barry Morrison observes, Baptists "have cherished the notion that God works unmediately in their midst."[151] This perspective is expressed in the Baptist notion of "soul competency." Every human being, Christian and non-Christian alike, has "the inalienable right of direct access to

God," and every believer, being "quickened by divine grace," is "fully 'competent' or capable of responding to God directly."[152] No individual person, such as a priest or pastor, is to be regarded as a mediary between the individual and God. Nor is any institution—namely, the church—to be relied upon for access to God. "Baptists, like other Protestants, affirm the autonomy of the individual soul and the priesthood of all believers," writes R. Wayne Stacy; "But unlike other Protestants, we Baptists are not just autonomous; we're belligerently autonomous!"[153] Each individual Christian is regarded as "competent" in spiritual matters. Thus, Baptist churches are governed democratically, believing that each church is "made up of converts with *equal spiritual standing.*"[154] Nevertheless, this does not mean that each member lives isolated from or in disregard for other members. As members of the priesthood of believers, all members of the local congregation are equal before God, have the right to direct access to God, and have the right and responsibility to participate, according to their gifts, in the decisions and work of the local church.[155] It is a Baptist ideal that "each Christian, having direct access to God through Christ, is his or her own priest and is also under obligation to become a priest for Christ in behalf of other persons."[156] Thus, the fundamental form of the church is the local church, voluntarily cooperating with other local churches while maintaining autonomy under the direct headship of Christ, and democratically facilitating the communion of the saints while not hindering each member's direct access to God. This voluntary cooperation often has been encoded in covenants.[157] Underlying this understanding of the form of the church are particular beliefs about the nature of and membership in the church.

Nature and membership of churches: Regenerate believers. Baptists often identify themselves with the "Believers' Church" groups within Protestantism. This title is indicative of the Baptist understanding of the nature of the church as including "all who profess faith in Christ and give evidence of that faith in their lives"—that is, "a company of believers in covenant with God and each other."[158] Furthermore, believing in Jesus Christ is inextricably linked with spiritual regeneration, and regeneration is synonymous with membership in the true church.[159] Erickson describes the church as "a fellowship of regenerate believers."[160] These are people who have been spiritually born anew through the Holy Spirit and have exercised trusting faith in Jesus Christ. The term *regenerate* is commonly used by Baptists to refer to two soteriological realities: regeneration and conversion. James P. Boyce writes, "Regeneration is the work of God, changing the heart of man by his sovereign will, while conversion is the act of man turning towards God with the new inclination thus given to his heart."[161] According to Ephesians 2:5, in regeneration sinners who are spiritually "dead" are "made . . . alive together with Christ." They are born again, "born of the Spirit" (Jn 3:5-6). There is "a change in the dominant affection of the soul" whereby "the ruling disposition, which was sinful, now becomes holy."[162] This new disposition is "exercised" in believing—that is, the act of repentant faith. As John 3:16 says, "God so loved the world that he gave his only Son, so that everyone who believes in him may not perish but have eternal life." Those who are regenerated and converted are, according to Colossians 1:13-14, "rescued . . . from the power of darkness and transferred . . . into the kingdom of his beloved Son, in whom we have redemption, the forgiveness of sins." Only those whose sins are thus forgiven, only those who are redeemed, are members of God's church, and only these should be members of a local church. Baptists do not claim that every member of every Baptist church is in fact regenerated. "However, the general consensus is," observes Norman, "that Baptist principles, when consistently applied, will theoretically exclude from church membership all but the converted."[163] In theory and in principle, the church is for regenerate believers only, and in practice, a local, democratic congregation that discerningly applies the New Testament description of believers will most closely approximate this ideal.

The Baptist emphasis on truth, noted in conjunction with the importance of theology, is seen again in connection with the doctrine of regeneration. God is the one who brings about regeneration, and truth is one of the instruments that God employs. According to Strong, the Holy Spirit "illuminate[s] the mind, so that it can perceive the truth. In conjunction with the change of man's inner disposition, there is an appeal to man's rational nature through the truth."[164] In discussing the work of the Holy Spirit in regeneration, Erickson, citing passages such as Matthew 13:13-15; Mark 8:18; and 1 Corinthians 2:11-14, highlights the importance of the work of the Spirit in overcoming the human "inability to recognize and understand the truth."[165] As James 1:18 says, "In fulfillment of his own purpose he gave us birth by the word of truth, so that we would become a kind of first fruits of his creatures" (see also Jn 15:3). And, this word of truth is the Word of God (1 Pet 1:23; 2 Pet 1:4; Heb 4:12; Eph 6:17). The church consists of those who are regenerate and the path to regeneration is belief in the truth. Thus it is fitting that the Baptist tradition, along with similar groups such as the Anabaptists, often is referred to as part of the "Believer's Church" tradition within Protestantism.

Because membership in a church is to be limited to those are regenerate, it is imperative to know how to identify such persons. Regeneration will be manifest in a life of holiness.[166] Erickson indicates that "purity and devotion are to be emphasized," and Grenz notes that "all the lofty phrases used in the New

Testament of 'the church' are to be true of each congregation of believers."[167] The New Hampshire Confession states that the "proper evidence" of regeneration "is found in the holy fruit which we bring forth to the glory of God."[168] Those who are regenerate will manifest this reality by believing the truth, trusting Jesus Christ for salvation from sin, giving verbal testimony to this, and living a life of obedience to God's directives set forth in the Bible. Thus, sanctification is the evidence of regeneration: only those who are regenerate are members of the universal church, and those who have experienced regeneration will manifest this in a sanctified life. Baptists seek churches whose members live holy lives characterized by regular attention to "the Word of God, self-examination, self-denial, watchfulness and prayer."[169]

Baptism. As we noted earlier, we must not let the name "Baptist" lead to a distorted or imbalanced understanding of the Baptist tradition. There is much more to Baptist theology than the affirmation of baptism.[170] Yet, as Tom Nettles says, "a Baptist church cannot exist where there is no regenerate church membership and no affirmation of believer's baptism. These are the ecclesiological *sine qua non*'s."[171] The practice of baptizing only believers in Jesus Christ is an "entirely logical" conclusion drawn from the conviction that the church consists of regenerate believers only.[172] Baptism is crucial to Baptists.

Character of baptism: An ordinance. For Baptists, water baptism and the Lord's Table are ordinances.[173] They are "outward rites which Christ has appointed to be administered in his church as visible signs of the saving truth of the gospel. They are signs, in that they vividly express this truth and confirm it to the believer."[174] Baptism is a symbolic act of obedience. It does not in any way convey God's saving grace to an individual.[175] Christ, in and through his own baptism by John, testified to the "binding obligation" upon his followers to be baptized.[176] A number of observers note that in recent decades an increasing number of Baptists use the term *sacrament* to refer to baptism and the Lord's Table.[177] This may be due in part to the influential book by the Baptist scholar G. R. Beasley-Murray, *Baptism in the New Testament,* in which he uses the term *sacrament* to refer to baptism.[178] However, Baptists continue to deny, for example, that "God's grace is limited to these rites or that the rites themselves guarantee the delivery of grace," and they affirm that "rather than [being] a means of grace . . . baptism is a *manifestation* of grace."[179] Baptism is a "sign" and a "symbol," with "no inherent connection between [the] sign and what it represents."[180] Thus, baptism continues to be described by Baptists in such a way that it makes most sense to retain, as Grenz does, the primacy of the term *ordinance.*[181]

Mode of baptism: Immersion. Obedience to the directives of the New Testament entails baptism by immersion, or complete submersion in water.[182] For

Baptists, immersion is the only mode of baptism fully consistent with both the Greek terminology and the symbolism of the New Testament. Baptist scholars have examined the use of βάπτω and βαπτίζω in the New Testament, and they conclude that these terms convey the meaning "to dip" or "to plunge" or "to immerse." To simply wash or sprinkle or pour is insufficient. Such actions do not fulfill the intent and directive of βάπτω or βαπτίζω.[183] Nothing in the New Testament usage of these terms suggests a "figurative" interpretation, so passages such as Matthew 28:19-20; John 4:1; and Galatians 3:27 are to be interpreted in terms of the "literal sense" of the "plain command" (related passages include Mt 3:6; Mk 1:5, 9; 7:4; Lk 11:38; 20:4).[184] The terminology of the New Testament indicates immersion.[185] Thus, the paradigmatic instances of baptism in the New Testament, such as those carried out by John the Baptist (Jn 3:23; Mk 1:10) and by Philip (Acts 8:36-39), are baptisms by immersion.[186]

Furthermore, the symbolism of the act demands immersion (see Rom 6:1-11; Col 2:11-12). Baptism is an act symbolizing the death and resurrection of Christ, "the great work of Christ" on our behalf.[187] But baptism does not testify only to the work of Christ accomplished in Jerusalem two thousand years ago; it also testifies to the believer being joined together with Christ in his death and resurrection. Baptism proclaims that the person being baptized has been regenerated through being united with the crucified and resurrected Savior.[188] Christ's body was laid in the tomb, and in baptism the believer's body is completely submerged in water. Christ bodily arose from the grave, and in baptism the believer, having been submerged, arises from the water. "If baptism is an enactment of the story of Jesus and our participation in that story," writes Grenz, "then immersion is its clearest symbol."[189] Only complete bodily immersion genuinely depicts Christ's work and the individual believer being united with Christ in that saving work.

Subjects of baptism: Believers. The only way one can be united with Christ in his death and resurrection is through faith. Only through trustingly believing in the work of Jesus Christ as the provision for the forgiveness of one's sins does one become spiritually regenerate. To be a Christian is to be a "believer," and to be a believer is to be regenerate, born again with the resurrection life of Christ. Baptism symbolizes or testifies to the fact that an individual has been born again through faith in Jesus Christ. "While faith is possible without baptism (i.e., salvation does not depend on one's being baptized), baptism is a natural accompaniment and the completion of faith"; it is itself "an act of faith and commitment."[190] Consequently, baptism is for believers, and for believers only. It "must be administered after faith, not prior to it, and . . . it must be the conscious, free, and voluntary act of the believer."[191] The Second London Confession, citing Mark 16:16 and Acts 8:36-37, states, "Those who do actually profess repentance towards God, faith in, and obedience, to our Lord Jesus, are the only proper subjects of this ordinance."[192] If baptism entails a public declaration of trusting faith in Jesus Christ, then, as Grenz indicates, "infant baptism simply cannot fulfill this function."[193]

This "believer's baptism" is consistent with the teaching and example of Christ and the apostles. As recorded in Matthew 28:19, Jesus directed his disciples to "make disciples of all nations, baptizing them [i.e., the ones who become disciples] in the name of the Father and of the Son and of the Holy Spirit," and according to Acts 8:12, when the Samaritans "believed Philip, who was proclaiming the good news about the kingdom of God and the name of Jesus Christ, they were baptized, both men and women" (see also Mt 3:2-3, 6; Acts 2:37-38, 41; 18:8; 19:4). In addition to this positive testimony of the New Testament is the absence of a single clear case of an individual being baptized apart from the exercise of faith.[194] Believer's baptism is also consistent with the nature of the church, which is understood as a company of regenerate persons (Jn 3:5; Rom 6:13). Indeed, the "logic" of the church as a body consisting of regenerate persons requires believer's baptism. A new believer should be baptized "with the least possible delay, after the candidate and the church have gained evidence that a spiritual change has been accomplished within."[195] Such spiritual change occurs only in the context of believing faith, and since infants and very young children are incapable of such faith, they should not be baptized.[196]

Conclusion: Freedom for Immediacy

It is neither prudent nor possible to reduce the essence of Baptist thought to a single "key" belief.[197] However, one of the motifs that runs throughout Baptist thought may be summarized in the phrase "freedom for immediacy." In both its method and outcomes, these "people of the Book" affirm and protect the freedom to be immediately, directly related to God through Christ.[198] People experience redemption as a result of God applying his truth directly to the heart and mind of individual persons. Thus redeemed and under the lordship of Christ, the believer is to be free to interpret the Bible apart from binding prescriptions of a creed, and apart from the demands of church or state. Under the guidance of the Holy Spirit and the tutelage of the Bible itself, the believer relates directly to God. The individual believer is free to contribute to the life of the local congregation, to participate in the democratic processes and the resulting ministries of this congregation. The local congregation is free to oversee its own affairs. No external or higher body, either ecclesial or governmental, has authority over the local congregation, which is free to conduct its affairs directly under the lordship of Christ.

FOR FURTHER STUDY

The endnotes contain citations of many useful resources, most of them written from within the Baptist tradition. A brief list of resources for further study follows here. Some of these resources consider the Baptist tradition in general, while others focus on history and/or theology.

Bibliographies

Brackney, William H. *A Genetic History of Baptist Thought: With Special Reference to Baptists in Britain and North America,* pp. 539-71. Macon, Ga.: Mercer University Press, 2004.

Starr, Edward C., ed. *A Baptist Bibliography.* 25 vols. Chester, Penn., and Rochester, N.Y.: American Baptist Historical Society, 1947-1976.

Reference Works

Allen, Clifton J., and Lynn E. May Jr., eds. *Encyclopedia of Southern Baptists.* 4 vols. Nashville: Broadman, 1958-1982.

Brackney, William H., ed. *Historical Dictionary of the Baptists.* Metuchen, N.J.: Scarecrow, 1999.

Leonard, Bill J., ed. *The Dictionary of Baptists in America.* Downers Grove, Ill.: InterVarsity Press, 1994.

Survey Resources

Brackney, William H. *A Genetic History of Baptist Thought: With Special Reference to Baptists in Britain and North America.* Macon, Ga.: Mercer University Press, 2004.

———. *The Baptists.* New York: Greenwood, 1988.

Leonard, Bill J. *Baptist Ways: A History.* Valley Forge, Penn.: Judson, 2003.

Primary Historical and Theological Resources

Baker, Robert A., ed. *A Baptist Sourcebook: With Particular Reference to Southern Baptists.* Nashville: Broadman, 1966.

Brackney, William H., ed. *Baptist Life and Thought: A Source Book.* Rev. ed. Valley Forge, Penn.: Judson, 1998.

George, Timothy, and Denise George, eds. *Baptist Confessions, Covenants, and Catechisms.* Nashville: Broadman & Holman, 1999.

Lumpkin, William L. *Baptist Confessions of Faith.* Rev. ed. Valley Forge, Penn.: Judson, 1969; reprint, 1989.

McBeth, H. Leon. *A Sourcebook for Baptist Heritage.* Nashville: Broadman, 1990.

Recent and Current Theological Explorations

Hendricks, William L. "Do We Need a New Confession of Faith?" *Perspectives in Religious Studies* 29, no. 4 (2002): 427-32.

Norman, R. Stanton. *More Than Just a Name: Preserving Our Baptist Identity.* Nashville: Broadman & Holman, 2001.

Review and Expositor 100, no. 4 (2003): 521-684. This issue of the journal includes a number of articles on Baptist theology and postmodernism, including Nancy L. DeClaissé-Wallford, "Postmodernity in Theology"; Steven R. Harmon, "The Authority of the Community (of All the Saints): Toward a Postmodern Baptist Hermeneutic of Tradition"; Timothy D. F. Maddox, "Scripture, Perspicuity, and Postmodernity"; and Dan R. Stiver, "Baptists: Modern or Postmodern?"

Shurden, Walter B. *The Baptist Identity: Four Fragile Freedoms.* Macon, Ga.: Smyth & Helwys, 1993.

Thompson, Philip E. "Re-envisioning Baptist Identity: Historical, Theological, and Liturgical Analysis." *Perspectives in Religious Studies* 27, no. 3 (2000): 287-302.

7 ■ Grace-Full Holiness and Holy Wholeness

WESLEYAN THEOLOGY

I saw, that "simplicity of intention, and purity of affection," one design in all we speak or do, and one desire ruling all our tempers, are indeed "the wings of the soul" without which she can never ascend to the mount of God. A year or two after, Mr. Law's Christian Perfection *and* Serious Call *were put into my hands. These convinced me, more than ever, of the absolute impossibility of being half a Christian; and I determined, through His grace, (the absolute necessity of which I was deeply sensible of) to be all-devoted to God, to give Him all my soul, my body, and my substance.*

John Wesley, *A Plain Account of Christian Perfection*[1]

Jesus, thine all victorious love shed in my heart abroad;
    Then shall my feet no longer rove, rooted and fixed in God.
Refining fire, go through my heart, illuminate my soul;
    Scatter thy life through every part, and sanctify the whole.
No longer then my heart shall mourn, while, purified by grace,
    I only for his glory burn, and always see his face.

Charles Wesley, untitled hymn text

All men need to be saved; all men can be saved; all men can know they are saved; all men can be saved to the uttermost.

Philip Watson, *The Message of the Wesleys*

Bill and I were standing on the sidewalk outside my apartment building. We had been good friends for several years. Although we came from different backgrounds, we shared the most important of commonalities—we were both followers of Jesus. He was the son of Methodist missionaries, and he had been steeped in the Wesleyan tradition since birth. On this particular afternoon we were having one of our many conversations about life and ministry and spiritual matters. The conversation moved into the subject of how Christians mature, and the way those who claim the identity "Christian" ought to live their lives. I do not remember all the details of the conversation, but I will never forget its crescendo. We were talking about the challenges of living a life that brings honor to God, and about struggling with temptation and sin. Speaking from my theology and experience, and seeking refuge for my failings, I said that certain kinds of troubling thoughts, feelings and actions were "only natural." To this my dear friend lovingly responded, "Precisely. They are only *natural*." He went on to describe his belief in and witness to the transformative, victorious life of holiness—a life to which Christ calls all his children and for which God empowers them through the work of the Holy Spirit. This new life of holiness is not natural, he said. It is, however, possible. And it is possible precisely because it is supernatural.

Context: Historical and Ecclesiastical Background

Historical origins and development. Rev. Samuel (1662-1735) and Susannah (1669-1742) Wesley nurtured their children in the Christian faith, within the context of the Church of England. Sons John (1703-1791) and Charles (1707-1788) were taught an Arminian Anglicanism, yet they were encouraged to be independent thinkers. They were encouraged by both parents to be persons of strong personal conviction and deep religious devotion.[2] Both of them were educated at Christ Church, Oxford University, and they were the central members of what came to be called the Holy Club at Oxford, from 1729 to 1735. During these years, with John the de facto leader, the members of the Holy Club met on a regular basis with the goal of deepening their own Christian faith and encouraging others to do the same. It was in this context that the term *Methodist* was first employed. The term originally was hurled at them by some who ridiculed the Holy Club's rigorous efforts, but Wesley adapted and adopted it to refer to those who live in accord with the "method" of life set forth in the Bible,[3] and because of the abiding influence of the teachings and practices of Wesley, the term *Wesleyan* came to identify those whose beliefs and practices, whatever their denominational affiliation, follow in the spirit of John Wesley.

In 1736, John Wesley traveled to Georgia, in the American colonies, under the auspices of the Society for the Propagation of the Gospel, an Anglican mission society. During his journey to America, and after his return to England, Wesley was impressed by the genuine and profound Christian piety of Moravians whom he met during passage. Less than two years after his journey to Georgia, he returned to England, profoundly discouraged over a mission regarded by many as "a disaster (to some, almost comical)," due to various blunders and failures.[4] Be that as it may, Wesley pressed on. After returning to England, he organized the first Methodist society (a voluntary association within the Church of England), at Fetter Lane in London, and he and Charles undertook itinerant ministries. On May 24 of that year, 1738, while attending a meeting on Aldersgate Street, John's heart was "strangely warmed," and he experienced "the change which God works in the heart through faith in Christ" as he pondered Luther's words in the preface to his commentary on Romans. At this point, Wesley recorded in his journal, "I felt I did trust in Christ, Christ alone for salvation; and an assurance was given me that He had taken away *my* sins, even *mine,* and saved *me* from the law of sin and death."[5] From this point onward, Wesley passionately pursued a life of holiness before God and called on others to do the same.

A variety of theological sources, mediated through family, church and travel, shaped Wesley early in life and subsequently influenced his theology. Ancient and medieval spiritual sources, such as Thomas à Kempis's *The Imitation of Christ,* linked Wesley to pre-Reformation thought. He embraced as his own the central teachings of the Protestant Reformation, such as justification by faith. From within post-Reformation Protestantism, Wesley was influenced by Puritanism, the Moravians, Pietism and Anglicanism, particularly its Arminian elements. He appreciated the Puritans' stress on moral earnestness and their insistence on single-minded purity in devotion. The Moravians sensitized Wesley to the inner workings of the Holy Spirit and the importance of fervent personal religious experience. Finally, although he had little direct knowledge of the writings of Arminius, Wesley enthusiastically embraced Arminian teachings as these were mediated through the Remonstrant movement and Arminian writers within the Church of England.[6] Perhaps the most significant component for Wesley of this Arminian perspective was its clear affirmation of the universal availability of divine grace.[7]

Luke Keefer suggests that Welsey's Arminianism "is implicit rather than explicit," and that "making Christians is his central concern; promoting Arminianism is secondary to it."[8] Given this qualification, it is true nonetheless that Wesley was a staunch proponent of Arminian views. His painful separation from his close associate George Whitefield (1714-1770) was precipitated over Arminian/ Calvinist theological differences. An affirmation of Arminian theology is set forth in, for example, an essay titled "The Question, 'What Is an Arminian?' Answered by a Lover of Free Grace,"[9] and in 1778 he established the *Arminian Magazine.* Intense exchanges with Calvinists over his Arminian views followed Wesley throughout his ministry.[10] Over the course of time, the magazine came to present a wide range of Wesleyan theological themes, but the original and guiding purpose was primarily to defend Arminian teaching on the Christian life. In one instance, Wesley summarizes Arminian teaching as "conditional predestination": God issued a conditional decree that those who believe will be saved; God offers this salvation through a grace that can be resisted by human free will; and those who receive this saving grace can "make shipwreck" of it, perishing forever.[11] The centrality of this type of Arminianism in Wesley and subsequent Wesleyan theology is such that it is not uncommon to refer to this theological stream as the Wesleyan-Arminian tradition.

In its earliest years, the Wesleyan movement was "spontaneous and diverse, full of energy and aspiration," fully within the Church of England, and "almost bereft of organization."[12] By the end of the eighteenth century, however, the Wesleyan movement in England was quite clearly defined, both organizationally and theologically. The year 1744 is generally regarded as the point at which the organizing conference for Methodism took place. In the years that followed, various Methodist societies developed into an interconnected network. In addition to these organizational developments, theological controversies precipitated further clarification and solidification of the theology of Wesley and his followers. Although he was indebted to the Moravians for sensitizing him to a religion of genuine, heartfelt faith, Wesley encountered irreconcilable differences with the Moravians. He believed, contrary to the Moravians, that there *are* "degrees of faith" commensurate with various degrees of Christian maturity and commitment, and that the sacraments *are* means by which we receive God's grace.[13] Even more significant was Wesley's dispute with Calvinists. Theological differences between Wesley and Whitefield came to a head in 1740-1741. Contrary to Calvinist teaching, Wesley denied predestination and, in Arminian fashion, affirmed that God's grace in the atonement of Christ is offered universally to all human beings. As Wesley writes in "Free Grace," "Thou drawest all men unto Thee, Grace doth to every soul appear; Preventing grace for all is free, And brings to all salvation near."[14] This controversy resulted in a separation between Whitefield and Wesley, and, within Methodism, between Calvinist Methodists and Wesleyan Methodists.[15]

During the middle of the eighteenth century, Methodist preaching and teaching on holiness or "purity of heart" intensified and flourished, and another theological controversy again served to deepen and solidify this theology.[16] During 1770-1771, Wesley engaged in an impassioned dispute with antinomians, who denied any relevance of Old Covenant law to the life of Christians. The dispute was over moral responsibility—or, in Wesley's understanding of antinomian views, irresponsibility. In contrast to the antinomians, Wesley stressed human responsibility, particularly the responsibility of the Christian to live a life characterized by works of love and faith issuing in holy action.[17] Furthermore, in the context of this controversy there emerged a person generally regarded as the first theologian of the Wesleyan movement, John Fletcher (1729-1785). His seven-volume *Checks to Antinomianism* further confirmed the theological differences between Wesleyan and Calvinist thought, and it reiterated and further developed Wesley's teaching on prevenient grace and on holiness.[18] One of Fletcher's emphases that proved influential on many later streams of Wesleyan thought was his use of the language of Pentecost to talk about Christian perfection or "perfect love."[19]

Although, as noted earlier, Wesley and Whitefield conducted missions to the American colonies in the 1730s, the beginning of Methodism as an identifiable movement in America is generally dated from the 1760s. The two earliest Methodist groups probably were those organized in Maryland, under the leadership of Robert Strawbridge (d. 1781), and in New York, under Thomas Webb (1724-1796) in 1766.[20] By 1769, there were approximately six hundred societies, concentrated in Maryland and Virginia. At this time, Wesley sent Richard Boardman (1738-1782) and Joseph Pilmore (1739-1825), as the first missionary preachers, to give guidance to the societies.[21] Yet, it was a missionary who arrived in 1771, Francis Asbury (1745-1816), who proved to be "the veritable father of American Methodism"[22] and "exercised the primary role of theological tutor for early American Methodism."[23] Thomas Coke (1747-1814), a close colleague of Wesley and the first bishop of the American Methodist Episcopal Church, also played a role in "confirming the general theological orientation in terms of the Wesleyan emphases."[24] Under Asbury's strong-willed leadership, Annual Conferences began in 1773, and the fundamental doctrinal teachings of British Wesleyanism were communicated to the American movement, as were the standards of Wesleyan teaching: Wesley's *Standard Sermons* (commonly referred to as *Sermons*) and *Explanatory Notes on the New Testament* (commonly referred to as *Notes*).[25]

Wesley opposed the colonies' revolutionary war. As a result, people associated with Wesley met with considerable suspicion and opposition in the colonies. Asbury was the only missionary who remained in America during the war, but for several years during this period he drastically reduced his involvement, relinquishing to American preachers much of the oversight of the movement. For much of the eighteenth century, the Methodist movement in America was essentially a missionary enterprise led largely by laypeople.[26] By 1784 the movement was sufficiently large and mature to formally organize as a denomination, the Methodist Episcopal Church. Early in the nineteenth century, African Americans began to assume roles of prominence within American Methodism. In response to segregationist and other demeaning practices, in 1787, Richard Allen (1760-1831) and another former slave, Absolom Jones, led a group of African Americans out of St. George's Methodist Church, Philadelphia, to form a separate congregation. Allen was ordained as a bishop in 1799, and under his leadership the African Methodist Episcopal Church gained official recognition as a distinct denomination in 1816. As Gayraud Wilmore observes, Allen embraced the "evangelical theology and policy" of Wesley's Methodism, combined with a particularly strong desire for "a church that would combine secular relevance with deep spirituality in a context of simplicity and spontaneity."[27] At its founding, the African Methodist Episcopal Church, numerically strong in Maryland and Virginia, had a membership of just under fifteen thousand, with eighty-three itinerant preachers and many lay preachers.[28] A similar series of events led to the formation of the African Methodist Episcopal Zion Church in 1821, under the leadership of founding bishop James Varick (c. 1750-1827).

In addition to some correspondence from Wesley, the Conference received his revised book of Sunday services and accepted as a doctrinal standard his twenty-four Articles of Religion, adding a twenty-fifth article affirming the independence of the country of the United States.[29] Thus, there was substantial and abiding theological continuity between British and American Wesleyanism. In addition to the official adoption, with little change, of doctrinal standards from British Methodism, the writings, for example, of second generation British Wesleyan theologians, such as Richard Watson's (1781-1833) *Theological Institutes* (1823) and Adam Clarke's (d. 1832) eight-volume Bible commentary (1810-1826), came to be widely used in the United States. Yet at the same time there were theological "modifications" that developed in America, giving to the classical Wesleyan emphases "an identifiable American cast."[30] Early North American Methodism emphasized the Holy Spirit's direct call upon individual persons to experience the graceful forgiveness of Christ and to live their lives in accord with his teachings. "There was an unusual convergence," notes Dennis Campbell, "between the evangelical theology of early American Methodism and the robust confidence of the people who populated the early republic. Methodism proclaimed a Christian gospel of grace and freedom that made sense in the untried, open, and optimistic society of the young nation."[31] The emphasis on Wesleyan theology as "a theology of salvation" and a theology of "equality, responsibility, and practical results" became even more pronounced in the congenial context of revivalism, frontier religion and "the free American spirit."[32] Robert Chiles observes that after 1810, the American leaders who began to replace the British "became increasingly dissatisfied with the oversimplifications of revivalism and the frontier. Reluctant merely to quote the primary Wesleyan authorities, these men display more independent theological judgment."[33] For much of the nineteenth century, Wesleyan thought in the United States was also shaped by a more-or-less ongoing encounter with Calvinism. Although the two sides never arrived at complete agreement, there were "modifications in their original positions bringing them closer and closer together" in their understandings of human being and of the role of human beings in the process of salvation.[34]

By the mid-1800s, Methodism was the fastest-growing church in America, having grown from eighteen thousand members in 1794 to 580,000 members in 1840.[35] Class meetings were one of the pillars of Methodism in the first half of the nineteenth century. Lay leaders met weekly with a group of no more than twelve people for fellowship, instruction, prayer and discipline. These groups were intended to supplement the ministry of a preacher who traveled most of the time. As itinerant ministers settled into localized pastorates, the groups declined. By the middle of the nineteenth century, camp meetings and revivalism contributed to the growth of ecclesiastical Methodism and Wesleyan-Holiness movements, as well as to the growth of other traditions.[36] Mid-century controversies over slavery challenged Methodism, as it did other denominations. For example, the Wesleyan Methodist Church, the first Holiness denomination in the United States, was formed in 1843 by abolitionist clergy and laity, and in 1846, the Methodist Episcopal Church—South was formed in the wake of a schism between north and south in the Methodist Episcopal Church two years earlier.

As for theology, one of the characteristics of the Wesleyan tradition that set it apart from other American theological traditions was its "unique emphasis on the universal prevenience of redemptive grace as constitutive of man's present moral responsibility."[37] Wilbur Fisk (1792-1839) and Asa Shinn (1781-1853) were among the American theologians who articulated a Wesleyan theology, including its disagreements with both Calvinism and universalism, in the early part of the nineteenth century. Furthermore, from approximately 1840 to 1890, both a "moralistic revision" and a "systematic integration" took place in Wesleyan thought.[38] The former occurred, in part, under the influence of Scottish commonsense philosophy, or "intuitional realism," which stressed personal free agency and "the ultimacy of moral and religious intuitions."[39] The systematic integration in America was led by theologian John Miley (1813-1895) and drew upon the writings of British theologian Richard Watson (1781-1833). The first American edition of Watson's *Theological Institutes* was published in 1829, and it proved to be "the standard authority" for Wesleyan theology beyond the middle of the nineteenth century.[40] His work later was superseded by that of Miley, professor of theology at Drew University, who published a two-volume systematic theology (1892-1894).

Miley's work may be seen as "the denouement" of nineteenth-century developments in Wesleyan theology, being consciously related to Arminian thought and employing free personal agency as the structuring principle.[41] In addition to Watson and his *Institutes,* another British theologian, William Burt Pope (1822-1903), was influential on American Wesleyan theology through his *Compendium of Christian Theology* (1880). Both Watson and Pope clearly affirmed the central emphases of Wesleyan Methodism, but their approach to the theological task constituted something of a departure. Explicit references to the Wesleys in their work are relatively few, and, with a view toward commending Wesleyan theology to a broader audience, these two theologians employed a more systematic and analytical, rather than experiential, approach.[42]

There was resistance, particularly within Holiness circles, to some of these theological developments, which were perceived as departures from traditional Wesleyan theology.[43] Concern arose over neglected doctrines, most notably Christian perfection, and over the increasing influence of "modernist" forms of thought.[44] Yet, as we will see, "although its primary legacy remains within the various Methodist denominations . . . the Wesleyan tradition has been redefined and reinterpreted as a catalyst for other movements and denominations," including Holiness and Pentecostal denominations.[45] A combination of these theological concerns, along with concerns over Christian practice and lifestyle, led to the formation of the National Camp meeting Association for the Promotion of Christian Holiness (NCAPCH) in 1867. The NCAPCH was begun by Methodist preacher-evangelists, and during its first several decades of existence, its primary work was to organize revival meetings. Over time, it developed into an association of Holiness churches.[46] These controversies over the importance and nature of holiness led to "a hardening of both language and temper" in Holiness preaching and teaching that eventually "muted," within Holiness movements, "the traditional Wesleyan emphasis on the growth of holiness that every Christian should enjoy."[47] They also contributed, along with slavery and other issues of Christian practice, to the establishment of new denominations, such as the Free Methodist Church of North America (1860).

As Barbara MacHaffie observes, women were particularly active within the Holiness stream of the Wesleyan tradition.[48] In *Holy Boldness: Women Preacher's Autobiographies and the Sanctified Self,* Susie Stanley documents the ways in which the experience of sanctification "changed Wesleyan/Holiness women's self-understanding, empowering them to challenge the claim that woman's sphere was in the private realm of domesticity, and motivated them to serve in the public sphere by preaching."[49] Of particular note is Phoebe Palmer (1807-1874), who "played a principle role in popularizing and promoting" Wesley's doctrine of sanctification in the United States. "Her theology of holiness," notes Stanley, "permeated sermons by holiness preachers and her language found its way into other women's autobiographies."[50] While holding to the essence of Wesley's view, in her *Entire Devotion to God* and other writings Palmer also modified it by eliminating the period of spiritual growth between conversion and sanctification, and by adding the act of complete consecration by "laying one's all on the altar of Christ" prior to sanctification.[51]

As the nineteenth century drew to a close, the theology of Methodism beyond the Holiness movements experienced "a major theological shift" as liberalism "caught up with the Methodists."[52] As references to John Wesley declined in the theological literature, appreciation for contemporary cultural sources—including evolutionary science, critical study of the Bible and various contemporary philosophies—increased.[53] Dennis Campbell observes that toward the end of the nineteenth century, professors at Methodist institutions, by and large, were influenced more by German research universities than by their Wesleyan or Anglican heritage. The work of a group of scholars who came to be known as the Boston Personalists constituted a noteworthy attempt to craft a distinctive tradition from within Methodism. Borden Parker Bowne (1847-1910), Albert C. Knudson (1873-1953) and Edgar Sheffield Brightman (1884-1953) led in the pursuit of an intellectual tradition that placed an emphasis on experience and on the personal, with respect to both human beings and God.[54] Methodist theology in the liberal spirit continued through at least the first third of the twentieth century. Its theological leaders included Harris F. Rall (1870-1964), Edwin Lewis (1881-1959) and Knudson. Georgia Harkness (1891-1979), one of Brightman's students, was a pioneering theologian, teacher and ecumenist. This liberal theology was resisted by Holiness Methodists, continuing their opposition to what they perceived to be a departure from genuinely Wesleyan theology. One observer suggests that in its "general character and spirit," liberal Methodist theology "had much more in common with the theology current in other denominations than it did with its own heritage."[55] Ironically, much the same could be said for Holiness-minded Methodists, as smaller, non-Methodist groups continued to emerge in the early and mid-twentieth century. Methodists who continued to stress the doctrine of Christian perfection and other Holiness teachings had much in common with, for example, the Church of the Nazarene, established in 1908. Leading Nazarene theologians included Aaron M. Hills (1848-1935) and H. Orton Wiley (1877-1961). Hills published the first Nazarene systematic theology, the two-volume *Fundamental Christian Theology,* in 1931, and Wiley's three-volume *Christian Theology* (1940-1943) was for decades a standard conservative Wesleyan systematic theology.

The mid-to-late twentieth century was characterized by a continuation or extension of many of the trends of the early part of the century. In fact, over the course of the twentieth century, a debate that had been with American Methodism "from the first" became increasingly evident: "a continuing debate between those who find [Methodism's] theological reason for being in the Wesleyan heritage and those who locate it in the theological expression of [Methodism's] current religious life."[56] Surveying the theological trends within Methodism through the nineteenth and twentieth centuries, Kenneth Cracknell and Susan White observe a "diminishing emphasis on evangelical Arminianism" extending to the "abandonment of John Wesley's theological ideas."[57] In non-Holiness Methodist circles there was a continued quest to be connected with historic Methodism while at the same time addressing contemporary themes and incorporating contemporary thought-forms. Mainline Methodist theologians wed Methodism with theological schools of thought such as neoorthodoxy, liberation theology, black theology, feminist theology, process theology and narrative theology, while at the same time seeking to address major societal issues such as race relations, poverty, and war and peace. At the same time, mainline Methodism was marked by "the rise of self-conscious caucuses designed to promote the interests of minority groups within the church," including African Americans, Hispanics, Asians and women.[58] Mergers of denominations over several decades culminated in the formation of the United Methodist Church (UMC) in 1968, uniting the Methodist Church (1939) and the Evangelical United Brethren (1946).

Many of the theologies that emerged during the latter part of the twentieth century were the product of appeals to what often is called the "Wesleyan quadrilateral." As chairperson of the Commission on Doctrine and Doctrinal Standards for the then-recently formed United Methodist Church (1968), Albert Outler (1908-1989) led in the formulation of a fourfold conceptualization of the sources and norms for theology: Scripture, tradition, reason and experience. In the decades that followed, many theologians who were seeking to create theologies that would more adequately reflect and address their distinctive sociocultural contexts appealed to experience or reason, rather than Scripture or tradition, as the starting point for doing theology, thereby being liberated from the commitments associated with the historic sources and norms.[59] By contrast, Holiness groups continued to take their theological start from Scripture and to emphasize a second, dramatic work of sanctifying grace subsequent to conversion and/or an emphasis upon Christian perfection. These differences with respect to both theological method and the conclusions issuing therefrom led to the formation of the Evangelical Church of North America in 1968, consisting of Evangelical United Brethren congregations that did not participate in the merger that formed the United Methodist Church. In the arena of scholarly theological work, Wesleyans gained a new voice with the founding of the Wesley Theological Society in 1965.

Dennis Campbell suggests, "Methodists tend to be 'structural fundamentalists' in regard to polity and open to a wide range of diversity ('live and let live') in regard to theology."[60] This tendency has led to a situation in which there is, according William Abraham, a "crisis which confronts Methodism as a theological tradition." Abraham remarks, "What is conspicuous about modern Methodist theology, in America at least, is its pluralism. It has been quite honestly confessed that any consensus there may have been in the past has broken down. Diversity, disagreement, and division are central facts of our theological life."[61] Indeed, the theological and ecclesiastical heritage stemming from the thought and work of the Wesleys is both rich and varied.

Diversity. The largest ecclesiastical body in the United States related to the Wesleyan tradition is the United Methodist Church (1968). Recalling the description of Robert Chiles, previously cited, it can be said that the predominant theology of the UMC is shaped by "the theological expression of its current religious life," though there are many individuals within the UMC who pursue a theology that is still self-consciously rooted "in the Wesleyan heritage."[62] The second largest Methodist denomination is the African Methodist Episcopal Church (1816). Other major African American denominations include the African Methodist Episcopal Zion Church (1821; present name officially adopted in 1848) and the Christian Methodist Episcopal Church (1870; present name officially adopted in 1954). The official doctrinal bases of these African American denominations include the Articles of Religion, and the theological character is similar to that of the United Methodist Church, although shaped by African American concerns and perspectives. All of these denominations are members of the World Council of Churches.

Another Methodist denomination of particular importance with reference to classical Wesleyan theology is the Free Methodist Church of North America (1860). In 1989, the Free Methodist Church of Canada became autonomous, becoming one of five general conferences in worldwide Methodism. From its beginnings, the Free Methodist Church (FMC) has emphasized both the teaching and practice of Christian holiness, including entire sanctification, and has sought to hold closely to the teachings of Wesley. The FMC is a member of the Christian Holiness Association.[63] By virtue of both its early historical origins and its size, Methodist expressions of the Wesleyan tradition are prominent in the remainder of this chapter.

The Wesleyan Church (1843), originally established as the Wesleyan Methodist Church of America, merged with the Pilgrim Holiness Church and adopted its present name in 1968. A member of the Christian Holiness Association, the Wesleyan Church emphasizes the doctrine of entire sanctification as a second experience following conversion. The Church of the Nazarene is considerably larger, but is another non-Methodist church and of a theological character similar to that of the Wesleyan Church. Established as the Pentecostal Church of the Nazarene in 1907, the Church of the Nazarene dropped "Pentecostal" from its name in 1919. The Church of the Nazarene is also a member of the Christian Holiness Association. The Salvation Army (late 1860s) is also counted among the members of the Christian Holiness Association that have Wesleyan roots.

Approach: Theological and Hermeneutical Method

Role of theology. As one inside observer puts it, "The Wesleyan tradition has not been accustomed to rigorous historical or theological debate and may have suffered from the lack of it."[64] Until recently, it was quite common among theologians who identify themselves as Wesleyan or Methodist to describe the Wesleyan heritage as one that is "nontheological," being "practical and evangelical instead."[65] Dennis Campbell makes the historical observation that, by and large, early Methodists "were not highly educated persons," and the leaders of the movement "were not sophisticated theologians."[66] Wesley himself has most often been viewed as a preacher-evangelist, not a theologian. As recently as 1996, the United Methodist *Book of Discipline* made the point that "while highly theoretical constructions of Christian thought make important contributions to theological understanding, we finally measure the truth of such statements in relation to their practical significance. Our interest is to incorporate the promises and demands of the gospel into our daily lives." The Wesleyan heritage is characterized by concern for "practical divinity."[67] At the same time, the mid- and late-twentieth century saw a marked increase in advanced exploration of distinctively Wesleyan theology, both historical and contemporary. Beginning around the time of the publication of George C. Cell's *The Rediscovery of Wesley* in 1935, Wesleyans began to look at their theological heritage—including John Wesley's vocation as theologian—more closely and to explore their theology more systematically. Wesley came to be acknowledged as, at the least, a "folk theologian,"[68] and more recently Wesleyan scholars such as Randy Maddox, Thomas Oden and Kenneth Collins have constructed more systematic analyses and presentations of Wesley's thought and of theological reflection in the spirit of the Wesleyan tradition.[69]

THE WESLEYAN TRADITION

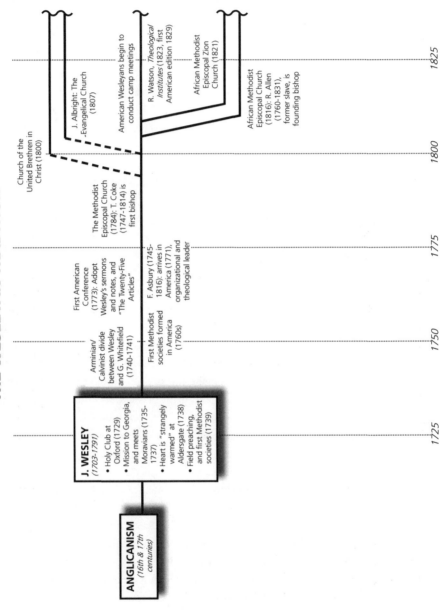

ANGLICANISM
(16th & 17th centuries)

J. WESLEY
(1703-1791)
- Holy Club at Oxford (1729)
- Mission to Georgia, and meets Moravians (1735-1737)
- Heart is "strangely warmed" at Aldersgate (1738)
- Field preaching, and first Methodist societies (1739)

Arminian/ Calvinist divide between Wesley and G. Whitefield (1740-1741)

First American Conference (1773): Adopt Wesley's sermons and notes, and "The Twenty-Five Articles"

First Methodist societies formed in America (1760s)

The Methodist Episcopal Church (1784): T. Coke (1747-1814) is first bishop

F. Asbury (1745-1816): arrives in America (1771), organizational and theological leader

Church of the United Brethren in Christ (1800)

J. Albright: The Evangelical Church (1807)

American Wesleyans begin to conduct camp meetings

R. Watson, *Theological Institutes* (1823, first American edition 1829)

African Methodist Episcopal Zion Church (1821)

African Methodist Episcopal Church (1816): R. Allen (1760-1831), former slave, is founding bishop

1725   1750   1775   1800   1825

THE WESLEYAN TRADITION (CONTINUED)

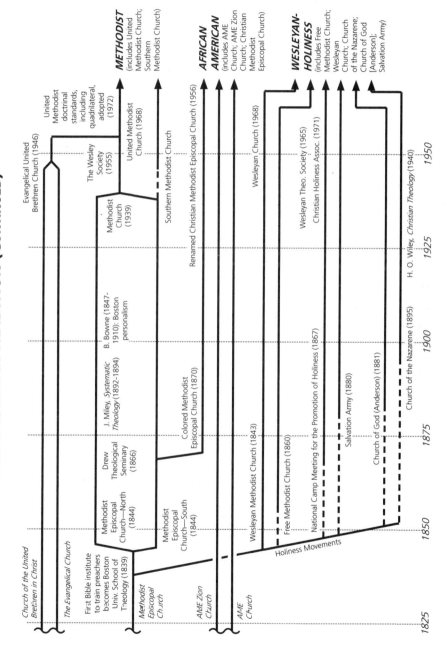

The Wesleyan tradition has been widely understood, both within and without, as primarily concerned with preaching the message of salvation and teaching the principles of holy Christian living. Theology is viewed as a secondary, if not tertiary, enterprise, motivated and directed by the practical concerns associated with Christian ministry. This fundamentally pragmatic orientation sometimes has led observers to suggest that Wesley and Wesleyans do not consider theology to be important. Increasingly, Wesleyan theologians are making the case that a serious interest in "good theology" is not necessarily synonymous with "academic" and "systematic," as these adjectives have commonly been used. From its beginnings, the Wesleyan tradition has been theologically concerned, while at the same time being equally, if not more, ministerially minded.[70]

Theological method. Allan Coppedge comments, "Not only is Wesley's work the standard for the content by which all subsequent Wesleyan theology must be judged, but it is also the standard with regard to the method by which theology is done."[71] Although not all Wesleyan theologians follow Wesley in the way Coppedge proposes, they do look to Wesley's way of doing theology for tutelage with respect to theological method. Within the North American Wesleyan tradition, one of the most significant methodological distinctives is appeal to the quadrilateral: Scripture, tradition, reason, experience. In fact, in theological circles the term *quadrilateral* is virtually synonymous with *Wesleyan.*[72]

The 1996 United Methodist *Book of Discipline* says that the preaching and teaching of the forebears of modern Methodism were "grounded in Scripture, informed by Christian tradition, enlivened by experience, and tested by reason."[73] Although Wesley himself never made explicit reference to a quadrilateral, many Wesleyan theologians agree that his sermons, for example, reveal that "Wesley characteristically appealed to Scripture, tradition, reason, and experience when he wanted to support or defend his theology."[74] In this, Wesley built upon his Anglican heritage by adding the appeal to experience to Anglicanism's appeal to Scripture, tradition and reason. Most Wesleyan theologians concur with regard to the identification of these four sources, but considerable differences arise among theological scholars and church leaders as to the relative authority of each of the sources and the relationship among them.[75] Some theologians weigh the four sources as being of equal authority, at least in principle.[76] For these theologians, any one or more of the sources may have a functional priority, even if only implicitly. Other theologians regard Scripture as being superior in authority to the other three. This latter position is most often associated with what is here regarded as classical Wesleyan theology.

Wesley refers to himself as *"homo unius libri,"* or "a man of one book."[77] That one book is the Bible. And for classical Wesleyans, Scripture is, as it was for Wesley, "the primary canon" for theology.[78] Bruce Birch notes, "Beginning with Wesley himself and extending to the Methodist societies established in this country over two hundred years ago, the Bible has been understood as the foundation for all Christian theology."[79] In classical Wesleyan theology Scripture is "the normative source by which all other sources of theology must be evaluated and tested."[80] The quadrilateral consists not of four "coordinate" sources, but of one primary source (Scripture) and three secondary or "subordinate" sources (tradition, reason, experience).[81] The United Methodist *Book of Discipline* instructs, "In theological reflection, the resources of tradition, experience, and reason are integral to our study of Scripture without displacing Scripture's primacy for faith and practice."[82] Accordingly, in *Methodist Doctrine,* Ted Campbell says, "The Bible is the *primary* source and authority for our faith, that is, no other authority can override the authority of God revealed in the Scriptures."[83] For all fundamental Christian teaching, Scripture is "the final standard."[84] As Wesley did before them, Wesleyan theologians use the three secondary sources as tools for the correct interpretation of Scripture.[85] In addition, the secondary sources may complement Scripture when it "does not give specific guidance but only general principles." On those issues that Scripture "does not make clear or address in detail," tradition, reason and experience are to be called upon as the sources for theological reflection.[86] In classical Wesleyan theology, theological statements based solely on the secondary sources are not to be considered requisite as fundamental to Christian faith. As George Lyons indicates, "Wesley and Wesleyans properly insist that whatever is not found in scripture is not to be made an article of faith."[87]

Wesley received from Anglicanism an appreciation for the value of church tradition. He had "a special appreciation for the tradition of the early church, the Ecumenical Councils, and the Anglican church."[88] The latter included the Thirty-Nine Articles, the *Book of Common Prayer* and the *Homilies.* All of these resources were valued because they disclosed the church's understanding of Scripture and the church's application of reason to the formulation of doctrine.[89] Wesley's interpretation of the Bible and formulation of theology were profoundly shaped by these resources, and they came to shape indirectly the Methodist tradition as it embraced a set of "standards" composed by Wesley. These standards are Wesley's *Sermons on Several Occasions,* his *Explanatory Notes on the New Testament* and his Articles of Religion. As Anglicans had done in their book of *Homilies,* Wesleyans adopted selected sermons by Wesley on a variety of topics—from justification by faith and Christian perfection, to the witness of the Holy Spirit and the education of children—that were to provide a "a model doctrinal standard for preaching."[90] Wesley's *Notes* provided a model for the translation and interpretation of Scripture, particularly the New Testament. The Articles were Wesley's adaptation of the Church of England's Thirty-Nine Articles of Religion.[91] Wesley's Articles have been influential on Wesleyan theology, both within and outside of Methodism.[92]

Reason, too, has a role to play in doing theology. "From the beginning," notes William Abraham, "Methodists were intentionally committed to Christian conference and reasoned argument."[93] Both Wesley and his heirs are "fully committed to the use of reason in religion." Reason is "invaluable in interpreting the essential truths of scripture and in understanding and discharging the duties of common life."[94] At the same time, classical Wesleyans recognize the not insignificant limitations of reason. Due to both human fallibility and, more important, sin and its effects, reason "cannot function as an independent source of revelation," and it cannot construct a theology. Nor can it produce Christian virtue.[95] Nonetheless, properly embraced as "a gift of prevenient grace," reason can "receive and grasp with some degree of comprehension that which is offered to faith."[96] Accordingly, in Wesleyan theology reason can help to structure and systematize, to guide the interpretation of Scripture, and to provide "the conceptual vehicles with which theological ideas are expressed."[97]

As we noted earlier, in addition to these three sources—Scripture, tradition, reason—acknowledged in Anglican theology, Wesley added a fourth: experience. "Christian experience played a most important rôle in [Wesley's] theology," oberves Harold Lindström. "Scripture was the obvious foundation to which he always referred, but it was interpreted in the light of experience."[98] The United Methodist *Book of Discipline* states, "In our theological task, we follow Wesley's practice of examining experience, both individual and corporate, for confirmations of the realities of God's grace attested in Scripture."[99] The role of experience should not be exaggerated, as has sometimes been the case with both critics and proponents of Wesleyan theology. For example, some within nineteenth-century Wesleyan revivalism "tended to forget . . . important distinctions" between the subjective experience of God and his salvation and the transcendent reality of that salvation.[100] Nonetheless, the distinctiveness of Wesley's method and that of his heirs resides more in their particular appeal to this source, more than the other three sources.[101] Experience is not to be understood as "emotion" or "feeling," but rather as a "medium for receiving reality, for participating in the real world."[102] For Wesley, this medium provides an essential, not merely useful, source for theology. It helps to clarify and, perhaps more important, to confirm the meaning of Scripture. According to Luke Keefer, for Wesley, "the truth of a doctrinal position was to be tested, at least in part, by its correspondence with Christian experience." Thus, when Wesley criticized the impact of Calvinist preaching, "he was doing more than questioning its pragmatic influence; he was challenging the very truthfulness of the doctrines involved."[103] Moreover, experience may complement or supplement the teaching of Scripture. Dunning approvingly comments, "Wesley derived his understanding of the substance (content) of his distinctive doctrine of Christian perfection from the scripture, but his understanding of the structure (circumstance) of the experience he derived from experience itself, since he did not find a clear-cut structural pattern in the Bible."[104] Thus, the three-legged stool of Anglicanism became the four-dimensional quadrilateral of Wesleyan theology. Appeal to experience is a defining characteristic of Wesleyan theological method.

In the Wesleyan quadrilateral, Scripture is the supreme standard for theology, while tradition, reason and experience serve theology primarily by informing the interpretation of Scripture. Yet, there are other principles and commitments that shape the classical Wesleyan reading of the Bible.[105] Apart from his understanding of the role of experience, Wesley's basic hermeneutical principles were similar to those of other Protestants of his time.[106] He sought the literal sense of the biblical text, and he used unambiguous passages to interpret those whose meaning is less clear. In a letter to Samuel Furly, Wesley writes, "The general rule of interpreting scripture is this: The literal sense of every text is to be taken, if it be not contrary to some other texts; but in that case the obscure text is to be interpreted by those which speak more plainly."[107] This "literal sense" does not exclude Scripture's "figurative or analogical use of language"; rather, it refers to "the plain sense of the text."[108] At the same time, the meaning of some texts is more "plain" than others, and those that are less clear need to be interpreted in the light of those that are more clear. Thus, Scripture is used to interpret Scripture.

In the Wesleyan tradition, using Scripture to interpret Scripture entails looking to the whole of Scripture and to Scripture as a whole for interpretive keys.[109] Dunning posits that in order to properly interpret individual passages, one must have some grasp of the "coherent unity" of the teaching of Scripture.[110] The hermeneutical key to this unity most commonly identified by Wesleyans is holiness.[111] As Timothy Smith points out, Wesley "came very early to believe that the only proper way to approach the scriptures, and the only means of grasping their unity, was through the hermeneutic of holiness that he derived from studying them."[112] Similarly, many Wesleyans read the Bible from the Genesis account of the Fall onward as "the story of God's plan and purpose to restore lost man to the divine plan for him." "Running through the Scriptures from beginning to end," observes Wilber Dayton, "is the theme that God desires the perfection of man."[113]

Theology: Characteristic Beliefs

"The Wesleyan tradition in America is far more than a theological expression," observes R. G. Tuttle, and "much of the clarity which marked the earlier movement has been lost."[114] Nonetheless, Wesleyans do have a long history of affirming what are sometimes referred to as "our doctrines," and the Wesleyan theological tradition is characterized by identifiable emphases, some would say norms.[115] Coppedge suggests three overarching themes for Wesleyan theology: God as Father, Christian holiness and God's grace.[116] Dunning proposes a threefold norm consisting of justification and sanctification by faith, prevenient grace and Christology.[117] Mildred Wynkoop sees love as the guiding theme and "dynamic" of Wesleyan theology.[118] These and other characteristic emphases center on a theology of salvation. From a classical Wesleyan perspective, "every doctrine should finally be evaluated in terms of its saving significance."[119] In *The Message of the Wesleys,* Philip Watson articulates an apt summary of Wesleyan theology in soteriological terms: "All men need to be saved; all men can be saved; all men can know they are saved; all men can be saved to the uttermost."[120] The discussion that follows here will consider the second and fourth components of this summary: "all men can be saved" and "all men can be saved to the uttermost."

Grace: Prevenient grace. Collins remarks, "The key theme in Wesley's theology, which not only ties his various doctrines together, but which also lies behind them as their source and context, is the grace of God. . . . The grace of God is over all," and Coppedge states, "Wesley's whole understanding of the order of salvation is dominated by this concept, beginning with prevenient grace and going all the way through to glorification."[121] Wesleyan theologians, from John Miley to John Cobb, assert that "at every point grace is primary," and that the affirmation of "a gracious help for all men" is "cardinal" in a Wesleyan system of theology.[122] The doctrine of grace is central to Wesleyan theology, and the doctrine of prevenient grace is integral to a theology of grace that is classically Wesleyan.[123]

Sin and grace. Wesleyan theology views human beings as sinners in need of God's grace. William Pope describes grace as "the love of the Triune God as it is displayed towards sinful man, helpless in his sin . . . mercy towards the guilty and help for the impotent soul."[124] Larry Shelton writes, "Grace is essentially God's love in action on behalf of sinful humanity. It is the favor of God bestowed freely and selflessly to work redemptively for all sinners. . . . It is unmerited love that is unrestricted in its universality."[125] This understanding of grace corresponds to a Wesleyan theology of human sinfulness.

According to Article 7 of the Twenty-Five Articles of Religion, original sin is "the corruption of the nature of every man . . . whereby man is very far gone from original righteousness, and of his own nature inclined to evil, and that continually."[126] This sinfulness entails both "the absence or perversion of the relationship in which man stood in the 'state of integrity'" and corruption "in every aspect of his being. . . . He is 'totally depraved.'"[127] The classical Wesleyan theology of human sinfulness is neither Pelagian nor Semi-Pelagian, both of which deny the necessity of divine grace for initiating the process of salvation. Rather, Wesleyan theology is Arminian with respect to its view of the universality of human sinfulness and the corresponding universal availability of enabling grace.[128] Jacob Arminius (1560-1609) was a Dutch Reformed theologian who rejected as deterministic the Calvinist theology of predestination and instead affirmed an increased role for the exercise of human will in the process of salvation. Miley asserts that "man is utterly evil; that all the tendencies and impulses of his nature are toward the evil; that he is powerless for any good, without a disposition to the good, and under a moral necessity of sinning." He goes on to suggest that the Arminian view of total depravity, properly understood, "differs little" from the Augustinian view.[129] Similarly, Taylor states, "Wesleyanism's doctrine of sin is Augustinian in respect to humanity's extensive, though not intensive, total depravity and moral inability. Apart from grace persons are unable, even disinclined, to turn to God."[130] The Arminian character of the Wesleyan view of the human situation consists in a distinctive understanding of human freedom—a freedom possessed by virtue of grace. "Wesleyanism is Arminianism," writes Wynkoop, "infused with the warmth and power of the Holy Spirit."[131]

Prevenient grace. Wesleyan theology is marked by what Ted Campbell calls "an optimism of divine grace." In fact, "what Methodists love to say about human nature and salvation," Campbell observes, is that God's grace is universally available, that is, available to every human being."[132] Pope comments, "The prevenient grace of the Spirit is exercised on the natural man: that is, on man as the Fall has left him. As the object of that grace man is a personality free and responsible."[133] Miley writes, "Man is fallen and corrupt in his nature, and therein morally helpless; but man is also redeemed and the recipient of a helping grace in Christ whereby he is invested with capabilities for a moral probation." He goes on to say, "The necessary grace for the present probation is an immediate benefit of the atonement, and the possession or the privilege of every man. This is the Arminian position."[134] Prevenient grace is "a universal benefit of the Atonement, removing the racial guilt related to Adam's sin, making all men salvable, assuring the salvation of infants and irresponsibles, and restoring a sufficient degree of moral ability to permit moral action in real freedom, either to respond to the convicting of the Spirit or to resist."[135] In sum, this grace is prevenient, helping and universal.

Wesley used the term *preventing* to describe this grace, and this terminology is employed in the Twenty-Five Articles.[136] However, the term *prevenient* has long been preferred among Wesleyan theologians. The word *prevenient* means "anticipatory" or "antecedent." Thus, "prevenient grace" means "the grace that comes before," referring to "God's activity prior to any human movement toward God."[137] Pope writes, "The propriety of the term Prevenient Grace, and the doctrine which it signifies, rests upon the general truth that salvation is altogether of the Divine lovingkindness."[138] In divine love, God aids human beings in their powerlessness. Pope observes that the "powerlessness of man" is "assumed in Scripture . . . the presupposition of the whole Bible"[139] Prevenient grace is not explicitly, "positively" articulated in Scripture, but it is implied, or stated "negatively," in many passages.[140] For example, Ephesians 2:1 describes human beings as "dead through . . . trespasses and sins," and John 15:5 indicates that, just as branches must be connected to the life-giving vine in order to bear fruit, "apart from [Christ] you can do nothing."[141] Human beings are in need of salvific help, and that help comes to us from God when we are utterly powerless to help ourselves.

Prevenient grace is, as noted above, a helping grace. It is part of the larger, divinely prompted work that Randy Maddox calls "responsible grace." Ultimately, God's grace enables, while not overriding, human responsibility.[142] Although the notion of irresistible grace is often cited as a point of contrast between the Calvinist and Wesleyan traditions (with Calvinists affirming it, and Wesleyans denying it), Wesleyan scholar Kenneth Collins points out that "since Wesley's doctrine of original sin underscores the notion of total depravity, it logically follows that 'irresistible grace' has to operate at least at some point in the Wesleyan way of salvation." And the point at which it operates is prevenient grace. This gracious restoration of the human faculties that make it possible for a person to embrace God's offer of salvation "cannot be refused."[143] Yet a person's embrace or rejection of this offer of salvation is a "responsible" one. Prevenient grace is a helping grace in that it restores human freedom, but it is not a coercive grace in that the offer of salvation can be refused. Prevenient grace helps, but it is "not, in and of itself, saving grace, even though it may become so if properly responded to."[144] In order for the divinely initiated salvific process to proceed, there must be a receptive response on the part of the human subject of this preparatory grace. Classical Wesleyan theology affirms that salvation is realized through "a cooperation, or synergism, between divine grace and the human will."[145] Passages such as Matthew 13:23; 1 Thessalonians 1:6; 2:13; Colossians 1:6; and especially 2 Corinthians 6:1 clearly evidence divine-human co-operation. The "understanding" that guides and the "affections" that move the human will are corrupted, but this enslavement to sin is "not absolute." Thus, prevenient grace "is not needed to restore to the faculty of will its power of orig-inating action: that has never been lost"; rather, this grace is needed to guide the intellect and move the affections in accord with God's will and God's ways.[146] Although not all human beings will respond to or cooperate with this prevenient grace of God, it is bestowed upon each and every person.

"Grace, being nothing other than God's love," writes Mildred Wynkoop, "is not selective."[147] Dunning says that the doctrine of prevenient grace "centrally expresses the Wesleyan commitment to the universality of the Atonement. . . . God offers himself to all men everywhere as a saving presence."[148] God's desire is that all people be saved, and through prevenient grace he makes all people savable, able to respond positively to him.[149] As John 1:9 indicates, there is a divine light that is given to every human being.[150] As we noted earlier, Wesleyan theology is marked by an optimism of grace. "We expect God to be at work in every human being," writes Ted Campbell, "whether Christians, followers of other religious traditions, atheists, whomever. Methodists trust that the 'free will' humans exercise, and whatever good human beings may actually do, are signs that God's grace is working in them."[151]

Holiness: Entire sanctification. Randy Maddox shows that in the thought of John Wesley, "it is God's *gracious* prevenience that effects faith in us, while our co-operant *responsibility* takes expression in loving deeds."[152] The call to a life of sanctified holiness, one manifestation of which is loving deeds, has al-ways been and continues to be one of the hallmarks of the Wesleyan tradition. In the preaching of John Wesley and the hymns of Charles Wesley, holiness was "the whole point of the Gospel."[153] Describing late-nineteenth-century Method-ism, John Miley writes, "The privilege of entire sanctification is at once so thor-oughly Scriptural and Wesleyan that from it there is among us only the rarest dissent."[154] And, at the turn to the twenty-first century, L. Gregory Jones ob-served, "Methodism's distinctive *charism* is 'holiness,' or, to use more specifi-cally Wesleyan terminology, 'scriptural holiness.'"[155] The gracious work of God enables us not only to exercise a freedom to receive eternal salvation in Christ, but also to be holy and to live a life of holiness here and now.

Sanctification. The conviction that "imputed righteousness must become im-parted righteousness" constitutes one of the distinctives of the Wesleyan tradi-tion.[156] People who embrace the gracious, saving work of Christ receive not only the gift of being regarded as holy, but also the gracious possibility of being holy. The Articles of Religion of the Wesleyan Methodist Church state, "Sanctification is that renewal of our fallen natures by the Holy Ghost, received through faith in Jesus Christ . . . whereby we are not only delivered from the guilt of sin, but are washed from its pollution, saved from its power, and are enabled, through grace, to love God with all our hearts, and to walk in his holy commandments blameless."[157] Holiness is "a moral or religious state," writes Miley, and sanctification is "a gracious work of God whereby that state is produced."[158] This state is experiential. The Christian can expect to have a conscious awareness of the sanctifying presence of God in Christ within. Furthermore, this experiential state is one of love. As 1 John 4:16 indicates, God is love, and to have God present and active in one's life cannot help but produce, by God's grace, a love for God and love for other people.[159]

In becoming holy, creatures who are fallen and sinful return to the state of righteousness in which human beings were originally created. Tuttle writes, "For the true Wesleyan, salvation is completed by a return to original righteousness, achieved by the work of the Holy Spirit,"[160] and Dunning states, "The great purpose of redemption is to restore man to the image of God. . . . The total process of sanctification . . . has as its objective the restoring of man to his original destiny."[161] In our original state, as created by God, we were without sin, and this perfection is the goal of sanctification.

Entire sanctification.[162] The Confession of Faith of the United Methodist Church affirms, "Entire sanctification is a state of perfect love, righteousness and true holiness which every regenerate believer may obtain by being delivered from the power of sin, by loving God with all the heart, soul, mind and strength, and by loving one's neighbor as one's self."[163] The Free Methodist Church's Articles of Religion teach that entire sanctification is "that work of the Holy Spirit, subsequent to regeneration, by which the fully consecrated believer, upon exercise of faith in the atoning blood of Christ, is cleansed in that moment from all inward sin and empowered for service."[164] This teaching is based on passages such as Ephesians 4:22, "You were taught to put away your former way of life, your old self, corrupt and deluded by its lusts, and to be renewed in the spirit of your minds, and to clothe yourselves with the new self, created according to the likeness of God in true righteousness and holiness," and 1 John 4:16-19, which reads in part, "God is love, and those who abide in love abide in God, and God abides in them. Love has been perfected among us in this: that we may have boldness on the day of judgment, because as he is, so are we in this world. There is no fear in love, but perfect love casts out fear. . . . And whoever fears has not reached perfection in love. We love because he first loved us."[165]

Entire sanctification, or Christian perfection, is realized through both the removal of sin from and the infusion of the love of God into the Christian.[166] The

Wesleyan Church, for example, teaches that in entire sanctification "the child of God is separated from sin unto God and is enabled to love God with all his heart and to walk blameless in all God's holy commandments."[167] In *A Contemporary Wesleyan Theology,* Dayton writes, "Entire sanctification is the act of God by which the human heart is cleansed from all sin and filled with love by the Holy Spirit who is given, through faith, to the fully consecrated believer."[168] Sin is "the great spoiler and perverter of humanity and of God's purpose for His people," and as such, purification from sin must take place if one is to actualize a transforming relationship with God.[169] The psalmist asks God to "cleanse" him so that he might be "whiter than snow" (Ps 51:7). Jesus teaches that the Father "prunes" the branches of the vine in order to make them more fruitful (Jn 15:2), and John assures us that "the blood of Jesus . . . cleanses us from all sin" (1 Jn 1:7).[170]

In conjunction with cleansing from sin, perfection entails the infusion of divine love. In fact, one of the synonyms for "entire sanctification" is "perfect love." Paul instructs that "God's love has been poured into our hearts through the Holy Spirit that has been given to us" (Rom 5:5), and God's will for us, as clearly set forth in the "first and greatest" commandment, is to "love the Lord your God with all your heart, and with all your soul, and with all your mind" (Mt 22:37). Thus, not surprisingly, God graciously "enable[s] us to love perfectly according to God's standard."[171] Love is "instilled in the heart in regeneration," and then it grows and develops in the process of sanctification, and becomes pure, unmixed with any unloving intentions, when Christian perfection is realized.[172] The grace of God is, in Georgia Harkness's words, "creatively redemptive, the power that works in us to make us perfect in love."[173] By God's grace, the perfected Christian lives "a holy life, dedicated fully to God through Christ."[174] "Entire sanctification," write Ted Campbell and Michael Burns, "denotes the sovereign reign of grace and the dominance of love in the life of a Christian."[175] As Thomas Oden observes, "There is no fated or absolute necessity that the regenerated life should remain arbitrarily bound by the power of sin, if God the Spirit is contextually offering grace sufficient to meet each and every successive temptation or challenge."[176]

What does this wholly holy life look like? The perfected Christian, cleansed from sin and infused with divine love, will, according to Miley, be characterized by "clearer spiritual discernment . . . easier victory over temptation . . . greater strength unto duty . . . intenser love . . . closer communion with God."[177] It is the spiritual perfection whereby a human being is "fully cleansed, renewed, and filled with God's Spirit" and enabled by God's gracious help to love both him and fellow human beings without any admixture of sinful affections.[178] This sanctified holiness is entire not only with respect to its degree or intensity, but also with respect to its scope: God's sanctifying work extends to human beings in all dimensions—body, soul and spirit. Commenting on 1 Thessalonians 5:23, Allan Coppedge writes, "God's work in the believer's total being—including his spirit, soul and body—is necessary to make the believer entirely holy. Paul is praying that God, in his creative role, will more fully make holy every part of the creature that he has made and already regenerated."[179]

Although this reality is referred to as *entire* sanctification or Christian *perfection,* classical Wesleyan theology does not presume that the process of transformation in the life of a perfected Christian is completed. Christian perfection does not endow one with "perfect judgment, complete wisdom, or full maturity of skills or perfection in performance."[180] Nor does entire sanctification mean that there is no room for further spiritual growth and change, or that one will never be tempted. Christian perfection is a perfection consistent with human finitude, consistent with "one's natural constitution." A Christian who is living in perfect love is still subject to making mistakes and is still subject to the limits of finitude, such as limited knowledge or understanding; however, his or her *intention* is one that is motivated by love of God and neighbor.[181] Moreover, whereas human intentions are conditioned by limited power, God's intentions are not. God's intention is that Christians should love God completely, and "it is within the *power* of God to bring about that which God intends."[182] "No limits can be set," writes Newton Flew, "to the moral or spiritual attainments of a Christian in the present life."[183]

Such perfection in feeble and fallen human beings may seem impossible, but not when understood as a gracious work of God. Christian perfection is possible by virtue of, and *only* by virtue of, God's power and grace.[184] Echoing Wesley, Dunning writes, "If God promises freedom from sin (perfection) either explicitly or implicitly in His Word, we may rest assured that it is a possibility within the divine power."[185] Christian perfection is a possibility in this life. It can be realized here and now. No one, no Christian, possesses the will or virtues to bring about a perfecting transformation of the self; rather, such transformation can come about only through the imparted grace of God. God not only graciously imputes or credits to Christians the righteousness and holiness of Christ, but also "imparts" or gives to Christians a righteousness and holiness of their own.[186] Not only does the Christian obtain the benefits of being considered righteous by virtue of being in Christ, but also, in sanctification the Christian is made, in fact, holy as "genuine changes [are] wrought in the human heart by transforming grace."[187] Paul urges, "Be transformed by the renewing of your minds, so that you may discern what is the will of God—what is good and acceptable and perfect" (Rom 12:2), and in 2 Corinthians 3:18 he encourages Christ-followers, saying that they "are being transformed" into the image of the glorified Lord. Peter exhorts, "As he who called you is holy, be holy yourselves in all your conduct; for it is written, 'You shall be holy, for I am holy'" (1 Pet 1:15-16; cf. Lev 11:44). It is God's will not only that we appear to be holy and be regarded by him as holy, but also that we actually *be* holy.

If there is to be entire sanctification, the Christian must respond in appropriate ways to the work that God has already done in her or his life. "A sensitive Christian," observes Harkness, "never ceases to wonder at the mystery and marvel of inflowing power that comes, all undeserved, from God's gracious love."[188] In keeping with the Arminian character of Wesleyan theology, the process of sanctification is seen as a "synergistic" one.[189] "Since Wesleyans do not believe that unconditional election or predestination is scriptural," writes Dayton, "they have all the more reason to believe that certain responses are necessary for the appropriation of grace." Just as an individual must respond to God in repentance and faith if the new birth is to be experienced, so also a Christian must respond to God in consecration and faith if Christian perfection is to be experienced.[190] The Christian who would be perfected must "walk not according to the flesh but according to the Spirit" (Rom 8:4). She or he must, by faith, "walk in the light" (1 Jn 1:7). This consecration entails a keen awareness of sin that yet remains and that is "of an inward, dispositional nature." This awareness is then accompanied by a heartfelt recognition of one's inability to rescue oneself from this sinfulness, and "mortification" or dying to sin. In addition to consecration, the path to perfection requires faith—that is, a confidence, that God can and will deliver one from sin.[191] Just as one must entrust oneself to God's salvific work in order to receive the gift of salvation, so one must entrust oneself to God's sanctifying work in order to receive the gift of Christian perfection.

Although Wesleyan theologians differ as to the usual sequence or pattern of God's perfecting work, most classical Wesleyans associate perfection with "a specific and definite act of God" distinct from conversion.[192] For example, in an article on "entire sanctification," Asbury Theological Seminary affirms that "God calls all believers to entire sanctification in a moment of full surrender and faith subsequent to their new birth in Christ."[193] The Church of the Nazarene teaches that entire sanctification is "wrought instantaneously by faith, preceded by entire consecration."[194] Some Wesleyans describe this work of God as a "second blessing" or "second work of grace."[195] Others refer to it as a "crisis" experience.[196] Many of the Wesleyan movements that are heirs of nineteenth-century American Holiness teachings specifically associate this second blessing with the baptism of the Holy Spirit.[197] According to the Articles of Faith of the Church of the Nazarene, entire sanctification "is wrought by the baptism with the Holy Spirit, and comprehends in one experience the cleansing of the heart from sin and the abiding indwelling presence of the Holy Spirit."[198] Similarly, the Wesleyan Church holds that "sanctification is wrought instantaneously when the believer presents himself a living sacrifice, holy and acceptable to God, through faith in Jesus Christ, being effected by the baptism with the Holy Spirit, who cleanses the heart from all inbred sin."[199] Joel 2:28-32 indicates that God will "pour out" his Spirit, and Acts 2:1-21 reports the sudden and dramatic coming of the Spirit. These passages, in conjunction with texts such as Acts 8:14-21; 9:3-9; 10:47; John 7:37-39; 20:22; Luke 24:48-49; Ephesians 1:3, clearly suggest an event that "is sufficiently specific and recognizable as to be called a crisis involving an instantaneous aspect."[200] Although there is an ongoing process of transformation, there is, writes Dunning, "an instantaneous moment"; and although one "may be dying to sin for some time . . . it is only at a particular point that one actually dies."[201]

What remains most important, however, is not the pattern of change, but the reality of transformation: the Christian does die to sin and actually lives a new life in Christ. The direction of the Christian life is toward Christlikeness, and this means toward holiness. By God's grace and power, the people of God will be the image of the God who is love. By God's grace and power, the people of God will be an image of the God who says, "Be holy as I am holy."

Conclusion: Grace-Full Holiness and Holy Wholeness

God's desire for all people is that they know him and his love, and that, as a result, they be transformed into glorious images of him. In order for this holy wholeness to be realized in a world of sin, God's grace must be shed abroad once again. This he has done. In response, Wesleyan Christians go out into nothing less than the entire world, their "parish," with nothing less than their practical divinity—a message of grace-full holiness. All people need to be saved, by God's grace all people can be saved, and this salvation can be wholly holy.

FOR FURTHER STUDY

The endnotes contain citations of many useful resources, most of them written from within the Wesleyan tradition. A brief list of resources for further study follows here. Some of these resources consider the Wesleyan or Methodist traditions in general, while others focus on history and/or theology.

Bibliographies

Eltschar, Susan M., ed. *Women in the Wesleyan and United Methodist Traditions: A Bibliography*. Madison, N.J.: General Commission on Archives and History, United Methodist Church, 1991.

Gray, C. Jarrett, Jr. *The Racial and Ethnic Presence in American Methodism: A Bibliography*. Madison, N.J.: General Commission on Archives and History, United Methodist Church, 1991.

Jones, Charles E., ed. *Guide to the Study of the Holiness Movement*. 2 vols. Metuchen, N.J.: Scarecrow, 1974.

Kirby, James E., Russell E. Richey and Kenneth E. Rowe. *The Methodists*, pp. 381-91. Westport, Conn.: Greenwood, 1996.

Miller, William C. *Holiness Works: A Bibliography*. Rev. ed. Kansas City, Mo.: Beacon Hill, 1986.

Rowe, Kenneth E., ed. *United Methodist Studies: Basic Bibliographies*. Nashville: Abingdon, 1998.

Reference Works

Harmon, Nolan B., ed. *Encyclopedia of World Methodism*. 2 vols. Nashville: United Methodist Publishing House, 1974.

Kostlevy, William, and Gari-Anne Patzwald, eds. *Historical Dictionary of the Holiness Movement*. Lanham, Md.: Scarecrow, 2001.

Survey Resources

Bucke, Emory S., ed. *The History of American Methodism*. 3 vols. New York: Abingdon, 1964.

Kirby, James E., Russell E. Richey and Kenneth E. Rowe. *The Methodists*. Westport, Conn.: Greenwood, 1996.

Norwood, Frederick A. *The Story of American Methodism: A History of the United Methodists and Their Relations*. Nashville: Abingdon, 1974.

Primary Historical and Theological Sources

Dayton, Donald W., ed. *The Higher Christian Life: Sources for the Study of the Holiness, Pentecostal, and Keswick Movements*. 48 vols. New York: Garland, 1985.

Wesley, John. *The Works of John Wesley*. Reprint ed. 14 vols. Grand Rapids: Zondervan, 1958.

———. *The Works of John Wesley*. Oxford: Clarendon, 1975-1983; Nashville: Abingdon, 1984-.

Recent and Current Theological Explorations

Cracknell, Kenneth, and Susan J. White. *An Introduction to World Methodism*. Cambridge: Cambridge University Press, 2005.

Marsh, Clive, et al., eds. *Unmasking Methodist Theology*. London: Continuum, 2004.

Meeks, M. Douglas, ed. *Trinity, Community, and Power: Mapping Trajectories in Wesleyan Theology.* Nashville: Kingswood, 2000.

Wesleyan Theological Society. *Wesleyan Theology in a Postmodern Era.* N.p.: Wesleyan Theological Society, 1999.

Yrigoyen, Charles, Jr., ed. *The Global Impact of the Wesleyan Traditions and Their Related Movements.* Lanham, Md.: Scarecrow, 2002.

8 ■ Rightly Dividing the Scriptures

DISPENSATIONAL THEOLOGY

To this end every curriculum study should be focused. Studies in theology, original languages, and history should contribute to the one ideal, namely, the knowledge of the Scriptures. There are social and pastoral problems concerning which a preacher should be instructed, but these are secondary compared to his call to minister the truth of God.

Lewis Sperry Chafer, *Systematic Theology*

Simply put, the basic unifying issue for all dispensationalists is that Israel is not the church.

Herbert W. Bateman IV,
in *Three Central Issues in Contemporary Dispensationalism*

Certainly, the goal [of theology] is not difference for its own sake but spiritual growth in faith and hope informed by the Scriptures and manifesting itself in love.

Craig Blaising, in *Dispensationalism, Israel and the Church*

My paternal grandparents were lifelong members of Plymouth Brethren assemblies in St. Louis, Missouri.[1] My father first professed Christ as Savior under the ministry of a Plymouth Brethren evangelist who preached in accord with Dispensational theology and who presented to my dad a comprehensive, diagrammatic overview of God's salvation plan for the ages. My mother, who came from a nonchurched home, came to faith in Christ as a child through the influence of a Plymouth Brethren assembly in her Chicago neighborhood. And my parents met at a summer Bible conference, where members of Plymouth Brethren assemblies gathered to become more firmly grounded in Dispensational biblical teaching. Among the treasured family heirlooms handed on to me is a well-worn, 1917 edition of the *Scofield Reference Bible*. "To William and Margaret with Christian love, June 15th, 1940" is written on the first page, along with the signatures of two members of one of the assemblies in St. Louis. This Bible was a wedding gift to my parents, and it is inscribed with a word of wisdom to the newlyweds, from the Word: "Trust in the LORD with all thine heart, and lean not unto thine own understanding. In all thy ways acknowledge Him, and He shall direct thy paths. Proverbs 3:5-6" (KJV).

Context: Historical and Ecclesiastical Background

Historical origins and development. The history of the Dispensational tradition of theology can be traced through four "generations."[2] The first generation began with John Nelson Darby (1800-1882) and flourished within the Brethren movement in the early- and mid-nineteenth century, sometimes called the "Formulative" era. The second generation included the Bible and prophecy conferences of the late-nineteenth century and the work of C. I. Scofield (1843-1921) and reached its zenith in the work of Lewis Sperry Chafer (1871-1952).[3] Some refer to this as the period of "Crystallization,"[4] while others, most notably Progressive Dispensationalists, often refer to this as "Classical" Dispensationalism.[5] A third generation flourished from the 1960s through the 1980s, and it includes the work of people such as Alva J. McClain (1888-1968), John F. Walvoord (1910-2002), J. Dwight Pentecost (b. 1915), Elliott E. Johnson and Charles C. Ryrie (b. 1925). The theology articulated by this generation is now sometimes referred to as "Traditional,"[6] prompted by the contrast with the subsequent generation that arose in the 1980s, Progressive Dispensationalism.[7] Those who have not embraced this Progressive expression would say that the third generation continues to embody the genuine theology of tradition.

Regardless of which of the current subtraditions they currently embrace, Dispensationalists widely regard John Nelson Darby as "the father of modern dispensational theology,"[8] and the nineteenth-century Brethren movement in England, of which Darby was a leader, as the context in which modern Dispensational thought was first systematized and promoted.[9] Like those in other traditions, Dispensationalists are eager to qualify and expand this description of their origins in a way that predates what is, in church-historical terms, the rather recent era of the early nineteenth century.[10] Yet, Dispensationalists clearly acknowledge the relatively recent emergence of the tradition as a systematized theology. For example, commenting on a central affirmation of Dispensationalism—the distinction between Israel and the church—Thomas McCall recently wrote that although this truth is taught in the New Testament, "it has been suppressed throughout most of church history."[11] Writing in the 1940s, Lewis Sperry Chafer observed, "Though predictive prophecy was made clear to the early Church, that great body of truth along with other vital doctrines was lost to view . . . [but] is becoming increasingly clear during these past two generations."[12] In recent years, a more common view of this pre-Darby history has been to suggest that "as a *system* of theology [Dispensationalism] is recent in origin," but that there are earlier historical references to "concepts" that were "eventually . . . systematized into dispensationalism."[13] Ryrie, for example, describes instances of Dispensational "concepts" (such as dividing history into a series of divine programs or covenantal periods) in the thought of a number of early church fathers, and then he traces these concepts into the twelfth century and the work of Joachim of Fiore, followed by his account of "a period of developing dispensationalism" in the seventeenth and eighteenth centuries.[14]

Although Dispensationalists have varying views of these premodern roots, or what Arnold Ehlert refers to as the "background,"[15] most Dispensationalists locate the origins of the tradition in the nineteenth century centered in the work of Darby and the Brethren movement in England.[16] Ehlert suggests that 1825 constitutes "the logical dividing-line between the old and the new dispensationalism," stating that by this year "there was a considerable literature to be found on the subject [of the doctrine of ages and dispensations], and the doctrine was well established as a theological concept."[17] Ryrie says, "Dispensationalism was first promoted through the study and teachings of John Nelson Darby."[18] Craig Blaising identifies the beginning of what he calls "classical" Dispensationalism with "the beginnings of the Brethren Movement in the early nineteenth century."[19] Steven Spencer refers to Darby as "the originator" of the Dispensational tradition,[20] and Larry Crutchfield states that Darby provided "the first, full, systematic expression of a dispensational interpretation of Scripture" and "set the stage and guided the way for the dispensational theology which was to follow him."[21]

John Nelson Darby was born, raised and educated in Ireland. He trained for the practice of law, and he became a lawyer in 1822. In the wake of a profound religious conversion, the following year he left the practice of law and pursued ordination in the Church of England. As his theology developed, particularly with reference to the nature of the church and the character of church life, he increasingly found himself at odds with church authorities. He left the Church of England sometime around 1827, settled in Dublin, Ireland, and entered into religious association with a group of Christians under the leadership of Edward Cronin, who shared many of Darby's views on the church and the Christian life.[22] By 1831, this group and a number of others began "breaking of bread" services centered on teaching of the Bible and celebration of the Lord's Table. During this same period, Darby moved to Plymouth, which throughout the

1830s and into the 1840s "was one of the chief centers of the [Brethren] movement." As many as eight hundred were in fellowship there.[23] Darby increasingly devoted himself to the ministry of this group, and in 1834, he helped found a newspaper, *The Christian Witness,* which served as an instrument for spreading the beliefs of this emerging Brethren group. In 1836, *The Christian Witness* published an essay by Darby titled "Apostasy of the Successive Dispensations," in which he clearly set forth for the first time in print a Dispensational perspective on the teachings of the Bible.[24]

Darby saw in the Scriptures successive periods in which the principles governing the relationship between God and human beings seemed to change. He wrote of these "dispensations" that they "all declare some leading principle or interference of God, some condition in which he has placed man, principles which in themselves are everlastingly sanctioned of God, but in the course of those dispensations placed responsibility in the hand of man for the display and discovery of what he was."[25] Although this understanding provided a structure within which to view the sweep of the history of redemption, it did not constitute the burden of Darby's teaching. A more fundamental concern was the proper understanding of the nature of the church and the character of the life and lives identified with it.[26] Influenced by his experience with what he perceived to be the apostate institutional church, Darby came to view the genuine church as a heavenly, essentially invisible reality—thus distinct and separate from the corrupted earthly "church"—whereas the nation of Israel constituted God's earthly, visible people.[27] This distinction between Israel and the church proves to be a central and abiding component throughout the history of Dispensational theology.

Darby personally carried Dispensational ideas beyond England to Germany, Italy, Switzerland, New Zealand, Canada and the United States through an itinerant ministry.[28] In the United States and Canada, Dispensationalism began to have a significant impact after the U.S. Civil War, not least through Bible and prophecy conferences that began in 1876 and flourished throughout the 1880s and 1890s.[29] Ryrie points out that these conferences were conceived not to promote Dispensational ideas per se, but rather to promote premillennialism,[30] Christian unity and Bible study. "Nevertheless," Ryrie writes, "these conferences inevitably did promote dispensationalism because of the insistence on the absolute authority of the Scriptures, the literal fulfillment of Old Testament prophecy, and the expectation of the imminent coming of Christ."[31]

Preeminent among these conferences, particularly from 1883 to 1897, was the Niagara Bible and Prophecy Conference, convened at Niagara on the Lake, Ontario. These conferences Herbert Bateman describes as "the catalyst for the spread of premillennial and dispensational thinking in North America."[32] Craig Blaising identifies two factors that made the Niagara conferences conducive to the development and expansion of Dispensationalism. Participants and attendees included people from a wide variety of churches and denominations, and the conferences sought "a visible experience of unity" within this diversity. Thus, the conferences provided a diverse exposure, beyond the Brethren movement, for Dispensational teachings. Second, at Niagara "the Bible was affirmed as the inspired Word of God, and instruction was to be based upon it alone." Whatever diversity has historically existed within Dispensationalism, these conjoined principles of a high view of the Bible as the divinely inspired Word of God and of teaching that is based on "the Bible alone" have always been foundational for Dispensationalists. Thus, whether or not various doctrinal views set forth at Niagara were explicitly Dispensational, the principles of biblical authority promulgated there could only reinforce, in some measure, the increasingly visible Dispensational school of thought. Blaising also indicates that in addition to the view of Scripture, the approach to the interpretation of the Bible taken at Niagara "left a lasting imprint on the hermeneutics of American dispensationalism."[33] This approach included the principles of christocentric interpretation whereby all passages are interpreted with reference to Christ, piety in interpretation whereby all Christians are guided by the Holy Spirit and grow in love for one another as they read the Bible, and inductive interpretation whereby "sectarian" interpretations are avoided. Last, but not least, "Niagara's employment of the notion of dispensations to develop and support premillennialism" served to advance the spread of a distinctively Dispensational approach to reading the Bible.[34]

The last Niagara conference was held in 1897, and although Bible and prophecy conferences had not ceased to convene, their impact had significantly diminished by the turn of the century. Nonetheless, Dispensational teachings had been introduced into American Protestantism through these conferences,[35] and within a decade another powerful vehicle for the dissemination of Dispensational Bible teaching emerged. The first edition of the *Scofield Reference Bible* was published in 1909, and it "popularized dispensationalism as much as any other single entity."[36] Blaising notes, "The *Scofield Reference Bible* became the Bible of Fundamentalism, and the theology of the notes approached confessional status in many Bible schools, institutes, and seminaries established in the early decades of this [the 20th] century."[37] The impact of this study Bible was so great that Scofield's particular understanding of premillennialism came to be known, until the 1940s, as "Scofieldism" and was "practically canonized in Bible schools, colleges and seminaries."[38]

After serving with distinction in the Civil War, Cyrus Ingerson Scofield studied and practiced law, first as a U.S. attorney and then in private practice in St. Louis. After a Christian conversion experience, he served pastorates in three congregations from 1882 to 1907. He then undertook Bible conference ministry in the United States and Great Britain, and in 1888 he published the widely read *Rightly Dividing the Word of Truth*. This brief book offered a popular, practical explanation of Dispensational, premillennial, pretribulational interpretation of the Bible. The *Scofield Reference Bible* was first published by Oxford University Press in 1909, and it was revised in 1917. Through clearly delineated notes, charts and other study aids, Scofield's Bible placed a clearly articulated Dispensational interpretation of the entire Bible into the hands of millions of laypeople. The nature and extent of the link between the thought of Darby and that of Scofield is not clear, with their writings manifesting both striking differences and significant similarities.[39] Darby and Scofield differed over, for example, the number and duration of dispensations. They were of similar mind, however, with regard to the principle of the "literal" interpretation of the Bible, the basic structure of dispensations, the outline of end-time events, and the prophetic futures of Israel and the church.[40] With regard to literal interpretation, in his introduction to the first edition of the *Scofield Reference Bible,* Scofield indicated that the prophetic books of the Bible had been "closed to the average reader by fanciful and allegorical schemes of interpretation." In its place, he argued for a literal interpretation—that is, reading words in the Bible, particularly in prophetic writings, in a plain and straightforward manner, just as they would be read if used in any other book. This became his "most well-known hermeneutical contribution."[41]

Although the significance of the influence of Scofield is difficult to underestimate, he was by no means the sole high-profile voice for Dispensationalism in the United States. In 1918, Clarence Larkin (1850-1924) published an elaborate work titled *Dispensational Truth, or God's Plan and Purpose in the Ages,* and three years later, *Rightly Dividing the Word,* a book based upon some of his sermons and lectures. Other ministers whose thought and work manifest the influence of Dispensationalism include D. L. Moody (1837-1899), Arno C. Gaebelein (1861-1945), James Inglis, James Hall Brookes (1830-1897), A. J. Gordon (1836-1895) and J. R. Graves (1820-1893).[42] In the 1920s and 1930s, Dispensationalism was influential enough that it constituted one side of a rift within the fundamentalist movement, the other side consisting largely of those within Reformed traditions, such as Presbyterian J. Gresham Machen. Among the most contested Dispensational teachings was, according to Blaising, "a fundamental contrast of God's relationship to the church in the present and future dispensations to his relationship to Jews and Gentiles in the past and future dispensations."[43] From a Reformed perspective, this historically recent interpretation of God's redemptive work was marked by too much discontinuity between Israel and the church, and between the Old and New Testaments.[44]

However, despite this quarrel within fundamentalism, Dispensational theology continued to develop in both substance and scope of influence. The reading of the Bible that Scofield had promulgated through the *Scofield Reference Bible* and correspondence courses now found more elaborate formulation and expression in the work of Lewis Sperry Chafer. Chafer was ordained as a Congregational minister in 1900, but in 1903, he became a Presbyterian and remained so the rest of his life. In 1914, he joined the faculty of the Philadelphia School of the Bible, newly founded by Scofield, and remained there until 1923, when he became pastor of Scofield Memorial Church in Dallas, Texas. Shortly after arriving in Dallas, Chafer began to work toward the establishment of a theological college, and in the fall of 1924, the Evangelical Theological College opened. In July of 1936, the name was changed to Dallas Theological Seminary, and Chafer served as president and professor of theology from the founding in 1924 until his death in 1952. Dallas Seminary is rightly regarded as perhaps the most noteworthy educational institution in the Dispensational tradition. In addition, many schools in the Bible institute movement advanced this theology, including Moody Bible Institute (Chicago), Philadelphia College of the Bible, the Bible Institute of Los Angeles and Multnomah School of the Bible (Portland, Oregon).

Chafer was Scofieldian in his theology, and the seminary he established was devoted to developing and handing on this theological tradition. In addition to founding Dallas Seminary, Chafer produced the first Dispensational systematic theology. This eight-volume work, published in 1948, is regarded by Dispensationalists as "the most developed form" of Scofieldian Dispensationalism.[45] Thus, as Ryrie puts it, "Scofield popularized; Chafer systematized."[46] Through his leadership of Dallas Seminary, his publications and his teaching, Chafer had a tremendous impact on the next generation of Dispensationalists. Among his students were John F. Walvoord, J. Dwight Pentecost and Charles C. Ryrie. Yet, Chafer's work in many respects marked the beginning of the end of the Scofieldian or "Crystalization" era.

Modifications in Scofieldian Dispensationalism clearly emerged by the 1960s, and many of these modifications found expression in Charles Ryrie's *Dispensationalism Today* (1965) and in a revised edition of the *Scofield Reference Bible* published in 1967.[47] Included among those who revised this Dispensational reference Bible and Scofield's version of Dispensationalism were

the students of Chafer mentioned above. Ryrie articulated a modified definition of "dispensation" and introduced new rationale for a number of beliefs,
including premillennialism. Other changes reduced, but by no means eliminated, some distinctions that had been articulated by Scofield and Chafer,
thereby in some measure lessening the discontinuities in the Dispensational
view of redemption history. These shifts toward greater continuity included,
for example, a more unified view of salvation across the various dispensations
and the dropping of the previously held distinction between "kingdom of
God" and "kingdom of heaven."

John Walvoord succeeded Chafer as president of Dallas Seminary in 1952,
a post that he then held for thirty-four years. Walvoord was a prolific author
of popular books, many of which expound the eschatological teachings of
Dispensationalism and their perceived relevance to current events.[48] J. Dwight
Pentecost taught Bible at Philadelphia College of the Bible from 1948 to 1955,
and then he taught Bible exposition at Dallas Seminary. He is the author of
Things to Come (1958),[49] which some Dispensationlists regard as "a definitive,
biblical treatment of the dispensational premillennial scheme of eschatology."[50] Charles C. Ryrie is the foremost Dispensational systematic theologian
of his generation. Apart from four years as president of Philadelphia College
of the Bible (1958-1962), Ryrie was professor of systematic theology at Dallas
Seminary for twenty-six years (1953-1958, 1962-1983). Having published more
than two dozen books, including *The Ryrie Study Bible* (1976) and *Basic Theology* (1986), Ryrie is often regarded as the leading theological voice of post-
Scofieldian Dispensationalism. In 1965, Ryrie published *Dispensationalism Today,* a response to criticisms and misrepresentations of Dispensationalism, and
a basic statement of the post-Scofieldian version of it. Ryrie here defines a dispensation as "a distinguishable economy in the outworking of God's purpose,"[51] and goes on to delineate his often-cited threefold *"sine qua non* of
dispensationalism": (1) maintaining the distinction between Israel and the
church (which Ryrie identifies as constituting "the essence of dispensationalism"); (2) consistently employing a "literal or plain" biblical hermeneutic,
which "does not spiritualize or allegorize"; and (3) affirming that God's underlying purpose in the world is to glorify himself.[52] In recent years some leading
Dispensational scholars have questioned the historical and theological accuracy of Ryrie's description of Dispensationalism, but for decades his presentation was regarded by many, both within and outside Dispensational circles, as
the standard description of the character of the tradition and the essence of
Dispensational theology.[53] In 1995, Moody Press published a revised edition
of Ryrie's book, under the abbreviated title *Dispensationalism,* in which he in-

teracts with more recent Dispensational perspectives, particularly those of Progressive Dispensationalism.

By the 1980s, what has come to be called Progressive Dispensationalism was emerging. In his 1981 presidential address to the Evangelical Theological Society, Kenneth L. Barker, who described himself as "a moderate dispensationalist," delineated as "false dichotomies" between the Old and New Testaments, attempting to give proper emphasis to the continuities in the Bible in the face of what he regarded as an excessive stress on the discontinuities.[54] In 1986, again in conjunction with the annual meeting of the Evangelical Theological Society, the first formal meeting of the Dispensational Study Group was convened, and this group proved to be a major arena for consideration of changing Dispensational views.[55] It was partly through discussions associated with this group that "Progressive" was adopted as the descriptor for this emerging version of Dispensationalism. While still recognizing distinctions between the covenants of the Old Testament and the New Covenant, and between Israel and the church, the term *Progressive* reflects a new emphasis on progressive fulfillment throughout the history of the dispensations of God's redemptive work—"continuity through progress: the progress of promissory fulfillment"—and on the continuities between God's peoples, namely Israel and the church.[56]

Progressive Dispensationalism has emerged as the predominant expression of the tradition for a significant number of scholars and students at historically Dispensational educational institutions, such as Dallas Theological Seminary and Talbot Seminary. Among the leading voices for Progressive Dispensationalism are theologians Craig Blaising (b. 1949) and Robert Saucy and New Testament scholar Darrell Bock. The Progressives view their emphasis on continuities within covenantal redemptive history and on continuities among the peoples of God—that is, Israel and the church—as both a more accurate reading of the Bible and as a legitimate development within, not a departure from, the Dispensational tradition.[57] In some other sectors of Dispensationalism, Progressive views are regarded as, at best, something less than genuine Dispensationalism and, at worst, a misinterpretation of the Bible.[58] Holding to what is today sometimes called Traditional Dispensationalism, the predominant understanding from the 1960s into the 1980s, are institutions such as Philadelphia College of the Bible and scholars such as theologian Charles Ryrie and biblical studies scholars Elliott E. Johnson and Robert Thomas.

Diversity. As the preceding history suggests, the single greatest distinction among subgroups within Dispensationalism currently is that between Traditionalist and Progressive views.[59] Throughout much of the twentieth century, there was another subtradition: Ultradispensationalism.[60] Like other Dispensationalists, Ultradispensationalists maintain a clear distinction between Israel and the church. Unlike other Dispensationalists, who generally regard the narrative of Acts 2 as recording the beginning of the church, Ultradispensationalists do not see the church beginning until the events recorded in Acts 9 or later. Moderate Ultradispensationalists, such as Charles F. Baker, J. C. O'Hair and Cornelius R. Stam, view the church as starting in Acts 9 or 13.[61] Extreme Ultradispensationalists, such as E. W. Bullinger (1837-1913), Charles Welch and Otis Q. Sellers, associate the beginning of the church with the record of Acts 28.[62] By virtue of this view, extreme Ultradispensationalists do not believe that the church should observe the Lord's Table, and within the biblical canon they regard only Paul's prison epistles as being directed primarily to the church. The congregations of Grace Bible Fellowship and Grace Bible College of Grand Rapids, Michigan, historically have promulgated Ultradispensationalist theology.

Unlike many of the traditions considered in this book, the diversity of Dispensationalism is encompassed essentially within evangelical and fundamentalist circles. One does not find a substantial Dispensational presence within, for example, either "liberal" or "mainline" denominations or educational institutions. Dispensational teaching touched a variety of ecclesiastical traditions through the late-nineteenth-century Bible and prophecy conferences, including Presbyterian, Episcopalian and Congregational. However, it was never predominant in any of these churches, and by the middle of the twentieth century "Baptists and non-denominational churches (especially 'Bible' churches) had become the most common ecclesiastical affiliations for dispensationalists."[63] Baptist denominations that are historically Dispensational include the General Association of Regular Baptists. Nondenominational and "independent" churches that are Dispensational in theology include Grace Gospel Fellowship and the congregations of the Independent Fundamental Churches of America. The Plymouth Brethren, the original ecclesiastical home of Dispensational theology, continues to be a movement that nurtures and is nurtured by Dispensational theology.

Educational institutions that historically have been committed to Dispensational theology include Briarcrest Bible College (Caronport, Saskatchewan), Dallas Theological Seminary, Emmaus Bible College (Dubuque, Iowa), Grace Theological Seminary (Winona Lake, Indiana), Moody Bible Institute (Chicago), Multnomah College of the Bible (Portland, Oregon), Philadelphia College of the Bible, Talbot Theological Seminary (La Mirada, California) and Western Seminary (Portland, Oregon).

THE DISPENSATIONAL TRADITION

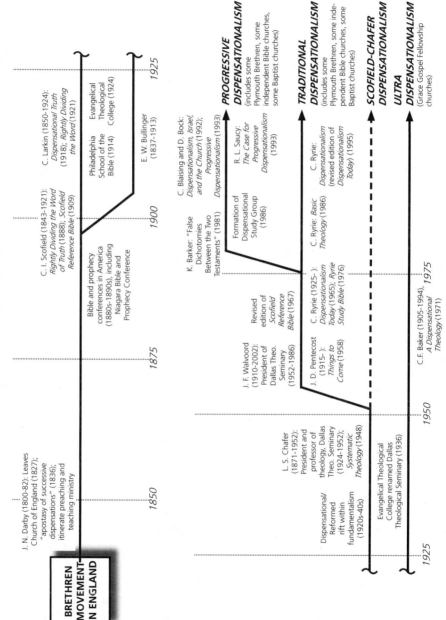

Approach: Theological and Hermeneutical Method

Role of theology. In the preface to his *Systematic Theology,* Lewis Sperry Chafer rhetorically asks, "What is the specific field of learning that distinguishes the ministerial profession if it is not the knowledge of the Bible and its doctrines?"[64] A persistent and pervasive desire to rightly interpret the Bible—the Bible in all of its parts and as a whole—is at the heart of the tradition. Simply put, for Dispensationalists, "the function of Systematic Theology is to unfold the Bible."[65] Theology—understood as Bible doctrine—is at the heart of Dispensationalism. This emphasis on Bible and theology is reflected in one of the distinctives of curriculum design at Dallas Theological Seminary. This seminary pioneered the four-year Master of Theology (Th.M.) degree for ministers. The Th.M. is one year longer than the conventional three-year Master of Divinity (M.Div.), and the reason for adding the additional year was to accommodate "additional emphasis in systematic theology, Hebrew and Old Testament exegesis, Greek and New Testament exegesis and Bible exposition."[66]

This singular devotion to Bible doctrine is not pursued, however, apart from a vigilant pursuit of a holy life and ministry. As noted above, among the concerns that were central to the father of Dispensationalism, J. N. Darby, was a concern with the nature of the church and church life. He was particularly burdened about the moral purity and spiritual holiness of those who would claim to be Christian.[67] This burden has accompanied the Dispensational theological tradition. Chafer asserts, "There can be no full or worthy apprehension of God's revealed truth by the Christian who is unscriptural or carnal. Hence the imperative of a yielded life."[68] In the twentieth century, Dispensationalism tended to flourish in ecclesiastical traditions, congregations and other ministries that pursued independence from larger denominational structures, motivated in part by a desire to have freedom to more purely conform doctrine and conduct to God's will as revealed in the Bible. An emphasis on separated, holy living, in accord with their understanding of biblical teaching, is characteristic of those contexts in which Dispensationalists' theology has most commonly flourished.[69]

Theological method. Dispensationalists have not written extensively about doctrinal or theological method per se, but they have written extensively about hermeneutical method. This is in keeping with the character of Dispensational theology as described above—theology is simply the unfolding of the Bible—and with the view of the sources of theology, particularly the Bible, as will be described below. In fact, it is not uncommon for Dispensationalists to maintain that "dispensationalism is not a theology but rather a method of interpretation helpful in grasping the progress of revelation in the Bible."[70]

C. I. Scofield instructs the readers of *Rightly Dividing the Word of Truth,* "The student is earnestly exhorted not to receive a single doctrine upon the authority of this book, but, like the noble Bereans (Acts 17:11), to search the *Scriptures* daily whether these things are so. No appeal is made to human authority. 'The anointing which ye have received of Him abideth in you, and *ye need not that any man teach you.*' (1 John 2:27)"[71] The Bible alone is the Word of God, and to heed the words of Scripture is not to follow a human authority or to receive human teaching, but rather to submit to the words of God. Thus, Scofield's disciple Lewis Sperry Chafer writes, "Systematic Theology must proceed on the basis of the belief that the Bible is, in all its parts, God's own Word to man."[72] In keeping with this belief, when Chafer delineates seven "essential requirements" for doing systematic theology, the first requirement is that "the inspiration and authority of the Scriptures are assumed."[73] Echoing this approach a generation later, Charles Ryrie states that "the belief in the truthfulness of the Bible is the basic presupposition," indeed "the watershed presupposition," of Christian theology.[74]

Historically, one of the ways in which this Dispensational devotion to the Bible has expressed itself in the doing of theology is that little conscious attention is given to the role of tradition. This is manifest in, for example, the methodological approach described by Chafer in his *Systematic Theology:*

> In this entire work on theology . . . all historical matter is omitted from the immediate discussion. . . . This is a constructive declaration of theology in its systematic form which is best not interrupted constantly with mere citation of past beliefs. In the plan followed in the Dallas Theological Seminary the student concludes his theological research with an extended course in the history of doctrine . . . and thus at a time when all the data on any aspect of truth is in view he may hope to see it in its true historical light.[75]

The theological process is protected from the premature influence of "mere" historical considerations until the truth is discerned, apart from the history of doctrine. The object of study for the theologian is "no less than the entire Bible," and "the boundaries of creeds and that limited body of truth which was recovered in the Reformation" should not render the theologian "bound by tradition or mere sectarian prejudice."[76]

This avoidance of tradition is reflected in, for example, the tensions between Reformed and Dispensational fundamentalists in the early and mid-twentieth century. As noted above, one of the most troubling points for many Reformed fundamentalists was the sharp Dispensational contrast between God's dealings with the nation of Israel in the Old Covenant and his dealings with the church

under the New Covenant. In analyzing the Dispensational posture in this dispute, Blaising suggests that "dispensationalists saw it as a tension between the
Bible and human tradition." The Dispensationalists regarded their views as
nothing other than "inductive summaries of Scripture," while the Reformed
views were thought to be distortions of scriptural teaching resulting from too
great an adherence to confessional loyalties.[77] Recently, another Dispensational
scholar, Stephen Spencer, has suggested that while previous generations of Dispensationalists did not consciously appeal to tradition, the degree of influence
of Scofield's thought and work "should nuance claims of Scripture's self-inter-
pretation, illustrating tradition's contribution."[78] Like so many Protestant traditions, the development of Dispensationalist theology has been significantly influenced by *its* tradition, even though tradition generally has not been formally
regarded as a source for theology.

Likewise, neither reason nor experience has been formally regarded as a
source for theology. The lack of conscious appeal to reason is another aspect
of the Dispensational inclination to emphasize hermeneutics rather than systematic theological method. Although Dispensationalists do not deny that their theology is reasonable or that reason is employed in arriving at theological conclusions, those conclusions are regarded not as the product of reason, but rather
as the exposition of the story and teachings of the Bible. As for personal experience, its role in theology is a derivative one rather than a formative one.[79] The
role of experience is not to reveal theological truth to us, but rather to be the
arena in which the truths taught in the Bible find their expression and impact.
Experience, understood as the way the Christian lives, both reactively and pro-
actively in relation to circumstances, is to be a reflection of the truths discerned
through careful biblical interpretation. And, as noted above, careful biblical interpretation is the heart of the Dispensational theological method.

Although the particulars of Dispensational hermeneutics are currently being
debated within the tradition, there is no debate within the tradition over the fundamental importance of biblical hermeneutics. Ryrie believes that "the consistency of one's hermeneutical principle is far more important than the defense
of one's theological system,"[80] and that, in the case of Dispensationalism, "the
hermeneutical principle is basic to the entire dispensational system. . . . It affects
everything."[81] Similarly, although Progressives disagree with Traditionalists on a
number of points regarding the history and nature of hermeneutics, as will be
seen below, they too continue to regard hermeneutics as being at the heart of
doing theology. One of the first books to explore and articulate Progressive Dispensational thought focuses specifically on "the hermeneutical reexamination of
the relationship between Israel and the church," and this largely because such

hermeneutical reexamination "contributes to the process of self-definition" within contemporary Dispensationalism.[82]

One commitment that shapes Dispensational hermeneutics is the belief that "although composed of many books, the Bible is a unity—one Book."[83] The Bible must be read and understood as a single, integrated whole. The sixty-six books of the Bible are marked by a divinely inspired unity, and rightly dividing the Scriptures entails a proper understanding of this unity. Scofield was of the conviction that "no particular portion of Scripture is to be intelligently comprehended apart from some conception of its place in the whole," and that existing approaches to studying the Bible were "fragmentary and disconnected." Consequently, he sought to display "the majestic, progressive order of the divine dealings of God with humanity, 'the increasing purpose' which runs through and links together the ages, from the beginning of the life of man to the end in eternity."[84] Chafer likewise states that the Bible "incorporates its every chapter and verse into its perfect unity and all its parts are interdependent. The mastery of any part necessitates the mastery of the whole."[85] More recently, both Ryrie and Progressive Dispensationalists seek to acknowledge the diversity and discontinuities within the Bible, but never at the expense of its unity. Darrell Bock, for example, writes that Scripture is to be read "as a canonical whole," and he indicates that Traditional Dispensationalists, such as Ryrie, share this concern.[86]

There are several views of the nature of the unity of Scripture. Scofield perceives a soteriological and christological unity, focusing on the person and work of Christ.[87] Ryrie proposes a doxological unity, consisting in the glorification of God.[88] A number of Dispensationalists have proposed a view of unity similar to that of Scofield in that it is christologically centered. For example, Elliott Johnson suggests that the continuity of the Bible "rests in the purpose of God that anticipated Christ and will be accomplished in Christ."[89] Blaising and other Progressives find canonical unity in "the goal of history, the kingdom of God . . . centered in the person and work of Jesus Christ."[90] Similarly, the doctrinal statement of Dallas Theological Seminary affirms that "all the Scriptures center about the Lord Jesus Christ in His person and work in His first and second coming, and hence . . . no portion, even of the Old Testament, is properly read, or understood unless it leads to Him."[91] Whatever diversity there is regarding the specific nature of the unity of Scripture, Dispensationalism is committed to interpreting the Bible both in light of and with a view toward displaying its integrated internal unity.

Since the mid-twentieth century, many Dispensationalists have cited the "literal" interpretation of the Bible as an identifying mark of the tradition.[92] According to Donald K. Campbell, "The insistence that the Bible must be interpreted literally" is a "foundational principle" of Dispensationalism,[93] and the second essential element in Ryrie's *sine qua non* of Dispensationalism is consistent literal interpretation.[94] According to Dwight Pentecost, literal interpretation "gives to each word the same exact meaning it would have in normal, ordinary, customary usage, whether employed in writing, speaking or thinking."[95] Dispensationalists sometimes refer to this literal approach as a "plain" or "normal" interpretation.[96] More often, literal interpretation is described by Dispensationalists, both Traditional and Progressive, as "grammatical-historical interpretation."[97] Thus, interpretation is not literal in the sense that it denies that the Bible sometimes employs figurative or symbolic language;[98] rather, "literal" interpretation, in Dispensationalism, means that "the meaning [of a Bible text] is determined by both grammatical and historical considerations."[99] Elliott Johnson indicates that literal interpretation "entails those meanings which the author intended to communicate in the expressions of the text (grammar) in the original setting (historical)."[100] Consequently, the interpretation of Scripture includes the study of etymology, lexicography and syntax, preferably with a working knowledge of the original biblical languages, as well as the historical setting in which a given book was written, including the author(s), location, occasion and audience.[101]

Dispensational writers also stress the importance of textual context, taking into consideration the concentric circles of biblical text surrounding the particular text being studied.[102] This attention to context, combined with belief in the unity of Scripture, manifests itself in attention to "the progressiveness of revelation."[103] A given verse or passage of Scripture must always be interpreted in terms of where it fits within the larger context or progression of divine revelation from Genesis to Revelation. Thus, for example, Dispensationalists seek to interpret the Old Testament in its own terms rather than allowing the New Testament to dictate the interpretation of the Old. "Dispensationalists have traditionally assumed," writes Johnson, "that the two testaments contribute in sequence to a view of progressive revelation." This progression is such that the Old Testament is interpreted on its own terms rather than being "reread" through the lens of conclusions drawn from the New Testament.[104] It is this belief in the importance of the progressive character of revelation that provides the rationale, at least in part, for the nomenclature "Progressive Dispensationalism" adopted by this recently emergent subtradition.

Alongside this attention to the progressive development of revelation is an equally vigilant attention to consistency in interpretation. In fact, many Dispensationlists believe that it is consistency in the application of literal, historical-grammatical hermeneutical principles rather than in the character of these principles themselves that distinguishes Dispensational methodology from other theological traditions. Ryrie writes, "Of course, literal interpretation is not the exclusive property of dispensationalists. . . . What, then, is the difference between the dispensationalist's use of this hermeneutical principle and the nondispensationalist's? The difference lies in the dispensationalist's claim to use the normal principle of interpretation *consistently* in *all* his study of the Bible."[105] Likewise, Thomas Ice, Dwight Pentecost, Robert Thomas and Mal Couch assert the importance of *consistent* application of the hermeneutic.[106] More recently, some Progressive Dispensationalists have rejected the notion that the principle of consistency in literal interpretation was a mark of Dispensationalism prior to the mid-twentieth century.[107]

In seeking to "work more integratively" with the diversity of the Bible, Progressive Dispensationalists advocate a "complementary" hermeneutic. Reflecting the Dispensational concern for the unity of Scripture and the progressive character of revelation, Progressives, such as Darrell Bock, propose that "what the New Testament gives us comes in alongside what God has already revealed in the Old Testament. . . . The New Testament indicates a complement to the Old Testament promises." The progress of revelation is such that "God can say more in his development of promises from the OT in the NT, but not less."[108] In the New Testament development of Old Testament promises, "both old and fresh associations are made."[109] There is both continuity and discontinuity. And, it is, according to Bock, the way in which one integrates various texts—the particular continuities and discontinuities that one identifies—rather than the character of the hermeneutical method per se that renders the differences among various systems of theology.[110]

Theology: Characteristic Beliefs

As we noted above, Dispensationalists often regard their tradition more in terms of a biblical hermeneutic than in terms of a set of specific theological doctrines. Blaising cautions against viewing Dispensationalism as, among other things, "a fixed set of confessional interpretations of Scripture."[111] Furthermore, there is an increasing recognition within Dispensationalism itself, particularly among Progressive Dispensationalists, that change and development have taken place, and that this has only increased the diversity within the tradition.[112] It is possible, nonetheless, to gain a better understanding of Dispensationalism and to see the doctrinal outworking of its history and methods by identifying theological loci that are frequently held forth as important by Dispensational theologians.

Based on Scofield's and Chafer's delineation of "well-defined time-periods" that together constitute "the divine program of the ages,"[113] one might argue that the concept and delineation of dispensations constitutes one, if not the, doctrinal distinctive of Dispensationalism. In 1965, Charles Ryrie described what many people, Dispensationalists and non-Dispensationalists alike, have understood to be the essential characteristics of Dispensationalism, and he clearly indicated that belief in dispensations was not one of them. As noted earlier, Ryrie's list of the indispensable components of Dispensationalism consisted in maintaining the distinction between Israel and the church, consistently employing a literal or historical-grammatical hermeneutic, and recognizing that the underlying purpose of God in the world is his own glory.[114] In his foreword to *Dictionary of Premillennial Theology,* editor Mal Couch posits "the distinctives of dispensational teaching" as the inspiration and inerrancy of the Bible, a consistent application of a literal or historical-grammatical hermeneutic, the progressive character of divine revelation, a recognition of distinct economies or dispensations over the course of biblical history, a particular understanding of the nature and sequence of eschatological events (e.g., pretribulational rapture), and a recognition that the ultimate goal of providence is to bring glory to God.[115] According to Willis and Master, the essentials of Dispensationalism are a proper understanding of the Davidic Covenant, the distinction between Israel and the church, and a literal, historical-grammatical hermeneutic.[116] In *Progressive Dispensationalism,* Blaising identifies "common features" of the Dispensational tradition: a high view of the authority of Scripture, the identification of successive dispensations throughout history, affirmation of the uniqueness and practical significance of the church, affirmation of the this-worldly relevance of biblical prophecy, belief in a future, premillennial return and rule of Jesus Christ, belief in the rapture of the church prior to the time of eschatological tribulation, and belief in an earthly and eternal future for the nation of Israel.[117] Steven Spencer, a Progressive Dispensationalist, observes that Dispensationalism "has consistently emphasized the authority of Scripture, discontinuities in the divine administration of history, the uniqueness of the church and of certain features of grace for the dispensation of the church (which began at Pentecost), the practical significance of the universal church, the theological relevance of biblical apocalyptic and prophecy, a futurist premillennialism, the imminent return of Christ, and a national future for Israel."[118] When, for the purposes of their book *Progressive Dispensationalism,* Blaising and Bock focus on a limited range of topics, they structure their discussion around dispensations, covenants and the kingdom of God.

For the purposes of this chapter, we will consider two of the recurring topics in these lists. The distinction between Israel and the church is often cited as an essential of Dispensationalism, and thus it warrants consideration here. And, the theology of biblical covenants, though not always explicitly evident, is a key to many of the theological concepts noted above.[119] An understanding of Dispensational beliefs regarding the biblical covenants reinforces the Israel/church distinction and provides a foundation for understanding other commonly held Dispensational beliefs regarding topics such as prophecy, premillennialism and the kingdom of God.

Israel and the church. If there is one theological tenet that Dispensationalists of all kinds repeatedly place at the heart of the tradition, it is the belief in the respective characters of and distinctions between the nation of Israel and the church. The doctrinal statement of Dallas Theological Seminary affirms that the church is "the body and bride of Christ, which began at Pentecost and is completely distinct from Israel," and the doctrinal statement of Philadelphia College of the Bible sets forth the same view.[120] In the first chapter of *Rightly Dividing the Word of Truth,* titled "The Jew, the Gentile, and the Church of God," Scofield writes, "It may safely be said that the Judaizing of the Church has done more to hinder her progress, pervert her mission, and destroy her spirituality, than all other causes combined."[121] In the opening chapter of his *Systematic Theology,* Chafer outlines twenty-four distinctions between Israel and the church, which are essential to recognizing the divine purpose of God.[122] Ryrie refers to this distinction as the "essence" and "touchstone" of Dispensationalism,[123] and Donald Campbell views it as "an essential mark."[124] In *The Case for Progressive Dispensationalism,* Robert Saucy writes, "The key distinctive of dispensational theology . . . is the recognition of Israel as a nation set apart from the other nations by God for the service of universal salvation for all peoples."[125] In the context of comparing Traditional and Progressive Dispensationalism, Herbert Bateman says, "Simply put, the basic unifying issue for all dispensationalists is that Israel is not the church."[126]

Basis of the distinction between Israel and the church. Dispensationalists affirm an abiding distinction between Israel and the church because that is what they believe the Bible teaches, as discerned through a responsible grammatical-historical reading. In *Israel in Prophecy,* John Walvoord observes that in the New Testament there is simply "no teaching that the nation of Israel as such becomes the church as such,"[127] and Progressive Dispensationalists agree.[128] Walvoord asks rhetorically whether Gentile Christians are ever designated "Israelites" in the Bible.[129] No, not even in the reference to "the Israel of God" in Galatians 6:16. This is not a reference to the present reality of the church, but rather an eschatological reference to "that body of ethnic Israel who are saved at the Messiah's return."[130]

Beyond arguments from silence—that is, the absence of verses equating the church with Israel—Dispensationalists note many instances of the expressed teaching of Scripture that undergird the distinction. Walvoord observes that "the word 'Israel' is used in the New Testament in the same sense as in the Old and . . . promises to Israel continue to be inviolate, including their future restoration."[131] Saucy concurs that the term *Israel* retains in the New Testament the same referent it had in the Old Testament: "the national ethnic people" of the Jews.[132] In the book of Acts (e.g., Acts 3:12; 4:8, 10; 5:21, 31, 35; 21:28) and elsewhere (e.g., Rom 9:3-5; 10:1), Israel is regarded as a distinct nation, separate from the church.[133] In other passages (e.g., Eph 2:12), "Gentiles as such are expressly excluded."[134] As Romans 9 indicates, Gentile Christians are "the spiritual seed of Abraham who received the promise of blessing to all nations which was to come through Abraham." However, "This does not mean . . . that they received the promises that came through Jacob to the nation of Israel."[135] The promises that God made to the nation of Israel have been and will continue to be honored and fulfilled by God as promises to Israel.

Romans 11 is regarded by Dispensationalists as one of the more important chapters of Scripture with regard to the distinction between Israel and the church. According to John Witmer, Romans 9—10 indicates that "God's personal righteousness and His provided righteousness for people has been displayed primarily in Israel's rejecting Christ and rebelling against God, and in God's choosing and turning to Gentiles in grace."[136] Yet, when we reach Romans 11, the theme is, according to Scofield and others, that "Israel has not been forever set aside,"[137] and Ryrie says, "In this chapter Paul assures us that God has not forgotten His people, the Jews, and His promises to them."[138] Both Scofield and Ryrie also make corresponding observations regarding the church, namely, that "Paul does not assert that the O.T. promises to Israel have been transferred to the largely Gentile Church."[139] Blaising writes, "God has not rejected His people (11:2). The hardening of Israel is partial and temporary (11:5),"[140] and J. Lanier Burns notes that the theme for Romans 11 is stated in verse 2: "God has not cast off his people whom he foreknew."[141] The promises made to Israel in the Old Testament are not annulled by God's creation of and work in the church reported in the New Testament. In this understanding, one clearly sees at work the Traditional Dispensational emphasis on a consistent literal hermeneutic, maintaining a consistent interpretation of "Israel" into and throughout the New Testament; and one sees the Progressive complementary hermeneutic in which Old Testament promises to Israel are maintained even while, in some respects, they are expanded to include the church.

Description of the distinction between Israel and the church. Although all Dispensationalists affirm an abiding distinction between Israel and the church, details as to the nature and extent of the distinction have been and continue to be debated.[142] In this regard, a historical development can be observed.[143] In the nineteenth century and through the first half of the twentieth, under the theological leadership of people such as Arno Gaebelein, Clarence Larkin, Scofield and Chafer, most Dispensationalists believed that there were two peoples of God, each with its own eternal sphere: the Jews were God's earthly people, and the church consisted of God's heavenly people. In *Rightly Dividing the Word of Truth,* for example, Scofield indicates that Israel and the church differ with respect to origin, calling, promise, worship, principles of conduct and future destiny.[144] By the 1950s, a shift or revision was developing through the work of people such as Alva McClain, Walvoord, Pentecost and Ryrie. In this revision, the eternal dimension of the distinction was dropped, so that it was no longer fundamentally a distinction between earthly and heavenly, but rather an organizational distinction between two groups of people. Recently, Progressive Dispensationalists have further reduced the discontinuity between Israel and the church, though they have not eliminated it. The church is not regarded as a redeemed group separate from and alongside Israel; rather, the church and Israel both share in "the same messianic kingdom of salvation history."[145] Yet, a distinction is maintained. The New Testament never teaches, says Blaising, that God's gracious work in and through the church constitutes "a *replacement* of the specific hopes of Israel," though they are *"compatible or complementary.*"[146] With other Dispensationalists, the Progressives continue to view the church as constituting "a *new manifestation of grace,* a new dispensation in the history of redemption."[147] Israel is not "swallowed up" into the church. National Israel has a future as national Israel. Saucy indicates that what distinguishes the church from Israel is not "spiritual realities," but rather the church's "lack of national characteristics." Israel was "formed and chosen as a nation among nations," whereas the church, while existing as an assembly, does not exist as a nation.[148] All of God's Old Covenant promises to Israel will be fulfilled in and through Israel.[149]

Significance of the distinction between Israel and the church. It is important that God's people glorify him by affirming and living in accord with God's revealed will, and the distinction between Israel and the church needs to be affirmed because this is what the Bible teaches. It is important to rightly divide the Word of Truth. The distinction needs to be recognized so that biblical principles and promises intended for Israel are not misapplied to the church. It is important that God's work in and for Israel be recognized, and that the church conduct itself in accord with God's purposes for the church. The distinction needs to be maintained so that Christians rightly discern and work in accord with God's unfolding eschatological, redemptive plan for the ages as revealed in the Bible. An important component in discerning God's eschatological plan for the ages, not least the roles of Israel and the church, is a proper understanding of the major biblical covenants.

The covenants. "Unless the promises made to Israel in their covenants are clearly understood, prophecy of future events will remain in a state of confusion."[150] Elliott Johnson says that the Old Testament covenants "frame in stable terms the outworking of God's purposes with man on earth and in history."[151] Blaising states that covenants constitute "the structure by which the history of redemption is carried out."[152] A correct literal interpretation of the biblical covenants provides a structure for understanding God's eternal plan.

The biblical covenants. A divine covenant can be defined as "a declaration by God concerning His voluntarily assumed responsibility in grace toward an individual, a family, a nation, or mankind as a whole."[153] God takes the initiative. God voluntarily and graciously makes the first move to redemptively engage people in spiritual need. God not only initiates this covenant relationship, but also is the one who will assure that the promises associated with the covenant will be fulfilled. Thus, the major biblical covenants are "unconditional," sometimes being referred to as "unilateral" or "grant" covenants.[154] Their fulfillment— their literal fulfillment—is ultimately dependent upon the one who initiated them, the God of Israel. Furthermore, the covenants were made with Israel. Israel was God's covenant people. Pentecost states that Israel's hopes were based on the "determinative covenants which God made with them," and that these covenants "confirmed certain national hopes and blessing and necessitate the preservation, continuity, and restoration of the nation if they are to be fulfilled literally."[155] This does not limit God's blessings or redemptive work to Israel, for God's desire is to redeem the world. Israel is, however, the nation through which God has promised to bring redemptive blessings to the world. As Blaising says, "The history of the covenants prior to Jesus Christ is the story of the divine promise to bless all life on earth—all nations and the people that compose them."[156] Dispensationalists take into consideration the entire range of biblical covenants, but the Abrahamic, Davidic and New Covenants are seen to be of particular significance.[157] These three covenants are at the heart of a proper understanding of God's unfolding eschatological plan, including, though not limited to, his will for Israel and the church.[158]

The Abrahamic Covenant. According to Genesis 15:18-19, God covenanted with Abram to give to his descendants a specific territory of land, the boundaries of which are delineated in the passage. This covenant is the formal formulation of the relationship described in Genesis 12:1-3, where God says to Abram, "Go from your country and your kindred and your father's house to the land that I will show you. I will make of you a great nation, and I will bless you, and make your name great, so that you will be a blessing. I will bless those who bless you, and the one who curses you I will curse; and in you all the families of the earth shall be blessed."[159] The Abrahamic Covenant is fundamental. It is "the foundational promise on which the other covenants depend."[160] "All subsequent covenant promises," writes Pentecost, "are reiterations, enlargements, and clarifications of parts of this original covenant made through Abraham with the nation and establish certain national promises and hopes."[161] And Blaising says, "The story of the Bible, from Abraham on, is the story of God's relationship with human beings as set forth in this covenant and developed from it as its features are expanded and detailed in subsequent revelation."[162]

The fulfillment of the Abrahamic Covenant is progressive over the course of redemptive history, and it entails promises pertaining to land, descendants and blessings.[163] The covenant was instituted with Abraham, but its fulfillment was not inaugurated with him.[164] That would wait. The "progressive confirmation and expansion [of the covenantal structure] tak[es] place in a succession of new dispensations which come into existence as subsequent covenants are revealed, inaugurated, and fulfilled in human experience."[165] And, being an unconditional covenant, the covenantal relationship between God and his people "remains in force through the generations, guiding the history of redemption to a blessed conclusion."[166] The people may be disobedient and disloyal to the covenant, and such offenses are punishable. However, the unconditional nature of the covenant means that the punishment will not abide forever, and God's promises will be fulfilled.[167] In and through Christ, the covenant "is and will be fulfilled."[168] The church does not replace Israel in the scheme of fulfillment; rather, those people who are the church participate in the fulfillment and share in the spiritual blessings of the covenant by virtue of being spiritual descendants of Abraham. Ultimately, as Genesis 12:1-3 and 15:18-19 indicate, the blessings of the covenant will extend to all nations and will include physical blessings, such as the land identified in Genesis 15. Thus, Saucy writes, "while there is in the present salvation in Christ a partial fulfillment of the spiritual blessing promised to all people through Abraham and his seed, many aspects of the promise remain to be fulfilled, especially those dealing with the 'great nation' seed and the 'land,' but also the final inheritance of spiritual salvation."[169] And Jesus' mediation of the blessings of the Abrahamic Covenant constitutes one dimension of his "Davidic ministry."[170]

The Davidic Covenant. Second Samuel 7:9-16 (cf. 1 Chron 17:4-15) records a message from God to David. Speaking on behalf of God, the prophet Nathan says to David,

> I will make for you a great name . . . And I will appoint a place for my people
> Israel and will plant them, so that they may live in their own place. . . . The LORD
> will make you a house. When your days are fulfilled and you lie down with your
> ancestors, I will raise up your offspring after you, who shall come forth from your
> body, and I will establish his kingdom. He shall build a house for my name, and I
> will establish the throne of his kingdom forever. . . . Your house and your kingdom
> shall be made sure forever before me; your throne shall be established forever.

This covenant "amplifies" the Abrahamic Covenant,[171] promising that David's
throne, lineage and kingdom will be without end.[172] According to Blaising, the
Davidic Covenant is both "*part* of the blessing" of the Abrahamic Covenant and
"the *means* by which" the Abrahamic blessings will come to pass.[173] The promise to bless the descendants of Abraham is fulfilled, in part, through a blessed
king in the Davidic line, and it is through this king that the Abrahamic blessing
for the many will be mediated.

In every generation, a descendant of David will be born who will possess
the qualifications to be king, and the Lord will, at his discretion, enthrone
them.[174] As Psalm 89:3-4 says, "You said, 'I have made a covenant with my chosen one, I have sworn to my servant David: "I will establish your descendants
forever, and build your throne for all generations.""" And, these promises certainly and literally will be fulfilled, for like the Abrahamic Covenant, the Davidic
Covenant is unconditional, ultimately dependent upon God for its fulfillment.
God provides the Christ, who is the Davidic king, the King of Israel.[175] The New
Testament teaches, says Saucy, that "the fulfillment of the Davidic Covenant begins in the coming of Jesus as the promised seed of David. . . . Through his victorious life, death, and resurrection Jesus has been exalted to the position of
highest honor and supreme authority at the right hand of God as the Messiah,
the Davidic king."[176] The fulfillment of the Davidic Covenant is an instance of
the already–not yet perspective of Scripture. Commenting on Psalm 89, Hugh
Ross writes, "Taken literally [this Psalm] supports the position that Christ is *now*
sitting on David's throne in heaven but *will* rule on his throne on earth."[177] The
fulfillment has already begun with the life, death and resurrection of Jesus; and
the fulfillment is not yet complete, awaiting the full reign of Christ over a messianic kingdom.[178] In that kingdom, as Psalm 132:17-18 says, the Lord "will cause
a horn to sprout up for David; I have prepared a lamp for my anointed one. His
enemies I will clothe with disgrace, but on him, his crown will gleam."

The New Covenant. This millennial kingdom will also be the scene of the ultimate fulfillment of the New Covenant. Jeremiah 31:33-34 indicates that the
Lord will make a covenant with Israel whereby he says, "I will put my law
within them, and I will write it on their hearts; and I will be their God, and they

shall be my people. . . . They shall all know me, from the least of them to the greatest, says the LORD; for I will forgive their iniquity, and remember their sin no more." In the eschatological future, God's redemptive work in, for and through Israel will be completed, as described in this covenant. There are, however, three different understandings among Dispensationalists as to how redemption history unfolds between the time of Jeremiah and the eschaton. The differences among these three views tend to center on differing concepts of the relationship among the biblical covenants and of the way the New Testament understands Old Testament teaching regarding the New Covenant.

Chafer, the "early" Charles Ryrie and others held that none of the benefits of this New Covenant would be applied to the church; rather, a second New Covenant, "a heavenly covenant for the heavenly people," was made with, and is now being fulfilled with respect to, the church.[179] The New Covenant referred to in Jeremiah 31 would be fulfilled in and its benefits applied only to Israel, and this would occur in the millennium. A second view is that there is only one New Covenant, but that there is a "two-fold application; one to Israel in the future and one to the church now."[180] In this view, the church is the beneficiary of some *spiritual* blessings under the New Covenant, but the comprehensive—both spiritual and physical—application and fulfillment of it will occur in the millennium, when all the promises to Israel as literally stated in the Old Testament are fulfilled.[181] More recently, Progressive Dispensationalists have advanced a third view, in which the New Covenant is seen as progressively expanding in its application and fulfillment from the time of the Old Testament and Israel, through the time of the New Testament and the church, and into the millennium, when it will be completely and finally fulfilled in both the church and Israel.[182] This progressive development honors and incorporates the provisions of the Abrahamic Covenant while nonetheless expanding to include the church.[183] The God of Abraham and David, the God of the Messiah Jesus Christ, will bring to completion the plan for the ages that he has begun.

Conclusion: Rightly Dividing the Scriptures

In an essay titled "Dispensationalism Tomorrow," Herbert Bateman remarks that Dispensationalism is "a tradition driven by a desire to be scriptural and a recognition that infallibility is what the text—not its interpreters—possesses."[184] Currently, this desire and recognition are manifest in the continuing formulation of Progressive Dispensationalism and in the discussion that this has precipitated within the tradition. Contrary to the stereotypes that associate Dispensationalism with extravagantly detailed eschatological charts, Dispensationalism continues to encompass a variety of repeatedly reexamined viewpoints. At the same time, there is continuity amidst this diversity. From the early Plymouth Brethren, to my grandparents who diligently studied their *Scofield Reference Bible,* to the work of scholars such as Dwight Pentecost and Charles Ryrie, to the Progressive Dispensationalists of today, the Dispensational tradition has sought to rightly divide the Scriptures. Through reverent and methodical study of the Bible, Dispensationalists seek to discern God's plan for the ages as revealed in the Scriptures. They have sought to know this plan so that they might live and minister in accord with it. Rightly dividing the Bible provides the foundation and guidance for rightly serving the God of the Bible.

FOR FURTHER STUDY

The endnotes contain citations of many useful resources, most of them written from within the Dispensational tradition. A brief list of resources for further study follows here. Some of these resources consider Dispensationalism in general, while others focus on history and/or theology.

Reference Works

Couch, Mal, ed. *Dictionary of Premillennial Theology.* Grand Rapids: Kregel, 1996.

Survey Resources

Blaising, Craig A., and Darrell L. Bock. *Progressive Dispensationalism.* Wheaton, Ill.: BridgePoint, 1993.

Ryrie, Charles. *Dispensationalism.* Rev. ed. Chicago: Moody, 1995.

Primary Historical and Theological Resources

Blaising, Craig A., and Darrell L. Bock, *Progressive Dispensationalism.* Wheaton, Ill.: BridgePoint, 1993.

Chafer, Lewis Sperry. *Systematic Theology.* 8 vols. Dallas: Dallas Seminary Press, 1947-1948.

Ryrie, Charles C. *Basic Theology.* Wheaton, Ill.: Victor, 1986.

Recent and Current Theological Explorations

Bateman, Herbert W., IV, ed. *Three Central Issues in Contemporary Dispensationalism: A Comparison of Traditional and Progressive Views.* Grand Rapids: Kregel, 1999.

Bigalke, Ron J. *Progressive Dispensationalism: An Analysis of the Movement and Defense of Traditional Dispensationalism.* Lanham, Md.: University Press of

America, 2005.

Blaising, Craig A., and Darrell L. Bock, eds. *Dispensationalism, Israel and the Church*. Grand Rapids: Zondervan, 1992.

Moore, Russell D. "Till Every Foe Is Vanquished: Emerging Sociopolitical Implications of Progressive Dispensational Eschatology," in *Looking into the Future: Evangelical Studies in Eschatology*, pp. 342-61. Edited by David W. Baker. Grand Rapids: Baker, 2001.

Saucy, Robert L. *The Case for Progressive Dispensationalism*. Grand Rapids: Zondervan, 1993.

9 ▪ The Spirit of Continuity

PENTECOSTAL THEOLOGY

It was the inductive study of the Bible that led the students at Bethel Bible school in Topeka, Kansas, in 1900, to expect a baptism in the Spirit with the accompanying sign of speaking in tongues. When they in fact experienced precisely what they thought the Bible was teaching, they were then able to affirm the continuity between Biblical concept and experiential reality.

William W. Menzies, in *Conference on the Holy Spirit Digest*

There is a continuity of the ways in which God works in the world from the time of the Resurrection to the Second Coming.

Gordon L. Anderson, "Pentecostal Hermeneutics: Part II"

Through the experience of the Holy Spirit, modern readers span the time and cultural differences between them and the ancient author. . . . The common experience of the ancient author and modern reader lies in their shared faith in Christ and in their walk in the Spirit, whom the exalted Lord poured out at Pentecost (Acts 2:33).

French L. Arrington, *Christian Doctrine: A Pentecostal Perspective*

We entered the school gymnasium a few minutes before the service was to begin. With our daughters between Nancy and me, we all took our seats on the folding chairs. The activity in the gathering crowd increased as people hurried to get to their seats and the worship leader walked onto the platform. With warmth and enthusiasm he welcomed the congregation to this time of praising the Lord. Suddenly, drums, saxophone, guitars, a piano and hundreds of voices broke into a fast-paced, upbeat song of praise, and the service was under way. People rose to their feet and enthusiastically burst out singing. When the first song was finished, the leader and many of the people earnestly praised God out loud with a heartfelt "Praise Jesus!" or "Praise you, Holy Spirit!" or "Thank you Father," and some seemed to be speaking in words and phrases that I did not understand. After a few words of inspiration and motivation from the leader, we launched into the next praise song. And so this opening portion of the service went, for twenty-five high-energy minutes. The nearly two hours we spent in that service were marked by joy and enthusiasm, just like, someone near us said, we see in the New Testament.

Context: Historical and Ecclesiastical Background

Historical origins and development. Pentecostalism is a twentieth-century phenomenon with roots in Wesleyan-Holiness and Higher Life movements of the nineteenth century.[1] There are other late-nineteenth-century Christian streams that, to varying degrees, influenced the shape of early Pentecostalism, such as restorationism, African American Christianity, millennialism and divine healing.[2] Yet, as historian Stanley Burgess notes, "virtually every concept as well as most of the vocabulary and imagery of twentieth-century Pentecostalism came from these Wesleyan-Holiness and Higher Life traditions."[3] Thus, although modern Pentecostalism developed into a formalized movement in the United States, its roots are in the United Kingdom.[4]

There was significant talk about and experience of the baptism in the Holy Spirit for at least a century before defining events unfolded in America at the beginning of the twentieth century. According to Pentecostal historian Vinson Synan, twentieth-century American Pentecostalism "was born in a holiness cradle," a cradle that began to rock in British Methodism during the eighteenth century.[5] It was here that the notion of a "second blessing"—a crisis experience subsequent to conversion—flourished. It was here that the "entire sanctification" of "Christian perfection" was taught and pursued.[6] Although the Holiness movements of the nineteenth century were quite diverse, most of them viewed this transformation of life in terms of a Wesleyan scheme of sanctification.[7] As the term *holiness* indicates, the people and organizations associated with these movements emphasized the radical transformation, both inward and outward, of those who claim to be Christian. In true Methodist fashion, holiness of life was most fully realized as the result of a second work of grace (entire sanctification), which is distinct from and subsequent to the first work of grace (regeneration). This second work of grace results in purity of heart and power for living the Christian life. Yet, the Holy Spirit is not bound by denominations.

A Presbyterian minister, Edward Irving (1792-1834), gave initial leadership to a charismatic renewal in the early 1830s. Encouraging the manifestation of New

Testament gifts, including speaking in tongues and prophecy, he established the Catholic Apostolic Church. Although Irving eventually was removed from a leadership role, in part because he never experienced speaking in tongues, the church continued well into the 1830s. By the 1870s, a variety of Higher Life movements flourished, most notably the Keswick movement.[8] This movement emerged in northwestern England in 1875 at the first meeting of the Keswick Convention for the Promotion of Scriptural Holiness. It shared with the Methodist-Holiness movement an emphasis on the importance of a second, sanctifying work of grace subsequent to conversion. However, whereas the Methodist-Holiness movement claimed that purity was the source of power, Keswick emphasized the indwelling presence of the Holy Spirit and did not teach the removal of the Christian's carnal nature.

Impulses from these movements came to "Pentecostal" fruition in a cluster of dramatic events in the opening years of the twentieth century. No single individual can be identified as the founder of the modern Pentecostal movement. Rather, "like the New Testament days, communication and instruction were carried on through letters, tracts, testimonies and, most importantly, through an ethos growing out of and centered in revivalistic, participatory, populist-oriented worship."[9] In the United States, this revivalistic, participatory, populist worship was spread throughout the nineteenth century through hundreds of camp meetings, and in 1867, the National Camp Meeting Association for the Promotion of Holiness was founded under the leadership of Methodist minister John Inskip (1816-1884). By the end of the century, the Holiness movement in America was so large and so fractured, largely due to differing views of the normative pattern of sanctification, that more than twenty denominations were founded during the 1890s. These included the Pentecostal Church of the Nazarene, the Pentecostal Holiness Church and the Fire-Baptized Holiness Church.[10]

Pentecostal historians identify a number of revivals that might be regarded as constituting the beginning of modern Pentecostalism, but two of these in particular launched people and theological ideas that proved formative in the beginning of the Pentecostal movement and the formulation of its theology: Topeka, Kansas, in 1901, and Los Angeles, California, in 1906.[11] In 1900, Charles Fox Parham (1873-1929) founded Bethel Bible College in Topeka, Kansas. Originally a minister in the Methodist Episcopal Church, he left the denomination in the late 1890s to become an independent Holiness preacher, proclaiming sanctification as a second work of grace, the reality of divine healing, and a third work, the baptism in the Holy Ghost. Within months of the first students' arrival at Bethel Bible College, an event took place that today is widely considered as constituting the beginning of modern Pentecostalism in North America.[12]

Parham instructed students to study the book of Acts in order to determine biblical teaching regarding evidence of baptism in the Holy Spirit. The students concluded that speaking in tongues, or "glossolalia,"[13] is the evidence. A few days later, during a New Year's watch-night service, Agnes N. Ozman (1870-1937), a student, asked Parham to lay hands on her and pray that she would be baptized in the Holy Spirit, and that this would be evidenced by speaking in tongues. Early in the morning of January 1, 1901, Agnes Ozman spoke in what was reported to be Chinese, a language unknown to her, and she spoke in Chinese exclusively for the next three days, being unable to speak or write in English.[14] With this event, the modern Pentecostal movement began.[15]

Other students prayed for and experienced baptism in the Holy Spirit, evidenced by speaking in tongues. Some time later, Parham himself had a similar experience. During the next four years, Parham undertook an itinerant preaching and revival ministry. In the fall of 1905, he established another school, the Bible Training School, in Houston, Texas. There he taught that baptism in the Holy Spirit is a "third experience," distinct in time and nature from the "second blessing" of sanctification.[16] Among the students at the school was an African American Baptist minister, William J. Seymour (1870-1922), who had embraced many Holiness teachings. Within a year, Seymour would be instrumental in the beginning of the landmark Azusa Street revival.

Edith Blumhofer points out that American Pentecostals, who find their roots in Topeka, Kansas, in 1901, are commonly referred to as "classical Pentecostals."[17] Further, Charles Parham's teachings proved to be seminal to the development of a distinctively Pentecostal theology. Parham has been called "the doctrinal father" of Pentecostalism, who "bequeathed to the Pentecostal movement its definitive hermeneutics, and consequently, its definitive theology and apologetics."[18] He was animated by the conviction that God intended "to repeat in contemporary America the awe-inspiring phenomena of early Christianity."[19] Central to Parham's theology were the beliefs that baptism in the Spirit is part of the normal Christian experience, and that speaking in tongues is the evidence of this Spirit baptism. Beginning with the events and teachings associated with Parham, this connection between Spirit baptism and glossolalia has "given identity and continuity to" the Pentecostal movement.[20]

The experiences and the interpretations of them that arose in Topeka gained reinforcement five years later in Los Angeles, where, at the Azusa Street Mission, a revival characterized by speaking in tongues and other "evidences" broke out. William Seymour, formerly a student at Parham's school in Texas, accepted an invitation to preach at the mission, and in January of 1906, he traveled to Los Angeles from his home in Houston. This son of former slaves, a man of humble spirit, began preaching in the home of Richard Asbury, on Bonnie Brae Street. Although he had never spoken in tongues before, on April 9, Seymour, and seven other people, did so at the mission. Soon the crowds were too large to be accommodated in the house, so Seymour obtained use of a larger, dilapidated facility at 312 Azusa Street, in a nonresidential area of Los Angeles. At this new location the revival grew in both fervor and numbers. Furthermore, the "numbers" transcended numerous social and cultural boundaries. Walter Hollenweger says that at Azusa Street "white bishops and black workers, men and women, Asians and Mexicans, white professors and black laundry women came together as equals."[21] This boundary-crossing, in addition to the dramatic and unusual nature of the religion preached and experienced, elicited the attention of both the secular press and the Protestant religious establishment—the former were curious, the latter, including both Holiness and mainline churches, were antagonistic.[22]

In October of 1906, Seymour's former teacher, Charles Parham, came to Azusa Street to preach. He was incensed by what he found. The forms and degrees of ecstatic behavior that characterized the meetings were, in his estimation, fanatical and not the work of the Holy Spirit. The people of Azusa Street bristled at Parham's critique, taking exception to his observations and eventually asking him to leave. Within five years of its beginning, the Pentecostal movement had gained a momentum and a character that left the founder alienated and on the fringes of the movement for the rest of his life. Yet, under Seymour's leadership the Azusa Street revival would last another three years, continuing into 1909, and, along with the events in Topeka, has come to be regarded as a revival to which "directly or indirectly, practically all of the pentecostal groups in existence can trace their lineage."[23] One historian describes Azusa Street as the "Grand Central Station" of the Pentecostal movement, with virtually all the key leaders of the early movement having some connection with the revival.[24] The most significant dimension of the revival and its teachings was the identification of tongues as *the* initial evidence of baptism in the Holy Spirit. Azusa Street was "the catalyst that congealed tongue-speaking into a fully defined doctrine."[25] And, Azusa Street was not the only place where Pentecostal revival was flourishing. From 1906 to 1909, Pentecostal experiences and teachings were advancing in Illinois, New York and large portions of the southern United States. Occasionally the revival spread in conjunction with the ministry of someone who had visited Azusa Street. For example, in November 1906, G. B. Cashwell traveled from North Carolina to Azusa Street, where he experienced the baptism in the Holy Spirit, and then he carried his report and the teaching about baptism in the Holy Spirit back to North Carolina as well as to a number of states throughout the south.[26]

The years following Azusa Street were marked not only by the rapid spread of Pentecostal experiences and teaching, but also by divisions, both racial and theological. The racial integration that was regarded by participants as one of the signs of God's blessing on the Azusa Street revival gradually dissolved.[27] With the ministry of Seymour and the demographics of Azusa Street in mind, Iain Mac-Robert summarizes the early history of Pentecostalism as consisting in "black birth, interracial infancy, and segregated childhood."[28] Divisions within the movement also emerged over specific points of theological teaching, complete with charges of heresy.[29] The first of these divisions was what one historian characterizes as "the sanctification schism."[30] Between 1906 and 1914 there was heated disagreement over the course or pattern of sanctification. Being true to Pentecostalism's Wesleyan roots, one side maintained that sanctification is a second and abrupt blessing, and to this they added the Pentecostal teaching of a third blessing, the baptism in the Holy Spirit. Thus, this constituted a three-step understanding of the course of the Christian life. In contrast with this there emerged a two-step view. This two-step account of the Christian life did not minimize the importance of sanctification, but it did deny that sanctification is a second work of grace distinct from and subsequent to conversion. Because, according to this view, sanctification is included along with conversion in the completed work of Christ at Calvary, this two-step account became known as the "Finished Work" view. This theology was embraced largely by those who entered Pentecostalism from non-Wesleyan-Holiness backgrounds. William Durham (1873-1912), of the North Avenue Mission in Chicago, first popularized Finished Work teaching.[31] He visited Azusa Street, experienced the baptism in the Holy Spirit, and returned to Chicago, where from 1907 until 1911 he aggressively promoted belief in two-step sanctification. Durham died in 1912, but significant numbers of people had already come to embrace this Finished Work view.

Divisions over the theology of sanctification came to be reflected in the young Pentecostal denominations. The Pentecostal-Holiness Church, the Church of God and the Church of God in Christ maintained the Holiness-rooted view of sanctification as a distinct, second work of grace, while many independent missions and assemblies embraced the Finished Work view of sanctification as a gradual two-step process beginning at conversion. The largest Pentecostal denomination, the Assemblies of God, reached something of a "compromise . . . acceptable to those of both persuasions" but nonetheless "disentangled itself further" from those who affirmed Holiness theology.[32] Today, approximately one-half of Pentecostals in the United States affirm three-step Holiness teaching and one-half affirm two-step Finished Work teaching.[33]

As the sides in the sanctification controversy were agreeing to disagree, another doctrinal schism disrupted the Pentecostal movement. This time it centered on a doctrine closer to more broadly defined Christian orthodoxy: the doctrine of the Trinity. By 1913, preachers within the movement were questioning, if not rejecting, traditional Trinitarian teaching. Among the most influential of these preachers was Frank J. Ewart (1876-1947). Ewart concluded that "Jesus" was the name of God, and that "Father," "Son" and "Holy Ghost" were simply ways of referring to different roles or functions of God, not to three persons of a Godhead. One conclusion drawn from this view was that any baptism performed in the name of "the Father, Son and Holy Spirit" was invalid. So, along with some colleagues, Ewart began to baptize (or rebaptize) people in the name of Jesus only. By the end of 1915, the Oneness movement was so strong that it had the potential to "take over" Pentecostalism.[34]

In 1916, largely in response to this controversy, the Assemblies of God drafted a Statement of Fundamental Truths. Until this time, some Pentecostal denominations, including the Assemblies of God, had been without creeds, if not anticreedal. Nonetheless, the theological issues were important enough and the popularity of "Jesus' Name" or Oneness doctrine was widespread enough that the General Council of the Assemblies of God chose to adopt a doctrinal statement that included a clear affirmation of traditional Trinitarian doctrine. Although the document covers the whole range of doctrine in seventeen articles, fully one-third of it is devoted to the article on "The Essentials As To The Godhead," a clear and detailed affirmation of the Godhead of three "persons."[35] The Statement of Fundamental Truths precipitated further division: rather than affirm this Trinitarian statement, 156 out of 585 preachers chose to leave the ranks of the Assemblies of God.[36] The following year, this defection was institutionalized with the establishment of another denomination, the Pentecostal Assemblies of the World. This "Jesus' Name" or "Oneness" Pentecostal group was begun under the leadership of an African American minister, Garfield T. Haywood (d. 1931). The denomination was racially mixed at the outset, but by 1924, the whites had left and formed the Pentecostal Ministerial Alliance.[37] Other Oneness groups arose, such as the Pentecostal Church, Incorporated, and the United Pentecostal Church, with many African American Pentecostals being associated with Oneness denominations. It is estimated that today, approximately one-fifth of Pentecostals in the United States stand within this unitarian tradition.[38]

Pentecostal scholar Russell Spittler offers an insightful analysis of these three theologically rooted events in the early history of Pentecostalism—the schisms over sanctification and the Trinity, and the creation of a statement of faith by the Assemblies of God. Spittler affirms that, as noted above, early Pentecostal theology emerged from nineteenth-century Holiness and Higher Life movements.

He goes on to say, "For this reason, Pentecostal theology in the first decades, say deep into the 1930s, had no reason to develop its own full-orbed doctrinal handbooks. The central belief, the baptism in the Holy Spirit, was set on top of the commonly accepted conservative Christian orthodoxy."[39] Thus, it is not surprising that differences over sanctification would emerge, for the doctrine of the baptism in the Holy Spirit constituted the distinctive and central point of theological reflection by Pentecostals. Sanctification, and particularly baptism in the Holy Spirit, was the focus of Pentecostal experience and theological thinking. If differences of opinion within the Pentecostal movement were going to emerge (and in what religious movement do significant differences not emerge?), the time, emotions and attention invested in Spirit baptism provided fertile ground for the development of diversity.[40] The lack of a perceived need to develop a full-orbed theology, due to the affirmation, in general, of Christian orthodoxy, combined with the commitment to a thoroughly Bible-based theology, contributed to reluctance on the part of Pentecostals to formulate comprehensive statements of faith—until a theological controversy struck at a core doctrine of that orthodox Christian theology. The emergence of Oneness theology, with its denial of the doctrine of the Trinity, was so strongly resisted because it violated the traditional, orthodox Christian beliefs that Pentecostals by and large affirmed. It was only when this happened that there was a reluctant willingness to draft a statement of faith. Corporately drafted statements of faith reflect the particular group and circumstances that prompted their creation, and the Assemblies of God's Statement of Fundamental Truths is no exception. The circumstance is reflected in the fact that, as noted earlier, approximately one-third of the text is devoted to the doctrine of God, most notably the doctrine of the Trinity. As for the distinctively Pentecostal character of the statement, this is largely limited to those portions that address sanctification and the work of the Holy Spirit. Apart from these features, the statement reflects, as Spittler puts it, "commonly accepted conservative Christian orthodoxy."[41]

The divisions within Pentecostalism solidified rather quickly, and the late-1920s through the 1940s was a relatively stable period in which the movement steadily grew numerically and flourished institutionally.[42] For example, by 1945, there were over forty Pentecostal Bible institutes. As Pentecostalism nurtured its second generation, and as the movement became more formally and elaborately organized, there emerged the need to more adequately elaborate the "doctrinal bare-bones" of the earlier period. There was "the need to recast the radical conversionism of the first generation into a form of theology that could help establish a range of more ordinary religious instruction suited to nurture the biological second-generation children that were being born into the Pentecostal faith."[43] It was during this period, in 1937, that the first standard, comprehensive Pentecostal theology text was published: Myer Pearlman's (1898-1943) *Knowing the Doctrines of the Bible*. And, it was during this period that Pentecostalism began to pursue a course that, as will be seen, has continued to both enrich and challenge Pentecostalism to this day: it increasingly embraced theological methods and views characteristic of non-Pentecostal conservative Christianity.

The 1950s saw new claims of a special divine "restoration" of pristine New Testament Christianity, echoing restoration claims in the opening years of the movement. In the 1960s and 1970s, Pentecostalism wrestled with the challenges, as well as the opportunities, posed by the burgeoning Charismatic movement[44] and forays by some Pentecostals into ecumenical dialogue.[45] The Charismatic movement, initially referred to by many people as "Neo-Pentecostalism," posed a challenge because while it shared Pentecostalism's emphasis upon personal holiness and the person and work of the Holy Spirit, it differed from Pentecostalism in at least two significant ways. First, although it emphasized and affirmed a variety of views of the baptism in the Holy Spirit, the Charismatic movement did not require speaking in tongues as the initial physical evidence of this. Second, unlike Pentecostalism, the Charismatic movement arose from and then penetrated mainline Protestant and Roman Catholic churches rather than, for the most part, forming its own denominations or independent local churches.[46] Thus, though closely akin to Pentecostalism, at two significant points the Charismatic movement posed challenges to Pentecostal theology and identity.

At the same time, as the Charismatic movement grew in numbers and influence, its emphasis upon personal holiness and on the person and power of the Holy Spirit meant that, at least in these respects, the Pentecostal movement had an increasingly powerful ally in its efforts to bring significant aspects of a message and experience of the Holy Spirit to an ever increasing number of people. During roughly the same period, a new initiative emerged from within the Pentecostal movement itself to engage in ecumenical interaction and relationships. As with the Charismatic movement, this initiative posed both challenge and opportunity. As has been noted, classical Pentecostalism is in most respects quite conservative theologically, and conservative Protestant groups, by and large, have been reluctant to enter into ecumenical relationships with mainline churches due to concerns regarding spiritual and theological integrity. Many Pentecostals shared this reluctance. Yet, following the initiatives of people such as David du Plessis (1905-1987), often referred to as "Mr. Pentecost," some Pentecostals entered into a variety of ecumenical conversations with both Protestants and Roman Catholics. These relationships were opportunities for Pentecostals to gain an even wider exposure for their distinctive form of Holy Spirit experience and belief.

The 1980s brought increased ethnic diversification, expansion of mission endeavors, and sometimes astonishing numerical growth worldwide. The numerical growth coincided with new challenges to Pentecostal identity, particularly in North America. As the Pentecostal movement grew in numbers and became more institutionalized in the decades prior to the 1980s, it also showed signs of increasing affinity both to the surrounding culture and to non-Pentecostal evangelicalism. For many decades, classical Pentecostalism was predominantly a working-class movement and often appealed to societally marginalized people. As is the case for most, if not all, traditions, its characteristic emphases were simultaneously the basis of both attraction and rejection. For example, commenting on the relationship of Mexican immigrants to Pentecostalism, Arlene Sánchez Walsh observes, "The spiritual gifts of tongues and healing were [in the early twentieth century] and remain two of the most important phenomena feeding the desire to become Pentecostal."[47] At the same time, "its very hallmark of glossolalia made it appear suspect in respectable society," while being repelled by mainstream culture was often taken to be "a badge of honor" by those within the tradition.[48] By the 1980s, significant and increasing numbers of Pentecostals and Pentecostal churches were located in the middle and upper classes of American society. Thus, being on the fringes of American culture was no longer necessarily an identifying badge of honor.[49]

Somewhat parallel to this development was the "evangelicalization" of Pentecostalism.[50] With Holy Spirit distinctives of belief and experience established, many Pentecostals devoted increased attention to the beliefs that they held in common with other conservative Protestants. Pentecostals differ as to whether this reflects a questionable desire for acceptance or a healthy broadening of Pentecostal perspectives, but in either case, the relationship between Pentecostals and evangelicals certainly is closer now than perhaps it has ever been. One symbol of this increasingly collegial relationship is the appointment of Ted Haggard as the president of the National Association of Evangelicals in 2003.[51] At the same time, the distinctively Pentecostal fires of Holy Spirit revival continue to burn in North America, as is evidenced by recent multiyear revivals in Toronto, Ontario, and Pensacola, Florida, that have attracted and impacted millions of people from all over the globe.[52]

Diversity. Over 320 Pentecostal denominations and church groups exist in the United States.[53] Most of these groupings reflect the developments and divisions outlined in the preceding account of the historical origins. Chronologically, Wesleyan-Holiness (or simply "Holiness"), Pentecostalism was the first

THE PENTECOSTAL TRADITION

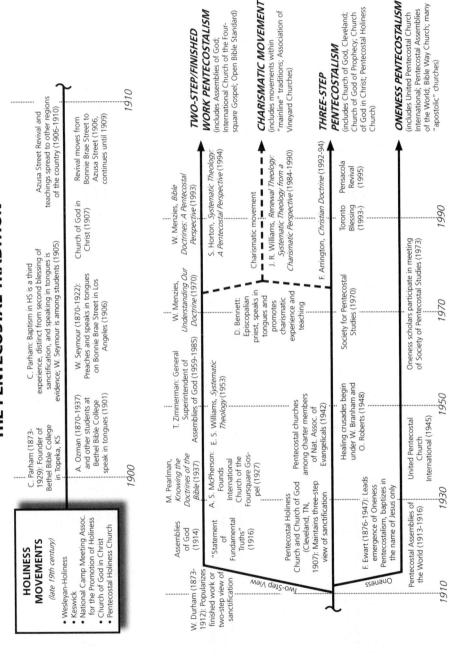

wave of Pentecostalism to emerge in the twentieth century. This form combines a Wesleyan understanding of sanctification with characteristic Pentecostal beliefs. Distinct from and subsequent to conversion (the first work of grace), there is a crisis of sanctification in which the sin nature is removed (the second work of grace), and subsequent to this second work one experiences the baptism in the Holy Spirit (the third work of grace). Denominations of this persuasion include the Church of God (Cleveland), the Church of God of Prophecy (Cleveland), the Church of God in Christ (Memphis), the Pentecostal-Holiness Church and Wesleyan Pentecostal churches.[54]

Finished Work Pentecostals view sanctification as both "positional and progressive."[55] In conversion one is positionally sanctified or regarded as a "saint" (the result of the first work of grace), thereby beginning a lifelong process of sanctification wherein one is actually transformed. Somewhere in this lifelong course of sanctification, the Christian is to experience the baptism in the Holy Spirit (the second work of grace). The Assemblies of God, the International Church of the Foursquare Gospel, the Pentecostal Church of God in America and the Open Bible Standard Churches are among the groups that hold this view. Largely because one of these denominations, the Assemblies of God, has been the predominant and most influential Pentecostal denomination, the Finished Work perspective will provide a good window into the Pentecostal tradition in the balance of this chapter.[56]

Jesus' Name or Oneness Pentecostals affirm a christologically unitarian understanding of God. They believe that there is one God, who is Jesus, and whose titles reflect three roles associated with references to Father, Son and Holy Spirit. For the most part, Oneness Pentecostals hold to a Finished Work view of sanctification. Churches within this subtradition include the United Pentecostal Church International, the Pentecostal Assemblies of the World, Bible Way churches and a variety of "Apostolic" churches.

Approach: Theological and Hermeneutical Method

Role of theology. Historically, Pentecostals have not been entirely uninterested in doctrine. Myer Pearlman's *Knowing the Doctrines of the Bible* was a standard theology text in Pentecostal circles for many years after its publication in 1937. In the introduction he writes, "Doctrinal knowledge is essential to the full development of Christian character. Strong beliefs make for strong character; clear-cut beliefs make for clear-cut convictions."[57] And, as noted earlier, when faced with theological controversy over the doctrine of the Trinity early in its history, the Assemblies of God formulated and adopted, albeit reluctantly, a statement of theological affirmations in which the full range of Christian doctrines were addressed in creedal form and Trinitarian matters were addressed in detail.[58] Yet, although Pentecostals have been active in ministry, ardent in evangelism and fervent in missions, they have not placed a high priority on formal theologizing.

By and large, Pentecostals have not invested much time and energy in sophisticated theological reflection and inquiry. As Raymond Pruitt puts it, "Worship, evangelism, and Christian service, have generally taken precedence over theology in our tradition, and that is as it should be." For, Pruitt continues, "the New Testament focused its energies on witnessing, worship, and work, and did not generally bother with setting down formal statements of doctrine until controversy made it necessary to resolve issues."[59] As one Pentecostal scholar points out, the "implicit values" of Pentecostalism include "personal experience, oral communication . . . spontaneity, otherworldliness, and scriptural authority," and these values, which typically do not create a context that encourages formal theological scholarship, "explain why little emphasis has been placed on the academic treatment of theology."[60] Furthermore, as noted earlier, Russell Spittler suggests that because Pentecostalism simply added its central theological tenet—baptism in the Holy Spirit—to otherwise widely accepted conservative Christian theology, it "had no reason to develop its own full-orbed doctrinal handbooks."[61]

In recent years there has been a growing emphasis on formal theological research and reflection in Pentecostalism. As Pentecostals have increased their involvement with Christians outside their own tradition, and as their institutions, including their educational institutions, have matured and become more culturally sophisticated, there has been an attendant interest and participation in academic theological scholarship by Pentecostal scholars. Some are calling for what they commend as "Informed Pentecostalism" and are asking Pentecostals to "make peace with the academy and understand that Jesus is Lord of learning, too."[62] In the early 1990s, Steven Land described Pentecostalism as being in "a period of theological adolescence where decisions are being made about how to use the parental inheritance, whom to court, marry and befriend, what vocation to pursue, and which kind of training and communication is most important for the future."[63] The fruit of this kind of emphasis on theological research and reflection can be seen in works such as Gordon Fee's *God's Empowering Presence: The Holy Spirit in the Letters of Paul* (1994); the *Dictionary of Pentecostal and Charismatic Movements,* edited by Stanley M. Burgess and Gary B. McGee (1988); Stanley Horton's *Systematic Theology: A Pentecostal Perspective,* edited by Horton with contributions from nineteen Pentecostal scholars (1994); Simon Chan's *Spiritual Theology: A Systematic Study of the Christian Life* (1998); the work of historians Edith Blumhofer and Grant Wacker; and the Journal of Pentecostal Theology Supplement Series, published by Sheffield Academic Press.[64]

The historical development of Pentecostal theology can be viewed in terms of four phases of theological work: definition, inculcation, defense and reflection.[65] From the beginning of the movement through the aftermath of the sanctification and Trinitarian controversies, the Pentecostal movement formulated and defined its theology in response to the "new experiences" of its participants. This included the initial definition of Pentecostal theology. After characteristic doctrinal positions were defined, theological writings were produced primarily for the purpose of instructing clergy, who generally received little formal training, and laypeople.[66] The concern was to inculcate or disseminate Pentecostal beliefs. Furthermore, many of these writings manifest a certain defensiveness. For example, in his *Systematic Theology,* Ernest S. Williams periodically devotes considerable space to quoting and responding to Calvinist criticisms of the Arminian-like views that he propounds.[67] This defensiveness has continued into the present and may have increased as more Pentecostal students have pursued advanced academic training and engaged non-Pentecostal scholarship. As Pentecostal scholar Roger Stronstad observed in 1993, "For the past twenty years or so Pentecostal scholars have been busy defining, explaining and defending Pentecostal hermeneutics and theology. For the most part this has been a defensive or a rear guard action."[68] Most recently, some Pentecostal scholars have moved beyond inculcation or defense to constructive or creative theological reflection, including hermeneutics.[69]

The function of Pentecostal theology is to shape the life of the Christian. Thus, "sound doctrine may be referred to as healthy doctrine. Healthy doctrine or healthy theology expresses itself through both increased knowledge of God and through motivation to live a consistent Christian lifestyle."[70] Theology is not an end in itself. The theologian, like every Christian, is to move beyond "doctrinal theory" to "a real experience" of the work of God.[71]

Theological method. In recent years, questions of theological methodology have become increasingly important to Pentecostal scholars. William Menzies remarks, "The heart of the theological battle today lies below the level of specific theological issues as such. It is the bedrock issue of *hermeneutics* itself. Inevitably, the real crux is that of *methodology.*"[72] There are some identifiable characteristics of the way in which Pentecostals do theology, but like theologians in a number of other traditions, until recently they have not self-consciously reflected, or at least have not written, about their method.[73]

Looking at both older and more recent Pentecostal theology books, we may observe several methodological characteristics, particularly with reference to the sources of theology. First, Pentecostal theologians strive to be thoroughly biblical. One can say that the Pentecostal approach to theology is "canonical."[74] The Bible is to be the basis for all theological affirmations. As French Arrington points out, "The starting point and very foundation for Pentecostal faith and praxis has been the biblical text."[75] Theology's task is primarily to gather all relevant Bible teaching on a particular topic. Myer Pearlman indicates that his book *Knowing the Doctrines of the Bible* is "guided by the questions: What do the Scriptures say (exposition), and what do the Scriptures mean (interpretation)?" Thus, for each doctrine "one must gather the references relating to it and place them in compartments (topics) and in smaller receptacles (sub-topics)."[76] This same affirmation of the Bible as "alone . . . the sufficient rule for faith and practice" characterizes recent Pentecostal theologies as well.[77] Writing in 1991, even before the emergence of works such as Chan's *Spiritual Theology,* Spittler observed, "For Pentecostals, 'systematic theology' is an elegant name for doctrine. And doctrine consists of a concise statement of biblical truth presented in a logical order and marked by gathered scriptural support."[78]

Second, Pentecostals place a great deal of emphasis on experience in the doing of theology. For example, Chan observes, "The central doctrine called 'baptism in the Spirit' is far richer in Pentecostal *experience* than in Pentecostal *explanation.*"[79] Historically, this emphasis on experience has been so pronounced that some Pentecostal scholars express concern that experience is given priority over the biblical text.[80] There is no doubt that in Pentecostal theology experience is looked to as an authoritative source. While Chan states that experience is not "the direct object of our intense gaze," he readily acknowledges that "Pentecostal experience is the lens through which we look at everything else."[81] In defending belief in the distinction between the reception of the Holy Spirit at conversion and a separate, subsequent infilling by the Spirit, E. S. Williams writes, "While the distinction may cause some perplexity for those who seek to understand this mystery through mental reasoning, no question remains with those who have entered and enjoy such experience."[82] More recently, Railey and Aker commend "an experience-certified theology,"[83] and Duffield and Van Cleave advise, "Do not substitute thinking for experiencing. When the Spirit comes in His fullness, no one needs to be told He is there."[84] This emphasis on experience combined with a commitment to the authority of the Bible has resulted in a tension in Pentecostal theology. "The Pentecostal movement has been accused of being an experience-centered movement, and indeed it is," note Duffield and Van Cleave, "but it is also a Bible-centered movement."[85] While being committed in principle to *sola scriptura,* Pentecostals have "struggled" to overcome "the temptation to elevate personal revelations and other spiritual manifestations to the same level" as the Bible.[86] Suspecting that appeals to experience have not always been properly regulated by the

Pentecostal commitment to Scripture, some Pentecostal scholars clearly affirm that "it is important to develop doctrine (teaching) from Scripture and not from human experience."[87] Thus, "all personal experiences must be checked and judged by Scripture."[88]

Third, in principle, Pentecostals regard neither reason nor tradition per se as significant sources for doing theology.[89] Early Pentecostals were "[i]mpatient with both tradition and creeds." Indeed, "[h]istorylessness was a badge of honor," and "many classical Pentecostals have evolved an anti-tradition rhetoric which consciously pits 'tradition' against the spontaneous and novel work of the Spirit."[90] Today Pentecostal theologians warn not to "substitute thinking for experiencing," and Assemblies of God scholars, for example, have wanted to avoid any suggestion that the Statement of Fundamental Truths in any way vies with Scripture for definitive authoritative status in the theological enterprise.[91] When doing theology, one must keep in mind Paul's warning in Colossians 2:8 and not allow "hollow and deceptive philosophy," rather than the Word, to capture one's mind. Just as one must not allow rational thought to override the plain truth that is in Scripture, so too one must not allow "human traditions" to get in the way of the fresh work of the Spirit now.

Upon turning to consideration of the biblical hermeneutics followed in Pentecostal theology, one finds that earlier Pentecostal theologians wrote little about hermeneutics, and that "Pentecostal hermeneutics has existed in an analytical vacuum the majority of its brief history."[92] Some Pentecostal scholars observe that the hermeneutic is a "pragmatic and intuitive interpretation," simply reading the Bible and setting forth its straightforward teachings with little conscious attention to the act of interpreting.[93] Scripture is to be interpreted "literally, or better, naturally."[94] Two convictions underlie and inform this "natural" hermeneutic. The first is a confidence that the Holy Spirit will, as he must, illumine and guide the interpreter. Pentecostal hermeneutics are "essentially *pneumatic,* or *charismatic.*"[95] The contemporary reader of Scripture needs the guidance and assistance of the Holy Spirit, just as the human authors of Scripture needed pneumatic guidance and assistance in order to fulfill their God-given task. As a result, Scripture is held to have, at least in some instances, multiple meanings. While looking for the literal or natural meaning of the Bible, Pentecostal interpreters are also open to having the "spiritual meaning" of a text revealed to them by the Holy Spirit.[96] Furthermore, "the Holy Spirit who inspired the writing of the Bible guides the mind and heart of the believer" (see Jn 16:13).[97] The Pentecostal pneumatic hermeneutic "finds its basis in the inspiration of Scripture."[98]

This recognition of the need for and confidence in the working of the Holy

Spirit today, just as he worked in biblical times, embodies a second important conviction: Pentecostal interpreters of Scripture believe in the continuity of God's presence and work in the world. All interpreters of the Bible bring theological presuppositions to their task. Perhaps the most important presupposition that Pentecostals bring is "the view that there is a continuity of the ways in which God works in the world from the time of the Resurrection to the Second Coming."[99] This confidence in continuity is particularly significant when it informs the interpretation of New Testament passages cited as the basis for distinctively Pentecostal beliefs (e.g., glossolalia as the manifestation of baptism in the Holy Spirit). One Pentecostal scholar refers to this as the "Pentecost as Pattern" hermeneutic. This hermeneutic looks to the events and experiences of Pentecost as recorded in the book of Acts as "the pattern for contemporary experience." One of the "essential distinctives" of Pentecostalism is the belief that the experience of the Christian today "should be identical to [that of] apostolic Christianity."[100]

One of the ways in which this confidence in continuity influences Pentecostal hermeneutics is the prominence given to, and a readiness to draw theological conclusions directly from, narrative portions of the book of Acts, as well as the Gospel of Luke. The line of hermeneutical thought goes something like this: here, in Acts and Luke, are recorded the experiences of the apostolic church; God works today as he did then (the principle of continuity); therefore, Christians are to expect that they will today have the same experiences as Christians did in apostolic times.[101] "From its inception," write Menzies and Menzies, "the Pentecostal movement has emphasized the narrative of Luke-Acts. It is evident that the distinctive features of Pentecostal theology—particularly its emphasis on a baptism in the Spirit distinct from conversion—are rooted in Luke-Acts." Luke had his own distinctive theology of the Spirit (a "charismatic" view), different from that of Paul (a "soteriological" view), and Luke's voice must be given equal consideration.[102] With regard to theological significance and contemporary normativity, Pentecostals basically make no distinction between descriptive and didactic portions of the Bible.[103]

David Nichols suggests that "the Pentecostal movement is now at a stage of maturity and depth so that it may discover and set forth its own ontology, epistemology, and hermeneutic, and thereby construct a proper Systematic Theology, worthy of the name Pentecostal."[104] This process has already begun. In recent years, Pentecostal scholars have begun to identify and reconsider these characteristics of classical Pentecostal theology: the tension between experience and the Bible; the neglect of (if not hostility toward) reason and tradition; the pragmatic and intuitive hermeneutic; and the pneumatic dimension of the interpretive process. Recent Pentecostal theological writings manifest changes in both principle and practice from the writings of earlier generations, and many of these changes reflect what some Pentecostal scholars regard as the "evangelicalization" of Pentecostalism.[105] As Pentecostals, particularly scholars, increasingly associate with evangelicalism in general, their way of reading the Bible and approaching the theological task increasingly reflects evangelical inclinations: greater concern that experience not have priority over the Bible; greater appreciation for the value of tradition and, especially, the value of reason; a more critically sophisticated hermeneutic; and, perhaps, less reliance on the Holy Spirit in the interpretive process.[106]

Thus, much of the recent discussion among Pentecostals about hermeneutical and methodological issues is part of a larger discussion about the distinctive characteristics of an authentically Pentecostal theology. In the past, when Pentecostal theologians have formulated comprehensive theologies, most often they have adapted approaches and structures from non-Pentecostal theologians. From a Pentecostal perspective, the results of this have been "at best, a mixed bag,"[107] and at worst "a total rejection of Pentecostal phenomena."[108] Now that Pentecostalism has matured, as Nichols suggests, and has more well-trained scholars than in the past, Pentecostals have begun more self-consciously to explore what it means to construct a distinctively "Pentecostal" theology. Some Pentecostal scholars think it either unnecessary or ill advised to construct a contemporary, distinctively Pentecostal theology;[109] others see such a contemporary, distinctively Pentecostal theology as long overdue.[110] While acknowledging this difference of opinion over where Pentecostal theology should go with respect to a particular type of systematic theological formulation, Pentecostal hermeneutical principles, in conjunction with the history of the movement and other methodological principles described above, leads Pentecostals to a number of distinctively characteristic beliefs.

Theology: Characteristic Beliefs

Although Pentecostalism, like other traditions, incorporates a diversity of theological beliefs, it nonetheless possesses what Spittler calls "a predictable set of theological beliefs."[111] In general, Pentecostals are sympathetic to Wesleyan-Arminian theology, but Pentecostal theology is not properly understood if regarded solely as a subset of Wesleyan-Arminian thought.[112] Classical Pentecostal theology is characterized by a "constellation of motifs"[113] sometimes referred to as "the fourfold Gospel."[114] This "constellation" of beliefs consists of salvation through faith in Jesus Christ; baptism in the Holy Spirit evidenced by speaking in tongues; the ready availability of divine healing; and the premillennial, imminent return of Jesus Christ.[115] Pentecostal beliefs regarding the first of these, salvation, are very similar to those of other traditions significantly influenced by Wesleyan-Arminian thought, and the fourth component, the return of Christ, is affirmed and defended in much the same way as in other premillennial traditions.[116] Furthermore, there are Pentecostal scholars who affirm that the "twin themes of Spirit-baptism and spiritual gifts have decisively marked the movement."[117] Thus, although particular beliefs about salvation and eschatology form part of the core of classical Pentecostal theology,[118] the present discussion will focus on two of the "fourfold" doctrines that are more clearly distinctive of Pentecostalism: baptism in the Holy Spirit evidenced by speaking in tongues, and the gift of divine healing.[119]

Baptism in the Holy Spirit.

Work of the Holy Spirit. The person and the work of the Holy Spirit constitute a central and pervasive emphasis in Pentecostal theology.[120] From a Pentecostal perspective, "the crucial point of demarcation between Pentecostals and other Christians is the unique Pentecostal emphasis on the person, work, and gifts of the Holy Spirit."[121] These loci of theology are "neglected" in other theological traditions, even though they occupy "the foremost rank of redemption truths" revealed in the Bible.[122] Pentecostals agree with much of what is said when non-Pentecostals discuss the Holy Spirit. What troubles them is what is *not* said.[123] Among those "neglected" topics is the baptism in the Holy Spirit. In particular, Pentecostals maintain that the baptism in the Holy Spirit is normative for Christians, that it is distinct from and subsequent to conversion, and that the initial evidence of Spirit baptism is speaking in tongues.

Importance of baptism in the Holy Spirit. It is difficult to overstate the degree of importance with which this doctrine is regarded by Pentecostals. For Pentecostals, "recovery of the doctrine and experience of being baptized in the Holy Spirit is comparable to the Reformation's recovery of the doctrine of justification by faith."[124] Chan observes, "Glossolalia and what it is believed to signify, baptism in the Spirit, are the most significant symbols of the Pentecostal movement. They are recognized in Pentecostal circles as the movement's most distinguishing marks."[125] In *Bible Doctrines,* Nelson proclaims that baptism in the Holy Spirit "is not a promise but '*the* promise,' the great mountain-peak promise which towers above all the rest of the Father's promises following the fulfillment of the promise of the Messiah."[126] According to Higgins, Dusing and Tallman, "The continuance of the Pentecostal baptism in the Spirit is the very heart of Pentecostalism. To compromise this issue is to give up the Pentecostal movement's reason for existence."[127]

Baptism in the Holy Spirit is "a new experience" in the life of a born-again Christian wherein the Spirit anoints and empowers him or her for service.[128] A Christian is one who is born again, "regenerated . . . a saint."[129] Having experienced regeneration, the Christian should then seek and expect to receive a "new dimension" of the Christian life, a "new experience of the Spirit."[130] The primary purpose of this baptism is to bestow divine empowerment for Christian service.[131] Although significantly increased personal holiness and greater joy in Christian living and worship may well result from this baptism, the primary result is to be equipped with the spiritual power necessary for effective ministry.[132] "The baptism of the Spirit," writes Pruitt, "is an enduement of power for victorious living and service, and is imperative for all believers who would be effective in service, and who would glorify Christ as He should be glorified."[133]

This baptism is available to all Christians. The only "prerequisite" for receiving the baptism is conversion, and the only "condition" for receiving is faith.[134] Even more, it is "intended to be the normal Divine provision for a fully adequate Christian work and witness,"[135] so it is to be desired and sought by all Christians. It is not enough to regard the baptism in the Holy Spirit as "nice, but not necessary; important but not vital to the life of the Church."[136] The baptism in the Spirit is not merely to be tolerated or even allowed for; rather, it is to be desired, sought after and prayed for, as it is an essential part of God's equipping of the church for the ministries that God has given to the church. And, "where the baptism of the Holy Spirit becomes seen as nice but not necessary," which often is the perspective of sympathetic non-Pentecostal Christians, "there the baptism in the Holy Spirit ceases to exist."[137]

Subsequence of baptism in the Holy Spirit. One of the essential tenets of classical Pentecostal theology is that the baptism in the Holy Spirit occurs subsequent to salvation. Pearlman says that the baptism is "in addition and subsequent to conversion,"[138] and Duffield and Van Cleave state that it is "an outpouring of the Spirit subsequent to salvation, and is not the impartation of spiritual life, but rather power for spiritual service."[139] This view is in accord with the Assemblies of God's Statement of Fundamental Truths, which asserts, "This experience is distinct from and subsequent to the experience of the new birth."[140] Some Pentecostal scholars speak of the "separability" of the baptism in the Holy Spirit from conversion, desiring to set aside questions of chronological sequence and to focus rather on the nature of the experience.[141]

The reason that there are no significant passages on baptism in the Spirit in the Pauline writings is that this baptism "was the normal experience of all first-century believers. All the people to whom [Paul] was writing were already filled with the Holy Spirit. So that was not a question."[142] This outpouring of the Spirit, both in Paul's time and today, is seen as a manifestation of the fulfillment of Joel 2:28-29, where God promises "I will pour out my spirit on all flesh," and also of the promises of the coming Spirit recorded by John the Evangelist in John 14:26; 15:26-27; 16:13. John the Baptist promises his followers that although he baptizes them with water, Jesus will baptize them "with the Holy Spirit and fire" (Mt 3:11; Mk 1:8; Lk 3:16; Jn 1:26, 33).

Narratives of the book of Acts are the foundation for the Pentecostal doctrine of the baptism in the Holy Spirit.[143] Five passages here are particularly important: Acts 2:1-13, the record of the day of Pentecost in Jerusalem; Acts 8:4-19, the "Samaritan Pentecost"; Acts 9:1-19, the conversion and calling of Paul; Acts 10:44-48, the "Gentile Pentecost"; and Acts 19:1-7, the "Ephesian Pentecost." In each of these pericopes Pentecostals see a record of the baptism in the Holy Spirit, and in each they find "evidence for the doctrine of subsequence."[144] Those gathered in Jerusalem on the Day of Pentecost were already followers of Jesus, and the verbal structure of Acts 2:1 indicates that the event recorded here constitutes the "completion" of a reality "begun at an earlier point."[145] In Samaria, those who received the baptism in the Holy Spirit had already "accepted the Word of God" (Acts 8:15) and "been baptized in the name of the Lord Jesus" (Acts 8:16). As for Paul, Ananias calls him "brother," and following Ananias's prayer on his behalf, Paul was then "filled with the Holy Spirit" (Acts 9:17). All of this took place subsequent to Paul's experience on the road to Damascus (Acts 9:3-8). The accounts of the Gentile and Ephesian Pentecosts, though less clear than the other accounts, also indicate subsequence. For example, the recipients of the baptism in the Spirit at Ephesus had been baptized "in the name of the Lord Jesus" (Acts 19:5) before they were baptized in the Spirit (Acts 19:6), and Paul would not have baptized them in the name of Jesus if he had not been confident that they were already converted.[146] The apostolic Christian experience was one that included the baptism in the Holy Spirit, and by virtue of the continuity of the Spirit's work in the world, the experience of today's Christians also is to include this baptism.

Initial evidence of baptism in the Holy Spirit. The affirmation of speaking in tongues, or glossolalia, as the initial evidence of baptism in the Spirit is "a hallmark of Pentecostal doctrine."[147] Pentecostal belief about evidentiary tongues is inextricably linked with the belief in the normativity of baptism in the Spirit subsequent to regeneration. William Menzies observes that the affirmation of this connection between baptism in the Holy Spirit and glossolalia has "given identity and continuity" to Pentecostalism from its beginnings into the present.[148] Pentecostal theologians themselves warn against a temptation, sometimes realized, to overemphasize tongues in and of itself rather than emphasizing the empowerment for which the baptism in the Holy Spirit is given.[149] Furthermore, they clearly state that glossolalia is the initial physical evidence, but not the only evidence, of baptism in the Holy Spirit. The Christian can also expect that there will be an increase in, for example, praise of God, power for service, joy, interest in the Bible and burden for the spiritually lost.[150]

Speaking in tongues may be defined as "the phenomenon of making sounds that constitute, or resemble, a language not known to the speaker."[151] Pentecostals maintain a distinction between tongues as a sign or initial evidence of baptism in the Spirit (see Acts 2:4) and tongues as a gift (see 1 Cor 12:4-10, 28).[152] Most Pentecostals regard both of these as being "the same in essence" yet "different in purpose and use."[153] Tongues *as a gift* is primarily intended to facilitate and enrich edification and worship. The Spirit distributes all gifts, including tongues, as he chooses (1 Cor 12:11). Thus, some Christians receive the gift of tongues, and some do not. Tongues *as a sign* has an evidentiary function, confirming to the Spirit-baptized believer that indeed the baptism in the Holy Spirit has been received.[154] Because baptism in the Spirit is intended for all Christians, tongues as a sign is intended for all Christians. Speaking in tongues, as evidence of baptism in the Holy Spirit, is "recognized in Scripture to be the privilege of all believers. It is both normal and normative."[155]

As they do with the doctrine of subsequent Spirit baptism, Pentecostals "go to the book of Acts for their proof" of the doctrine of tongues.[156] The verses most commonly cited come from the same passages consulted with respect to subsequence: Acts 2:4, 11, 39; 9:17; 10:44-46; 19:1-7. Acts 2:4 reports that all who were filled with the Spirit on the Day of Pentecost (and this included "all of them") "began to speak in other languages, as the Spirit gave them ability." Furthermore, according to some Pentecostal scholars, the continuation of this phenomenon into the present is indicated by Peter's statement that the promise of the Holy Spirit is "for you, for your children, and for all who are far away" (Acts 2:39). In this interpretation, Christians throughout history and into the present are included in the reference to those who are "far away."[157] In Acts 9:17, although it is reported that Paul is filled with the Spirit, speaking in tongues is not explicitly referred to. However, Paul reports in 1 Corinthians 14:18 that he speaks in tongues. From this, Pentecostals conclude that since Paul did report speaking in tongues, and since there is a pattern of glossolalia accompanying baptism in the Spirit, "it is reasonable to conclude that, following the pattern, Paul began to speak in tongues when he was filled with the Spirit."[158] Acts 10:44-46 reports that the believers who accompanied Peter knew that the Gentiles had been baptized in the Holy Spirit, "for they heard them speaking in tongues and extolling God." Lastly, Acts 19:6-7 reports that Paul baptized the new believers at Ephesus with water and then laid his hands on them and prayed for them, with the result that "the Holy Spirit came upon them, and they spoke in tongues and prophesied."

Explaining why this important matter of evidentiary tongues is not reported more frequently in Acts, Wyckoff says that "speaking in tongues was the normal, expected experience of all New Testament believers who were baptized in the Holy Spirit. . . . Because of this, Luke felt no need to point out tongues speaking every time he discussed an instance of the experience."[159] More important, in every instance where the results of baptism in the Spirit are described in Acts, "there is always an immediate, supernatural, outward expression . . . an ecstatic speaking in a language that the person has never learned."[160] Because of the conviction that the Spirit continues to work today just as then, Spirit baptism will today be evidenced initially by speaking in such an unknown language.

Gift of divine healings.

Gifts of the Holy Spirit. It is wonderful that the Holy Spirit confirms this baptism with the capacity to speak in unknown languages, and that he endues individual Christians with power for ministry. Yet, the Holy Spirit does even more. The baptism in the Holy Spirit is "the door" or "the gateway" to even more divine blessings.[161] The Holy Spirit gives good "gifts" to the church. These gifts of the Spirit may be described as "supernatural abilities imparted by the Spirit for special ministries,"[162] such as those listed in 1 Corinthians 12:28-30. Spiritual gifts are not exclusively "spiritual"; rather, they incorporate realities both "spiritual" and "natural."[163] Yet spiritual gifts are not to be equated with "human talents." A gift of knowledge, such as discernment, will grant a degree of understanding and insight beyond any merely natural knowledge. A gift of power, such as the gift of miracles, will enable the accomplishment of feats not possible through human means alone. A gift of communication, such as the gift of prophecy, will grant to a local church a degree of understanding not otherwise available. Christians are to employ their natural talents and abilities in the service of the church, but spiritual gifts will always be the principal means through which God builds the church.[164] This being the case, these gifts are "not adornment or frills, but essential functions which the Church must exercise if she is to be what her Lord requires her to be."[165]

Because spiritual gifts are for the church, the church, not individual Christians, is the recipient of the Holy Spirit's gifts. Gifts are given "to the Church as a whole."[166] Thus, no individual ought to claim to "possess" a gift.[167] Menzies and Horton remark that an "individual in the congregation may develop a ministry featuring one or more of the gifts, but none are to be considered one's private property, for the Spirit dispenses His ministrations for the benefit of the Church 'just as he determines' (1 Cor 12:11; 14:12, 32)."[168] This churchly character of spiritual gifts means that they are not something to be used for the pleasure of the person through whom they are given to the church, nor are they to be used as a tool to bring about the sanctification of an individual Christian.[169] These blessings may be by-products of the proper stewardship of gifts, but the proper stewardship or use of gifts is employing them for ministry and service *to others*. Pearlman states that the purpose of gifts is "building up the church of God through the instruction of believers and the winning of converts."[170] Teaching, edification, worship and evangelism are the kinds of tasks to which the use of gifts is to be committed.

Divine healings. The gift of divine healing is "supernaturally ministering health to the sick, through prayer."[171] Among the gifts of the Spirit, belief in gifts of divine healing occupies a place of prominence in many Pentecostal circles. It is the only gift explicitly set forth in the Assemblies of God's Statement of Fundamental Truths,[172] and, writing in 1948, P. C. Nelson observed, "The Pentecostal people, one hundred per cent strong, accept the doctrine of divine healing, and nearly all of them have proved it in their own bodies."[173]

Properly speaking, the gift of healing is *gifts* of healing. In his wisdom and power, God grants many gifts in order that the diverse needs of specific persons and situations may be met, and Pentecostal authors point out that in the Greek text of the New Testament, references to both "gifts" and "healings" are in the plural.[174] There is some difference of belief among classical Pentecostals as to whether or not God intends to bring healing in all cases of illness. Nelson says, "It is God's will to heal all the sick, for Jesus and the apostles healed all that came to them for healing (Mt 8:16; Acts 5:12-19)."[175] Others indicate that not all cases of sickness will be remedied through a gift of divine healing (biblical examples include 2 Kings 13:14; 2 Cor 4:10-12, 16-17; 12:7-9; Gal 4:13-15; 2 Tim 4:20). Healing is, according to them, a "privilege" and not a "right," and there is always the possibility that, in accord with God's own plan, an individual will be called upon to suffer for the sake of Christ and the gospel.[176] But those of both persuasions— God intends to heal all physical afflictions, and God does not necessarily intend to heal all afflictions—agree that divine healing is part of the salvific work of God. Vernon Purdy states, "The Bible's teaching of healing parallels its teaching of salvation."[177] Thus, "God's normative will is to heal the sick."[178]

Several beliefs undergird Pentecostal confidence with respect to divine healing. First, the healing God of the Old Testament and Jesus the healer of the New Testament are the same yesterday, today and forever. As testified to in Exodus 15:26, God is the God "who heals you." Simply put, "it is God's nature to heal," and God's nature does not change.[179] The Gospels report many instances of Jesus healing, and, like his Father, Jesus the healer is the same today as he was in New Testament times. Divine healing is another manifestation of the continuity of the work of God in this world. Second, healing is one facet of the holistic salvation provided by God in Christ. Salvation extends to all dimensions of human being, including the physical dimension.[180] The benediction recorded in 1 Thessalonians 5:23 reads, "May the God of peace himself sanctify you *entirely;* and may your spirit and soul *and body* be kept sound and blameless at the coming of our Lord Jesus Christ." Pentecostals proclaim "the whole gospel for the whole person."[181] Third, healing is provided for in the atoning work of Christ. Pentecostals believe that "deliverance from sickness is provided for in the atonement, and is the privilege of all believers."[182] Sickness, in any and all forms, is a work of the devil, and as such it is a target of the work of Christ (see 1 Jn 3:8). Healing is in the atonement "in the sense that Christ came to destroy the works of Satan. Sickness and death are the results of sin, and sickness is a manifestation of sin in the world. . . . Jesus came to destroy the works of Satan, and this was done in His atoning work at Calvary, and in His resurrection."[183] Texts of Scripture often cited in this regard are found in Isaiah 53; Matthew 8; and 1 Peter 2.[184]

Isaiah 53:4-5 reads, "Surely he has borne our infirmities and carried our diseases [or, 'sorrows']; yet we accounted him stricken, struck down by God, and afflicted. But he was wounded for our transgressions, crushed for our iniquities; upon him was the punishment that made us whole, and by his bruises we are healed." According to many Pentecostal interpreters, the term "infirmities," חֳלִי *(ḥŏlî),* "primarily refers to physical disease and secondarily to sin," and the term "sorrows," מַכְאֹב *(mak'ōb),* taken literally, means physical "pain."[185] The suffering of Christ on the cross was physical, and the healing that we enjoy as a result of that suffering includes healing that is physical. An important New Testament echo of this passage is found in Matthew 8:17. It is particularly important here because in this text one finds "a *sensus plenior* interpretation" of Isaiah 53. A *sensus plenior* interpretation identifies a meaning intended by God but unknown to the original human author. The New Testament often provides a key of this kind to the Old Testament.[186] Commenting on Jesus casting out demons and curing people who were physically sick, Matthew writes, "This was to fulfill what had been spoken through the prophet Isaiah, 'He took our infirmities and bore our diseases.'" This text is taken as indicating the "physical" interpretation of Isaiah 53:4-5: the divine healing of people, including physical healing, can be realized because Jesus the Messiah took upon himself, and thus took away from God's followers, "infirmities" and "diseases," including physical afflictions.[187] Peter writes, "He himself bore our sins in his body on the cross, so that, free from sins, we might live for righteousness; by his wounds you have been healed" (1 Pet 2:24). Commenting on this verse, Pentecostal scholars reject any "alien dichotomy between the spiritual and physical dimensions of human existence," affirming that the healing referred to here is physical, bodily just as the bearing of sins was "in his body."[188] Furthermore, Duffield and Van Cleave point out that the Greek word ἰάομαι, translated as "heal," "always speaks of physical healing in the New Testament, and always in connection with healing of physical ailments."[189] The blessed hope of the Christian includes the resurrection and glorification of the body. The physical healings of today are "a first installment" of this future redemption.[190] There is a continuity to the holistic redemptive work of God, continuing from the past, in the present and into the future.

Conclusion: The Spirit of Continuity

Pentecostal Christians, like many in other Christian traditions, firmly believe that God is the same yesterday, today and forever. However, in a manner unlike most other Christians, they further believe that the way that God works through his Holy Spirit, the way this work manifests itself in the lives of his people, and the way his people experience this work are the same yesterday, today and forever. The Holy Spirit may be seen as the Spirit of Continuity, and the proper way to read and apply the Bible is to do so in a spirit of continuity. The God-produced experiences of the early church, as recorded in the book of Acts, provide patterns for all God-followers in all ages. Thus, an approach to Christian theology and life that is guided by the spirit of continuity will discern rightly the truth about and the present-day workings of the Spirit of Continuity in the baptism in the Holy Spirit, evidenced in speaking in tongues, and in supernatural gifts, such as healing. These and other divine enablements will empower God's people today, just as they did in the early church, to "be [Christ's] witnesses in Jerusalem, and in all Judea and Samaria, and to the ends of the earth" (Acts 1:8).

FOR FURTHER STUDY

The endnotes contain citations of many useful resources, most of them written from within the Pentecostal tradition. A brief list of resources for further study follows here. Some of these resources consider Pentecostalism in general, while others focus on history and/or theology.

Bibliographies

Bundy, David D. "Bibliography and Historiography of Pentecostalism in the

United States," in *The New International Dictionary of Pentecostal and Char-ismatic Movements*, pp. 382-417. Edited by Stanley M. Burgess and Eduard M. Van der Maas. Rev. ed. Grand Rapids: Zondervan, 2000.

Synan, Vinson. *The Holiness-Pentecostal Tradition: Charismatic Movements in the Twentieth Century*, pp. 299-328. Grand Rapids: Eerdmans, 1997.

Reference Work

Burgess, Stanley M., and Eduard M. Van der Maas, eds. *The New International Dictionary of Pentecostal and Charismatic Movements*. Rev. ed. Grand Rap-ids: Zondervan, 2000.

Survey Resources

Anderson, Allan. *An Introduction to Pentecostalism: Global Charismatic Theol-ogy*. Cambridge: Cambridge University Press, 2004.

Synan, Vinson. *The Holiness-Pentecostal Tradition: Charismatic Movements in the Twentieth Century*. Grand Rapids: Eerdmans, 1997.

Primary Historical and Theological Resources

Dayton, Donald W., ed. *The Higher Christian Life: Sources for the Study of the Holiness, Pentecostal, and Keswick Movements*. 48 vols. New York: Garland, 1985.

Recent and Current Theological Explorations

Archer, Kenneth J. *A Pentecostal Hermeneutic for the Twenty-First Century: Spirit, Scripture and Community*. London: T & T Clark, 2004.

Ma, Wonsuk, and Robert P. Menzies, eds. *Pentecostalism in Context: Essays in Honour of William W. Menzies*. Journal of Pentecostal Theology Supplement Series 11. Sheffield: Sheffield Academic Press, 1997.

Macchia, Frank. *Baptized in the Spirit: A Global Pentecostal Theology*. Grand Rapids: Zondervan, 2006.

Martin, David. *Pentecostalism: The World Their Parish*. Malden, Mass.: Black-well, 2002.

Nañez, Rick M. *Full Gospel, Fractured Minds?* Grand Rapids: Zondervan, 2006.

Shaull, Richard, and Waldo Cesar. *Pentecostalism and the Future of the Christian Churches: Promises, Limitations, Challenges*. Grand Rapids: Eerdmans, 2000.

Yong, Amos. *The Spirit Poured Out on All Flesh: Pentecostalism and the Possibil-ity of Global Theology*. Grand Rapids: Baker, 2005.

10 ▪ Conclusion

THEOLOGICAL TRADITIONS
AND CHRISTIAN HOSPITALITY

Above all, maintain constant love for one another, for love covers a multitude of sins. Be hospitable to one another without complaining. Like good stewards of the manifold grace of God, serve one another with whatever gift each of you has received.

1 Peter 4:8-10

Is not doctrine exactly contradictory to whatever we might associate with hospitality and truth? Is not dogma the very enemy of hospitality and truth?

Reinhold Hütter, in *Practicing Theology*

Strange as it may seem, it is still true, that those who fail to understand other churches than their own are not the people who care intensely about theology, but the theological dilettantes . . . while those very men who have found themselves forced to confront a clear, thorough-going, logical sic et non find themselves allied to each other in spite of all contradictions, by an underlying fellowship and understanding, even in the cause which they handle so differently and approach from such painfully different angles. But that cause, it may be, is nothing else than Jesus Christ and the unity of the Church.

Karl Barth, *The Church and the Churches*

We live in an era in which we are called upon by leaders, in both society and church, to live together in harmony and, at the same time, to recognize and celebrate diversity. As frustrating as this combination may sometimes seem, it is difficult to deny the fundamental validity and importance of each of these two summons, and of their beauty when authentically combined. The church, the body of Christ, is both one and many, both united and diverse. Recognizing that the realization of a Christ-honoring combination of unity and diversity has often eluded Christians—not least in the realm of theology—this chapter commends the virtue and practice of Christian hospitality as an easy yoke (cf. Mt 11:29-30) and a faithful guide.

The Challenge of Divisions Within Christianity

This book surveys just eight ecclesio-theological traditions of Protestant theology: Lutheran, Anabaptist, Reformed, Anglican, Baptist, Wesleyan, Dispensational and Pentecostal. Obviously, there are more traditions within Protestantism, not to mention those within Roman Catholic and Eastern Orthodox Christianity. The existence of so many traditions is troubling to an increasing number of people. These traditions, and the denominations in which many of them are lived out, are seen by many as the embodiment of sinful division within the church. "It is clear," writes John Frame, "that all denominational division has been due to sin somewhere. . . . The birth of a denomination is always attended by sin."[1] This book is not primarily about denominations and denominationalism, but it is safe to say that many of the attitudes and perspectives of the so-called postdenominational era are held also in regard to classical traditions of theology. This multiplicity of theological traditions is seen as sinful.

Two sins are most often cited: one against the church, and one in relation to the world beyond the church. The existence of so many traditions within Christianity is often identified with schism—dividing the one body of Christ.[2] The apostle Paul teaches that God has brought the parts of the body together in such a way that "there may be no dissension within the body, but the members may have the same care for one another" (1 Cor 12:25), and to many people, the existence of various traditions is a prime example of this "dissension." In addition to constituting a sin against the church, the multiplicity of traditions is viewed as constituting a sin against the world. These divisions undermine the church's witness to the world. Perhaps the most oft-cited passage in this regard is Jesus' prayer recorded in John 17. Three times in this context he prays to the Father that his followers would "be one as we are one," and in John 17:23 this desire is tied to the witness to the Father's love and work through the Son, as he prays that "they may become completely one, so that the world may know that you have sent me and have loved them even as you have loved me." Against this backdrop, traditions within Christianity are viewed as, above all else, divisions, and such divisions are regarded by some as contradicting the message of reconciling love that the church is trying to take into the world.

These schismatic and undermining divisions are often said to be the result of an inordinate attention to theology, or what Paul Avis refers to as *confessionalism*—"a hardening of confessional identity into a defensive attitude of self-justification."[3] One manifestation of the reaction against this perceived divisive emphasis on theology is the reduction in length and the simplification of doctrinal statements. This could be referred to as a minimalist trend in confessional theology. Such minimalism can be found among churches (both independent and denominational), parachurch organizations and explicitly ecumenical endeavors. For example, at its founding in 1981, the denomination in which I am a member, the Evangelical Presbyterian Church (EPC), adopted a comparatively brief statement of Essentials of the Faith in conjunction with the traditional confessional document of the Presbyterian tradition, the lengthy Westminster Confession. The Essentials of the Faith lacks almost all of the distinctively Reformed and Calvinistic elements of the Westminster Confession, thereby enabling many people who do not hold these historically characteristic Reformed and Presbyterian beliefs to be at home in the EPC.[4] The statements of faith of many parachurch organizations include affirmations of major tenets of historic Christian faith, but they are crafted so as to avoid identification with any particular tradition of theology. The National Association of Evangelicals (NAE) is an ecumenical organization, within evangelical purview, and its statement of faith exemplifies a form of minimalism. The NAE statement lacks, for example, the explicit affirmation of a number of doctrines that are historically central to "evangelical" belief, such as the affirmation of God as Creator, the sinfulness of all human beings and justification by faith in Jesus Christ.

Most, if not all, of the moves toward theological minimalism are motivated, at least in part, by a desire to cast a wider net. The goal is quite simple, and clearly commendable: minimizing theological particulars opens the doors to a wider range of theological views, and thus a wider range and larger number of people, both from within the community of Christian faith and, potentially, from outside the household of faith. This kind of theological minimalism is a response to the adverse effects of the existence of diverse traditions. It is a response to "the sin of schism" and the accompanying impairment of Christian witness.[5]

A "Both/And" Approach to Unity and Diversity Within Christianity

Inherently sinful divisions? Divisions within the body of Christ that stem from sinful attitudes or actions are a shameful blight on the church. God's design and desire, as reflected in Jesus' prayer recorded in John 17, is that under the headship of Jesus Christ all of God's spiritual children be "one." And, it is all too often the case that this divine desire is not realized, either internally (i.e., in mind and heart) or externally (i.e., in relationships), among God's people. In the face of this reality, I propose here that the unity of the church, and thereby its health and mission, would be advanced through a revised understanding of the phenomenon of traditions and the application of principles of Christian hospitality to relationships among Christians of various traditions. It is understandable, and right, that Christians should be wary of the diversity of traditions. The history of Christianity provides too many cautionary tales of differences turning into divisions, of traditions becoming the occasion for sectarianism. However, must this always and necessarily be the case? Is it possible to envision the church as characterized by both unity and diversity, both particularity and unity? Is it possible for someone to both stand within a tradition and stand with other Christians outside that tradition? Such a "both/and" view of the church is not only possible, but is also, I propose, the proper and the most realistic and constructive view.[6]

Diversity or difference should not necessarily be equated with sinful division or schism. It is a mistake to regard the various traditions of Christian theology as inherently constituting the primary roadblock to greater unity in the body of Christ. "Diversity in the church is not a problem to be overcome," observes John Franke, "but rather a gift of the Holy Spirit."[7] Furthermore, in an era when values such as diversity and multiculturalism are being advanced, it is ironic that so many North American churches and Christians are pursuing a supposedly generic, "just plain" Christianity. These responses to the existential reality of a divided Christianity are understandable and, in most instances, well intended. Many times, these responses are prompted by good motives such as a love for the body of Christ and a desire to see as many people as possible welcomed into this body. However, the assertion that diversity, and the accompanying recognition of boundaries (more on this below), is incompatible with unity reflects an inappropriate and unrealistic "either-or" way of thinking. This either-or approach tends to view the differences and diversity embodied in various traditions of Christianity as inherently and necessarily constituting sinful division or schism. There must be, this thinking goes, either the absence of substantial diversity and difference among churches or there is, by definition, sinful division. Moreover, in the pursuit of greater unity in the face of these sinful divisions, this either-or approach can unwittingly encourage a uniformity that is substituted for genuine Christian unity or a form of organizational commonality achieved through the avoidance of substantive theological commitment. None of these approaches—eliminating differences, pursuing uniformity, avoiding substantive theological commitment—nor any combination of them provides a basis for genuine Christian unity, much less constitutes a substitute for it.

Both unity and diversity. A more realistic, honest and constructive perspective on the diversity of Christian traditions can and should be attained through a revised historical and theological understanding of the church—a both/and understanding. The church is, and ought to be, characterized by both unity and diversity.

Existentially and experientially, the church is diverse and divided. (Ironically, this is likely something on which most Christians can agree.) The question then becomes how this diversity and these divisions ought to be viewed. We noted above that some people view both diversity and divisions as inherently sinful. However, the *incarnational character of Christianity necessarily entails historical particularity*. The Son of God *came to earth* and modeled for us a way to live *here and now*. In addition to being a transcendent religion, Christianity is an immanent and incarnational religion, and incarnational religion is antithetical to ahistorical, gnostic religion. North Americans may be particularly prone to this form of religion, which, even when in Christian garb, is "essentially private, acultural and ahistorical."[8] This is precisely the approach manifest in the pursuit of "just plain Christianity." To the extent that this gnostic approach is characteristic of churches' teaching and practice, churches deny the radically historical and incarnational character, and thereby the particularlity, of Christian religion. "The *ekklesia* is the place," observes Thomas Oden, "where Christ is becoming embodied in history."[9] This historical and incarnational character means that expressions of Christianity in this world will always be marked by *particularity*. Incarnated Christianity will always reflect particular people's encounter with Christ and their particular understanding of how one is to live as a Christian. Christianity believed and lived in this world will always reflect the particular place and time of those who believe it and live it. Expressions of Christianity in this world will always be finite or limited, as is everything in this world other than God himself. Christianity, believed and lived in *this* world, will inevitably embody selected portions or dimensions of God and of his will for humankind. Thus, incarnated Christianity—the only kind of Christianity there can be—will always be marked by particularity, and particularity entails being marked by *boundaries*.

Boundaries and unity. As discussed here, boundaries consist in identifying characteristics that distinguish one Christian tradition from another. Some might think that the existence of boundaries is inherently inconsistent with the unity of the church, but this is not necessarily the case.[10] *The recognition of the existence of boundaries is not synonymous with denying the unity of the body of Christ or the universality of the truth of Christianity.* Boundaries can be nothing more or less than one manifestation of incarnational particularity. Ontologically the church *is* one, as Paul's discussions of the body of Christ clearly indicate, and missionally all churches are called to desire and work to more fully realize this unity, in accord with the desire of Jesus as expressed in John 17. "There is," as Paul writes, "one body and one Spirit, just as you were called to the one hope of your calling, one Lord, one faith, one baptism, one God and Father of all," and Christians, individually and collectively, are to witness to this reality in word and deed (Eph 4:4-5). Genuine Christian unity consists in the *ontological reality* of many individuals belonging to one body by virtue of being related to the head of that body, Jesus Christ; authentic unity in this world does not consist in uniformity or commonality achieved through radically reducing substantive theological commitments. Christian unity both flows from and is expressed in a disposition of heart and mind combined with actions wherein Christians, individually and collectively, eagerly recognize, respect, encourage, learn from, and work with sisters and brothers in Christ by virtue of their shared redemptive relationship with Jesus Christ. Genuine Christianity does not issue from the pursuit of some supposedly traditionless, generic form of "just plain Christianity." Christian unity "need not mean that all churches come to resemble each other more and more until they are indistinguishable."[11] The mark of Christian unity is love for Christ, the Head of all, and for all those who are members of the body of Christ; it is not agreement with them in every matter of theology and practice. John Franke correctly observes, "The unity of the church is not to be found in full agreement concerning all the teachings and practices of the church but rather in the living presence of Christ in the church."[12] Thus, Christian love does not, and should not be interpreted to, require sameness achieved through the abandonment of all differences, including differences in theology. Rather, this love is like all other genuine loves in that it respects "the other" as the other and then reaches across boundaries to embrace the other. The pursuit of genuine Christian unity includes working to eliminate divisions, but not working to eliminate diversity. As Oliver O'Donovan observes, Christians' "universal communion in the truth of the gospel will not come about by the denial of denominational traditions, but only by the critical appropriation and sharing of them."[13]

Recognition of boundaries does not invalidate claims regarding this oneness, nor does it necessarily undermine the pursuit of the greater realization of unity.[14] Rather, *the recognition of boundaries is integral to the recognition of the incarnational character of Christianity, and as such it provides a most appropriate and realistic perspective for thinking about Christian diversity and unity.* Christianity embodied in this world has always been and will always be, in some respects, particular and limited by virtue of the nature of earthly human existence. And, from within this God-created context of particularity, Christians have and will continue to formulate and proclaim their theological beliefs.[15] Traditions that are Christian take the Bible seriously. The Bible speaks about many subjects, including, for example, the nature and work of God, the nature of the created order, the nature and spiritual state of human being, God's desires and design for creation, and God's desires and design for humanity, both individually and corporately. This is just a truncated summary of some of the substance of theology, but even in this scant distillation it is self-evident that these are matters of import, matters of consequence. Ironically, as D. G. Hart observes, one of the biblical texts that sometimes provides a rationale for the kind of "wider net" mindset that pursues theological minimalism, the commission in Matthew 28:18-20, includes the often neglected directive to teach followers of Christ to obey "all" or "everything" that he commanded.[16] This hardly seems like a summons to theological minimalism. Christians rightly ask legitimate questions and come to hold firm yet differing beliefs about a wide variety of important matters. These differing yet firm beliefs—these theologies—deserve to be taken seriously and need to be taken seriously if the unity that is pursued is to be genuinely Christian.

The eschatological "already–not yet." Finally, this both/and approach to unity and diversity must be viewed in light of another hyphenated guide: the "already–not yet" of salvation history. The church and its history must always be viewed in its eschatological context. As enacted in the Lord's Table, Christians are to be mindful of what God has already accomplished in this world even as they look forward to a yet future culmination of that redemptive work. God has established his church. God has called and continues to call a people to be his own, and the individuals who make up this people *are* one people. The reality of this oneness will be fully and gloriously manifest in the eschatological marriage feast of the Lamb, and it will be a oneness with diversity. People of all times and places, people of all languages and races—and people who are reconciled to God in Christ but who held differing theologies—will be united in worship of their one Lord. This redemption history is not yet fulfilled. Those who are reconciled to God in Christ do not yet fully experience and express their common worship of the one Lord, though one day they will. The church does not yet fully experience or express the unity in which it exists, but one day it will. With this recognition, there is no question as to the direction in which the church should be moving. All Christians ought to be working toward the full experience and expression of unity in Jesus Christ. This pursuit is not optional. It is an obligatory opportunity and a privileged challenge. And, in light of the incarnational and particular character of Christianity at this point in God's redemptive work (i.e. at the present time), this trajectory toward unity will be manifest not in the eradication of all differences, diversity and boundaries, but in a grace-full reach and embrace from an incarnationally particular location amidst diversity.

A Call to Christian Theological Hospitality

The call to Christian hospitality. The present era of "already–not yet" calls
for Christians to exercise hospitality. Thomas Oden suggests, "A kind of ecumenical hospitality is required to welcome guests from other church traditions
that they may teach us what they can out of their particular historical experience."[17] We recognized above the ontological reality of the unity of the body of
Christ, and the too frequent experiential reality of divisions. We have noted the
incarnational particularity of Christianity, as well as God's desire and the Christian eschatological assurance of the full realization of unity in Christ. This state
of affairs issues a summons to Christian hospitality. The existence of diverse traditions within Protestantism, and also within the larger Christian community, is
an occasion for hospitality, and the fact that these are traditions *within Christianity* means that this hospitality will include, rather than bypass, attention to
Christian belief and theology.

Christians are supposed to be hospitable. The apostle Peter writes, "Above
all, maintain constant love for one another, for love covers a multitude of sins.
Be hospitable to one another without complaining. Like good stewards of the
manifold grace of God, serve one another with whatever gift each of you has
received" (1 Pet 4:8-10). The hospitality to which Peter here refers is most likely
that of Christians welcoming other Christians into their homes. This could have
been groups of Christians gathering for fellowship and worship, or individual
travelers in need of bed and board. Peter's exhortation is akin to the apostle
Paul's call to "extend hospitality to strangers" (Rom 12:13), and to the instruction
by the author of Hebrews to "show hospitality to strangers" (Heb 13:2). Extending an Old Testament virtue (see, e.g., Gen 18—19; Josh 2; 1 Sam 25) in a self-
consciously New Covenant way, the community of followers of Jesus Christ was
to be, and to a significant degree was, characterized by hospitality. This is not
surprising when one notes that this virtue is grounded in a reality common to
both the Old and New Testaments: the one true God. In *Making Room: Recovering Hospitality as a Christian Tradition,* Christine Pohl observes, "Our hospitality both reflects and participates in God's hospitality."[18] God's people are to
be hospitable because God is hospitable. When we are hospitable to others, it
is because God was first hospitable to us. "A life of hospitality begins in worship," Pohl writes, "with a recognition of God's grace and generosity. Hospitality
is not first a duty and responsibility; it is first a response of love and gratitude
for God's love and welcome to us. Although it involves responsibility and faithful performance of duties, hospitality emerges from a grateful heart."[19] Commenting on the call in Hebrews 13:2 to "show hospitality to strangers," William
Lane correctly notes that hospitality is "first and foremost an attitude, not an ac-

tion," and this attitude is love.[20] Like all works of grace, this attitude has its origin in God. We love because God first loved us. God loved us, and if we are genuinely grateful, our gratitude will find expression in both the attitude and actions of love. We extend hospitality because God first extended hospitality to us. God showed us hospitality, and if we are genuinely grateful, we will show hospitality to others.

Particularity, God's hospitality and Christian traditions. The basis, then, of all Christian hospitality is God's hospitality to us. God gives the gift of new life in Christ through his initiative, and in the process he also adopts us into his family and more fully discloses himself and his ways. One of the good gifts that accompany being reconciled to God in Christ is the gift of a particular community of faith. When God extends his hospitality by adopting someone as one of his spiritual children, that child enters into the family of God. As a result, each child has the privilege of entering into meaningful relationship with some of the other members of this family. The boundary implied here by reference to "some" members of the family is not one of sinful sectarianism, but rather a reflection of limitations associated with incarnate finitude and particularity. Although every Christian is in fact related to every other Christian by virtue of sharing membership in the one body of Christ, it is simply impossible for any one member to existentially enter into meaningful relationship with all the members of this family. It is, however, possible—and not only possible, but an obligatory privilege—to pursue substantive and meaningful relationship with some of one's sisters and brothers in Christ. Thus, at its root and properly understood, identification with and participation in a particular Christian tradition is one of God's good gifts.

Identification with a particular community of faith does not constitute commitment to a tradition *as* a tradition. This identification and participation are not to be the expression of loyalty to a tradition for the sake of the tradition. Rather, the opportunity to share in the life of a particular community of faith is part of the hospitality that God extends to us. "By tracing one's personal roots and grounding one's identity in some collectivity with a shared past," notes Gerda Lerner, "one acquires stability and the basis for community."[21] As such, that community of faith—from, for example, small group to local congregation to denominational fellowship—can and should serve as a home, not a fortress, from which and within which hospitality can be extended to those who are members of other communities of Christian faith, as well as those who are not members of any community of faith. Part of God's hospitality is the gift of community, and one should welcome others into that community and serve them through it.

Another gift of God's hospitality is a fuller understanding of God and his ways. God's people have the privilege of exploring and reflecting on his self-disclosures and other revelations, particularly the Holy Scriptures of the Bible. With varying degrees of formality and sophistication, God's people formulate and hold beliefs—often called "theology"—that encapsulate this understanding. In addition to knowledge about God that is available through universal revelation, God reveals himself more fully to those who are his spiritual children. These spiritual children are, by God's grace and under the guidance of the Holy Spirit, inclined and enabled to more fully explore, understand and appreciate God's self-disclosure. As a result of divine renewal of mind and spirit, that which would otherwise be regarded as foolishness is received as divine wisdom (1 Cor 1:18-25). Through a new respect for and desire to know the Word of God, God's children come to new understandings and knowledge through study of the Scriptures, which he has provided. In the effort to "take captive every thought" and to live lives worthy of God by bringing the truth of his Word to bear upon all of life, those who follow Christ over time develop more expansive and amplified understandings of God and his ways (2 Cor 10:5). This growth in knowledge and understanding is characteristic of both individual Christians and communities of faith. This growth in knowledge and understanding occurs within individual lifetimes and across centuries of tradition. It occurs both through formal, intentional study and as an unintended byproduct of Christians simply seeking to follow Christ in daily life in the light of Scripture. And this growth is a good gift from God. None of this is meant to suggest that complete or perfect knowledge is attained. No individual or community exhaustively or unerringly apprehends the truth about God and his ways. However, God does give to his children who seek it, both individually and corporately, a deeper and richer understanding of him and his will. This understanding, and the theological beliefs that accompany it, can and should guide one's life and be shared with other members of Christ's body.[22] A tradition of theology that flows from God's preemptive hospitality is a good gift and, as are all good gifts received from his hand, a resource for, not an enemy of, Christian hospitality.

The Character of Christian Hospitality

Hospitality that issues from God's love for us, and from our love for God and others, has a distinctive and complex character. It is distinctive in that it is grounded in God's love in Christ; it is complex in that it consists in a combination of attitudes and a combination of practices. When rightly understood and embodied, these attitudes and practices reflect something of the complexity of God and his ways, and they render hospitality potent in the complex world in which it is practiced. Hospitality, including theological hospitality, can be understood through an adaptation of what Miroslav Volf refers to as "differentiation" and "embrace." As will be seen below, both are together imperative—both differentiation and embrace.[23]

Differentiation—but not exclusion. Christian hospitality acknowledges and seeks to maintain appropriate boundaries, and in this respect it entails differentiation. Volf clearly distinguishes between creative, life-affirming differentiation and sinful, life-denying exclusion. Exclusion does not consist in an appropriate identification and maintenance of boundaries. Rather, exclusion entails the attempt to do away with "the other" through *either* separating *or* binding. In separating, the one supposedly extending hospitality disconnects from the one to whom the hospitality is extended, with the result that interdependence is broken and the supposed helper becomes instead a domineering sovereign. If someone is a sister or brother in Christ, theological tradition is not a legitimate basis for separating oneself from that person in this domineering way. On the other hand, in binding, all separation and distinction are eradicated in such a way that "the other then emerges as an inferior being who must either be assimilated by being made like the self or be subjugated to the self."[24] Firm adherence to a tradition of theology is no excuse for binding another—that is, for regarding Christians in other theological traditions as inferior Christians. When such binding occurs, one feels the need to make every effort either to assimilate the other to one's own tradition or to be sure that the influence of other traditions is kept under the control of one's own tradition. Theological beliefs should not be used as justification for a posture of exclusion—a posture of either separating or binding—with respect to other members of the body of Christ. These same theological beliefs will, however, be an occasion for differentiation.

Differentiation consists in *both* separating *and* binding. As Volf observes,

> The human self is formed not through a simple rejection of the other—through a binary logic of opposition and negation—but through a complex process of "taking in" and "keeping out." We are who we are not because we are separate from the others who are next to us, but because we are both separate and connected, both distinct and related; the boundaries that mark our identities are both barriers and bridges.[25]

In contrast to boundaries of exclusion, boundaries of differentiation are a necessity in this world. They have life-affirming functions. Boundaries of differentiation help define who we are. Identity, whether individual or collective, entails an awareness of difference. Such awareness is not, and should not be regarded as, the sole factor constituting identity, but it is a necessary dimension of it. This awareness of difference is a necessary condition for a life that is something other than narcissistic. Such awareness enables us to recognize and respect the other as someone other than oneself. It is a necessary step on the way to honoring the uniqueness and importance of other people, or of other theological traditions. This awareness can become, of course, an occasion for disrespecting the other, but this is not inherent in an awareness of otherness. Apart from this awareness there would be no perception of the need to reach out and across boundaries, while with it there is, at the least, the occasion for reaching out. The goal of hospitality is not to achieve identification, but rather to serve the other in a way that helps the other while respecting them for who they are, and this requires the maintenance of appropriate boundaries. Boundaries help define who we are, and the boundaries of Christian traditions help define us as Christians here and now.

For centuries Christians have found ecclesiological and theological homes among a rich diversity of traditions, including those considered in this book. When Christians, whether individually or corporately, incarnate the life of Christ in this world, that incarnated life will be particular. It will be within certain boundaries. There needs to be much careful discussion and discernment with respect to where those boundaries fall and whether or not the boundaries are being appealed to in ways that are divisive and exclusionary. But, boundaries there are and must be. Life in Christ in this world is never "just plain." It is always incarnated in particular ways at a particular place at a particular time by particular people. A proper sense of identity consists in an awareness of this particularity, and, *as long as this is combined with the gracious embrace of hospitality,* there is no sin in being comfortable with particularity and boundaries.

Being "at home" in an ecclesio-theological tradition is a good gift from God. Having such a home provides a wonderful setting from which to extend hospitality—hospitality both to those who are fellow members of the body of Christ and to those who are not. Such a home provides a place of clarity and identity, and as a result, guests can have a sense of where they are and whom they are with. Such a home is a place where hosts are not unduly distracted by confusion of identity or lack of unity, and so they can attend to their guests without undue self-consciousness or defensiveness. And, recognizing that all of us also need to be the recipients of the hospitality of others, such a home is a place to which one can return after having enjoyed the hospitality of others. Feminist scholar Mary D. Pellauer rightly observes, "Theological reflection . . . requires a certain *tradition,* a body of material in continuity with which the newcomer explores the terrain of the faith and life she or he shares with the predecessors—whether to extend its known boundaries or simply to dwell comfortably and with a certain assurance even in the midst of doubts."[26] Boundaries, when regarded in terms of Christian hospitality, are necessary and good.

The pursuit of a fuller manifestation of Christian unity should not consist in the attempt to create a generic church (or, ironically, many generic churches). Christian unity consists not in a generic homogeneity, but in a unity that embraces incarnated particularities. The summons to ecclesio-theological hospitality does not consist in, for example, calling upon Dispensationalists to abandon their basic theological commitments and affirm ones that they do not see in Scripture in order to enter into some form of organizational identification with Pentecostals. Rather, the call to ecclesio-theological hospitality is in keeping with the longing and command for Christian unity that is characteristic of the New Testament: worship the one Lord of all, and love one another. The relationships between Anabaptists and Anglicans, between Lutherans and Baptists, should not be characterized primarily by inattention to or the abandonment of deeply held theological convictions (although, if someone within one of these traditions concludes that such change is warranted, there should be the freedom to pursue this possibility). Rather, their relationships should be characterized by patience, kindness, humility, perseverance and rejoicing in the truth (1 Cor 13:4-7).

Not only do boundaries help define who we are, but also the recognition and maintenance of boundaries constitutes a necessary condition for effective and sustainable hospitality. Without boundaries, hospitality is impossible. People in "helping professions" know this. If they are to be of help, therapists, nurses, ministers and doctors must establish and maintain appropriate boundaries between themselves and the people they serve. Would-be helpers will be of little use if they lose a sense of their own identity and completely identify with the person they hope to assist. The same is true of those who extend hospitality. "Boundaries or guidelines," writes Pohl, "protect guests, maintain communal identity and commitments, and preserve workers."[27] Maintaining appropriate boundaries is in the best interest of hospitality and those to whom it is extended. Volf wisely notes, "Vilify all boundaries, pronounce every discrete identity oppressive, put the tag 'exclusion' on every stable difference—and you will have aimless drifting instead of clear-sighted agency, haphazard activity instead of moral engagement and accountability and, in the long run, a torpor of death instead of a dance of freedom."[28] To be sure, one must seek wisdom to discern between differentiation (which is necessary and appropriate) and disrespect (which is neither necessary nor appropriate), and there must be vigilance in not allowing the maintenance of appropriate boundaries to become an excuse for a failure to reach out across difference. Yet, in order for the virtue of hospitality to be exercised, there must be the strength of identity that is grounded in differentiation combined with the commitment to use that strength to extend hospitality to the other.

Embrace: Strangers and divine hospitality. Christian hospitality transcends boundaries, extending grace and generosity to the stranger. In this way it incarnates embrace. Hospitality "reflects and anticipates God's welcome."[29] Christian hospitality consists in both differentiation and embrace. In hospitality, the host becomes the one through whom the Father reaches across boundaries to embrace and give gracious gifts to the stranger. Differentiation, including the existence of boundaries, must be maintained, but only in conjunction with embrace. Scripture is replete with references to the distinct yet overlapping images of those who are different, those who are "other"—the stranger, the sojourner, the foreigner, the alien, the pilgrim.[30] These "others" are both unfamiliar and foreign. This history of otherness, of strangeness and stranger-ness, illustrates the fact that strangers need a place to be, whether for short-term rest or for long-term residence. The stranger is worthy of embrace. Hospitality extends the embrace of welcome. Christian hospitality extends the embrace of Christ's welcome.

Hospitality is first and foremost an attitude, and as an attitude it is first and foremost love. How does love regard and respond to a stranger in need of embrace? Those moved by the love of God that issues in hospitality recognize that they themselves are strangers. "This person is a Christian," writes Augustine, "who, even in his own house and in his own country, acknowledges himself to be a stranger."[31] Furthermore, such people recognize that they are strangers who have been embraced by God. The apostle John states, "In this is love, not that we loved God but that he loved us. . . . We love because he first loved us" (1 Jn 4:10, 19; see also Rom 15:7). This is self-awareness of an un-self-centered kind. This is self-awareness *coram Deo* ("before God"). When faced by a stranger, those who extend the embrace of hospitality have a keen awareness of God's hospitality toward them. Furthermore, this awareness includes not only a proper sense of who they are (namely, strangers) and what God has done (embraced them), but also an awareness that what they have to offer in hospitality is ultimately from God. In embracing the stranger, what does one give but that which one has been given? All we have comes from the gracious provision sent to us by our Father in heaven (see Deut 8:1-18; Eph 2:8-10; Jas 1:17). With regard to ecclesio-theological traditions, this means that whatever measure of truth is apprehended and articulated by the tradition has been received, ultimately, from God. This is one embodiment of what it means to "love because he first loved us"—we can give because God has given to us. We are equipped for hospitality by virtue of the divine hospitality that has already been extended to us.

As we noted earlier, one dimension of God's hospitality to us is the opportunity to enter into an identifiable community of faith. However, in order for identification with a particular Christian tradition to manifest itself as a good gift from God (which it is), this identification must be combined with an embracing grace that extends across boundaries to those brothers and sisters in Christ who are not "at home" in this same tradition. The impetus for this kind of embrace begins with the awareness of having been first embraced by God. Although a person now may be at home in a particular Christian community, this is only because God first reached out to that person when he or she was a stranger. Whatever blessings one might enjoy by virtue of identifying with a particular Christian community of faith, these blessings are a gift from God. They are not of one's own doing, so that no one can boast and no one should hoard. Rather, the resources of a particular community of faith, including its theological resources, should be shared with and used for the good of others. One's community of faith should be viewed not as a fortress, but as a home base from which to serve others.

In addition to the awareness of being recipients of God's initiating hospitality, those who use their ecclesio-theological home as an occasion for hospitality have an awareness that they continue to stand in need of God's gracious hospitality, an awareness that they continue to be a stranger in this world. One's particular understanding and incarnation of faith is not exhaustive of the Christian faith. It is not perfect. It is not definitive. It is a work of grace and a work in progress. Baptists and Wesleyans who reach out to embrace Christian sisters and brothers in Presbyterian and Anglican traditions know that within this world and within the church they themselves are strangers.

The love of God that issues in hospitality entails not only an awareness of one's self as stranger, but also a proper awareness of the other as stranger. Christians ought to regard brothers and sisters in other traditions of Christianity not as opponents, but as fellow *strangers*. Although these co-members of the body of Christ are nothing less than sisters and brothers in the faith, they are strangers to one another when a lack of knowledge and understanding or a lack of appreciation and respect stands between them. And, when this is the case, they are best regarded as *fellow* strangers. All those who are reconciled to God in Christ are members of the body of Christ. As such, those who are strangers by virtue of being yet unknown and belonging to other ecclesio-theological traditions are nonetheless members of the same household of faith in Christ and thus fellow strangers. They are also fellow strangers by virtue of the fact that, as noted earlier, those who extend hospitality to others are themselves strangers. Those who extend theological hospitality to people in other

Christian traditions do so neither because they, unlike their guests, already have all theological truth and thus have nothing to learn (i.e., separating) nor because they need to work to bring others into conformity with their tradition (i.e., binding). Rather, those who extend theological hospitality do so with the awareness that they themselves are also in need of learning more. They extend hospitality as from one stranger to another. In fact, they are aware of the possibility that the stranger may prove to be a messenger of God. The exhortation to hospitality by the author of Hebrews includes the disclosure that in hosting strangers some have "entertained angels without knowing it" (Heb 13:2).[32] Something akin to this is perhaps even more likely when the stranger is a member of the body of Christ.[33] Anglicans who enter into genuine conversation with Dispensationalists, or Pentecostals who enter into conversation with Lutherans, may actually gain a new and more thoroughly biblical understanding of the church and of life in Christ.

The Potential of Theological Hospitality

The crossing of boundaries always entails both risks and benefits, and crossing boundaries of Christian theological traditions is no exception. It is only appropriate, then, to identify the potential losses and gains associated with theological hospitality.

Potential risks of theological hospitality. Entering into substantive interaction with members of a Christian tradition different from one's own can unsettle one's sense of identity.[34] When Methodists and Baptists engage in sustained and meaningful theological conversation or cooperate in some ministry endeavor, there is the possibility that people's own theological beliefs will be challenged, if not changed. Furthermore, their view of the beliefs held by persons from the other tradition may be similarly challenged or changed. Such changes can be unsettling, leading to something of an identity crisis. "By welcoming strangers," writes Pohl, "the community's identity is always being challenged and revised, if only slightly. While this is often enriching, it can occasionally stretch a place beyond recognition."[35] Indeed, as noted in the introductory chapter, historians and theologians in a number of traditions have given increased attention to questions of identity, sometimes using precisely the language of "identity crisis" to describe what has happened within their traditions during the last half of the twentieth century.[36] Churches and denominations that once had a clear sense of who they were and what they believed have become increasingly uncertain or fragmented as a result, at least in part, of increased interaction with Christians of other traditions or attempts to draw into their communities people from more diverse backgrounds. There are, for example, Baptist churches that are accepting into membership people who have not been baptized. Some Mennonite fellowships are struggling with whether one can support government war efforts and still be authentically Mennonite. There are churches within classically Pentecostal denominations that do not emphasize or publicly encourage speaking in tongues as the initial physical evidence of baptism in the Holy Spirit. Whether or not one thinks that such changes are for the good, the point here is that such challenges and changes strike at some of the defining marks of these traditions and, as a result, can be very unsettling. Pohl observes, "The practice of hospitality challenges the boundaries of a community while it simultaneously depends on that community's identity to make a space that nourishes life."[37] Some may consider the chance of an "identity crisis," like those described above, as a risk too great to take.

A second and related risk associated with theological hospitality is that of division within one's own community of faith. Ironically, the pursuit of a fuller realization of Christian unity with members of other Christian traditions can result in fragmentation within one's own tradition. If members of an Anglican congregation and members of an independent Bible church that is Dispensational in its theology enter into sustained conversation or some form of joint mission, some members of the Anglican congregation may find considerable affinity with aspects of Dispensational theology and the life of the Bible church while other members of the Anglican community will experience no such affinity and become more deeply appreciative of the Anglican way. These kinds of differences within a community of faith can prove troubling, if not divisive, and some will find this risk too great to take even for the sake of ecclesio-theological hospitality and a greater realization of Christian unity.

These two risks—identity crises and division—can be reduced by the adoption of the both/and perspective on Christian unity proposed above. The pursuit of greater Christian unity should be marked by both differentiation and embrace— or, at this point in our discussion it might be helpful to refer to embrace and differentiation. Christians entering into sustained engagement with persons of other Christian traditions should not feel compelled to abandon fundamental theological beliefs, though some may choose to do so. Embrace takes place only where there is differentiation, and differentiation can and should be an occasion for the divine work of embrace. The risk of identity crises and division within a community of faith will be reduced when the expectations assumed and the agenda pursued do not focus on eliminating all difference and diversity, but rather encourage patient understanding of and love for those with whom one differs. That said, the fact is that the risks remain, and they should not be dealt with by denying that they exist. Having acknowledged these risks, we need to ask the question "Should Christian communities of faith nonetheless venture into theological hospitality?"

An affirmative response to this question is already implicit in that this book (and perhaps the reading of it) is an exercise in theological hospitality. This being the case, one must then ask, "How can the pursuit of theological hospitality be justified in light of the risks, and what, if any, are the benefits?" First, the importance of the both/and approach of embrace and differentiation must not be underestimated. Christians, whether individuals or churches, should not be encouraged to pursue a greater realization of the oneness of the body of Christ *primarily by means of the avoidance or elimination of all theological distinctives.* Such an approach may foster an unhealthy loss of identity and *undermine an appropriate sense of theological conviction and integrity.* The Bible has much to say, and its interpretation and application to life, both individual and corporate, are important tasks that, despite differences among Christians, ought to be pursued with vigor, seriousness and integrity. Oneness should not be pursued through ignoring or bypassing theology. The pursuit of greater oneness in Christ *through a divine and gracious embrace across the boundaries of differences* can lead to a more authentic oneness while reducing the risk of an unhealthy loss of either identity or theological integrity. Furthermore, by applying this same principle not only between communities of faith but *within* communities of faith, we further reduce the risk of division within a particular community. Ironically, some of the most divisive theological exchanges take place between Christians who identify with the same Christian tradition or who belong to the same local congregation. The spirit of gracious embrace that ought to characterize relationships among Christians of various traditions ought also to characterize those who are co-members in a particular Christian community.

The "both/and" of differentiation and embrace is a theologically sound principle that can shape theological hospitality in a way that minimizes, though will never eliminate, the most significant risks associated with it. And, the measure of risk that remains should not deter one from the venture of theological hospitality. The call of the Christian life is not a call to safety—that is, no risk—but rather is a call to pursue the abundant life found in and through Jesus Christ, and part of that abundant life is the greater realization of the oneness of God's people, the body of Christ.

Benefits of theological hospitality. In addition to acknowledging the risks, it is essential that we also note the benefits of Christian hospitality "across" traditions. The exercise of theological hospitality honors God's will and desire, as expressed in Christ's prayer that his followers "be one." The sincere and responsible venture into theological hospitality constitutes one dimension of obedience to God—a benefit, if such terminology is appropriate, in and of itself. As is so often the case, obedience to God entails humility. In the case of theological hospitality, humility entails admitting that one's theology is neither complete nor free of errors. "Self-criticism of a tradition," writes Martin Marty, "is a key to the practice of hospitality."[38] No tradition of Christian theology can claim comprehensive and perfectly accurate knowledge of and conformity to the Word of God. Whatever the theological understanding of an individual Christian or the richness of the heritage of an ecclesio-theological tradition, there is always room for improvement. Such fallibility is often acknowledged, at least in principle, but theological hospitality requires acting upon this humility. Whether one is the host or the guest, theological hospitality entails recognizing oneself as a stranger and entering into mutual conversation, including conversation about matters on which traditions differ. In return, this action holds the prospective benefit of improving one's theology and, as a result, strengthening one's foundation for Christian life and ministry.

Theological improvements may take various forms, from filling in gaps to rectifying imbalances, and even to correcting errors. For example, through engagement with Pentecostal Christians, Dispensational Christians may come to affirm and thereby experience a greater range of work by the Holy Spirit than they would apart from such engagement. Through extending hospitality to Anglican Christians, a Baptist church may come a fuller understanding of the grace of God that comes to his people through the Lord's Supper. Through candid interaction with Anabaptists, Presbyterian Christians may revise their understanding of the relationship between Christians and society, including civil government. For each of these examples, one could, of course, posit a parallel yet inverse direction of influence. Pentecostal Christians could revise their understanding of the Holy Spirit in light of engagement with Dispensational Christians, some Anglicans might modify their understanding of the Lord's Supper by virtue of the hospitality of Baptists, and Anabaptist Christians may come to view their relationship to civil authority a bit differently as result of their interaction with Presbyterians. Such mutual benefit is what can be hoped for and expected. At the same time, genuine humility means being open to and celebrating improvement in one's own theology whether or not there is a corresponding change in the theology of one's conversation partner.[39]

Furthermore, in addition to obeying Christ's call to pursue greater oneness and improving one's theology through bringing it into closer accord with the Word of God, the exercise of theological hospitality can move Christians toward a greater realization of the oneness of the body of Christ. Beyond obedient pursuit—worthy in itself—hospitality can lead to a greater actualization of the oneness of the people of God. Emboldened by a combination of Christian love, theological conviction and humble openness to the other, those who participate in theological hospitality may find themselves attaining a greater awareness of beliefs already held in common, a greater degree of shared belief through revisions in theology, or a greater respect for and commitment to each other as fellow members of the one body of Christ despite—and, perhaps, because of— theological differences. Any such developments are nothing less than steps toward the fulfillment of Jesus' prayer in John 17. Pohl writes, "Part of our ability to sustain hospitality in the midst of an unjust and disordered world comes from putting our small efforts into a larger context. God is at work in the world, and our little but significant moves participate in that work."[40] Participation in theological hospitality is rightly understood as participation in God's continuing work of building his church as one people of God in this world. Christians who are Baptist or Pentecostal, Wesleyan or Reformed, Lutheran or Dispensational, Anglican or Anabaptist, are all members of God's church in this world by virtue of being reconciled to God in Jesus Christ. Regardless of tradition, all who are adopted by God and fellow heirs with Christ are adopted into the one family of God (see Rom 8:15-17; Gal 4:4-7; Eph 1:5). Rather than being "strangers and aliens" in relation to one another, they are "citizens with the saints and also members of the household of God" (see Eph 2:19). Jesus' prayer for unity was neither misguided nor unheard. God is at work building a more united church (Mt 16:18; 1 Cor 3:10-11; Eph 2:19-22; 1 Pet 2:4-5), and sincere participation in theological hospitality is one form of participation in this work.

In *A Contemporary Anabaptist Theology: Biblical, Historical, Constructive*, Thomas Finger provides a helpful example of theology done in the spirit of both particularity and universality. As the book's title indicates, Finger writes from a self-consciously and unapologetically Anabaptist location. While the book is an exercise in constructive theology, explicit engagement with the history of Anabaptism and its theologies is woven throughout, and the selection and ordering of topics, as well as the discussion thereof, reflect the Anabaptist tradition. At the same time, Finger desires to engage in theology in a way that advances the thought and life of the one body of Christ. He suggests, "Diversities, of course, are valuable, particularly when they contribute insights from marginalized Christian families. . . . But if theology simply revels in particularities, can churches form a vision strong, clear and unified enough to interact with today's globalizing forces? Not, I propose, unless theology's traditional quest for universal affirmations also plays a role."[41] In the face of divisions between, for example, Roman Catholics and Protestants, marginalized groups and majority groups, liberals and conservatives, Finger audaciously proposes that his particular tradition can contribute to the pursuit of unifying, and thereby empowering, theological reflection. "In today's culture," he writes, "which prizes particularity yet where many tendencies press swiftly toward globality, an unlikely, very particular Christian communion, the Anabaptists, can aid theology in addressing both dimensions."[42] The work of the Wesleyan Holiness Study Project provides another example of serious theological work that seeks to combine particularity with universality. This initiative brings together scholars from ten denominations to engage in fresh theological reflection that is self-consciously grounded in the Wesleyan-Holiness tradition and, at the same time, offered to the worldwide Church with the specific desire that their work be used to encourage greater unity among Christians of all traditions.[43] Yet another example is *Feminist and Womanist Essays in Reformed Dogmatics,* edited by Amy Plantinga Pauw and Serene Jones. Here the editors and contributors write "out of the conviction that Reformed traditions offer resources to nourish feminist and womanist concerns, and that these concerns offer a way of carrying forward Reformed traditions."[44] The work of theology in the service of the church will be greatly advanced as more theologians in other traditions engage in constructive theology in the spirit of both particularity and universality modeled by these scholars and initiatives.

Finally, both the act and the fruit of theological hospitality will advance the witness to God in the world and, by God's grace and power, draw others toward Christ. This, too, is in accord with Jesus' prayer. As we noted earlier, Jesus prayed for unity among his followers "to let the world know" that the Father had sent him and loved them, and that as a result they might believe in him (John 17:21-23). The unity that is realized is not exclusively, nor even primarily, for the benefit of Christians (though it certainly is a blessing), but rather is for the glory of God and the benefit of those who are not yet members of the household of God. Substantive and respectful theological dialogue between Baptists and Wesleyans, Lutherans and Pentecostals, Reformed and Anabaptists, or Anglicans and Dispensationalists is noteworthy. Unfortunately, it is noteworthy, at least in part, because it stands in stark contrast to the sinful divisiveness that has so often characterized ecclesio-theological traditions of Christianity. Christians of various traditions joining together in grace-filled yet substantive theological conversation or mission is a wonderful witness to the world. And, even if such joint ventures themselves are not publicly recognized, the long-term results will strengthen the people of God for the work of God in the world. The world will know that we are Christians not by how little theology we passionately hold, but by how much we love. The world will see divinely inspired love and acceptance at work when Christians incarnate love and acceptance by embracing each other across boundaries of difference.

Epilogue

SOME FRUIT OF THEOLOGICAL HOSPITALITY

M y faith and life have been enriched through studying and experiencing some of the wide-ranging diversity within Protestant Christianity, only a portion of which has been considered in the present work. Though not recounted here, to my benefit this journey has also included engagement with Eastern Orthodox and Roman Catholic Christians. Through reading texts, participating in worship services, conversing with clergy and laity, and simply enjoying Christian friendship and fellowship, I have gained an appreciation for many Protestant traditions.

I have enjoyed my exercise in theological hospitality and have attempted to keep in mind the posture of a learner described in the introductory chapter, frequently asking the question, "What lessons can I learn about Christian faith and life?" As I have reflected upon my encounters with the traditions, not surprisingly I have come away with both lessons of dissent and lessons of assent. There are beliefs and practices that I have observed and, based on my encounter, have determined that I would not affirm or adopt. These dissenting appraisals often were accompanied by a confirmation or reaffirmation of beliefs and practices that I already embraced. Thus, the contrast with views different from my own, views from which I decided to dissent, proved instructive. At the same time, there are beliefs and practices that led me into lessons of assent. Once again, the differences between the traditions and my previously held views proved instructive, though in this case prompting me to revise my own theology or practice. As will sometimes be apparent in the few pages that follow, some of these lessons have been drawn from doctrines or dimensions of the traditions beyond those explicitly considered in the preceding chapters.

It is risky to offer abridged comments about someone else's faith tradition, particularly when those comments are evaluative. Nonetheless, in the spirit of the risks of hospitality addressed in the concluding chapter, I offer here some reflections on lessons I have learned to date. I begin with four overarching lessons that have arisen from comparing the traditions.

First, I have been struck by the fact that the traditions studied here share a significant number of fundamental theological commitments in common. As noted in the introductory chapter, due to the selectivity applied in the preceding chapters, this commonality is not clearly reflected in the descriptions of the traditions. However, all of the classical expressions of Protestant Christianity affirm, each in its own way, basic doctrines such as the Trinity, the humanity and deity of Jesus Christ, the human need for salvation, the salvific work of Christ, the accompanying works of the Holy Spirit, the importance of the church, and the certainty of God's ultimately victorious reign in and through Jesus Christ. This body of shared belief should not be taken for granted and should be celebrated.[1]

Second, these common areas of belief are to a significant degree the fruit of two formal or methodological commonalities: commitments to the Bible and to the application of biblical truth. Despite the stereotypes of each tradition and the corresponding jokes that are made—sometimes in jest, sometimes not—about the idiosyncrasies of each tradition, the fact is that the classical streams of all of the traditions studied here affirm the authority of the Bible and seek to formulate theology that is true to Scripture. None of the Protestant traditions in principle place any source of theology above, much less against, the Bible, and all of them want their theology to be formulated in accord with Scripture. They also view the ultimate purpose of the theological enterprise as being the transformation of Christians and the empowerment of the church. None of these traditions encourages theological understanding solely for the purpose of increased knowledge. Theology is to be practical, and theological work is incomplete until the truth of theology is applied to the lives of God's people, both individually and corporately. This was not a surprise, but this belief in the importance and value of theology applied to Christian life was impressed upon me once again.

Third, tracing the progress of Protestant traditions through a pair of cultural upheavals in the United States brought a renewed and more poignant awareness that Christianity is a historical, incarnated faith. Timeline diagrams such as those in the preceding chapters cannot adequately convey the wrenching divisions that separated Christians black and white, North and South, beginning in the 1840s and continuing, in some cases, into today. And, this fresh awareness of the historical character of Christian faith was further reinforced as I traced the paths of Christian traditions through the 1960s and beyond. The many contextual theologies that emerged and continue to develop—feminist, African American, womanist, Asian American, ecological and postmodern, to name but a few—are a reminder of the necessity for the members of each generation to engage their time with an appropriate combination of change and continuity. These contextual theologies are not prominent in the preceding chapters, in part because in many instances they transcend or bypass, rather than build or elaborate upon, the traditions considered here. In many instances, the existential and contextual factors that give rise to these theological movements have an equal or greater role in shaping the theology than do the explicitly theological commitments that have historically shaped the traditions described in the preceding chapters. This is one of the reasons for some of the "identity crises" noted in the introductory and concluding chapters. The impact that the dramatic cultural changes since the mid-twentieth century on the landscape of Christian traditions, like the upheavals of the mid-nineteenth century, reminded me once again of the inescapable call to live one's beliefs in *this* world, not some other world. The stories of how these traditions—both those that are a century or more old and those that are more recently emergent—will relate to each other is only beginning to be written.

A fourth overarching observation reflects an unanticipated outcome for me. I could not help but be struck by the importance of the church and churches. Both the nature and task of theology and the substance of the beliefs that result from it are intimately tied to the reality of Christian community. As I have surveyed the various traditions, attempting to discern the methods and doctrines that constitute the distinctives of each tradition, I have been struck by how often ecclesiology was part of the mix. Whether one considers, for example, the guidance from confessions in the Lutheran hermeneutic, or Baptist concern for preserving the purity and autonomy of churches, or Anabaptist emphasis on community, God's corporate people loom large in the classical traditions of Protestantism. In these traditions, theology is important to the church and the churches, and the church and the churches are important in theology. As a result, I come away from this study with a new level of respect and appreciation for the church.

Having noted these four general lessons, I will now offer a brief response to each of the traditions considered in this book, describing my own lessons of dissent and assent.

I do not share with Lutheran Christians their particular sacramental understanding of baptism and the Lord's Supper. However, although I thereby do not concur with the teaching of the Lutheran confessions on this, as well as some other matters, I do appreciate the commitment to being guided by confessional heritage in both biblical interpretation and theological formulation. Furthermore, I share with many Christians a tendency to live according to a *psychology* of works righteousness even though I do not cognitively affirm a *theology* of works righteousness—and from my first reading years ago of Martin Luther's *The Freedom of the Christian* through the present day, I continue to be challenged and helped by the classical Lutheran emphasis on salvation by grace alone.

The Anabaptist tradition is, in my estimation, often too separatist-minded with respect to the broader confessional heritage of the church and, at times, with respect to society at large. However, my view of this tradition has changed over the years, and my appreciation for it has grown. I am increasingly challenged by the counterworldly peacemaking call of the Anabaptist tradition, as well as the Gospels-centered hermeneutic and christocentric theology behind this call. Moreover, the Anabaptist emphasis on Christian community, including the importance of community in biblical interpretation and theological reflection, is a rich resource for Christian engagement in and with postmodern culture.

Although (or, perhaps, because) my personal commitments are with the Reformed tradition, I observe here a tendency to underestimate the present and powerful work of the Holy Spirit, and the supernatural joy and victory that result from this work. Even though Reformed churches unapologetically affirm the doctrine of the Trinity, the "third person" is sometimes hard to find. Yet, at the heart of my attraction to and continuance in this tradition is a realistic assessment of the fallen human condition combined with the guiding affirmation of the glory, sovereignty and grace of God. Furthermore, grounded in a recognition of the ways in which this sovereignty is manifest in God's general revelation and common grace, the Reformed tradition continues to robustly affirm the life of the Christian mind and engagement with culture.

As someone who values in-depth theological discourse combined with strength of theological conviction, I am sometimes disappointed with Anglican reluctance to be "too detailed" or "too dogmatic" with respect to doctrine. I am challenged, however, by the value that Anglican Christians place on the unity and catholicity of the church. (This is a value that I seek to honor, in an admittedly modest way, in this book.) Furthermore, I have often experienced spiritual refreshment through *The Book of Common Prayer* and been nourished in worship services conducted under its tutelage. I also appreciate the value that Anglicanism places upon the aesthetic in Christian spirituality, both individual and corporate.

I am sometimes troubled by the Baptist tendency to cultivate an individualistic spirit. This manifests itself with respect to both the way individual Christians view their relationship to the church (or, more true to the Baptist heritage, church*es*) and the way individual local congregations view their relationship to the greater body of Christ. Yet, much of my life has been spent in close personal and professional relationships with Baptist Christians, and I have been encouraged and challenged by their affirmation of the priesthood of all believers. Additionally, I have seen enough ritualistic Christianity to be grateful for the Baptist emphasis on "a personal relationship" with Jesus Christ, and have witnessed enough ecclesiastical politics to recognize a measure of wisdom in the Baptist mistrust of ecclesiastical hierarchy.

The Wesleyan tradition is too optimistic, I believe, with respect to the human condition and human potential. This is true of the view of human beings, both apart from redemptive renewal in Christ by the Holy Spirit and in the context of this redemptive renewal. Yet, this same optimism, viewed in its context of the loving and supernatural work of God, challenges me to move toward a greater longing for and aspiration to a life of holiness. I am also challenged by the model of social action and the significant ministries of women that have characterized the history of the Methodist and Holiness traditions.

Dispensational theology has too often promoted what I consider to be an unhealthy disjuncture within the people of God. While Christians must acknowledge that the history of the church is painfully punctuated by distrust, disrespect and even hatred of Jews, the Dispensational view of the Jews as a special people has often led to a disjointed view of the single New Covenant community in Christ, both Jew and Gentile, both present and future. Furthermore, Dispensational teaching on the eschatological *future* has often provided the rationale for a lack of concrete Christian engagement with *present* societal and cultural affairs. Having said this, I must also say that Christians who affirm Dispensational theology have, in general, demonstrated an extraordinary respect for the Scriptures and a fervent desire to formulate a theology that is thoroughly biblical. This pursuit of a thoroughly biblical theology is marked by a confidence in the internal unity and coherence of the Bible combined with confidence in the correspondence between the teachings of the Bible and events in the world.

Pentecostalism, in general, appears to continue to struggle with an unhealthy neglect, if not distrust, of rigorous theological study, and when this tradition does engage in such theological reflection, "experience" often seems to play a more determinative role than it should. Additionally, these tendencies contribute to an imbalance wherein the Holy Spirit is sometimes given a prominence disproportionate to that given to Jesus and the Father. Nonetheless, we Christians who stand outside the Pentecostal tradition would do well to reconsider the roles that experience and narrative biblical texts (such as those in Acts) play in our theological method. We may find that we should give those texts more attention than we do, and that we should acknowledge the role that experience in fact plays in our theologies. As for the Holy Spirit, some non-Pentecostal traditions could attain a more genuinely Trinitarian, as opposed to binitarian, theology by giving due honor to the "third person."

For these and other lessons learned I am thankful, with the hope that such learning might continue for the rest of my earthly journey with Christ in his church.

Notes

Chapter 1: Introduction

[1] Contrary to a currently popular belief, this type of identification with a particular Christian tradition is not necessarily bad (as I will argue below).

[2] Susan M. Felch, "'In the Chorus of Others': M. M. Bakhtin's Sense of Tradition," in *The Force of Tradition: Response and Resistance in Literature, Religion, and Cultural Studies,* ed. Donald G. Marshall (Lanham, Md.: Rowman & Littlefield, 2005), p. 58.

[3] For Roman Catholicism, see, for example, Kevin O. Johnson, *Expressions of the Catholic Faith: A Guide to the Teachings and Practices of the Catholic Church* (New York: Ballantine, 1994); Richard P. McBrien, *Catholicism,* rev. ed. (San Francisco: HarperSanFrancisco, 1994); and *A New Catechism: Catholic Faith for Adults,* trans. Kevin Smyth (New York: Crossroad, 1988). For Eastern Orthodoxy, see Kallistos Ware, *The Orthodox Way,* rev. ed. (Crestwood, N.Y.: St. Vladimir's Seminary Press, 1995); Vladimir Lossky, *Orthodox Theology: An Introduction* (Crestwood, N.Y.: St. Vladimir's Seminary Press, 1978); and Daniel B. Clendenin, *Eastern Orthodox Christianity: A Western Perspective,* 2nd ed. (Grand Rapids: Baker, 2003).

[4] Within most, if not all, of these traditions there are those who argue that their tradition has its origins in Jesus, the apostles, and the New Testament church rather than in historical persons and events of the sixteenth century or later. However, without denying that Jesus and the New Testament church are foundational, or that the sixteenth century can be properly understood only in the context of the fifteen centuries that preceded it, scholars from within each of these traditions acknowledge a later historical emergence of the traditions as distinct, historically identifiable movements within the church.

[5] Leo Driedger and Leland Harder, eds., *Anabaptist-Mennonite Identities in Ferment,* Occasional Papers 14 (Elkhart, Ind.: Institute of Mennonite Studies, 1990); Thomas F. Torrance et al., "Debating Reformed Identity," *Reformed Review* 54.1 (Autumn 2000): 5-56; Stephen H. Applegate, "The Rise and Fall of the Thirty-Nine Articles: An Inquiry into the Identity of the Protestant Episcopal Church in the United States," *Historical Magazine of the Protestant Episcopal Church* 50 (December 1981): 409-21; Timothy George, "Conflict and Identity in the Southern Baptist Convention: The Quest for a New Consensus," in *Beyond the Impasse? Scripture, Interpretation, and Theology in Baptist Life,* ed. Robison B. James and David S. Dockery (Nashville: Broadman, 1992), pp. 195-214. Questions of "identity" will be addressed more fully in the concluding chapter.

[6] For example, R. Wayne Stacy writes, "It is notoriously difficult to speak with authority on any

282 Notes to Pages 20-26

issue of 'Baptist theology.' For, indeed, there is no such thing as the 'Baptist theology.' There are only Baptists' theologies. Even given Baptist diversity, however, one can find some common features to Baptist thinking" ("Baptism," in *A Baptist's Theology,* ed. R. Wayne Stacy [Macon, Ga.: Smyth & Helwys, 1999], p. 154).

[7]In part because classical traditions of theology have been, by and large, closely linked to the life of the church, theology is formulated and expressed in diverse forms, including, for example, devotional literature, liturgy, music, preaching and poetry. These resources are, for the most part, beyond the scope of the present book, but they constitute rich resources for pursuing a more comprehensive engagement with the traditions considered here.

[8]Studies seeking to chart the influence of Dispensationalism include Peter E. Prosser, *Dispensationalist Eschatology and Its Influence on American and British Religious Movements,* Texts and Studies in Religion 82 (Lewiston, N.Y.: Edwin Mellen, 1999); Timothy P. Weber, *Living in the Shadow of the Second Coming: American Premillennialism, 1875-1982* (Chicago: University of Chicago Press, 1987).

[9]Clodovis Boff, "Epistemology and Method of the Theology of Liberation," in *Mysterium Liberationis: Fundamental Concepts of Liberation Theology,* ed. Ignacio Ellacuriá and Jon Sobrino (Maryknoll, N.Y.: Orbis, 1993), pp. 66-69.

[10]Stanley J. Grenz and Roger E. Olson, *Who Needs Theology? An Invitation to the Study of God* (Downers Grove, Ill.: InterVarsity Press, 1996), pp. 24-35.

[11]Though beyond the scope of this book, theology also finds expression through other vehicles such as music, sermons, devotional literature, and poetry, to name some.

[12]See, for example, Barbara H. MacHaffie, *Her Story: Women in Christian Tradition* (Philadelphia: Fortress, 1986), p. 68.

[13]Anthony J. Carter, *On Being Black and Reformed: A New Perspective on the African-American Christian Experience* (Phillipsburg, N.J.: P & R, 2003), p. 73.

[14]The early years of an ecclesio-theological tradition are uniquely formative. These years typically generate defining and identifying characteristics that in some form abide as long as the tradition is recognized as a tradition.

[15]Henry was director of the Institute for Ecumenical and Cultural Research, St. John's University, Collegeville, Minnesota, during my residence at the Institute, and he shared this and other words of wisdom during the early stages of the writing of this book.

[16]Harold T. Lewis, "Whose Tradition?" in *Theological Education for the Future,* ed. Guy F. Lytle (Cincinnati: Forward Movement, 1988), p. 53.

[17]Jaroslav Pelikan describes a shift during the eighteenth and nineteenth centuries "from a static definition (and consequent rejection) of continuity to a wistfully romantic portrayal of change and loss to an innovative effort at a redefinition of continuity that embraces change," and challenges "the modern enthronement of historical change as the primary category by which to understand doctrines and creeds" (*Credo: Historical and Theological Guide to Creeds and Confessions of Faith in the Christian Tradition* [New Haven: Yale University Press, 2003], pp. 32, 33).

[18]On continuity in theology, see Pelikan, *Credo,* pp. 7-34; and R. P. C. Hanson, *The Continuity of Christian Doctrine* (New York: Seabury, 1981).

[19]Marva Dawn, *Talking the Walk: Letting Christian Language Live Again* (Grand Rapids: Brazos, 2005), p. 14.

[20]For example, Maurice Wiles, *The Making of Christian Doctrine* (Cambridge: Cambridge University Press, 1967); *The Remaking of Christian Doctrine* (Philadelphia: Westminster Press, 1978); Karlfried Froehlich, "Problems of Lutheran Hermeneutics," in *Studies in Lutheran*

Hermeneutics, ed. John Reumann, Samuel H. Nafger and Harold H. Ditmanson (Philadelphia: Fortress, 1979), p. 131.

[21]See, for example, David P. Scaer, "How Do Lutheran Theologians Approach the Doing of Theology Today?" in *Doing Theology in Today's World: Essays in Honor of Kenneth S. Kantzer,* ed. John D. Woodbridge and Thomas E. McComiskey (Grand Rapids: Zondervan, 1991), pp. 201-2.

[22]The use of "minority/majority" language with reference to theological traditions is not without its problems, because with the exception of denominational votes (which themselves sometimes are seen as less than representative of "the people in the pews") on matters of doctrine and polity, we do not have mathematical statistics on the history and current status of specific traditions of theological belief. That said, it is very common for people within a particular tradition, including scholars of the tradition, to talk in terms of minority/majority views. For example, Richard Taylor writes, "We must resist any covert insinuation . . . that holiness is in any sense a maverick emphasis instead of the heart of the Christian faith—even if it has not always been seen as such by the majority of Christendom" ("Historical and Modern Significance of Wesleyan Theology," in *A Contemporary Wesleyan Theology: Biblical, Systematic, and Practical,* ed. Charles W. Carter, 2 vols. [Grand Rapids: Zondervan, 1983], 1:57-58). Speaking of those who are guided by historical confessions of faith, George Lindbeck observes, "Even if they are a small minority, they function as the church's conscience" ("Ecumenical Directions and Confessional Construals," *Dialog* 30 [spring 1991]: 119).

[23]Readers who are interested in a more complete introduction to the principles of theological hospitality may choose to read the concluding chapter before turning to the chapters on the various traditions.

[24]As already suggested, I am of the belief that for Christians who seek to live the Christian life in communion with other Christians (which clearly is God's design), there is no such thing as "traditionless" Christianity. If you participate in the life of a community of Christians that has spanned more than one generation, you are part of a tradition, regardless of how "contemporary" or "nontraditional" or "Bible only" that community claims to be.

Chapter 2: A Gospel of Grace

[1]For a recent discussion of Luther's place in the Lutheran tradition, see Eric W. Gritsch, *A History of Lutheranism* (Minneapolis: Fortress, 2002), pp. 257-60.

[2]Martin Luther, *Luther's Works,* vol. 26, *Lectures on Galatians, 1535,* ed. and trans. Jaroslav Pelikan (St. Louis: Concordia, 1963), p. 9.

[3]Eric W. Gritsch, *Fortress Introduction to Lutheranism* (Minneapolis: Fortress, 1994), p. 4.

[4]Eric W. Gritsch and Robert W. Jenson, *Lutheranism: The Theological Movement and Its Confessional Writings* (Philadelphia: Fortress, 1976), p. 4.

[5]In the preface to his commentary on Romans, Luther writes, "This epistle is really the chief part of the New Testament, and is truly the purest gospel" (*Luther's Works,* vol. 35, *Word and Sacrament,* ed. E. Theodore Bachmann [Philadelphia: Fortress, 1960], p. 365).

[6]Ibid., p. 368.

[7]E. Theodore Bachmann and Mercia Brenne Bachmann, *Lutheran Churches in the World: A Handbook* (Minneapolis: Augsburg, 1989), p. 29; Günther Gassmann and Scott Hendrix, *Fortress Introduction to the Lutheran Confessions* (Minneapolis: Fortress, 1999), p. 37. Gritsch and Jenson refer to the Augsburg Confession as "The Lutheran Magna Carta" (*Lutheranism,* p. 23).

[8]The Greek word *gnōsios* means "authentic." Gnesio-Lutherans claimed to be, unlike the Philippists, genuinely or authentically Lutheran.

[9]Gritsch, *Introduction to Lutheranism,* p. 26.

[10]Gritsch and Jenson, *Lutheranism,* p. 29; Gassmann and Hendrix, *Lutheran Confessions,* p. 45.

[11]Gritsch and Jenson, *Lutheranism,* p. 30

[12]Formula of Concord, in *The Book of Concord: The Confessions of the Evangelical Lutheran Church,* ed. Robert Kolb and Timothy J. Wengert (Minneapolis: Fortress, 2000), p. 486.

[13]Gassmann and Hendrix, *Lutheran Confessions,* p. 47.

[14]Gritsch, *Introduction to Lutheranism,* p. 38.

[15]Ibid., pp. 44-46.

[16]Abdel Wentz, *A Basic History of Lutheranism in America* (Philadelphia: Muhlenberg, 1955), p. 23.

[17]Gritsch, *Introduction to Lutheranism,* p. 56.

[18]E. Theodore Bachmann, "Churches of North America," in *Lutheran Churches of the World,* by Lutheran World Federation (Minneapolis: Augsburg, 1957), p. 140.

[19]Immigrants sometimes referred to Europe as the "Old World"; see Gritsch, *Introduction to Lutheranism,* p. 40.

[20]Wentz, *Lutheranism in America,* p. 61. Wentz does qualify this observation with "for better or worse."

[21]Conrad Bergendoff, *The Church of the Lutheran Reformation: A Historical Survey of Lutheranism* (St. Louis: Concordia, 1967), p. 193; also L. DeAne Lagerquist, *The Lutherans,* Denominations in America 9 (Westport, Conn.: Greenwood Press, 1999), p. 12.

[22]Gritsch, *Introduction to Lutheranism,* p. 57.

[23]Charles P. Arand, *Testing the Boundaries: Windows to Lutheran Identity* (St. Louis: Concordia, 1995), p. 25.

[24]Gritsch, *Introduction to Lutheranism,* p. 58. Although Lutherans did migrate to some southern states, Richard Dickenson notes that, at least comparatively speaking, Lutheranism "was not numerically strong in the slave states" (*Roses and Thorns: The Centennial Edition of Black Lutheran Mission and Ministry in the Lutheran Church—Missouri Synod* [St. Louis: Concordia, 1977], p. 20).

[25]Frank S. Mead and Samuel S. Hill, *Handbook of Denominations in the United States,* 9th ed. (Nashville: Abingdon, 1990), p. 139; also Bergendoff, *Church of the Lutheran Reformation,* p. 231. Gritsch observes that divisions over issues related to the Civil War "impeded the progress of assimilation, increased immigration, and helped maintain ties to Europe" (*Introduction to Lutheranism,* p. 63).

[26]Arand, *Testing the Boundaries,* p. 25.

[27]Gritsch, *Introduction to Lutheranism,* p. 61; see also p. 63.

[28]Dickinson, *Roses and Thorns,* pp. 27-31.

[29]Eugene Fevold, "Coming of Age, 1875-1900," in *The Lutherans in North America,* ed. E. Clifford Nelson (Philadelphia: Fortress, 1975), p. 289; also Arand, *Testing the Boundaries,* p. 152.

[30]Wentz, *Lutheranism in America,* p. 106.

[31]This was published in English as *Christian Dogmatics,* 3 vols. (St. Louis: Concordia, 1950-1953). Prior to the publishing of this English-language edition, one of Pieper's students, John T. Mueller, published an abbreviated version in English: *Christian Dogmatics* (St. Louis: Concordia, 1934). Mueller referred to his work as an "epitome" of Pieper's *Dogmatik.*

[32]Gassmann and Hendrix, *Lutheran Confessions,* pp. 186-87.

[33]For discussion of this polarity and the contested theological issues, see E. Clifford Nelson, *Lutheranism in North America, 1914-1970* (Minneapolis: Augsburg, 1972), p. 161; Gritsch, *Introduction to Lutheranism,* pp. 62-64; Fevold, "Coming of Age," pp. 291, 314-25; Arand, *Testing the Boundaries,* pp. 21-24.

[34]Arand, *Testing the Boundaries,* p. 14.

[35]See Wentz, *Lutheranism in America,* pp. 66-67; Nelson, *Lutheranism in North America;* Gritsch, *Introduction to Lutheranism,* pp. 62-64.

[36]Gritsch, *Introduction to Lutheranism,* p. 92. For a detailed discussion of the Federation, see Bachmann and Bachmann, *Lutheran Churches,* pp. 29-41.

[37]For a schematic overview, see "Cooperation and Consolidation among Lutherans in 20th-Century USA," in Bachmann and Bachmann, *Lutheran Churches,* pp. 584-85.

[38]Fred W. Meuser, "Facing the Twentieth Century, 1900-1930," in Nelson, *The Lutherans in North America,* pp. 381-84.

[39]E. Clifford Nelson, "The New Shape of Lutheranism, 1930-," in Nelson, *The Lutherans in North America,* p. 457; also Arand, *Testing the Boundaries,* pp. 205-6.

[40]Nelson, "New Shape of Lutheranism," p. 471; for an overview of the issues and factions from a Neo-Lutheran perspective, see pp. 458-62.

[41]Arand, *Testing the Boundaries,* p. 14.

[42]David P. Scaer, "How Do Lutheran Theologians Approach the Doing of Theology Today?" in *Doing Theology in Today's World: Essays in Honor of Kenneth S. Kantzer,* ed. John D. Woodbridge and Thomas E. McComiskey (Grand Rapids: Zondervan, 1991), p. 200.

[43]Carl E. Braaten, *Principles of Lutheran Theology* (Philadelphia: Fortress, 1983), p. x.

[44]Scaer, "Lutheran Theologians," p. 200.

[45]Braaten, *Principles of Lutheran Theology,* p. 39.

[46]George Lindbeck, "Ecumenical Directions and Confessional Construals," *Dialog* 30 (spring 1991): 120-22. Charles Arand, a Missouri-Synod Lutheran scholar, offers a similar analysis, describing two "diametrically opposite views of the nature of confessions": historical and biblical-theological (*Testing the Boundaries,* p. 17).

[47]Samuel H. Nafzger, "America's Lutherans: What They Believe," *Christianity Today* 33 (November 3, 1989): 25.

[48]Lindbeck, "Ecumenical Directions," p. 123. Lindbeck makes his observations in a discussion of contemporary Lutheran views of ecclesiology and ecumenicity, but his analysis of the conflicting views within Lutheranism have a wider applicability than issues of ecumenicity alone. For a recent proposal regarding a way to transcend the polarity described by Lindbeck, see David G. Truemper, "The Lutheran Confessional Writings and the Future of Lutheran Theology," in *The Gift of Grace: The Future of Lutheran Theology,* ed. Niels Henrik Gregersen et al. (Minneapolis: Fortress, 2005), pp. 131-44.

[49]Bachmann and Bachmann, *Lutheran Churches,* pp. 588-89.

[50]Ibid., p. 607.

[51]For descriptions of these, see ibid., pp. 585-610.

[52]Nelson correctly cautions that the various "*theological* camps" within Lutheranism cannot always be directly or strictly correlated with denominational or "*organizational* constellations" (*Lutheranism in North America,* p. 78).

[53]Bachmann, "Churches of North America," p. 176.

[54]Heinrich Schmid, *Doctrinal Theology of the Evangelical Lutheran Church,* trans. Charles A. Hay and Henry E. Jacobs, 3rd ed. (Philadelphia: United Lutheran Publication House, 1899; reprint, Minneapolis: Augsburg, 1961).

[55]Carl E. Braaten and Robert W. Jenson, eds., *Christian Dogmatics,* 2 vols. (Minneapolis: Fortress, 1984).

[56]To date this multivolume work includes David P. Scaer, *Christology* (Fort Wayne: International Foundation for Lutheran Confessional Research, 1989); Kurt E. Marquart, *The Church and Her*

Fellowship, Ministry, and Governance (Fort Wayne, Ind.: International Foundation for Lutheran Confessional Research, 1990); John R. Stephenson, *Eschatology* (Fort Wayne: Luther Academy, 1993); David P. Scaer, *Baptism* (St. Louis: Luther Academy, 1999); and John R. Stephenson, *The Lord's Supper* (St. Louis: Luther Academy, 2003).

[57]Nafzger, "America's Lutherans," p. 22.

[58]David Scaer begins an essay on Lutheran theological method by stating, "Lutheran theology is derived from Holy Scripture, but it is also normed or regulated by the ancient, catholic creeds and the Lutheran Confessions from the sixteenth century" ("Lutheran Theologians," p. 197).

[59]See David P. Daniel and Charles P. Arland, *A Bibliography of the Lutheran Confessions,* Sixteenth Century Bibliographies 28 (St. Louis: Center for Reformation Research, 1988), which is 216 pages in length.

[60]See, for example, Carl Braaten's typology of "repristination," "liberal nonconfessionalism," "hypothetical confessionalism," "anti-confessional biblicism" and "constructive confessionalism" (*Principles of Lutheran Theology,* pp. 29-31), George Lindbeck's typology of "Lutheranism as a confessional movement" ("Ecumenical Directions," pp. 120-22), and David Scaer's essay "How Do Lutheran Theologians Approach the Doing of Theology Today?" (pp. 197-225).

[61]J. A. O. Preus III, "Lutheran Identity Is Insistence on Truth," *Dialog* 16 (fall 1977): 292-95.

[62]Pieper, *Christian Dogmatics,* 1:104-5.

[63]Mueller, *Christian Dogmatics,* p. 64.

[64]Nafzger, "America's Lutherans," p. 25; Braaten, *Principles of Lutheran Theology,* p. 35.

[65]Braaten, *Principles of Lutheran Theology,* p. 4.

[66]Edmund Schlink, *Theology of the Lutheran Confessions,* trans. Paul F. Koehneke and Herbert J. A. Bouman (Philadelphia: Fortress, 1961), p. 27; see also Schmid, *Doctrinal Theology,* p. 27.

[67]Brief Statement of the Doctrinal Position of the Missouri Synod, Article 2 (*EARRC,* 1:148).

[68]Pieper, *Christian Dogmatics,* 1:3; see also Schmid, *Doctrinal Theology,* p. 39.

[69]Brief Statement of the Doctrinal Position of the Missouri Synod, Article 1 (*EARRC,* 1:148).

[70]Henry E. Jacobs, *A Summary of the Christian Faith* (Philadelphia: General Council Publication House, 1913), p. 5. Jacobs does allow that experience can be "an important element in the interpretation of doctrines, in so far as it declares the presence and power of the Holy Spirit in applying God's Word." In support of his view he cites 1 John 4:1-2; Galatians 1:8; Acts 17:11.

[71]Pieper, *Christian Dogmatics,* 1:156.

[72]Jacobs, *Christian Faith,* p. 11; also Schmid, *Doctrinal Theology,* p. 30.

[73]Scaer, "Lutheran Theologians," p. 210; also Schmid, *Doctrinal Theology,* p. 25.

[74]Scaer, "Lutheran Theologians," p. 210. One indication of how highly the confessional sources are regarded is Scaer's allowance that they may actually "supplement," not merely "confirm," Scripture.

[75]Scaer, "Lutheran Theologians," p. 201.

[76]Confession [of the Lutheran Church—Missouri Synod], Article 2 (*EARRC,* 1:148). Article 1 identifies the Old and New Testaments of the Bible as "the written Word of God." See also Scaer, "Lutheran Theologians," pp. 199, 204. By contrast, the Evangelical Lutheran Church in America affirms the unaltered Augsburg Confession and Luther's Small Catechism as "true witnesses to the Gospel," and the Apology of the Augsburg Confession, the Smalcald Articles, Luther's Large Catechism and the Formula of Concord as "further valid interpretations of the confession of the Church" (Confession of Faith [of the Evangelical Lutheran Church in Amer-

ical], Sections 5 and 6 [*EARRC*, 2:119]).

[77]Gassmann and Hendrix, *Lutheran Confessions*, p. 54; Arand, *Testing the Boundaries*, p. 15.

[78]Scaer, "Lutheran Theologians," p. 208. Interestingly, Scaer allows for Lutherans doing theology "without reference to their confessions" when theology is being done in a "non-Lutheran setting" or "ecumenical context."

[79]Schlink, *Lutheran Confessions*, p. 33.

[80]Horace Hummel, "Are Law and Gospel a Valid Hermeneutical Principle?" *Concordia Theological Quarterly* 46, nos. 2-3 (1982): 202. Braaten likens the confessions to "a signpost or compass" and "a map for . . . exegetical explorations through the Scriptures" (*Principles of Lutheran Theology*, pp. 34-35).

[81]Schlink, *Lutheran Confessions*, pp. 29, 33, 35. In addition, some classical Lutherans believe that the confessions also convey the *principles of* biblical interpretation. See Ralph A. Bohlmann, "Confessional Biblical Interpretation: Some Basic Principles," in *Studies in Lutheran Hermeneutics*, ed. John Reumann, Samuel H. Nafzger and Harold H. Ditmanson (Philadelphia: Fortress, 1979), pp. 190-208; cf. Lutheran Council in the USA, *The Function of Doctrine and Theology in Light of the Unity of the Church* (New York: Lutheran Council in the USA, 1978), p. 12. For a contrary view, see Karlfried Froehlich, "Problems of Lutheran Hermeneutics," in Reumann, Nafzger and Ditmanson, *Lutheran Hermeneutics*, pp. 129-30.

[82]Scaer, "Lutheran Theologians," p. 197. For a discussion of differences among Lutherans specifically on the role of the confessions in biblical interpretation and presentations by persons representing a variety of perspectives, see Lutheran Council in the USA, *Function of Doctrine and Theology*.

[83]Nelson, *Lutheranism in North America*, p. 79; see also Braaten, *Principles of Lutheran Theology*, p. xiii. Nelson indicates that Missouri Synod Lutherans, the prime example of "repristination," prefer the term "real confessionalism" or "strict confessionalism."

[84]Harold H. Ditmanson, "Perspectives on the Hermeneutics Debate," in Reumann, Nafzger and Ditmanson, *Lutheran Hermeneutics*, p. 94.

[85]Scaer, "Lutheran Theologians," pp. 197-98.

[86]Ibid., p. 202.

[87]Braaten, *Principles of Lutheran Theology*, p. 27.

[88]Following Robert Kolb and James A. Nestingen, eds., *Sources and Contexts of the Book of Concord* (Minneapolis: Fortress, 2001), p. xii; Warren A. Quanbeck, "The Confessions and Their Influence upon Biblical Interpretation," in Reumann, Nafzger and Ditmanson, *Lutheran Hermeneutics*, p. 19.

[89]Braaten suggests, "Luther's most revolutionary principle of interpretation was the insistence on the literal, historical, and philological exposition of the Scriptures. He thereby rejected the allegorical method of exegesis which had been practiced to excess since Origen" (*Principles of Lutheran Theology*, p. 9).

[90]Meg H. Madson, "Hermeneutics and Theological Method," *Journal of Ecumenical Studies* 23, no. 3 (1986): 532.

[91]Bohlmann, "Confessional Biblical Interpretation," pp. 194-95.

[92]Robert Kolb, *The Christian Faith: A Lutheran Exposition* (St. Louis: Concordia, 1993), p. 231.

[93]Formula of Concord, II: "Solid Declaration," VII.45 (Kolb and Wengert, *Book of Concord*, pp. 600-601).

[94]Brief Statement of the Doctrinal Position of the Missouri Synod, Article 2 (*EARRC*, 1:148).

[95]Bohlmann, "Confessional Biblical Interpretation," p. 205.

[96]Ditmanson, "Hermeneutics Debate," p. 78.

[97]Ibid. Hummel observes, "Our hermeneutical circle is traditionally expressed in terms of 'Scripture as its own interpreter.' . . . While we commonly underscore one half of our hermeneutical circle, namely, that our doctrines are based on Scripture, the other half often fails to receive equal stress, namely, that they all double back as hermeneutical guides to the proper understanding of relevant biblical texts" ("Law and Gospel," p. 196).

[98]Jacobs, *Christian Faith*, p. 213.

[99]Eric W. Gritsch, "Lutheran Teaching Authority: Historical Dimensions and Ecumenical Implications," *Lutheran Quarterly* 25 (November 1973): 383.

[100]Quanbeck, "Confessions and Their Influence," p. 185.

[101]Madson, "Hermeneutics and Theological Method," p. 530.

[102]Apology of the Augsburg Confession, 4.5-6 (Kolb and Wengert, *Book of Concord*, p. 121).

[103]Pieper, *Christian Dogmatics*, 1:78.

[104]Hummel, "Law and Gospel," pp. 185, 191; see also Nafzger, "America's Lutherans," p. 25; Gerhard O. Forde, "The Formula of Concord, Article V: End or New Beginning?" *Dialog* 15 (summer 1976): 189.

[105]See Scaer, "Lutheran Theologians," pp. 213, 215; Schlink, *Lutheran Confessions*, pp. xxii, 27; Ditmanson, "Hermeneutics Debate," p. 78; Braaten, *Principles of Lutheran Theology*, p. 34; Madson, "Hermeneutics and Theological Method," pp. 530-31.

[106]Apology of the Augsburg Confession, Article 4.36-39 (Kolb and Wengert, *Book of Concord*, p. 126).

[107]Gassmann and Hendrix, *Lutheran Confessions*, p. 59.

[108]Lindbeck, "Ecumenical Directions," p. 121. Lindbeck contrasts this view with what he refers to as "denominational church" Lutherans, for whom "the Lutheran Reformation was constitutive of a reconstituted *ecclesia* rather than a corrective movement of renewal within the Western church."

[109]Scaer, "Lutheran Theologians," p. 206.

[110]This dimension of Lutheran theology is notably manifest in the inclusion of the Apostles' Creed, the Nicene Creed and the Athansian Creed—referred to as the "Three Chief Symbols"—in *The Book of Concord.*

[111]For example, Carl Braaten, *Justification: The Article by Which the Church Stands or Falls* (Minneapolis: Fortress, 1990); J. A. O. Preus III, "Justification by Faith: The *Articulus Stantis et Cadentis Ecclesiae*," in *And Every Tongue Confess: Essays in Honor of Norman Nagel on the Occasion of His Sixty-fifth Birthday,* ed. Gerald S. Krispin and Jon D. Vieker (Dearborn, Mich.: Nagel Festschrift Committee, 1990), pp. 264-82; Gritsch and Jenson, *Lutheranism,* p. 36; Scaer, "Lutheran Theologians," p. 214; Karl L. Barth, "Cardinal Principles of Lutheranism and 'Evangelical Theology,'" *Concordia Journal* 7, no. 2 (1981): 251; Pieper, *Christian Dogmatics,* 2:513; Madson, "Hermeneutics and Theological Method," p. 530. Cf. Oswald Bayer, "Justification: Basis and Boundary of Theology," in *By Faith Alone: Essays on Justification in Honor of Gerhard O. Forde,* ed. Joseph A. Burgess and Marc Kolden (Grand Rapids: Eerdmans, 2004), p. 69 and passim.

[112]Nafzger, "America's Lutherans," p. 22. Barth identifies these three as the "cardinal principles of Lutheranism" ("Cardinal Principles," pp. 50-51).

[113]Braaten, *Principles of Lutheran Theology*, pp. xiii-xiv. The "two kingdoms" doctrine articulates the Lutheran understanding of the Christian's rights and responsibilities to the state and other earthly institutions, and to the kingdom of heaven.

[114]There is also the recognition that Lutherans disagree over the precise meaning and implications of justification by faith. Braaten goes so far as to suggest that, ironic as it may be, Luth-

erans are "confused and void of inner harmony on this doctrine" (*Justification,* p. 22; see also p. 12).

[115]Preus, "Justification by Faith," p. 112; see also Pieper, *Christian Dogmatics,* 2:404.

[116]Braaten, *Justification,* p. 7; see also Gritsch and Jenson, *Lutheranism,* pp. vii, 6, 36.

[117]Luther, *Lectures on Galatians,* p. 283.

[118]Gassmann and Hendrix, *Lutheran Confessions,* p. 82.

[119]Augsburg Confession, Article 4.1-2 (Kolb and Wengert, *Book of Concord,* pp. 38, 40). Cited are Romans 3:21-26; 4:5.

[120]Preus, "Justification by Faith," p. 273; see also Mueller, *Christian Dogmatics,* p. 79; W. H. T. Dau, "The Heritage of Lutheranism," in *What Lutherans Are Thinking: A Symposium on Lutheran Faith and Life,* ed. Edward C. Fendt (Columbus, Ohio: Wartburg Press, 1947), p. 21.

[121]Bayer, "Justification," p. 68.

[122]Pieper, *Christian Dogmatics,* 1:139-40; also 2:404, 513. Pieper cites 1 Corinthians 2:2 in conjunction with Acts 20:27; 10:43.

[123]Brief Statement of the Doctrinal Position of the Missouri Synod, Article 17 (*EARRC,* 1:150).

[124]Schmid, *Doctrinal Theology,* p. 424; also Schlink, *Lutheran Confessions,* p. 9. Pieper states, "Δικαιουν is always used in the New Testament in the declaratory, the forensic sense" (*Christian Dogmatics,* 2:525).

[125]Schlink, *Lutheran Confessions,* pp. 91-92.

[126]Ibid., pp. 92, 95; also Jacobs, *Christian Faith,* pp. 207-8. Cf. Pieper's view that "the forgiveness of sins constitutes the entire justification, not merely part of it" (*Christian Dogmatics,* 2:537).

[127]Kolb, *The Christian Faith,* pp. 161-62. Cf. Jacobs's view that "justification itself is entirely external" (*Christian Faith,* p. 211), and Pieper's view of justification as synonymous with "objective reconciliation" (*Christian Dogmatics,* 2:398-400).

[128]Schlink, *Lutheran Confessions,* p. 94.

[129]Wanda Deifelt, "The Relevance of the Doctrine of Justification," in *Justification in the World's Context,* ed. Wolfgang Grieve, LWF Documentation 45 (Geneva: Lutheran World Federation, 2000), p. 37.

[130]Formula of Concord, II: "Solid Declaration," 11.8 (Kolb and Wengert, *Book of Concord,* p. 642).

[131]Mueller, *Christian Dogmatics,* p. 246.

[132]Nafzger, "America's Lutherans," p. 22.

[133]Gassmann and Hendrix, *Lutheran Confessions,* p. 54.

[134]Pieper, *Christian Dogmatics,* 2:422.

[135]Kolb, *The Christian Faith,* p. 159.

[136]Gassmann and Hendrix, *Lutheran Confessions,* pp. 83-84.

[137]Augsburg Confession, Article 20.23 (Kolb and Wengert, *Book of Concord,* p. 56).

[138]Apology of the Augsburg Confession, Articles 4.110, 4.116 (Kolb and Wengert, *Book of Concord,* p. 139); Brief Statement of Doctrinal Position of the Missouri Synod, Article 10 (*EARRC,* 1:149).

[139]Pieper, *Christian Dogmatics,* 2:423, 437-38.

[140]Nafzger, "America's Lutherans," p. 23.

[141]Apology of the Augsburg Confession, Article 4.50 (Kolb and Wengert, *Book of Concord,* p. 128).

[142]Pieper, *Christian Dogmatics,* 2:423.

[143]Augsburg Confession, Article 20.26 (Kolb and Wengert, *Book of Concord,* p. 57).

[144]Apology of the Augsburg Confession, Article 4.46 (Kolb and Wengert, *Book of Concord,* p. 127).

[145]Apology of the Augsburg Confession, Article 4.48 (Kolb and Wengert, *Book of Concord,* p. 128 n. 77).

[146]Pieper, *Christian Dogmatics,* 2:422.

[147]Barth, "Cardinal Principles," p. 55.

[148]Kolb, *The Christian Faith,* p. 163.

[149]Pieper, *Christian Dogmatics,* 2:402.

[150]Nafzger, "America's Lutherans," p. 24.

[151]Schlink, *Lutheran Confessions,* p. 97.

[152]Ibid., p. 96.

[153]Schmid, *Doctrinal Theology,* p. 492.

[154]Gassmann and Hendrix, *Lutheran Confessions,* p. 83.

[155]Smalcald Articles, Part 3, Article 8.10 (Kolb and Wengert, *Book of Concord,* p. 323).

[156]As David Lotz points out, in Luther's writings "Word of God" is most often synonymous with "*gospel,* with the spoken Word, the oral proclamation of Christ." The Word of God "as gospel" is "proclamation of God's gracious acceptance of sinners for Christ's sake" ("*Sola Scriptura:* Luther on Biblical Authority," *Interpretation* 35, no. 3 [1981]: 261).

[157]Jacobs, *Christian Faith,* pp. 322-23.

[158]Schlink, *Lutheran Confessions,* p. 182.

[159]See Hummel's comments on the significance of Lutheran "sacramentology" (Hummel, "Law and Gospel," p. 197).

[160]Gassmann and Hendrix, *Lutheran Confessions,* p. 93.

[161]Ibid.

[162]Kolb, *The Christian Faith,* p. 229.

[163]Ibid., p. 235.

[164]Jacobs describes these as "a divine institution," "an earthly element" and "a special heavenly gift." He identifies the last as "the Word" (*Christian Faith,* pp. 315-16).

[165]Augsburg Confession, Article 9.1-2 (Kolb and Wengert, *Book of Concord,* p. 42). At least one Lutheran author goes so far as to state that it is "of higher necessity than the Lord's Supper" (Jacobs, *Christian Faith,* p. 324).

[166]Schlink, *Lutheran Confessions,* p. 150.

[167]Gassmann and Hendrix, *Lutheran Confessions,* p. 99; see also Schlink, *Lutheran Confessions,* p. 151.

[168]Kolb, *The Christian Faith,* p. 215.

[169]Small Catechism, 4.10 (Kolb and Wengert, *Book of Concord,* p. 359).

[170]Small Catechism, 4.7-8 (Kolb and Wengert, *Book of Concord,* p. 359).

[171]Augsburg Confession, Article 9.1-2 (Kolb and Wengert, *Book of Concord,* p. 42).

[172]Apology of the Augsburg Confession, Article 9.2 (Kolb and Wengert, *Book of Concord,* p. 184).

[173]Kolb, *The Christian Faith,* p. 223. The importance of this point is seen in Kolb's observation that "argument over the interpretation of these passages [Mt 28:19; Acts 16:33] will avail little so long as one presumes that Baptism is fundamentally a human action and that infants do not need to have a relationship with God established through Baptism" (ibid., pp. 224-25).

[174]Ibid., p. 219; also pp. 224, 225.

[175]Ibid., p. 225.

[176]Nafzger, "America's Lutherans," p. 24.

[177]Kolb, *The Christian Faith,* p. 223.

[178]Notice that in John 3:15 this life is referred to as "eternal life."

[179]Schlink, *Lutheran Confessions*, pp. 181-83. Confirmation is an "implication" of baptism. Its purpose is "to help Christians realize Baptism's gracious benefits" ("The Confirmation Ministry Task Force Report," in Robert L. Conrad et al., *Confirmation: Engaging Lutheran Foundations and Practices* [Minneapolis: Fortress, 1999], p. 268).

[180]Kolb, *The Christian Faith*, p. 216.

[181]Gassmann and Hendrix, *Lutheran Confessions*, p. 100.

[182]Augsburg Confession, 10.1 (Kolb and Wengert, *Book of Concord*, p. 44).

[183]Apology of the Augsburg Confession, Article 10.4 (Kolb and Wengert, *Book of Concord*, pp. 184-85).

[184]For example, Kolb, *The Christian Faith*, p. 232; Schmid, *Doctrinal Theology*, p. 555; Schlink, *Lutheran Confessions*, pp. 159, 169; Mueller, *Christian Dogmatics*, p. 510.

[185]Several Lutheran authors use the term "presuppositions" (e.g., Schlink, *Lutheran Confessions*, p. 193; Kolb, *The Christian Faith*, p. 230). A case could be made that these "presuppositions" are the other, neglected half of the hermeneutical circle spoken of by Hummel: doctrinal conclusions that have been arrived at and are then applied to explaining Scripture interpretations that support belief in the real presence ("Law and Gospel," p. 196).

[186]Schlink, *Lutheran Confessions*, p. 159.

[187]Kolb, *The Christian Faith*, pp. 231-32.

[188]Gassmann and Hendrix, *Lutheran Confessions*, p. 120.

[189]Formula of Concord, I: "Epitome," VII.6-7 (Kolb and Wengert, *Book of Concord*, p. 505).

[190]See Mueller, *Christian Dogmatics*, p. 524.

[191]Ibid., p. 521; see also Kolb, *The Christian Faith*, pp. 230-31.

[192]Kolb, *The Christian Faith*, pp. 231, 233; Schlink, *Lutheran Confessions*, p. 172.

[193]Schmid, *Doctrinal Theology*, p. 555; Mueller, *Christian Dogmatics*, p. 521.

[194]Kolb, *The Christian Faith*, p. 232. The New Testament Greek word μυστήριον ("mystery" [e.g., Eph 5:32; 1 Tim 3:16]) often was translated into Latin as *sacramentum*, and subsequently was applied to certain rites of the church.

[195]Kolb, *The Christian Faith*, p. 237.

[196]Smalcald Articles, III.vi.1 (Kolb and Wengert, *Book of Concord*, p. 320).

[197]Formula of Concord, I: "Epitome," VII.16 (Kolb and Wengert, *Book of Concord*, p. 506).

[198]Formula of Concord, I: "Epitome," VII.20 (Kolb and Wengert, *Book of Concord*, p. 506); Small Catechism, VI.8 (Kolb and Wengert, *Book of Concord*, p. 363); Mueller, *Christian Dogmatics*, pp. 508, 534-36; Formula of Concord, I: "Epitome," VII.19 (Kolb and Wengert, *Book of Concord*, p. 506); Schlink, *Lutheran Confessions*, p. 163; and Schmid, *Doctrinal Theology*, p. 557. Citing forgiveness of sins as "the foremost gift of the Supper," Mueller lists the following "concomitant" blessings: "the strengthening of faith, the union with Christ and with His spiritual body, the Church, growth in sanctification, furtherance in love toward God and the neighbor, increase in patience and in the hope of eternal life, greater joy in confessing Christ" (*Christian Dogmatics*, p. 536).

[199]Schlink, *Lutheran Confessions*, p. 163.

[200]Gassmann and Hendrix, *Lutheran Confessions*, p. 119; Mueller, *Christian Dogmatics*, p. 507.

[201]Mueller, *Christian Dogmatics*, p. 508.

[202]Having just referred to "God's free grace," Michael Root writes, "The church is called to proclaim and mediate that grace and to shape its life in accord with that grace" ("The Lutheran Churches," in *The Christian Church: An Introduction to the Major Traditions*, ed. Paul Avis [London: SPCK, 2002], p. 208).

Chapter 3: Faith for Radical Community

[1]C. Arnold Snyder, "Beyond Polygenesis: Recovering the Unity and Diversity of Anabaptist Theology," in *Essays in Anabaptist Theology,* ed. H. Wayne Pipkin (Elkhart, Ind.: Institute of Mennonite Studies, 1994), p. 2.

[2]In 1995, an entire issue of the *Mennonite Quarterly Review* (vol. 69, no. 3) was dedicated to a reconsideration of and reflections upon Bender's views.

[3]Harold S. Bender, *The Anabaptist Vision* (Scottdale, Penn.: Herald, 1944). This booklet is based upon Bender's 1943 presidential address to the American Society of Church History.

[4]C. Arnold Snyder, *Anabaptist History and Theology: An Introduction* (Kitchener, Ont.: Pandora, 1995), pp. 3-5; Cornelius J. Dyck, *An Introduction to Mennonite History,* 3rd ed. (Scottdale, Penn.: Herald, 1993), p. 34.

[5]Roland H. Bainton, "The Left Wing of the Reformation," in *Studies on the Reformation,* Collected Papers in Church History, Series 2 (Boston: Beacon, 1963), pp. 119-29; George H. Williams, *The Radical Reformation,* 3rd ed. (Kirksville, Mo.: Sixteenth Century Journal Publishers, 1992).

[6]Wilbert Shenk, "A Traditioned Theology of Mission," in *What Mennonites Are Thinking, 2000,* ed. Merle Good and Phyllis P. Good (Intercourse, Penn.: Good Books, 2000), p. 242; John Driver, *Radical Faith: An Alternative History of the Christian Church,* ed. Carrie Snyder (Kitchener, Ont.: Pandora, 1999), p. 18.

[7]In 1994, Arnold Snyder commented, "I am not entirely sure that historical and theological *monogenesis* [as in Bender's work] has really given way as a descriptive historical and theological model. . . . It is my impression . . . that polygenesis has been dealt with, in the North American Mennonite Church at least, more by a stubborn refusal to acknowledge its existence than by an effort to reflect upon, incorporate, and assimilate its disturbing findings. Most Mennonite pastors, and the vast majority of Mennonite church members, for example, appear not to be aware of the fact that their Anabaptist parents in the faith disagreed profoundly amongst themselves on crucial theological issues" ("Beyond Polygenesis," p. 6).

[8]James M. Stayer, Werner O. Packull and Klaus Depperman, "From Monogenesis to Polygenesis: The Historical Discussion of Anabaptist Origins," *Mennonite Quarterly Review* 49, no. 2 (1975): 83-121.

[9]Snyder, "Beyond Polygenesis," pp. 8-9. In this article Snyder argues that having described Anabaptist origins in this way, scholars now must attempt a more adequate interpretation of the subsequent development of Anabaptism. For an alternative to the polygenesis view, see Abraham Friesen, *History and Renewal in the Anabaptist/Mennonite Tradition,* Cornelius H. Wedel Historical Series 7 (North Newton, Kans.: Bethel College, 1994).

[10]See, for example, Donald B. Kraybill and Carl F. Bowman, *On the Backroad to Heaven: Old Order Hutterites, Mennonites, Amish, and Brethren* (Baltimore: Johns Hopkins University Press, 2001).

[11]For a critique of Snyder, see J. Denny Weaver, *Becoming Anabaptist: The Origin and Significance of Sixteenth-Century Anabaptism,* 2nd ed. (Scottdale, Penn.: Herald, 2005), pp. 216-20, 223-31.

[12]William Estep writes, "The Mennonites occupy a position of unusual importance in the Free Church movement: first, as preservers of the basic insights of sixteenth-century Anabaptism, and second, as transmitters of these concepts via influence and direct stimulus upon English Separatism, particularly the Baptists" (*Anabaptist Beginnings [1523-1533]: A Source Book,* ed. William R. Estep, Bibliotheca humanistica et reformatorica 16 [Nieuwkoop: de Graaf, 1976], p. 4).

[13]Snyder, *Anabaptist History and Theology,* p. 2.

[14]Ibid., p. 53.

[15]Dyck, *Introduction to Mennonite History,* p. 37.

[16]Snyder, *Anabaptist History and Theology,* p. 53.

[17]Ibid., p. 54; also Dyck, *Introduction to Mennonite History,* p. 38.

[18]William R. Estep, *The Anabaptist Story: An Introduction to Sixteenth-Century Anabaptism,* 3rd ed. (Grand Rapids: Eerdmans, 1996), p. 14.

[19]Driver, *Radical Faith,* p. 183.

[20]Dyck, *Introduction to Mennonite History,* p. 37.

[21]Snyder, *Anabaptist History and Theology,* p. 56.

[22]Ibid., p. 55. Snyder makes the following observation in regard to Anabaptist historiography and the peasant revolt: "It is at this point that Harold Bender's depiction of Swiss Anabaptist origins has been substantially revised. . . . The Swiss Anabaptist movement began as a grass-roots, alternative movement of popular reform, not as a separatist and thoroughly pacifist movement. . . . Swiss Anabaptism in 1525 . . . was not uniformly pacifist, apolitical, or sep-aratist, even among the 'Grebel circle'" (ibid., pp. 57, 59).

[23]Driver, *Radical Faith,* p. 174.

[24]Snyder, *Anabaptist History and Theology,* p. 60.

[25]Ibid.

[26]The ban was corporate discipline of believers who had fallen into serious sin. It often in-cluded their separation from fellowship or excommunication. The stated goal was "that we may all in one spirit and in one love break and eat from one bread and drink from one cup" (Schleitheim Confession, Article 2 [*MCF,* p. 80]).

[27]Rejection of "the sword" is synonymous with nonresistance. Later Mennonite thought often would also include in this rejection separation from involvement with civil government.

[28]Snyder, *Anabaptist History and Theology,* pp. 61-62.

[29]Ibid., p. 51.

[30]Frank H. Epp, *Mennonites in Canada, 1786-1920: The History of a Separate People* (Toronto: Macmillan of Canada, 1974), p. 30.

[31]Snyder, *Anabaptist History and Theology,* p. 93. The best-known descriptions of persecution and martyrdom are those found in the many editions of the seventeenth-century book *The Bloody Theater, or, Martyr's Mirror,* by Thieleman J. van Braght, and vividly illustrated by Jan Luyken. See also John B. Toews, *Journeys: Mennonite Stories of Faith and Survival in Stalin's Russia* (Winnipeg: Kindred Productions, 1998); C. Arnold Snyder, "Martyrdom: The Baptism in Blood," in *Following in the Footsteps of Christ: The Anabaptist Tradition* (Maryknoll, N.Y.: Orbis, 2004), pp. 159-83.

[32]Dyck, *Introduction to Mennonite History,* pp. 41-43; Snyder, *Anabaptist History and Theol-ogy,* pp. 67-69.

[33]Dyck, *Introduction to Mennonite History,* p. 42.

[34]Ibid.

[35]Snyder, *Anabaptist History and Theology,* p. 79; Dyck, *Introduction to Mennonite History,* p. 42.

[36]Dyck, *Introduction to Mennonite History,* p. 46.

[37]Snyder, *Anabaptist History and Theology,* p. 150.

[38]Ibid., p. 153. The other groups did not entirely disappear. Dyck describes the many contro-versies and divisions that occurred among the northern Mennonites in the later-sixteenth and early-seventeenth centuries. He also suggests a variety of contributing factors, including in-

tolerance resulting from strong emphases on both purity and deep conviction of belief that often accompany persecution and the vagaries of life for those living as refugees. See Dyck, *Introduction to Mennonite History,* pp. 122-27.

[39]Dyck, *Introduction to Mennonite History,* p. 47.

[40]Ibid., p. 158.

[41]Those who live under or in the shadow of persecution, as so many Anabaptists did, rarely have the luxury of time and place for sustained, formal theological reflection.

[42]Dyck, *Introduction to Mennonite History,* pp. 129, 158.

[43]Ibid., p. 166.

[44]Ibid., p. 151.

[45]This had two contrasting impacts. The Anabaptists' agricultural and business skills sometimes led civil authorities to welcome the Anabaptists into their jurisdiction; on the other hand, these same attributes sometime led citizens to resent their presence.

[46]Dyck, *Introduction to Mennonite History,* p. 167.

[47]Ibid., pp. 386-87.

[48]Epp, *Mennonites in Canada,* p. 43; Dyck, *Introduction to Mennonite History,* p. 196.

[49]Dyck, *Introduction to Mennonite History,* p. 198.

[50]Epp, *Mennonites in Canada,* p. 56.

[51]For a description of Canadian developments, see ibid., pp. 233-300.

[52]Dyck, *Introduction to Mennonite History,* p. 417.

[53]J. Howard Kauffman and Leo Driedger, *The Mennonite Mosaic: Identity and Modernization* (Scottdale, Penn.: Herald, 1991), p. 190.

[54]The first Mennonite school for higher theological education was Wadsworth Institute. It operated in Wadsworth, Ohio, from 1868 to 1878, offering three years of study of the Bible, largely in German. See S. F. Pannebecker, "Wadsworth Mennonite School," in *The Mennonite Encyclopedia: A Comprehensive Reference Work on the Anabaptist-Mennonite Movement,* ed. Harold S. Bender et al., 5 vols. (Hillsboro, Kans.: Mennonite Brethren Publishing House; Scottdale, Penn.: Herald, 1955-1990), 4:866-67.

[55]Kauffman and Driedger, *Mennonite Mosaic,* pp. 189-90.

[56]Rodney J. Sawatsky, "The Quest for a Mennonite Hermeneutic," *Conrad Grebel Review* 11 (winter 1993): 5.

[57]Kauffman and Driedger, *Mennonite Mosaic,* p. 32.

[58]Dyck indicates that among the factors prompting them to leave Russia were increased pressure (or at least a perceived increase in pressure) to serve in the military, increasing pressures to "assimilate," need for more farmland and "an inability to deal creatively with the problems of a changing society" (*Introduction to Mennonite History,* p. 207). See also Epp, *Mennonites in Canada,* pp. 183-206.

[59]Lydia Harder, "Power and Authority in Mennonite Theological Development," in *Power, Authority, and the Anabaptist Tradition,* ed. Benjamin W. Redekop and Calvin W. Redekop (Baltimore: Johns Hopkins University Press, 2001), p. 82.

[60]Dyck, *Introduction to Mennonite History,* p. 211.

[61]Ibid., p. 407.

[62]Ibid.

[63]C. Norman Kraus, "Shifting Mennonite Theological Orientations," in Driedger and Harder, *Anabaptist-Mennonite Identities in Ferment,* p. 32. Kraus also points out that this emergent denominationalism became a means whereby the various groups within Anabaptism could "define and organize their own denominational identities vis-à-vis one another."

[64]Dyck, *Introduction to Mennonite History,* p. 409.

[65]Shenk, "Traditioned Theology of Mission," p. 245.

[66]In *The Mennonite Encyclopedia,* see Herman Bontranger, "South America," 5:128-30; Amzie Yoder, "Central America," 5:843-46.

[67]Dale R. Stoffer, "Nonconformity: Archaic Ideal or Timeless Essential?" in *Anabaptist Currents: History in Conversation with the Present,* ed. Carl F. Bowman and Stephen L. Longenecker (Camden, Maine: Penobscot, 1995), p. 206; Dyck, *Introduction to Mennonite History,* p. 413.

[68]Kauffman and Driedger, *Mennonite Mosaic,* p. 32.

[69]Ibid., p. 33.

[70]Thomas N. Finger, *Christian Theology: An Eschatological Approach,* 2 vols. (Scottdale, Penn.: Herald, 1985-1989), 1:85.

[71]Marlin Jeschke, "How Mennonites Have Done and Should Do Theology," in *Explorations of Systematic Theology,* ed. Willard Swartley, Occasional Papers 7 (Elkhart, Ind.: Institute of Mennonite Studies, 1984), p. 9.

[72]James W. McClendon Jr., *Systematic Theology,* 3 vols. (Nashville: Abingdon, 1986-2000), 1:20.

[73]Walter Klaassen, *Anabaptism: Neither Catholic nor Protestant* (Waterloo, Ont.: Conrad, 1973), p. 37. Robert Friedmann comments that "theology was not the manifest concern of the brethren and was bypassed wherever possible" (*The Theology of Anabaptism: An Interpretation* [Scottdale, Penn.: Herald, 1973], p. 20). See also Shenk, "Traditioned Theology of Mission," pp. 244-45.

[74]Jeschke, "How Mennonites Have Done and Should Do Theology," p. 10.

[75] J. Denny Weaver, *Anabaptist Theology in the Face of Postmodernity: A Proposal for the Third Millennium,* C. Henry Smith Series 2 (Telford, Penn.: Pandora; Scottdale, Penn.: Herald, 2000), p. 17. Weaver offers a succinct summary of the emergence of Anabaptist engagement with systematic theology (ibid., pp. 23-25).

[76]Friedmann, *Theology of Anabaptism,* p. 19; Klaassen, *Neither Catholic nor Protestant,* p. 37.

[77]Finger, *Christian Theology,* 1:85; Jeschke, "How Mennonites Have Done and Should Do Theology," p. 9.

[78]C. Norman Kraus, preface to *Evangelicalism and Anabaptism,* ed. C. Norman Kraus (Scottdale, Penn.: Herald, 1979), p. 7. John Howard Yoder observes that Anabaptism "was not the unfolding of a new *logical* or *theological* position, but rather expressed a different concern for integrity in *practice"* ("Hermeneutics of the Anabaptists," in *Essays on Biblical Interpretation: Anabaptist-Mennonite Perspectives,* ed. Willard Swartley, Text-Reader Series 1 [Elkhart, Ind.: Institute of Mennonite Studies, 1984], p. 12).

[79]McClendon, *Systematic Theology,* 1:25.

[80]Jeschke, "How Mennonites Have Done and Should Do Theology," p. 10.

[81]Commenting on the history of the Anabaptist movement, particularly the history of persecution against it, Jeschke suggests, "Professional theologizing is thus not essential to survival of the church (witness the church in the USSR today). Still such theologizing is a desirable and useful task for the church to engage in" ("How Mennonites Have Done and Should Do Theology," p. 9).

[82]Friedmann, *Theology of Anabaptism,* p. 20.

[83]Marlin E. Miller, "America's Anabaptists: What They Believe," *Christianity Today* 34 (October 22, 1990): 30. Similarly, Thomas Finger writes, "Life-oriented, practical Mennonites have seldom felt a need for extraordinarily *comprehensive* systems of theology" ("Is 'Systematic Theology' Possible from a Mennonite Perspective?" in Swartley, *Explorations of Systematic The-*

ology, p. 43). See also Kauffman and Driedger, *Mennonite Mosaic,* p. 188; Kraus, *Evangelicalism and Anabaptism,* p. 180.

[84]Klaassen, *Neither Catholic nor Protestant,* p. 10; see also John Christian Wenger, *The Doctrines of the Mennonites* (Scottdale, Penn.: Mennonite Publishing House, 1950), pp. 26-27; and John D. Roth, *Beliefs: Mennonite Faith and Practice* (Scottsdale, Penn.: Herald, 2005), pp. 29-30.

[85]Finger, "Is 'Systematic Theology' Possible?" pp. 42-43.

[86]Klaassen, *Neither Catholic nor Protestant,* pp. 79-80.

[87]For example, compare Leonard Gross, "The Doctrinal Era of the Mennonite Church," *Mennonite Quarterly Review* 60, no. 1 (1986): 83-103, with A. James Reimer, "Mennonite Theological Self-Understanding, the Crisis of Modern Anthropocentricity, and the Challenge of the Third Millennium," in *Mennonite Identity: Historical and Contemporary Perspectives,* ed. Calvin W. Redekop and Samuel J. Steiner (New York: University Press of America, 1988), pp. 13-39.

[88]Friedmann, *Theology of Anabaptism,* pp. 21-22. See also Thomas N. Finger, *A Contemporary Anabaptist Theology: Biblical, Historical, Constructive* (Downers Grove, Ill.: InterVarsity Press, 2004), pp. 9-12; Snyder, "Beyond Polygenesis," pp. 11-12.

[89]Finger, *Christian Theology,* 1:85.

[90]Friedmann, *Theology of Anabaptism,* p. 22.

[91]See *MCF,* p. 19.

[92]Reimer, "Mennonite Theological Self-Understanding," p. 21; see also p. 29.

[93]*Confession of Faith in a Mennonite Perspective* (Scottdale, Penn.: Herald, 1995).

[94]Klaassen, *Neither Catholic nor Protestant,* p. 45. For a window into the way in which Mennonites struggled to bring this fusion to bear upon race relations, see Le Roy Belcher, *The Black Mennonite Church in North America, 1886-1986* (Scottdale, Penn.: Herald, 1986).

[95]Klaassen, *Neither Catholic nor Protestant,* pp. 46-47; see also Daniel Kauffman, ed., *Doctrines of the Bible: A Brief Discussion of the Teachings of God's Word* (Scottdale, Penn.: Herald, 1928), pp. 15, 17. Cf. John Christian Wenger, *Introduction to Theology: An Interpretation of the Doctrinal Content of Scripture, Written to Strengthen a Childlike Faith in Christ* (Scottdale, Penn.: Herald, 1954), p. 5.

[96]Friedmann, *Theology of Anabaptism,* pp. 36-37.

[97]Howard John Loewen, "The Mission of Theology: Reflections on the Structure of Theology from a Believers' Church Perspective," in Swartley, *Explorations of Systematic Theology,* p. 97.

[98]Kauffman, *Doctrines of the Bible,* p. 136.

[99]*Confession of Faith in a Mennonite Perspective,* Article 4 (pp. 22-23).

[100]See Finger, "Is 'Systematic Theology' Possible?" p. 47.

[101]Friedmann, *Theology of Anabaptism,* p. 36.

[102]Bernhard Rothmann, "Restitution," quoted in *Anabaptism in Outline: Selected Primary Sources,* ed. Walter Klaassen (Scottdale, Penn.: Herald, 1981), p. 149.

[103]For example, *MCF,* p. 47.

[104]C. Norman Kraus, "Anabaptism and Evangelicalism," in Kraus, *Evangelicalism and Anabaptism,* p. 180.

[105]For example, a descriptive paragraph on the title page of Wenger's *The Doctrines of the Mennonites,* published in 1950, indicates that the contents of the book are "correlated with" the Schleitheim Confession (1527), the Dordrecht Confession (1632), the Christian Fundamentals (1921), the Shorter Catechism (1690), the Waldeck Catechism (1778) and Roosen's Catechism (1702).

[106]See Wenger, *Doctrines of the Mennonites,* which correlates its presentation of doctrine with Anabaptist confessional and catechetical documents, which are reproduced in appendices.

[107]Willard Swartley observes that over the course of the history of Anabaptism there has been an "increasing readiness to acknowledge that interpretation should be held accountable to faith, both confessionally and traditionally" ("Afterword: Continuity and Change in Anabaptist-Mennonite Interpretation," in Swartley, *Essays on Biblical Interpretation,* p. 326).

[108]Stuart Murray, *Biblical Interpretation in the Anabaptist Tradition* (Kitchener, Ont.: Pandora, 2000), p. 48.

[109]J. Denny Weaver, "Response," in Driedger and Harder, *Anabaptist-Mennonite Identities in Ferment,* p. 30.

[110]For summary overviews of the development of Anabaptist hermeneutics, see Snyder, *Anabaptist History and Theology,* pp. 159-60; Swartley, "Afterword," pp. 326-27.

[111]*Confession of Faith in a Mennonite Perspective,* Article 4 (pp. 22, 24).

[112]See Snyder, *Anabaptist History and Theology,* p. 7.

[113]Klaassen, "Anabaptist Hermeneutics," p. 10.

[114]Klaassen, *Neither Catholic nor Protestant,* pp. 79-80; Yoder, "Hermeneutics of the Anabaptists," pp. 21-22; J. Denny Weaver, *Becoming Anabaptist* (Kitchener, Ont.: Herald, 1987), pp. 118-19.

[115]Barbara J. MacHaffie, *Her Story: Women in Christian Tradition* (Philadelphia: Fortress, 1986), p. 71.

[116]A. J. Klassen, "Discipleship in a Secular World," in *Consultation on Anabaptist-Mennonite Theology,* ed. A. J. Klassen (Fresno, Calif.: Council of Mennonite Seminaries, 1970), p. 108. The context of Klassen's observation makes it clear that the hermeneutic community is synonymous with genuine Christian community.

[117]Murray, *Biblical Interpretation,* p. 189.

[118]Klassen, "Discipleship in a Secular World," p. 108.

[119]Walter Klaassen, "Anabaptist Hermeneutics: Presuppositions, Principles and Practice," in Swartley, *Essays on Biblical Interpretation,* p. 6. See also Weaver, "Response," p. 30. As will be seen below, Christ's teachings are central to a proper understanding of all of Scripture.

[120]Snyder, *Anabaptist History and Theology,* p. 161.

[121]Finger suggests, "Believers' churches have historically kept the interplay between Word and Spirit alive in a way that Protestant orthodoxy generally has not" (*Christian Theology,* 1:86). For an overview of the role of the Spirit in early Anabaptist hermeneutics, see Snyder, *Anabaptist History and Theology,* pp. 162-72.

[122]Klaassen, "Anabaptist Hermeneutics," p. 5.

[123]MacHaffie, *Her Story,* p. 71.

[124]For example, *Confession of Faith in a Mennonite Perspective,* Article 4 (pp. 21, 23).

[125]Weaver, *Becoming Anabaptist,* 2nd ed., p. 172.

[126]Beulah S. Hostetler, *American Mennonites and Protestant Movements: A Community Paradigm,* Studies in Anabaptist and Mennonite History 28 (Scottdale, Penn.: Herald, 1987), p. 221.

[127]Klaassen, "Anabaptist Hermeneutics," p. 8. Comparing early Anabaptists with "Reformed" theologians, Klaassen observes that the Reformed gave greater credence to the Old Testament.

[128]Yoder, "Hermeneutics of the Anabaptists," p. 26.

[129]Mennonite Confession of Faith, Article 2 (*MCF,* p. 73). The immediate context—Article 2 in its entirety—makes it clear that here the Old Covenant is synonymous with the Old Testament, and the New Covenant is synonymous with the New Testament. For other references

to the relationship as one of fulfillment, see, for example, Dyck, *Introduction to Mennonite History,* p. 146; Wenger, *Doctrines of the Mennonites,* p. 48.

[130]Kauffman affirms that the Old Testament was "taken away" so that the New Testament could be established as the Christian's "only rule" (*Doctrines of the Bible,* p. 150). Wenger emphasizes his view that the Old Testament was *"done away,"* and that New Testament teaching constitutes the basis for *"every church ordinance and the entire ethic of the Christian"* (*Doctrines of the Mennonites,* p. 48). In reviewing the history of North American confessions, Loewen observes that there is a progressive overall decrease in the frequency of references to the Old Testament (*MCF,* p. 34). See also Weaver, *Becoming Anabaptist,* 2nd ed., p. 172.

[131]Klaassen, *Neither Catholic nor Protestant,* p. 79.

[132]Klaassen, "Anabaptist Hermeneutics," pp. 7-8.

[133]*Confession of Faith in a Mennonite Perspective,* Article 4 (pp. 21, 24). See also Wenger, *Introduction to Theology,* pp. 33-34.

[134]Snyder, "Beyond Polygenesis," p. 16. See also J. Denny Weaver, "Mennonite Theological Self-Understanding: A Response to A. James Reimer," in Redekop and Steiner, *Mennonite Identity,* pp. 50-52. Cf. Friedmann, *Theology of Anabaptism,* pp. 45-46.

[135]Shorter Catechism (Wenger, *Doctrines of the Mennonites,* pp. 92-96).

[136]Wenger, *Doctrines of the Mennonites,* p. 96.

[137]Snyder, *Footsteps of Christ,* p. 139.

[138]Bender, *Anabaptist Vision,* p. 21.

[139]Wenger, *Doctrines of the Mennonites,* p. 62.

[140]Kauffman, *Doctrines of the Bible,* p. 470.

[141]Friedmann, *Theology of Anabaptism,* p. 44.

[142]Kauffman, *Doctrines of the Bible,* p. 473.

[143]Shorter Catechism (Wenger, *Doctrines of the Mennonites,* p. 92). In discussing the nature of the church (Question 12), the catechism states that it consists in those who "through faith in Jesus Christ, have withdrawn from a sinful world and submitted in obedience to the Gospel, not to live any more to themselves, but to Christ, in true humility."

[144]Christian Fundamentals, Article 10 (Wenger, *Doctrines of the Mennonites,* p. 89). Although this statement reflects the spirit of separation that characterized a number of Fundamentalist traditions in the United States in the early twentieth century, it nonetheless constitutes one expression in a long line of Anabaptist statements on separation from the world.

[145]*Confession of Faith in a Mennonite Perspective,* Article 17 (p. 65).

[146]Harry Loewen, introduction to *Why I Am a Mennonite: Essays on Mennonite Identity,* ed. Harry Loewen (Kitchener, Ont.: Herald, 1988), p. 17.

[147]Bender, *Anabaptist Vision,* p. 28. Other Anabaptist writers refer to "two worlds," "two realms" or "two kingdoms" (e.g., Friedmann, *Theology of Anabaptism,* pp. 41, 45; Wenger, *Introduction to Theology,* p. 316).

[148]Friedmann, *Theology of Anabaptism,* p. 38.

[149]Wenger, *Doctrines of the Mennonites,* pp. 56-57.

[150]Bender, *Anabaptist Vision,* pp. 27-28.

[151]Snyder, *Footsteps of Christ,* p. 185.

[152]Finger, *Contemporary Anabaptist Theology,* p. 232.

[153]Kauffman, *Doctrines of the Bible,* pp. 495-99.

[154]Wenger, *Introduction to Theology,* p. 317.

[155]*Confession of Faith in a Mennonite Perspective,* Article 23 (p. 86); also Article 17 (p. 65) and the commentaries on Articles 10, 23. Additional confessional statements of the principle of

separation are found in the Schleitheim Confession, Articles 4, 6; and the Mennonite Confession of Faith, preamble and Article 16.

[156]Wenger, *Introduction to Theology*, pp. 317, 315.

[157]Finger, *Contemporary Anabaptist Theology*, p. 158. There are, for Finger, three intertwined dimensions. In conjunction with the personal and communal there is also the missional, extending beyond the community into the world.

[158]Snyder, *Footsteps of Christ*, p. 187.

[159]Friedmann, *Theology of Anabaptism*, p. 43.

[160]Bender, *Anabaptist Vision*, p. 27.

[161]Finger, *Christian Theology*, 2:238; see also 1:88.

[162]Ibid., 2:238; also Bender, *Anabaptist Vision*, p. 26.

[163]Finger, *Christian Theology*, 1:88.

[164]Friedmann, *Anabaptist Theology*, p. 43.

[165]In the most traditional and conservative communities, this discipline may range from "brotherly admonition" to "the ban"—that is, exclusion from the community (Friedmann, *Theology of Anabaptism*, p. 43). The ban has been a disciplinary provision within Anabaptism from its earliest days. See, for example, the second article of the Schleitheim Confession. See also Finger, *Contemporary Anabaptist Theology*, pp. 227-33.

[166]Finger, *Christian Theology*, 2:238.

[167]This phraseology associating "peace" and "nonresistance" was first used in 1943 by Bender in his original essay on "The Anabaptist Vision." According to Ted Koontz, through the influence of Bender's essay the term "nonresistance" "became the most common way to speak of traditional Mennonite ways of understanding our peace commitment" ("Grace to You and Peace: Nonresistance as Piety," *Mennonite Quarterly Review* 69, no. 3 [1995]: 354 n. 1).

[168]According to Koontz, "No theological theme is more central to the Anabaptist Vision or to the historical identity of Mennonites than what H. S. Bender in his famous essay of 1943 called 'an ethic of love and nonresistance'" ("Grace to You and Peace," p. 354; see also Bender, *Anabaptist Vision*, p. 31). Loewen refers to this as a "most central emphasis" ("Mission of Theology," p. 103).

[169]Koontz refers to nonresistance as "something historically central to Mennonite identity" ("Grace to You and Peace," p. 355). Klaassen says that nonresistance has been "an important identity symbol for Mennonites for so long" (*Anabaptism in Outline*, p. 265).

[170]Schleitheim Confession, Article 4 (*MCF*, p. 80).

[171]Dordrecht Confession, Article 14 (*MCF*, p. 68). Also cited here are Romans 12:14; 1 Peter 3:9. More recent confessional statements of nonresistance include the Mennonite Confession of Faith, Articles 18, 19; and *Confession of Faith in a Mennonite Perspective*, Article 22 (p. 81).

[172]See, for example, the appeals to Isaiah's and Micah's references to beating swords into ploughshares, cited above.

[173]Wenger, *Doctrines of the Mennonites*, p. 48.

[174]Klaassen, *Anabaptism in Outline*, p. 265.

[175]Roth, *Beliefs*, p. 44.

[176]Mennonite Confession of Faith, Article 18 (*MCF*, p. 77). See also Schleitheim Confession, Article 6 (*MCF*, p. 80), and *Confession of Faith in a Mennonite Perspective*, Articles 17, 22 (pp. 65, 81).

[177]Kauffman, *Doctrines of the Bible*, p. 507.

[178]Vernard Eller, "Beliefs," in *The Church of the Brethren: Past and Present*, ed. Donald F. Durnbaugh (Elgin, Ill.: Brethren Press, 1971), p. 47.

[179]Donald B. Kraybill, "Yieldedness and Accountability in Traditional Anabaptist Communities,"

in Bowman and Longenecker, *Anabaptist Currents,* pp. 274-75.

[180]Wenger argues that in distinction from most, if not all, Protestants, Anabaptists neither neglect nor explain away New Testament passages that teach "unqualified love for and nonresistance to evil men" (e.g., Mt 5:38-48; Lk 6:27-36; Jn 18:36; Rom 12:17-21; 1 Thess 5:15; 1 Pet 2:20-23; 3:8-9). Anabaptists interpret these passages "in an absolute sense." They teach a love manifest in turning the other cheek, and this is what disciples are to do (*Doctrines of the Mennonites,* p. 34).

[181]Klaassen, *Anabaptism in Outline,* p. 266.

[182]*Confession of Faith in a Mennonite Perspective,* commentary on Article 22 (p. 82).

[183]*Confession of Faith in a Mennonite Perspective,* Article 22 (p. 81).

[184]See, for example, John D. Unruh, *In the Name of Christ: A History of the Mennonite Central Committee and Its Service, 1920-1951* (Scottdale, Penn.: Herald, 1952); Paul Toews, *Mennonites in American Society, 1930-1970: Modernity and the Persistence of Religious Community* (Scottdale, Penn.: Herald, 1996).

Chapter 4: To the Glory of God and God Alone

[1]John H. Leith, *An Introduction to the Reformed Tradition: A Way of Being the Christian Community,* rev. ed. (Atlanta: John Knox, 1981), p. 34; cf. Jack Rogers, *Reading the Bible and the Confessions—The Presbyterian Way* (Louisville: Geneva, 1999), p. 56.

[2]I. John Hesselink, *On Being Reformed: Distinctive Characteristics and Common Misunderstandings* (Ann Arbor, Mich.: Servant, 1983), p. 6; M. Eugene Osterhaven, *The Spirit of the Reformed Tradition* (Grand Rapids: Eerdmans, 1971), pp. 172-74.

[3]Leith, *Reformed Tradition,* p. 8; Donald K. McKim, introduction to *Major Themes in the Reformed Tradition,* ed. Donald K. McKim (Grand Rapids: Eerdmans, 1992), p. xiv.

[4]McKim, introduction to *Major Themes,* p. xiv; Leith, *Reformed Tradition,* p. 34.

[5]Hesselink, *On Being Reformed,* p. 8.

[6]Ibid., pp. 93-94; Leonard J. Coppes, *Are Five Points Enough? The Ten Points of Calvinism* (Manassas, Va.: Reformation Educational Foundation, 1980), p. x; Stephen E. Smallman, "What Is a Reformed Church?" *Presbyterion* 8, no. 1 (1982): 2. When referring to theological schools of thought in particular, the term *Covenant* could be added to this list. See Mark W. Karlberg, "Doctrinal Development in Scripture and Tradition: A Reformed Assessment of the Church's Theological Task," *Calvin Theological Journal* 30, no. 2 (1995): 416.

[7]Richard Muller, "How Many Points?" *Calvin Theological Journal* 28, no. 2 (1993): 426.

[8]Leith, *Reformed Tradition,* p. 34.

[9]Charles Miller, "The Spread of Calvinism in Switzerland, Germany, and France," in *The Rise and Development of Calvinism,* ed. John H. Bratt (Grand Rapids: Eerdmans, 1971), p. 36; Leith, *Reformed Tradition,* p. 34.

[10]John T. McNeill, *The History and Character of Calvinism* (London: Oxford University Press, 1967), pp. 38-50.

[11]Ibid., pp. 67-71.

[12]Ibid., pp. 49-55, 65-66.

[13]Miller, "Spread of Calvinism," p. 33.

[14]John Calvin, *Institutes of Christian Religion: 1536 Edition,* trans. Ford L. Battles, rev. ed. (Grand Rapids: Eerdmans, 1986).

[15]David Fergusson, "The Reformed Churches," in *The Christian Church: An Introduction to Its Major Traditions,* ed. Paul Avis (London: SPCK, 2002), p. 20.

[16]McNeill, *History and Character,* Part II, "Calvin and the Reformation in Geneva," pp. 165-70.

[17]Bard Thompson, *Humanists and Reformers: A History of the Renaissance and Reformation* (Grand Rapids: Eerdmans, 1996), p. 502.

[18]Leith, *Reformed Tradition*, p. 37.

[19]Miller, "Spread of Calvinism," p. 52.

[20]The precise meaning of this nickname, "Huguenots," is unknown. It may mean "confederates." The first Calvinists to come to North America were Huguenots who came to the New World under the leadership of Gaspard de Coligny in 1555. Their mission was to establish a settlement that would be "a place of refuge" for Huguenots. In this they did not succeed, the people eventually abandoning many of their religious beliefs as well as their dream for the settlement (McNeill, *History and Character*, p. 331).

[21]Miller, "Spread of Calvinism," pp. 46, 49.

[22]Hesselink, *On Being Reformed*, p. 7. This estimate may reflect a Dutch Reformed perspective. Within Presbyterian circles, this stature probably is attributed to the Westminster Confession.

[23]Miller, "Spread of Calvinism," p. 47.

[24]Leith, *Reformed Tradition*, p. 38.

[25]McNeill, *History and Character*, p. 266.

[26]Leith, *Reformed Tradition*, pp. 41-42.

[27]John R. H. Moorman, *A History of the Church in England*, 3rd ed. (London: Adam & Charles Black, 1973), pp. 186, 190.

[28]Leith, *Reformed Tradition*, p. 42.

[29]McNeill, *History and Character*, p. 293.

[30]Ibid., p. 295.

[31]Ibid., p. 299.

[32]See William D. Maxwell, *John Knox's Genevan Service Book, 1556: The Liturgical Portions of the Genevan Service Book Used by John Knox While a Minister of the English Congregation of Marian Exiles at Geneva, 1556-1559* (Edinburgh: Oliver & Boyd, 1931; reprint, Westminster: Faith Press, 1965). Calvin's *The Forme of Prayers and Ministration of the Sacraments* was published in Geneva in 1556, with the first Scottish edition being published in 1562 and enlarged in 1564.

[33]Richard A. Muller, *After Calvin: Studies in the Development of a Theological Tradition* (Oxford: Oxford University Press, 2003).

[34]Leith, *Reformed Tradition*, p. 38. Leith observes, "While the Synod of Dort has sometimes become a symbol of extreme Calvinism, it actually sought to arrive at a consensus of the sixteenth-century Reformed community" (ibid., p. 39). See also McNeill, *History and Character*, p. 265.

[35]The Remonstrants were followers of the thought of Arminius, and they affirmed what they took to be a more significant role for human will. This order, beginning with election, is the order in which these five doctrines are presented under the five "Heads" of the Canons of the Synod of Dordt, and it reflects the logic and relationship among these five as understood at Dordt (Canons of the Synod of Dordt [*EARRC*, 1:173-84]). One popular way of referring to these points is through the English-language acronym TULIP: Total depravity, Unconditional election, Limited atonement, Irresistible grace, Perseverance of the saints.

[36]Miller suggests that the Westminster Confession and the Heidelberg Catechism constitute "the greatest creedal statements of Calvinism" ("Spread of Calvinism," p. 28).

[37]Leith, *Reformed Tradition*, p. 42.

[38]Ibid., p. 45.

[39]Ibid., p. 47; also McNeill, *History and Character*, p. 337.

[40]George M. Marsden, "Reformed and American," in *Reformed Theology in America*, ed. David F.

Wells (Grand Rapids: Baker, 1985), p. 3.

[41]Ibid., pp. 4, 5.

[42]Randall H. Balmer and John R. Fitzmier, *The Presbyterians,* Denominations in America 5 (Westport, Conn.: Greenwood Press, 1993), p. 24.

[43]McNeill, *History and Character,* pp. 362-63. These three works constitute the first three volumes in a critical edition of Edwards's works, which is in progress (*The Works of Jonathan Edwards,* 23 vols. [New Haven: Yale University Press, 1957-]).

[44]John Saillant, *Black Puritan, Black Republican: The Life and Thought of Lemuel Haynes (1753-1833)* (New York: Oxford University Press, 2003), p. 4. For an introduction to the history of Presbyterianism in relationship to African Americans, see Gayraud W. Wilmore, *Black and Presbyterian: The Heritage and the Hope* (Philadelphia: Geneva, 1983); on the Reformed Church in America, see Noel Leo Erskine, *Black People and the Reformed Church in America* (Lansing, Ill.: Reformed Church Press, 1978).

[45]McNeill, *History and Character,* p. 365.

[46]Eugene P. Heideman, "The Americanization of Reformed Confessions," *Perspectives* 6 (June 1991): 13-14.

[47]For example, in 1742, the Philadelphia Baptist Convention adopted the London Confession (1677), which is basically a modified version of the Westminster Confession (Leith, *Reformed Tradition,* p. 46).

[48]Miller, "Spread of Calvinism," pp. 40-44, 57; Leith, *Reformed Tradition,* p. 40.

[49]Gordon J. Spykman, *Reformational Theology: A New Paradigm for Doing Dogmatics* (Grand Rapids: Eerdmans, 1992), p. 6. Kuyper founded the Free University, a distinctively Calvinist institution, in 1880, and he taught in its seminary. He also led an influential political party, and in 1901, he was made Prime Minister of the Netherlands. These types of initiatives were the outworking of Kuyper's notion of sphere sovereignty, whereby each major sphere of society possessed its own God-given value and rights. See Abraham Kuyper, *Lectures on Calvinism* (Grand Rapids: Eerdmans, 1953); idem, *Principles of Sacred Theology* (Grand Rapids: Eerdmans, 1954); see also Vincent Bacote, *The Spirit in Public Theology: Appropriating the Legacy of Abraham Kuyper* (Grand Rapids: Baker, 2005).

[50]Spykman, *Reformational Theology,* p. 6.

[51]See, for example, Henry Zwaanstra, "Louis Berkhof," in Wells, *Reformed Theology in America,* pp. 166-67. A compendium of Bavinck's *Gereformeerde Dogmatiek* subsequently was published as *Magnalia Dei* (1909), and this abridgment was translated into English, by Henry Zylstra, as *Our Reasonable Faith* (Grand Rapids: Eerdmans, 1956). The first two of the original four volumes recently have been translated and published in English under the title *Reformed Dogmatics* (Grand Rapids: Baker, 2003).

[52]McNeill, *History and Character,* p. 366.

[53]As Marsden points out, "These divisions were not confined to Presbyterianism, although they took their clearest shape among them" ("Reformed and American," p. 6).

[54]Ibid., pp. 5-6.

[55]Morton Smith, "The Southern Tradition," in Wells, *Reformed Theology in America,* pp. 196, 198.

[56]Ibid., p. 200.

[57]Marsden, "Reformed and American," p. 7.

[58]See Mark A. Noll, "The Princeton Theology," in Wells, *Reformed Theology in America,* pp. 15-24.

[59]Morton Smith observes that "Princeton Theology" was originally brought to Princeton from Virginia by Archibald Alexander, who had been at Liberty Hall Academy in Virginia ("The Southern Tradition," p. 193).

[60]Spykman, *Reformational Theology,* p. 37. Dutch Reformed theology came to influence Princeton through the Dutch-born scholar Geerhardus Vos, who taught biblical theology at Princeton from 1893 to 1932 (Robert W. Godfrey, "The Westminster School," in Wells, *Reformed Theology in America,* p. 95).

[61]James D. Bratt, "The Dutch Schools," in Wells, *Reformed Theology in America,* p. 141.

[62]In 1938, the name of the Presbyterian Church of America was changed to the Orthodox Presbyterian Church.

[63]McNeill, *History and Character,* pp. 380-81. A large number of Presbyterian churches did not join the union, instead forming the Presbyterian Church of Canada.

[64]Augustus Hopkins Strong, *Systematic Theology: A Compendium and Commonplace-Book Designed for the Use of Theological Students,* rev. ed., 3 vols. (Philadelphia: American Baptist Publication Society, 1907-1909).

[65]Spykman, *Reformational Theology,* p. 3.

[66]Fred H. Klooster, "Louis Berkhof," in *Handbook of Evangelical Theologians,* ed. Walter A. Elwell (Grand Rapids: Baker, 1993), pp. 107-8.

[67]Herman Hoeksema, *Reformed Dogmatics* (Grand Rapids: Reformed Free Publishing Association, 1966).

[68]G. C. Berkhouwer, *Studies in Dogmatics,* 14 vols. (Grand Rapids: Eerdmans, 1952-1976). See also Gary L. Watts, "G. C. Berkhouwer," in Elwell, *Handbook of Evangelical Theologians,* pp. 193-208.

[69]Dennis Voskuil, "Neoorthodoxy," in Wells, *Reformed Theology in America,* p. 256.

[70]Ibid., p. 257.

[71]James Montgomery Boice, "The Future of Reformed Theology," in Wells, *Reformed Theology in America,* p. 300.

[72]Alisdair I. C. Heron, "Confessional Continuity in the Reformed Family of Churches," in *Reformiertes Erbe: Festschrift für Gottfried W. Locher zu seinem 80. Geburtstag,* ed. Heiko A. Oberman et al., 2 vols. (Zurich: Theologischer Verlag, 1993), 2:148.

[73]Alan P. F. Sell, "The Reformed Family Today: Some Theological Reflections," in McKim, *Major Themes,* p. 436.

[74]See Boice, "Future of Reformed Theology," p. 300; Heron, "Confessional Continuity," 2:148; Sell, "Reformed Family Today," p. 436.

[75]Joel R. Beeke and Sinclair B. Ferguson, eds., *Reformed Confessions Harmonized* (Grand Rapids: Baker, 1999).

[76]Jean-Jacques Bauswein and Lukas Vischer, eds., *The Reformed Family Worldwide: A Survey of Reformed Churches, Theological Schools, and International Organizations* (Grand Rapids: Eerdmans, 1999), pp. 516-40.

[77]Not all denominations that are "United" in name are the result of this type of merger. For example, neither of the denominations that merged to form the United Methodist Church (the Methodist Church and the Evangelical United Brethren) was Reformed, and the United Brethren in Christ was not formed through a merger and is Arminian in theology.

[78]Hesselink, *On Being Reformed,* p. 106; Edward A. Dowey Jr., "Always to Be Reformed," in *Always Being Reformed: The Future of Church Education,* ed. John C. Purdy (Philadelphia: Geneva, 1985), p. 16; John Van Engen, "The Problem of Tradition in the Christian Reformed Church," *Calvin Theological Journal* 20, no. 1 (1985): 84.

[79]See Heron, "Confessional Continuity," 2:149. Another informative illustration of this is given in the following account of the nineteenth-century Dutch immigrant theologian Foppe Ten Hoor: "Most striking, perhaps, is Ten Hoor's very act of addressing [a wide range of] cultural concerns precisely in his role as professor of systematic theology at the Christian Reformed

seminary in Grand Rapids. That the post brought with it this license, even mandate, to speak to any and all issues and that no office in the entire community held more prestige attest to the priority of place the Dutch Reformed have given theology" (Bratt, "Dutch Schools," p. 135).

[80]Leith, *Reformed Tradition,* p. 89.

[81]Spykman, *Reformational Theology,* p. 4.

[82]Hesselink, *On Being Reformed,* p. 106.

[83]Heron, "Confessional Continuity," 2:150.

[84]Fred H. Klooster, "How Reformed Theologians 'Do Theology' in Today's World," in *Doing Theology in Today's World: Essays in Honor of Kenneth S. Kantzer,* ed. John D. Woodbridge and Thomas E. McComiskey (Grand Rapids: Zondervan, 1991), p. 247.

[85]Hesselink, *On Being Reformed,* p. 102.

[86]Klooster, "Reformed Theologians," p. 247.

[87]John Calvin, *Institutes of the Christian Religion,* ed. John T. McNeill, trans. Ford L. Battles, 2 vols. (Philadelphia: Westminster Press, 1960), §1.6.2.

[88]McNeill, *History and Character,* p. 73.

[89]Louis Berkhof, *Introduction to Systematic Theology* (Grand Rapids: Eerdmans, 1932; reprint, Grand Rapids: Baker, 1979), p. 59.

[90]Donald K. McKim, *Introducing the Reformed Faith: Biblical Revelation, Christian Tradition, Contemporary Significance* (Louisville: Westminster John Knox, 2001), p. 12.

[91]Calvin, *Institutes,* §1.7.4 (cf. §1.8.1-13).

[92]Otto Weber, *Foundations of Dogmatics,* trans. Darrell L. Guder, 2 vols. (Grand Rapids: Eerdmans, 1983), 1:312.

[93]Smallman, "What Is a Reformed Church?" p. 4.

[94]H. Henry Meeter, *The Basic Ideas of Calvinism,* rev. Paul A. Marshall, 6th ed. (Grand Rapids: Baker, 1990), p. 28.

[95]Charles Hodge, *Systematic Theology,* reprint ed. (Grand Rapids: Eerdmans, 1977), 1:152.

[96]Ibid., 1:183. With regard to worship, many within the Reformed tradition seek to follow the "regulative principle"—that is, "Whatever is not commanded is forbidden." In order to be included in corporate worship, each element must not merely be free of contradiction with Scripture, but must have scriptural warrant. See, for example, Westminster Confession, Chapter 21, Paragraph 1 (*BCCPC,* §6.101); John M. Frame, "Some Questions about the Regulative Principle," *Westminster Theological Journal* 54, no. 2 (1992): 357.

[97]Klooster, "Reformed Theologians," p. 239.

[98]Westminster Confession, Chapter 1, Paragraph 6 (*BCCPC,* §6.006).

[99]J. F. Peter, "The Place of Tradition in Reformed Theology," *Scottish Journal of Theology* 18, no. 2 (1965): 296-97.

[100]Ibid., p. 298.

[101]George S. Hendry, "The Place and Function of the Confession of Faith in the Reformed Church," in *The New Man: An Orthodox and Reformed Dialogue,* ed. John Meyendorff and Joseph McClelland (New Brunswick, N.J.: Agora Books, 1973), p. 31.

[102]L. Berkhof, *Introduction to Systematic Theology,* p. 64; cf. p. 60.

[103]Peter, "Place of Tradition," p. 300.

[104]Hendry, "Place and Function of the Confession," p. 31; see also McKim, *Introducing the Reformed Faith,* p. 7.

[105]Smallman, "What Is a Reformed Church?" p. 4.

[106]L. Berkhof, *Introduction to Systematic Theology,* p. 64.

[107]Dowey, "Always to Be Reformed," p. 13.

[108]Canons of the Synod of Dordt, Conclusion (*EARRC,* 1:183).

[109]Hendry, "Place and Function of the Confession," p. 31.

[110]Hodge, *Systematic Theology,* 1:184.

[111]Donald McKim, "Foundational Issues," in McKim, *Major Themes,* p. 1.

[112]Dowey, "Always to Be Reformed," p. 13.

[113]Hans-Helmut Esser, "The Authority of the Church and Authority in the Church According to the Reformed Tradition," in *Theological Dialogue Between Orthodox and Reformed Churches,* ed. Thomas F. Torrance, 2 vols. (Edinburgh: Scottish Academic Press, 1985), 1:51.

[114]Kuyper, *Lectures on Calvinism,* p. 16; see also Karl Barth, *The Theology of the Reformed Confessions,* trans. Darrell J. Guder and Judith J. Guder (Louisville: Westminster John Knox, 2002), pp. 7-16.

[115]Presbyterian Church (U.S.A.), "The Confessional Nature of the Church," in McKim, *Major Themes,* p. 25; see also McKim, *Introducing the Reformed Faith,* pp. 8-9.

[116]Compare, for example, the emphasis on change seen in B. A. Gerrish, ed., *Reformed Theology for the Third Christian Millennium* (Louisville: Westminster John Knox, 2003), with the confidence in the abiding value of confessions evident in Beeke and Ferguson, *Reformed Confessions Harmonized.*

[117]Eberhard Busch, "The Closeness of the Distant: Reformed Confessions after 1945," in *Toward the Future of Reformed Theology,* ed. David Willis and Michael Welker (Grand Rapids: Eerdmans, 1999), p. 515.

[118]Jan Rohls, *Reformed Confessions: Theology from Zurich to Barmen,* trans. John Hoffmeyer (Louisville: Westminster John Knox, 1998), p. 9; see also B. A. Gerrish, introduction to Gerrish, *Reformed Theology,* p. 4.

[119]Busch, "Closeness of the Distant," pp. 514-15. See also Robert Benedetto, Darrell L. Guder and Donald K. McKim, introduction to *Historical Dictionary of the Reformed Churches,* Historical Dictionaries of Religions, Philosophies, and Movements 24 (Lanham, Md.: Scarecrow, 1999), pp. xlviii-xlix.

[120]Meeter, *Basic Ideas of Calvinism,* p. 41.

[121]L. Berkhof, *Introduction to Systematic Theology,* p. 72.

[122]Meeter, *Basic Ideas of Calvinism,* p. 41.

[123]This phraseology is adapted from the title of a book by Reformed philosopher Nicholas Wolterstorff, *Reason Within the Bounds of Religion,* 2nd ed. (Grand Rapids: Eerdmans, 1984). See also Hendrik Hart, John Vander Hoeven and Nicholas Wolterstorff, eds., *Rationality in the Calvinian Tradition* (Lanham, Md.: University Press of America, 1983).

[124]Howard L. Rice, *Reformed Spirituality: An Introduction for Believers* (Louisville: Westminster John Knox, 1991), p. 18.

[125]L. Berkhof, *Introduction to Systematic Theology,* p. 67.

[126]Alister E. McGrath, *Christian Spirituality: An Introduction* (Oxford: Blackwell, 1999), p. 96.

[127]Anthony J. Carter, *On Being Black and Reformed: A New Perspective on the African-American Christian Experience* (Phillipsburg, N.J.: P & R, 2003), pp. 14-15. Carter continues by saying, "I am convinced that such theology is best articulated and maintained within the Reformed theological tradition."

[128]Presbyterian Church (U.S.A.), "Confessional Nature of the Church," p. 26. This does not mean that the confessions are beyond questioning. This document continues, "On the other hand they are free . . . to be open to hear a new and perhaps different word from the living Lord the standards confess, and to examine critically the church's teachings in the light of further

study of Scripture."

[129]Edward A. Dowey Jr., "Confessional Documents as Reformed Hermeneutic," *Journal of Presbyterian History* 61, no. 1 (1983): 96.

[130]Westminster Confession, Chapter 1, Paragraph 9 (*BCCPC,* §6.009); see also Second Helvetic Confession, Chapter 2, Paragraph 1 (*BCCPC,* §5.010).

[131]Richard B. Gaffin, "Systematic Theology and Biblical Theology," *Westminster Theological Journal* 38, no. 2 (1976): 294-97.

[132]Louis Berkhof, *Principles of Biblical Interpretation,* 2nd ed. (Grand Rapids: Baker, 1952), p. 165.

[133]Dowey, "Confessional Documents," p. 94.

[134]Hesselink, *On Being Reformed,* p. 102. See, for example, Heinrich Heppe, *Reformed Dogmatics Set Out and Illustrated from the Sources,* rev. and ed. Ernst Bizer, trans. G. T. Thomson (London: George Allen & Unwin, 1950), pp. 282-319, 371-409, 581-89; discussions of the "covenant of works," the "covenant of redemption" and the "covenant of grace" in many Reformed systematic theologies (e.g., Louis Berkhof, *Systematic Theology,* 4th ed. [Grand Rapids: Eerdmans, 1941], pp. 262-301; Hodge, *Systematic Theology,* 2:117-22, 354-77); M. Eugene Osterhaven, "Covenant Theology," in *Evangelical Dictionary of Theology,* ed. Walter A. Elwell, 2nd ed. (Grand Rapids: Baker, 2001), pp. 301-3.

[135]See Ben Warburton, *Calvinism: Its History and Basic Principles, Its Fruits and Its Future, and Its Practical Application to Life* (Grand Rapids: Eerdmans, 1955), p. 13.

[136]L. Berkhof, *Principles of Biblical Interpretation,* p. 160.

[137]Meeter, *Basic Ideas of Calvinism,* pp. 15-18.

[138]Hesselink, *On Being Reformed,* pp. 108-11. See also Carter, *Black and Reformed,* p. 12; Albert Wolters, "Dutch Neo-Calvinism: Worldview, Philosophy and Rationality," in Hart, Vander Hoeven and Wolterstorff, *Rationality in the Calvinian Tradition,* pp. 113-31.

[139]Benedetto, Guder and McKim, introduction to *Historical Dictionary of the Reformed Churches,* p. xlix.

[140]Hesselink, *On Being Reformed,* p. 2. It is also important to note that those who emphatically acknowledge the diversity within the Reformed tradition (e.g., Donald McKim, John Leith) nonetheless see enough continuity and coherence that they also celebrate, write about and identify themselves with what they refer to as "the Reformed tradition."

[141]Ibid., pp. 94-111.

[142]Some of these are Kuyper, *Lectures on Calvinism,* pp. 9-40; Coppes, *Are Five Points Enough?* Meeter, *Basic Ideas of Calvinism,* especially pp. 15-23, 43-48; Leith, *Reformed Tradition,* especially pp. 70-88, 96-112; Bauswein and Vischer, *Reformed Family Worldwide,* pp. 26-33; Warburton, *Calvinism;* Sell, "Reformed Family Today," p. 435; Rogers, *Reading the Bible,* pp. 57-58; Van Engen, "Problem of Tradition," p. 87; R. C. Sproul Jr., ed., *After Darkness, Light: Distinctives of Reformed Theology* (Phillipsburg, N.J.: P & R, 2003); Philip Graham Ryken, *What Is a True Calvinist?* (Phillipsburg, N.J.: P & R, 2002).

[143]R. C. Sproul Jr., *"Soli Deo Gloria,"* in Sproul, *After Darkness, Light,* p. 191.

[144]Carter, *Black and Reformed,* pp. 102-3, 16.

[145]Hesselink, *On Being Reformed,* p. 97.

[146]TULIP: Total depravity, Unconditional election, Limited atonement, Irresistible grace, Perseverance of the saints. Although there are theologians who have written books expounding these five points (e.g., Daniel N. Steele and Curtis C. Thomas, *The Five Points of Calvinism— Defined, Defended, Documented* [Phillipsburg, N.J.: P & R, 1963]), theologians seeking a more adequate understanding of Reformed theology (e.g., Muller, "How Many Points?" p.

426) adamantly argue that it would be "a major error—both historically and doctrinally—if the five points of Calvinism were understood either as the sole or even as the absolutely primary basis for identifying someone as holding the Calvinistic or Reformed faith." See also Coppes, *Are Five Points Enough?* Miller, "Spread of Calvinism," p. 27; Sell, "Reformed Family Today," p. 435. Roger Nicole writes, "Salvation is of the Lord! This is the theme of Scripture and of the five points of Calvinism" ("The 'Five Points' and God's Sovereignty," in *Our Sovereign God: Addresses Presented to the Philadelphia Conference on Reformed Theology, 1974-1976,* ed. James M. Boice [Grand Rapids: Baker, 1977], p. 36). See also Bavinck, *Our Reasonable Faith,* p. 130.

[147]Hesselink, *On Being Reformed,* pp. 108-9; Sell, "Reformed Family," p. 435.

[148]Bavinck, *Our Reasonable Faith,* p. 130.

[149]The selection of these two loci is also in keeping with Catherine Gonzalez's delineation of the three "distinctive emphases" of the Reformed tradition: the sovereignty of God, the grace of God, sanctification ("God," in *Encyclopedia of the Reformed Faith,* ed. Donald K. McKim [Louisville: Westminster John Knox, 1992], p. 155).

[150] Thomas F. Torrance, "The Distinctive Character of the Reformed Tradition," *Reformed Review* 54:1 (autumn 2000): 5; also M. Eugene Osterhaven, response to Torrance, ibid., p. 29.

[151]*The Constitution of the Presbyterian Church (U.S.A.), Part 2, Book of Order* (Louisville: Office of the General Assembly of the Presbyterian Church [U.S.A.], 2004), §G-2.0500.

[152]Bavinck, *Our Reasonable Faith,* pp. 130-31.

[153]Quoted in Osterhaven, *Spirit of the Reformed Tradition,* p. 101.

[154]Gonzalez, "God," p. 147. See also Meeter, *Basic Ideas of Calvinism,* pp. 17-18, 22-23, 43-44; Heron, "Confessional Continuity," 2:151.

[155]Weber, *Foundations of Dogmatics,* 1:512. For other affirmations of the doctrine of God, particularly the sovereignty of God, as the preeminent doctrine in Reformed thought, see Paul T. Fuhrmann, *God-Centered Religion: An Essay Inspired by Some French and Swiss Protestant Writers* (Grand Rapids: Zondervan, 1942), p. 23 and passim; Heron, "Confessional Continuity," 2:154-55; Balmer and Fitzmier, *The Presbyterians,* p. 5; Kuyper, *Lectures on Calvinism,* p. 46.

[156]L. Berkhof, *Systematic Theology,* p. 43; see also Barth, *Reformed Confessions,* p. 85.

[157]Hoeksema, *Reformed Dogmatics,* p. 48.

[158]These three by no means exhaust the Reformed understanding of God, but they are among the more common major descriptors.

[159]See, for example, Heidelberg Catechism, Question 6 (*BCCPC,* §4.006); Westminster Confession, Chapter 4, Paragraph 1 (*BCCPC,* §6.022); Beeke and Ferguson, *Reformed Confessions Harmonized,* pp. 36-40.

[160]Spykman, *Reformational Theology,* p. 147.

[161]Hodge, *Systematic Theology,* 1:562.

[162]Bavinck, *Our Reasonable Faith,* pp. 166-67.

[163]Hodge, *Systematic Theology,* 1:558.

[164]Spykman, *Reformational Theology,* p. 149.

[165]Hodge, *Systematic Theology,* 1:558.

[166]Westminster Confession, Chapter 4, Article 1.

[167]Bavinck, *Our Reasonable Faith,* p. 168.

[168]L. Berkhof, *Systematic Theology,* pp. 76-79.

[169]Bavinck, *Our Reasonable Faith,* p. 182.

[170]Hendrikus Berkhof, *Christian Faith: An Introduction to the Study of the Faith,* trans. Sierd

Woudstra, rev. ed. (Grand Rapids: Eerdmans, 1986), p. 215.

[171]The answer to Question 11, "What are God's works of providence?" in the Westminster Shorter Catechism is, "God's works of providence are his most holy, wise, and powerful preserving and governing of all his creatures, and all their actions" (*BCCPC,* §7.011). On the creation-providence connection, see Heidelberg Catechism, Questions 26, 27 (*BCCPC,* §§4.026, 4.027); Westminster Confession, Chapter 5, Paragraph 1 (*BCCPC,* §6.024).

[172]Spykman, *Reformational Theology,* p. 272.

[173]Belgic Confession, Article 13.

[174]Bavinck, *Our Reasonable Faith,* p. 169; see also pp. 177, 182.

[175]Ibid., p. 178.

[176]Westminster Confession, Chapter 5, Article 1.

[177]G. C. Berkouwer, *The Providence of God,* trans. Lewis B. Smedes, Studies in Dogmatics (Grand Rapids: Eerdmans, 1952), p. 68.

[178]Spykman, *Reformational Theology,* p. 276.

[179]Ibid., p. 273.

[180]McKim, *Introducing the Reformed Faith,* p. 41.

[181]Spykman, *Reformational Theology,* p. 160.

[182]Bavinck, *Our Reasonable Faith,* p. 182; see also Berkouwer, *Providence of God,* p. 35.

[183]Gonzalez, "God," p. 155; Westminster Confession, Chapter 8, Paragraphs 1, 3, 5, 8 (*BCCPC,* §§6.043, 6.045, 6.047, 6.050).

[184]Carter, *Black and Reformed,* p. 45.

[185]Calvin, *Institutes,* §2.15.3-5; Westminster Confession, Chapter 8, Paragraph 1 (*BCCPC,* §6.043).

[186]Calvin, *Institutes,* §2.15.4.

[187]Marsden, "Reformed and American," p. 11.

[188]George W. Stroup, "Grace," in McKim, *Encyclopedia of the Reformed Faith,* p. 161.

[189]Hoeksema, *Reformed Dogmatics,* p. 111. L. Berkhof highlights the significance of grace for the hermeneutical analogy of faith (*Principles of Biblical Interpretation,* pp. 54, 164-65).

[190]L. Berkhof, *Systematic Theology,* p. 427.

[191]Hoeksema, *Reformed Dogmatics,* p. 109.

[192]Kuyper, *Lectures on Calvinism,* p. 53.

[193]Other terms for this are "ordinary providence" or "general providence" (e.g., Robert L. Reymond, *A New Systematic Theology of the Christian Faith* [Nashville: Thomas Nelson, 1998], p. 399).

[194]L. Berkhof stresses the fact that "natural blessings" should not be taken for granted or regarded simply as "there"; rather, they are "manifestations of the *grace* of God to man in general" (*Systematic Theology,* p. 435).

[195]Ibid., pp. 435-36.

[196]Spykman, *Reformational Theology,* pp. 320-21.

[197]Richard J. Mouw, *He Shines in All That's Fair: Culture and Common Grace* (Grand Rapids: Eerdmans, 2001). Mouw includes discussion of some of the differences within the Reformed tradition, particularly the Dutch Reformed tradition, concerning the theology of common grace.

[198]L. Berkhof, *Systematic Theology,* p. 435.

[199]Heidelberg Catechism, Question 60 (*BCCPC,* §4.060).

[200]Nicole, "The 'Five Points' and God's Sovereignty," p. 35.

[201]Hesselink, *On Being Reformed,* p. 95; see also James Montgomery Boice and Philip G. Ryken, *The Doctrines of Grace: Rediscovering the Evangelical Gospel* (Wheaton, Ill.: Crossway, 2002).

[202]This order reflects the infralapsarian view, which holds that God's decision regarding election is *subordinate* to the decision to create a world subject to the fall into sin. The supralapsarian view, on the other hand, holds that God made the decision regarding election *prior* to the decision to create such a world. Infralapsarianism has been the predominant view within the Reformed tradition. For a recent discussion, see "'Infra-' Versus 'Supra-,'" in Mouw, *He Shines in All That's Fair,* pp. 53-74. For Calvin's view of election, see *Institutes,* §§3.21.1-7, 3.22.1-11, 3.23.1-14.

[203]Canons of the Synod of Dordt, Head 1, Articles 6, 7, 10 (*EARRC,* 1:173-74).

[204]Canons of the Synod of Dordt, Head 2, Article 3 (*EARRC,* 1:176). On election as grace, see also Weber, *Foundations of Dogmatics,* 2:438; Cornelius Plantinga Jr., *A Place to Stand: A Study of Ecumenical Creeds and Reformed Confessions* (Grand Rapids: Board of Publications of the Christian Reformed Church, 1981), pp. 70-71.

[205]Calvin, *Institutes,* §2.16.2.

[206]Hodge makes the point that "Christ is truly, not figuratively, a Priest" (*Systematic Theology,* 2:464).

[207]Canons of the Synod of Dordt, Head 2, Article 8 (*EARRC,* 1:176-77).

[208]For example, Reymond, *New Systematic Theology,* pp. 671-702; Hodge, *Systematic Theology,* 2:544-62; L. Berkhof, *Systematic Theology,* pp. 367-99.

[209]Calvin, *Institutes,* §2.16.2.

[210]Canons of the Synod of Dordt, Heads 3/4, Article 1 (*EARRC,* 1:178).

[211]Westminster Confession, Chapter 6, Paragraph 2 (*BCCPC,* §6.032).

[212]Calvin, *Institutes,* §2.16.1-4.

[213]Canons of the Synod of Dordt, Heads 3/4, Article 12 (*EARRC,* 1:179).

[214]Hodge, *Systematic Theology,* 2:688.

[215]Stroup, "Grace," p. 347.

[216]Hodge, *Systematic Theology,* 2:688.

[217]L. Berkhof, *Systematic Theology,* p. 545. Berkhof's summary is virtually a quotation of the Westminster Confession, Chapter 17, Paragraph 1 (*BCCPC,* §6.081). See also Calvin, *Institutes,* §3.24.7.

[218]Canons of the Synod of Dordt, Head 5, Article 3 (*EARRC,* 1:181).

[219]H. Berkhof, *Christian Faith,* p. 480.

[220]Hesselink, *On Being Reformed,* pp. 94-95.

[221]Canons of the Synod of Dordt, Head 5, Articles 3-6 (*EARRC,* 1:181).

[222]Shirley Heeg, response to Thomas F. Torrance and Alan P. F. Sell, *Reformed Review* 54:1 (autumn 2000): 49.

Chapter 5: The Spirit of a *Via Media*

[1]J. Robert Wright, "Anglicanism, Ecclesia Anglicana, and Anglican: An Essay on Terminology," in *The Study of Anglicanism,* rev. ed. Stephen Sykes, John Booty and Jonathan Knight (London: SPCK; Philadelphia: Fortress, 1998), p. 479; see also Paul Avis, *Anglicanism and the Christian Church: Theological Resources in Historical Perspective,* 2nd ed. (London: T & T Clark, 2002), p. 344.

[2]Wright, "Anglicanism," p. 424.

[3]C. P. Price, "The Identity and Viability of the Anglican Tradition," *St. Luke's Journal of Theology* 23, no. 4 (1980): 251. As Sykes, Booty and Knight point out, this choice is "controversial" (preface to the first edition of *Study of Anglicanism,* p. xi; cf. Wright, "Anglicanism," p. 426). Stephen Neill describes five ways in which Anglicans view the significance and weigh the

merits of the sixteenth-century English Reformation (*Anglicanism,* rev. ed. [Hammond-sworth, U.K.: Penguin, 1960], pp. 31-32).

[4]Sykes, Booty and Knight, preface to the first edition of *Study of Anglicanism,* p. xii.

[5]Ibid., p. xiii.

[6]William P. Haugaard, "From the Reformation to the Eighteenth Century," in Sykes and Booty, *Study of Anglicanism,* p. 3.

[7]On the history of the church in England prior to the sixteenth century, see John R. H. Moorman, *A History of the Church in England,* 2nd ed. (London: Adam & Charles Black, 1967), pp. 3-157.

[8]Haugaard, "Reformation to the Eighteenth Century," p. 4.

[9]Ibid., p. 10. Haugaard indicates that "political" here refers "not only to civil matters, but to wider human relations as they reflect the varied aspects of community life, religious practices, convictions, and church structures."

[10]Ibid., p. 7.

[11]W. Taylor Stevenson, "Lex Orandi—Lex Credendi," in Sykes and Booty, *Study of Anglicanism,* p. 175.

[12]Paul E. More, "The Spirit of Anglicanism," in *Anglicanism: The Thought and Practice of the Church of England, Illustrated from the Religious Literature of the Seventeenth Century,* ed. Paul E. More and Frank L. Cross (London: SPCK, 1962), p. xix; cf. Haugaard, "Reformation to the Eighteenth Century," pp. 11-12.

[13]Haugaard, "Reformation to the Eighteenth Century," p. 11.

[14]Moorman, *Church in England,* pp. 177-78.

[15]Haugaard, "Reformation to the Eighteenth Century," p. 13.

[16]Marion J. Hatchett, "Prayer Books," in Sykes and Booty, *Study of Anglicanism,* p. 122.

[17]Stevenson, "Lex Orandi—Lex Credendi," p. 175.

[18]Michael Ramsey, *The Anglican Spirit,* ed. Dale Coleman (Cambridge, Mass.: Cowley, 1991), p. 14.

[19]Haugaard, "Reformation to the Eighteenth Century," p. 13.

[20]Ramsey, *Anglican Spirit,* p. 14.

[21]See Moorman, *Church in England,* pp. 191-98; Haugaard, "Reformation to the Eighteenth Century," p. 8.

[22]Moorman, *Church in England,* pp. 199, 200.

[23]See "The Act of Supremacy, 1559" and "The Act of Uniformity, 1559," in *Documents of the English Reformation,* ed. Gerald Bray (Minneapolis: Fortress, 1994), pp. 318-28, 329-34; also Moorman, *Church in England,* pp. 200-201.

[24]See "The Elizabethan Injunctions, 1559," in Bray, *Documents of the English Reformation,* pp. 335-48; also Moorman, *Church in England,* p. 201.

[25]See "The Injunctions of Elizabeth, AD 1559," in *Documents Illustrative of English Church History,* ed. Henry Gee and William J. Hardy (London: Macmillan, 1910; reprint, New York: Kraus, 1966), pp. 417-42.

[26]Haugaard, "Reformation to the Eighteenth Century," p. 9.

[27]Ramsey, *Anglican Spirit,* p. 18.

[28]G. W. H. Lampe, "The Revision of the Articles," in *The Articles of the Church of England,* by J. C. de Satgé et al. (London: Mowbray, 1964), p. 97.

[29]Bray, *Documents of the English Reformation,* p. 285.

[30]Lampe, "Revision of the Articles," p. 97. For the text of the Thirty-Nine Articles, see Bray, *Documents of the English Reformation,* pp. 284-311; also "Articles of Religion" (*BCPEC,* pp. 867-

76). The significance and interpretation of the Thirty-Nine Articles will be considered in the section on theological method and tradition.

[31]Moorman, *Church in England,* p. 212.

[32]See ibid., pp. 222-24; Haugaard, "Reformation to the Eighteenth Century," pp. 9-10; Alister E. McGrath, *In the Beginning: The Story of the King James Bible and How It Changed a Nation, a Language, and a Culture* (New York: Anchor, 2001).

[33]Haugaard, "Reformation to the Eighteenth Century," p. 22.

[34]Moorman, *Church in England,* p. 240.

[35]"The Preface to The Book of Common Prayer, 1662," in Bray, *Documents of the English Reformation,* p. 560.

[36]Felix R. Arnott, "Anglicanism in the Seventeenth Century," in More and Cross, *Anglicanism,* p. lxxii.

[37]Perry Butler, "From the Eighteenth Century to the Present Day," in Sykes and Booty, *Study of Anglicanism,* p. 44.

[38]Although "Caroline" refers to the period of the reigns of Charles I (1625-49) and Charles II (1660-1685), the term "Caroline Divines" is not limited in its reference to theologians who wrote during that period. These theologians, most of them bishops, included Lancelot Andrewes (1555-1626) and William Laud (1573-1645). Latitudinarians pursued a tempered, moderating course, deemphasizing dogmatic theological statements, ecclesiastical organization and liturgical formalities. In their emphasis on the role of reason in theology, they had affinity with the Cambridge Platonists. See Moorman, *Church in England,* pp. 233-37.

[39]Arnott, "Anglicanism," p. lxxii.

[40]Francis Fletcher, chaplain for the explorer Sir Francis Drake, conducted a service at what is now Drake's Bay, near San Francisco (Raymond W. Albright, *A History of the Protestant Episcopal Church* [New York: Macmillan, 1964], p. 13).

[41]Ibid., pp. 47, 123. Cf. David Hein and Gardiner Shattuck's description of circumstances that lead to the conclusion that "seventeenth-century Virginia did not prove to be a congenial place in which to establish or support English religious institutions" (*The Episcopalians,* Denominations in America 11 [Westport, Conn.: Praeger, 2004], pp. 13, 15-16).

[42]Albright, *Protestant Episcopal Church,* pp. 15, 20.

[43]Robert Webber, "Protestant Episcopal Church in the U.S.A.," in *Dictionary of Christianity in America,* ed. Daniel G. Reid et al. (Downers Grove, Ill.: InterVarsity Press, 1990).

[44]Ibid., p. 950.

[45]See William B. Williamson, "Episcopalians," in *An Encyclopedia of Religions in the United States: One Hundred Religious Groups Speak for Themselves,* ed. William B. Williamson (New York: Crossroad, 1992), p. 121.

[46]Because *Episcopalian* is a commonly used term in the United States, while *Anglican* is used in Canada and among some smaller Anglican denominations in the United States, and because the Episcopal Church (formerly the Protestant Episcopal Church in the United States of America) is an integral part of the worldwide Anglican communion, the terms *Episcopal* and *Anglican* will be considered virtually synonymous in discussion of the Anglican tradition in the United States.

[47]Butler, "Eighteenth Century to the Present Day," pp. 31, 32.

[48]Ibid., p. 32. Evangelicals were among those at the forefront of resistance to Deism. For example, in 1731, William Law (1686-1761) published *The Case of Reason* in response to the Matthew Tindal's *Deistic Christianity as Old as Creation* (1730), and in 1736, Joseph Butler (1692-1752), bishop of Durham, published his apologetic classic, *The Analogy of Religion,*

Natural and Revealed, to the Constitution and Course of Nature (1736).

[49]Butler, "Eighteenth Century to the Present Day," p. 33.

[50]Webber, "Protestant Episcopal Church," p. 950. Following the War for Independence, Anglicanism was eventually disestablished in all these jurisdictions.

[51]Albright, *Protestant Episcopal Church,* p. 113.

[52]Ibid., p. 113; Webber, "Protestant Episcopal Church," p. 950.

[53]Albright, *Protestant Episcopal Church,* p. 123.

[54]Webber, "Protestant Episcopal Church," p. 950.

[55]Don S. Armentrout and Robert B. Slocum, eds., *Documents of Witness: A History of the Episcopal Church, 1782-1985* (New York: Church Hymnal, 1994), p. 1.

[56]Albright, *Protestant Episcopal Church,* p. 135.

[57]W. J. Hankey, "Canon Law," in Sykes and Booty, *Study of Anglicanism,* p. 203.

[58]Armentrout and Slocum, *Documents of Witness,* p. 1.

[59]Webber, "Protestant Episcopal Church," p. 950.

[60]Albright, *Protestant Episcopal Church,* p. 140; see also p. 124.

[61]Ibid., p. 140.

[62]For a summary of the changes, see Hatchett, "Prayer Books," p. 131.

[63] Hein and Shattuck, *The Episcopalians,* p. 25; the second quotation is from Henry May, *The Enlightenment in America* (New York: Oxford University Press, 1976), p. 66, quoted by Hein and Shattuck.

[64]Hein and Shattuck, *The Episcopalians,* pp. 25-26.

[65]Butler, "Eighteenth Century to the Present Day," pp. 29, 35. The foundational figures in the Oxford Movement included John Keble (1792-1866), John Henry Newman (1801-1890), Richard Hurrell Froude (1803-1836) and Edward Bouverie Pusey (1800-1882). The early phases of the Oxford Movement are also referred to as "Tractarianism," after essays published by proponents in a series titled Tracts for the Times.

[66]Ibid., pp. 34-35, 37.

[67]Moorman, *Church in England,* pp. 392, 394; Butler, "Eighteenth Century to the Present Day," p. 41.

[68]As in England, evangelicals organized in order to counter the influence of the Oxford Movement, establishing the Protestant Episcopal Society for the Promotion of Evangelical Knowledge in 1848 (Albright, *Protestant Episcopal Church,* p. 189).

[69]Ibid., p. 237; Robert W. Prichard, *A History of the Episcopal Church* (Harrisburg, Penn.: Morehouse, 1991), p. 144.

[70]Albright, *Protestant Episcopal Church,* p. 239.

[71]Stephen H. Applegate, "The Rise and Fall of the Thirty-Nine Articles: An Inquiry into the Identity of the Protestant Episcopal Church in the United States," *Historical Magazine of the Protestant Episcopal Church* 50 (December 1981): 414-15; Albright, *Protestant Episcopal Church,* pp. 302-3.

[72]This was precipitated by a request for such a conference from John Travers Lewis, bishop of Ontario, in 1865.

[73]Neill, *Anglicanism,* p. 431.

[74]Butler, "Eighteenth Century to the Present," p. 40.

[75]Neill, *Anglicanism,* p. 431.

[76]The four articles affirmed (1) the authority of the Bible as the "rule and ultimate standard of faith," (2) the Apostles' Creed and the Nicene Creed, (3) the sacraments of baptism and the Lord's Supper, and (4) the historic episcopate. Further consideration of these articles will be

given in the second and third sections of the present chapter. The text of the Lambeth reso-lution on the Quadrilateral is reproduced in a number of sources, including *The Book of Com-mon Prayer;* see "The Chicago-Lambeth Quadrilateral" (*BCPEC,* pp. 876-78); see also J. Robert Wright, ed., *Quadrilateral at One Hundred: Essays on the Centenary of the Chicago-Lambeth Quadrilateral, 1886/88-1986/88,* Anglican Theological Review Supplementary Series 10 (Cin-cinnati: Forward Movement Publications; London: Mowbray, 1988).

[77]Huntington's seminal ideas can be found in his *The Church-Idea; an Essay Toward Unity* (New York: E. P. Dutton, 1870).

[78]Prichard, *History of the Episcopal Church,* p. 157.

[79]Robert W. Prichard, "The Place of Doctrine in the Episcopal Church," in *Reclaiming the Faith: Essays on Orthodoxy in the Episcopal Church and the Baltimore Declaration,* ed. Ephraim Radner and George R. Sumner (Grand Rapids: Eerdmans, 1993), pp. 14, 38.

[80]Albright, *Protestant Episcopal Church,* p. 346. See also Prichard, *History of the Episcopal Church,* p. 188; Butler, "Eighteenth Century to the Present Day," pp. 44-46.

[81]Prichard observes that the affirmation of the creeds "gave a peculiar character" to these con-troversies in the Episcopal Church. Scholars could "question the literal reading of the Old Tes-tament with impunity," but "when they began to question the literal truth of passages from the Apostles' and Nicene creeds . . . trouble instantly followed" (Prichard, *History of the Epis-copal Church,* pp. 206-7).

[82]Applegate observes that the official adoption of Huntington's Quadrilateral and the attendant setting aside of the Articles, at the 1910 Convention of the Protestant Episcopal Church, are indicative of "the basic liberalizing tendencies within theology at that time" ("Rise and Fall," p. 420). A 1925 proposed draft of the Episcopal *Book of Common Prayer* did not include the Thirty-Nine Articles, but the version finally adopted in 1928 reinstated them as a result of strong opposition to the earlier proposal (Prichard, *History of the Episcopal Church,* p. 211). The 1979 version of *The Book of Common Prayer* includes the Thirty-Nine Articles, but in a newly created section, "Historical Documents of the Church." This compromise proved to be quite controversial, with critics viewing this as a de facto rejection of them.

[83]Prichard, "Place of Doctrine," p. 35.

[84]Prichard, *History of the Episcopal Church,* p. 230. For examples of Neoorthodox thought, see the six volumes of "The Church's Teaching Series," published by Seabury Press (1949-1955). For "radical" theology, see Paul M. van Buren, *The Secular Meaning of the Gospel: Based on an Analysis of Its Language* (London: SCM, 1963); John A. T. Robinson, *Honest to God* (Phil-adelphia: Westminster Press, 1963).

[85]Prichard, "Place of Doctrine," p. 40.

[86]David E. Sumner, *The Episcopal Church's History: 1945-1985* (Wilton, Conn.: Morehouse-Barlow, 1987), p. 193; Prichard, *History of the Episcopal Church,* p. 278.

[87]Hein and Shattuck, *The Episcopalians,* p. 147.

[88]Harold T. Lewis, "By Schisms Rent Asunder? American Anglicanism on the Eve of the Millen-nium," in *A New Conversation: Essays on the Future of Theology and the Episcopal Church,* ed. Robert B. Slocum (New York: Church Publishing, 1999), p. 12.

[89]Charles Hefling, "On Being Reasonably Theological," in Slocum, *New Conversation,* pp. 51, 53. Hefling also cites the Anglo-Catholic emphasis on liturgy, rather than doctrine, as another contributing factor.

[90]Henry Chadwick, "Tradition, Fathers and Councils," in Sykes and Booty, *Study of Anglican-ism,* p. 96.

[91]W. S. F. Pickering, *Anglo-Catholicism: A Study in Religious Ambiguity* (London: Routledge,

1989), p. 141.

[92]W. Taylor Stevenson, "Is There a Characteristic Anglican Theology?" in Sykes and Booty, *Study of Anglicanism,* p. 24.

[93]A. M. Allchin, "The Understanding of Unity in Tractarian Theology and Spirituality," in *Tradition Renewed: The Oxford Movement Conference Papers,* ed. Geoffrey Rowley (Allison Park, Penn.: Pickwick, 1986), p. 232.

[94]Sumner, *Episcopal Church's History,* p. 107. In light of Anglicanism's pursuit of inclusive unity and the grounding of that pursuit in a book of "common" prayer, Gayraud Wilmore observes a historical irony: "the tenor of the preaching and the formality of the services . . . were not amenable to most blacks," resulting in considerably fewer African Americans entering the Episcopal church than less formal church traditions (*Black Religion and Black Radicalism: An Interpretation of the Religious History of African Americans,* 3rd ed. [Maryknoll, N.Y.: Orbis, 1998], p. 115).

[95]This delineation of types is an adaptation of a typology employed by Peter Toon in an essay on the Thirty-Nine Articles and the Homilies; see Peter Toon, "The Articles and Homilies," in Sykes and Booty, *Study of Anglicanism,* p. 137. Cf. Webber's reference to "evangelicals, charismatics, liberals, and Anglo-Catholics" ("Protestant Episcopal Church," p. 951), and E. Clowes Chorley's mid-twentieth-century delineation of "the Evangelical; the High Church; the early Church; the Broad Church; the Anglo-Catholic; the Ritualistic; the Low Church; the Liberal Evangelical, and the Liberal Catholic" (*Men and Movements in the American Episcopal Church* [New York: Scribner, 1946], p. v).

[96]For a history of Anglo-Catholic Episcopalianism in America, through the 1928 revision of *The Book of Common Prayer,* see George E. DeMille, *The Catholic Movement in the American Episcopal Church,* 2nd ed. (Philadelphia: Church Historical Society, 1950). For a description of Anglo-Catholicism, see "What Is Anglo-Catholicism?" in Pickering, *Anglo-Catholicism,* pp. 13-40.

[97]Neill, *Anglicanism,* p. 31.

[98]Sumner, *Episcopal Church's History,* p. 154.

[99]Webber, "Protestant Episcopal Church," pp. 949-50.

[100]For most of the denomination's history, the official name has been, and continues to be, the Protestant Episcopal Church in the U.S.A. In 1967, the General Council adopted an official alternative name, the Episcopal Church.

[101]Stephen Sykes, *The Integrity of Anglicanism* (New York: Seabury, 1978), p. v.

[102]Robert Hannaford, "Ecclesiology and Communion," in *The Future of Anglicanism,* ed. Robert Hannaford (Leominster: Gracewing, 1996), p. 56.

[103]Some Anglicans would even suggest that theology per se is tertiary, behind liturgical worship and ministry/social action.

[104]Louis Weil, "The Gospel in Anglicanism," in Sykes and Booty, *Study of Anglicanism,* pp. 63-64.

[105]See D. R. G. Owen, "Is There an Anglican Theology?" in *The Future of Anglican Theology,* ed. M. Darrol Bryant, Toronto Studies in Theology 17 (Toronto: Edwin Mellen, 1984), p. 3. Stevenson questions whether one can even talk of a distinctive Anglican method ("Characteristic Anglican Theology," pp. 15-17).

[106]Stevenson, "Characteristic Anglican Theology," p. 24; see also p. 25.

[107]Weil, "Gospel in Anglicanism," pp. 60, 63. Consequently, some Anglicans regard corporate worship as "the principle arena not only of supplication and praise but also of theological experimentation and formulation," thereby fostering ongoing change and development in

theology. (Stevenson, "Lex Orandi—Lex Credendi," pp. 174, 186.)

[108]Sykes, *Integrity of Anglicanism*, p. 93.

[109]Chadwick, "Tradition, Fathers and Councils," p. 96.

[110]Likewise the Chicago-Lambeth Quadrilateral (*BCPEC*, p. 877).

[111]An Outline of the Faith, Commonly Called the Catechism (*BCPEC*, p. 853). (Hereafter, this document will be referred to as "Catechism.")

[112]The Ordination of a Bishop (*BCPEC*, p. 513).

[113]Articles of Religion, Article 7 (*BCPEC*, p. 869). The canon delineated here includes 1 Esdras and 2 Esdras in the canon of the Old Testament, and it identifies fourteen apocryphal books as being "read for example of life and instruction in manners" but not to be used "to establish any doctrine."

[114]Articles of Religion, Article 6 (*BCPEC*, p. 868).

[115]F. A. Peake, "The Anglican Ethos," in Bryant, *Future of Anglican Theology*, p. 30.

[116]W. H. Griffith Thomas, *The Principles of Theology: An Introduction to the Thirty-nine Articles*, 3rd ed. (London: Church Book Room Press, 1945), p. 284.

[117]Ramsey, *Anglican Spirit*, p. 24.

[118]Articles of Religion, Article 34 (*BCPEC*, p. 874).

[119]Francis White, *A Treatise of the Sabbath-Day* (London: R. Badger, 1635), quoted in More and Cross, *Anglicanism*, p. 8 (no. 2).

[120]Ramsey, *Anglican Spirit*, p. 26; cf. Kenneth A. Locke, "Antiquity as a Guide to Orthodoxy? A Critical Appraisal of Newman's Via Media," in Hannaford, *Future of Anglicanism*, pp. 18-30.

[121]Catechism (*BCPEC*, p. 851); see also Chicago-Lambeth Quadrilateral (*BCPEC*, p. 877). The Athanasian Creed is also cited in the Catechism (1979), although it does not have the prominence or consistent affirmation throughout the Anglican communion that the Apostles' and Nicene Creeds have. Along with the Athanasian Creed, the Chalcedonian definition of the person of Christ is included among the "Historical Documents" in *BCPEC*, pp. 864-65.

[122]Articles of Religion, Article 20 (*BCPEC*, p. 871).

[123]Ramsey, *Anglican Spirit*, p. 26. Ramsey observes that in England the appeal to antiquity came to be associated with Arminian theology and High Church, sacramental liturgical practices.

[124]Chadwick, "Tradition, Fathers and Councils," p. 96.

[125]For example, see "Anglican Standards," in Sykes and Booty, *Study of Anglicanism*, pp. 119-215; "Standards of Faith," in More and Cross, *Anglicanism*, pp. 119-95.

[126]The Homilies are two collections of sermons from the sixteenth-century, composed and compiled for use by clergy. The authors include such leading figures as Thomas Cranmer, Edmund Bonner, John Jewel and Matthew Parker. The Homilies are commended in Article 35 of the Thirty-Nine Articles. The third homily in the first collection was of particular significance, being specifically commended in Article 11 of the Thirty-Nine Articles as "an authoritative exposition" of the doctrine of justification.

[127]Ordinals are the rites, including affirmations and commitments made by the candidate, governing the ordaining and consecrating of bishops, priests and deacons. See *BCPEC*, pp. 511-55.

[128]See ibid., pp. 843-62.

[129]*Divine* is a Middle English term for a cleric or theologian; it does not attribute any form of deity to those to whom it is applied. John Booty describes these figures as "theological writers whose works have been widely regarded as, in some sense, standards not only for faith and doctrine but also for public worship and personal spirituality." There is not an authoritative list, but "there are some whose names would most likely be found on most lists, di-

vines whose names appear in calendars of lesser feasts, those whose works are most often anthologized" ("Standard Divines," in Sykes and Booty, *Study of Anglicanism,* p. 163). For suggested listings, see the chapter by Booty cited here, and, though limited to the sixteenth and seventeenth centuries, More and Cross, *Anglicanism,* especially pp. 785-811.

[130]Canon law is the body of ecclesiastical rules or laws that govern the church in matters of faith and polity.

[131]H. R. McAdoo, *Anglican Heritage: Theology and Spirituality* (Norwich: Canterbury, 1991), p. 11.

[132]A. S. McGrade, "Reason," in Sykes and Booty, *Study of Anglicanism,* p. 106. McGrade and Ramsey readily acknowledge that it is easier to indicate what the role of reason is not, as opposed to positively stating what it is (McGrade, "Reason," p. 107; Ramsey, *Spirit of Anglicanism,* p. 30).

[133]Avis, *Anglicanism and the Christian Church,* p. 337.

[134]Ramsey, *Anglican Spirit,* p. 30.

[135]Paul Avis, "The Churches of the Anglican Communion," in *The Christian Church: An Introduction to the Major Traditions,* ed. Paul Avis (London: SPCK, 2002), p. 136.

[136]Benjamin Whichcote, *Several Discourses,* Discourse XXIII, quoted in More and Cross, *Anglicanism,* p. 213 (no. 90). I learned of this passage in Ramsey, *Anglican Spirit,* p. 31. Whichcote was one of the Cambridge Platonists, who were enthusiastic and confident about the role that reason was to play in theology.

[137]Experience per se as it relates to theological method in classical Anglican theology is not discussed. Experience conceived of in corporate terms is sometimes alluded to in discussions of the church and tradition, and the "pragmatic" demand that Anglican theology "work" is sometimes cited as deterrent to more sophisticated systematic theological reflection among Anglicans. See More, "Spirit of Anglicanism," pp. xxxiii-xxxvii; Sykes, *Integrity of Anglicanism,* pp. 75-79.

[138]Owen, "Anglican Theology," p. 3.

[139]Sykes, *Integrity of Anglicanism,* pp. 87-88. An excerpt from the 1948 Lambeth report is included in the appendix of Sykes's book (ibid., pp. 112-14).

[140]Ramsey, *Anglican Spirit,* p. 18. Cf. James E. Griffiss, "A Hope for Theology in the Episcopal Church," in Slocum, *New Conversation,* pp. 201-12.

[141]Ferderick H. Borsch, "All Things Necessary to Salvation," in *Anglicanism and the Bible,* ed. Frederick H. Borsch, Anglican Study Series (Wilton, Conn.: Morehouse-Barlow, 1984), p. 220.

[142]Articles of Religion, Article 20 (*BCPEC,* p. 871).

[143]Francis J. Hall, *Theological Outlines,* rev. Frank H. Hallock, 3rd ed. (Milwaukee: Morehouse, 1933), p. 232.

[144]Chadwick, "Tradition, Fathers, and Councils," p. 94.

[145]Catechism (*BCPEC,* pp. 853-54).

[146]More, "Spirit of Anglicanism," p. xxix. More was describing sixteenth- and seventeenth-century Anglicanism in particular, but it is also an apt description of subsequent classical Anglican thought. See John 14:25-26; 15:26; 16:13-15.

[147]Stevenson, "Lex Orandi—Lex Credendi," p. 186.

[148]Sykes, *Integrity of Anglicanism,* p. 91.

[149]See Tim Bradshaw, "The Christological Centre of Anglicanism," in Hannaford, *Future of Anglicanism,* pp. 90-103.

[150]Articles of Religion, Article 7 (*BCPEC,* p. 869).

[151]Ramsey, *Anglican Spirit,* pp. 25-26.

[152]Avis, "Churches of the Anglican Communion," pp. 132-33.

[153]Neill, *Anglicanism,* p. 417. Cf. Rowan Williams's suggestion that "it is not true that there is no distinctive Anglican doctrine. But the discovery of it may require some patience in reading and attending to a number of historical strands, in order to watch the way in which distinctiveness shows itself." (*Anglican Identities* [Cambridge, Mass.: Cowley, 2003], p. 1).

[154]Williamson, "Episcopalians," p. 121; see also Weil, "Gospel in Anglicanism," p. 63.

[155]See Slocum, *New Conversation,* especially chapters by Gardiner Shattuck Jr., Charles Hefling, Paul Zahl, J. Robert Wright and James Griffiss.

[156]Neill, *Anglicanism,* p. 418. Peake also refers to Anglicanism as an "attitude," as well as "a frame of mind, an ethos" ("Anglican Ethos," p. 29).

[157]Stevenson, "Characteristic Anglican Theology," p. 18; see also Stevenson, "Lex Orandi—Lex Credendi," p. 177.

[158]Owen, "Anglican Theology," p. 3.

[159]Ramsey, *Anglican Spirit,* p. 19.

[160]Neill, *Anglicanism,* pp. 422-23. See also Price, "Identity and Viability," p. 258; Williamson, "Episcopalians," p. 122.

[161]Williams, *Anglican Identities,* pp. 4-5, 7-8.

[162]Neill, *Anglicanism,* pp. 422-23. See also Price, "Identity and Viability," p. 258; Williamson, "Episcopalians," p. 122.

[163]Both from within and without the Anglican communion, some suggest that, especially since the mid-nineteenth century, "in their love of comprehension, the Anglican Churches have drawn their boundaries with too great laxity" (Neill, *Anglicanism,* p. 426).

[164]Chadwick, "Tradition, Fathers and Councils," p. 96. Chadwick cites *The Book of Common Prayer* and the English Ordinal as embodying this.

[165]Seeing church and sacrament, with baptism constituting the "foundational sacrament," as integral to the Anglican tradition, Avis propounds a "baptismal paradigm of ecclesiology" (*Anglicanism and the Christian Church,* p. 354).

[166]More, "Spirit of Anglicanism," pp. xxxvi, xxxviii; Sykes, *Integrity of Anglicanism,* pp. ix, 76-77, 85; Williamson, "Episcopalians," p. 121; Robert B. Slocum, "The Saving Role of Participation in Anglican Ecclesiology," paper presented at the annual meeting of the Mid-West Region of the American Academy of Religion, St. Paul, Minnesota, 13 April 1996.

[167]Francis J. Hall, *The Church and the Sacramental System,* Dogmatic Theology 8 (New York: Longmans, Green, 1920; reprint, New York: American Church Union, 1967), p. 288.

[168] Ibid., p. 289.

[169]Marianne H. Micks, *Introduction to Theology,* rev. ed. (New York: Seabury, 1983), pp. 47-48.

[170]Hall, *Church and the Sacramental System,* pp. 288-89.

[171]Sykes, *Integrity of Anglicanism,* pp. ix, 85.

[172]Articles of Religion, Article 19 (*BCPEC,* p. 871).

[173]Catechism (*BCPEC,* p. 854).

[174]Hall, *Theological Outlines,* p. 221; see also Thomas, *Principles of Theology,* p. 267.

[175]On "the organic church," see T. A. Lacey, *The Anglo-Catholic Faith,* Faiths: Varieties of Christian Expression, 2nd ed. (London: Methuen, 1926), pp. 73-88.

[176]Micks, *Introduction to Theology,* p. 52.

[177]Some Anglican theologians deny such a distinction, affirming only a visible church; see, for example, Hall, *Theological Outlines,* p. 224.

[178]Prayers of the People, Form V (*BCPEC,* p. 391).

[179]Even those Anglicans who place considerable emphasis on the reality of the invisible church, such as Griffith Thomas, believe that "membership in the invisible Church will naturally ex-

press itself in membership in the visible Church," and that "the members of the body of Christ are rightly to be sought for in the visible Churches, for the true Church at present can only manifest itself in the form of visible communities" (Thomas, *Principles of Theology,* pp. 269, 277).

[180]Hall, *Theological Outlines,* pp. 223-24.

[181]Richard Hooker, *The Folger Library Edition of the Works of Richard Hooker,* ed. W. Speed Hill, vol. 1., *Of the Laws of Ecclesiastical Polity: Preface and Books I-IV,* ed. Georges Edelen (Cambridge, Mass.: Belknap Press of Harvard University Press, 1977), §3.1.14 (p. 205).

[182]Hall, *Theological Outlines,* p. 224.

[183]Articles of Religion, Article 26 (*BCPEC,* p. 873). See also Hall, *Theological Outlines,* p. 223.

[184]Joseph Hall, *A Plain and Familiar Explication, by Way of Paraphrase, of All the Hard Texts of the Whole Divine Scripture of the Old and New Testament* (1633), quoted in More and Cross, *Anglicanism,* p. 44 (no. 19).

[185]Articles of Religion, Article 26 (*BCPEC,* p. 873).

[186]See Hall, *Theological Outlines,* pp. 229, 233.

[187]Catechism (*BCPEC,* p. 854); cf. For the Unity of the Church, Collect (*BCPEC,* pp. 204-5), and Prayers for the People, Form V (*BCPEC,* p. 389). See also Hall, *Church and the Sacramental System,* pp. 168-224.

[188]Ramsey, *Anglican Spirit,* p. 119.

[189]Ibid.

[190]Lacey, *Anglo-Catholic Faith,* p. 80.

[191]Catechism (*BCPEC,* p. 855).

[192]For the Mission of the Church, Collect, (*BCPEC,* p. 206); see also Prayers of the People, Form V (*BCPEC,* p. 390). Gayraud Wilmore notes a tragically ironic distortion of this principle in the history of the appropriation of the Anglican tradition in America. He observes, "The attitude [toward slavery] of the Episcopalians may be deduced from the fact that, unlike the Presbyterians, they were not divided between North and South during the Civil War. Although the Anglicans were the first to evangelize the African slaves, the Protestant Episcopal Church, which succeeded it in the independent nation, catered to its southern constituency in the interest of preserving the unity of the denomination" (*Black Religion and Black Radicalism,* p. 116).

[193]See Catechism (*BCPEC,* p. 855); Hall, *Theological Outlines,* pp. 232-36.

[194]The Ministry, in Catechism (*BCPEC,* p. 855). Their ministry is "to represent Christ and his Church; to bear witness to him wherever they may be; and, according to the gifts given them, to carry on Christ's work of reconciliation in the world; and to take their place in the life, worship, and governance of the Church" (ibid.). On the authority of laypeople, see Stephen Sykes, "Authority in Anglicanism, Again," in Bryant, *Future of Anglican Theology,* pp. 189-90.

[195]Preface to the Ordination Rites (*BCPEC,* p. 510); For Those to Be Ordained, Collect (*BCPEC,* p. 205); Hall, *Theological Outlines,* p. 222.

[196]Preface to the Ordination Rites (*BCPEC,* p. 510).

[197]The Examination, in The Ordination of a Bishop (*BCPEC,* p. 517).

[198]The Ministry, in Catechism (*BCPEC,* p. 855).

[199]See Chicago-Lambeth Quadrilateral (*BCPEC,* p. 878); also Albright, *Protestant Episcopal Church,* pp. 229-30. Cf. Sykes, *Integrity of Anglicanism,* p. 84.

[200]David L. Edwards, *What Anglicans Believe in the Twenty-First Century* (London: Mowbray, 2000), p. 92.

[201]Ramsey, *Anglican Spirit,* p. 128.

[202]Hall, *Theological Outlines,* pp. 229-30.

[203]More, "Spirit of Anglicanism," pp. xxxv-xxxvi.

[204]William Beveridge, "Christ's Presence with His Ministers," quoted in More and Cross, *Anglicanism,* p. 372 (no. 159). Cf. John Pearson, *An Exposition of the Creed,* Article XI, quoted in More and Cross, *Anglicanism,* pp. 30-31 (no. 13).

[205]*BCPECUSA,* p. 552.

[206]Ramsey, *Anglican Spirit,* p. 128.

[207]This is an adaptation of five views of the apostolicity of the church articulated by Ramsey (*Spirit of Anglicanism,* p. 126).

[208]Sykes, *Integrity of Anglicanism,* p. 84.

[209]Avis, *Anglicanism and the Christian Church,* p. 353.

[210]This is an adaptation of terminology used by Hall, *Church and the Sacramental System,* p. 282.

[211]Articles of Religion, Article 25 (*BCPEC,* p. 872).

[212]Catechism (*BCPECUSA,* p. 572); Catechism (*BCPEC,* p. 857).

[213]Hall, *Church and the Sacramental System,* p. 313.

[214]See Hooker, *Laws of Ecclesiastical Polity,* §V.57.5.

[215]Catechism (*BCPECUSA,* p. 572); Thomas, *Principles of Theology,* p. 348.

[216]Catechism (*BCPEC,* p. 857).

[217]Chicago-Lambeth Quadrilateral (*BCPEC,* p. 878).

[218]Alf Härdelin, "The Sacraments in the Tractarian Spiritual Universe," in Rowell, *Tradition Renewed,* p. 85.

[219]Hall, *Church and the Sacramental System,* p. 321.

[220]Articles of Religion, Article 26 (*BCPEC,* p. 873). Cf. Hall on the "intention" of the minister (*Church and the Sacramental System,* pp. 319-20).

[221]Hall, *Church and the Sacramental System,* pp. 316, 320-21.

[222]Articles of Religion, Article 25 (*BCPEC,* p. 872). See 1 Cor 11:27-30; Heb 4:2.

[223]Thomas, *Principles of Theology,* p. 357; see also Hall, *Church and the Sacramental System,* p. 316.

[224]Catechism (*BCPEC,* p. 858); Catechism (*BCPECUSA,* p. 572); Chicago-Lambeth Quadrilateral (*BCPEC,* p. 878). Within Anglicanism, a sacramental regard for the five other rites is most common among Anglo-Catholics. Among those who regard these five rites as sacramental, baptism and the Lord's Supper are often regarded as the "major" or "great" sacraments. See "Other Sacramental Rites," in Catechism (*BCPEC,* pp. 860-61); Hall, *Church and the Sacramental System,* pp. 299-301, 315. Note that neither baptism nor the Lord's Supper, nor any of the other five rites, is referred to in the Apostles' Creed; baptism is affirmed in the Nicene Creed.

[225]Linda Moeller, "Baptism: Rite of Inclusion or Exclusion?" in *Leaps and Boundaries: The Prayer Book in the 21st Century,* ed. Paul V. Marshall and D. Lesley Northup (Harrisburg, Penn.: Morehouse, 1997), p. 81.

[226]John Hacket, *Christian Consolations,* Chapter 5, quoted in More and Cross, *Anglicanism,* p. 425 (no. 178).

[227]Catechism (*BCPEC,* p. 858).

[228]Edwards, *What Anglicans Believe,* p. 72.

[229]Articles of Religion, Article 27 (*BCPEC,* p. 873).

[230]Catechism (*BCPECUSA,* p. 572); Catechism (*BCPEC,* p. 858).

[231]The Baptismal Covenant (*BCPEC,* p. 307; also pp. 306, 308). See also The Ministration of Holy

Baptism (*BCPECUSA*, pp. 274, 276, 278-80).

[232]Articles of Religion, Article 27 (*BCPEC*, p. 873).

[233]Catechism (*BCPEC*, p. 858); see also The Baptism (*BCPEC*, p. 308).

[234]Hall, *Church and the Sacramental System*, p. 326.

[235]Catechism (*BCPEC*, p. 858); see also Hall, *Church and the Sacramental System*, pp. 326-27.

[236]Articles of Religion, Article 27 (*BCPEC*, p. 873); Hall, *Church and the Sacramental System*, pp. 326-27.

[237]Catechism (*BCPEC*, pp. 858-59).

[238]Though not a high sacramentalist, Thomas sets forth seven points in support of infant baptism (*Principles of Theology*, pp. 377-78).

[239]Article 27 of the Thirty-Nine Articles affirms the baptism of young children as "most agreeable with the institution of Christ" (*BCPEC*, p. 873). See also Matthew 28:19.

[240]The Catechism indicates that names for this include "Holy Eucharist," "Lord's Supper," "Holy Communion," "Divine Liturgy," "Mass" and "Great Offering" (Catechism [*BCPEC*, p. 859]).

[241]Hall, *Church and the Sacramental System*, p. 292.

[242]Holy Communion—Rite One (*BCPEC*, p. 334); Catechism (*BCPEC*, p. 859). Neither the Apostles' Creed nor the Nicene Creed makes reference to the Eucharist.

[243]Catechism (*BCPEC*, p. 859).

[244]The Holy Eucharist—Rite One (*BCPEC*, p. 335); Holy Communion (*BCPECUSA*, p. 81).

[245]The Holy Eucharist—Rite One (*BCPEC*, p. 338); Holy Communion (*BCPECUSA*, pp. 82, 83).

[246]The Holy Eucharist—Rite One (*BCPEC*, p. 339); The Holy Eucharist—Rite Two (*BCPEC*, p. 365).

[247]Articles of Religion, Article 28 (*BCPEC*, p. 873).

[248]Holy Communion (*BCPECUSA*, p. 81).

[249]Catechism (*BCPEC*, pp. 859-60).

[250]The Holy Eucharist—Rite One (*BCPEC*, p. 339).

[251]Transubstantiation is the belief that the substance, though not the perceivable characteristics, of the bread and wine in the Lord's Supper changes to that of the body and blood of Christ. See Articles of Religion, Article 28 (*BCPEC*, p. 873). Cf. *Report of the Anglo-Catholic Congress: London, 1927; Subject: The Holy Eucharist* (Milwaukee: Morehouse, 1927).

[252]Ramsey, *Anglican Spirit*, p. 20.

[253]The Holy Eucharist—Rite One (*BCPEC*, pp. 316-17).

[254]Ramsey, *Anglican Spirit*, p. 20.

Chapter 6: Freedom for Immediacy

[1]For a brief survey of views, see Bill J. Leonard, *Baptist Ways: A History* (Valley Forge, Penn.: Judson Press, 2003), pp. 10-15.

[2]William H. Brackney, *The Baptists* (New York: Greenwood, 1988), p. xvii. One example of a history written from this perspective is John T. Christian's *A History of the Baptists* (Nashville: Sunday School Board of the Southern Baptist Convention, 1922). Baptist historian Robert Torbet refers to this as an unscientific, "apologetic and polemical" approach (*A History of the Baptists*, rev. ed. [Valley Forge, Penn.: Judson Press, 1963], p. 19).

[3]Leon McBeth, "Baptist Beginnings," *Baptist History and Heritage* 15, no. 4 (1980): 65; idem, *The Baptist Heritage: Four Centuries of Baptist Witness* (Nashville: Broadman, 1987), p. 61.

[4]For example, Thomas Armitage, *A History of the Baptists, Traced by Their Vital Principles and Practices, from the Time of Our Lord and Saviour Jesus Christ to the Year 1889* (New York: Bryan, Taylor: 1889).

[5]For example, Brackney, *The Baptists,* pp. 3-10; Bruce L. Shelley, "Baptist Churches in U.S.A," in *Dictionary of Christianity in America,* ed. Daniel G. Reid et al. (Downers Grove, Ill.: InterVarsity Press, 1990), pp. 110-11; McBeth, *Baptist Heritage,* p. 21.

[6]See McBeth, *Baptist Heritage,* p. 21; Timothy George, "The Reformation Roots of the Baptist Tradition," *Review & Expositor* 86, no. 1 (1989): 9-22.

[7]Duane A. Garrett and Richard Melick Jr., eds. *Authority and Interpretation: A Baptist Perspective* (Grand Rapids: Baker, 1987), p. 7. Similarly, Brackney observes that there is "no date, no place, and no person" that can be referred to as "the locus classicus" of the Baptist tradition (Brackney, *The Baptists,* p. xvii). See also Leonard, *Baptist Ways,* p. 10. On Southern Baptists in particular, see Paul A. Basden, ed., *Has Our Theology Changed? Southern Baptist Thought Since 1845* (Nashville: Broadman & Holman, 1994), p. 331.

[8]Brackney, *The Baptists,* p. 3.

[9]William R. Estep, "The English Baptist Legacy of Freedom and the American Experience," in *Pilgrim Pathways: Essays in Baptist History in Honour of B. R. White,* ed. William H. Brackney, Paul S. Fiddes and John H. Y. Briggs (Macon, Ga.: Mercer University Press, 1999), p. 267.

[10]Brackney, *The Baptists,* p. 5.

[11]Estep, "English Baptist Legacy," p. 267.

[12]Brackney, *The Baptists,* pp. 3-5.

[13]Ibid.

[14]James E. Tull, *Shapers of Baptist Thought* (Valley Forge, Penn.: Judson Press, 1972; reprint, Macon, Ga.: Mercer University Press, 1984), p. 30.

[15]For analyses of the phases of Smyth's theological development, see Jason K. Lee, *The Theology of John Smyth: Puritan, Separatist, Baptist, Mennonite* (Macon, Ga.: Mercer University Press, 2003); Tull, *Shapers of Baptist Thought,* pp. 29, 19-30.

[16]Estep, "English Baptist Legacy," p. 268.

[17]Brackney, *The Baptists,* pp. 5-6.

[18]McBeth, *Baptist Heritage,* p. 42.

[19]Torbet, *History of the Baptists,* pp. 42-43; McBeth, *Baptist Heritage,* p. 44.

[20]Brackney suggests that the London Confession is one of the three determinative events for the shaping of Baptist identity. The other two events are the establishment of the Baptist Missionary Society in 1792 and the formation of the Baptist Bible Union in 1923 (*The Baptists,* p. xix).

[21]For an introduction to, and the text of, the London Confession and other Baptist confessional documents, see William L. Lumpkin, ed., *Baptist Confessions of Faith,* rev. ed. (Valley Forge, Penn.: Judson Press, 1969. (Hereafter referred to as *BCF.*)

[22]Brackney, *The Baptists,* p. 7.

[23]McBeth, *Baptist Heritage,* pp. 98, 99.

[24]George, "Reformation Roots," p. 11; see also William R. Estep, "Biblical Authority in Baptist Confessions of Faith, 1610-1963," in *The Unfettered Word: Southern Baptists Confront the Authority-Inerrancy Questions,* ed. Robinson B. James (Waco, Tex.: Word, 1987), p. 169.

[25]McBeth, *Baptist Heritage,* p. 98.

[26]Timothy George, introduction to *Baptist Confessions, Covenants, and Catechisms,* ed. Timothy George and Denise George (Nashville: Broadman & Holman, 1999), p. 15. For a representative collection of historic covenants, see ibid., pp. 171-224.

[27]Brackney, *The Baptists,* p. 9; McBeth, *Baptist Heritage,* p. 148.

[28]William H. Brackney, ed., *Baptist Life and Thought: A Source Book,* rev. ed. (Valley Forge, Penn.: Judson Press, 1998), p. 97; Timothy George, "The Future of Baptist Theology," in

Theologians of the Baptist Tradition, ed. Timothy George and David S. Dockery (Nashville: Broadman & Holman, 2001), p. 2.

[29]William H. Brackney, ed., *Baptist Life and Thought, 1600-1980: A Source Book* (Valley Forge, Penn.: Judson Press, 1983), p. 16; cf. Brackney's observation elsewhere that socioeconomically, "on the whole, the early Baptists in the Colonies improved on the lot of their 'hole-in-the-wall' brethren in England, while still carrying a stigma of dissent" (*The Baptists,* p. 11).

[30]George, "Future of Baptist Theology," p. 2.

[31]Brackney, *Baptist Life and Thought,* rev. ed., p. 109.

[32]Ibid., p. 125.

[33]McBeth, *Baptist Heritage,* p. 124.

[34]Ibid., p. 136.

[35]Brackney, *The Baptists,* pp. 10-11; McBeth, *Baptist Heritage,* pp. 137-43. McBeth includes a fourth church, in Kittery, Maine.

[36]One practice where differences were evident was the laying of hands on new converts. General Baptists demanded conformity to six foundational principles set forth in Hebrews 6:1-2: "repentance from dead works, and faith toward God, instruction about baptisms, laying on of hands, resurrection of the dead, and eternal judgment." Consequently, they were sometimes known as Six-Principle Baptists. The Particular Baptists did not practice the laying of hands on converts, and thus sometimes they were called Five-Point Baptists (McBeth, *Baptist Heritage,* p. 139).

[37]Brackney, *The Baptists,* pp. 11-13; McBeth, *Baptist Heritage,* pp. 144-47.

[38]Brackney, *Baptist Life and Thought,* p. 16.

[39]By the end of the eighteenth century, Baptists were the second largest tradition in America, next to the Methodists. The Baptists had about 750 churches, with approximately eighty thousand members (Brackney, *The Baptists,* pp. 13, 96). See also Estep, "English Baptist Legacy," p. 278.

[40]Brackney, *Baptist Life and Thought,* p. 96.

[41]Estep, "English Baptist Legacy," p. 278.

[42]Brackney, *Baptist Life and Thought,* rev. ed., p. 106.

[43]James M. Washington, *Frustrated Fellowship: The Black Baptist Quest for Social Power* (Macon, Ga.: Mercer University Press, 1986), p. 20.

[44]Barbara J. MacHaffie, *Her Story: Women in Christian Tradition* (Philadelphia: Fortress, 1986), p. 71.

[45]Gayraud S. Wilmore, *Black Religion and Black Radicalism: An Interpretation of the Religious History of African Americans,* 3rd ed. (Maryknoll, N.Y.: Orbis, 1998), p. 104.

[46]Estep, "English Baptist Legacy," p. 281.

[47]One of the reasons for this concentration of activity and strength in Philadelphia was greater religious toleration, as there was no official religion in this region, unlike the situation in the New England colonies.

[48]Brackney, *The Baptists,* p. 14.

[49]Ibid., p. 15.

[50]These churches came to be known as Primitive, Hard Shell or Old School Baptists.

[51]Edwin S. Gaustad, "Toward a Baptist Identity in the Twenty-First Century," in *Discovering Our Baptist Heritage: The Papers of the Baptist Heritage Education Conference,* ed. William H. Brackney (Valley Forge, Penn.: American Baptist Historical Society, 1985), p. 90; Brackney, *Baptist Life and Thought,* rev. ed., p. 125.

[52]*BCF,* p. 361; Estep, "Biblical Authority," p. 173. Cf. Thomas J. Nettles, new preface to *By His*

Grace and for His Glory: A Historical, Theological, and Practical Study of the Doctrines of Grace in Baptist Life (Lake Charles, La.: Cor Meum Tibi, 2002), pp. 8-10.

[53]New Hampshire Confession, Articles 3, 6, 7 (*BCF,* pp. 362-63).

[54]Brackney observes that state conventions became representative of "a peculiar ethos which strengthened bonds of a socio-political type more than those ties which had originally given birth to the idea" (*The Baptists,* p. 17).

[55]Leroy Fitts, *A History of Black Baptists* (Nashville: Broadman, 1985), p. 24.

[56]Brackney, *The Baptists,* p. 17.

[57]George, "Future of Baptist Theology," p. 3.

[58]Brackney, *The Baptists,* pp. 18-19.

[59]E. Y. Mullins, "The Testimony of Christian Experience," in *The Fundamentals: A Testimony to the Truth,* 4 vols. (Los Angeles: Bible Institute of Los Angeles, 1917), 4:314-23; J. J. Reeve, "My Personal Experience with the Higher Criticism," in ibid., 1:348-68; Charles B. Williams, "Paul's Testimony to the Doctrine of Sin," in ibid., 3:25-39.

[60]Walter Rauschenbusch, *A Theology for the Social Gospel* (New York: Macmillan, 1917).

[61]For example, two Baptist groups formed as the result of withdrawals from the Northern Baptist Convention (NBC). The General Association of Regular Baptists was formed by Fundamentalists in 1932 as a result of the liberal orientation of theological education and the doctrinal ambiguity characterized the NBC, and the Conservative Baptist Association was established in 1947 largely as a result of doctrinal permissiveness in the appointment of missionaries by the Foreign Mission Society of the NBC (Brackney, *The Baptists,* p. 19). For a survey of late-nineteenth-century Black feminist theology, within what Evelyn Brooks refers to as "the context of the liberalization of theology," see her essay "The Feminist Theology of the Black Baptist Church, 1880-1900," in *Class, Race, and Sex: The Dynamics of Control,* ed. Amy Swerdlow and Hannah Lessinger (Boston: G. K. Hall, 1983), pp. 31-59.

[62]George, "Future of Baptist Theology," p. 5.

[63]George, introduction to *Baptist Confessions, Covenants, and Catechisms,* p. 13.

[64]For an introduction to the two major sides of this controversy, see the "conservative" Thomas J. Nettles and Russell Moore, eds., *Why I Am a Baptist* (Nashville: Broadman & Holman, 2001), and the "moderate" Cecil P. Stanton Jr., *Why I Am a Baptist: Reflections on Being Baptist in the 21st Century* (Macon, Ga.: Smyth & Helwys, 1999). See also Fisher Humphreys, *The Way We Were: How Southern Baptist Theology Has Changed and What It Means to Us All,* rev. ed. (Macon, Ga.: Smyth & Helwys, 2002).

[65]Brackney, *The Baptists,* pp. 20-21.

[66]David S. Dockery, "Baptist Theology and Theologians," in *Baptist Theologians,* ed. Timothy George and David S. Dockery (Nashville: Broadman, 1990), p. 685. This chapter offers a helpful introduction to the ebb and flow of theology within the Baptist tradition, focusing on specific theologians.

[67]Dwight A. Moody, "Contemporary Theologians Within the Believers' Church," in *The People of God: Essays on the Believers' Church,* ed. Paul Basden and David S. Dockery (Nashville: Broadman, 1991), p. 350. Similarly, Walter Shurden observes that diversity "flows naturally from the Baptist preoccupation with the right of choice" (*The Baptist Identity: Four Fragile Freedoms* [Macon, Ga.: Smyth & Helwys, 1993], p. 3).

[68]Baptist Jubilee Advance, "Baptist Distinctives and Diversities and Disagreements and Differences of Emphasis among Baptists," in Shurden, *Baptist Identity,* p. 73. This document was drafted in 1964, with participation by representatives of six major Baptist groups: Baptist Federation of Canada, American Baptist Convention, National Baptist Convention, Inc., North

American Baptist General Conference, Seventh Day Baptist General Conference and Southern Baptist Convention.

[69]Diversity within the Baptist tradition is not only theological, but also, as noted earlier, "regional" and "racial/ethnic." The focus of the present discussion is the theological dimensions of the diversity.

[70]Some of the theological descriptions of denominations, associations and conventions that follow are drawn from Frank S. Mead and Samuel S. Hill, *Handbook of Denominations,* 9th ed. (Nashville: Abingdon, 1990), pp. 34-58.

[71]Evidenced in, for example, the Philadelphia Confession (1742).

[72]For example, George, "Reformation Roots," p. 15; William L. Lumpkin, "The Nature and Authority of Baptist Confessions of Faith," *Review & Expositor* 76, no. 1 (1979): 23; Nettles, *By His Grace and For His Glory.* Cf. Doyle L. Young, "The Doctrine of Salvation: Baptist Views," *Southwestern Journal of Theology* 35, no. 2 (1993): 10-11.

[73]The New Hampshire Confession constituted the basis for the Southern Baptist Convention's Baptist Faith and Message (see *BCF,* pp. 391-92). Recent writings by Thomas Nettles *(By His Grace and For His Glory)* and Timothy George ("Reformation Roots") are representative of a reassertion of an unambiguously Calvinist theology, at least with respect to anthropology and aspects of soteriology, among some Southern Baptists.

[74]In 1917, Baptist theologian E. Y. Mullins wrote, "We are learning to discard both names [i.e., "Calvinist" and "Arminian"] and to adhere more closely than either to the Scriptures, while retaining the truth in both systems" (*The Christian Religion in Its Doctrinal Expression* [Philadelphia: Judson Press, 1917], p. vii).

[75]This terminology is adapted from George M. Marsden, *Fundamentalism and Modern Culture* (Grand Rapids: Eerdmans, 1980).

[76]William H. Brackney, "African American Baptists: Prolegomenon to a Theological Tradition," in *The Quest for Liberation and Reconciliation: Essays in Honor of J. Deotis Roberts,* ed. Michael Battle (Louisville: Westminster John Knox, 2005), p. 165.

[77]Moody, "Contemporary Theologians," p. 333.

[78]Timothy George, "Conflict and Identity in the Southern Baptist Convention: The Quest for a New Consensus," in *Beyond the Impasse? Scripture, Interpretation, and Theology in Baptist Life,* ed. Robison B. James and David S. Dockery (Nashville: Broadman, 1992), p. 202. George's comment is about Southern Baptists, but it can be fittingly applied to Baptists in general.

[79]See Brackney, *The Baptists,* pp. 26-27, 145, 263; McBeth, *Baptist Heritage,* pp. 302-7, 509-11.

[80]Dockery, "Baptist Theology and Theologians," pp. 685-94. A revised edition of this book has been published as *Theologians of the Baptist Tradition* (Nashville: Broadman & Holman, 2001). Recent comprehensive systematic theologies by authors who identify in some significant way with the Baptist tradition include Millard J. Erickson, *Christian Theology,* 2nd ed. (Grand Rapids: Baker, 1998); James L. Garrett, *Systematic Theology: Biblical, Historical, and Evangelical,* 2 vols. (Grand Rapids: Eerdmans, 1990); Stanley J. Grenz, *Theology for the Community of God* (Grand Rapids: Eerdmans, 2000); Wayne A. Grudem, *Systematic Theology: An Introduction to Biblical Doctrine* (Grand Rapids: Zondervan, 1994); Gordon R. Lewis and Bruce A. Demarest, *Integrative Theology,* 3 vols. (Grand Rapids: Zondervan, 1996).

[81]For example, Erickson, *Christian Theology,* pp. 30-31; Garrett, *Systematic Theology,* 1:12-15; Grudem, *Systematic Theology,* p. 18; Stanley J. Grenz and Roger Olson, *Who Needs Theology? An Invitation to the Study of God* (Downers Grove, Ill.: InterVarsity Press, 1996); John L. Dagg, *A Manual of Theology* (Charleston, S.C.: Southern Baptist Publication Society, 1857;

reprint, Harrisonburg, Va.: Gano Books, 1982), pp. 13-18; James P. Boyce, *Abstract of Systematic Theology* (Philadelphia: American Baptist Publication Society, 1887; reprint, n.p.: Christian Gospel Foundation, 1979), p. 7; Augustus H. Strong, *Systematic Theology* (Valley Forge, Penn.: Judson Press, 1907), pp. 15-19; Mullins, *Christian Religion,* pp. 16-17; Walter T. Conner, *Revelation and God: An Introduction to Christian Doctrine* (Nashville: Broadman, 1936), pp. 20-22.

[82]L. Russ Bush and Thomas J. Nettles, *Baptists and the Bible,* rev. ed. (Nashville: Broadman & Holman, 1999), p. 358. This emphasis on the importance of truth is another link of continuity to John Smyth, who, according to Jason Lee, instilled in his followers "the belief that they were to pursue truth relentlessly" (*Theology of John Smyth,* p. 293; see also p. 289).

[83]Erickson, *Christian Theology,* p. 30.

[84]Grenz, *Theology for the Community of God,* p. 11.

[85]Dagg, *Manual of Theology,* p. 18. Many nineteenth- and early-twentieth-century Baptist theologians taught that truth is the means by which the Holy Spirit brings about regeneration. See, for example, Dagg, *Manual of Theology,* p. 278; Boyce, *Abstract of Theology,* p. 375-77; Strong, *Systematic Theology,* p. 811; Mullins, *Christian Religion,* p. 378.

[86]Strong, *Systematic Theology,* p. 808.

[87]Ibid., p. 16.

[88]At the same time, theological work is not to be understood exclusively as a quest for the truth. Timothy George writes, "Theology is about more than getting our doctrine correct; in its most basic and comprehensive sense, it is about being rightly related to God" ("Renewal of Baptist Theology," in George and Dockery, *Baptist Theologians,* p. 14). See also Baptist Jubilee Advance, "Baptist Distinctives and Diversities," p. 73.

[89]Brackney, *The Baptists,* p. xviii.

[90]Second London Confession (*BCF,* p. 248).

[91]William Estep decries this as a misguided move toward "bibliolatry" ("Biblical Authority," pp. 155-76), but whatever one's assessment, the fact remains that Scripture has pride of place in most Baptist confessional statements.

[92]James Leo Garrett Jr., "Sources of Authority in Baptist Thought," *Baptist History and Heritage* 13 (July 1978): 43. Eric Ohlmann observes, "Baptist confessions of faith regularly refer to the bible as the supreme or sole source of faith and practice. And in reaction to developments such as historical criticism, they have increasingly shifted to the expression, '*sole* source of faith and practice" ("Baptists and Evangelicals," in *The Varieties of American Evangelicalism,* ed. Donald W. Dayton and Robert K. Johnston [Downers Grove, Ill.: InterVarsity Press, 1991], p. 154).

[93]Garrett, *Systematic Theology,* 1:181-82.

[94]Lewis and Demarest, *Integrative Theology,* 1:29.

[95]For example, Erickson, *Christian Theology,* p. 23; Grudem, *Systematic Theology,* p. 15; Garrett and Melick, *Authority and Interpretation,* p. 7; Brackney, *The Baptists,* p. 23; Shurden, *Baptist Identity,* pp. 63, 103; Dagg, *Manual of Theology,* pp. 21, 40-41; Boyce, *Abstract of Theology,* p. 6; Strong, *Systematic Theology,* pp. 27, 33.

[96]For an introduction to these documents and their role in Baptist life and thought, see William Brackney, *A Genetic History of Baptist Thought: With Special Reference to Baptists in Britain and North America* (Macon, Ga.: Mercer University Press, 2004), pp. 7-63; George, introduction to *Baptist Confessions, Covenants, and Catechisms,* pp. 1-18; Lumpkin, "Nature and Authority of Baptist Confessions"; Estep, "Biblical Authority"; idem, "Baptists and Authority: The Bible, Confessions, and Conscience in the Development of Baptist Identity," *Review & Expos-*

itor 84, no. 4 (1987): 599-615; Thomas J. Nettles, "Creedalism, Confessionalism, and the Baptist Faith and Message," in *The Unfettered Word: Southern Baptists Confront the Authority-Inerrancy Question,* ed. Robison B. James (Waco, Tex.: Word, 1987), pp. 138-54. In the context of recent controversies in the Southern Baptist Convention, some "conservatives" and "moderates" have differed over the use of confessions, with conservatives (e.g., Nettles, George) giving more credence to the use of confessions than do moderates (see, e.g., James's introduction to the chapter by Nettles in *The Unfettered Word*).

[97]Brackney, *Genetic History of Baptist Thought,* p. 528; also p. 63.

[98]George, "Future of Baptist Theology," p. 4.

[99]Estep, "Biblical Authority," p. 157.

[100]Estep, "Baptists and Authority," pp. 600-601.

[101]George, introduction to *Baptist Confessions, Covenants, and Catechisms,* p. 3.

[102]Lumpkin, "Nature and Authority of Baptist Confessions," p. 28.

[103]George, introduction to *Baptist Confessions, Covenants, and Catechisms,* p. 3.

[104]Preamble of *Baptist Faith and Message* (1925; 1963) (*BCF,* p. 392).

[105]Bush and Nettles, *Baptists and the Bible,* p. 358.

[106]Cf. the remarks of W. N. Clarke, who asks, "Is Christianity a book-religion?" and responds by saying, "It is not. . . . The Christian revelation was not made in a book, or in writing, or by diction, but in life and action, especially by the living Christ. It was not given in order to be written out" (*An Outline of Christian Theology,* 6th ed. [New York: Scribner, 1899], p. 20).

[107]One of the clearest recent statements of this principle is found in Grudem, *Systematic Theology,* pp. 23-26.

[108]McBeth, *Baptist Heritage,* p. 63; Brackney, *The Baptists,* p. xviii.

[109]Moody, "Contemporary Theologians," p. 350. This observation was made about seven contemporary Baptist theologians, but is also applicable to Baptist theologians of previous generations (e.g., Boyce, *Abstract of Theology,* pp. 3, 7; Strong, *Systematic Theology,* pp. 2, 15).

[110]Robison B. James, introduction to James, *The Unfettered Word,* p. 142.

[111]Similarly, Nettles, "Creedalism," p. 144. Cf. Dagg, *Manual of Theology,* p. 21; Strong, *Systematic Theology,* pp. 25-29; Mullins, *Christian Religion,* pp. 27-28.

[112]Examples of hermeneutics texts written by Baptists include A. Berkeley Mickelsen, *Interpreting the Bible* (Grand Rapids: Eerdmans, 1963); Bernard Ramm, *Protestant Biblical Interpretation,* 3rd ed. (Grand Rapids: Baker, 1970); Bruce Corley, Steve Lemke and Grant Lovejoy, *Biblical Hermeneutics,* 2nd ed. (Nashville: Broadman & Holman, 2002); William W. Klein, Craig L. Blomberg and Robert L. Hubbard Jr., *Introduction to Biblical Interpretation,* rev. ed. (Nashville: Thomas Nelson, 2004).

[113]John J. Kiwiet, "The Baptist View of the Church: A Personal Account," *Southwestern Journal of Theology* 31, no. 2 (1989): 14.

[114]L. Russ Bush, "On Taking the Bible Literally," in Garrett and Melick, *Authority and Interpretation,* p. 81. Bush does not elaborate on these "rules" here. For a discussion of the grammatical-historical method from a Baptist perspective akin to Bush's, see William B. Tolar, "The Grammatical-Historical Method," in *Biblical Hermeneutics: A Comprehensive Introduction to Interpreting Scripture,* ed. Bruce Corley, Steve W. Lemke and Grant I. Lovejoy, 2nd ed. (Nashville: Broadman & Holman, 2002), pp. 21-38.

[115]Although not always explicitly stated, these principles are often clearly implied. Cf. comments by a number of Baptist scholars about the absence of statements concerning certain beliefs that were simply "assumed" in some Baptist confessions (see Estep, "Biblical Authority," p. 175; Garrett, "Sources of Authority," p. 41; Eric H. Ohlmann, "The Essence of the Bap-

tists: A Reexamination," *Perspectives in Religious Studies* 13, no. 4 [1986]: 100).

[116]Dale Moody, *The Word of Truth: A Summary of Christian Doctrine Based on Biblical Revelation* (Grand Rapids: Eerdmans, 1981), p. 3.

[117]For example, Albert R. Mohler Jr., "Being Baptist Means Conviction," in Nettles and More, *Why I Am a Baptist,* p. 64; James T. Draper Jr., "What Is a Baptist?" in ibid., pp. 56-57; Mullins, *Christian Religion,* p. 4; Ellis A. Fuller, "Why Baptists?" *Review & Expositor* 48, no. 1 (1951): 20.

[118]Kiwiet, "Baptist View of the Church," p. 14. In this, Kiwiet sees the Baptists as "following their Anabaptist forerunners."

[119]Justice C. Anderson, "Old Baptist Principles Reset," *Southwestern Journal of Theology* 31, no. 2 (1989): 7; see also L. G. Champion, "The Baptist Doctrine of the Church in Relation to Scripture, Tradition and the Holy Spirit," *Foundations* 2 (1959): 30; Mullins, *Christian Religion,* p. 28. Commenting on The First London Confession (1644), Estep observes, "Of the more than three hundred Scripture references, only forty-five are from the Old Testament, and these are never allowed to stand alone without corroborating New Testament references" ("Biblical Authority," p. 167).

[120]Conner, *Revelation and God,* p. 91; cf. p. 100. Conner says that the Old Testament is "a partial and preparatory revelation which finds its significance in Christ. The Old Testament is everywhere a forward-looking book" (ibid., p. 94).

[121]Basden, *Has Our Theology Changed?* p. 332.

[122]Duane A. Garrett, "Inerrancy as a Principle of Biblical Hermeneutics," in Garrett and Melick, *Authority and Interpretation,* p. 68.

[123]Stan Norman, "Distinctively and Unashamedly Baptist," in Nettles and More, *Why I Am a Baptist,* p. 186; and Russell D. Moore, "Baptist after All: Resurgent Conservatives Face the Future," in ibid., pp. 243-44.

[124]C. Penrose St. Amant, "Perspectives in Our Baptist Heritage," in Brackney, *Discovering Our Baptist Heritage,* p. 11.

[125]Garrett, "Inerrancy as a Principle," p. 68. Paul Basden suggests, "The only theological boundaries have been the broad parameters of historic Christian orthodoxy, generally interpreted as following in the tradition of the Church Fathers, the Reformers, the Pietists, and the Puritans" (*Has Our Theology Changed?* p. 331). Much of the recent debate about appeals to confessional statements has centered on whether or not such appeals hinder the free exercise of soul competency in biblical interpretation and resulting theological belief.

[126]John L. Dagg, *Manual of Theology, Second Part: A Treatise on Church Order* (Charleston, S.C.: Southern Baptist Publication Society, 1858; reprint, Harrisonburg, Va.: Gano Books, 1982), p. iii.

[127] Brackney, *Genetic History of Baptist Thought,* p. 1.

[128]Humphries, *The Way We Were,* pp. 133-44.

[129]This "identity crisis" has been particularly visible in the context of denominational controversies. For some responses to this, see Humphreys, *The Way We Were;* Thomas J. Nettles, "Being Baptist: We Must Not Sell It Cheap," in Nettles and More, *Why I Am a Baptist,* pp. 3-18; R. Stanton Norman, *More Than Just a Name: Preserving Our Baptist Identity* (Nashville: Broadman & Holman, 2001); idem, *The Baptist Way: Distinctives of a Baptist Church* (Nashville: Broadman & Holman, 2005); George, "Reformation Roots," pp. 13, 19; Anderson, "Old Baptist Principles Reset," p. 5; Ohlmann, "Essence of the Baptists," p. 83; William H. Brackney, "'Commonly, (Though Falsely) Called . . .': Reflections on the Search for Baptist Identity," *Perspectives in Religious Studies* 13, no. 4 (1986): 67-69.

[130]Brackney, *Genetic History of Baptist Thought,* p. 528. Elsewhere, Brackney suggests that there is a "continuity" of Baptist thought, and yet that connecting the first century of Christianity with contemporary Baptist beliefs "remains a compelling problem for Baptists" ("Baptists and Continuity," in *Distinctively Baptist: Essays on Baptist History,* ed. Marc A. Jolley and John D. Pierce [Macon, Ga.: Mercer University Press, 2005], pp. 41-58).

[131]Brackney suggests, "It matters not whether the foe is the truly pagan or a different form of Christian expression; most Baptists are not by nature given to compromise" (*The Baptists,* p. xix; see also p. 21). Ohlmann notes that the "sectarian trait has waned some among baptists in America, but it has not been lost. One can take a dissenter out of sectarianism, but not sectarianism out of a dissenter. . . . The sectarian mentality is still very apparent in baptist thought" ("Baptists and Evangelicals," p. 150). See also George, "Renewal of Baptist Theology," p. 13.

[132]See, for example, Humphries, *The Way We Were,* pp. 35-49, 117-28; Baptist Jubilee Advance, "Baptist Distinctives and Diversities," pp. 68-73; Robison B. James, "Beyond Old Habits and on to a New Land," in James and Dockery, *Beyond the Impasse?* p. 120; Strong, *Systematic Theology,* pp. 890-91; Edgar Y. Mullins, *The Axioms of Religion: A New Interpretation of the Baptist Faith* (Philadelphia: American Baptist Publication Society, 1908), p. 74; Brackney, *The Baptists,* p. 21; Torbet, *History of the Baptists,* p. 17; McBeth, *Baptist Heritage,* p. 61; Lumpkin, "Nature and Authority of Baptist Confessions," pp. 23-24; Anderson, "Old Baptist Principles Reset," pp. 6-9; Ohlmann, "Essence of the Baptists," 85-93. Fisher Humphries observes, "The distinctively Baptist beliefs are all related to the two general ideas of church life and freedom" (*The Way We Were,* p. 111).

[133]Timothy George cites ecclesiology and baptism as the two classically Baptist distinctives ("Future of Baptist Theology," p. 9).

[134]Norman, "Distinctively and Unashamedly Baptist," p. 183; Bill J. Leonard, "The Church," in Basden, *Has Our Theology Changed?* pp. 159-60. Leonard describes the debate over this contention.

[135]For example, Shelley, "Baptist Churches in U.S.A.," p. 110.

[136]George, "Renewal of Baptist Theology," p. 23. See also McBeth, *Baptist Heritage,* pp. 35, 75; Kiwiet, "Baptist View of the Church," p. 14.

[137]Ernest F. Kevan writes, "It is a popular misunderstanding about Baptists to think that their chief concern is with the administration of baptism. The convictions of Baptists are based primarily upon the spiritual nature of the church, and the practice of believers' baptism arises only as a corollary of this and in the light of the NT teaching" ("The Baptist Tradition," in *Evangelical Dictionary of Theology,* ed. Walter A. Elwell [Grand Rapids: Baker, 1984], p. 122). See also Anderson, "Old Baptist Principles Reset," p. 8; Champion, "Baptist Doctrine of the Church," pp. 30-31.

[138]Dagg, *Treatise on Church Order,* p. 100.

[139]Ibid., pp. 125, 128, 133; see also T. Furman Hewitt, "The Church," in *A Baptist's Theology,* ed. R. Wayne Stacy (Macon, Ga.: Smyth & Helwys, 1999), pp. 117-18.

[140]Brackney, *The Baptists,* p. xviii.

[141]Draper, "What Is a Baptist?" p. 55.

[142]Strong, *Systematic Theology,* p. 889. Strong later states that, in the New Testament, "The church was never so large that it could not assemble" (ibid., p. 891).

[143]The Baptist Heritage Commission, "Towards a Baptist Identity: A Statement Ratified by The Baptist Heritage Commission in Zagreb, Yugoslavia, July, 1989," in *Faith, Life and Witness: The Papers of the Study and Research Division of The Baptist World Alliance 1986-1990,* ed.

William H. Brackney and Ruby J. Burke (Birmingham, Ala.: Samford University Press, 1990), p. 147.

[144]Erickson, *Christian Theology,* p. 1043.

[145]Dagg, *Treatise on Church Order,* pp. 130-31.

[146]Strong, *Systematic Theology,* p. 898; also p. 926. Strong indicates that it is a "fundamental principle" of Baptist polity "that there is no authority on earth above that of the local church" (ibid., p. 927).

[147]Baptist Heritage Commission, "Towards a Baptist Identity," p. 147.

[148]Washington, *Frustrated Fellowship,* p. 203.

[149]See Baptist Jubilee Advance, "Baptist Distinctives and Diversities," p. 71; Ralph A. Herring et al., "Baptist Ideals," in Shurden, *Baptist Identity,* p. 109.

[150]Anderson says, "The collective corollary of the personal priesthood of the believer is the autonomy of the local congregation" ("Old Baptist Principles Reset," p. 9).

[151]Barry D. Morrison, "Tradition and Traditionalism in Baptist Life and Thought: The Case of the Lord's Supper," in *Memory and Hope: Strands of Canadian Baptist History,* ed. David T. Priestly (Waterloo, Ont.: Wilfrid Laurier University Press, 1996), p. 48.

[152]George, "Renewal of Baptist Theology," p. 15. The doctrine of soul competency also undergirds the Baptist commitment to the separation of church and state. See Timothy George, "The Priesthood of All Believers," in Basden and Dockery, *The People of God,* pp. 85-87.

[153]R. Wayne Stacy, "Baptism," in Stacy, *A Baptist's Theology,* p. 154.

[154]Lewis and Demarest, *Integrative Theology,* 3:273.

[155]Roy T. Edgemon, *The Doctrines Baptists Believe* (Nashville: Convention, 1988), p. 89.

[156]Herring et al., "Baptist Ideals," p. 106.

[157]See Paul S. Fiddes, "'Walking Together': The Place of Covenant Theology in Baptist Life Yesterday and Today," in Brackney, Fiddes and Briggs, *Pilgrim Pathways,* pp. 52-55; Charles W. DeWeese, *Baptist Church Covenants* (Nashville: Broadman, 1990); George and George, *Baptist Confessions, Covenants, and Catechisms,* pp. 14-16.

[158]Grudem, *Systematic Theology,* p. 856; and Grenz, *Theology for the Community of God,* p. 47.

[159]For example, Strong, *Systematic Theology,* p. 897; Hewitt, "The Church," p. 119. Baptism by immersion is also usually a requirement for membership in a local church.

[160]Erickson, *Christian Theology,* p. 1059. See also Brackney, "African American Baptists," pp. 168-69; Norman, "Distinctively and Unashamedly Baptist," p. 184.

[161]Boyce, *Abstract of Systematic Theology,* p. 374.

[162]Strong, *Systematic Theology,* p. 804. Dagg refers to this as a "moral" change, and "change in the character" (*Manual of Theology,* pp. 277-78).

[163]Norman, "Distinctively and Unashamedly Baptist," p. 184.

[164]Strong, *Systematic Theology,* p. 822. See also Boyce, *Abstract of Theology,* pp. 375-77; Dagg, *Manual of Theology,* pp. 278, 284; Mullins, *Christian Religion,* p. 378. Baptist theologians often also make the point that regeneration does *not* come about through baptism or the Lord's Supper.

[165]Erickson, *Christian Theology,* p. 274.

[166]Dagg, *Manual of Theology,* p. 277; Strong, *Systematic Theology,* pp. 818-19.

[167]Erickson, *Christian Theology,* p. 1059; Grenz, *Theology for the Community of God,* p. 468.

[168]New Hampshire Confession, Article 7 (*BCF,* p. 364).

[169]New Hampshire Confession, Article 10 (*BCF,* p. 365). This list is neither exhaustive nor definitive, but it does give a sense of what kinds of things Baptists associate with a sanctified life.

[170]It is interesting to note, for example, that James Boyce, in his *Abstract of Systematic Theology,*

does not include chapters on baptism or the Lord's Supper, and that Edgar Mullins devotes only two full pages to baptism in *The Christian Religion in Its Doctrinal Expression* (see pp. 375, 383, 427).

[171]Nettles, *By His Grace and For His Glory,* p. 27.

[172]Baptist Heritage Commission, "Towards a Baptist Identity," p. 147.

[173]Second London Confession, Article 28.1 (*BCF,* p. 290).

[174]Strong, *Systematic Theology,* p. 930.

[175]Baptist Jubilee Advance, "Baptist Distinctives and Diversities," p. 70; Brackney, *Baptists,* p. xviii; Mullins, *Christian Religion,* p. 427.

[176]Strong, *Systematic Theology,* p. 932. Strong goes on to say, "In continuing the practice of baptism through his disciples (John 4:1-2), and in enjoining it upon them as part of a work which was to last to the end of the world (Mt. 28:19-20), Christ manifestly adopted and appointed baptism as the invariable law of the church."

[177]For example, Lewis and Demarest, *Integrative Theology,* 3:286; Bruce Rumbold, "Theological Reflection on the Practice of the Ordinances," in Brackney and Burke, *Faith, Life and Witness,* p. 431. Grudem uses the terms "ordinance" and "sacrament" interchangeably, and suggests that the distinction is not a significant one (*Systematic Theology,* p. 966).

[178]George R. Beasley-Murray, *Baptism in the New Testament* (London: Macmillan, 1962), pp. 216-26, 262-66.

[179]Rumbold, "Theological Reflection," p. 431; Lewis and Demarest, *Integrative Theology,* 3:287; Stacy, "Baptism," p. 164.

[180]Erickson, *Christian Theology,* p. 1110.

[181]Grenz, *Theology for the Community of God,* p. 515; see also Stacy, "Baptism," p. 165.

[182]The Second London Confession states, "Immersion, or dipping of the person in water, is necessary to the due administration of this ordinance" (Article 29.4 [*BCF,* p. 291]).

[183]For example, Lewis and Demarest, *Integrative Theology,* 3:289-90; Erickson, *Christian Theology,* pp. 1113-14.

[184]Dagg, *Treatise on Church Order,* p. 14; see also pp. 21-22.

[185]Grenz, *Theology for the Community of God,* p. 530; Dagg, *Treatise on Church Order,* pp. 23-31, 35; Strong, *Systematic Theology,* pp. 933-35.

[186]Lewis and Demarest, *Integrative Theology,* 3:290; Erickson, *Christian Theology,* p. 1113.

[187]Dagg, *Treatise on Church Order,* p. 38.

[188]William L. Hendricks, "Baptism: A Baptist Perspective," *Southwestern Journal of Theology* 31, no. 2 (1989): 26; Strong, *Systematic Theology,* p. 931; Herring et al., "Baptist Ideals," p. 108.

[189]Grenz, *Theology for the Community of God,* p. 531; see also Grudem, *Systematic Theology,* p. 969.

[190]Erickson, *Christian Theology,* p. 1110.

[191]Stacy, "Baptism," p. 64.

[192]Second London Confession, Article 29.2 (*BCF,* p. 291).

[193]Grenz, *Theology for the Community of God,* p. 529.

[194]Erickson, *Christian Theology,* p. 1113.

[195]Strong, *Systematic Theology,* p. 950.

[196]There is no universally agreed upon minimum age for baptism among Baptists. Many churches begin considering children as candidates somewhere between the ages of seven and twelve. It was not uncommon for older theological works to include a lengthy rebuttal of infant baptism (e.g., Strong, *Systematic Theology,* pp. 951-59). McBeth offers this summary of Baptist arguments against infant baptism: "The New Testament nowhere teaches that in-

fants should be baptized or gives examples of infants being baptized; baptism is not related to circumcision, so the fact that infants were circumcised in the Old Testament in no wise proves that infants should be baptized; the New Testament does teach that believers are to be baptized, but since infants cannot yet believe they cannot be truly baptized; that nature of faith and baptism are such that they require a personal decision and commitment that infants are incapable of making" (*Baptist Heritage,* p. 81).

[197]Ohlmann correctly rejects this kind of reductionism ("Essence of the Baptists," p. 85).

[198]Walter Shurden states, "The one word that comes closer than any other to capturing the historic Baptist identity is the word 'freedom'" (*Baptist Identity,* p. 55). See also Brackney, *Genetic History of Baptist Thought,* pp. 2, 536; Baptist Jubilee Advance, "Baptist Distinctives and Diversities," p. 72; Moody, "Contemporary Theologians," p. 350; cf. Nettles, *By His Grace and For His Glory,* p. 27. For other proposals regarding the essence or central distinctive of Baptist theology, see Ohlmann, "Essence of the Baptists," pp. 85-86, 93, 99, 103; Brackney, "Reflections on the Search," pp. 79-80; Fuller, "Why Baptists?" pp. 16-17; Anderson, "Old Baptist Principles Reset," p. 6.

Chapter 7: Grace-Full Holiness and Holy Wholeness

[1]Cf. Wilber T. Dayton, "Entire Sanctification: The Divine Purification and Perfection of Man," in *A Contemporary Wesleyan Theology: Biblical, Systematic, and Practical,* ed. Charles W. Carter, 2 vols. (Grand Rapids: Zondervan, 1983), 1:524-25.

[2]Maldwyn Edwards, "John Wesley," in *A History of the Methodist Church in Great Britain,* ed. Rupert Davies and Gordon Rupp, 4 vols. (London: Epworth, 1965-1988), 1:38-39.

[3]Ibid., 1:44.

[4]R. G. Tuttle, "Wesleyan Tradition," in *Dictionary of Christianity in America,* ed. Daniel G. Reid et al. (Downers Grove, Ill.: InterVarsity Press, 1990), p. 1243.

[5]John Wesley, *Journal,* May 24, 1738, in *The Works of John Wesley,* vol. 18, *Journals and Diaries I (1735-38),* ed. W. Reginald Ward and Richard P. Heitzenrater (Nashville: Abingdon, 1988), p. 250. For analysis by contemporary Wesleyan scholars of the nature and significance of the Aldersgate event, see Randy L. Maddox, ed., *Aldersgate Reconsidered* (Nashville: Kingswood, 1990).

[6]Richard S. Taylor, "Historical and Modern Significance of Wesleyan Theology," in Carter, *Contemporary Wesleyan Theology,* 1:62-64; Luke Keefer, "Characteristics of Wesley's Arminianism," *Wesleyan Theological Journal* 22, no. 1 (1987): 89.

[7]Ted A. Campbell, *Methodist Doctrine—The Essentials* (Nashville: Abingdon, 1999), p. 51.

[8]Keefer, "Characteristics of Wesley's Arminianism," pp. 92, 97; see also p. 95.

[9]John Wesley, "The Question, 'What Is an Arminian?' Answered by a Lover of Free Grace," in *The Works of John Wesley,* reprint ed., 14 vols. (Grand Rapids: Zondervan, 1958), 10:358-61.

[10]See E. Gordon Rupp, "Son of Samuel: John Wesley, Church of England Man," in *The Place of Wesley in the Christian Tradition,* ed. Kenneth E. Rowe (Metuchen, N.J.: Scarecrow, 1976), p. 55.

[11]Wesley, "The Question, 'What Is an Arminian?'" pp. 358-61; see also Taylor, "Historical and Modern Significance," p. 63. With respect to the "conditional" character of Wesley's view of God's saving work, Allan Coppedge notes the importance of God's foreknowledge as to who will respond to the gospel in faith (*John Wesley in Theological Debate* [Wilmore, Ky.: Wesley Heritage, 1987], pp. 24, 132-34).

[12]Frederick A. Norwood, *The Story of American Methodism: A History of the United Methodists and Their Relations* (Nashville: Abingdon, 1974), p. 31.

[13]Ibid., pp. 37, 48.

[14]John Wesley, "Free Grace," *Poetics,* 3:94, in *John Wesley's Theology: A Collection from His Works,* ed. Robert W. Burtner and Robert E. Chiles (New York: Abingdon, 1954; reprint, Nashville: Abingdon, 1982), p. 189. Wesley's term "preventing grace" is synonymous with the subsequent Wesleyan term "prevenient grace."

[15]David C. Shipley, "The European Heritage," in *The History of American Methodism,* ed. Emory S. Bucke, 3 vols. (New York: Abingdon, 1964), 1:33-35; Norwood, *Story of American Methodism,* p. 38.

[16]Timothy L. Smith, "A Historical and Contemporary Appraisal of Wesleyan Theology," in Carter, *Contemporary Wesleyan Theology,* 1:83-84.

[17]Shipley, "European Heritage," pp. 38-39.

[18]Smith, "Historical and Contemporary Appraisal," p. 86.

[19]Ibid., pp. 86-87.

[20]Norwood, *Story of American Methodism,* pp. 65-69.

[21]Ibid., p. 72.

[22]Ibid., p. 73.

[23]Leland Scott, "The Message of Early American Methodism," in Bucke, *History of American Methodism,* 1:335.

[24]Ibid.

[25]Thomas C. Oden, *Doctrinal Standards in the Wesleyan Tradition* (Grand Rapids: Zondervan, 1988), p. 30; Frank Baker, "The Doctrines in the *Discipline:* A Study of the Forgotten Theological Presuppositions of American Methodism," *Duke Divinity School Review* 31 (winter 1966): 40; Norwood, *Story of American Methodism,* p. 76. Cf. Daniel N. Berg, "The Theological Context of American Wesleyanism," *Wesleyan Theological Journal* 20, no. 1 (1985): 45.

[26]Norwood, *Story of American Methodism,* pp. 65-67, 85-87.

[27]Gayraud S. Wilmore, *Black Religion and Black Radicalism: An Interpretation of the Religious History of African Americans,* 3rd ed. (Maryknoll, N.Y.: Orbis, 1998), p. 105.

[28]Norwood, *Story of American Methodism,* p. 74.

[29]Wesley's Sunday service book is based on the Anglican *Book of Common Prayer,* and his twenty-four Articles are an abbreviated and slightly modified version of the Church of England's Thirty-Nine Articles of Religion.

[30]Robert E. Chiles, *Theological Transition in American Methodism: 1790-1935* (New York: Abingdon, 1965), pp. 38-39, 42, 47; also Berg, "Theological Context of American Wesleyanism," p. 45. On the history of theological developments within American Methodism, in addition to Chiles and Berg, see Thomas A. Langford, *Practical Divinity: Theology in the Wesleyan Tradition,* rev. ed., 2 vols. (Nashville: Abingdon, 1998-1999), 1:160-228; Oden, *Doctrinal Standards;* John L. Peters, *Christian Perfection and American Methodism* (New York: Abingdon, 1956).

[31]Dennis M. Campbell, introduction to *Doctrines and Disciplines,* ed. Dennis M Campbell, William B. Lawrence and Russell E. Richey (Nashville: Abingdon, 1999), p. 6.

[32]Chiles, *Theological Transition in American Methodism,* pp. 42-43. See also Berg, "Theological Context of American Wesleyanism," p. 45; Norwood, *Story of American Methodism,* p. 224; Scott, "Early American Methodism," 1:308.

[33]Chiles, *Theological Transition in American Methodism,* p. 43.

[34]Ibid., p. 45.

[35]Tuttle, "Wesleyan Tradition," p. 1244. Not surprisingly, this growth was accompanied by the establishment of a number of denominations, including the Newly-Formed Methodist Confer-

ence (1807; subsequently, the Evangelical Association [1816]), the African Methodist Episcopal Church (1816), the African Methodist Episcopal Zion Church (1821), the Methodist Protestant Church (1830), the United Brethren (1841), the Wesleyan Methodist Connection (1843), the Methodist Episcopal Church, South (1846) and the Free Methodist Church of North America (1860).

[36]Norwood, *Story of American Methodism,* pp. 129-32, 311-12.

[37]Scott, "Early American Methodism," 1:357.

[38]Chiles, *Theological Transition in American Methodism,* p. 52.

[39]Ibid., p. 50; and Scott, "Early American Methodism," 1:352-53.

[40]Norwood, *Story of American Methodism,* p. 226.

[41]Chiles, *Theological Transition in American Methodism,* pp. 59-60. Other systematic theologies included Miner Raymond, *Systematic Theology* (Cincinnati: Cranston & Curts, 1877-1879); Thomas O. Summers, *Systematic Theology: A Complete Body of Wesleyan-Arminian Divinity Consisting of Lectures on the 25 Articles of Religion,* 2 vols. (Nashville: Publishing House of the Methodist Episcopal Church—South, 1888).

[42]Kenneth Cracknell and Susan J. White, *An Introduction to World Methodism* (Cambridge: Cambridge University Press, 2005), pp. 114-15.

[43]For one historian's accounting of the theological continuities between Wesley and nineteenth-century Holiness thought, see Smith, "Historical and Contemporary Appraisal," pp. 92-94.

[44]Peters, *Christian Perfection and American Methodism,* p. 191. For women's views of perfection, see Susie C. Stanley, *Holy Boldness: Women Preachers' Autobiographies and the Sanctified Self* (Knoxville: University of Tennessee Press, 2002), pp. 89-91.

[45]Tuttle, "Wesleyan Tradition," p. 1243.

[46]Subsequently, the association changed its name to the National Holiness Association, and later, in 1971, to the present name, the Christian Holiness Association.

[47]Smith, "Historical and Contemporary Appraisal," p. 90.

[48]Barbara J. MacHaffie, *Her Story: Women in the Christian Tradition* (Minneapolis: Fortress, 1986), p. 109.

[49]Stanley, *Holy Boldness,* p. 1.

[50]Ibid., pp. 69-70.

[51]Ibid., pp. 70-71; see also Amy Oden, ed., *In Her Own Words: Women's Writings in the History of Christian Thought* (Nashville: Abingdon, 1994), p. 282.

[52]Kenneth E. Rowe, introduction to Rowe, *Place of Wesley,* p. 2.

[53]Chiles, *Theological Transition in American Methodism,* p. 61; see also Thomas A. Langford, "Constructive Theology in the Wesleyan Tradition," in *Wesleyan Theology Today: A Bicentennial Theological Consultation,* ed. Theodore Runyon (Nashville: Kingswood, 1985), p. 56. Norwood observes that "the pietistically inclined" United Brethren and Evangelicals were less influenced by these currents than were the Methodists (*Story of American Methodism,* p. 426).

[54]Campbell, introduction to *Doctrines and Disciplines,* p. 8.

[55]Chiles, *Theological Transition in American Methodism,* pp. 71-72.

[56]Ibid., p. 25.

[57]Cracknell and White, *Introduction to World Methodism,* pp. 113-16.

[58]Norwood, *Story of American Methodism,* pp. 432-33.

[59]Campbell, introduction to *Doctrines and Disciplines,* pp. 10-14.

[60]Ibid., p. 14.

[61]William J. Abraham, "The Wesleyan Quadrilateral," in Runyon, *Wesleyan Theology Today,* p. 119.

[62]For critique of the UMC's relationship to its theological heritage by one who is self-consciously rooted in the Wesleyan heritage, see Thomas Oden, *Requiem: A Lament in Three Movements* (Nashville: Abingdon, 1995).

[63]The Christian Holiness Association (CHA), the descendant of the National Campmeeting Association for the Promotion of Christian Holiness, is the oldest ecumenical structure for Holiness denominations and groups. Begun by Methodist revivalists in 1867, the CHA currently includes both Wesleyan and non-Wesleyan (e.g., Brethren in Christ, Evangelical Friends Alliance [Quakers]) members.

[64]Oden, *Doctrinal Standards,* p. 17. Cf. Norwood, *Story of American Methodism,* pp. 223-24, 232; Emory S. Bucke, introduction to Bucke, *History of American Methodism,* 1:xiii.

[65]Chiles, *Theological Transition in American Methodism,* pp. 22-23.

[66]Campbell, introduction to *Doctrines and Disciplines,* p. 7.

[67]*The Book of Discipline of the United Methodist Church, 1996* (Nashville: United Methodist Publishing House, 1996), Paragraph 63, Section 4, p. 74; Paragraph 60, Section 1, p. 43.

[68]Wesley scholar Albert Outler is credited with coining this phrase. See his comments in *John Wesley,* ed. Albert C. Outler, Library of Protestant Thought (New York: Oxford University Press, 1964), pp. vii, 119, 135, 473; see also idem, "The Place of Wesley in the Christian Tradition," in Rowe, *Place of Wesley,* p. 13.

[69]See Randy L. Maddox, *Responsible Grace: John Wesley's Practical Theology* (Nashville: Kingswood, 1994); Thomas C. Oden, *John Wesley's Scriptural Christianity: A Plain Exposition of His Teaching on Christian Doctrine* (Grand Rapids: Zondervan, 1994); Kenneth J. Collins, *The Scripture Way of Salvation: The Heart of John Wesley's Theology* (Nashville: Abingdon, 1997); idem, *John Wesley: A Theological Journey* (Nashville: Abingdon, 2003). On the history of attempts to systematize Wesley's thought, Theodore Runyon observes, "Every attempt to reduce Wesley to a system (Fletcher, Watson, Miley, Wiley, etc.) has failed to do justice to one aspect or another of his thought" (introduction to *Wesleyan Theology Today,* p. 1).

[70]Norwood, *Story of American Methodism,* pp. 224, 232.

[71]Allan Coppedge, "How Wesleyans Do Theology," in *Doing Theology Today's World,* ed. John D. Woodbridge and Thomas E. McComiskey (Grand Rapids: Zondervan, 1991), p. 267; see also p. 285.

[72]Abraham points out that although the quadrilateral currently occupies "a pivotal place" in North American Methodist theology, in part because it provides an agreed upon "context" or "criteria" for Christian faith in the midst of pluralism, "there has been little if any interest in the quadrilateral within British Methodism" ("Wesleyan Quadrilateral," p. 119).

[73]*Book of Discipline of the United Methodist Church, 1996,* Paragraph 60, Section 1, p. 39.

[74]Abraham, "Wesleyan Quadrilateral," p. 120; see also H. Ray Dunning, *Grace, Faith, and Holiness: A Wesleyan Systematic Theology* (Kansas City, Mo.: Beacon Hill, 1988), p. 77. For an in-depth study of Wesley and the quadrilateral, see Donald A. D. Thorsen, *The Wesleyan Quadrilateral: Scripture, Tradition, Reason and Experience as a Model of Evangelical Theology* (Lexington: Emeth, 2005).

[75]Campbell suggests that "in fact there is no agreement, and cannot be, as to exactly how these multiple norms actually function for theology" (introduction to *Doctrines and Disciplines,* p. 13).

[76]See Durwood Foster, "Wesleyan Theology: Heritage and Task," in Runyon, *Wesleyan Theology Today,* p. 31.

[77]Coppedge, "How Wesleyans Do Theology," p. 269.

[78]Abraham, "Wesleyan Quadrilateral," p. 120; see also John Miley, *Systematic Theology,* 2 vols.

(New York: Hunter & Eaton; Cincinnati: Cranston & Stowe, 1892-1894), 1:12, 46.

[79]Bruce C. Birch, "Biblical Theology: Issues in Authority and Hermeneutics," in Runyon, *Wesleyan Theology Today,* p. 127; see also Coppedge, "How Wesleyans Do Theology," p. 271.

[80]Dunning, *Grace, Faith, and Holiness,* p. 76; see also Smith, "Historical and Contemporary Appraisal," p. 82.

[81]Coppedge, "How Wesleyans Do Theology," pp. 270, 279; also Abraham, "Wesleyan Quadrilateral," p. 120.

[82]*Book of Discipline of the United Methodist Church, 1996,* Paragraph 63, Section 4, p. 80; see also the analysis in Charles Yrigoyen Jr., *Belief Matters: United Methodism's Doctrinal Statements* (Nashville: Abingdon, 2001), p. 124.

[83]Campbell, *Methodist Doctrine,* p. 36.

[84]Oden, *Doctrinal Standards,* p. 21; also George Lyons, "Hermeneutical Bases for Theology: Higher Criticism and the Wesleyan Interpreter," *Wesleyan Theological Journal* 18, no. 1 (1983): 67.

[85]Coppedge, "How Wesleyans Do Theology," p. 278; Abraham, "Wesleyan Quadrilateral," p. 120.

[86]Coppedge, "How Wesleyans Do Theology," pp. 279, 273.

[87]Lyons, "Hermeneutical Bases for Theology," p. 67; see also Oden, *Doctrinal Standards,* p. 21.

[88]Coppedge, "How Wesleyans Do Theology," p. 275.

[89]Abraham, "Wesleyan Quadrilateral," p. 120; Coppedge, "How Wesleyans Do Theology," p. 275.

[90]Oden, *Doctrinal Standards,* p. 22; see also pp. 31-33. See *The Standard Sermons in Modern English,* ed. Kenneth C. Kinghorn, 3 vols. (Nashville: Abingdon, 2002-2003).

[91]In recent times, considerable discussion has taken place among some Methodists as to whether or not the *Sermons* and *Notes* are of the same abiding significance as the Articles. For example, see the exchange between Richard P. Heitzenrater, who argues that by the beginning of the nineteenth century Wesley's *Sermons* and *Notes* were not legal standards in Methodism, and Thomas C. Oden, who affirms that they remained legal standards (Heitzenrater, "At Full Liberty: Doctrinal Standard in Early American Methodism," and Oden, "What Are 'Established Standards of Doctrine'?" in *Doctrine and Theology in The United Methodist Church,* ed. Thomas A. Langford [Nashville: Abingdon, 1991], pp. 109-24, 125-42). See also Oden, *Doctrinal Standards.*

[92]For example, Dunning, *Grace, Faith, and Holiness,* p. 83; cf. Miley, *Systematic Theology,* 1:12-13.

[93]William J. Abraham, *Waking from Doctrinal Amnesia: The Healing of Doctrine in the United Methodist Church* (Nashville: Abingdon, 1995), p. 14.

[94]Abraham, "Wesleyan Quadrilateral," p. 121.

[95]Ibid. Cf. Miley, *Systematic Theology,* 1:39-40, 43.

[96]Dunning, *Grace, Faith, and Holiness,* p. 85; idem, "Systematic Theology in a Wesleyan Mode," *Wesleyan Theological Journal* 17, no. 1 (1982): 20.

[97]Dunning, *Grace, Faith, and Holiness,* pp. 85-86.

[98]Harald Lindström, *Wesley and Sanctification: A Study in the Doctrine of Salvation* (London: Epworth, 1946; reprint, Nappanee, Ind.: Francis Asbury, 1996), p. 5.

[99]*Book of Discipline of the United Methodist Church, 1996,* Paragraph 63, Section 4, p. 78.

[100]Theodore Runyon, "What Is Methodism's Theological Contribution Today?" in Runyon, *Wesleyan Theology Today,* p. 3; cf. Smith, "Historical and Contemporary Appraisal," pp. 77, 80-81.

[101]Martin Schmidt, "Wesley's Place in Church History," in Rowe, *Place of Wesley,* p. 79. Schmidt writes "from a Lutheran perspective," but his work on Wesley's life and thought is highly regarded among Wesleyan scholars.

[102]Runyon, "Methodism's Theological Contribution," p. 12. Runyon refers to experience as "the" means of perceiving and participating in the real world.

[103]Keefer, "Characteristics of Wesley's Arminianism," p. 91.

[104]Dunning, *Grace, Faith, and Holiness,* p. 92.

[105]Lyons perceives that "there is no generally agreed upon or distinctively Wesleyan hermeneutic" ("Hermeneutical Bases for Theology," p. 63); see also Birch, "Biblical Theology," p. 127.

[106]Lyons, "Hermeneutical Bases for Theology," pp. 65, 72; Coppedge, "How Wesleyans Do Theology," p. 272.

[107]John Wesley, letter to Samuel Furly, 10 May 1755; quoted in Shipley, "European Heritage," 1:30.

[108]Coppedge, "How Wesleyans Do Theology," p. 272.

[109]Runyon, introduction to *Wesleyan Theology Today,* p. 2.

[110]Dunning, *Grace, Faith, and Holiness,* p. 75; see also Coppedge, "How Wesleyans Do Theology," p. 282.

[111]In addition to holiness, Coppedge identifies two other "overarching themes" that provide the "hermeneutical norms" by which Wesley interprets the Bible, as his followers also ought to do: God as Father, and God's grace ("How Wesleyans Do Theology," p. 282). Dunning proposes that "the New Testament's use of the Old Testament provides the most productive clue to an adequate hermeneutical theory," and that this use suggests that the "'new hermeneutic' in terms of which the Christian must read his Old Testament" is the life and work of Christ, particularly his suffering and death on the cross (*Grace, Faith, and Holiness,* pp. 590, 594, 627).

[112]Smith, "Historical and Contemporary Appraisal," pp. 77, 87; also Dayton, "Entire Sanctification," p. 522.

[113]Dayton, "Entire Sanctification," p. 523. For some Wesleyans, the New Testament has a hermeneutical priority over the Old Testament, with the former providing interpretive guidance for reading the latter; yet, holiness is still the most common hermeneutical key (see ibid., p. 563; Dunning, *Grace, Faith, and Holiness,* p. 590) .

[114]Tuttle, "Wesleyan Tradition," p. 1244.

[115]Oden, *Doctrinal Standards,* p. 11; Coppedge, "How Wesleyans Do Theology," p. 282; H. Ray Dunning, "Perspective for a Wesleyan Systematic Theology," in Runyon, *Wesleyan Theology Today,* pp. 51-52; idem, *Grace, Faith, and Holiness,* p. 47.

[116]Coppedge, "How Wesleyans Do Theology," pp. 282-86.

[117]Dunning, "Systematic Theology in a Wesleyan Mode," pp. 18-21; idem, *Grace, Faith, and Holiness,* p. 47.

[118]Mildred B. Wynkoop, *Theology of Love: The Dynamic of Wesleyanism* (Kansas City, Mo.: Beacon Hill, 1972).

[119]Dunning, "Perspective for a Wesleyan Systematic Theology," p. 51. For Dunning, "saving" entails both initial salvation (e.g., justification) and continuing salvation (i.e., sanctification).

[120]Philip S. Watson, *The Message of the Wesleys: A Reader of Instruction and Devotion* (New York: Macmillan, 1964), p. 35. Numerous Wesleyan writers approvingly cite this passage from Watson, including Taylor, "Historical and Modern Significance," p. 55; A. Raymond George, "Foundation Documents of the Faith: IX. Methodist Statements," *Expository Times* 91 (1980):

262; Norwood, *Story of American Methodism*, p. 47.

[121]Collins, *Scripture Way of Salvation*, p. 19; Coppedge, "How Wesleyans Do Theology," p. 284. See also M. Douglas Meeks, "The Future of the Methodist Theological Traditions," in *The Future of the Methodist Theological Tradition*, ed. M. Douglas Meeks (Nashville: Abingdon, 1985), p. 25; Dunning, *Grace, Faith, and Holiness*, p. 338; Norwood, *Story of American Methodism*, p. 48.

[122]John B. Cobb Jr., *Grace and Responsibility: A Wesleyan Theology for Today* (Nashville: Abingdon, 1995), p. 108; Miley, *Systematic Theology*, 2:244.

[123]For analyses of a theological shift from free grace to free will within major sectors of American Methodism, see Chiles, *Theological Transition in American Methodism*, pp. 186-87; Berg, "Theological Context of American Wesleyanism," p. 48.

[124]William Pope, *A Compendium of Christian Theology*, 2nd ed., 3 vols. (New York: Phillips & Hunt, 1882), 2:359.

[125]R. Larry Shelton, "Initial Salvation: The Redemptive Grace of God," in Carter, *Contemporary Wesleyan Theology*, 1:485. Among the biblical passages cited by Shelton are Titus 2:11; 1 Corinthians 16; 2 Corinthians 8; 9:8; Galatians 2:9, 19-21; Romans 3:24.

[126]The Articles of Religion of the Methodist Church (*BDUMC*, p. 61). This document is the Twenty-Five Articles of Religion.

[127]Dunning, *Grace, Faith, and Holiness*, p. 290.

[128]Kenneth J. Grider, *A Wesleyan-Holiness Theology* (Kansas City, Mo.: Beacon Hill, 1994), p. 35; Campbell, *Methodist Doctrine*, p. 51.

[129]Miley, *Systematic Theology*, 2:243.

[130]Taylor, "Historical and Modern Significance," p. 65.

[131]Mildred Bangs Wynkoop, *Foundations of Wesleyan Arminian Theology* (Kansas City, Mo.: Beacon Hill, 1967), p. 68.

[132]Campbell, *Methodist Doctrine*, p. 50.

[133]Pope, *Compendium of Christian Theology*, 2:363.

[134]Miley, *Systematic Theology*, 2:246-47.

[135]Taylor, "Historical and Modern Significance," p. 64.

[136]Article 8 of the Twenty-Five Articles reads, "We have no power to do good work, pleasant and acceptable to God, without the grace of God by Christ preventing us, that we may have a good will, and working with us, when we have that good will" (*BDUMC*, p. 61).

[137]Dunning, *Grace, Faith, and Holiness*, p. 338.

[138]Pope, *Compendium of Christian Theology*, 2:360.

[139]Ibid.

[140]Pope also writes, "It is not so much in single passages as in the constant tenor of Scripture that we gather the spontaneous freedom of the grace that provided salvation" (*Compendium of Christian Theology*, 2:361).

[141]Pope also cites Zechariah 4:6; 2 Corinthians 3:5; Romans 5:6, 8, 10.

[142]Maddox, *Responsible Grace*, p. 19.

[143]Collins, *Scripture Way of Salvation*, pp. 43-44.

[144]Dunning, *Grace, Faith, and Holiness*, p. 158.

[145]Shelton, "Initial Salvation," p. 485. See also Barry L. Callen, "A Mutuality Model of Conversion," in *Conversion in the Wesleyan Tradition*, ed. Kenneth J. Collins and John H. Tyson (Nashville: Abingdon, 2001), pp. 146-48; Dunning, *Grace, Faith, and Holiness*, p. 430, on "synergism"; Thomas C. Oden, *Systematic Theology*, vol. 3, *Life in the Spirit* (New York: HarperCollins, 1992), p. 230; Pope, *Compendium of Christian Theology*, 2:364-65, on "co-operation."

[146]Pope, *Compendium of Christian Theology*, 2:364; cf. Dunning, *Grace, Faith, and Holiness*, p. 339.

[147]Wynkoop, *Theology of Love*, p. 154.

[148]Dunning, *Grace, Faith, and Holiness*, p. 339.

[149]Taylor, "Historical and Modern Significance," p. 64.

[150]Michael Lodahl, *The Story of God: Wesleyan Theology and Biblical Narrative* (Kansas City, Mo.: Beacon Hill, 1994), p. 45.

[151]Campbell, *Methodist Doctrine*, pp. 51, 55.

[152]Maddox, *Responsible Grace*, p. 176.

[153]Dayton, "Entire Sanctification," p. 522.

[154]Miley, *Systematic Theology*, 2:370.

[155]L. Gregory Jones, "What Makes 'United Methodist Theology' Methodist?" in Campbell, Lawrence and Richey, *Doctrines and Disciplines;* see also Lodahl, *Story of God,* p. 192.

[156]Tuttle, "Wesleyan Tradition," p. 1243.

[157]Articles of Religion of the Wesleyan Methodist Church, Article 13 (*EARRC,* 1:309).

[158]Miley, *Systematic Theology*, 2:354.

[159]Lodahl, *Story of God,* p. 28.

[160]Tuttle, "Wesleyan Tradition," p. 1243.

[161]Dunning, *Grace, Faith, and Holiness,* p. 478; see also Lindström, *Wesley and Holiness,* p. 123.

[162]Virtual synonyms include "Christian perfection," "perfect love," "heart purity," "Christian holiness" and "fullness of the blessing." See, for example, Articles of Faith of the Church of the Nazarene, Article 10 (*EARRC,* 1:289).

[163]Confession of Faith of the Evangelical United Brethren Church, Article 11 (*BDUMC,* pp. 69-70). Although this document is still labeled as being "of the Evangelical United Brethren," it was adopted by the United Methodist Church in 1968.

[164]Articles of Religion of the Free Methodist Church, Article 13 (*EARRC,* 1:297); see also Articles of Faith of the Church of the Nazarene, Articles 5, 10 (*EARRC,* 1:289).

[165]Other passages cited here with reference to Christian perfection are Leviticus 20:7-8; John 14:16-17; 17:19; Acts 1:8; 2:4; 15:8-9; Romans 5:3-5; 8:12-17; 12:1-2; 1 Corinthians 6:11; 12:4-11; Galatians 5:22-25; 1 Thessalonians 4:7; 5:23-24; 2 Thessalonians 2:13; Hebrews 10:14.

[166]Dunning, *Grace, Faith, and Holiness,* p. 479. Some Wesleyans, such as the Church of the Nazarene, speak of the "eradication" of sin. We are to "Be perfect . . . as [our] heavenly Father is perfect" (Mt 5:48), and this perfection cannot come to pass as long as there is sin in our lives. However, it is possible, Nazarenes affirm, for the love of God to expel "all disposition to sin" (Stan Ingersol, "Church of the Nazarene," in *An Encyclopedia of Religions in the United States: One Hundred Religious Groups Speak for Themselves,* ed. William B. Williamson [New York: Crossroad, 1992], p. 227).

[167]Daniel L. Burnett, "Wesleyan Church," in Williamson, *Encyclopedia of Religions,* p. 234.

[168]Dayton, "Entire Sanctification," p. 521.

[169]Ibid., p. 529; see also Dunning, *Grace, Faith, and Holiness,* p. 455; Miley, *Systematic Theology,* 2:365.

[170]Other passages cited in this connection include Acts 2:1-4; 15:9; 1 John 3:8; Psalm 51:2; Isaiah 1:18; Malachi 3:2-3; Exodus 29:36; Matthew 8:3; 15:13; James 4:8.

[171]Dayton, "Entire Sanctification," p. 533.

[172]Dunning, *Grace, Faith, and Holiness,* p. 465.

[173]Georgia Harkness, *Beliefs That Count* (New York: Abingdon, 1961), p. 82.

[174]Dayton, "Entire Sanctification," p. 529.

[175]Ted A. Campbell and Michael T. Burns, *Wesleyan Essentials in a Multicultural Society* (Nashville: Abingdon, 2004), p. 85.

[176]Oden, *Life in the Spirit*, p. 228.

[177]Miley, *Systematic Theology*, 2:363.

[178]Dayton, "Entire Sanctification," pp. 532-33.

[179]Allan Coppedge, *Portraits of God: A Biblical Theology of Holiness* (Downers Grove, Ill.: InterVarsity Press, 2001), p. 82.

[180]Dayton, "Entire Sanctification," p. 532.

[181]Lodahl, *Story of God*, pp. 195-97; Collins, *Scripture Way of Salvation*, p. 182.

[182]Campbell, *Methodist Doctrine*, pp. 61-62.

[183]R. Newton Flew, *The Idea of Christian Perfection: An Historical Study of the Christian Ideal for the Present Life* (London: Oxford University Press, 1934), p. 416.

[184]Dayton, "Entire Sanctification," pp. 521, 563.

[185]Dunning, *Grace, Faith, and Holiness*, p. 464.

[186]Dayton, "Entire Sanctification," p. 529.

[187]Ibid., pp. 563-64.

[188]Harkness, *Understanding the Christian Faith* (New York: Abingdon, 1947), p. 21.

[189]Dunning, *Grace, Faith, and Holiness*, p. 466.

[190]Dayton, "Entire Sanctification," p. 564.

[191]Dunning, *Grace, Faith, and Holiness*, p. 466.

[192]Dayton, "Entire Sanctification," p. 563.

[193]Statement of Faith of Asbury Theological Seminary [Article 7], Entire Sanctification (*EARRC*, 2:166).

[194]Articles of Faith of the Church of the Nazarene, Article 10 (*EARRC*, 1:289).

[195]Dayton, "Entire Sanctification," p. 521; Miley, *Systematic Theology*, 2:357, 368-69; Tuttle, "Wesleyan Tradition," p. 1244.

[196]Dayton, "Entire Sanctification," pp. 543, 545, 552; Burnett, "Wesleyan Church," p. 234.

[197]Bergs observes, "The baptism of the Holy Ghost is introduced to American Wesleyanism and tied to the doctrine of sanctification by Asa Mahan and Oberlin theology" ("Theological Context of American Wesleyanism," p. 53). Even among Wesleyans who do not associate perfection with baptism in the Holy Spirit, God's sanctifying work is viewed as being a work of the Holy Spirit.

[198]Articles of Faith of Church of the Nazarene, Article 10 (*EARRC*, 1:289); see also Article 5 (*EARRC*, 1:289).

[199]Burnett, "Wesleyan Church," p. 234.

[200]Dayton, "Entire Sanctification," p. 543.

[201]Dunning, *Grace, Faith, and Holiness*, pp. 465-66.

Chapter 8: Rightly Dividing the Scriptures

[1]Historically, Plymouth Brethren have referred to a local congregation as an "assembly" or "chapel."

[2]One of the characteristics of "generations" that makes it an apt image is the recognition that generations overlap. At any given point in history, a tradition may simultaneously find expression through two, three or more generations.

[3]In recognition of differences between Darby and Scofield, some might divide this phase into two phases: Pre-Scofield, and Scofield and Chafer.

[4]For example, Mark L. Bailey, "Dispensational Definitions of the Kingdom," in *Integrity of*

Heart and Skillfulness of Hands: Biblical and Leadership Studies in Honor of Donald K. Campbell, ed. Charles H. Dyer and Roy B. Zuck (Grand Rapids: Baker, 1994), p. 202.

[5]For example, Craig A. Blaising and Darrell L. Bock, "Dispensationalism, Israel and the Church: Assessment and Dialogue," in *Dispensationalism, Israel and the Church: The Search for Definition,* ed. Craig A. Blaising and Darrell L. Bock (Grand Rapids: Zondervan, 1992), p. 379.

[6]For example, this is the terminology adopted by Bateman in *Three Central Issues in Contemporary Dispensationalism: A Comparison of Traditional and Progressive Views,* ed. Herbert W. Bateman IV (Grand Rapids: Kregel, 1999). By contrast, Progressive Dispensationalists usually refer to this third generation as embodying "Revised" Dispensationalism, emphasizing what the Progressives view as significant changes introduced into Dispensationalism by this generation, or "Essentialist" Dispensationalism, emphasizing the tendency to reduce Dispensationalism to certain "essentials," most notably those delineated by Charles Ryrie in his influential book *Dispensationalism Today* (Chicago: Moody Press, 1965; rev. ed., 1995). Carl Sanders observes that from its earliest days "a degree of flexibility has existed within the movement," and that "this diversity means that later forms of dispensationalism should not be assumed to be definitional of dispensationalism, even when connected to important figures like Scofield, Chafer, or Ryrie" (*The Premillennial Faith of James Brookes: Reexamining the Roots of American Dispensationalism* [Lanham, Md.: University Press of America, 2001], p. 142).

[7]Each of the traditions presented in this book has gone through significant, often traumatic, changes, and all of them currently are wrestling, to varying degrees, with questions of identity. Nonetheless, perhaps more clearly and emphatically than any of these others, Dispensationalism recently has witnessed the emergence of a new development: Progressive Dispensationalism. The emergence of Progressive Dispensationalism is fairly recent (1980s), yet it is gaining ever increasing influence in historically Dispensational circles. Progressive Dispensational scholars have already begun to produce a noteworthy body of literature; yet, there continue to be respected voices and significant numbers of Dispensationalists, particularly outside of academic contexts, who have not yet embraced the Progressive version. The emergence of Progressive Dispensationalism, and its precursors, will be included below in the review of the history of Dispensationalism. However, it is important at this point to take note of this contemporary debate because the history of the tradition, the theological and interpretive methods of the tradition, and the characteristic teachings of the tradition are being contested. Given this situation, the present chapter incorporates perspectives from both Traditional and Progressive expressions of Dispensationalism.

[8]Larry V. Crutchfield, preface to *Origins of Dispensationalism: The Darby Factor* (Lanham, Md.: University Press of America, 1992).

[9]Charles Ryrie, *Dispensationalism,* rev. ed. (Chicago: Moody Press, 1995), p. 67.

[10]For example, Ryrie responds to "the charge of recency" by chronicling early, pre-Darby formulations of Dispensational concepts (*Dispensationalism,* pp. 62-67), and Arnold Ehlert traces "the roots of foundations" of the tradition "far back into antiquity" (*A Bibliographic History of Dispensationalism* [Grand Rapids: Baker, 1965], pp. 23-46).

[11]Thomas S. McCall, "Israel and the Church: The Differences," in *Dictionary of Premillennial Theology,* ed. Mal Couch (Grand Rapids: Kregel, 1996), p. 194.

[12]Lewis Sperry Chafer, *Systematic Theology,* 8 vols. (Dallas: Dallas Seminary Press, 1947-1948), 1:xxxiii.

[13]Ryrie, *Dispensationalism,* pp. 63, 65.

[14]Ibid., pp. 63-67. See also Mal Couch, foreword to Couch, *Dictionary of Premillennial Theology.*

[15]Ehlert, *Bibliographic History,* p. 22.

[16]For a description of this by a non-Dispensationalist, see Timothy Weber, *Living in the Shadow of the Second Coming: American Premillennialism, 1875-1982,* rev. ed. (Chicago: University of Chicago Press, 1987), p. 17.

[17]Ehlert, *Bibliographic History,* pp. 47, 33.

[18]Charles Ryrie, "Update on Dispensationalism," in *Issues in Dispensationalism,* ed. Wesley R. Willis and John R. Master (Chicago: Moody Press, 1994), p. 16.

[19]Craig A. Blaising, "Contemporary Dispensationalism," *Southwestern Journal of Theology* 36, no. 2 (1994): 6; see also idem, "Changing Patterns in American Dispensational Theology," *Wesleyan Theological Journal* 29, nos. 1-2 (1994): 149.

[20]Steven R. Spencer, "Dispensationalism," in *The Encyclopedia of Christianity,* ed. Erwin Fahlbusch et al., trans. Geoffrey W. Bromiley (Grand Rapids: Eerdmans, 1999-), 1:854-55.

[21]Crutchfield, *Origins of Dispensationalism,* pp. 206, 207.

[22]Henry A. Ironside, *A Historical Sketch of the Brethren Movement,* rev. ed. (Neptune, N.J.: Loizeaux, 1985), p. 12.

[23]Ibid., p. 25.

[24]J. N. Darby, "The Apostasy of the Successive Dispensations," in *The Collected Writings of J. N. Darby,* ed. William Kelly, reprint ed., 34 vols. (Sunbury, Penn.: Believer's Bookshelf, 1971), 1.1:124-30; see also Ehlert, *Bibliographic History,* pp. 47-49.

[25]J. N. Darby, *The Collected Writings of J. N. Darby,* 34 vols. (London: G. Morrish, 1867), 2:568, quoted in Ryrie, *Dispensationalism,* p. 69.

[26]See "J. N. Darby's Own Account of the Origin of the Movement," in Ironside, *Brethren Movement,* Appendix A, pp. 181-87.

[27]Spencer, "Dispensationalism," p. 854; see also Ryrie, *Dispensationalism,* p. 145; Crutchfield, *Origins of Dispensationalism,* p. 11. Spencer goes on to point out that as Dispensationalism made its way into America, many fundamentalists embraced the distinction between Israel and the church but "discarded [Darby's] fundamental doctrine, the apostasy of the organized church," instead being committed to "purifying or restoring an organized Christianity, whether denominational or not" ("Dispensationalism," pp. 1-2).

[28]Ryrie, *Dispensationalism,* p. 68; also Mark A. Noll, *A History of Christianity in the United States and Canada* (Grand Rapids: Eerdmans, 1992), p. 377.

[29]Weber, *Living in the Shadow,* pp. 16-17.

[30]Premillennialism is the belief that "Christ will return to earth, (this return is also known as the Second Coming) literally and bodily, before the millennial ages begins and that, by His presence, a kingdom will be instituted over which He will reign." This reign will last one thousand years, and hence is referred to as "the millennium" (Bobby Hayes, "Premillennialism," in Couch, *Dictionary of Premillennial Theology,* p. 311).

[31]Ryrie, *Dispensationalism,* p. 146. In his book on James Brookes, Carl Sanders highlights the significance of premillennialism: "Dispensationalism in its earliest history was fundamentally premillennialism, and viewed itself as such. Its roots in America are the antebellum premillennialist movement" (*Premillennial Faith of James Brookes,* p. 140).

[32]Herbert W. Bateman IV, "Dispensationalism Yesterday and Today," in Bateman, *Three Central Issues,* p. 43 n. 1. See also Craig A. Blaising, "Dispensationalism: The Search for Definition," in Blaising and Bock, *Dispensationalism, Israel and the Church,* p. 16.

[33]Blaising, "Dispensationalism: The Search for Definition," pp. 17-18.

[34]Ibid., p. 20.

[35]See Weber, *Living in the Shadow,* pp. 26-28.

[36]Ryrie, "Update on Dispensationalism," p. 18.

[37]Blaising, "Dispensationalism: The Search for Definition," p. 21.

[38]Ibid., p. 23. See also Spencer, "Dispensationalism," p. 855.

[39]Crutchfield, *Origins of Dispensationalism,* pp. 206-8; David J. MacLeod, "Walter Scott: A Link in Dispensationalism Between Darby and Scofield?" *Bibliotheca Sacra* 153 (April-June 1996): 155-78; Ryrie, *Dispensationalism,* p. 69.

[40]Crutchfield, *Origins of Dispensationalism,* p. 206.

[41]Stephen R. Spencer, "Scofield, C(yrus). I.," in *Dictionary of Major Bible Interpreters,* ed. Donald K. McKim (Downers Grove, Ill.: InterVarsity Press, 1998), p. 612.

[42]Craig A. Blaising, "The Extent and Varieties of Dispensationalism," in *Progressive Dispensationalism,* by Craig A. Blaising and Darrell L. Bock (Wheaton, Ill.: BridgePoint, 1993), p. 10.

[43]Blaising, "Dispensationalism: The Search for Definition," p. 22.

[44]Blaising observes, "Neither side comprehended, much less appreciated, the phenomena of dispensationalism as a *developing* subtradition in American evangelicalism. The label *dispensationalism* was itself a victim of the hermeneutical problem and further masked the historical reality of the movement" (ibid.).

[45]Spencer, "Dispensationalism," p. 855.

[46]Ryrie, "Update on Dispensationalism," p. 19.

[47]This analysis follows that of Blaising and reflects a Progressive Dispensational perspective on this chapter of the history of Dispensationalism ("Dispensationalism: The Search for Definition," p. 28). Traditionalists probably would dispute the degree of change portrayed in Blaising's description; Blaising suggests that the Traditionalists "generally did not gain a historical understanding of the tradition or the transition they had undergone" (ibid., p. 29).

[48]John D. Hannah, "John F. Walvoord," in *Handbook of Evangelical Theologians,* ed. Walter A. Elwell (Grand Rapids: Baker, 1993), p. 242.

[49]J. Dwight Pentecost, *Things to Come: A Study in Biblical Eschatology* (Grand Rapids: Zondervan, 1964).

[50]Paul P. Enns, "J. Dwight Pentecost," in Couch, *Dictionary of Premillennial Theology,* p. 294.

[51]Ryrie, *Dispensationalism Today,* p. 29.

[52]Ibid., pp. 44-46.

[53]Blaising, who is among those who have most rigorously critiqued Ryrie's book, states, "The importance of this work for the self-understanding of late twentieth-century dispensationalism cannot be overstated" ("Dispensationalism: The Search for Definition," p. 23).

[54]Kenneth L. Barker, "False Dichotomies Between the Testaments," *Journal of the Evangelical Theological Society* 25, no. 1 (1982): 3-16.

[55]For a brief sketch of the early history of this group, see Ronald T. Clutter, "Dispensational Study Group: An Introduction," *Grace Theological Journal* 10, no. 2 (1989): 123-24.

[56]Blaising and Bock, "Dispensationalism, Israel and the Church," pp. 380-81.

[57]Craig Blaising has offered the most comprehensive articulation of this perspective to date. See, for example, his "Dispensationalism: The Search for Definition"; "The Extent and Varieties of Dispensationalism"; "Changing Patterns in American Dispensational Theology"; "Contemporary Dispensationalism." Robert Saucy describes Progressive Dispensationalism as a revision of "classic" Dispensationalism (*The Case for Progressive Dispensationalism: The Interface Between Dispensational and Non-Dispensational Theology* [Grand Rapids: Zondervan, 1993], pp. 8-9).

[58]For example, Ryrie writes, "Progressives wish to call their teachings 'developments' within dispensationalism, so that they can still call themselves dispensationalists, but they clearly seem to include changes (that is, essential differences from dispensationalism)" (*Dispensa-*

tionalism, p. 70). See also ibid., pp. 69, 162, 167, 178; idem, "Update on Dispensationalism," pp. 18, 97.

[59]For informative presentations and responses by both Progressives and Traditionalists, see Bateman, *Three Central Issues.*

[60]See Charles Ryrie, "Dispensationalism," in Couch, *Dictionary of Premillennial Theology,* pp. 97-98; Paul Enns, *The Moody Handbook of Theology* (Chicago: Moody Press, 1989), pp. 523-24.

[61]For an example of a moderate Ultradispensationalist theology, see Charles F. Baker, *A Dispensational Theology* (Grand Rapids: Grace Bible College Publications, 1971).

[62]For examples of extreme Ultradispensationalist theology, see E. W. Bullinger, *The Apocalypse, or, "The Day of the Lord,"* 3rd ed. (London: Eyre & Spottiswoode, 1935); idem, *Selected Writings* (London: Lamp Press, 1960; reprint, Lafayette, Ind.: Truth for Today Bible Fellowship, 1991); Charles H. Welch, *The Apostle of the Reconciliation, or, The Dispensational Position of the Acts and the Ministry and the Epistles of Paul* (London: F. P. Brininger, 1923; reprint, London: Berean Publishing Trust, 1959).

[63]Spencer, "Dispensationalism," p. 855.

[64]Chafer, *Systematic Theology,* 1:v.

[65]Ibid., 1:viii.

[66]"A Brief History of Dallas Theological Seminary," <http://www.dallasseminary.edu/visitors/about_dts/brief_history.html>.

[67]See, for example, Darby's "Considerations on the Nature and Unity of the Church of Christ" and "On the Apostasy: What Is Succession a Succession Of?" in *The Collected Writings of J. N. Darby,* 1.1:20-35, 112-23.

[68]Chafer, *Systematic Theology,* 1:113.

[69]I admittedly, though without hesitation, make these comments based not on documentable research but on my experience with people and ministries in the Dispensational tradition. Without claiming that I agree with Dispensational theology or that those who affirm it always live up to all the moral and spiritual teachings in Dispensational circles, I have always been impressed with the high personal standards that are set and the seriousness with which they are pursued.

[70]Frank E. Gaebelein, foreword to Ryrie, *Dispensationalism Today,* p. 8; see also Barker, "False Dichotomies," pp. 3-4. This perspective has also been expressed to me in a number of conversations with friends who would identify themselves as Dispensationalists. Cf. the rejection of this view in Dale S. DeWitt, *Dispensational Theology in America During the Twentieth Century* (Grand Rapids: Grace Bible College Publications, 2002), pp. 6-9.

[71]C. I. Scofield, *Rightly Dividing the Word of Truth* (New York: N. P. Scofield, n.d.), p. 6.

[72]Chafer, *Systematic Theology,* 1:21.

[73]Ibid., 1:7.

[74]Charles C. Ryrie, *Basic Theology* (Wheaton, Ill.: Victor, 1986), p. 16.

[75]Chafer, *Systematic Theology,* 1:xxxvii.

[76]Ibid., 1:11.

[77]Blaising, "Dispensationalism: The Search for Definition," p. 21.

[78]Spencer, "Scofield," p. 614.

[79]Cf. Chafer's warnings about twisting or molding Scripture "to make it conform to one's preconceived notions" (*Systematic Theology,* 1:119).

[80]Ryrie, *Dispensationalism,* p. 101.

[81]Ibid., p. 146; see also p. 79; and Elliott E. Johnson, "Theology and Exegesis," in *Basic Theology: Applied,* ed. Wesley Willis et al. (Wheaton, Ill.: Victor, 1995), pp. 57, 59-60.

[82]Blaising, "Dispensationalism: The Search for Definition," pp. 33-34. In their second book, *Progressive Dispensationalism,* Blaising and Bock again devote strategic attention to hermeneutics, with Bock contributing two chapters to this before moving into an exposition of Progressive Dispensational theology.

[83]E. Shuyler English, *A Companion to the New Scofield Reference Bible* (New York: Oxford University Press, 1972), p. 19.

[84]Scofield, introduction to 1909 edition, *Scofield Reference Bible,* rev. ed. (New York: Oxford University Press, 1917), p. iii; and preface to *Scofield Reference Bible,* rev. ed., p. v. See also English, *Companion to the New Scofield Reference Bible,* pp. vii, 19.

[85]Chafer, *Systematic Theology,* 1:36; see also 1:xxx, 29, 114.

[86]Bock identifies this as a matter of concern to both Progressives and Traditionalists ("Hermeneutics of Progressive Dispensationalism," in Bateman, *Three Central Issues,* p. 86).

[87]Scofield, preface to *Scofield Reference Bible,* rev. ed., p. v.

[88]Ryrie, *Dispensationalism,* pp. 93-95, 165.

[89]Elliott Johnson, "Hermeneutics and Dispensationalism," in *Walvoord: A Tribute,* ed. Donald K. Campbell (Chicago: Moody Press, 1982), p. 251.

[90]Blaising, "Dispensationalism: The Search for Definition," p. 33.

[91]Doctrinal Statement of Dallas Theological Seminary, Article 1 (*EARRC,* 1:567).

[92]Thomas Ice identifies two meanings of the term *literal* as employed by Dispensationalists. One use refers to the hermeneutical system as a whole, and Ice identifies this as macroliteralism. The term *literal* can also refer to the determination of whether or not a particular word, phrase or genre is to be interpreted connotatively (figurative) or denotatively (literal), and he identifies this as microliteralism ("Dispensational Hermeneutics," in Willis and Master, *Issues in Dispensationalism,* pp. 32-33). The present discussion deals with "literal" in the first sense, referring to a hermeneutical system.

[93]Donald K. Campbell, "The Church in God's Prophetic Program," in *Essays in Honor of J. Dwight Pentecost,* ed. Stanley D. Toussaint and Charles H. Dyer (Chicago: Moody Press, 1986), p. 154; see also Robert P. Lightner, *Evangelical Theology: A Survey and Review* (Grand Rapids: Baker, 1986), pp. 23-24.

[94]Ryrie, *Dispensationalism,* p. 40; see also p. 80.

[95]Pentecost, *Things to Come,* p. 9; see also Ryrie, *Dispensationalism,* p. 80.

[96]For example, Ryrie, *Dispensationalism,* pp. 80, 82; *Basic Theology,* pp. 110, 114-15. See also Howard P. McKaughan, "The Importance of Context in Biblical Interpretation," in Willis et al., *Basic Theology: Applied,* p. 53.

[97]For example, Darrell L. Bock, "Why I Am a dispensationalist with a Little 'd'," *Journal of the Evangelical Theological Society* 41, no. 3 (1998): 388.

[98]See, for example, Pentecost, *Things to Come,* pp. 12-13, 39-44. Ryrie suggests that literal interpretation "might also be designated 'plain' interpretation so that no one receives the mistaken notion that the literal interpretation rules out figures of speech. Symbols, figures of speech, and types are all interpreted plainly in this method, and they are in no way contrary to literal interpretation" (*Dispensationalism,* pp. 80-81).

[99]Pentecost, *Things to Come,* p. 9; see also Ryrie, *Dispensationalism,* p. 80. Cf. Blaising, "Extent and Varieties of Dispensationalism," p. 27.

[100]Elliott E. Johnson, "A Traditional Dispensational Hermeneutic," in Bateman, *Three Central Issues,* p. 65.

[101]See, for example, Chafer, *Systematic Theology,* 1:115-19; Pentecost, *Things to Come,* pp. 34-44; Ryrie, *Basic Theology,* pp. 114-15.

[102]See McKaughan, "Importance of Context," pp. 46-53; also Chafer, *Systematic Theology,* 1:117; Pentecost, *Things to Come,* p. 36.

[103]Ryrie, *Basic Theology,* p. 114.

[104]Elliott E. Johnson, "Covenants in Traditional Dispensationalism," in Bateman, *Three Central Issues,* p. 123. Cf. Ryrie, *Basic Theology,* p. 17, where he argues, in part based on the progression of revelation, that in formulating doctrine the New Testament "has greater priority" than the Old Testament.

[105]Ryrie, *Dispensationalism,* p. 82; see also pp. 90-91, 101, 147, 158. In the context of talking about progressive revelation, Ryrie writes, "Classic dispensationalism is a result of consistent application of the basic hermeneutical principle of literal, normal, or plain interpretation. No other system of theology can claim this" (ibid., p. 85). More recently, Ryrie reaffirms "consistent literal interpretation" as an "essential" of Dispensationalism ("Update on Dispensationalism," p. 26). See also Ryrie, *Basic Theology,* pp. 113, 115.

[106]Ice, "Dispensational Hermeneutics," pp. 32, 35, 45; Pentecost, *Things to Come,* p. 64; Robert L. Thomas, "The Hermeneutics of Progressive Dispensationalism," *The Master's Seminary Journal* 6, no. 2 (1995): 94; Couch, foreword to Couch, *Dictionary of Premillennial Theology,* p. 9.

[107]For example, Bock, "Why I Am a dispensationalist with a Little 'd'," pp. 388-89; cf. Bateman, "Dispensationalism Yesterday and Today," p. 37. Cf. DeWitt's proposal for "adaptive literalism with stable continuity of meaning" (*Dispensational Theology in America,* pp. 101-31).

[108]Bock, "Why I Am a dispensationalist with a Little 'd'," p. 390. For a more comprehensive presentation of hermeneutics from a Progressive perspective, see Blaising and Bock, *Progressive Dispensationalism,* pp. 57-105.

[109]Bock, "Hermeneutics of Progressive Dispensationalism," p. 89.

[110]Bock, "Why I Am a dispensationalist with a Little 'd'," p. 388.

[111]Craig A. Blaising, "Developing Dispensationalism (Part 2): Development of Dispensationalism by Contemporary Dispensationalists," *Bibliotheca Sacra* 145 (July-September 1988): 255-56.

[112]For example, Saucy, *Case for Progressive Dispensationalism,* p. 8; see also Bateman, "Dispensationalism Yesterday and Today," p. 23. By contrast, Ryrie approvingly cites non-Dispensationalist Clarence Bass's observation (in *Backgrounds to Dispensationalism* [Grand Rapids: Eerdmans, 1960], p. 128) that "the basic elements, and hermeneutical pattern, of Darby's eschatology persist unchanged in contemporary dispensationalism" ("Update on Dispensationalism," p. 17).

[113]See Chafer, *Systematic Theology,* 1:xi-xxxviii.

[114]Ryrie, *Dispensationalism,* pp. 30-40; see also *Dispensationalism Today,* pp. 44-47.

[115]Couch, foreword to *Dictionary of Premillennial Theology,* pp. 9-10.

[116]Willis and Master, *Issues in Dispensationalism,* p. 14.

[117]Blaising, "Extent and Varieties of Dispensationalism," pp. 13-21; see also idem, "Contemporary Dispensationalism," pp. 5-6, 13; "Changing Patterns in American Dispensational Theology," pp. 163-64.

[118]Spencer, "Dispensationalism," p. 854.

[119]I appreciate the assistance of my colleague Dr. M. Daniel Carroll R. in helping me to gain a proper appreciation for the importance of the biblical covenants in Dispensational thought.

[120]Doctrinal Statement of Dallas Theological Seminary, Article 13 (*EARRC,* 1:569); Doctrinal Position of Philadelphia College of the Bible, Article 11 (*EARRC,* 2:389).

[121]Scofield, *Rightly Dividing the Word of Truth,* p. 17.

[122]Chafer, *Systematic Theology,* 1:xiv-xx; see also 4:29-35, 47-53, 127-33.

[123]Ryrie, *Dispensationalism,* pp. 41, 123.

[124]Campbell, "Church in God's Prophetic Program," p. 149.

[125]Saucy, *Case for Progressive Dispensationalism,* p. 221.´

[126]Herbert W. Bateman IV, "Dispensationalism Tomorrow," in Bateman, *Three Central Issues,* p. 308; see also pp. 37-38, 309, 313.

[127]John F. Walvoord, *Israel in Prophecy* (Grand Rapids: Zondervan, 1962), p. 57.

[128]See, for example, Saucy, *Case for Progressive Dispensationalism,* p. 207.

[129]Walvoord, *Israel In Prophecy,* p. 58.

[130]S. Lewis Johnson Jr., "Paul and 'The Israel of God': An Exegetical and Eschatological Case-Study," in Toussaint and Dyer, *Essays in Honor of J. Dwight Pentecost,* p. 192. See also Charles C. Ryrie, *The Ryrie Study Bible* (Chicago: Moody Press, 1978), p. 1778, note on Galatians 6:16; Donald K. Campbell, "Galatians," in *The Bible Knowledge Commentary,* ed. John F. Walvoord and Roy B. Zuck, 2 vols. (Wheaton, Ill.: Victor, 1985), 2:611; Saucy, *Case for Progressive Dispensationalism,* p. 201.

[131]Walvoord, *Israel In Prophecy,* p. 55.

[132]Saucy, *Case for Progressive Dispensationalism,* p. 207.

[133]Walvoord, *Israel in Prophecy,* p. 56.

[134]Ibid., pp. 56-57.

[135]Ibid., p. 58.

[136]John Witmer, "Romans," in Walvoord and Zuck, *Bible Knowledge Commentary,* 2:482.

[137]Scofield, *Scofield Reference Bible,* rev. ed., p. 1204 n. 2 (on Rom 11:1).

[138]Ryrie, *Ryrie Study Bible,* p. 1717, note on Romans 11:1-36.

[139]Ibid.

[140]Craig A. Blaising, "The Kingdom of God in the New Testament," in Blaising and Bock, *Progressive Dispensationalism,* p. 269.

[141]J. Lanier Burns, "The Future of Ethnic Israel in Romans 11," in Blaising and Bock, *Dispensationalism, Israel and the Church,* p. 190.

[142]This analysis is affirmed by a Traditional Dispensationalist, Stanley Toussaint, in "Israel and the Church of a Traditional Dispensationalist," in Bateman, *Three Central Issues,* p. 227.

[143]See ibid., pp. 228-29; also Blaising, "Extent and Varieties of Dispensationalism."

[144]Scofield, *Rightly Dividing the Word of Truth,* p. 9.

[145]Saucy, *Case for Progressive Dispensationalism,* p. 9. See also Blaising, "Extent and Varieties of Dispensationalism," pp. 49-51, 53-54; idem, "Contemporary Dispensationalism," pp. 11-12.

[146]Blaising, "Kingdom of God in the New Testament," p. 267.

[147]Blaising, "Extent and Varieties of Dispensationalism," p. 49.

[148]Saucy, *Case for Progressive Dispensationalism,* p. 210.

[149]See Blaising, "Extent and Varieties of Dispensationalism," p. 49; Bock, "Hermeneutics of Progressive Dispensationalism," p. 98; idem, response to Elliott E. Johnson, "A Traditional Dispensational Hermeneutic," in Bateman, *Three Central Issues,* p. 156; J. Lanier Burns, response to Stanley Toussaint, "Israel and the Church of a Traditional Dispensationalist," in Bateman, *Three Central Issues,* p. 253.

[150]Lewis Sperry Chafer, *Systematic Theology,* ed. John F. Walvoord, abridged ed., 2 vols. (Wheaton, Ill.: Victor, 1988), 2:411.

[151]Johnson, "Covenants in Traditional Dispensationalism," p. 121.

[152]Blaising, "The Fulfillment of the Biblical Covenants Through Jesus Christ," in Blaising and

Bock, *Progressive Dispensationalism,* p. 199.

[153]English, *Companion to the New Scofield Reference Bible,* p. 55.

[154]For example, English, *Companion to the New Scofield Reference Bible,* p. 55; Rick Bowman, "Covenants, The," in Couch, *Dictionary of Premillennial Theology,* p. 72; Pentecost, *Things to Come,* p. 534, idem, "The Biblical Covenants and the Birth Narratives," in Campbell, *Walvoord: A Tribute,* p. 257; Johnson, "Covenants in Traditional Dispensationalism," p. 122.

[155]Pentecost, *Things to Come,* p. 535.

[156]Craig Blaising, "The Structure of the Biblical Covenants: The Covenants Prior to Christ," in Blaising and Bock, *Progressive Dispensationalism,* p. 172.

[157]The delineation of the major covenants varies. For example, Scofield identifies eight covenants: Edenic, Adamic, Noahic, Abrahamic, Mosaic, Palestinian, Davidic, New (*Scofield Reference Bible,* rev. ed. [New York: Oxford University Press, 1917], see notes on Genesis 1:28 and Hebrews 8:8). Bowman identifies six covenants: Noahic, Mosaic, Abrahamic, Palestinian, Davidic, New ("Covenants," p. 73). Pentecost identifies four covenants: Abrahamic, Palestinian, Davidic, New ("Biblical Covenants," p. 257). The covenants found on all lists, including those of Progressive Dispensationalists, are the Abrahamic, Davidic and New.

[158]Chafer, *Systematic Theology,* abridged ed., 2:418.

[159]Johnson, "Covenants in Traditional Dispensationalism," p. 125.

[160]Chafer, *Systematic Theology,* abridged ed., 2:414; see also Blaising, "Structure of the Biblical Covenants," p. 172 (cf. p. 140).

[161]Pentecost, *Things to Come,* p. 534.

[162]Blaising, "Structure of the Biblical Covenants," p. 172; see also p. 135.

[163]Johnson, "Covenants in Traditional Dispensationalism," p. 125; Chafer, *Systematic Theology,* abridged ed., 2:413; Bowman, "Covenants," p. 73; Saucy, *Case for Progressive Dispensationalism,* p. 42.

[164]Johnson, "Covenants in Traditional Dispensationalism," pp. 126-27.

[165]Blaising, "Structure of the Biblical Covenants," p. 140. Of particular interest among these subsequent covenants are the Mosaic, Davidic and New Covenants (see ibid., pp. 140-73).

[166]Ibid., p. 135.

[167]Ibid., pp. 132-33.

[168]Blaising, "Fulfillment of the Biblical Covenants," p. 193.

[169]Saucy, *Case for Progressive Dispensationalism,* p. 58.

[170]Blaising, "Structure of the Biblical Covenants," pp. 193-94.

[171]Arnold G. Fruchtenbaum, "Davidic Covenant," in Couch, *Dictionary of Premillennial Theology,* p. 87. Fruchtenbaum focuses specifically on amplification of the "seed" aspect of the Abrahamic Covenant. See also Eugene H. Merrill, "2 Samuel," in Walvoord and Zuck, *Bible Knowledge Commentary,* 1:464; Saucy, *Case for Progressive Dispensationalism,* p. 63.

[172]Bowman, "Covenants," p. 73; see also Pentecost, "Biblical Covenants," p. 260; Fruchtenbaum, "Davidic Covenant," pp. 86-87.

[173]Blaising, "Structure of the Biblical Covenants," p. 166.

[174]Johnson, "Covenants in Traditional Dispensationalism," p. 130.

[175]Blaising, "Structure of the Biblical Covenants," p. 175.

[176]Saucy, *Case for Progressive Dispensationalism,* p. 80.

[177]Hugh P. Ross, "Psalms," in Walvoord and Zuck, *Bible Knowledge Commentary,* 1:858.

[178]Saucy, *Case for Progressive Dispensationalism,* p. 80.

[179]Chafer, *Systematic Theology,* 7:98-99; also 4:325-28. See also Pentecost, *Things to Come,* p. 124; "early" Ryrie in *The Basis of the Premillennial Faith* (Neptune, N.J.: Loizeaux, 1953), pp.

115-25. See Matthew 26:28; Mark 14:24; Luke 22:20; Hebrews 8:6; 9:15; 10:29; 13:20.

[180]Pentecost, *Things to Come,* p. 123. See also Rodney Decker, "New Covenant, Dispensational Views of the," in Couch, *Dictionary of Premillennial Theology,* pp. 280-83.

[181]Charles H. Dyer, "Jeremiah," in Walvoord and Zuck, *Bible Knowledge Commentary,* 1:1172. Dyer here cites the following New Testament passages with respect to the New Covenant: 2 Corinthians 3:6; Hebrews 8:6-13; 9:15; 12:22-24. See also Bowman, "Covenants," p. 73.

[182]Saucy, *Case for Progressive Dispensationalism,* p. 139.

[183]Blaising, "Structure of the Biblical Covenants," pp. 155-59.

[184]Bateman, "Dispensationalism Tomorrow," p. 308.

Chapter 9: The Spirit of Continuity

[1]Vinson Synan, "Pentecostalism: Varieties and Contributions," *Pneuma* 9, no. 1 (1987): 32.

[2]Edith Blumhofer sheds further light on "how multifaceted Pentecostal backgrounds are," while stressing the "restorationist yearning" (*Restoring the Faith: The Assemblies of God, Pentecostalism, and American Culture* [Urbana: University of Illinois Press, 1993], pp. 11-42). See also Iain MacRobert, *The Black Roots and White Racism of Early Pentecostalism in the USA* (New York: St. Martin's Press, 1988); Donald Dayton, *Theological Roots of Pentecostalism* (Metuchen, N.J.: Scarecrow, 1987; Grand Rapids: Zondervan, 1987), pp. 36-38; Walter J. Hollenweger, *Pentecostalism: Origins and Developments Worldwide* (Peabody, Mass.: Hendrickson, 1997), p. 202.

[3]Stanley M. Burgess, "Cutting the Taproot: The Modern Pentecostal Movement and Its Traditions," in *Spirit and Renewal: Essays in Honor of J. Rodman William,* ed. Mark W. Wilson, Journal of Pentecostal Theology Supplement Series 5 (Sheffield, U.K.: Sheffield Academic Press), p. 57; see also Russell P. Spittler, "Theological Style Among Pentecostals and Charismatics," in *Doing Theology in Today's World,* ed. John D. Woodbridge and Thomas E. McComiskey (Grand Rapids: Zondervan, 1991), p. 296. Vinson Synan also notes the significance of nineteenth century "attempts . . . to restore tongues and other gifts of the Spirit to the prominent place they once held in the early church," most notably the work of Edward Irving, of London, England ("The Role of Tongues as Initial Evidence," in Wilson, *Spirit and Renewal,* p. 70; cf. Dayton, *Theological Roots,* p. 167).

[4]Vinson Synan, *The Holiness-Pentecostal Movement in the United States* (Grand Rapids: Eerdmans, 1971), p. 217. See also Gordon Strachan, "Theological and Cultural Origins of the Nineteenth Century Pentecostal Movement," in *Essays on Apostolic Themes,* ed. Paul Elbert (Peabody, Mass.: Hendrickson, 1985), pp. 144-57. In addition to the Wesleyan and Keswick movements described below, another important early manifestation was the Welsh revival of 1904.

[5]Vinson Synan, *The Holiness-Pentecostal Tradition: Charismatic Movements in the Twentieth Century* (Grand Rapids: Eerdmans, 1997), p. 106.

[6]Vinson Synan, *The Century of the Holy Spirit: 100 Years of Pentecostal and Charismatic Renewal, 1901-2001* (Nashville: Thomas Nelson, 2001), pp. 2-3.

[7]See Melvin E. Dieter, *The Holiness Revival of the Nineteenth Century,* 2nd ed., Studies in Evangelicalism 1 (Lanham, Md.: Scarecrow, 1996), pp. 2-5, 15-128.

[8]See William A. Raws, *Monitoring the Movement of God: A History of America's Keswick* (Whiting, N.J.: America's Keswick, 2000); John C. Pollock, *The Keswick Story* (Chicago: Moody Press, 1964); Charles E. Jones, *A Guide to the Study of the Pentecostal Movement,* 2 vols., ATLA Bibliography Series 6 (Metuchen, N.J.: Scarecrow, 1983), 1:251-52.

[9]Steven J. Land, *Pentecostal Spirituality: A Passion for the Kingdom,* Journal of Pentecostal Theology Supplement Series 1 (Sheffield, U.K.: Sheffield Academic Press, 1993), p. 19.

[10]Synan, *Century of the Holy Spirit,* pp. 34, 99.

[11]Other important early revivals include those in Cherokee County, North Carolina (1890s); Zion City, Illinois (1904); and Houston, Texas (1905). See David D. Bundy, "Bibliography and Historiography of Pentecostalism in the United States," in *The New International Dictionary of Pentecostal and Charismatic Movements,* ed. Stanley M. Burgess and Eduard M. Van der Maas, rev. ed. (Grand Rapids: Zondervan, 2000), pp. 382-417.

[12]Synan, *Holiness-Pentecostal Tradition,* p. 91.

[13]The term "glossolalia" is derived from two Greek words: *glossa* ("tongue") and *lalia* ("talking").

[14]Synan, *Holiness-Pentecostal Tradition,* p. 91.

[15]Roger Stronstad says that Parham is "the father of Pentecostalism, Topeka, Kansas the locus of Pentecostalism, and Agnes Ozman the first Pentecostal" ("Trends in Pentecostal Hermeneutics," *Paraclete* 22, no. 3 [1988]: 1).

[16]Synan, *Holiness-Pentecostal Tradition,* pp. 93-94.

[17]Blumhofer, *Restoring the Faith,* p. 2. Roman Catholic ecumenical scholar Kilian McDonnell coined the term "classical Pentecostalism" to refer to "that which was present in the Pentecostal churches founded since 1900 and to distinguish it from charismatic renewal in the historic churches" (Cecil M. Robeck, "McDonnell, Kilian," in Burgess and Van der Maas, *New International Dictionary of Pentecostal and Charismatic Movements,* p. 853).

[18]Synan, *Holiness-Pentecostal Tradition,* p. 165; Stronstad, "Trends in Pentecostal Hermeneutics," p. 1.

[19]Blumhofer, *Restoring the Faith,* p. 44.

[20]William W. Menzies, "The Methodology of Pentecostal Theology: An Essay on Hermeneutics," in Elbert, *Essays on Apostolic Themes,* p. 2; see also Synan, "Role of Tongues," p. 71.

[21]Walter J. Hollenweger, foreword to MacRobert, *Black Roots and White Racism,* p. xiii.

[22]For an analysis of opposition to the revival, see Synan, *Century of the Holy Spirit,* pp. 61-63.

[23]Synan, *Holiness-Pentecostal Tradition,* p. 105; see also Blumhofer, *Restoring the Faith,* pp. 56-62.

[24]Douglas Jacobsen, *Thinking in the Spirit: Theology of the Early Pentecostal Movement* (Bloomington: University of Indiana Press, 2003), p. 24.

[25]Synan, *Holiness-Pentecostal Tradition,* pp. 111-12.

[26]Blumhofer, *Restoring the Faith,* pp. 71-84; Synan, *Holiness-Pentecostal Tradition,* pp. 118-28.

[27]See Gayraud S. Wilmore, *Black Religion and Black Radicalism: An Interpretation of the Religious History of African Americans,* 3rd ed. (Maryknoll, N.Y.: Orbis, 1998), pp. 182-83. Arlene M. Sánchez Walsh indicates that she "took note of the socioeconomic reality in post-Azusa Street Pentecostalism and found that its claims to racial utopia were baseless" (*Latino Pentecostal Identity: Evangelical Faith, Self, and Society* [New York: Columbia University Press, 2003], p. 1).

[28]MacRobert, *Black Roots and White Racism,* pp. 77-89.

[29]For an exploration of the interrelationship between the racial and theological divisions, see ibid., pp. 60-77.

[30]Robert M. Anderson, *Vision of the Disinherited: The Making of American Pentecostalism* (New York: Oxford University Press, 1979), pp. 153-75.

[31]On Durham and the Finished Work controversy, see Blumhofer, *Restoring the Faith,* pp. 80-81, 125; Synan, *Holiness-Pentecostal Tradition,* pp. 150-56.

[32]Blumhofer, *Restoring the Faith,* pp. 126-27. Synan interprets the Assemblies of God position a bit differently, suggesting that their doctrinal formulation "became the model of the subsequent 'finished work' denominations that coalesced after 1914" (*Holiness-Pentecostal Tradition,* p. 155).

[33]Synan, *Holiness-Pentecostal Tradition,* p. 165.

[34]Ibid., p. 159.

[35]The complete text of the 1916 version of the Statement of Fundamental Truths is reproduced in William W. Menzies and Stanley M. Horton, *Bible Doctrines: A Pentecostal Perspective* (Springfield, Mo.: Logion, 1993), pp. 263-66.

[36]Synan, *Holiness-Pentecostal Tradition,* p. 160.

[37]The present discussion is concerned primarily with theological divisions. However, associated with theological divisions over Trinitarian and "Oneness" doctrines was another type of division that was a significant factor in the history of Pentecostalism: racial division, primarily between blacks and whites. See Anderson, *Vision of the Disinherited,* pp. 176-94; Synan, *Holiness-Pentecostal Tradition,* pp. 167-86.

[38]Synan, *Holiness-Pentecostal Tradition,* p. 165.

[39]Spittler, "Theological Style," p. 296. Blumhofer offers a similar description, referring to Assemblies of God theology of the 1920s and 1930s as "fundamentalism with a difference" (*Restoring the Faith,* p. 5).

[40]Jacobsen observes, "Pentecostals may have had a common point of contact in the Azusa revival, but that did not mean they all experienced the Azusa revival in the same way or saw eye to eye on all the details (or even all the core beliefs) of Pentecostal faith" (*Thinking in the Spirit,* p. 10).

[41]Spittler, "Theological Style," p. 296.

[42]W. W. Menzies is referring to the Assemblies of God in particular, but these terms may also legitimately be applied to Pentecostalism in general. See William W. Menzies, *Anointed to Serve: The Story of the Assemblies of God* (Springfield, Mo.: Gospel Publishing House, 1971).

[43]Douglas Jacobsen, "Knowing the Doctrines of Pentecostals: The Scholastic Theology of the Assemblies of God, 1930-55," in *Pentecostal Currents in American Protestantism,* ed. Edith L. Blumhofer, Russell P. Spittler and Grant Wacker (Urbana: University of Illinois Press, 1999), p. 92.

[44]The present chapter focuses on Pentecostalism. The two movements, Pentecostalism and the Charismatic movement, are related yet distinct. Recognition of this distinction means that here I will not appeal to, for example, J. Rodman Williams's *Renewal Theology: Systematic Theology from a Charismatic Perspective,* 2 vols. (Grand Rapids: Zondervan, 1988-1990). There are extensive bodies of literature specifically on both the Charismatic movement and the relationship between Pentecostalism and the Charismatic movement. For an excellent guide to this research, see Charles E. Jones, *The Charismatic Movement: A Guide to the Study of Neo-Pentecostalism, with an Emphasis on Anglo-American Sources,* ATLA Bibliography Series 30, 2 vols. (Metuchen, N.J.: Scarecrow, 1995).

[45]See Blumhofer, *Restoring the Faith,* pp. 222-38; Cecil M. Robeck Jr., "Pentecostals and Ecumenism in a Pluralistic World," in *The Globalization of Pentecostalism: A Religion Made to Travel,* ed. Murray W. Dempster, Byron D. Klaus and Douglas Petersen (Oxford: Regnum, 1999), pp. 338-62; David du Plessis and Bob Slosser, *A Man Called Mr. Pentecost* (South Plainfield, N.J.: Bridge, 1977).

[46]The Vineyard movement, which emerged from the ministry of Rev. John Wimber in the 1980s, is regarded by many as the first Charismatic denomination.

[47]Sánchez Walsh, *Latino Pentecostal Identity,* p. 20.

[48]David G. Roebuck and Karen C. Mundy, "Women, Culture, and Post–World War Two Pentecostalism," in *The Spirit and the Mind: Essays in Informed Pentecostalism,* ed. Terry L. Cross and Emerson B. Powery (Lanham, Md.: University Press of America, 2000), p. 194.

[49]Some observers point to the appointment of John Ashcroft as U.S. attorney general as a quintessential symbol of this shift in Pentecostalism's social location.

[50]See Peter D. Hocken, "A Charismatic View on the Distinctiveness of Pentecostalism," in *Pentecostalism in Context: Essays in Honour of William W. Menzies,* ed. Wonsuk Ma and Robert P. Menzies, Journal of Pentecostal Theology Supplement Series 11 (Sheffield, U.K.: Sheffield Academic Press, 1997), p. 101; Hollenweger, *Pentecostalism,* p. 19.

[51]Pentecostal scholars are often cited as the major influence in this phenomenon, the suggestion being that in their pursuit of academic respectability they have adopted and advanced non-Pentecostal views. Peter Hocken seeks to revise this analysis, suggesting that "a major reason for the evangelicalization of the Pentecostals were evangelists and missionaries, not scholars; and that when they needed to formulate their doctrine, they fell back on evangelical formulations" ("Charismatic View," p. 101).

[52]The Toronto revival began at what was then a congregation of the Vineyard movement, and it continued under the leadership of John Arnott. The revival in Pensacola began in 1995 at the Brownsville Assembly of God under the leadership of pastor John Kilpatrick and evangelist Steve Hill (Synan, *Century of the Holy Spirit,* p. 12). At the same time, some Pentecostal scholars are offering friendly critique and pointing to signs of increasing "spiritual fatigue" and theological dissatisfaction within the tradition. See, for example, Simon Chan, *Pentecostal Theology and the Christian Spiritual Tradition,* Journal of Pentecostal Theology Supplement Series 21 (Sheffield, U.K.: Sheffield Academic Press, 2000), pp. 8-11; Blumhofer, *Restoring the Faith,* pp. 264-74; William W. Menzies and Robert P. Menzies, *Spirit and Power: Foundations of Pentecostal Experience* (Grand Rapid: Zondervan, 2000), p. 9.

[53]J. Gordon Melton, ed., *Encyclopedia of American Religions,* 7th ed. (Detroit: Gale Research, 2003), pp. 433-528.

[54]Jones indicates that the small, fringe "signs-following" groups (e.g., groups that practice snake handling or the drinking of poison) generally affirm the Holiness Pentecostal viewpoint (*Study of the Pentecostal Movement,* 1:406-9).

[55]Cecil M. Robeck, "Pentecostal Churches," in *New 20th-Century Encyclopedia of Religious Knowledge,* ed. J. D. Douglas, 2nd ed. (Grand Rapids: Baker, 1991), p. 646.

[56]For a brief description of reasons for using the Assemblies of God to illustrate the larger Pentecostal movement, see Blumhofer, *Restoring the Faith,* pp. 2, 264-65. See also Synan, *Century of the Holy Spirit,* p. 124.

[57]Myer Pearlman, *Knowing the Doctrines of the Bible* (Springfield, Mo.: Gospel Publishing House, 1937), p. ix. He also indicates the importance of doctrinal knowledge for rendering an "answer" to people's questions about "existence," "safeguard[ing] against error" and providing a pedagogical resource (ibid., pp. x-xi).

[58]Furthermore, in 1979, the Assemblies of God established a permanent Commission on Doctrinal Purity, in part out of a belief that "careful attention should be given to the prevention of proliferation of unscriptural teachings in [the] Fellowship" (*Minutes of the Thirty-Eighth General Assembly of the Assemblies of God* [Springfield, Mo.: Assemblies of God, 1979], p. 26). For a Oneness Pentecostal perspective, see Nathaniel A. Urshan, "The Importance of Truth" and "Why a Symposium on Doctrinal Truths," in *Symposium on Oneness Pentecostalism,* by Nathaniel A. Urshan et al. (Hazelwood, Mo.: Word Aflame, 1990), pp. 11-18, 21-32.

[59]Raymond M. Pruitt, *Fundamentals of the Faith* (Cleveland: White Wing, 1981), p. 2.

[60]Gary B. McGee, "Historical Background," in *Systematic Theology: A Pentecostal Perspective,* ed. Stanley M. Horton (Springfield, Mo.: Logion, 1994), p. 21. McGee may here be following

Russell Spittler, "Implicit Values in Pentecostal Missions," *Missiology: An International Review* 16, no. 4 (1988): 409-24; idem, "Theological Style," p. 294.

[61]Spittler, "Theological Style," p. 296.

[62]Donald N. Bowdle, "Informed Pentecostalism: An Alternative Paradigm," in Cross and Powery, *The Spirit and the Mind,* pp. 9-19.

[63]Land, *Pentecostal Spirituality,* p. 29.

[64]These authors and works are cited here simply as illustrative of a much larger body of literature produced by Pentecostal scholars. See the bibliographies in these works, as well as the sources cited in the present chapter.

[65]This analysis is informed by French L. Arrington's identification of three periods in the development of Pentecostal hermeneutics: definition, defense and reflection ("Hermeneutics, Historical Perspectives on Pentecostal and Charismatic," in *Dictionary of Pentecostal and Charismatic Movements,* ed. Stanley M. Burgess and Gary B. McGee [Grand Rapids: Regency Reference Library, 1988], pp. 376-89; cf. Frank D. Macchia, "Theology, Pentecostal," in Burgess and Van der Maas, *New International Dictionary of Pentecostal and Charismatic Movements,* pp. 1121-23).

[66]Representative of this period are works such as Pearlman, *Knowing the Doctrines of the Bible;* Ernest S. Williams, *Systematic Theology,* 3 vols. (Springfield, Mo.: Gospel Publishing House, 1953); P. C. Nelson, *Bible Doctrines,* rev. ed. (Springfield, Mo.: Gospel Publishing House, 1948). A key example of the early definition of doctrine is the Assemblies of God's Statement of Fundamental Truths (1916). Since the adoption of this document, there has been a lineage of theology texts that are structured in accord with the articles of the Statement, including Nelson, *Bible Doctrines;* William W. Menzies, *Understanding Our Doctrine* (Springfield, Mo.: Gospel Publishing House, 1980); and Menzies' book as revised and expanded by Stanley M. Horton (*Bible Doctrines: A Pentecostal Perspective*).

[67]For example, Williams, *Systematic Theology,* 2:157-211, and corresponding notes.

[68]Roger Stronstad, "Pentecostal Hermeneutics: A Review Essay of Gordon D. Fee, *Gospel and Spirit,*" *Pneuma* 15, no. 2 (1993): 219. A recent example of this defensiveness is John W. Wyckoff's chapter "The Baptism in the Holy Spirit" in Horton, *Systematic Theology,* pp. 423-55.

[69]For example, Simon Chan, *Spiritual Theology: A Systematic Study of the Christian Life* (Downers Grove, Ill.: InterVarsity Press, 1998); Land, *Pentecostal Spirituality;* Menzies, "Methodology of Pentecostal Theology"; Howard M. Ervin, "Hermeneutics: A Pentecostal Option," in Elbert, *Essays on Apostolic Themes,* pp. 23-35; Timothy B. Cargal, "Beyond the Fundamentalist-Modernist Controversy: Pentecostals and Hermeneutics in a Postmodern Age," *Pneuma* 15, no. 2 (1993): 163-87; Richard D. Israel, Daniel E. Albrecht and Randal G. McNally, "Pentecostals and Hermeneutics: Texts, Rituals and Community," *Pneuma* 15, no. 2 (1993): 137-61; Mark D. McLean, "Toward a Pentecostal Hermeneutic," *Pneuma* 16, no. 2 (1994): 35-56; Roger Stronstad, "Pentecostal Experience and Hermeneutics," *Paraclete* 26, no. 1 (1992): 14-30; idem, "Trends in Pentecostal Hermeneutics"; Arden C. Autry, "Dimensions of Hermeneutics in Pentecostal Focus," *Journal of Pentecostal Theology* 3 (1993): 29-50; Kenneth J. Archer, "Pentecostal Hermeneutics: Retrospect and Prospect," *Journal of Pentecostal Theology* 8, no. 2 (1996): 63-81; Veli-Matti Kärkkäinen, "Pentecostal Hermeneutics in the Making: On the Way from Fundamentalism to Postmodernism," *Journal of the European Pentecostal Theological Association* 18 (1998): 76-115; Macchia, "Theology, Pentecostal," including the bibliography (pp. 1140-41).

[70]James L. Hennesy, foreword to *An Introduction to Theology: A Classical Pentecostal Perspective,* ed. John R. Higgins, Michael L. Dusing and Frank D. Tallman (Dubuque, Iowa: Kendall Hunt, 1993), p. ix.

[71]Williams, *Systematic Theology*, 3:57.

[72]Menzies, "Methodology of Pentecostal Theology," p. 4.

[73]Given the more "popular" character of most Pentecostal theology texts published before the 1980s, it is not surprising that they do not include discussions of methodology. In his *Systematic Theology* (1953), E. S. Williams does include a brief introductory chapter that features some discussion of methodologically related matters. Yet, even many of the more recent, more substantial texts (e.g., Guy P. Duffield and Nathaniel M. Van Cleave, *Foundations of Pentecostal Theology* [Los Angeles: L.I.F.E. Bible College, 1983]) do not include a chapter dedicated to methodological issues. There is a consideration of methodological issues in James H. Railey Jr. and Benny C. Aker, "Theological Foundations," in Horton, *Systematic Theology*, pp. 39-60.

[74]Railey and Aker, "Theological Foundations," p. 42. They suggest a fivefold typology of theological systems, based on the system's basis of authority. Three "external" forms of authority are "canonical" (the Bible), "theological" (tradition) and "ecclesiastical" (the church); two "internal" forms of authority are "experience" and "reason."

[75]French L. Arrington, "The Use of the Bible by Pentecostals," *Pneuma* 16, no. 1 (1994): 101.

[76]Pearlman, *Knowing the Doctrines*, pp. xii, xi.

[77]Railey and Aker, "Theological Foundations," p. 46.

[78]Spittler, "Theological Style," p. 297. Spittler also observes that biblical studies and exegesis, rather than systematic theology, have proven to be the disciplines where Pentecostal scholars have made the greatest early advances with respect to doctoral studies and scholarly publications (ibid., pp. 300-301).

[79]Chan, *Spiritual Theology*, p. 10.

[80]In a passage that frequently has been cited and commented on by Pentecostal scholars, Gordon Fee says, "In general the Pentecostals' experience has preceded their hermeneutics. In a sense, the Pentecostal tends to exegete his experience" ("Hermeneutics and Historical Precedent—A Major Problem in Pentecostal Hermeneutics," in *Perspectives on the New Pentecostalism,* ed. Russell P. Spittler [Grand Rapids: Baker, 1976], p. 122).

[81]Chan, *Spiritual Theology*, p. 71. See also Menzies and Menzies, *Spirit and Power*, p. 209; Jacobsen, *Thinking in the Spirit*, pp. 3-5.

[82]*Systematic Theology*, 3:39; see also Nelson, *Bible Doctrines*, p. 88.

[83]Railey and Aker, "Theological Foundations," p. 59.

[84]Duffield and Van Cleave, *Foundations of Pentecostal Theology*, p. 315.

[85]Ibid., p. 27.

[86]McGee, "Historical Background," p. 25.

[87]Menzies and Horton, *Bible Doctrines*, p. 205.

[88]John R. Higgins, "God's Inspired Word," in Horton, *Systematic Theology*, p. 83; see also Railey and Aker, "Theological Foundations," p. 40.

[89]See Burgess, "Cutting the Taproot," p. 64. More recently, many Pentecostal theologians (e.g., Railey and Aken, "Theological Foundations," pp. 45-46) have been much more open to self-consciously drawing upon reason and tradition in doing theology.

[90]Blumhofer, *Restoring the Faith*, pp. 13-14; and Chan, *Pentecostal Theology*, p. 22.

[91]Yet the Statement of Fundamental Truths has often been looked to for determining and ordering the loci of theology.

[92]Stronstad, "Trends in Pentecostal Hermeneutics," p. 3. Despite the fact that there was essentially no conscious reflection on or about the hermeneutic, the existence and importance of the hermeneutic cannot be denied. As Stronstad goes on to note, "This pragmatic hermeneutic

became the bulwark of Pentecostal apologetics and the pillar of classical Pentecostalism which . . . remained inviolate until recently."

[93]Gerald T. Sheppard, "Pentecostals and the Hermeneutics of Dispensationalism: The Anatomy of an Uneasy Relationship," *Pneuma* 6, no. 2 (1984): 22. See also Wyckoff, "Baptism in the Holy Spirit," pp. 435-36; Spittler, "Theological Style," p. 312.

[94]Duffield and Van Cleave, *Foundations of Pentecostal Theology,* p. 544. The context of their observation is a discussion of the interpretation of biblical prophecy in particular; however, their words provide an apt description of the classical Pentecostal perspective on interpretation in general.

[95]Arrington, "Hermeneutics, Historical Perspectives," p. 382a.

[96]Arrington, "Use of the Bible," p. 104.

[97]Railey and Aker, "Theological Foundations," p. 39.

[98]Arrington, "Hermeneutics, Historical Perspectives," p. 382a.

[99]Gordon L. Anderson, "Pentecostal Hermeneutics: Part II," *Paraclete* 28, no. 2 (1994): 21; see also Matthew S. Clark et al., *What Is Distinctive About Pentecostal Theology?* (Pretoria: University of South Africa, 1989), p. 28. Some Pentecostals press the continuity back beyond the time of the resurrection through the entirety of the Old Testament.

[100]Stronstad, "Trends in Pentecostal Hermeneutics," pp. 2-4.

[101]Recently, some Pentecostal scholars appeal not to the principle of continuity, but to analyses of the book of Acts that they believe demonstrate that Luke's purposes were not only historical but also theological. Noteworthy in this regard is Roger Stronstad, *The Charismatic Theology of St. Luke* (Peabody, Mass.: Hendrickson, 1984).

[102]Menzies and Menzies, *Spirit and Power,* pp. 43, 49-61.

[103]Cargal, "Fundamentalist-Modernist Controversy," p. 185.

[104]David R. Nichols, "The Search for a Pentecostal Structure in Systematic Theology," *Pneuma* 16, no. 2 (1994): 57.

[105]Cargal, "Fundamentalist-Modernist Controversy," p. 182.

[106]For example, Higgins, Dusing and Tallman set forth what they refer to as a "Pentecostal-Evangelical" theology, attempting to reflect both "a contemporary Evangelical position and a classical Pentecostal perspective" (*Introduction to Theology,* p. xi).

[107]Nichols, "Search for a Pentecostal Structure," p. 57.

[108]McLean, "Toward a Pentecostal Hermeneutic," p. 37; see also p. 50.

[109]For example, Israel, Albrecht and McNally, "Pentecostals and Hermeneutics," p. 161.

[110]For example, Cargal, "Fundamentalist-Modernist Controversy"; Nichols, "Search for a Pentecostal Structure"; Stronstad, "Pentecostal Experience and Hermeneutics"; Sheppard, "Pentecostals and the Hermeneutics of Dispensationalism."

[111]Spittler, "Theological Style," p. 294.

[112]With some variations, this observation is made by a number of Pentecostal scholars (e.g., Synan, *Holiness-Pentecostal Movement,* p. 217; Railey and Aker, "Theological Foundations," p. 50; Higgins, Dushing and Tallman, *Introduction to Theology,* p. 107). A good classical illustration of these Wesleyan-Arminian sympathies is found in E. S. Williams's *Systematic Theology,* where he does not hesitate to spar with John Calvin and approvingly cite John Wesley and John Miley.

[113]Dayton, *Theological Roots,* p. 20.

[114]See Grant Wacker, "Bibliography and Historiography of Pentecostalism," in Burgess and McGee, *Dictionary of Pentecostal and Charismatic Movements,* p. 72b; Dayton, *Theological Roots,* pp. 20-22, 173. The "fourfold" imagery is incorporated into the name of the church

that emerged from the ministry of Aimee Semple McPherson (1890-1994), the International Church of the Foursquare Gospel.

[115]Cf. William Faupel's cautions about "reductionism" in identifying the distinctives of Pentecostalism ("The Function of 'Models' in the Interpretation of Pentecostal Thought," *Pneuma* 2, no. 1 [1980]: 71).

[116]On the difficulties of Pentecostal theology's dependence upon another system of premillennial theology, see Sheppard, "Pentecostals and the Hermeneutics of Dispensationalism."

[117]Robert P. Menzies, "Spirit-Baptism and Spiritual Gifts," in Ma and Menzies, *Pentecostalism in Context*, p. 48.

[118]Wacker, "Bibliography and Historiography," p. 73a. It should be noted that there are scholars outside the Pentecostal tradition who argue that eschatology constitutes "the integrating core of the Pentecostal message" (see Burgess, "Cutting the Taproot," p. 60 n. 6).

[119]Arrington suggests that the "two primary Pentecostal doctrines" are baptism in the Holy Spirit occurring subsequent to conversion, and tongues as the initial evidence of this experience ("Hermeneutics, Historical Perspectives," p. 384b). Stronstad agrees with this, adding a third: "the conviction that contemporary experience should be identical to apostolic Christianity" ("Trends in Pentecostal Hermeneutics," p. 2).

[120]In this discussion, baptism "of" the Holy Spirit refers to the work of the Spirit in conversion, while baptism "in" or "with" the Holy Spirit refers to a subsequent work (see Higgins, Dusing and Tallman, *Introduction to Theology*, p. 144). Other phrases that are more or less synonymous with "baptism in the Holy Spirit" include references to being filled with the Holy Spirit, receiving the Spirit, the Spirit being poured out, the Spirit falling upon someone, and the Spirit coming upon someone (see Wyckoff, "Baptism in the Holy Spirit," pp. 426-27).

[121]Synan, "Pentecostalism: Varieties and Contributions," p. 32.

[122]Pearlman, *Knowing the Doctrines*, p. 277; see also Mark D. McLean, "The Holy Spirit," in Horton, *Systematic Theology*, p. 375. The first sentence of Wyckoff's chapter on baptism in the Holy Spirit, in *Systematic Theology* edited by Horton, is "Many systematic theology works do not include a chapter specifically on the subject of the baptism in the Holy Spirit" ("Baptism in the Holy Spirit," p. 423).

[123]Menzies, "Methodology of Pentecostal Theology," p. 1; Donald R. Wheelock, "Spirit Baptism in American Pentecostal Thought" (Ph.D. diss., Emory University, 1983), p. 167.

[124]Wyckoff, "Baptism in the Holy Spirit," p. 454.

[125]Chan, *Pentecostal Theology*, p. 13.

[126]Nelson, *Bible Doctrines*, p. 72; see also pp. 91-92.

[127]Higgins, Dusing and Tallman, *Introduction to Theology*, p. 157. See also Menzies, "Methodology of Pentecostal Theology," p. 2; Wheelock, "Spirit Baptism," pp. 155, 168; Spittler, "Theological Style," p. 293. Article 5 of the Assemblies of God's Statement of Fundamental Truths reads, "All believers are entitled to and should ardently expect and earnestly seek the promise of the Father, the baptism in the Holy Ghost and fire, according to the command of our Lord Jesus Christ. . . . This experience is distinct from and subsequent to the experience of the new birth (Acts 8:12-17; 10:44-46; 11:14-16; 15:7-95)." *Minutes of the Forty-fifth General Assembly of the Assemblies of God* (Springfield: Assemblies of God, 1993), p. 129.

[128]Higgins, Dusing and Tallman, *Introduction to Theology*, p. 144. See also Pearlman, *Knowing the Doctrines*, pp. 310, 312-13; Duffield and Van Cleave, *Foundations of Pentecostal Theology*, p. 307; Menzies and Horton, *Bible Doctrines*, p. 124.

[129]Menzies and Horton, *Bible Doctrines*, p. 124.

[130]Higgins, Dusing and Tallman, *Introduction to Theology*, pp. 157, 144.

[131]Williams, *Systematic Theology,* 3:47.

[132]Menzies and Horton, *Bible Doctrines,* p. 123; Wyckoff, "Baptism in the Holy Spirit," pp. 447-49; Duffield and Van Cleave, *Foundations of Pentecostal Theology,* p. 308; Williams, *Systematic Theology,* 3:47.

[133]Pruitt, *Fundamentals of the Faith,* p. 293.

[134]Wyckoff, "Baptism in the Holy Spirit," p. 453. Some Pentecostal theologians do elaborate on the prerequisites or conditions for receiving the baptism, describing an "active, obedient faith" (Menzies and Horton, *Bible Doctrines,* p. 130), or identifying a list of "conditions" (e.g., prayer, yielding, water baptism, deep sense of need) that ordinarily precede the baptism (Wyckoff, "Baptism in the Holy Spirit," p. 451; Duffield and Van Cleave, *Foundations of Pentecostal Theology,* pp. 313-14).

[135]Duffield and Van Cleave, *Foundations of Pentecostal Theology,* p. 313.

[136]McLean, "Toward a Pentecostal Hermeneutic," p. 37; see also p. 50.

[137]McLean, "The Holy Spirit," p. 389 n. 29.

[138]Pearlman, *Knowing the Doctrines,* p. 310.

[139]Duffield and Van Cleave, *Foundations of Pentecostal Theology,* p. 277.

[140]Statement of Fundamental Truths, Article 7 (*MGAAG,* p. 129).

[141]For example, Wyckoff, "Baptism in the Holy Spirit," p. 431.

[142]Menzies and Horton, *Bible Doctrines,* p. 127. Wyckoff suggests, "The Old Testament and the Gospels prophesy concerning it and look forward to it; the Epistles assume the experience and therefore only occasionally refer to it indirectly" ("Baptism in the Holy Spirit," p. 428). See also Pearlman, *Knowing the Doctrines,* p. 313.

[143]Arrington, "Hermeneutics, Historical Perspectives," p. 384b.

[144]Ibid., p. 385a; cf. Wyckoff, "Baptism in the Holy Spirit," p. 430.

[145]Higgins, Dusing and Tallman, *Introduction to Theology,* p. 146. They state that this interpretation is indicated by the "use of the verb *[symplēraō]* as a present passive infinitive with *ento* [*sic*] (when)," which usage is "peculiar to Luke in order to designate the arriving of a particular period of point of time."

[146]Ibid., p. 153.

[147]Ibid., p. 149.

[148]Menzies, "Methodology of Pentecostal Theology," p. 2; see also Synan, "Pentecostalism: Varieties and Contributions," p. 32. Article 8 of the Assemblies of God's Statement of Fundamental Truths reads, "The baptism of believers in the Holy Ghost is witnessed by the initial physical sign of speaking with other tongues as the Spirit of God gives them utterance (Acts 2:4)" (*MGAAG,* p. 130). Synan observes, "While some charismatics are coming closer to a near initial evidence position, some Pentecostals are wavering on the question, especially among teachers and students in evangelical seminaries" ("Role of Tongues," p. 79).

[149]Williams, *Systematic Theology,* 3:51-52; Wyckoff, "Baptism in the Holy Spirit," pp. 449-50; Duffield and Van Cleave, *Foundations of Pentecostal Theology,* p. 322; Higgins, Dusing and Tallman, *Introduction to Theology,* p. 157.

[150]Wyckoff, "Baptism in the Holy Spirit," p. 442; Duffield and Van Cleave, *Foundations of Pentecostal Theology,* pp. 322-23.

[151]Russell P. Spittler, "Glossolalia," in Burgess and Van der Maas, *New International Dictionary of Pentecostal and Charismatic Movements,* pp. 670-76.

[152]Pearlman, *Knowing the Doctrines,* p. 326.

[153]Menzies and Horton, *Bible Doctrines,* p. 134.

[154]McLean indicates that the experience of evidentiary tongues "removes an individual's ambi-

guity in respect to her or his place in the body of Christ" ("The Holy Spirit," p. 389 n. 30).

[155]Hardy W. Steinberg, "Initial Evidence of the Baptism in the Holy Spirit," in *Conference on the Holy Spirit Digest: A Condensation of Plenary Sessions and Seminars of the Conference on the Holy Spirit in Springfield, Missouri, August 16-18, 1982,* ed. Gwen Jones, 2 vols. (Springfield, Mo.: Gospel Publishing House, 1983), 1:41. Steinberg here cites 1 Corinthians 14:5.

[156]Williams, *Systematic Theology,* 3:267 n. 1.

[157]Wyckoff, "Baptism in the Holy Spirit," pp. 445-46.

[158]Higgins, Dusing and Tallman, *Introduction to Theology,* p. 155.

[159]Wyckoff, "Baptism in the Holy Spirit," p. 441.

[160]Pearlman, *Knowing the Doctrines,* p. 313.

[161]Menzies and Menzies, *Spirit and Power,* p. 189. Cf. Menzies, "Spirit-Baptism and Spiritual Gifts," wherein he argues for a revision of the "gateway" view, suggesting that Spirit-baptism is the "gateway" to a subset or "special cluster of gifts described by Paul, the prophetic-type gifts which are associated with special revelation and inspired speech" (pp. 58-59).

[162]Pearlman, *Knowing the Doctrines,* p. 320.

[163]Higgins, Dusing and Tallman, *Introduction to Theology,* p. 133.

[164]Menzies and Horton, *Bible Doctrines,* p. 169.

[165]Pruitt, *Fundamentals of the Faith,* p. 310.

[166]Menzies and Horton, *Bible Doctrines,* p. 166; cf. Pearlman, *Knowing the Doctrines,* p. 324.

[167]Menzies and Horton, *Bible Doctrines,* pp. 207-8. Pruitt suggests that the gifts are "mediated through individuals, but they belong to the Spirit in that they have their source in Him, are operated by Him, and are for the glory of God and the edifying of the Church" (*Fundamentals of the Faith,* p. 312).

[168]Menzies and Horton, *Bible Doctrines,* p. 166.

[169]Pentecostal writers recognize the potential for misuse of gifts and offer principles for the regulation of the use of gifts (e.g., Pearlman, *Knowing the Doctrines,* pp. 328-29).

[170]Pearlman, *Knowing the Doctrines,* p. 320; see also Williams, *Systematic Theology,* 3:67.

[171]Pearlman, *Knowing the Doctrines,* p. 323; cf. Higgins, Dusing and Tallman, *Introduction to Theology,* pp. 196-98.

[172]Statement of Fundamental Truths, Article 12 (*MGAAG,* pp. 131).

[173]Nelson, *Bible Doctrines,* p. 121.

[174]For example, David Lim, "Spiritual Gifts," in Horton, *Systematic Theology,* p. 466; Williams, *Systematic Theology,* 3:71; Menzies and Horton, *Bible Doctrines,* p. 166; Pruitt, *Fundamentals of the Faith,* pp. 315-16.

[175]Nelson, *Bible Doctrines,* p. 123.

[176]Menzies and Horton, *Bible Doctrines,* p. 200; see also Higgins, Dusing and Tallman, *Introduction to Theology,* p. 213.

[177]Vernon Purdy, "Divine Healing," in Horton, *Systematic Theology,* p. 489; see also Duffield and Van Cleave, *Foundations of Pentecostal Theology,* p. 389.

[178]Purdy, "Divine Healing," p. 521.

[179]Menzies and Horton, *Bible Doctrines,* p. 193.

[180]Nelson, *Bible Doctrines,* pp. 48-49.

[181]Purdy, "Divine Healing," p. 490.

[182]Statement of Fundamental Truths, Article 12 (*MGAAG,* pp. 131). The denial of this, circumscribing the atonement to spiritual realities alone, is the result of the influence of pagan Hellenistic and Platonic philosophies (see Purdy, "Divine Healing," pp. 500, 503). Pentecostals believe not only that healing is available to all, but also that, as needed, all Christians can

and should participate in community prayer on behalf of the sick (see James 5:14-16).

[183]Pruitt, *Fundamentals of the Faith,* p. 316; see also Nelson, *Bible Doctrines,* p. 123.

[184]See also Hosea 3:1-5; 13:4, 14; 14:4; Numbers 21:9; and the fulfillment of these recorded in John 3:14-16.

[185]Purdy, "Divine Healing," p. 505.

[186]Ibid.

[187]See Menzies and Horton, *Bible Doctrines,* p. 198.

[188]Purdy, "Divine Healing," p. 503.

[189]Duffield and Van Cleave, *Foundations of Pentecostal Theology,* p. 391.

[190]Purdy, "Divine Healing," p. 509. See Romans 8:23; Matthew 10:7-8; Hebrews 2:3-4; 6:5.

Chapter 10: Conclusion

[1]John M. Frame, *Evangelical Reunion: Denominations and the Body of Christ* (Grand Rapids: Baker, 1991), p. 38; see also Karl Barth, *The Church and the Churches,* new ed. (Grand Rapids: Eerdmans, 2005), pp. 29, 37.

[2]See, for example, Frame, *Evangelical Reunion,* p. 38.

[3]Paul Avis, "Keeping Faith with Anglicanism," in *The Future of Anglicanism,* ed. Robert Hannaford (Leominster: Gracewing, 1996), p. 7. Avis contrasts this confessionalism with *confessional identity*—"the healthy recognition that one belongs to an historical church . . . which is an essential prerequisite of any meaningful ecumenical dialogue."

[4]The Essentials of the Faith is accompanied by a note referring the reader to the Westminster Confession for a fuller elaboration of the doctrines set forth, but in at least some churches within the EPC, it is clear that the Essentials of the Faith, not the Westminster Confession, is the guiding document. Interestingly, during a lunch break while writing this chapter of the book, I was approached by a student who wanted to discuss the pros and cons of his historically Baptist church's deliberations over whether or not to divide their doctrinal statement into two categories: "essential" and "traditional" beliefs. The strategy would be to require staff and leaders to affirm both categories, while membership would require adherence to the "essentials" only, thereby facilitating membership for Christians who do not hold to distinctively Baptist beliefs such as believer's baptism by immersion.

[5]C. S. Lewis's *Mere Christianity* (New York: Macmillan, 1952) is often cited in support of a minimalist or reductionist theological agenda. However, Lewis's extensive body of work hardly supports such a notion, and, though not always recognized, his writings clearly reflect an Anglican (and catholic) approach to Christian theology and life.

[6]For a recent discussion of the importance of "both/and" thinking in theology, see Roger E. Olson, *The Mosaic of Christian Belief: Twenty Centuries of Unity and Diversity* (Downers Grove, Ill.: InterVarsity Press, 2002), pp. 11-27.

[7]John R. Franke, *The Character of Theology: An Introduction to Its Nature, Task, and Purpose* (Grand Rapids: Baker, 2005), p. 191.

[8]Rodney Clapp, *A Peculiar People: The Church as Culture in a Post-Christian Society* (Downers Grove, Ill.: InterVarsity Press, 1996), p. 34. Many forms of early gnostic religion taught a spirit-matter dualism and were characterized by an accompanying tendency to devalue or flee from earthly, material reality.

[9]Thomas Oden, *Systematic Theology,* vol. 3, *Life in the Spirit* (New York: HarperCollins, 1992), p. 287; see also the rest of his discussion of "The Church as Body of Christ" (ibid., pp. 287-97).

[10]Some have suggested that Christians focus exclusively on "the center" or "the core" of belief *instead of* boundaries. In keeping with the both/and principle, it is suggested here that con-

scious attention to both of these—a foundational center and boundaries—is the most realistic and profitable approach to Christian unity and diversity.

[11]Paul Avis, *Anglicanism and the Christian Church: Theological Resources in Historical Perspective* (London: T & T Clark, 2002), p. 347. With a view toward postmodern concerns, Avis goes on to say, "An undifferentiated totality, an ecumenical soup, would be even more ideologically suspect than the present plurality of distinct communions with their patently defensive boundaries of identity. There must be another way of discovering our solidarity in Christ without sacrificing the identity constituted by our tradition, our time-tested way of being Christians together in a particular community" (ibid.).

[12]Franke, *Character of Theology*, p. 192.

[13]Oliver O'Donovan, *On the Thirty-nine Articles: A Conversation with Tudor Christianity*, Latimer Monographs (Exeter: Paternoster, 1986), p. 10, quoted in Mark A. Noll, *Confessions and Catechisms of the Reformation* (Grand Rapids: Baker, 1991), p. 13.

[14]For a thought-provoking discussion of a boundary—in this case, baptism in the Baptist tradition—as serving both exclusion and inclusion, see Paul S. Fiddes, *Tracks and Traces: Baptist Identity in Church and Theology*, Studies in Baptist History and Thought 13 (Carlisle: Paternoster, 2003), pp. 125-56.

[15]See "The Creedal and Confessional Imperative" and "Confession of Faith as Doctrine," in Jaroslav Pelikan, *Credo: Historical and Theological Guide to Creeds and Confessions of Faith in the Christian Tradition* (New Haven: Yale University Press, 2003), pp. 35-92; Ellen T. Charry, *By the Renewing of Your Minds: The Pastoral Function of Christian Doctrine* (New York: Oxford University Press, 1997); Stanley J. Grenz and Roger E. Olson, *Who Needs Theology? An Invitation to the Study of God* (Downers Grove, Ill.: InterVarsity Press, 1996), pp. 9-35, 50-67, 134-48; and several of the essays in John J. Davis, ed., *The Necessity of Systematic Theology*, 2nd ed. (Grand Rapids: Baker, 1980).

[16]D. G. Hart, *Deconstructing Evangelicalism: Conservative Protestantism in the Age of Billy Graham* (Grand Rapids: Baker, 2004), p. 189.

[17]Oden, *Life in the Spirit*, p. 312.

[18]Christine D. Pohl, *Making Room: Recovering Hospitality as a Christian Tradition* (Grand Rapids: Eerdmans, 1999), p. 172.

[19]Ibid.

[20]William L. Lane, *Hebrews 9-13*, Word Biblical Commentary 47B (Dallas: Word, 1991), p. 512.

[21]Gerda Lerner, *Why History Matters: Life and Thought* (New York: Oxford University Press, 1997), p. 118. Lerner is not speaking here specifically about communities of religious faith, but her observations are applicable nonetheless.

[22]The same can be said for other aspects of the life and ministry of Christians. Recognizing that they are good gifts that ultimately flow from God's hospitality to us, Christians should extend hospitality through sharing, for example, their corporate worship, their ministry strategies, their material resources and their personnel.

[23]See Miroslav Volf, *Exclusion and Embrace: A Theological Exploration of Identity, Otherness, and Reconciliation* (Nashville: Abingdon, 1996), pp. 65-67.

[24]Ibid., p. 67.

[25]Ibid., p. 66. The degree of emphasis that I place here on diversity may be somewhat stronger than that of Volf, but the basic principle of "both/and" is the same.

[26]Mary D. Pellauer, *Toward a Tradition of Feminist Theology: The Religious Social Thought of Elizabeth Cady Stanton, Susan B. Anthony, and Ann Howard Shaw*, ed. Jerald C. Brauer and Martin E. Marty, Chicago Studies in the History of American Religion 15 (Brooklyn, N.Y.: Carl-

son, 1991), p. 306.

[27]Pohl, *Making Room,* p. 139.

[28]Volf, *Exclusion and Embrace,* pp. 64-65.

[29]Pohl, *Making Room,* p. 187.

[30]Early in the biblical narrative human beings become alienated and wanderers when Adam and Eve rebel against God and must leave the garden (Gen 3:17-24). Abraham was both patriarch and pilgrim (Gen 12:1-9). Generations of the children of Israel were strangers in strange lands (Gen 15:13). During his itinerant life in this world Jesus was "not of this world" (Jn 8:23). Peter regards those who follow Jesus as "exiles" in the world (1 Pet 1:1, 17). Recounting a long history of those who have modeled faith in God, the author of Hebrews commends them for their recognition that they were "strangers and foreigners on the earth" (Heb 11:13).

[31]Augustine of Hippo, "Sermon 61," in *Homilies on the Gospels,* Nicene and Post-Nicene Fathers 1.6, p. 446, quoted in Amy Oden, "God's Household of Grace," in *Ancient and Postmodern Christianity: Paleo-Orthodoxy in the 21st Century,* ed. Kenneth Tanner and Christopher A. Hall (Downers Grove, Ill.: InterVarsity Press, 2002), p. 44.

[32]This is congruent with the divine identification commended in Proverbs: "Those who oppress the poor insult their Maker, but those who are kind to the needy honor him," and "Whoever is kind to the poor lends to the LORD, and will be repaid in full" (Prov 14:31; 19:17; see also 17:5). Indeed, Jesus so identifies with those who are hungry or thirsty or strangers or without clothes or sick or imprisoned that he tells his followers, "Just as you did it to one of the least of these who are members of my family, you did it to me" (Mt 25:40). Jesus identifies with those in need, and, in a manner appropriate to who we are, so should we.

[33]There is debate as to whether Jesus' reference to "the least of these brothers of mine" or "members of my family" in Matthew 25:40 is a universal reference to all needy human beings or is a more limited reference to disciples of Christ. I am inclined to the latter understanding, with the recognition that the principle of generosity could justifiably be extrapolated to others outside the household of faith. See Donald A. Hagner, *Matthew 14-28,* Word Biblical Commentary 33B (Dallas: Word, 1995), pp. 744-45.

[34]Martin Marty observes that "hospitality brings with it dangers . . . associated with the stranger: it can be both too threatening *and* too alluring" (*When Faiths Collide* [Malden, Mass.: Blackwell, 2005], p. 137). In this book Marty addresses relationships among various religions, but much of the chapter on "The Risk of Hospitality" is readily applicable to intramural relationships among traditions of Christianity (ibid., pp. 124-48).

[35]Pohl, *Making Room,* p. 136.

[36]Among Baptists, for example, see William Brackney, "Baptists and Continuity," in *Distinctively Baptist: Essays on Baptist History,* ed. Marc A. Jolley and John D. Pierce (Macon, Ga.: Mercer University Press, 2005), pp. 41-58; Fiddes, *Tracks and Traces,* pp. 1-20; Fisher Humphreys, *The Way We Were: How Southern Baptist Theology Has Changed and What It Means to Us All,* rev. ed. (Macon, Ga.: Smyth and Helwys, 2002); R. Stanton Norman, *The Baptist Way: Distinctives of a Baptist Church* (Nashville: Broadman & Holman, 2005); Timothy George, "The Reformation Roots of the Baptist Tradition," *Review & Expositor* 86, no. 1 (1989): 19; Justice C. Anderson, "Old Baptist Principles Reset," *Southwestern Journal of Theology* 31, no. 2 (1989): 5; Eric H. Ohlmann, "The Essence of the Baptists: A Reexamination," *Perspectives in Religious Studies* 13, no. 4 (1986): 83; idem, "'Commonly, (Though Falsely) Called . . .': Reflections on the Search for Baptist Identity," *Perspectives in Religious Studies* 13, no. 4 (1986): 67-69. With respect to Lutheranism, see Carl Braaten, *Principles of Lutheran*

Theology (Philadelphia: Fortress, 1983), p. 29; idem, *Justification: The Article by Which the Church Stands or Falls* (Minneapolis: Fortress, 1990), pp. 1-3; Gerhard Forde, "Radical Lutheranism," *Lutheran Quarterly*, n.s., 1, no. 1 (1987): 5, 8, 12. On the Mennonite tradition, see Leo Driedger and Leland Harder, eds., *Anabaptist-Mennonite Identities in Ferment*, Occasional Papers 14 (Elkhart, Ind.: Institute of Mennonite Studies, 1990); Howard J. Kauffman and Leo Driedger, *The Mennonite Mosaic: Identity and Modernization* (Scottdale, Penn.: Herald, 1991); Calvin W. Redekop and Samuel J. Steiner, eds., *Mennonite Identity: Historical and Contemporary Perspectives* (New York: University Press of America, 1988); Arnold Snyder, "Beyond Polygenesis: Recovering the Unity and Diversity of Anabaptist Theology," in *Essays in Anabaptist Theology*, ed. H. Wayne Pipkin (Elkhart, Ind.: Institute of Mennonite Studies, 1994), pp. 1-33. Similarly, consider the current debate between "Traditional" and "Progressive" Dispensationalists, such as Herbert W. Bateman IV, ed., *Three Central Issues in Contemporary Dispensationalism: A Comparison of Traditional and Progressive Views* (Grand Rapids: Kregel, 1999); Craig A. Blaising, "Dispensationalism: The Search for Definition," in *Dispensationalism, Israel and the Church,* ed. Craig A. Blaising and Darrell L. Bock (Grand Rapids: Zondervan, 1992), pp. 13-34; Wesley R. Willis and John R. Master, eds., *Issues in Dispensationalism* (Chicago: Moody Press, 1994).

[37]Pohl, *Making Room,* p. 130.

[38]Marty, *When Faiths Collide,* p. 129. Anthony Carter helpfully distinguishes between "wrong" and "incomplete" (*On Being Black and Reformed: A New Perspective on the African-American Christian Experience* [Phillipsburg, N.J.: P & R, 2003], pp. 73-75.

[39]Pohl writes, "The temptation to use hospitality for advantage remains an important issue today because we tend to be so instrumental in our thinking, so calculating, so aware of costs and benefits. . . . Hospitality is rich with blessing but such benefits come as gifts, and we must be wary of efforts to turn hospitality into some form of commercial exchange" (*Making Room,* p. 144). Theological hospitality should be entered into not primarily with a view toward the "advantage" to be gained by convincing the other of one's theological perspective (though this is not to be shunned, either), but with a humble openness to "gifts" that may take a variety of forms, including greater understanding of and respect for Christians of other traditions, improvements in one's own theology, as well as the gift of someone embracing some of one's own theological beliefs.

[40]Ibid., p. 184.

[41]Thomas N. Finger, *A Contemporary Anabaptist Theology: Biblical, Historical, Constructive* (Downers Grove, Ill.: InterVarsity Press, 2004), p. 11.

[42]Ibid., pp. 12-13. Another Anabaptist scholar, J. Denny Weaver, similarly argues for a theology that is at once both distinctly Anabaptist and of universal relevance for the church (*Anabaptist Theology in the Face of Postmodernity* [Telford, Penn.: Pandora, 2000], p. 27). For a Reformed reflection on this, see Alan P. F. Sell, "Reformed Identity: A Non-Issue of Catholic Significance" *Reformed Review* 54:1 (Autumn 2000): 17-27.

[43]Scholars from the following denominations are participating: Church of the Nazarene, Free Methodist Church, Missionary Church, United Methodist Church, Brethren in Christ, International Church of the Foursquare Gospel, Christian and Missionary Alliance, Salvation Army, Church of God (Anderson, Ind.), Church of God in Christ, International Pentecostal Holiness Church, and Shield of Faith. The combination of Wesleyan/Methodist and Pentecostal denominations is a manifestation of the historical-theological connection between these traditions. Publications sponsored by the Wesleyan Holiness Study Project are in preparation.

[44]Amy Plantinga Pauw and Serene Jones, eds., *Feminist and Womanist Essays in Reformed Dogmatics* (Louisville: Westminster John Knox, 2006), p. x.

Epilogue

[1]For an interesting example of a "celebration" of this oneness, see J. I. Packer and Thomas Oden, *One Faith: The Evangelical Consensus* (Downer Grove, Ill.: InterVarsity Press, 2004).

Subject Index

Scripture Index